A Survey of Agricultural Economics Literature
VOLUME 2

The three volumes in *A Survey of Agricultural Economics Literature* have been prepared by and published for the American Agricultural Economics Association. The general editor of the survey volumes is Lee R. Martin.

Volume 1, *Traditional Fields of Agricultural Economics, 1940s to 1970s.* Lee R. Martin, editor.

Farm Management and Production Economics, 1946-70 by Harald R. Jensen.

The Analysis of Productive Efficiency in Agricultural Marketing: Models, Methods, and Progress by Ben C. French.

Policy for Commercial Agriculture, 1945-71 by G. E. Brandow.

Postwar Policies Relating to Trade in Agricultural Products by D. Gale Johnson.

Agricultural Price Analysis and Outlook by William G. Tomek and Kenneth L. Robinson.

Agricultural Finance and Capital Markets by John R. Brake and Emanuel Melichar.

Technical Change in Agriculture by Willis Peterson and Yujiro Hayami.

Volume 2, *Quantitative Methods in Agricultural Economics, 1940s to 1970s.* George G. Judge, Richard H. Day, S. R. Johnson, Gordon C. Rausser, and Lee R. Martin, editors.

Volume 3, *Economics of Welfare, Development, and Natural Resources in Agriculture, 1940s to 1970s.* Lee R. Martin, editor.

Economics of Rural Poverty by D. Lee Bawden and W. Keith Bryant.

Rural People, Communities, and Regions. George S. Tolley, coordinator. "Economic Bases for Growth" by Clark Edwards. "Rural Development: Problems and Prospects" by Dean Jansma, Hays Gamble, Patrick Madden, and Rex Warland. "Population Distribution: Migration and Settlement Patterns" by Marion Clawson and Philip E. Graves.

Agriculture in Economic Development. "Africa" by Carl Eicher. "Asia" by John W. Mellor. "Latin America" by G. Edward Schuh.

Natural Resources by Emery N. Castle, Maurice M. Kelso, Herbert H. Stoevener, and Joe B. Stevens.

Philosophic Foundations of Agricultural Economics Thought by Glenn L. Johnson.

Organization and Performance of Agricultural Markets by Peter Helmberger, Gerald R. Campbell, and William D. Dobson.

A
SURVEY OF
AGRICULTURAL
ECONOMICS
LITERATURE

VOLUME 2

Quantitative Methods in Agricultural Economics, 1940s to 1970s

George G. Judge, Richard H. Day, S. R. Johnson, Gordon C. Rausser, and Lee R. Martin, editors

Published by the University of Minnesota Press, Minneapolis,
for the American Agricultural Economics Association

Copyright © 1977 by the American Agricultural
Economics Association. All rights reserved.
Printed in the United States of America at
The North Central Publishing Company, St. Paul
Published by the University of Minnesota Press,
2037 University Avenue Southeast, Minneapolis, Minnesota 55455,
and published in Canada by Burns & MacEachern Limited,
Don Mills, Ontario

Library of Congress Catalog Card Number 77-77439

ISBN 0-8166-0818-0

The University of Minnesota is an equal
opportunity educator and employer

Contents

Foreword xi

Introduction xv

PART I. Estimation and Statistical Inference in Economics

Estimation and Statistical Inference in Economics,
by *George G. Judge* 3
The Pre-1940 Period   4
The Decade of the 1940s   6
The Decade of the 1950s   8
The Decade of the 1960s   16
The First Half of the 1970s   25
The Future   32
Concluding Remarks   34
References   35

Discussion of George G. Judge's *Estimation and Statistical Inference
in Economics*, by *Richard J. Foote* 50
References   53

PART II. Economic Optimization in Agricultural and Resource Economics

On Economic Optimization: A Nontechnical Survey,
by *Richard H. Day* 57
Optimization Models   58

Parametric Programming and Comparative Static Analysis   67

Duality   70

Algorithms   71

Efficiency and Games   74

Decomposition and Coordination   76

Multiple Goals   77

Risk and Uncertainty   78

Dynamic Optimization   80

Recursive Optimization   83

On the Normative Content of Optimizing   84

Concluding Remarks   85

References   86

Optimization Models in Agricultural and Resource Economics,
    by *Richard H. Day and Edward Sparling* 93

Food and Diet   95

Farm and Agribusiness Management   96

Farm Firm Development   100

Production Response   101

Interregional and Spatial Economics   103

Natural Resources   106

Agricultural Development Problems   108

References   112

Agricultural Production Function Studies,
    by *Roger C. Woodworth* 128

Aggregate Production Functions   130

Production Functions for Crop Production   131

Production Functions for Animal and Poultry Production   137

Assessment   139

Future Outlook and Research Needs   142

References   144

PART III. Systems Analysis and Simulation in Agricultural
and Resource Economics

Systems Analysis and Simulation: A Survey of Applications in
    Agricultural and Resource Economics, by *S. R. Johnson
    and Gordon C. Rausser*. 157

Historical Perspective   158

Nomenclature   160

Systems Concepts   163

    Types of Systems   164

    Modeling Objectives   166

    Systems Analysis   168

    Systems Synthesis   169

    Systems Design   170

Model Representation   171

    Classes of Models   171

    Construction of Models   172

    Adaptive Models   176

    Tractability   182

Simulation   183

    Analogs   183

    Verification   185

    Validation   186

    Experimentation   191

    Artificial Intelligence and Heuristic Methods   196

    Interpretation   198

Applications of Systems Analysis and Simulation   201

    Games and Gaming   202

    Firm and Process   206

    Market or Industry Models   212

    Aggregate Models   218

    Development Models   224

    Resource Models   228

Critique and Appraisal   235

Tables of General References and Surveys   239

Notes   280

References   281

PART IV. Agricultural Economic Information Systems

Developments in Agricultural Economic Data, by *M. L. Upchurch* 305

    The Setting for Agricultural Data   305

    The Census of Agriculture   310

    Survey Methods   312

        Developments in Theory   312

        Changes in Sampling Methods   314

Methods of Crop Forecasting   316
Current Commodity Statistics   317
   Crop and Livestock Statistics Reports   317
   Commodity Supply and Utilization Data   319
   Price Statistics and Indexes   322
   Market News   323
Farm Data   325
   Farm Income and Expenditures   325
   Enterprise Budgets   326
   Farm Costs and Returns Data Series   327
   Agricultural Sectors of National Input-Output Models   327
   Farm Output, Input, and Productivity   329
   Farm Population   330
Production Resources and Costs   331
   Finance   331
   Credit Institutions   333
   Farm Real Estate   334
   Machinery and Equipment   335
   Fertilizer   336
   Feed   337
   Pesticides   338
   Farm Labor   339
   Insurance   341
Marketing   341
   Market Basket Statistics   342
   Marketing Bill Data   343
   Related Statistical Series   344
Data on Farm-Related Business   345
Food Consumption and Nutrition   346
   Food Consumption and Related Data   346
   The Index of Supply and Utilization   350
   The Nutritive Value of Diets in the United States   351
Natural Resource Economic Data   352
   Land Use   352
   Land Tenure   354
   Inventory of Conservation Needs   355
   Soil Surveys   355
   Water   356

Forests   357

Weather Indexes   358

Airphotos   360

Remote Sensing   360

International Data   361

The World Census of Agriculture   362

Annual Country Statistics   363

World Food Data   363

Rural Area Development   364

Rural Poverty   364

Rural Housing   365

Health   366

Local Governments   367

The Future   368

Technical Developments in Agricultural Estimates Methodology,
by *Harry C. Trelogan, C. E. Caudill, Harold F. Huddleston,
William E. Kibler, and Emerson Brooks* 373

History of Methodology for Agricultural Statistics before 1940   373

Technical Developments in
Agricultural Estimates Methodology, 1940-50   377

Technical Advances in Agricultural
Statistical Methodology, 1950-70   381

Crop Yield Estimates and Forecasts   383

Multiple Frame Estimation Theory   384

Advances in Automatic Data Processing   385

Future Possibilities for Technological Advances   385

Assessment of the Current Agricultural Data Base: An Information
System Approach, by *James T. Bonnen* 386

The Current State of Our Information Systems   387

Conceptual Obsolescence in Agricultural Data   387

The Census of Agriculture   389

Statistics for Rural Society   392

Institutional Obsolescence   392

Vested Interests in Data   393

Empiric Failure in Design and Collection of Data   394

Data, Analysis, and Information: A Paradigm   395

The Nature of Data and Data Systems   395

The Nature of Information   397
Analysis as a Function of Information   397
The Imperative of Information System Design   398
The Design and Management of Information Systems   399
Development and Information   400
Economic Structure and Information   401
The Dysfunctional Behavior
    of the Actors — A Systems Management Problem   402
Conclusion   405
Notes   407

Rural Economic and Social Statistics, by *W. Keith Bryant*. 408
The Demand for Economic and Social Statistics   410
The Supply of Economic and Social Statistics   413
Suggestions for Improvement of the Statistical System   416
Conclusion   418
Notes   420

Appendix (Part IV). A Brief Review of the Literature
    by Subject Category 421
Information Systems and Purposes   422
Theoretical and Operational Concepts   422
Data Collection Methods   423
Evaluations of Methodology   424
Evaluations of Information Systems, Programs, Concepts, and Data   424
Information and Data Needs   425
Reports of Advisory Committees   426
Relationship between Agricultural
    Economic Data and National Economic Data   426
Explanations and Illustrations of Data Series   426
Evaluative Techniques   427
Economic Forecasting Models   427
Foreign Agricultural Economic Information   427

References (Part IV) 428

Epilogue 467

Foreword

In March 1968 C. E. Bishop, president of the American Agricultural Economics Association, appointed a committee to investigate the need for a major survey of the agricultural economics literature published from the 1940s to the 1970s. The committee found that an extensive assessment of this body of literature would indeed be of value to research workers, teachers, extension workers, and graduate students in agricultural economics; teachers, research workers, and graduate students in economics and economic statistics, sociology, geography, political science, and anthropology; and teachers, research workers, and graduate students in technical agriculture. In the end the committee was assigned the responsibility for planning the project and commissioning authors to prepare the papers.

The members of the committee were Glenn L. Johnson (Michigan State University), M. M. Kelso (University of Arizona), James E. Martin (Virginia Polytechnic Institute), M. L. Upchurch (Economic Research Service of the United States Department of Agriculture), and Lee R. Martin, chairman (University of Minnesota). Early in 1969 James E. Martin resigned from the committee, and several new members—John P. Doll (University of Missouri), Peter G. Helmberger (University of Wisconsin), J. Patrick Madden (Pennsylvania State University), and Edward W. Tyrchniewicz (University of Manitoba)—were appointed.

As its first step, the committee tentatively identified the fields to be covered and commissioned highly regarded members of the profession to draw up outlines of the coverage to be undertaken in the different fields. These outlines were used in the selection of economists to prepare the surveys and in negotiating agreements with prospective authors. Once the surveys were prepared, the committee again obtained assistance from highly competent members of the profession to make critical, constructive evaluations of each survey draft. In the case of the preparation of outlines and the review of papers, the committee sought to strike a representative balance among differing viewpoints in each field. For the preparation of the papers themselves, the committee obtained the services of outstanding agricultural economists with special competence in the respective fields.

In connection with the papers published in this volume, substantial assistance was provided by the following individuals:

PART I. Estimation and Statistical Inference in Economics. *Preparation of outline:* John P. Doll and Oscar R. Burt. *Review of paper:* Richard J. Foote and Wayne A. Fuller.

PART II. On Economic Optimization: A Nontechnical Survey. *Preparation of outline:* John P. Doll and Oscar R. Burt. *Review of paper:* Verner G. Hurt. **Optimization Models in Agriculture and Resource Economics.** *Review of paper:* Oscar R. Burt. **Agricultural Production Function Studies.** *Review of paper:* Chester B. Baker, Harold O. Carter, John C. Crecink, Lee M. Day, Richard J. Edwards, Irving F. Fellows, Burton L. French, Earl O. Heady, George D. Irwin, Earl W. Kehrberg, Luther H. Keller, W. W. McPherson, D. D. Mason, Ronald L. Mighell, Frank Orazen, G. A. Peterson, W. B. Sundquist, Earl R. Swanson, and W. D. Toussaint.

PART III. Systems Analysis and Simulation in Agricultural and Resource Economics. *Preparation of outline:* S. R. Johnson and Gordon C. Rausser. *Review of outline:* Ludwig Eisgruber, Earl Fuller, Tom Manetsch, Thomas H. Naylor, and Warren H. Vincent. *Review of paper:* Oscar R. Burt, Ludwig Eisgruber, Albert N. Halter, and Thomas H. Naylor.

PART IV. Developments in Agricultural Economic Data. *Preparation of outline:* Earl Houseman, Fred Abel, and Harry C. Trelogan. *Review of outline:* James T. Bonnen, James P. Cavin, Wayne Dexter, Clark Edwards, and Warren Grant. *Review of paper:* James T. Bonnen, James P. Cavin, Karl A. Fox, and Nathan M. Koffsky. **Technical Developments in Agricultural Estimates Methodology.** *Review of paper:* Lee R. Martin. **Assessment of the Current Agricultural Data Base: An Information System Approach.** *Review of paper:* George G. Judge and Lee R. Martin. **Rural Economic and Social Statistics.** *Review of paper:* James T. Bonnen, George G. Judge, Lee R. Martin, and Luther G. Tweeten.

This list includes only the official reviewers who acted on behalf of the association and the committee. Many other individuals who assisted the authors of the papers in various ways are cited in the notes preceding each paper. The authors were urged to incorporate into their papers the comments and suggestions provided by the respective reviewers, but final decisions about the content of the papers were left to the discretion of the authors.

The Committee on Publication of Postwar Literature Review arranged for publication of the three-volume set of literature reviews. The members of this committee are Emerson M. Babb (chairman), J. P. Madden, Lee R. Martin, and John C. Redman. Neil Harl provided valuable assistance in the publication phase to both committees.

On behalf of the members of the association and the Literature Review Committee I wish to express sincere gratitude to the authors of the papers in this volume and the the advisors, reviewers, and others who participated in the planning and implementation of the project as a whole.

Finally, I would like to direct readers' attention to current literature reviews of some closely related fields of agricultural economics—reviews that both complement and supplement the reviews in this volume and the two companion volumes. The following reviews have been published in an Australian journal, *Review of Marketing and Agricultural Economics*:

> G. Weinschenck, W. Henrichsmeyer, and F. Aldinger (1969). "The Theory of Spatial Equilibrium and Optimal Location in Agriculture: A Survey." 37:3-70.
>
> Ulf Renborg (1970). "Growth of the Agricultural Firm: Problems and Theories." 38:51-101.
>
> John L. Dillon (1971). "An Expository Review of Bernoullian Decision Theory in Agriculture: Is Utility Futility?" 39:3-80.
>
> Roger W. Gray and David J. S. Rutledge (1971). "The Economics of Commodity Futures Markets: A Survey." 39(4):57-108.
>
> Harold F. Breimyer (1973). "The Economics of Agricultural Marketing: A Survey." 41:115-165.
>
> Jock R. Anderson (1974). "Simulation: Methodology and Application in Agricultural Economics." 42:3-55.

An additional article commissioned by the *Review of Marketing and Agricultural Economics* but not yet published is "Public Utility Pricing" by David Gallagher.

Another important set of literature reviews in agricultural economics is being published in the British *Journal of Agricultural Economics*. To date the following review articles have been published:

G. H. Peters (1970). "Land Use Studies in Britain: A Review of the Literature with Special Reference to Applications of Cost-Benefit Analysis." 21:171-214.

D. S. Thornton (1973). "Agriculture in Economic Development." 24:225-287.

T. E. Josling (1974). "Agricultural Policies in Developed Countries: A Review." 25:229-264.

C. S. Barnard (1975). "Data in Agriculture: A Review with Special Reference to Farm Management Research, Policy and Advice in Britain." 26:289-333.

D. I. Bateman (1976). "Agricultural Marketing: A Review of the Literature of Marketing Theory and Selected Applications." 27:171-225.

Also worthy of note is Marguerite C. Burk's 1967 "Survey of Interpretations of Consumer Behavior by Social Scientists in the Postwar Period," *Journal of Farm Economics* 49:1-31.

Lee R. Martin
Survey Editor

June 1977

Introduction

In the evolution of modern economics from nineteenth-century political economy many have expressed the ideas that "(1) mathematics, however useful it may have proved in the physical sciences, can play no essential role in the development of the social sciences because the phenomena studied are somehow different—'human beings are not amenable to mathematical law'— and (2) the judgment and intuition of the skilled investigator are fundamentally more useful in the social sciences than mathematical formulas based on quantitative observation" (Arrow [1951]). In a letter in 1906 Alfred Marshall advised A. L. Bowley to "use mathematics as a shorthand language rather than as an engine of inquiry."

In the face of these propositions perhaps we should ask why Bowley ignored Marshall's advice and went on to write a treatise restating the basic postulates of economics in mathematical form and why economists should try to measure "things." What does measuring accomplish that nonmeasuring does not? It is costly to obtain measurements. Are the returns from the efforts worth the cost?

It is important to realize that in order to explain the relations among so-called economic variables, economics has become essentially a general theory of choice. Moreover, in situations where the choices of individuals are reciprocally dependent, we have been forced to develop a general theory of strategy. Consequently, one ultimate purpose of economic research is to generate in-

Note: Some of the material in this section is based on Judge [1968].

formation that may be used to improve economic decision making or strategy formation. A consumer seeks the best way to buy. A firm seeks the best way to produce. A government seeks the best way to regulate. As Dreze [1972] has noted, these decisions are typically made under uncertainty and formal analysis of the problems reflects the *states*, which describe the environment; the *consequences*, which describe what happens to the decision maker; and the *acts*, which are functions that assign a consequence to each state. A decision involves the choice of a "best" element from a set of acts.

As the "decision machine" runs on information, we might say, following Marschak [1953], that "knowledge is useful if it helps us make the best decisions." For most decision problems it is not enough to know that certain variables are related, because in the economic sphere the rallying cry seems to be that "everything depends on everything else." This means that if information is to be useful in a decision context we must understand the fundamental structural aspects of the problem, we must know in what direction the relationship runs, and we must be able to estimate *how much* or at least the probability of how much. Thus, cardinal and ordinal measurements appear operationally necessary.

Given the need for quantitative knowledge in economics, how do we go about capturing it? In the history of science two approaches have been employed in the search for knowledge: (1) postulation or logical argument, and (2) experimentation or measurement. The structure of the search process for

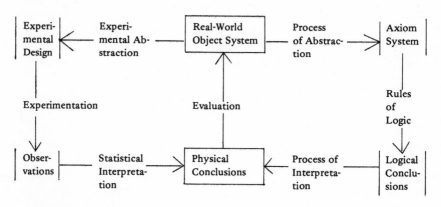

The role of postulation and experimentation in the search for knowledge. (Adapted from Thrall, Coombs, and Raiffa [1954].)

both routes to knowledge is given in the accompanying diagram. The two routes have been used individually and in combination. Moreover, they are tied together in the sense that conclusions or hypotheses reached via the logical route form the basis for experimental models.

From the standpoint of economics the way to knowledge through the logical route noted in the diagram is clear: *economic theory* and *mathematical economics* are the result. The logical route, of course, only gives us the consequences of the axiom system and tells us nothing about the truth or falsity of the knowledge relative to real-world phenomena. Alternatively, the measurement or experimentation route provides a basis (1) for refuting, refining, or modifying the axiom set of conclusions reached by the logical route and (2) for attaching signs, numbers, and reliability statements to events so that they can be used as a basis for decisions.

The experimental restrictions in the search for knowledge become apparent at the left side of the diagram. Experiments give reproducible knowledge, and within the framework of the experimental design the outcome of an experiment can be forecast. Even though the objectives of the economist are the same as those of the engineer or the physicist (for example, to estimate or predict the effects of a change in structure), the economist's models for the most part are of a nonexperimental nature and his data are like those of the meteorologist. As Marschak [1950] observed, the economist is usually asked to estimate the impact of a change in the mechanism which produces his data, and none of these changes can be produced beforehand in a laboratory experiment. Data are thus generated according to society's experimental design, and the economist can observe the outcome but can affect that outcome very little. This situation means, according to Marschak [1950], that "economic data are generated by systems of economic relations that are in general stochastic, simultaneous and dynamic. Occurring jointly, these three properties give rise to unsolved problems of statistical inference from the observed data to the relations. Yet these very relations constitute economic theory and knowledge of them is needed for economic practice."

In addition, we know so little about the mechanisms at work in the economic sphere that there is enormous arbitrariness in any specification. Economic theory provides several alternative models for explaining economic behavior and does not really help to narrow the range of hypotheses. Furthermore, passively generated data, for which we cannot control variables and isolate relations, are often consistent with a variety of hypotheses. This means that there is considerable difficulty in discriminating among alternative hypotheses and some question about whether our theories can be tested and whether the quantitative results have validity for any broader body of data.

Given these pitfalls, should we despair and take our alphas, betas, and imaginary numbers and go home? The papers contained in this volume provide a historical answer to this question and make suggestions of possible future responses in the areas of both theory and practice.

In the first essay Judge reviews attempts over the last three decades to cope with the problems of measurement in economics and discusses within the context of a time path the analytical methods developed and employed in analyzing and learning from economic data. Noting the early contributions to measurement in economics, the essay starts with a detailed review of attempts in the 1940s to develop statistical models and procedures for estimation and inference that are consistent with the endogenous nature of economic data. The refinement of these procedures in the 1950s is discussed and their application in estimating the parameters of a variety of micro and macro economic regulations is reviewed. The period of the 1960s is viewed as an era in which economists concentrated on the question of how to make systematic use of both sample and external (prior) information in learning from economic data. In this period the theory and practice of econometrics helped to make transparent the estimation and inferential implications of both sampling theory and Bayesian approaches in searching for quantitative economic knowledge. The early 1970s are viewed as a period in which the search for estimators that are appropriate for economic decision problems was continued, in which the estimators proposed under a range of measures of goodness were superior to traditional estimators, and in which systems analysis and control theory provided a framework for joining the separate problems of estimation, optimization, and design of experiments. The chapter closes with a discussion of the contributions of econometrics of the science of economics and the identification of some of the changes in econometric models and tools likely in the decades ahead.

In the second paper Day reviews developments since the 1950s in optimization theory and methods that underlie much of the applied work in agricultural and resource economics. Day begins with a brief discussion of the relationships among classical, neoclassical, and modern theories of economizing. The point of view established and alluded to throughout the paper is that modern concepts of optimization incorporate, unify, and generalize the seminal insights of the classical and neoclassical founders of economic theory. The remainder of the paper is divided into sections that summarize the basic concepts and provide key references to the following topics: alternative optimization models, parametric programming and comparative statics, the duality of choice and imputation, economizing or optimization algorithms, economic efficiency and games, decomposition and coordination of complex economic decisions, economizing with multiple goals, risk and uncertainty, dynamic or intertemporal optimization, recursive optimization or suboptimizing with feedback, and the relationship between optimization and economic behavior. In the last section we are reminded that optimality is a logical property of formal models; whether or not it is a meaningful characteristic of human behavior is of course a subjective matter. This reservation becomes stronger when we contemplate the difficulty of extending the concept of intertemporal optimality to resource allocation problems that ultimately involve future generations, whose preferences are yet to be formed. The epilogue, however, emphasizes that, subject to such reservations, optimization theory and methods occupy key roles in the understanding and control of human economic affairs.

This paper is followed by Day and Sparling's survey of optimization models in agricultural and resource economics. They begin by recalling von Thünen's classic development of marginalist and budgeting principles in the context of optimal farm management. The introduction is followed by a survey of selected contributions to economic analysis in the following areas: food and nutrition, farm and agribusiness management, farm growth and development, production response studies at national and regional levels, spatial economics, natural resource management, and agricultural development problems in less developed countries. This survey illustrates the extensive and varied applications of the spectrum of optimization concepts and methods outlined in the preceding chapter.

Building on the previous chapters, Woodworth assesses applied research concerned with developing optimum conditions in farm production. Starting with the historical background, he presents an overview of the broad range of production function studies in agriculture, including studies of farms and marketing firms that use cross-section or time series data. The major emphasis of Woodworth's chapter is an assessment of production function studies relating inputs to crop and livestock production. These studies, which reached a peak in numbers of projects and general interest in the 1950s, brought about a unique degree of multidisciplinary cooperation among plant and animal scientists, statisticians, and economists.

Johnson and Rausser review the applications and developments of an approach more recent in origin than econometrics or optimization. Systems analysis and the simulation of systems models has become a popular method of studying economic problems and the generation of information about economic relationships. With the advent of the modern computer the possibility of operating and monitoring the outcomes of large models has become a reality. Taking advantage of this technology, the early workers in the system and simulation area used comparatively detailed models to study a wide range of economic problems. The approach was and is characterized by the use of highly flexible models based on various sources of prior and sample information and operated in an exploratory manner.

Applications of systems and simulation concepts are grouped in six categories defined on the basis of research areas in agricultural and resource economics. These include gaming, firm and process, market and industry, aggregate, economic development, and resource models. The review focuses on the method of model formulation, corroboration of models with the systems they are designed to represent, model type, and simulation method. Noteworthy developments in methods which have occurred in agricultural economics are identified.

As the systems and simulation approach is new, a major portion of the chapter is devoted to a review of the method itself. This is necessary to provide a framework for reviewing the applications. The discussion makes it apparent that the flexibility of the approach is paid for in research results which are highly personalized. It is interesting that not only the process of depersonalizing model formulation but also the specialization of models to particular systems and the simulation of systems models lead directly to problems in the theory of optimal control. Research strategies based on the notion of systems and simulation modeling can thus be viewed as crude approximations to the solution of the control problems. Nevertheless, viewing systems analysis and simulation in this context provides a basis for identifying common threads in the various approaches to quantitative economic problems; useful insights on these approaches might be modified to augment their potential value.

In the concluding chapters Upchurch, Trelogan and his colleagues, Bonnen, and Bryant trace out and interpret from different points of view the development in agricultural economic data since World War II. Emphasis is placed on the recurring national statistical series most often used by agricultural economists. Much of the periodic statistical data originated before World War II. The agricultural depression of the 1920s and the urgent economic problems of the 1930s led pioneers in the profession to seek data that would help them describe, diagnose, analyze, and test economic relationships. The problems of the 1940s brought special demands for additional kinds of data and for more reliable data. For example, rationing of food during the war made apparent the need for better knowledge of food consumption, and rationing of farm machinery prompted further development of data on resources used in production. Requirements for price support programs led to refinements in data on prices received and paid by farmers. These developments and others provided the raw material for expanded economic analyses. During the past three decades improved methods of collecting and processing data have increased the accuracy, capacity, and reliability of the information available to decision makers. For the future, it appears that remote sensing, computers, improved sampling techniques, and other technology will make possible important improvements in collecting and analyzing data. More important to the usefulness of the information, however, will be new concepts and definitions of the food and fiber industry and its parts, different populations for demographic data, and different problems for agricultural economists.

Over recent decades there has been a growing separation of the agricultural economic analyst from the agricultural statistician. This compartmentalization or specialization accounts in part for the relative scarcity of articles on data in our literature, and it may have contributed to the dissatisfaction many agricultural economists now feel toward much of their data. A substantial change may occur in the decade ahead. Bonnen's paper builds on this theme and traces some of the impacts of the greater specialization and organizational fragmentation on information system design and the corresponding difficulties of maintaining a coherent, integrated information system. Bonnen further points to some growing obsolescence of the concepts which serve as the basis of our data system and the corresponding measurements. Even though knowledge of the uncertainty surrounding the possible payoffs or losses for a range of agricultural decisions was often repressed by policy action during much of the period since World War II, Bonnen concludes that, for today's decision needs, we have undervalued our agricultural information system. Consequently, we have not invested adequately in some subsystems and we have allowed others to decay seriously. Because the returns to careful decisions about data and information appear to be high, the case is made for each agricultural economist, and perhaps especially for those in academia, to take more responsibility in shoring up the conceptual underpinnings of the agricultural information system and in keeping those underpinnings in close harmony with the dynamic sector.

In the area of economic and social statistics Bryant notes the increasing resources allocated to social experiments and experimental design, to basic data collection, to the training of economists in statistical measurement and data collection techniques, and to training in working with longitudinal panel data. He makes some suggestions on how to accelerate the process of bringing the information system for the rural sector closer to what is needed for improved decision making. He concludes optimistically that the 1980s may become the "data decade."

In the epilogue an attempt is made to combine the contributions in the various areas and to assess their joint impacts on the discipline of economics and the subject matter area of agricultural economics.

References

Arrow, K. J. [1951], "Mathematical Models in the Social Sciences." In *The Policy Sciences*, D. Lerner and H. D. Lasswell, eds. Stanford: Stanford University Press.

Dreze, J. H. [1972]. "Econometrics and Decision Theory." *Econometrica* 40:1-18.

Judge, G. G. [1968]. "The Search for Quantitative Economic Knowledge." *Am. J. Agr. Econ.* 50:1703-1717.

Marschak, J. [1950]. "Statistical Inference in Economics." In *Statistical Inference in Dynamic Economic Models*, T. C. Koopmans, ed. New York: Wiley.

Marschak, J. [1953]. "Economic Measurement for Policy and Prediction." In *Studies in Econometric Methods*, W. C. Hood and T. C. Koopmans, eds. New York: Wiley.

Thrall, R. M., C. H. Coombs, and R. L. Davis [1954]. *Decision Processes*. New York: Wiley.

Part I. Estimation and Statistical Inference in Economics

This essay is dedicated to those members of the economics and statistics faculties at Iowa State University who during the 1940s and 1950s did so much to make statistical inferences an operational tool in economics and to give meaning and context to the phrase "measurement with theory."

Dennis Aigner, George E. Brandow, John P. Doll, Richard J. Foote, Wayne A. Fuller, Stanley R. Johnson, George W. Ladd, Lee R. Martin, Gordon C. Rausser, Earl R. Swanson, Takashi Takayama, Gerhard Tintner, Thomas D. Wallace, Fred V. Waugh, and Arnold Zellner read an earlier draft of this paper and made a larger number of useful comments, many of which in one way or another found their way into the final copy.

G. G. J.

Estimation and Statistical Inference in Economics

George G. Judge
Professor of Economics
University of Illinois, Urbana-Champaign

This essay is focused on attempts over the last three decades to cope with the problem of measurement in economics. In particular, it is directed to a review of analytical methods developed and employed in analyzing and learning from economic data. To some extent, it is a report of an experiment—an experiment in nonexperimental model building. The achievements realized through a systematic use of economic and statistical models, methods, and data give empirical content to economic theory and practice and bring out clearly the complementarity between theory and measurement, and these achievements have made economics a leader of the nonexperimental sciences. Therefore, it is with great pleasure that I take this intellectual trek through time.

Perhaps during the first half of this century it was possible to summarize, as many tried to do, the theory and method of economics, but I doubt if any economist in his right mind would attempt to do so today. The virtual explosion of knowledge over the past few decades has made this impossible. My task is only to review a subset of quantitative economic knowledge, but in this area the pace of development is so rapid I have a feeling that if I do not hurry and finish this paper I too shall be accused of not being in my right mind.

This literature review is a brief, personal, partially documented statement of one man's view of the development of econometric theory and applications and cannot and should not be considered exhaustive or all-inclusive. Rather, it is only a subjective sampling of some of the creative analytical and empirical work done over the last thirty years. Others who have looked back over the field and have viewed with alarm and pointed with pride, as they emphasized various aspects of the evolution of econometrics, include Tintner [1966], Wold [1969], Leser [1968], and Klein [1971]. Since the econometric methods and applications I will discuss cut across subject matter areas, I have chosen time as a frame on which to hang and contrast the developments. Other subject matter survey papers have been commissioned that will include detailed reviews of applied econometric results, and for this reason I have been very selective in the application references noted.

The Pre-1940 Period

At the close of the 1930s economists had available to them the following tools in their search for knowledge: an economic theory developed over the decennia which included, among other things, the general equilibrium theory of Walras, the partial equilibrium theories of Marshall, and the aggregative economic theory of Keynes; a steady flow of economic data from the developed countries; the elements of classical statistical theory and scientific method that appeared sometime between 1880 and 1920 and developed under the influence of such men as Pearson [1938] and Fisher [1935]; the concept of least squares estimation supported by a theory that dates back to around 1800 and owes its conceptual base to Gauss [1821] and Legendre [1805]; and the wonderful statistical tool known as multiple correlation and regression (Ezekiel [1930]). Armed with these tools, economists and statisticians in the twentieth century, after the casual empiricism of the nineteenth century, made systematic and scientific use of statistical data (1) to give empirical content to economic theory by refuting, refining, or modifying the conclusions reached from abstract reasoning, and (2) to estimate the parameters of demand, supply, production, cost, consumption, and investment relations so they could be used as a basis for decision making.

Although linear statistical models and estimators have existed since 1800, the lack of the currently fashionable sampling theory concepts of gauging the statistical consequences of model misspecification and comparing the performance of estimators via defined properties or risk functions caused the early applied econometricians little or no pain at all. By and large, the following linear statistical model or a slightly transformed variant was the workhorse of the day:

(1) $y = X\beta + u$

where y, called a dependent variable, was a $(T \times 1)$ vector of observations, X was a $(T \times K)$ matrix of observations on K independent (usually nonstochastic) variables, β was the (K × 1) vector of unknown parameters (coefficients), and u, called the error term, was a (T × 1) vector of unobservable (normal) random variables with mean zero and scalar identity covariance $\sigma^2 I_T$. It was not until the 1930s that the statisticians and some workers in applied economics became very precise about the stochastic assumptions underlying the error term. The Gauss-Markoff Theorem, specified and proved by Aitken [1934] and by David and Neyman [1938], resulted in the conclusion that out of the class of *linear unbiased* estimators the least squares estimator, $\hat{\beta} = (X'X)^{-1} X'y$, was best (minimum variance). Also, under the quadratic loss measure of goodness for evaluating estimator performance that is so popular today, the least squares estimator is minimax (minimizes the maximum expected loss over the parameter space β).

The statistical study of demand, which started with Moore [1914], culminated with Schultz's classic work *The Theory and Measurement of Demand* [1938]. Schultz's work was concerned with making use of economic theory, mathematical economics, the regression statistical model (1), and the data of the day in specifying and estimating the parameters of the demand relations for agricultural commodities. Ezekiel, Bean, Warren, Pearson, and the Workings were important contributors to the development of demand analysis in the 1920s and 1930s. In his paper "What Do Statistical 'Demand Curves' Show?" E. J. Working [1926] looked at this activity which made use of data passively generated by society and questioned the possibility of deducing statistically the Cournot-Marshall demand curve when only the coordinates of intersection of the demand and supply relations were given for a series of points in time. In addition, the least squares approach to estimation was a method in which different estimates were obtained for a given parameter, depending on which variable was chosen to play the dependent role. Demand theory unfortunately gave little help on this problem since it was stated in functional terms and hence treated all variables symmetrically. Investigators faced the multiple-parameter dilemma and reacted to the problem by reporting two relations for each commodity analyzed—one for price and one for quantity.

On the supply side, the focus was on agricultural commodities and much of the work concerned single equation economic and statistical models, involving the variables acreage and lagged price. This work was summarized by Black [1924] in an article in the *Journal of Farm Economics*, and several years later Bean [1929] published his famous article, "The Farmers' Response to Price."

Also during the 1920s and 1930s Black, Jensen, Spillman, and others attempted to estimate production functions for the technical units and pro-

cesses in agriculture, and Cobb and Douglas [1928] worked on industry relations. Dean [1936] specified and estimated statistical cost functions, and
Bressler [1942] and his associates were generating the data for and estimating
cost-output functions. Stone and Stone [1938-39] made a statistical study of
the macro consumption function, and S. Kuznets [1935] and Tinbergen
[1938] used statistical evidence to reject Clark's accelerator model of investment.

As the first forty years of this century came to a close, attempts were being made to deal with the endogenous generation of economic data, and multi-
relation models came to the foreground in econometric research. Wright
[1934] put forth the method of path analysis to reflect interdependencies in
social processes. Frisch [1934] extended his work to complete regression systems, and Tinbergen [1939] developed his macroeconomics model for the
Netherlands and the United States. About the same time Leontief [1937]
completed the work started by the Physiocrats in the eighteenth century and
developed input-output analysis to make it possible to take into account the
interdependence between the sectors of an economy and permit structural
analysis. Although they could not satisfactorily solve the puzzle, many investigators during this period were aware of the conceptual problems of using
single equation regression models, and in order to patch up the regression
method they proposed and applied a variety of procedures such as canoni-
cal correlation (Hotelling [1936]), the variate difference method (Tintner
[1940]), confluence analysis (Frisch [1934]), principal components (Hotelling [1933] and Girschick [1936]), and weighted regression (Koopmans
[1937]).

The Decade of the 1940s

The early 1940s marks the beginning of the era of modern econometrics. The
conceptual problems raised by E. J. Working [1926], Frisch [1934], Tinbergen [1938], and others emphasized among other things that economic data
are generated by systems of economic relations that are stochastic, dynamic,
and simultaneous and pointed to the many unsolved problems of statistical
inference, from the observed data to the relations. It was fully realized that if
the results of econometric ventures were to reflect desired properties in estimation and inference, there must be consistency between the statistical model employed and the sampling model by which the data were generated.

In formulating statistical models consistent with the way economic data
are visualized as being generated, a milestone was reached in 1943 when two
articles were published in *Econometrica* by Haavelmo [1943] and Mann and
Wald [1943], and Haavelmo wrote a monograph entitled *The Probability Ap-*

proach to Econometrics [1944]. Haavelmo converted the economist's simultaneous equation model to a statistical model by assuming a random disturbance for each equation and specifying the distribution of these random variables. This specification resulted in the following so-called simultaneous system of equations statistical model:

(2) $Y\Gamma + XB = U$

where Y is a T × G matrix of jointly determined or endogenous variables, Γ is a G × G matrix of parameters, X is a T × K matrix of exogenous and predetermined variables, B is a K × G matrix of parameters, and U is a T × G matrix of disturbances or, in the early language, latent variables or shocks. Classical assumptions were made about the stochastic properties of the disturbances and thus, $E(u_j) = 0$, for j = 1, 2, . . ., G, and $E(u_j u_i') = \sigma_{ji} I_T$ for j, i = 1, 2, . . ., G, and the G × G symmetric and positive semidefinite variance-covariance matrix Σ. Since Γ is assumed to be nonsingular, the structural equation statistical model (2) was also expressed in the statistically equivalent "reduced form" format.

(3) $Y = -XB\Gamma^{-1} + U\Gamma^{-1} = X\Pi + V.$

Mann and Wald suggested a large sample solution to the estimation problem arising from the new systems of equations formulation. Marschak and Andrews [1944] pointed out the simultaneous nature of production decisions leading to the determination of input levels in the production function. Anderson and Rubin [1949] developed the "limited information" maximum likelihood estimators for estimating the parameters of an equation in a system of equations and derived corresponding large sample properties and statistical tests. Koopmans [1949] faced up to the problem first raised by Working [1926] and developed, with the aid of zero linear restrictions on Γ, B, and Σ, necessary and sufficient conditions for identifying each mathematical equation as a definite economic relation and discriminating between alternative competing structures. Vining and Koopmans [1949] debated the question of measurement without theory as one goes about searching for knowledge. Marschak [1947, 1953] made clear the need for structural estimation if the results were to be useful for policy purposes and suggested decision models for making use of empirical results. In two important articles which appeared in the *Journal of Farm Economics* Cooper [1948] made clear the role of the econometric model in inference and D. G. Johnson [1948] discussed the use of econometric models in the study of agricultural policy. The work of the 1940s, which was based squarely on economic and statistical theory, was to a large extent centered in the Cowles Commission at the University of Chicago. A monograph edited by Koopmans [1950] summarized the state of the tools of quantitative knowledge after the developments of the 1940s.

Girshick and Haavelmo [1947] beautifully integrated economic theory and inferential statistics in their classic five-equation model concerned with the demand for food. Haavelmo] 1947] made use of a system of equations in estimating the parameters of the consumption function. Klein [1950] completed his work on a sophisticated macroeconometric model of the United States economy. Judge [1949], under the direction of Hurwicz and Thompson, completed a simultaneous systems of equations analysis of the feeder cattle sector; Ogg [1949], working with Hildreth, completed a simultaneous equation analysis of the production relation for a sample of firms; French [1950] made a statistical analysis of the demand for meat; and G. Johnson [1952] made a statistical analysis of the burley tobacco sector. Computational burdens with the new techniques were significant since the desk calculator was still the main tool of the "estimators." Anyone who has inverted a 10×10 matrix on a hand calculator can attest to the reality of this computing restriction and to the impossibility of the data dredging and mining activities that many currently engage in.

At the end of the 1940s Samuelson published his book on the *Foundations of Economic Analysis* [1948], Von Neumann and Morgenstern [1947] introduced the profession to game theory, Wald [1950] alerted us to statistical decision theory, Dantzig [1951a, 1951b] developed the simplex algorithm for use with linear optimizing models, and Koopmans [1951] and his cohorts were putting together the conceptual basis for the activity analysis approach to price and allocation problems in economics. Each of these creative efforts had a significant impact on the demand for and structure of econometric efforts in the 1950s and 1960s. Economists interested in agriculture were leaders in applying the new statistical procedures for estimation and prediction, and at the end of this period there was great optimism that we were on the road to making mathematical economics and econometrics into tools that would serve the needs and aspirations of the discipline and society.

The Decade of the 1950s

As the decade opened, Haavelmo's view [1943] of endogenous data generation was questioned by Wold [1956]. Wold proposed the recursive or causal chain economic and statistical models which were characterized by a triangular Γ matrix of coefficients for the endogenous variables and diagonal covariance matrix Σ. The term "single equation or least square bias" became firmly implanted in the literature (Bronfenbrenner [1953]). The argument of single versus simultaneous system of equations estimators was launched and reasons were advanced why single equation techniques were or were not satisfactory for a wide variety of agricultural commodities or sectors (Bentzel and Hanson [1954], Fox [1953], Foote [1955a], G. Kuznets [1955]). Hood and Koopmans [1953] published their book on studies in econometrics, and Tintner [1952] and Klein [1953] published textbooks which gathered together the theory and practice of the techniques that today we call econometrics. Most economics and agricultural economics departments with an emphasis on graduate work introduced a course or courses in econometrics. "How to" handbooks appeared (Foote [1958], Friedman and Foote [1955]), and there was hardly an agricultural commodity that was not statistically analyzed as Hildreth and Jarrett [1955], Judge [1954], Nordin, Judge, and Wahby [1954], Fox [1951], Foote [1952, 1953a, 1953b, 1955b], E. J. Working [1954], Rojko [1953, 1957a, 1957b], Cromarty [1959a, 1959b, 1962], Meinken [1953, 1955], Harlow [1960], King [1958], Gerra [1959a, 1959b], Shuffett [1954], and many others (for example, Buchholz, Judge, and West [1962]) specified and estimated systems of equations. These econometric ventures, which involved systems of behavioral, technical, definitional, and institutional equations, did much to increase our understanding of the economic process and institutions underlying each of the agricultural sectors, the interactions among the agricultural sectors, and to a limited degree the interactions between the agricultural sector and the other sectors of the economy. In addition, the econometric results sometimes generated numbers that were useful for choice purposes at one or more of the structural decision-making levels. At the macro or economy level almost every major country had one or more simultaneous equation models constructed, estimated, and used, with perhaps the Dutch being the most conscientious in using econometric results for economic policy and planning purposes.

Chernoff and Divinsky [1953] specified the "full maximum likelihood method," which in contrast to the limited information system used information concerning the structure and data from all of the variables in the system. Unfortunately, since the estimating equations involved were nonlinear, with this procedure numerical methods had to be used for solution purposes, and in the 1950s the method was impractical.

As an alternative estimator for the parameters of an equation in a system of equations, Theil [1954] and Basmann [1957] proposed the generalized classical or two-stage least squares estimator, and Theil [1954] the k-class estimator. In this procedure an equation from the system of equations (2) was written as

(4a) $$y_j = [Y_j \; X_j] \begin{bmatrix} \gamma_j \\ B_j \end{bmatrix} + u_j = Z_j \delta_j + u_j$$

or equivalently as

$$(4b) \qquad y_j = [E(Y_j), X_j] \begin{bmatrix} \gamma_j \\ B_j \end{bmatrix} + (Y_j - E(Y_j)) \gamma_j + u_j.$$

Since the expectation operator makes the observation matrix $[E(Y_j), X_j]$ non-stochastic, the reduced form equation (3) may be used to estimate the unknown $E(Y_j)$ and then least squares may be applied to the resulting equation to yield a consistent estimator.

The addition of these estimators to the econometrician's tool chest meant that we had reached the stage of multiple parameters estimates for any given economic model, and just as early econometricians had asked the question "Which regression?" we now had to ask "Which estimator?" The choice of estimator question was a difficult one since for the system of equations estimators only the asymptotic properties were available, and many estimators were asymptotically equivalent. For economists who usually have to work with small samples of data, however, finite sample results are essential. In order to get some idea of the performance of the alternative estimators in finite samples, simulation or sampling experiments were proposed and carried through by Ladd [1957], Wagner [1958], Neiswanger and Yancey [1959], Summers [1965], and others for certain specialized models, some of which involved measurement and specification errors. The progress via this route was slow, and at its 1958 winter meetings the Econometric Society sponsored a panel discussion under the pleading title, "Simultaneous Equation Estimators—Any Verdict Yet?" At that time the final verdict was not in (and in some respects it still is not in). In the 1950s the electronic computer became a reality and put system of equations estimators within the reach of the individual researcher.

The decade of the 1940s made us acutely aware of the necessity for consistency between the assumptions underlying economic and statistical models. When models are correctly specified and sufficiently simple, statistical theory provides procedures for obtaining point and interval estimates and evaluating the performance of various linear estimators. Unfortunately, we seldom work with true models and a method was not available for drawing inferences based on "false" models. Because statistical theory provided inferential statements conditioned on true models and investigators in the main were working with false models, a large amount of effort was devoted to if-then types of questions: if relevant variables are omitted from an equation, what is the impact on the properties of the estimates and how will the inferences be distorted (Griliches [1957], Theil [1957])? If the disturbances are autocorrelated and, for example, the disturbance u_t of (1) follows a first-order autoregressive scheme $u_t = \rho u_{t-1} + e_t$ where e_t has mean zero and scalar identity covariance, how will the efficiency of the estimator be affected and how can we mitigate the impact of this specification error (Hildreth and Liu [1960], Cochrane and Orcutt [1949], Durbin and Watson [1950, 1951])? What is the inferential impact of not fulfilling the assumption of the disturbances being identically (homoscedasticity) as well as independently distributed? What are the implications of stochastic rather than fixed regressors? What are the statistical implications of using variables that contain a measurement error (Durbin [1954])?

Since some progress was being made in formulating statistical models to cope with the simultaneous and stochastic nature of economic data, attention was directed to the dynamic aspects of economic models and data. The question of how to specify models consistent with the dynamic characteristics of economic data led to the consideration of the autoregressive case and the specification of somewhat ad hoc distributed lag economic models based on vague notions such as inertia and habit formation and their attendant problems of estimation. The work of Koyck [1954], Cagan [1956], and Nerlove [1958a, 1958b, 1958c] stand out in this development and their formulations led to the application of the distributed lag model (Nerlove and Addison [1958]) with emphasis on estimating the short-run and long-run parameters of behavior patterns. The conventional distributed lag model as a variant of (1) may be written as

$$(5a) \qquad y_t = \beta \sum_{j=0}^{\infty} \lambda^j x_{t-j} + u_t$$

where $|\lambda| < 1$. Subtracting from (5a), λy_{t-1}, yields

$$(5b) \qquad y_t = \beta x_t + \lambda y_{t-1} + u_t - \lambda u_{t-1},$$

which is used for estimation purposes. This result, (5b), is also consistent with the behavioral hypothesis of adaptive expectations. There were several techniques for estimating β and λ (for example, Koyck [1954] and Klein [1958]), some of which were not consistent or asymptotically efficient. The practical difficulties of distinguishing between different lag schemes when using nonexperimental data were early recognized and to a large extent the problem still exists today.

In the demand area, in addition to the commodity analyses already alluded to, Stone [1954] estimated a system of expenditure functions which satisfied various theoretical conditions, Frisch [1959] developed a scheme for computing cross elasticities of substitution, and Brandow [1961] completed his work concerned with the interrelations among demands for farm products. There was a feeling during this decade, well expressed by T. W. Schultz, that we had made more progress in capturing the parameters of demand relations than had been made with those for supply relations. This realization generated a flurry of activity led by W. Cochrane [1955], Nerlove [1958c], and others, and the debate of positive versus normative supply response functions began.

Questions relating to the economic and statistical impact of using aggregate economic data and relations have an early origin and intuitively most analysts feel that aggregation involves a loss of information. An important work in this area was the book by Theil [1954], *Linear Aggregation of Economic Relations*, in which he dealt with the problem of interpreting the parameters of macro relations estimated from aggregate data, when the observed data are generated from a set of micro relations. One of his major results, assuming the micro coefficients are constant, was that when macro variables are obtained by simple aggregation (the aggregate result postulated to hold independently of the micro relations), the expectation of the macro coefficient estimator will depend on a complicated combination of corresponding and noncorresponding micro coefficients. This result may be seen in terms of (1) by writing the micro statistical model as

$$(6a) \qquad y_i = X_i \beta_i + u_i, \text{ for } i = 1,2 \ldots,N,$$

where the usual definitions hold for y_i, X_i and u_i. If by simple aggregation we use the macro variables $Y = \frac{1}{N} \sum_i y_i$ and $\chi = \frac{1}{N} \sum_i X_i$, the statistical model $Y = \chi\beta + u$, with usual definitions for the variables and the least squares estimator, then

$$(6b) \qquad E(\hat{\beta}) = E[(\chi'\chi)^{-1}\chi'Y] = (\chi'\chi)^{-1}\chi'(\frac{1}{N}\sum_i X_i\beta_i) \neq \frac{1}{N}\sum_i \beta_i.$$

Given this result, Theil [1954] raised the question of whether we should abolish the macro models and estimates. Alternatively, Klein [1953] showed that when the macro and micro relations are derived so that they are consistent, then the macro variables are weighted averages of the micro coefficients. If the weights are stable over time, then no aggregation bias results. The usual case, however, is for the weights to change over time. Grunfeld and Griliches [1960] answered no to the question "Is aggregation necessarily bad?" but the outcome was as many had suspected—the question should have been answered yes (Zellner [1962b]). It is interesting to note that in spite of the discouraging words of Theil, Klein, and Zellner, during the 1950s macroeconometric model building and estimation continued at full pace.

Given the questionable virtue of the macro data, in the 1950s much effort by persons such as Orcutt, Greenberger, Korbel, and Rivlin [1961] went into specifying a framework for and actually generating more complete micro data over time. Data panels and banks were set up and sample surveys were conducted to capture these data. From the point of view of estimation, this expanded data base made it imperative to develop estimating methods which would permit the combining of cross-section and time series data. In the 1950s covariance analysis, usually through the use of dummy (zero-one) variables, provided the major estimating technique, although extraneous estimators were being talked about and actually applied by Tobin [1950] and others.

Much econometric activity in estimating production and cost functions was evident during this decade. Heady and Baker [1954], in an article on resource adjustments to equate productivities in agriculture, exemplified the techniques employed in estimating the parameters of aggregate production and the uses to which they were put. Swanson [1956], in an article concerned with the optimum size of business, gave a good example of some of the problems of empirical production function analysis. Hoch [1958], Mundlak [1961], and others investigated the sampling properties of conventional parameter estimates of production functions for total farm or nonexperimental situations. Assuming that the income share accruing to each production factor is equal or proportionate to the respective output elasticity, Solow [1957] estimated (and started the debate about how to measure) the impact of technical progress on output or growth.

Concern over the richness of macro data or relations also raised questions about the necessity of generating data via controlled experiments. Within this context it was realized by Heady and Dillon [1961] and others that, in estimating production functions, if we were to trace out the parameters of the production surface in order to estimate isoproduct and production possibility relations, data from controlled experiments would be necessary. This generated work on the appropriate experimental design to employ (Heady and Dillon [1961]) and the actual applications of these designs to generate the experimental data.

At about the same time many questions were being raised about the use of passively generated data in estimating the parameters of price-consumption response relations. This led Godwin [1952], Brunk [1958], Franzmann and Judge [1957], and others to design and carry out controlled experiments in retail markets and to develop parameter estimates for an array of commodity response relations. Questions about the generalizability of these results to a wider range of data were raised, and by the end of the decade the generation and use of experimental price-consumption data trended downward.

Friedman [1957] put forth his permanent income hypothesis and separated income and consumption for behavior purposes into the unobservable permanent and transitory components. Houthakker [1958], Eisner [1958], Nerlove [1958d], and others investigated the implications of this framework and how to measure these nonobservable variables and to test the permanent income hypothesis in Friedman's consumption function model.

Given the development in the 1950s of various linear and nonlinear decision and simulation models under certainty and uncertainty (Batchelor [1959-64]) and the evolution of operations research and management science, the need for hard quantitative knowledge at all structural decision levels was emphasized and econometrics started serving these new masters.

In spite of the rapid pace of developments in theory and application, econometrics was, as the decade ended, an essay in persuasion. The alternative choices or permutations regarding the model, method, and data facing an investigator were many (Booth and Judge [1956]), and in many cases one had the feeling in reading an article or bulletin that the investigator had searched over a variety of models, methods, and data to find a set of numbers satisfying a theory or his own intuition. In some examples of data dredging the investigator reported many alternative results and in a sense appealed to the reader to make a choice among the possibilities. In the 1950s, as in the 1940s, economists interested in agriculture took the lead in applying and sharpening the new and old econometric tools. Many of these results were seldom if ever used for decision purposes.

The Decade of the 1960s

If the role of the economic model (the prototype of the sampling model that generated the data) in determining appropriate statistical models became evident in the 1940s and 1950s, the 1960s made us aware of the necessity of developing statistical models which (1) provide systematic ways of combining sample and a priori information and (2) are appropriate for economic decision problems—the fruit of an idea introduced by Wald [1950] in the 1940s. As some have implied, in a sense the respectability of probability as a state of mind was reestablished. It was suggested that if econometric models are constructed and estimated as a source of information for decision making or choice, the theory of statistical decision, based on an analysis of losses due to incorrect decisions, can and should be used. In addition, it was argued that, since nonexperimental observations are the main data source of the economist, the criterion of using performance in repeated trials, and thus, unobserved samples as a basis for rationalizing sampling theory approaches, should be questioned.

For economic data, which are by and large nonexperimental in nature, the statistical decision theory problem is that of making the "best" decision on the basis of a given set of data, when θ, the true state of the world (parameter), is unknown. A number of solutions have been proposed and used for this statistical decision problem. Traditionally, the class of decision rules (estimators) is typically restricted to those that are linear and unbiased, and in conventional estimation theory where a quadratic loss function is assumed, this approach leads to minimum variance unbiased estimators. In spite of the near godly stature of unbiasedness that one gets from economic literature, the notion of unbiasedness, although intuitively plausible, is an arbitrary restriction and has no connection with the loss due to incorrect decisions and is thus unsatisfactory from a decision theory point of view. In any event, as the decision theorists note, the conventional sampling theory approach does not always lead to an optimal decision rule (estimator) and, as W. Fisher [1962] and Zellner [1972] have shown, may not in some cases satisfy even certain minimal properties.

As a means of facing up to some of these objections, the use of Bayes's rule for handling inference and decision problems was revived and developed in the 1960s. If we let $p(y,\theta)$ denote the joint probability density function of the observation vector y and the parameter vector θ and use the definition of conditional probability for y and θ which implies $p(\theta/y)p(y) = p(y/\theta)p(\theta)$, we may write the posterior probability density function for the parameter vector θ, given the sample information as

(7) $p(\theta|y) = p(y|\theta)p(\theta)/p(y) \propto p(y|\theta)p(y)$

where α denotes proportionality. Equation (7) is a statement of Bayes's rule or the principle of inverse probability, and in this approach the decision maker's prior information about the state of the world or parameter θ is combined with the sample information y to make the "best decision." Within the context of (7) it is assumed that the investigator's information or uncertainty about some parameter θ can be summarized in a prior probability function $p(\theta)$. This information is then combined with the sample density function $p(y|\theta)$ to yield a posterior probability density function $p(\theta|y)$. Then, given a loss function, say $L = L(\theta,\hat{\theta})$, which reflects the losses due to an incorrect estimation, the Bayesian choice of a point estimate $\hat{\theta}$ is the one that minimizes the expected loss, where the posterior distribution of θ is used in the expectation, i.e.,

(8) $\underset{\hat{\theta}}{\text{Min}}\ E[L(\hat{\theta},\theta)] = \underset{\hat{\theta}}{\text{Min}} \int L(\hat{\theta},\theta)p(\theta|y)d\theta.$

Thus, the posterior probability density function combines both prior and sample information, and it is this distribution which is employed in estimation and to make inferences about the parameters.

Given this framework and building on the work of Jeffreys [1961] and Savage [1954], Raiffa and Schlaifer [1961], Drèze [1962], and Zellner [1971] and his associates developed a Bayesian formulation of the regression model with extensions to cover the problems of autocorrelated erros, distributed lags, errors in the variables, prediction and decision, and multiple equation systems. One problem of applying Bayesian decision theory is the need to find a set of prior distributions rich enough to incorporate the investigator's knowledge but simple enough to be algebraically tractable. Modern methods of numerical analysis, however, have done much to change the definition of what is tractable. Much of the theory and practice of Bayesian inference in econometrics which took place in the sixties has been summarized in a recent book by Zellner [1971], and some of the elements of the debate still raging between the Bayesians and the non-Bayesians are contained in articles by Zellner [1972] and Rothenberg [1972]. One major restriction on the application of Bayesian estimation and inference procedures to variants of the linear statistical model is the almost complete nonavailability of viable computer programs.

Within the spirit of combining prior and sample information, several sampling theory estimators were developed for the regression model, and the alternative specifications have been analyzed and applied:

(i) When the prior knowledge concerning an individual or group of coefficient(s) is exact in nature, for the linear regression statistical model (1), this external information or hypothesis may appear as $R\beta = r$, where R is a $(J \times K)$ matrix of known elements with rank J and r is a $(J \times 1)$ vector of known elements (hypotheses). Under this specification the methods and test statistics proposed by Wilks [1947], Tintner [1940], and Chipman and Rao [1964] may be employed. Either the conventional likelihood ratio test or the Toro-Vizcarrondo and Wallace [1968] or Wallace [1972] tests may be used with this model for deciding when, under a mean square error or squared error loss criterion, the restricted least squares estimator on possibly incorrect, although exact, prior information is superior to the conventional estimator using only sample data.

(ii) If the prior information on an individual coefficient or group of coefficients is of a statistical nature, the stochastic linear hypotheses or prior information may be specified for statistical model (1) as $r = R\beta + v$, where r is a $(J \times 1)$ mean vector of known constants, R is a $(J \times K)$ matrix of known constants, v is a $(J \times 1)$ unobservable normally distributed random vector with mean δ, which is usually assumed to be zero, and covariance $\sigma^2 v$. Under this specification, i.e., stochastic linear hypotheses with known finite mean and variance, the methods and test statistics proposed by Durbin [1953], Theil and Goldberger [1961], and Theil [1963], which make use of Aitken's generalized least squares technique, may be employed to estimate the parameters and test the compatibility of the prior and sample information. It should be noted that this estimator yields the same results as the mean of the limiting distribution for the Bayesian formulation assuming a locally uniform prior for β and σ^2.

(iii) When the prior knowledge is less complete and information exists only in the form of inequality restraints, $R\beta \leq r$, where all symbols have been previously defined, one possibility when placing a prior upper and lower bound on a coefficient is to specify a mean and variance for the parameter which would give a very low probability to values outside this range. Under this specification, the resulting information could be used in the same way as Theil and Goldberger [1961] use prior knowledge of a statistical type and Aitken's generalized least squares estimator could be applied. Alternatively, when the prior information consists of linear inequality restraints on the individual coefficients or combinations thereof, following Zellner [1963] and Judge and Takayama [1966], the problem may be specified and solved as a quadratic programming problem. The minimum absolute deviations (linear programming) estimator whose properties have been analyzed by Ashar and Wallace [1963], Blattberg and Sargent [1971], and Smith and Hall [1972] is still another alternative specification for handling the linear inequality parameter restriction problem.

These Bayesian and non-Bayesian formulations (Judge and Yancey [1969]) permit the investigator to take account of prior information about the unknown parameters that exist via the routes of postulation, experimentation, or "revelation." When a certain minimum amount of information is available concerning the structure of the relation(s), these estimators, either through restrictions or other outside information, may offer one way of coping with the troublesome problem of multicollinearity. The sampling properties of the inequality restricted least squares estimator are yet to be established, but initial Monte Carlo sampling studies, such as those by Thornber [1967] and Lee, Judge, and Zellner [1970], yield encouraging results relative to its performance. Both the Bayesian and sampling theory estimating methods can handle the cases for a multivariate regression system and a simultaneous equation system.

In deriving new estimators during the decades of the 1950s and 1960s the standard practice appears to have been: (1) to change the statistical model, (2) to change the prior information or the way to use prior information, or (3) to change the loss function or measure of goodness. Although not all of the inferential and philosophical problems in this area were solved in the 1960s, these procedures appear to offer promise in our search for "optimum" estimators and suggest systematic ways for proceeding as we attempt to learn from experience and data.

In the early 1960s Graybill's book [1961] on linear statistical models was published and provided the theoretical base and format for the econometric texts of this era. The volumes by Johnston [1963] and Goldberger [1964] were the two outstanding textbooks of the period, and their appearance along with other econometric texts had much impact on the quality of instruction and the level of the econometric sophistication of students.

In the 1960s systems analysis and control theory provided a framework for combining into one package automatic or adaptive control, estimation, prediction, and some utility functional or optimality criterion (Pontryagin et al. [1962], Aoki [1967]) and thus the possible joining of optimization, estimation, and the design of experiments. These methods, especially in the discrete form, suggested, for example, ways to deal with the effects of lags and uncertainty on the conduct of stabilization policy and permitted one basis for following up the early contributions of Phillips [1954]. Bayesian methods, as outlined by W. Fisher [1962], Zellner and Geisel [1968], and Prescott [1967] provide a systematic way of handling control problems since they permit optimal, computable solutions which use both prior and past sample information, take account of uncertainty about parameter values, make use of new information as it becomes available, and, in an experimental design sense, provide a basis for making settings for the control variables.

Meanwhile in the area of classical sampling theory Zellner and Theil [1962], within the two-stage least squares framework, specified the system of simultaneous equations as

$$(9) \quad \begin{bmatrix} y_1 \\ y_2 \\ \cdot \\ \cdot \\ \cdot \\ y_G \end{bmatrix} = \begin{bmatrix} Z_1 & 0 & \dots & 0 \\ 0 & Z_2 & & 0 \\ \cdot & & \cdot & \\ \cdot & & & \cdot \\ 0 & 0 & \dots & Z_G \end{bmatrix} \begin{bmatrix} \delta_1 \\ \delta_2 \\ \cdot \\ \cdot \\ \cdot \\ \delta_G \end{bmatrix} + \begin{bmatrix} u_1 \\ u_2 \\ \cdot \\ \cdot \\ \cdot \\ u_G \end{bmatrix} \quad \text{or} \quad y = Z\delta + u,$$

where $Z_j = [Y_j, X_j]$ and $\delta_j = [\gamma_j, \beta_j]$ were defined in conjunction with (4). Each u_j is assumed to have a zero mean vector with the conventional covariance $E[u_j u_k'] = \sigma_{jk} I$ and covariance matrix $E[uu'] = X \otimes I$, where $\otimes$ represents the Kronecker product symbol. With proper transformations relative to the system of equations (9), involving X, the observation matrix of all of the exogenous and predetermined variables in the system, and use of the Aitken least squares procedure applied to the resulting set of equations, Zellner and Theil [1962] developed the three-stage least squares estimator

$$(10) \quad \hat{\delta} = [Z'(\Sigma^{-1} \otimes X(X'X)^{-1}X')Z]^{-1} Z'(\Sigma^{-1} \otimes X(X'X)^{-1}X')y.$$

Since Σ is normally unknown, Zellner and Theil suggested estimating it from the two-stage least squares residuals. It should perhaps be noted that two-stage least squares is nothing more than the application of Aitken's generalized least squares to (9), when the equations are appropriately transformed, and three-stage least squares involves the double application of the Aitken generalized least squares procedure.

Nagar [1962] widened the class of system of equations estimators to include the double k-class variety. Rothenberg and Leenders [1964] developed the method of linearized maximum likelihood and investigated some properties of the alternative system of equations estimators. Several Monte Carlo sampling studies (Cragg [1966, 1967, 1968], Summers [1965]) and analytical studies (Basmann [1957, 1965], Dhrymes [1965], Kabe [1964], Richardson [1968], Sawa [1969], Madansky [1964]) were completed, and we have gradually learned a little more about the finite sample properties of alternative system of equations estimators. The debate on the appropriate statistical model and methods for prediction purposes was fed by Waugh's provocative article [1961] on the place of least squares in econometrics.

Shortly before and to some extent in conjunction with his three-stage least squares work, Zellner [1962a] formulated an Aitken type estimator for handling the following sets of regression equations of the form of (1):

$$
(11) \quad
\begin{bmatrix} y_1 \\ y_2 \\ . \\ . \\ . \\ y_M \end{bmatrix}
=
\begin{bmatrix}
X_1 & 0 & \dots & 0 \\
0 & X_2 & \dots & 0 \\
. & & & . \\
. & & & . \\
. & & & . \\
0 & 0 & \dots & X_M
\end{bmatrix}
\begin{bmatrix} \beta_1 \\ \beta_2 \\ . \\ . \\ . \\ \beta_M \end{bmatrix}
+
\begin{bmatrix} u_1 \\ u_2 \\ . \\ . \\ . \\ u_M \end{bmatrix}
$$

where the equations are disturbance related with a covariance matrix consistent with (9) and the regressors vary over equations. For this seemingly unrelated regression model Zellner developed a test for aggregation bias and some small sample properties.

Work continued on how to detect and mitigate such specification errors as autocorrelation and heteroscedasticity and even the old multicollinearity problem took on new interest. In particular, Lancaster [1968], Goldfeld and Quandt [1965], Glejser [1969], and Rutemiller and Bowers [1968] advanced the topic of estimation in a heteroscedastic regression model; Koerts [1967], Theil [1965, 1968], Kadiyala [1968], Durbin [1970a, 1970b], Tiao and Zellner [1964], and Rao and Griliches [1969] contributed procedures and tests for autocorrelation; Farrar and Glauber [1967], Silvey [1969], and Toro-Vizcarrondo and Wallace [1968] contributed procedures and tests for handling multicollinearity.

Interest in and use of some of the multivariate techniques developed in the 1930s was revived. Discriminant analysis and linear probability functions which permit the measurement of the effect of continuous variables on group membership were reviewed by Ladd [1966] and were used, for example, by Ladd [1967] to analyze the objectives of fluid milk cooperatives, by Adelman and Morris [1968] to explore the forces affecting a country's prospects for development, and by J. Fisher [1962] to study the purchase of durable goods. Factor analysis and principal components, inductive procedures that are used to develop (among other things) hypotheses from data, were reviewed by Scott [1966] and used by Baumer, Brandt, Jacobson, and Walker [1969] to study psychological and attitudinal differences between milk purchasers, and by Massey, Frank, and Lodahl [1968] to study various measures of consumer purchasing power.

In regard to enriching the data base by using both time series and cross-section data, Balestra and Nerlove [1966], Mundlak [1961], Wallace and Hussain [1969], and Maddala [1971] specified a components of error model whereby the regression error is assumed to be composed of three independent components—one with time, one with the cross-section, and one overall component in both the time and cross-section dimensions. Nerlove [1971] investigated, by Monte Carlo procedures, the properties of various estimators within this context and proposed a two-round estimation procedure. Chetty [1968] reformulated the cross-section/time series problem along Bayesian lines. Swamy [1971], in contrast to conventional fixed coefficient models, recognized the heterogeneity of behavior among individuals and over time (i.e., the invariance of parameter systems), by developing the random coefficient statistical model and analyzed estimation procedures for it. Within the framework of the conventional linear statistical model (1) this model may be written as

$$(12) \qquad y_i = X_i(\bar{\beta} + \eta_i) + u_i, \text{ for } i = 1, 2, \ldots, N,$$

where $\bar{\beta}$ is the mean vector of the unknown coefficients, the η_i are additive independent and identical distributed random variables with mean zero and covariance σ^2 if $i = i'$ and zero otherwise. Hildreth and Houck [1968] and Griffiths [1970] extended the results of a variant of this statistical model. Zellner [1967] analyzed the statistical implications of the aggregation problem within the context of the random coefficient statistical model.

In classical estimation and inference in econometrics a population is postulated which is assumed to be characterized by a density function whose parameters are unknown but fixed. A sample of observations is captured and used as the basis for estimation and statistical inferences about the unknown parameters. In economics one frequently encounters a situation where the sample consists of single observations on different random variables. A sequence of such random variables is called a stochastic process and spectral analysis consists of examining various aspects of the stochastic process when its random variables have been given a representation in the frequency domain. This tool of frequency domain analysis, which has also been referred to under topics such as harmonic, Fourier, and periodogram analysis, is based on the idea of decomposing a stochastic process into a number of orthogonal components, each of which is associated with a given frequency (Granger and Hatanaka [1964], Nerlove [1964], Fishman [1969]). These methods are in general possible when the variance and covariances are time independent. Cross-spectral methods which deal with relations between variables are of great importance to economists but at this time are the least developed. Since modern computers can easily handle these techniques, a large number of researchers have made use of spectral procedures in the time series modeling of economic phenomena (Dhrymes [1971, pp. 383-484]), and spectral methods have been extended to such areas as estimating time domain distributed lag models (Dhrymes [1971, pp. 263-325], Fishman [1969]) and evaluating the dynamic properties of structural systems of equations (Howrey [1971]). Rausser and Cargill [1970] give a survey of spectral analysis, discuss its relationship to Fourier and periodogram analysis, and apply the procedures to the study of broiler cycles.

The distributed lag or autoregressive model (5) with moving average error continued to enjoy considerable use in empirical work. Fuller and Martin [1961] considered a distributed lag model with autocorrelated errors and suggested a consistent estimator. Griliches [1967] surveyed the work in this area during the 1950s and early 1960s, concentrating his emphasis on estimating distributed lags in the form of difference equations. Since this time emphasis has shifted to estimation of distributed lags under more general stochastic assumptions about the disturbance (Hannan [1967], Amemiya and Fuller [1967], Dhrymes [1971], Fishman [1969], Hall [1971], Jorgenson [1966]), constraining the lag function to belong to a family controlled by a few parameters (parametrization) and/or treating the least squares estimates so that adjacent lag coefficients lie close to one another (smoothing). In the linear parametrization area the idea of fitting polynomials to a series of coefficients, which can be dated back to Irving Fisher, was identified as the pre-Almon [1965] approach and became the dominant method of modern empirical work in distributed lags. The work of Ladd and Tedford [1959] reflects one pre-Almon application of this procedure in the agricultural economics literature. An alternative to making exact parametric restrictions is a probabilistic (Bayesian) characterization of the lag distribution which has been proposed by Leamer [1970] and Shiller [1970]. In closing this discussion we should note the work of Box and Jenkins [1970] on time series models from the class of discrete linear stochastic processes of integrated autoregressive moving average form and the work of Aigner [1971b] in integrating this work with that of econometrics. The autoregressive moving average (ARMA) model may be written as

(13) $$y_t = \phi_1 y_{t-1} + \phi_2 y_{t-2} + \ldots + \phi_p y_{t-p} + u_t + \theta_1 u_{t-1} + \ldots + \theta_q u_{t-q},$$

where y_t is a stochastic process defined on integral time points and generated autoregressively. The residual in (13) is defined as a moving average of well-behaved random variables, u_{t-j}, which are assumed to be identically and independently distributed. The regression function (13) is used in estimating the parameters of the y_t process. Estimation techniques permit a y_t process which is both stationary and nonstationary to be accommodated. An early application of this procedure in the form of a multiplicative seasonal model, by Leuthold [1970], provided the basis for evaluating forecasts of a structural model of the hog market.

The econometric dimensions of the consumer's problem of how to allocate income to M commodities, given prices and income, was pushed forward on the theoretical, estimation, and testing fronts. Some of the major econometric contributors to the problem of estimation of demand parameters under consumer budgeting that give empirical content to the ideas of Frisch [1959], Gorman [1959], and Strotz [1959] include Barten [1968], Theil [1967, 1971], DeJanvry, Bieri, and Nuñez [1972], Powell [1966], and Boutwell and Simmons [1968].

One important activity in the 1960s was the econometric study of investment behavior which developed from empirical comparisons of alternative determinants of producer behavior. This work is important here since it has provided an important basis for the development of new econometric techniques for representing the time structure of economic behavior. Some of the contributors in this area include Meyer and Kuh [1957], Eisner and Strotz [1963], Griliches, Modigliani, Grunfeld, and especially Jorgenson [1971].

The dynamic and stochastic nature of economic data led several writers to suggest that economic observations may be viewed as being generated by a stochastic process—that is, a process that develops in time or space according to probabilistic laws. This proposition led to the use of a first-order stationary Markov process as the appropriate probability model when the observation at any time is the category in which an observation falls. The object of this type of analysis is to use the time-ordered movements of micro data as a basis for estimating the transition probability system where the transition probabilities p_{ij}, which are associated with a change from state i (s_i) to state j (s_j) for the discrete random variable X_t (t = 0,1,2, . . .,T) are generated under the assumption that $X_{t-1} = s_i$ and $X_t = s_j$, and

(14) $$\Pr(X_t = s_j | X_{t-1} = s_i) = P_{ij}(t) = P_{ij}, \text{ for all } t.$$

The parameters of the probability system, the P_{ij}, are used as a basis for summarizing the dynamic characteristics of the data, predicting future outcomes and the long-run equilibrium of the system. This type of model has found many applications ranging from the work of Goodman [1965] on gauging social mobility to that of Adelman [1958], Judge and Swanson [1962], Preston and Bell [1961], Steindl [1965], and Hallberg [1969] on the size distribution of firms. One problem in making use of this model is that in many cases the data for the micro units are not available and only their aggregate counterparts (proportions in each state) exist. In order to use the aggregate data as a basis for estimating the behavior system for the micro data (transition probabilities), Miller [1952] and later Telser [1963] formulated the problem within the least squares framework and assumed the sample observations were generated by the following stochastic relation:

$$(15) \qquad X_j(t) = \sum_i X_i(t-1) P_{ij} + u_j(t), \text{ for } i, j = 1, 2, \ldots, r.$$

Building on this work Lee, Judge, and Zellner [1970] developed restricted least squares, maximum likelihood and Bayesian estimators of the transition probabilities. Simulated sampling studies with these estimators have shown that each of the estimators perform well when the aggregate data are generated by a first-order Markov process, although the Bayesian estimator, using a multivariate beta prior, appears to yield the best performance.

Growth theory received much emphasis during the decade of the 1960s and since the aggregate production function, which expresses the basic relationship among output, employment, and capital stock, is the engine for most of the models searching for the golden rule of accumulation, this relation provided the basis for a large number of studies on technical change and growth. As a replacement for the Cobb-Douglas specification which implies a unitary elasticity of substitution between the factors, Arrow, Chenery, Minhas, and Solow [1961] proposed the constant elasticity of substitution (CES) production function

$$(16) \qquad Z = [\beta K^{-\rho} + \alpha L^{-\rho}]^{h/\rho} u,$$

where Z is output, K is capital, and L is labor, which permitted the elasticity of substitution to lie between zero and one; Dhrymes [1965] developed statistical tests for the CES production function; Revankar [1966] proposed a generalized production function which permits variable returns to scale; and Newman and Read [1961] and Ferguson and Pfouts [1962] proposed a production function that would permit variable factor shares. These specifications result in relations which are nonlinear functions of the parameter, and conventional estimation methods fail because alternative estimators lead to the problem of solving a system of nonlinear equations. Because of this result, various attempts have been made to circumvent the problem of nonlinear estimation methods (Kmenta [1967], Bodkin and Klein [1967], and Tsang [1971]). Aigner and Chu [1968] questioned the conventional rationale used in estimating the parameters of production functions and developed and applied procedures for estimating the frontier of a production function. Meanwhile, the old problems of multicollinearity, aggregation bias, specification error, how to isolate the impacts of management and technical progress, and the question of the meaning to be attached to the parameters of macro production functions were still unsolved.

During the 1960s interest and work continued in the area of macroeconometric models (Nerlove [1966], Hallberg [1972]) and produced such outcomes as the SSRC-Brookings (Griliches [1968]), FRB-MIT-Penn (Rasche and Shapiro [1968]), and St. Louis (Anderson and Carlson [1970]) specifications. The first two of these models entailed the cooperative efforts of the theorist, applied economist, statistician, mathematician, and computer scientist in the job of model specification, estimation, and modeling. These models involved several industrial sectors, of which agriculture was one, and the national income accounting and input-output systems were combined in the specification. Thus, these efforts continued the tendency to increase the size of the macroeconometric models by a finer disaggregation of the major macro variables. Monetary sectors were added as monetary policy became more in vogue. Nonlinear systems were estimated and solved. As a sign of the times in terms of working with these econometric models, Zellner [1970a] did a paper on "The Care and Feeding of Econometric Models." The macroeconometric models were used by Goldberger [1959], Evans and Klein [1967], Fromm and Taubman [1968], and others for ex ante forecasting. Perhaps it should be noted at this point that there are three equivalent forms for a given econometric model. The structural and reduced form equation alternatives are well known and the reduced form is more convenient that the structural equations for calculating the effects of the exogenous changes on the endogenous variables. When lagged endogenous variables appear in the model, the reduced form equations are not sufficient for impact analysis purposes, and Theil and Boot [1962] use equations which are obtained by eliminating all lagged endogenous variables from the reduced form. This leads to what they term impact, interim, and total multipliers that may be used in describing the generation of the endogenous variables.

As the models got bigger, the debate between the big and the small specifications gathered steam. Within this context Cooper and Nelson [1971] compared the FRB-MIT Penn 171-equation model, the St. Louis 8-equation model, and the simple Box-Jenkins autoregressive moving average model for ex post and ex ante prediction of six endogenous variables and found that no single model or predictor could be said to dominate the others. Given this result, they suggested a convex combination of the estimates as one superior alternative. However, the debate continues, and Klein [1971] and others talk of models in the 1,000-equation range. The timid during this period continued to ask where one is to get the data base to support the parameter space for these larger and larger ventures. Unfortunately, they were not swamped with either the data or the answers to the query. At this stage, perhaps the greatest payoff is, as it was in the 1950s, in the building of the models and the identification of conceptual, data, estimation, and nonlinear system solution needs.

One break from the past, where it was conventional to toss econometric results to the masses with a plea for their use by somebody, at some place, and at some time, was to set up and carry through simulation experiments in order to see if the outcomes of the estimated systems were consistent with observed behavior and expected results. This further testing of our models through modeling did much to improve the usefulness of the results and raise the interesting philosophical question of whether simulation procedures, which iterate on parameter systems, may not be one meaningful way to capture unknown parameters or systems. Elsewhere in this volume Johnson and Rausser discuss some of the formal attempts to estimate unknown parameters on the basis of simulated results. Much of the macroeconometric estimation and modeling was made possible by advances in computer technology. What seemed beyond the reach of estimation and analysis in the 1940s and 1950s became accepted practice in the 1960s.

Since the econometric machine runs on data, we will close this section by noting that as the 1960s ended we were well on our way to creating large data banks of economic statistics, using remote access computer consoles, and we were starting to discuss seriously and to design large-scale controlled experiments as a basis for understanding existing or potential economic processes and institutions.

The First Half of the 1970s

As the decade of the 1970s began, the rapid pace of econometric developments started in the 1940s and 1950s continued. Methods for estimating economic relations and testing economic hypotheses were refined and extended. The use of Bayesian estimation and inference in econometrics was firmly established and no longer had to be justified anew each time it was mentioned or applied. Many schools introduced Bayesian techniques in their econometric and economic theory courses. From an applications standpoint the lack of computer programs to handle the various data-generating processes and marginal prior densities still remained, although work currently under way at the University of Chicago (Zellner) and the Center for Operations Research and Econometrics (Drèze) will narrow if not eliminate this gap. Recent contributions to Bayesian inference in econometrics were summarized in a book (in honor of Savage) edited by Fienberg and Zellner [1974]. Several econometric texts were completed (Theil [1971], Kmenta [1971], Dhrymes [1970], Malinvaud [1970], Walters [1970], Johnston [1971], Aigner [1971a], and others), and in contrast to the situation in the 1950s the teacher and student have almost unlimited material for texts and references.

Analytical work concerning the finite sample properties of systems of equations estimators made headway in a number of special cases. Sawa [1972] evaluated the finite sample moments of the k-class estimators for $0 \leqslant k \leqslant 1$ and developed numerical calculations of the mean square error and the bias for specific cases. Mariano [1972, 1973] obtained necessary and sufficient conditions for the existence of even moments of the two-stage least squares estimator and approximated the distribution function of the two-stage least squares estimator up to the terms whose order of magnitude are $1/\sqrt{n}$, where n is the sample size, Mariano and Sawa [1972] developed the exact finite sample distribution of the limited information maximum likelihood estimator when the structural equation being estimated contains two endogenous variables and is identifiable in a complete system of linear stochastic equations. Hendry [1976] explored the possibility that a simple formula could be obtained which encompassed most systems of equations and emphasized close similarities in the face of apparent diversities. Hendry concluded that most simultaneous equation estimators are really only different numerical methods for solving an expression for the full information estimator. This result helps to clarify the asymptotic equivalences of the various estimators, while permitting the alternative numerical variants to yield very different finite sample properties.

Within the context of the classical linear regression model the detection of autocorrelated errors continued to be a matter of concern, and new test statistics were proposed which had the advantage of having distributions independent of the design matrix. Durbin [1970a, 1970b] developed a test wherein the residuals are based on estimates of the parameters obtained from a derived set of regressors. Abrahamse and Louter [1971] developed a test statistic based on a new class of estimators for the disturbance vector. Berenblut and Webb [1973] developed what they called a g test statistic which is more powerful than the Durbin and Watson [1951] test for high values of autocorrelation. The tables in Durbin and Watson [1951] can be used in making the bounds for the new statistic. Smith [1973] reviewed sampling studies of autocorrelation and distribution lag models and concluded that most of the techniques used are comparable in their performance patterns for small samples.

Box and Jenkins [1970] techniques for time series analysis were applied and evaluated, and one of the interesting and promising developments in the area centered around the analysis of dynamic simultaneous equation models within the context of general linear multiple time series processes. Zellner and Palm [1973], building on the idea that if a set of variables is generated by a multiple time series process it is often possible to solve for the processes generating individual variables, showed that if a multiple time series process is appropriately specified we can obtain the usual dynamic simultaneous equation model in structural form and then the associated reduced form and transfer functions can be derived.

Interest in optimal decisions under uncertainty continued to grow at an exponential rate and econometricians constructed models of markets in which participants act optimally over time subject to uncertainty. A survey article by Nerlove [1972] demonstrated both the level of interest and unsolved problems faced by researchers in this area. In the theory of the firm the firm's forecasts of prices play a role in generating an actual series of equilibrium prices, and it was this point that led Muth [1961] to define a rational expectation forecasting rule where the probability distribution of anticipated prices is the same as those actually generated by anticipations. Lucas and Prescott [1971] assumed that expectations of firms are rational in that anticipated price at time t is the same function of the random disturbances as is the actual price. Grossman [1975] synthesized the rational expectations theory with Bayesian econometric theory to develop econometric models of competitive markets subject to uncertainty and derived optimal estimators of the parameters of the Cobb-Douglas production function and the equilibrium predictor of future prices. Rausser [1971] and Just [1972] formally incorporated variables associated with risk and uncertainty in the estimation of lag relationships pertaining to investment behavior and/or supply response. Lucas and Prescott [1974] applied these procedures in the equilibrium search and unemployment area. Obviously work that is going on in this area has important implications for specifying econometric models under uncertainty and for econometric forecasting.

In most econometric models it is customary to assume that the parameters are stationary or time invariant. Most economic systems are not time constant, however, and the response parameters do change over time. The time varying parameter problem received much attention in the early 1970s under the following three main theoretical structures: random coefficient models, systematic nonrandom variation models, and Kalman-filter models. In 1973 the National Bureau of Economic Research sponsored a symposium on time varying parameter structures, and the papers were published in the October 1973 issue of the *Annals of Economic and Social Measurement*. The procedures discussed in the various papers offer much that can improve the econometrician's approach to the fixed coefficient limitation of conventional econometric models.

One of the problems that characterizes most econometric ventures pertains to measurement and observation errors. In most statistical models such as (1) and (2) it is assumed that errors occur in the equations and that the variables are measured without error. Unfortunately, most data that we generate or that are generated for us do not have this quality and instead of the true y and x we must work with the observed approximate measurements y^* and χ^*. Thus, if we consider two variables, the measurement error of the observed variables may be represented as

(17) $\chi^* = X + \delta$ and $y^* = y + \xi$

where δ and ξ are the vectors of the error in the variables. The statistical model now contains both errors in the variables and errors in the equation and the relationship between the observable variables for the general case may be written as

(18) $y^* = \chi^*\beta + u + \Delta\beta + \xi.$

Errors in the variables, as is well known, cause conventional estimators to give both biased and inconsistent results. Out of the procedures proposed to cope with the measurement error problem, the method of instrumental variables, which dates back to the 1930s, has probably been the most widely used. Excellent survey articles on the errors in the variables model covering the period from 1940 to 1970 may be found in Madansky [1959], Moran [1971], and Malinvaud [1970]. In making use of one of the alternative consistent estimators when measurement errors are suspected, the investigator is usually uncertain whether the virtue of consistency in his finite sample is sufficient to outweigh the increased variance from the use of instrumental variables. As an approach to this problem Feldstein [1973] suggested and evaluated alternative procedures for balancing the loss of efficiency in instrumental variables estimators against the potential gain of reduced bias. Fuller [1972] investigated the properties of the estimators of errors in the variables model when the covariance matrix is estimated. Unobservable variables, such as permanent and transitory income, are a special case of the errors in the variables model and are the subject of studies by Zellner [1970b] and Goldberger [1972]. Zellner considered a regression model containing a single unobservable variable and, for the practical situation where the variances are unknown, developed an operational version of generalized least squares where sample variances replace their unknown population counterparts. In customary Zellner fashion he also proposed a Bayesian analysis of the model. Goldberger [1972], building on the work of Zellner, developed a maximum likelihood procedure for the unobservable independent variable problem. The revival of econometric interest in the errors in the variables problem and realization of the possibility of identification and efficient estimation in unobservable variable models have contributed to the development of a unified statistical methodology (Goldberger [1971]) for the social sciences. Geracci [1976] examined the identification and estimation of simultaneous models which contain errors in both the equations and the variables.

In regard to sampling theory estimators, the inferential problem of making use of preliminary tests of significance, a problem first emphasized by Bancroft [1944], received new attention in the 1970s. This problem arises since in much of the work in economic measurement there is uncertainty about the agreement between the sampling model that generated the data and the statistical model that is employed for estimation and inference purposes. Statistical theory provides estimator properties and inferential statements conditioned on true models, whereas post-data model construction, by making use of preliminary tests of significance based on the data in hand, constitutes a rejection of the concept of true models. Two-stage procedures which yield an estimate after a preliminary test of significance make the estimation procedure dependent on the outcome of a test of hypothesis and lead to preliminary test or sequential estimators. Within the context of the general linear statistical model (1), the pretest estimator may be expressed as

$$(19) \qquad \hat{\hat{\beta}} = I_{(0,c)}\,(\omega)\hat{\beta} + I_{[c,\infty)}\,(\omega)b$$

where ω is the usual test statistic from making use of likelihood ratio procedures, $\hat{\beta}$ is the general linear hypothesis estimator of β (restricted least squares estimator or the sampling theory prior information estimators), b is the least squares estimator of β, $I_{(0,c)}\,(\omega)$, and $I_{[c,\infty)}\,(\omega)$ are indicator functions which are one if ω falls in the interval subscripted and zero otherwise, and c is the critical level of the test or the statistical significance level chosen. Although this estimator is widely used by workers in applied economics, little is known of the sampling properties of the estimator and the possible distortion of subsequent inferences when preliminary tests of significance are performed. Bancroft [1964], Sclove, Morris, and Radhakrishnan [1972], Ashar [1970], and Kennedy and Bancroft [1971] studied, usually for special cases, the properties of the resulting statistics in terms of their mean values and mean square errors and contrasted the forward and backward selection and sequential deletion model building procedures. Bock, Judge, and Yancey [1973a], building on the work of Bancroft and Sclove and using a squared error loss measure, derived analytically the risk for the preliminary test estimator (PTE) for the general case, showed that there are points in the parameter space where the risk of the PTE exceeds that of the conventional estimator and developed the conditions necessary for the risk of the PTE to be equal to or less than that of the conventional estimator under squared error loss. Bock, Yancey, and Judge [1973b] derived the sampling properties of the PTE and considered the sampling information of the PTE under a generalized mean square error criterion. Judge, Yancey, and Bock [1973] and Yancey, Judge, and Bock [1974] extended the mean square error test of Toro-Vizcarrondo and Wallace [1968] to include stochastic linear hypotheses and developed the properties of the stochastic PTE (i.e., the sampling properties of Theil's mixed regression estimator [1963] when the compatibility test statistic is used).

At the same time that work on the preliminary test estimator was going on, renewed interest emerged in Stein-rule estimators, which lie outside of the class of linear unbiased estimators. Stein [1956] showed the conventional least squares estimator of the multivariate mean (with components greater than two) was inadmissible under the squared error loss measure of goodness. James and Stein [1961] showed that in estimation under square error loss if the number of regressors or hypotheses for the general linear regression model is equal to or greater than three ($K \geqslant 3$) and c^* fulfills the conditions $0 \leqslant c^* < 2(J-2)(T-K)/(T-K+2)K$, then the Stein-rule estimator

$$(20) \qquad \beta^* = (1 - c^*/\omega)(b-\hat{\beta}) + \hat{\beta} = b - c^*/\omega(b-\hat{\beta})$$

dominates (is uniformly superior to) the conventional least squares estimator. The optimal choice of c^* was shown to be $(T-K)(J-2)/(T-K+2)K$.

Baranchik [1964] showed that the positive part version of the Stein-rule estimator

$$(21) \qquad \beta^+ = I_{(0,c^*)}(\omega)(1 - c^*/\omega)(b-\hat{\beta}) + \hat{\beta},$$

which implies $\beta^+ = \hat{\beta}$ if $\omega \leqslant c^*$ and $\beta^+ = \beta^*$ if $\omega > c^*$, dominates the original James and Stein estimator β^*. Strawderman [1971] developed, for the case when the number of parameters involved was greater than five, an estimator that was admissible and minimax. Sclove, Morris, and Radhakrishnan [1972] showed that the estimator

$$(22) \qquad \beta^{++} = I_{(c,\infty)}(\omega) \beta^+,$$

which is a modified version of the James and Stein-Baranchik positive part Stein-rule estimator, dominates the preliminary test estimator (19) and is thus uniformly superior over the entire range of the parameter values. Bock [1975] generalized the results for the above estimators for cases usually found in practice. Zellner and Vandaele [1972] developed Bayesian interpretations of and alternatives to the preliminary test and Stein-rule estimators. Hill [1975] investigated the problem of the inadmissibility of the usual multivariate estimator of a multivariate location parameter and presented a unified approach to estimation and hypothesis testing which is based directly on the concept of subjective probability. Lindley [1968] considered the analysis of data under the regression model and argued that the form of the analysis should depend on the use to be made of the results; in his approach to the variable choice problem he made use of ideas from decision theory. Although some problems remain (e.g., for the sampling theory estimators the optimal level of the test), we now have a much better idea of the sampling performance of a wide range of old and new estimators, and this should pay off in terms of improved procedures for sequential model building and learning from data.

The work on post-data model evaluation or discriminating among alternative admissible economic and statistical models has continued. Some of the hypothesis and decision rule procedures referred to earlier have implications for post-data model evaluation and choice. Dhrymes et al. [1972] surveyed the alternative and to some extent ad hoc procedures for the parametric evaluation of econometric models and noted the unsatisfactory nature of econometric practice and the state of the art. Beale [1970] summarized many of the most commonly used regression model building procedures, many of which are based only on intuitive appeal, and lends support to the backward stepwise method of variable elimination. Kennedy and Bancroft [1971] consider the forward selection and sequential deletion model building procedures and via numerical sampling experiments study the relative efficiency of the two procedures and recommend significance levels to use in confronting the best subset problem. Much work has been done using Bayesian procedures for comparing alternative models, and some of the productive efforts that stand out in this context are Box and Hill [1967], Geisel [1970], Thornber [1966], and Zellner [1971]. An excellent survey of these and other procedures for model selection is given in Gaver and Geisel [1973]. In spite of these advances in both the Bayesian and non-Bayesian areas, much remains to be done since we know little of (1) the sensitivity of these procedures to specification errors, (2) the finite sample behavior of these procedures, and (3) the implications for multiple equation models.

In the 1970s, in addition to adding to the stock of econometric tools, much effort went into evaluating through error analysis and impact multipliers the performance of ongoing econometric models specified and estimated in the 1960s and 1970s. Some of the major macroeconometric models include the Bureau of Economic Analysis Model, the Brookings Model, the University of Michigan Model, the Data Resources, Inc., Model, the Fair Model, the Federal Reserve Bank of St. Louis Model, the MIT-Pennsylvania-SSRC Model, the Wharton Mark III and Anticipation Version Model, the Stanford University Model, the Wharton Annual Model, and the Cornell University Model. Descriptions and evaluations of each of these models are given in the *International Economic Review* (June 1974, October 1974, and February 1975 issues) and in Fromm [1973] and Fromm and Klein [1976]. Each of the models offers a different approximation to reality and each has its own characteristics and insights. No one model appears to dominate. As Nelson [1972] puts it, "some combination of the models is needed for effective interpretation of movements of the important economic variables." While not wanting to add to the critical voices surrounding the specification and estimation of econometric models and the uses to which they are put, may I suggest we perhaps expect too much from these quantitative ventures. Because of the nature of the models most are designed for short-run forecasting purposes. If this is true perhaps, as Lucas [1973] suggests, the model characteristics which lead to forecasting success are unrelated to quantitative policy evaluation and simulations involving these traditional models can in principle provide no useful information about the actual consequences of alternative economic policies.

The Economic Research Service of the United States Department of Agriculture continued to improve the econometric models underlying the economic information it provides on near-term agricultural outlook and long-run projections. The various models and efforts of the price analysis and forecast group are well described in a paper by Boutwell and his colleagues [1976]. Two symposiums involving ERS and university researchers in the econometric area were held in 1975 and 1976 to consider cooperative efforts in developing, implementing, and using an ongoing comprehensive econometric model of the United States agricultural sector.

The Future

Having enumerated some of the elements and events in the econometric set which help us to determine where we have been and where we are, let us now turn to the future and engage in a little ex ante prediction as it relates to econometrics.

Unfortunately, most of the problems of measurement in economics that have been raised over the last half century remain. Although we more clearly understand the inferential implications of what we do when "measuring with or without theory," the models and methods that we have developed and the questions that remain suggest that we are only at the beginning of our science. If the paths we have taken and the successes we have achieved are in any way a prologue, it seems apparent that we will continue to refine and develop our economic and statistical models to cope with the special problems of our sample data and the decision problems for which the results are to be used. We will continue to improve our knowledge of the finite sample properties of sampling theory estimators and learn more of the implications and possibilities for combining prior and sample information for the purposes of estimation, prediction, and control. Nonlinear estimators and their stochastic properties and random coefficient statistical models will be further developed and become standard equipment in the econometrician's tool chest. We will improve by both sampling theory and Bayesian procedures our ability to handle the distributed lag estimation problem and to transform the distributed lag model into the frequency domain. The progress to date in the area of post-data model evaluation, while to a large degree ad hoc and unsatisfactory in nature, warrants an optimistic forecast that the development and extension of useful selection methods will continue. Computer programs for alternative Bayesian estimators will become available and the use of Bayesian inference, estimation, and decision processes will grow rapidly in our search for "optimal" actions (estimators). There will continue to be a significant growth in the average level of sophistication of economists with respect to econometric techniques, and perhaps ten years from now everyone will be at least a residual Bayesian. The gap or lag between theory and analytical tools and application should continue to narrow.

The communalities between problems and methods in the social sciences will become more apparent, and we will move toward a unified set of quantitative techniques which we hope will preclude a situation in which the tools and techniques of one discipline are rediscovered twenty-five years later in another (Hauser and Goldberger [1971]). We will gradually learn that quantitative tools are less specialized than the people who use them, and we will start to make use of state space representations of our econometric models and such far-afield procedures as linear filter and prediction theory (Kalman [1960]) that have been developed by engineers to cope with the problem of estimation in dynamic systems which involve unobservable variables and non-time-constant parameters.

Dynamic and stochastic decision models will grow in sophistication and usefulness, and econometrics will serve as a foundation stone in the development of operational routines for a formal analysis of decision problem under uncertainty. The use of structural modeling and simulation procedures will continue to grow very rapidly and especially the modeling of macroeconometric models will increase in importance as a tool to gauge the relative performance of alternative estimators and models and to help us understand the results. Future methods and models will, as they become more appropriate for economic decision problems under uncertainty, continue to emphasize the use of systems or stochastic control theory which combines in one package automatic or adaptive control, estimation, prediction, and some optimality criterion (Drèze [1972]).

The acquisition or generation of appropriate data will continue to be a problem, but since the model builders and the model users are now beginning to coordinate their efforts, there are many reasons to be optimistic in regard to an improvement in quantity, form, and accuracy. Quantitative economists will realize that federal collection agencies will not supply many of their data needs and new institutional arrangements will be specified and implemented for acquiring the research data we need. One hopeful sign is that we are finally generating data from large social experiments (for example, the experiments in New Jersey, North Carolina, and Iowa involving the negative income tax proposal). Thus over the next ten years we should see a flow of much more usable experimental and survey-generated data, where data design is integrated with use, and the situation relative to social statistics, where currently we know more about the population of hogs and cows than the population of people, will be improved. Central files of data and prior research results will be stored with ready access to the researcher via remote terminals. When this information is combined with econometric programs and remote terminals, the individual researcher, department, or institute will have ready access to large-scale systems now available to only a few.

Finally, since mathematical economics is one of the foundation stones of econometrics, we note that much of our modern economic theory is a theory of position and not of movement. This means that in order to have a conceptual base for many of the major problems facing society we must develop a more workable theory of change which is concerned with a feedback system involving leads, lags, and expectations, with intertemporal relations among phenomena and the dynamic mechanism of transmitting impulses. As Nerlove [1972] has noted, dynamic economics is still in large part a thing of the future. Econometric procedures now available or on the horizon, along with more and better data and computing possibilities, provide the ingredients appropriate for evaluating economic hypotheses and for accumulating a system of uniformities in the form of mathematical economic theory which will permit us to understand better the dynamic characteristics of economic processes and institutions and to develop a more adequate theory of quantitative economic policy evaluation.

Concluding Remarks

We are now at the end of a very inadequate tour. When I finished putting together these words and other symbols, I was impressed by how hard the problems were and how far we have come. The last thirty years have been a very important experiment in nonexperimental model building and the current interdisciplinary focus in academia has only helped to emphasize that our achievements in econometric theory and applications have made economics a leader of the social sciences. Economists interested in agriculture have had a significant role over time in testing the new methods of estimation and inference and in many cases modifying, sharpening, and extending them. The list of econometricians who cut their teeth on agricultural data, or who at least did some work on agricultural problems during their careers, is indeed an impressive one. Agricultural economics will continue to be an important testing ground for econometric work, but its uniqueness in this respect will diminish as economists get a better break at the funding table and the general economics departments continue to develop their research programs.

In a post-industrial society theoretical and empirical knowledge in economics will become a primary source of innovation and policy analysis, and academic economic research, where this knowledge is codified and tested, will assume a task greater than it has carried through history. In spite of past performances and the importance of the charge for the future, econometrics will continue to have its social and other critics and to be under suspicion to some. Some may feel that we continue to work or fiddle with the properties of esoteric estimators while the world burns and people suffer. Others may hold that we are out to violate man's sacred beliefs and deal him the final moral insult by developing schemes to manipulate or control human behavior and that we are hard at work on a set of structural equations which will capture the relevant behavioral mechanisms or processes and make the "understand, predict, and control" trichotomy operational. Our response to the charges of irrelevance and impiety and our future performance as a science will ultimately depend on how well we fulfill the prescriptive goal of helping peoples and their governments to satisfy their social, cultural, and economic aspirations. This goal is best served by a science that provides an understanding of the regularities of economic life and a framework for using this information as a basis for decision making and choice. In the quest for this kind of a science of economics the continued development and application of tools of econometric analysis are essential.

References

Abrahamse, A. P. J., and A. S. Louter [1971]. "On a New Test for Autocorrelation in Least Squares Regression." *Biometrika* 58:53-60.

Adelman, I. G. [1958]. "A Stochastic Analysis of the Size Distribution of Firms." *J. Am. Stat. Assoc.* 53:893-904.

Adelman, I. G., and C. T. Morris [1968]. "An Econometric Model of Socio-economic and Political Change in Underdeveloped Countries." *Am. Econ. Rev.* 58:1184-1218.

Aigner, D. J. [1971a]. *Basic Econometrics.* Englewood Cliffs, N.J.: Prentice-Hall.

———— [1971b]. "A Compendium on Estimation of the Autoregressive-Moving Average Model from Time Series Data." *Int. Econ. Rev.* 12:348-371.

Aigner, D. J., and S. F. Chu [1968]. "On Estimating the Industry Production Function." *Am. Econ. Rev.* 53:826-839.

Aitken, A. C. [1934]. "On Least Squares and Linear Combinations of Observations." *Proc. Royal Soc. Edin.* 55:42-48.

Almon, S. [1965]. "The Distributed Lag between Capital Appropriations and Expenditures." *Econometrica* 33:178-196.

Amemiya, T., and W. Fuller [1967]. "A Comparative Study of Alternative Estimators in a Distributed Lag Model." *Econometrica* 35:509-529.

Andersen, L. C., and K. M. Carlson [1970]. "A Monetarist Model for Economic Stabilization." *Federal Reserve Bank of St. Louis Review* 52:7-25.

Anderson, T. W., and H. Rubin [1949]. "Estimation of the Parameters of a Single Equation in a Complete System of Stochastic Equations." *Annals of Math. Stat.* 20:46-63.

Aoki, M. [1967]. *Optimization of Stochastic Systems.* New York: Academic Press.

Arrow, K. J., H. B. Chenery, B. S. Minhas, and R. M. Solow [1961]. "Capital Labor Substitution and Economic Efficiency." *Rev. Econ. and Stat.* 43:225-250.

Ashar, V. G. [1970]. "On the Use of Preliminary Tests in Regression." Unpublished Ph.D. dissertation, North Carolina State University, Raleigh.

Ashar, V. G., and T. D. Wallace [1963]. "A Sampling Study of Minimum Absolute Deviations Estimators." *Operations Research* 11:747-758.

Balestra, P., and M. Nerlove [1966]. "Pooling Cross Section and Time Series Data in the Estimation of a Dynamic Model: The Demand for Natural Gas." *Econometrica* 34:585-612.

Bancroft, T. A. [1944]. "On Biases in Estimation Due to the Use of Preliminary Tests of Significance." *Annals of Math. Stat.* 15:190-204.

———— [1964]. "Analysis and Inference for Incompletely Specified Models Involving the Use of Preliminary Test(s) of Significance." *Biometrics* 20:427-442.

Baranchik, A. J. [1964]. *Multiple Regression and Estimation of the Mean of a Multivariate Normal Distribution.* Stanford University Technical Report 51.

Barten, A. P. [1968]. "Estimating Demand Equations." *Econometrica* 36:213-251.

Basmann, R. L. [1957]. "A Generalized Classical Method of Linear Estimation of Coefficients in a Structural Equation." *Econometrica* 25:77-83.

———— [1965]. "A Tchebychev Inequality for the Convergence of a Generalized Classical Linear Estimator, Sample Size Being Fixed." *Econometrica* 33:608-618.

Batchelor, J. [1959-64]. *Operations Research: An Annotated Bibliography.* 4 vols. St. Louis: St. Louis University Press.

Baumer, E. F., W. K. Brandt, R. E. Jacobson, and F. E. Walker [1969]. *Dimensions of Consumer Attitudes in Fluid Milk Purchases.* Ohio Agricultural Research Bulletin 1028.

Beale, E. M. L. [1970]. "Note on Procedures for Variable Selection in Multiple Regression." *Technometrics* 12:909-914.

Bean, L. H. [1929]. "The Farmers' Response to Price." *J. Farm Econ.* 11:368-385.

Bentzel, R., and B. Hanson [1954]. "On Recursiveness and Interdependency in Economics Models." *Rev. Econ. Studies* 22:53.

Berenblut, I. I., and G. I. Webb [1973]. "A New Test for Autocorrelated Errors in the Linear Regression Problem." *J. Royal Stat. Soc.* (Series B) 35:33-50.

Black, J. D. [1924]. "Elasticity of Supply of Farm Products." *J. Farm. Econ.* 6:145-155.

Blattberg, R., and T. Sargent [1971]. "Regression with Non-Gaussian Stable Disturbances: Some Sampling Results." *Econometrica* 39:501-511.

Bock, M. E. [1975]. "Minimax Estimators of the Mean of a Multivariate Normal Distribution." *Annals of Statistics* 3:209-218.

Bock, M. E., G. G. Judge, and T. A. Yancey [1973a]. "Some Comments on Estimation
in Regression after Preliminary Tests of Significance." *J. Econometrics* 1:191-
200.

Bock, M. E., T. A. Yancey, and G. G. Judge [1973b]. "Properties of Some Preliminary
Test Estimators in Regression Using a Quadratic Loss Criterion." *J. Am. Stat.
Assoc.* 68:109-116.

Bodkin, R. G., and L. R. Klein [1967]. "Nonlinear Estimation of Aggregate Production
Functions." *Rev. Econ. and Stat.* 49:28-44.

Booth, E. J. R., and G. G. Judge [1956]. "The Impact of the Choice of Model on Measurements of Economic Behavior." *J. Farm Econ.* 38:570-583.

Boutwell, W., C. Edwards, R. Haidecker, H. Hogg, W. Kost, J. Penn, J. Roop, and L.
Quance [1976]. "Comprehensive Forecast and Projection Models in ERS."
Agr. Econ. Res. 28:41-51.

Boutwell, W. K., Jr., and R. L. Simmons [1968]. "Estimation of Demand for Food and
Other Products Assuming Ordinally Separable Utility." *Am. J. Agr. Econ.* 50:366-
378.

Box, G. E. P., and W. J. Hill [1967]. "Discriminating among Mechanistic Models." *Technometrics* 9:57-71.

Box, G. E. P., and G. M. Jenkins [1970]. *Time Series Analysis, Forecasting and Control.*
San Francisco: Holden-Day.

Brandow, G. E. [1961]. *Interrelations among Demands for Farm Products and Implications for Control of Market Supply.* Pennsylvania State University Bulletin 680.

Bressler, R. G. [1942]. *Economies of Scale in the Operation of Country Milk Plants.*
New England Research Council Technical Bulletin, Boston.

Bronfenbrenner, J. [1953]. "Sources and Sizes of Least Squares Bias in a Two Equation
Model." In *Studies in Econometric Method*, W. C. Hood and T. C. Koopmans,
eds. New York: Wiley. Pp. 221-235.

Brunk, M. E. [1958]. "Use of Experimental Design in Marketing Research." *J. Farm
Econ.* 40:1237-1246.

Buchholz, H. E., G. G. Judge, and V. I. West [1962]. *A Summary of Selected Estimated
Behavioral Relations for Agricultural Products.* University of Illinois Research Report 57.

Cagan, P. [1956]. "The Monetary Dynamics of Hyperinflation." In *Studies in the Quantity Theory of Money*, M. Friedman, ed. Chicago: University of Chicago Press. Pp.
25-117.

Cargill, T. F. [1971]. "Early Applications of Spectral Methods to Economic Time Series." Paper presented at meeting of Western Economic Association, Vancouver,
British Columbia.

Chernoff, H., and N. Divinsky [1953]. "The Computation of Maximum-Likelihood Estimates of Linear Structural Equations." In *Studies in Econometric Method*, W. C.
Hood and T. C. Koopmans, eds. New York: Wiley. Pp. 236-269.

Chetty, V. K. [1968]. "Pooling of Time Series and Cross Section Data." *Econometrica*
36:279-290.

Chipman, J. S., and M. M. Rao [1964]. "The Treatment of Linear Restrictions in Regression Analysis." *Econometrica* 32:198-209.

Cobb, C. W., and P. H. Douglas [1928]. "A Theory of Production." *Am. Econ. Rev.* 18: 139-165.

Cochrane, D., and G. H. Orcutt [1949]. "Application of Least Squares Regression to Relationships Containing Auto-Correlated Error Terms." *J. Am. Stat. Assoc.* 44:32-61.

Cochrane, W. W. [1955]. "Conceptualizing the Supply Relation in Agriculture." *J. Farm Econ.* 37:1161-1176.

Cooper, G. [1948]. "The Role of Econometric Models in Econometric Research." *J. Farm Econ.* 30:101-116.

Cooper, J. R., and C. R. Nelson [1971]. "The Ex Ante Prediction Performance of the St. Louis and FTB-MIT-Penn Econometric Models." Unpublished paper, University of Chicago.

Cragg, J. G. [1966]. "On the Sensitivity of Simultaneous-Equations Estimators to the Stochastic Assumptions of the Models." *J. Am. Stat. Assoc.* 61:136-151.

―――― [1967]. "On the Relative Small-Sample Properties of Several Structural-Equation Estimators." *Econometrica* 35:89-110.

―――― [1968]. "Some Effects of Incorrect Specification on the Small-Sample Properties of Several Simultaneous-Equation Estimators." *Int. Econ. Rev.* 9:63-86.

Cromarty, W. A. [1959a]. "An Econometric Model for United States Agriculture." *J. Am. Stat. Assoc.* 54:556-574.

―――― [1959b]. "The Farm Demand for Tractors, Machinery and Trucks." *J. Farm Econ.* 41:323-331.

―――― [1962]. *Predicting the Impact of Alternative Government Programs on the Wheat and Feed-Livestock Economies*. Michigan State University Agricultural Experiment Station Technical Bulletin 286.

Dantzig, G. B. [1951a]. "Maximization of a Linear Function of Variables Subject to Linear Inequalities." In *Activity Analysis of Production and Allocation*, T. C. Koopmans, ed. New York: Wiley. Pp. 339-347.

―――― [1951b]. "The Programming of Interdependent Activities: Mathematical Model." In *Activity Analysis of Production and Allocation*, T. C. Koopmans, ed. New York: Wiley. Pp. 19-32.

David, F. N., and J. Neyman [1938]. "Extension of the Markoff Theorem on Least Squares." *Stat. Research Memoirs* 2:105-116.

Dean, J. [1936]. "Statistical Determination of Costs with Special Reference to Marginal Costs." *Studies Bus. Adm.* 7:132-154.

DeJanvry, A. J., J. Bieri, and A. Nuñez [1972]. "Estimators of Demand Parameters under Consumer Budgeting." *Am. J. Agr. Econ.* 54:422-430.

De Leeuw, F., and E. M. Gramlich [1968]. "The Federal Reserve-MIT Econometric Model." *Federal Reserve Bulletin*, pp. 11-40.

Dhrymes, P. J. [1965]. "Some Extensions and Tests for the CES Class of Production Functions." *Rev. Econ. and Stat.* 47:357-366.

―――― [1970]. *Econometrics*. New York: Harper and Row. Pp. 272-277.

―――― [1971]. *Distributed Lags: Problems of Estimation and Formulation*. San Francisco: Holden-Day.

Dhrymes, P. J., E. Howrey, S. Hymans, J. Kmenta, E. Leamer, R. Quandt, J. Ramsey, H. Shapiro, and V. Zarnowitz [1972]. "Criteria for Evaluation of Econometric Models." *Annals of Econ. and Social Measurement* 1:291-324.

Drèze, J. [1962]. *The Bayesian Approach to Simultaneous Equations Estimation*. Northwestern University Technological Institute Research Memorandum 67.

———— [1972]. "Econometrics and Decision Theory." *Econometrica* 40:1-18.

Duesenberry, J. S., G. Fromm, L. R. Klein, and E. Kuh [1965]. *The Brookings Quarterly Econometric Model of the United States.* Chicago: Rand McNally.

Durbin, J. [1953]. "A Note on Regression When There Is Extraneous Information about One of the Coefficients." *J. Am. Stat. Assoc.* 48:799-808.

———— [1954]. "Errors in Variables." *Rev. Int. Stat. Institute* 22:23-32.

———— [1970a]. "An Alternative to the Bounds Test for Testing for Serial Correlation in Least-Squares Regression." *Econometrica* 38:422-429.

———— [1970b]. "Testing for Serial Correlation in Least-Squares Regression When Some of the Regressors Are Lagged Dependent Variables." *Econometrica* 38:410-421.

Durbin, J., and G. S. Watson [1950]. "Testing for Serial Correlation in Least Squares Regression, I." *Biometrika* 37:409-428.

———— [1951]. "Testing for Serial Correlation in Least-Squares Regression, II." *Biometrika* 38:159-178.

Eisner, R. [1958]. "The Permanent Income Hypothesis: Comment." *Am. Econ. Rev.* 48:972-990.

Eisner, R., and R. H. Strotz [1963]. "Determinants of Business Investment." In *Impacts of Monetary Policy*, Eisner and Strotz, eds. Englewood Cliffs, N.J.: Prentice-Hall.

Evans, M. K., and L. R. Klein [1967]. *The Wharton Econometric Forecasting Model.* Philadelphia: University of Pennsylvania Press.

Ezekiel, M. [1930]. *Methods of Correlation Analysis.* New York: Wiley.

Farrar, D. E., and R. R. Glauber [1967]. "Multicollinearity in Regression Analysis: The Problem Re-visited." *Rev. Econ. and Stat.* 49:92-107.

Feldstein, M. [1973]. "Errors in the Variables: A Consistent Estimator with Smaller MSE in Finite Samples." Harvard Institute of Economics Research Paper 275.

Ferguson, C. E., and R. W. Pfouts [1962]. "Aggregate Production Functions and Relative Factor Shares." *Int. Econ. Rev.* 3:328-337.

Fienberg, S., and A. Zellner [1974]. *Studies in Bayesian Econometrics and Statistics in Honor of L. J. Savage.* Amsterdam: North-Holland.

Fisher, J. [1962]. "An Analysis of Consumer Goods Expenditures." *Rev. Econ. and Stat.* 44:64-71.

Fisher, R. A. [1935]. *Design of Experiments.* London: Oliver and Boyd.

Fisher, W. D. [1962]. "Estimation in Linear Decision Models." *Int. Econ. Rev.* 3:1-29.

Fishman, G. S. [1969]. *Spectral Methods in Econometrics.* Cambridge: Harvard University Press.

Foote, R. J. [1953a]. "A Four-Equation Model of the Feed-Livestock Economy and Its Endogenous Mechanisms." *J. Farm Econ.* 35:44-61.

———— [1953b]. *Statistical Analyses Relating to the Feed-Livestock Economy.* USDA Technical Bulletin 1070.

———— [1955a]. "A Comparison of Single and Simultaneous Equation Techniques." *J. Farm Econ.* 37:975-990.

———— [1955b]. "Surveys of Econometric Results in Agriculture—Demand and Price." *J. Farm Econ.* 37:197-205.

———— [1958]. *Analytical Tools for Studying Demand and Price Structures.* USDA Agr. Handbook 146.

Foote, R. J., J. W. Klein, and M. Clough [1952]. *The Demand and Price Structure for Corn and Total Feed Concentrates.* USDA Technical Bulletin 1061.

Fox, K. A. [1951]. "Relations between Prices, Consumption, and Production." *J. Am. Stat. Assoc.* 46:323-333.
——— [1953]. *The Analysis of Demand for Farm Products.* USDA Technical Bulletin 1081.
Franzmann, J. R., and G. G. Judge [1957]. "Estimation of Response Relationships for Eggs." *J. Farm Econ.* 39:927-935.
French, B. L. [1950]. "The Statistical Determination of the Demand for Meat." Unpublished M.S. thesis, Iowa State College.
Friedman, J., and R. J. Foote [1955]. *Computational Methods for Handling Systems of Simultaneous Equations.* USDA Agr. Handbook 94.
Friedman, M. [1957]. *A Theory of the Consumption Function.* Princeton: Princeton University Press.
Frisch, R. [1934]. *Statistical Confluence Analyses by Means of Complete Regression Systems.* Oslo University Institute of Economics.
——— [1959]. "A Complete Scheme for Computing All Direct and Indirect Cross Demand Elasticities in a Model with Many Sectors." *Econometrica* 27:177-196.
Fromm, G. [1973]. "Implications to and from Economic Theory in Models of Complex Systems." *Am. J. Agr. Econ.* 55:259-271.
Fromm, G., and L. Klein [1976]. "NBER/NST Model Comparison Seminar: An Analysis of Results." *Annals of Econ. and Social Measurement* 5:1-28.
Fromm, G., and P. T. Taubman [1968]. *Policy Simulations with an Econometric Model.* Washington: Brookings Institution.
Fuller, W. A. [1972]. "Some Properties of Estimators for the Errors in Variables Model." Unpublished paper, Iowa State University.
Fuller, W. A., and J. E. Martin [1961]. "The Effects of Autocorrelated Errors on the Statistical Estimation of Distributed Lag Models." *J. Farm Econ.* 43:71-82.
Gauss, C. F. [1821]. "On the Theory of Least Squares." Translation appears in Technical Report #5, *Statistics Techniques Research Group.* Princeton: Princeton University Press.
Gaver, K. M., and M. S. Geisel [1973]. "Discriminating among Alternative Models: Bayesian and Non-Bayesian Methods." In *Frontiers of Econometrics*, Paul Zarembka, ed. New York: Academic Press.
Geisel, M. S. [1970]. "Comparing and Choosing among Parametric Statistical Models: A Bayesian Analysis with Macroeconomic Applications." Unpublished Ph.D. dissertation, University of Chicago.
Geracci, V. J. [1976]. "Identification of Simultaneous Equation Models with Measurement Errors." *J. Econometrics* 6:263-284.
Gerra, M. J. [1959a]. "An Econometric Model of the Egg Industry." *J. Farm Econ.* 41:284-301.
——— [1959b]. *The Demand, Supply, and Price Structure for Eggs.* USDA Agr. Handbook 1204.
Girshick, M. A. [1936]. "Principal Components." *J. Am. Stat. Assoc.* 31:519-536.
Girshick, M. A., and T. Haavelmo [1947]. "Statistical Analysis of the Demand for Food: Examples of Simultaneous Estimation of Structural Equations." *Econometrica* 15:79-110.
Glejser, H. [1969]. "A New Test for Heteroskedasticity." *J. Am. Stat. Assoc.* 64:316-323.
Godwin, M. R. [1952]. *Consumer Response to Varying Prices for Florida Oranges.* Florida Experiment Station Bulletin 508.

Goldberger, A. S. [1959]. *Impact Multipliers and Dynamic Properties of the Klein-Goldberger Model*. Amsterdam: North-Holland.

—— [1964]. *Econometric Theory*. New York: Wiley.

—— [1971]. "Econometrics and Psychometrics: A Survey of Communalities." *Psychometrika* 36:83-107.

—— [1972]. "Maximum Likelihood Estimation of Regression Containing Unobservable Variables." *Int. Econ. Rev.* 13:1-15.

Goldberger, A. S., and T. Gameletsos [1970]. "A Cross-Country Comparison of Consumer Expenditure Patterns." *European Econ. Rev.* 1:357-400.

Goldfeld, S. M., and R. E. Quandt [1965]. "Some Tests for Homoscedasticity." *J. Am. Stat. Assoc.* 60:539-547.

Goodman, L. A. [1965]. "On the Statistical Analysis of Mobility Tables." *Am. J. Sociology* 70:564-585.

Gorman, W. M. [1959]. "Separable Utility and Aggregation." *Econometrica* 27:469-481.

Granger, C. W. J., and M. Hatanaka [1964]. *Spectral Analysis of Economic Time Series*. Princeton: Princeton University Press.

Graybill, F. A. [1961]. *An Introduction to Linear Statistical Models*. New York: McGraw-Hill.

Griffiths, W. E. [1970]. "Estimation of Regression Coefficients Which Change over Time." Unpublished Ph.D. dissertation, University of Illinois, Urbana-Champaign.

Griliches, Z. [1957]. "Specification Bias in Estimates of Production Functions." *J. Farm Econ.* 39:8-20.

—— [1967]. "Distributed Lags: A Survey." *Econometrica* 35:16-49.

—— [1968]. "The Brookings Model Volume: A Review Article." *Rev. Econ. and Stat.* 50:215-234.

—— [1973]. "Errors in Variables and Other Nonobservables." Harvard Research Paper, Economics Department, Harvard University Press.

Grossman, S. [1975]. "Rational Expectation and the Econometric Modeling of Markets Subject to Uncertainty: A Bayesian Approach." *J. Econometrics* 3:255-272.

Grunfeld, Y., and Z. Griliches [1960]. "Is Aggregation Necessarily Bad?" *Rev. Econ. and Stat.* 42:1-13.

Haavelmo, T. [1943]. "The Statistical Implications of a System of Simultaneous Equations." *Econometrica* 11:1-12.

—— [1944]. "The Probability Approach in Econometrics." Supplement, *Econometrica* 12:1-118.

—— [1947]. "Methods of Measuring the Marginal Propensity to Consume." *J. Am. Stat. Assoc.* 42:105-122.

Hall, R. E. [1971]. "A Survey of Recent Work on the Estimation of Distributed Lags." Paper prepared for NBER-NSF seminar on time series and distributed lags.

Hallberg, M. C. [1969]. "Projecting the Size Distribution of Agricultural Firms." *Am. J. Agr. Econ.* 51:289-302.

—— [1972]. "Macroeconometric Models: A Survey of Applications." Unpublished paper, Pennsylvania State University.

Hannan, E. J. [1967]. *Time Series Analysis*. London: Methuen.

Harlow, A. A. [1960]. "The Hog Cycle and the Cobweb Theorem." *J. Farm Econ.* 42: 842-853.

Hauser, R. M., and A. S. Goldberger [1971]. "The Treatment of Unobservable Variables in Path Analysis." In *Sociological Methodology*, H. L. Costner, ed. San Francisco: Jassey-Boss.

Heady, E. O., and C. B. Baker [1954]. "Resource Adjustments to Equate Productivities in Agriculture." *Southern Econ. J.* 21:36-52.

Heady, E. O., and J. L. Dillon [1961]. *Agricultural Production Functions.* Ames: Iowa State University Press.

Hendry, D. F. [1976]. "The Structure of Simultaneous Equations Estimators." *J. Econometrics* 4:51-88.

Hildreth, C., and J. P. Houck [1968]. "Some Estimators for a Linear Model with Random Coefficients." *J. Am. Stat. Assoc.* 63:584-595.

Hildreth, C., and F. G. Jarrett [1955]. *A Statistical Study of Livestock Production and Marketing.* New York: Wiley.

Hildreth, C., and J. Y. Liu [1960]. *Demand Relations with Autocorrelated Disturbances.* Michigan State University Agricultural Experiment Station Technical Bulletin 276.

Hill, B. M. [1975]. "On Coherence, Inadmissibility and Inference about Many Parameters in the Theory of Least Squares." In *Studies in Bayesian Econometrics and Statistics,* S. E. Fienberg and A. Zellner, eds. Amsterdam: North-Holland.

Hoch, I. [1958]. "Simultaneous Equation Bias in the Context of the Cobb-Douglas Production Function." *Econometrica* 26:566-578.

Hood, W. C., and T. C. Koopmans [1953]. *Studies in Econometric Method.* New York: Wiley.

Hotelling, H. [1933]. "Analysis of Complex Statistical Variables into Principal Components." *J. Educational Psychology* 24:417-429.

——— [1936]. "Relations between Two Sets of Variants." *Biometrika* 28:321-377.

Houthakker, H. S. [1958]. "The Permanent Income Hypothesis." *Am. Econ. Rev.* 48: 396-404, 48:991-993.

Howrey, E. [1971]. "Stochastic Properties of the Klein-Goldberger Model." *Econometrica* 39:73-87.

James, W., and C. Stein [1961]. "Estimation with Quadratic Loss." *Proceedings of Fourth Berkeley Symposium on Mathematical Statistics and Probability,* vol. I, *Contributions to the Theory of Statistics,* Jerzy Neyman, ed. Berkeley: University of California Press. Pp. 361-379.

Jeffreys, H. [1961]. *Theory of Probability.* 3rd ed. Oxford: Clarendon Press.

Johnson, D. G. [1948]. "The Use of Econometric Models in the Study of Agricultural Policy." *J. Farm Econ.* 30:117-130.

Johnson, G. [1952]. *Burley Tobacco Control Programs: Their Over-All Effect on Production and Prices, 1933-50.* Kentucky Agricultural Experiment Station Bulletin 580.

Johnston, J. [1971]. *Econometric Methods.* New York: McGraw-Hill.

Joregenson, D. W. [1966]. "Rational Distributed Lag Functions." *Econometrica* 34: 135-149.

——— [1971]. "Econometric Studies of Investment Behavior: A Review." Harvard Institute of Economic Research Discussion Paper 204.

Judge, G. G. [1949]. "Determinants of the Extent and Type of Cattle Feeding in Iowa." Unpublished M.S. thesis, Iowa State University.

——— [1954]. *Econometric Analysis of the Demand and Supply Relationships for Eggs.* Storrs Agricultural Experiment Station Bulletin 307.

Judge, G. G., and E. R. Swanson [1962]. "Markov Chains: Basic Concepts and Suggested Uses in Agricultural Economics." *Australian J. Agr. Econ.* 6:49-61.

Judge, G. G., and T. Takayama [1966]. "Inequality Restrictions in Regression Analysis." *J. Am. Stat. Assoc.* 61:166-181.

Judge, G. G., and T. A. Yancey [1969]. "The Use of Prior Information in Estimating the Parameters of Economic Relationships." *Metroeconomica* 21:97-140.

Judge, G. G., T. A. Yancey, and M. E. Bock [1973]. "Properties of Estimators after Preliminary Tests of Significance When Stochastic Restrictions Are Used in Regression." *J. Econometrics* 1:29-47.

Just, R. E. [1972]. "Econometric Analysis of Production Decisions with Government Intervention: The Case of California Field Crops." Unpublished Ph.D. dissertation, University of California, Berkeley.

Kabe, D. G. [1964]. "On the Exact Distributions of the GCL Estimators in a Leading Three-Equation Case." *J. Am. Stat. Assoc.* 59:881-894.

Kadiyala, K. R. [1968]. "A Transformation Used to Circumvent the Problem of Autocorrelation." *Econometrica* 36:93-96.

Kalman, R. E. [1960]. "A New Approach to Linear Filtering and Prediction Problems." *J. Basic Engineering* 82:34-45.

Kennedy, W. J., and T. A. Bancroft [1971]. "Model Building for Prediction in Regression Based upon Repeated Significance Tests." *Annals of Math. Stat.* 42:1273-1284.

King, G. A. [1958]. *The Demand and Price Structure for Byproduct Feeds.* USDA Technical Bulletin 1183.

Klein, L. R. [1950]. *Economic Fluctuations in the United States.* New York: Wiley.

—— [1953]. *A Textbook of Econometrics.* Evanston, Ill.: Row, Peterson.

—— [1958]. "The Estimation of Distributed Lags." *Econometrica* 26:553-565.

—— [1971]. "Whither Econometrics?" *J. Am. Stat. Assoc.* 66:415-421.

Kmenta, J. [1967]. "On Estimation of the CES Production Function." *Int. Econ. Rev.* 8:180-189.

—— [1971]. *Elements of Econometrics.* New York: Macmillan.

Koerts, J. [1967]. "Some Further Notes on Disturbance Estimates in Regression Analysis." *J. Am. Stat. Assoc.* 62:169-186.

Koopmans, T. C. [1937]. *Linear Regression Analysis in Economic Time Series.* Haarlem: Haarlem Press.

—— [1949]. "Identification Problems in Economic Model Construction." *Econometrica* 17:125-144.

—— [1951]. *Activity Analysis of Production and Allocation.* New York: Wiley.

——, ed. [1950]. *Statistical Inference in Dynamic Economic Models.* New York: Wiley.

Koyck, L. M. [1954]. *Distributed Lags and Investment Analysis.* Amsterdam: North-Holland.

Kuznets, G. [1955]. "Survey of Econometric Results in Agriculture: Discussion." *J. Farm Econ.* 37:235-236.

Kuznets, S. [1935]. "Relations between Capital Goods and Finished Products in the Business Cycle." In *Essays in Honor of Wesley Clair Mitchell.* New York: Columbia University Press. Pp. 211-267.

Ladd, G. W. [1957]. "Effects of Shocks and Errors in Estimation." *J. Farm Econ.* 38:485-495.

—— [1966]. "Linear Probability Functions and Discriminant Functions." *Econometrica* 34:873-885.

—— [1967]. *An Analysis of Ranking Dairy Bargaining Cooperative Objectives.* Iowa State Experiment Station Bulletin 550.

Ladd, G. W., and J. Tedford [1959]. "A Generalization of the Working Method for Estimating Long-Run Elasticities." *J. Farm Econ.* 40:221-233.

Lancaster, T. [1968]. "Grouping Estimators on Heteroscedastic Data." *J. Am. Stat. Assoc.* 63:182-191.

Leamer, E. E. [1970]. "Distributed Lag Analysis with Informative Prior Distributions." Harvard Institute of Economic Research Discussion Paper 147.

Lee, T. C., G. G. Judge, and A. Zellner [1970]. *Estimating the Parameters of the Markov Probability Model from Aggregate Time Series Data*. Amsterdam: North-Holland.

Lee, T. C., and S. K. Seaver [1971]. "A Simultaneous-Equation Model of Spatial Equilibrium." *Am. J. Agr. Econ.* 53:63-70.

Legendre, A. M. [1805]. "On the Method of Least Squares." In *A Source Book in Mathematics*, D. E. Smith, ed. New York: Dover, 1959.

Leontief, W. W. [1937]. "Interrelations of Prices, Outputs, Savings and Investment." *Rev. Econ. and Stat.* 19:109-144.

Leser, C. E. V. [1968]. "A Survey of Econometrics." *J. Royal Stat. Soc.* (Series A) 131: 530-566.

Leuthold, R. M. [1970]. "Forecasting Daily Hog Prices and Quantities: A Study of Alternative Forecasting Techniques." *J. Am. Stat. Assoc.* 65:90-107.

Lindley, D. V. [1968]. "The Choice of Variables in Multiple Regression." *J. Royal Stat. Soc.* (Series B) 30:31-66.

Lucas, R. E. [1973]. "Econometric Policy Evaluation: A Critique." Unpublished paper, Carnegie-Mellon University (Economics).

Lucas, R., and E. Prescott [1971]. "Investment under Uncertainty." *Econometrica* 29: 659-682.

—— [1974]. "Equilibrium Search and Employment." *J. Econ. Theory* 5:188-209.

Madansky, A. [1959]. "The Fitting of Straight Lines When Both Variables Are Subject to Error." *J. Am. Stat. Assoc.* 54:173-205.

—— [1964]. "On the Efficiency of Three-Stage Least-Squares Estimation." *Econometrica* 32:51-56.

Maddala, G. S. [1971]. "The Use of Variance Components Models in Pooling Cross Section and Time Series Data." *Econometrica* 39:341-358.

Malinvaud, E. [1970]. *Statistical Methods in Econometrics*. Amsterdam: North-Holland.

Mann, H. B., and A. Wald [1943]. "On the Statistical Treatment of Linear Stochastic Difference Equations." *Econometrica* 11:173-220.

Mariano, R. S. [1972]. "The Existence of Moments of the Ordinary Least Squares and Two-Stage Least Squares Estimators." *Econometrica* 40:643-652.

—— [1973]. "Approximations to the Distribution Functions of the Ordinary Least-Squares and Two-Stage Least-Squares Estimations in the Case of Two Included Endogenous Variables." *Econometrica* 41:67-77.

Mariano, R. S., and T. Sawa [1972]. "The Exact Finite Sample Distribution of the Limited Information Maximum Likelihood Estimators." *J. Am. Stat. Assoc.* 67:59-63.

Marschak, J. [1947]. "Economic Structure, Path, Policy, and Prediction." *Am. Econ. Rev.* 37:81-84.

—— [1953]. "Economic Measurements for Policy and Prediction." In *Studies in Econometric Method*, W. C. Hood and T. C. Koopmans, eds. New York: Wiley. Pp. 1-26.

Marschak, J., and W. H. Andrews [1944]. "Random Simultaneous Equations and the Theory of Production." *Econometrica* 12:143-205.

Massey, W. F., R. E. Frank, and T. Lodahl [1968]. *Purchasing Behavior and Personal Attributes*. Philadelphia: University of Pennsylvania Press.

Meinken, K. W. [1953]. *The Demand and Price Structure for Oats, Barley, and Sorghum Grains.* USDA Technical Bulletin 1080.
—— [1955]. *The Demand and Price Structure for Wheat.* USDA Technical Bulletin 1136.
Meyer, J., and E. Kuh [1957]. *The Investment Decision.* Cambridge: Harvard University Press. Pp. 6-35.
Miller, G. A. [1952]. "Finite Markov Processes in Psychology." *Psychometrika* 17:149-167.
Moran, P. A. P. [1071]. "Estimating Structural and Functional Relations." *J. Multivariate Analysis* 1:232-255.
Moore, H. L. [1914]. *Economic Cycles: Their Law and Cause.* New York: Macmillan; reprinted 1967 by A. M. Kelly.
Mundlak, Y. [1961]. "Empirical Production Function Free of Management Bias." *J. Farm Econ.* 43:45-56.
Muth, J. F. [1961]. "Rational Expectations and the Theory of Price Movements." *Econometrica* 24:315-335.
Nagar, A. L. [1962]. "Double K-Class Estimators of Parameters in Simultaneous Equations and Their Small Sample Properties." *Int. Econ. Rev.* 3:168-188.
Neiswanger, W. A., and T. A. Yancey [1959]. "Parameter Estimates and Autonomous Growth." *J. Am. Stat. Assoc.* 54:389-402.
Nelson, C. R. [1972]. "The Prediction Performance of the FRB-MIT-Penn Model of U.S. Economy." *Am. Econ. Rev.* 62:902-917.
Nerlove, M. [1958a]. *The Dynamics of Supply: Estimation of Farmers' Response to Price.* Baltimore: Johns Hopkins Press.
—— [1958b]. *Distributed Lags and Demand Analysis for Agricultural and Other Commodities.* USDA Agr. Handbook 141.
—— [1958c]. "Distributed Lags and Estimation of Long-Run Supply and Demand Elasticities: Theoretical Considerations." *J. Farm Econ.* 40:301-311.
—— [1958d]. "The Implications of Friedman's Permanent Income Hypothesis for Demand Analysis." *Agr. Econ. Res.* 10:1-14.
—— [1964]. "Spectral Analysis of Seasonal Adjustment Procedures." *Econometrica* 32:241-286.
—— [1966]. "A Tabular Survey of Macro-Econometric Models." *Int. Econ. Rev.* 7:127-175.
—— [1971]. "Further Evidence on the Estimation of Dynamic Economic Relations from a Time Series of Cross Sections." *Econometrica* 39:359-382.
—— [1972]. "Lags in Economic Behavior." *Econometrica* 40:221-252.
Nerlove, M., and W. Addison [1958]. "Statistical Estimation of Long-Run Elasticities of Supply and Demand." *J. Farm Econ.* 40:861-880.
Newman, P. K., and R. C. Read [1961]. "Production Functions with Restricted Input Shares." *Int. Econ. Rev.* 2:127-133.
Nordin, J. A., G. G. Judge, and O. Wahby [1954]. *Application of Econometric Procedures to the Demands for Agricultural Products.* Iowa State College Research Bulletin 410.
Ogg, W. E. [1949]. "A Study of Maladjustment of Resources in Southern Iowa." Unpublished Ph.D. dissertation, University of Chicago.
Orcutt, G. J., M. Greenberger, J. Korbel, and A. M. Rivlin [1961]. *Microanalysis of Socio-Economic Systems: A Simulation Study.* New York: Harper.
Pearson, K. [1938]. *The Grammar of Science.* New York: Dutton.

Phillips, A. W. [1954]. "Stabilization Policy in a Closed Economy." *Econ. J.* 64:290-323.
Pontryagin, L. S., V. G. Boltyanskii, R. V. Gamkrelidze, and E. F. Mischenko [1962]. *The Mathematical Theory of Optimal Processes.* New York: Interscience.
Powell, A. [1966]. "A Complete System of Consumer Demand Equations for the Australian Economy Fitted by a Model of Additive Preferences." *Econometrica* 34: 661-675.
Prescott, E. C. [1967]. "Adaptive Decision Rules for Macro Economic Planning." Unpublished Ph.D. dissertation, Carnegie-Mellon University.
Preston, L. E., and E. J. Bell [1961]. "The Statistical Analysis of Industry Structure: An Application to Food Industries." *J. Am. Stat. Assoc.* 56:925-932.
Raiffa, H. A., and R. S. Schlaifer [1961]. *Applied Statistical Decision Theory.* Boston: Harvard University.
Rao, P., and Z. Griliches [1969]. "Small-Sample Properties of Several Two-Stage Regression Methods in the Context of Auto-Correlated Errors." *J. Am. Stat. Assoc.* 64: 253-272.
Rasche, R. H., and H. T. Shapiro [1968]. "The FRB-MIT Econometric Model: Its Special Features." *Am. Econ. Rev.* 58:123-149.
Rausser, G. C. [1971]. "Dynamic Econometric Model of the California-Arizona Orange Industry." Unpublished Ph.D. dissertation, University of California, Davis.
Rausser, G. C., and T. F. Cargill [1970]. "The Existence of Broiler Cycles: An Application of Spectral Analysis." *Am. J. Agr. Econ.* 52:109-121.
Revankar, N. S. [1966]. "The Constant and Variable Elasticity of Substitution Production Functions: A Comparative Study in United States Manufacturing Industries, Part I." Paper presented at the annual meeting of the Econometric Society, University of Wisconsin Social Systems Research Institute.
Richardson, D. H. [1968]. "The Exact Distribution of a Structural Coefficient Estimator." *J. Am. Stat. Assoc.* 63:1214-1226.
Rojko, A. S. [1953]. "An Application of the Use of Economic Models to the Dairy Industry." *J. Farm Econ.* 35:834-849.
——— [1957a]. *The Demand and Price Structure for Dairy Products.* USDA Technical Bulletin 1168.
——— [1957b]. "Econometric Models for the Dairy Industry." *J. Farm Econ.* 39:323-338.
Rothenberg, T. J. [1972]. "The Bayesian Approach and Alternatives in Econometrics." In *Frontiers of Quantitative Knowledge,* M. D. Intriligator, ed. Amsterdam: North-Holland. Pp. 194-210.
Rothenberg, T. J., and C. T. Leenders [1964]. "Efficient Estimation of Simultaneous Equations Systems." *Econometrica* 32:57-76.
Rutemiller, H. C., and D. A. Bowers [1968]. "Estimation in a Heteroscedastic Regression Model." *J. Am. Stat. Assoc.* 63:552-557.
Samuelson, P. A. [1948]. *Foundations of Economic Analysis.* Cambridge: Harvard University Press.
Savage, L. J. [1954]. *The Foundations of Statistics.* New York: Wiley.
Sawa, T. [1969]. "The Exact Sampling Distribution of Ordinary Least Squares and Two-Stage Least Squares Estimators." *J. Am. Stat. Assoc.* 64:923-937.
——— [1972]. "Finite Sample Properties of the K-Class Estimators." *Econometrica* 40: 653-680.
Schipper, L. [1964]. *Consumer Discretionary Behavior: A Comparative Study in Alternative Methods of Empirical Research.* Amsterdam: North-Holland.

Schultz, H. [1938]. *The Theory and Measurement of Demand*. Chicago: University of Chicago Press.

Sclove, S. L., C. Morris, and R. Radhakrishnan [1972]. "Non-optimality of Preliminary-Test Estimators for the Multinormal Mean." *Annals of Math. Stat.* 43:1481-1490.

Scott, J. T. [1966]. "Factor Analysis and Regression." *Econometrica* 34:552-562.

Shiller, R. [1970]. "The Use of Prior Distributions in Distributed Lag Estimation." Massachusetts Institute of Technology, Economics Discussion Paper.

——— [1973]. "A Distributed Lag Estimator Derived from Smoothed Priors." *Econometrics* 41:775-788.

Shuffett, D. M. [1954]. *The Demand and Price Structure for Selected Vegetables*. USDA Technical Bulletin 1105.

Silvey, S. D. [1969]. "Multicollinearity and Imprecise Estimation." *J. Royal Stat. Soc.* (Series B) 31:539-552.

Smith, R., and T. Hall [1972]. "A Comparison of Maximum Likelihood Versus BLUE Estimates." *Rev. Econ. and Stat.* 54:186-190.

Smith, V. K. [1973]. "A Tabular Review of Sampling Studies with Problems of Autocorrelation and Distributed Lag Models." *International Statistical Rev.* 41:341-350.

Solow, R. M. [1957]. "Technical Change and the Aggregate Production Function." *Rev. Econ. and Stat.* 39:312-320.

Stein, C. [1956]. "Inadmissibility of the Usual Estimator for the Mean of a Multivariate Normal Distribution." *Proceedings of the Third Berkeley Symposium on Mathematical Statistics and Probability*, vol. I. *Contributions to the Theory of Statistics*, Jerry Neyman, ed. Berkeley: University of California Press. Pp. 197-206.

Steindl, J. [1965]. *Random Processes and the Growth of Firms*. New York: Hafner.

Stone, J. R. N. [1954]. "Linear Expenditure Systems and Demand Analysis." *Econ. J.* 64:511-527.

Stone, J. R. N., and M. W. Stone [1938-39]. "The Marginal Propensity to Consume: A Statistical Investigation." *Rev. Econ. Studies* 6:1-24.

Strawderman, W. E. [1971]. "Proper Bayes Minimax Estimators of the Multivariate Normal Mean." *Annals of Math. Stat.* 42:385-388.

Strotz, R. H. [1959]. "The Utility Tree — A Correction and Further Appraisal." *Econometrica* 27:482-488.

Summers, R. [1965]. "A Capital Intensive Approach to the Small-Sample Properties of Various Simultaneous Equation Estimators." *Econometrica* 33:1-41.

Swamy, P. A. V. B. [1971]. "Statistical Inference in Random Coefficient Regression Models." *Lecture Notes in Operations Research and Mathematical Systems*, vol. 55. Heidelberg: Springer-Verlag.

Swanson, E. R. [1956]. "Determining Optimum Size of Business from Production Functions." In *Research Productivity, Returns to Scale and Farm Size*, E. O. Heady, G. L. Johnson, and L. S. Hardin, eds. Ames: Iowa State College Press.

Telser, L. G. [1963]. "Least Squares Estimates of Transition Probabilities." In *Measurement in Economics*. Stanford: Stanford University Press.

Theil, H. [1954]. *Linear Aggregation of Economic Relations*. Amsterdam: North-Holland.

——— [1957]. "Specification Errors and the Estimation of Economic Relationships." *Rev. Int. Stat. Institute* 25:41-51.

——— [1963]. "On the Use of Incomplete Prior Information in Regression Analysis." *J. Am. Stat. Assoc.* 58:401-414.

———— [1965]. "The Analysis of Disturbances in Regression Analysis." *J. Am. Stat. Assoc.* 60:1067-1079.

———— [1967]. *Economics and Information Theory.* Amsterdam: North-Holland.

———— [1968]. "A Simplification of the BLUS Procedure for Analyzing Regression Disturbances." *J. Am. Stat. Assoc.* 63:242-251.

———— [1971]. *Principles of Econometrics.* New York: Wiley.

Theil, H., and J. C. G. Boot [1962]. "The Final Form of Econometric Equations Systems." *Rev. Int. Stat. Institute* 30:136-152.

Theil, H., and A. S. Goldberger [1961]. "On Pure and Mixed Statistical Estimation in Economics." *Int. Econ. Rev.* 2:65-78.

Thornber, E. H. [1966]. "Applications of Decision Theory of Econometrics." Unpublished Ph.D. dissertation, University of Chicago.

———— [1967]. "Finite Sample Monte Carlo Studies: An Autoregressive Illustration." *J. Am. Stat. Assoc.* 62:801-818.

Tiao, G. C., and A. Zellner [1964]. "Bayesian Analysis of the Regression Model with Autocorrelated Errors." *J. Am. Stat. Assoc.* 59:763-778.

Tinbergen, J. [1938]. "Statistical Evidence on the Accelerator Principle." *Economica* 10:164-176.

———— [1939]. *Statistical Testing of Business Cycle Theories.* Vols. 1 and 2. Geneva: League of Nations.

Tintner, G. [1940]. *The Variate Difference Method.* Bloomington: Bloomington Press.

———— [1952]. *Econometrics.* New York: Wiley.

———— [1966]. "Some Thoughts about the State of Econometrics." In *The Structure of Economic Science: Essays on Methodology,* S. R. Krupp, ed. Englewood Cliffs, N.J.: Prentice-Hall.

Tobin, J. [1950]. "A Statistical Demand Function for Food in the U.S.A." *J. Royal Stat. Soc.* (Series A) 113:113-141.

Toro-Vizcarrondo, C., and T. D. Wallace [1968]. "A Test of the Mean Square Error Criterion for Restrictions in Linear Regression." *J. Am. Stat. Assoc.* 63:558-572.

Tsang, H. [1971]. "A Generalized Neoclassical Production Function." Unpublished Ph.D. dissertation, University of Illinois.

Vining, R., and T. C. Koopmans [1949]. "Methodological Issues in Quantitative Economics." *Rev. Econ. and Stat.* 32:77-94.

Von Neumann, J., and O. Morgenstern [1947]. *Theory of Games and Economic Behavior.* Princeton: Princeton University Press. (Second edition now available.)

Wagner, H. [1958]. "A Monte Carlo Study of Estimates of Simultaneous Linear Structural Equations." *Econometrica* 26:117-133.

Wald, A. [1950]. *Statistical Decision Functions.* New York: Wiley.

Wallace, T. D. [1972]. "Weaker Criteria for Tests for Linear Restrictions in Regression." *Econometrica* 40:689-698.

Wallace, T. D., and A. Hussain [1969]. "The Use of Error Components Models in Combining Cross Section with Time Series Data." *Econometrica* 37:55-72.

Walters, A. A. [1970]. *An Introduction to Econometrics.* New York: Norton.

Waugh, F. V. [1961]. "The Place of Least Squares in Econometrics." *Econometrica* 29:386-396.

Wilks, S. S. [1947]. *Mathematical Statistics.* Princeton: Princeton University Press.

Wold, H. O. [1956]. "Causal Inference from Observational Data: A Review of Ends and Means." *J. Roy. Stat. Soc.* (Series A) 119:28-61.

———— [1969]. "Econometrics as Pioneering in Nonexperimental Model Building." *Econometrica* 37:369-381.

Working, E. J. [1926]. "What Do Statistical 'Demand Curves' Show?" *Quart. J. Econ.* 41:212-235.

———— [1954]. *The Demand for Meat*. Chicago: Institute of Meat Packing.

Wright, S. [1934]. "The Method of Path Coefficients." *Annals of Math. Stat.* 5:161-215.

Yancey, T. A., G. G. Judge, and M. E. Bock [1974]. "A Mean Square Error Test When Stochastic Restrictions Are Used in Regression." *Communications in Statistics* 8: 755-768.

Zellner, A. [1962a]. "An Efficient Method of Estimating Seemingly Unrelated Regressions and Tests for Aggregation Bias." *J. Am. Stat. Assoc.* 57:348-368.

———— [1962b]. *On the Questionable Virtue of Aggregation*. Social Systems Research Institute Workshop Paper 6202.

———— [1963]. "Decision Rules for Economic Forecasting." *Econometrica* 31:111-130.

———— [1967]. *Aggregation: A New Approach to an Old Problem*. University of Chicago, Mathematical Economics Center Workshop Paper.

———— [1970a]. "The Care and Feeding of Econometric Models." Paper prepared for Seventeenth Annual Midwest Conference on Statistics for Decision. University of Chicago Graduate School of Business, Selected Paper 35.

———— [1970b]. "Estimation of Regression Relationships Containing Unobservable Variables." *Int. Econ. Rev.* 11:441-454.

———— [1971]. *An Introduction to Bayesian Inference in Econometrics*. New York: Wiley.

———— [1972]. "The Bayesian Approach and Alternatives in Econometrics." In *Frontiers of Quantitative Knowledge*, M. D. Intriligator, ed. Amsterdam: North-Holland. Pp. 178-195.

Zellner, A., and M. S. Geisel [1968]. "Sensitivity of Control to Uncertainty and Form of the Criterion Function." In *The Future of Statistics*, D. G. Watts, ed. New York: Academic Press.

Zellner, A., and F. Palm [1973]. "Time Series Analysis and Simultaneous Equation Models." H. G. B. Alexander Foundation Paper, University of Chicago.

Zellner, A., and N. S. Revankar [1969]. "Generalized Production Functions." *Rev. Econ. Studies* 36:241-250.

Zellner, A., and H. Theil [1962]. "Three-Stage Least Squares: Simultaneous Estimation of Simultaneous Equations." *Econometrica* 30:54-78.

Zellner, A., and W. Vandaele [1974]. "Bayes-Stein Estimators for the K Means, Regression and Simultaneous Equation Models." In *Studies in Bayesian Econometrics and Statistics*, S. Fienberg and A. Zellner, eds. Amsterdam: North-Holland.

Discussion of George G. Judge's
Estimation and Statistical
Inference in Economics

Richard J. Foote
Professor of Agricultural Economics
Texas Technological University

My first knowledge of this field was obtained at Iowa State in 1936 when, as a graduate assistant, I was asked by Professor Geoffrey Shepherd to work with J. Russell Ives in an attempt to show the relation between graphic and mathematical regression analysis. After much work, and a transfer to the old Bureau of Agricultural Economics in the USDA in Washington, we developed a paper which we submitted to the *Journal of Farm Economics*. The editors of the *Journal* replied that it was an excellent paper but that they felt it should be submitted to the *Journal of the American Statistical Association*. In the meantime we had decided that it should be consigned to the wastebasket!

In about 1940 the USDA hired a mathematical statistician, M. A. Girshick, to work on the measurement of clothing sizes for children. I told Girshick that the graphic method yielded approximation to the true mathematical partial relations. He said, "You are wrong." I said, "I am sorry, sir, but I know I am right." So he said, "I will prove that you are wrong." After five minutes of what to him was simple algebra, he proved that I was right. So he became interested in the problem and showed that the Bean [1929] method of successive approximation is a geometric equivalent of a mathematical iterative approach that converges to the true least squares regressions. Problems arise at times because, if the independent variables are highly correlated, the initial estimates of the regressions probably will deviate widely from the true partial

Note: Richard J. Foote is now teaching agricultural economics at the University of Dar es Salaam, Morogoro, Tanzania.

regressions and the speed of convergence is very slow. Thus in such cases the graphic analyst is apt to stop long before he reaches the true slopes. These conclusions were published by Foote and Ives [1941] in a mimeographed BAE report. Since the distribution of this report was limited, the conclusions were restated in an article by Foote [1953].

In the meantime, serious questions were raised by agricultural economists about whether multiple regression could be used to measure economic relations. The argument was advanced that these methods had been developed to apply to experimental data and could be used only with such data. At a conference on price analysis at the 1936 annual meeting of the American Farm Economic Association, Sturges [1937, p. 699] said: "our current attitude toward correlation constants, whether of mathematical or of graphical derivation, is one of skepticism, or at best, of uncertainty. With a decade or more of none-too-successful economic forecasting behind us we rightfully wonder if a high correlation coefficient or a low standard error of estimate is really any basis for assurance that our forecast, or inference as to the future, will be sufficiently correct for practical needs. Our inferences as to the future are being based very largely upon our own personal opinion of what 'common sense' consists and not upon a thoughtful, but purely objective, consideration of the data as a sample from an infinite universe. Probability, in its precise sense, is seldom a factor in our inferences."

A year or so later Sturges left the Bureau of Agricultural Economics, returned to farming, and has not been heard from since. Some time later George Judge gave up and turned to linear programming, but the references cited by him relating to the 1970s suggest that he has returned to the fold. Still later economists in the USDA became involved with the logistics of food allocation and supply for agricultural commodities during World War II and forgot about theoretical problems relating to multiple regression.

In 1946 I was employed by a consulting firm to develop price analyses to predict where prices would go when ceilings were removed. This was a challenge because historic data on free-market prices ended in 1941, and predictions were needed for 1946-47. Armed with desk calculators, two clerks and I worked for six months and developed least squares regressions for ten or so commodities that saved our client millions of dollars by telling the client whether to go long or short in futures contracts. This restored my faith in the application of regression analysis to economic data.

In 1950 I returned to the USDA in Washington. Karl Fox introduced me to the simultaneous equations approach and, with the help of Klein [1953], I learned to use this fascinating new tool. Our first model was developed from a notion formulated by Bob Post, who had been writing material for *Wheat Situation* (a quarterly report by the USDA Economic Research Service on market intelligence, outlook, and policy for wheat) for twenty years or more. Highly experienced clerks worked for six months on desk calculators to fit the model by limited information. Fortunately, the coefficients seemed reasonable. The rationale for the model was described by Meinken [1955], and Foote and Weingarten [1956] showed how this and a related model could be used as a guide to price-support policy.

Other models worthy of mention that came out of the USDA during the period were those by Rojko [1957] on dairy products and by Gerra [1959] on eggs, and later models by Harlow [1962] on hogs and by Hee [1967] on potatoes. George Kuznets and I attempted to develop methods of analysis for consumer panel data on citrus and related products (Kuznets and Foote [1954]), but little of practical value was completed.

In 1957 I joined a newly formed consulting firm that wished to emphasize application of econometric methods to price forecasting. Harry Eisenpress, who had done much of the programming on the Census method of seasonal adjustment, joined IBM at about this time to develop a full information program for their computers. We fitted models by full information relating to Maine potatoes, eggs (including the yolk/albumen/whole egg complex), and cocoa beans and products. The egg model was a dud. As a last resort, I used what now would be called a first-round equation. But the cocoa model was a great success. The model we presented to our clients was bearish. The clients argued that the price trend, if one prevailed, could only be up. Within six months, the price had dropped by 30 percent! I have been told that the model has predicted several other major turning points, some of which were missed by the trade.

Making and losing money occupied my time for the next several years. As they say, "Those who can, do; those who can't, teach." So I ended up as a professor at Texas Tech. Somehow I learned about three-stage least squares. The Thornber and Zellner computer program [1965], adapted for the IBM 360/50, was obtained from the USDA in Washington. I had traded on the pork belly futures market and was convinced that a system of equations was needed to predict these prices. A graduate student fitted quarterly models by three-stage least squares as a term paper, and we then obtained a grant from the United States Commodity Exchange Authority to refine them. The results were published in two articles (Foote, Craven, and Williams [1972] and Foote, Williams, and Craven [1973]). The models gave useful price forecasts outside the period of fit for a year and a half.

What can we conclude from my experiences and Judge's excellent review? First, successful models have been formulated and fitted despite all the theoretical objections and the fact that one generally must work with poor data and small samples. To fit good models, one must have access to sound knowledge about how the particular sector operates and a certain minimum volume of acceptable data. Second, based on my research, methods that have been shown to be best by Monte Carlo studies—namely, full information and three-stage least squares—also seem to give the best results in applied work. Third, the need exists for sound research to adapt these methods and to develop other methods of this type as decision-making tools both for industry and government. This, I believe, is generally recognized, although many economists may doubt that existing methods are practical. Fourth, progress will continue to be made, first by mathematicians who develop and refine the methodology and then, perhaps much later, by those of us who work in applied areas. As noted by Judge, the electronic computer has been of immense value in the application of some of the newer techniques.

References

Bean, L. H. [1929]. "A Simplified Method of Graphic Curvilinear Correlation." *J. Am. Stat. Assoc.* 24:286-397.

Foote, R. J. [1953]. "The Mathematical Basis for the Bean Method of Graphic Multiple Correlation." *J. Am. Stat. Assoc.* 48:778-788.

Foote, R. J., J. A. Craven, and R. R. Williams, Jr. [1972]. "Quarterly Models to Predict Cash Prices of Pork Bellies." *Am. J. Agr. Econ.* 54:603-610.

Foote, R. J., and J. R. Ives [1941]. *The Relation of the Method of Graphic Correlation to Least Squares.* United States Bureau of Agricultural Economics, Statistics and Agriculture No. 1.

Foote, R. J., and H. Weingarten [1956]. "How Research Results Can Be Used to Analyze Alternative Governmental Policies." *Agr. Econ. Res.* 8:33-43.

Foote, R. J., R. R. Williams, Jr., and J. A. Craven [1973]. *Quarterly and Shorter-Term Price Forecasting Models Relating to Cash and Futures Quotations for Pork Bellies.* USDA Technical Bulletin 1482.

Gerra, M. J. [1959]. *The Demand, Supply, and Price Structure for Eggs.* USDA Technical Bulletin 1204.

Harlow, A. A. [1962]. *Factors Affecting the Price and Supply of Hogs.* USDA Technical Bulletin 1274.

Hee, O. [1967]. *Demand and Price Analysis for Potatoes.* USDA Technical Bulletin 1380.

Klein, L. R. [1953]. *A Textbook of Econometrics.* Evanston: Row, Peterson.

Kuznets, G. M., and R. J. Foote [1954]. "The Demand for Citrus Products." Abstract, *J. Am. Stat. Assoc.* 49:361-362.

Meinken, K. W. [1955]. *The Demand and Price Structure for Wheat.* USDA Technical Bulletin 1136.

Rojko, A. S. [1957]. *The Demand and Price Structure for Dairy Products.* USDA Technical Bulletin 1168.

Sturges, A. [1937]. "The Use of Correlation in Price Analysis." *J. Farm Econ.* 19:699-706.

Thornber, H., and A. Zellner [1965]. *Program for Computing Two- and Three-Stage Least Squares Estimates and Associated Statistics.* University of Wisconsin, Social Systems Research Institute, Systems Formulation and Methodology Workshop Paper 6308. Revised July 1965.

Part II. Economic Optimization in Agricultural and Resource Economics

This paper is dedicated to Geoffrey S. Shepherd, exemplary scholar and developer of economies and economists. Edward Sparling assisted in the preparation of the section on risk and uncertainty and the bibliography. The paper was written while the author was a visiting professor at the Mathematics Research Center, University of Wisconsin.

R. H. D.

On Economic Optimization:
A Nontechnical Survey

Richard H. Day
Professor of Economics
University of Southern California, Los Angeles

For at least two centuries economic principles have involved three fundamental concepts. First, individual or group behavior can be explained—at least in part—as the result of pursuing one's advantage. Second, a given system of individuals or nations may possess a kind of harmony or equilibrium when each individual or nation pursues its own advantage. Third, if the environment is properly structured, the working of an economy may bring about individual optima and group equilibria. As early as Cournot [1838], these ideas began to receive an explicit mathematical treatment. It was Cournot who first used calculus to analyze the three classical notions of optimum, equilibrium, and process in markets. The methods that he initiated dominated analytical economics for over a century. The more or less definitive form of this neoclassical, marginalist economics was established by Jevons [1871], Marshall [1890], and Walras [1874] and culminated with Hicks's *Value and Capital* [1939] and Samuelson's *Foundations of Economic Analysis* [1948].

From the vantage point of our generation it is clear that something substantial was lost in the neoclassical mathematization of classical economic thought. The issue involves alternative assumptions about the underlying structure of choices and its role in bringing about compatibility between individual optimization and group equilibrium. It is now clear, thanks to Samuelson [1949, 1959a, 1959b] and others, that some of the classical ideas—for example, the theory of rent (Malthus, West) and the theory of trade (Ricardo, Mill)—are most naturally expressed by means of linear programming models, a postneoclassical development. But this linear programming structure could not be accommodated in the "smooth" neoclassical world. With the advent of Arrow and Debreu's analysis [1954] of general equilibrium this problem was overcome. Classical linearities and inequalities could be incorporated into the general economic optimization framework. Thus, modern optimization theory not only helps to mathematize and illustrate classical ideas, it makes it possible to identify the fundamental unity in two centuries of economic thought.

The transition to the modern period began to occur even before the closing of the neoclassical system by Hicks and Samuelson. The catalysts for this include Leontief, Von Neumann, and Wald. Leontief's input-output or interindustry model [1928, 1936] and Von Neumann's growth model [1937, 1945] captured essential features of classical thought and through the use of algebra forced a shift away from the calculus of the neoclassical school. The game theory of Von Neumann [1928] and Von Neumann and Morgenstern [1944] made possible a profound new formalization of the multiperson joint optimization problem inherent in economics and introduced the axiomatic method and topology. Wald [1936, 1951] contributed the first rigorous proof of the existence of general equilibrium among economic optimizing individuals. The full impact of this reorientation came at mid-century when the duality of constrained optimization and economic valuation was established by Gale, Kuhn, and Tucker [1951] and Kuhn and Tucker [1951] and when efficient optimization algorithms were discovered. Especially because of Dantzig's simplex method [1949] for linear programming, optimization became a tool for planners as well as a theory for economists. Further background material relating optimization concepts to the history of economic thought will be found in Samuelson [1948], Koopmans [1951], Dorfman, Samuelson, and Solow [1958], and Leontief [1960].

During the past two decades modern optimization theory and methods have continued to develop, and at the same time their effective application has spread to a growing variety of important applied problems. The literature is indeed by now so vast as to preclude a comprehensive survey. In this overview, therefore, we shall present a nontechnical summary of the most important concepts involved in these developments for economic theory and applied analysis. The applications of optimization theory to problems in agricultural and resource economics are reviewed elsewhere in this volume (see "Optimization Models in Agricultural and Resource Economics" by Richard H. Day and Edward Sparling).

Optimization Models

For a very long time the mathematical development of theoretical and applied economics was severely circumscribed by the limited class of optimization model types with which it could cope. Though many fundamental barriers remain, the breakthroughs just recalled resulted in a spectrum of operational optimizing models. This spectrum can be broken down according to the components of an optimization model which we will outline. Various important examples are then illustrated. Next, the concept of infinite programming is used to show how the classical and neoclassical optimization approaches are related. Remarks on the distinction between problems and models conclude the chapter.

The following more or less standard definitions will facilitate our discussion: "Optimizing" is finding a best choice among possible or feasible alternative choices. An "optimization model" is a specific formalization of a problem in terms of its comparable alternatives, the criterion for comparing alternatives, and the feasible alternatives. A "mathematical optimization model" consists of a "choice space," which is the set of comparable alternatives, an "objective function," which describes how alternatives are to be compared, and a "feasible region," which is a subset of the choice space and contains those alternatives that are eligible for choice. The feasible region is usually — though not always — defined by equations or inequality constraints.

The choice space. Virtually all economic optimization models involve real linear spaces in which each comparable choice may be represented by a vector of real variables. If the dimension of the choice space is finite, so that the number of choice variables is finite, we have a finite-dimensional optimization model. Otherwise the model is called infinite-dimensional. If each variable or component in the choice space can take on any real value, we have "continuous" or "real" optimization; if each variable may take on only discrete values, we have "discrete" or "integer" optimization. If some variables are discrete while others are continuous, we have "mixed integer" optimization. According to the type of choice space, then, we may distinguish six types of optimization models as summarized in the following outline.

Optimization Models by Type of Choice Space

1. Finite-dimensional optimization
   - 1.1 Continuous or real variables
   - 1.2 Discrete or integer variables (integer programming)
   - 1.3 Continuous *and* discrete variables (mixed integer programming)
2. Infinite-dimensional optimization
   - 2.1 Continuous variables
   - 2.2 Discrete variables
   - 2.3 Continuous *and* discrete variables

The linear and quadratic programming problems and the neoclassical optimizing fall in category 1.1. The transportation problem is an example of category 1.2. Models including increasing returns to scale utilize category 1.3. Optimal control and dynamic programming models are often defined for an infinite future and provide examples of category 2.1. Categories 2.2 or 2.3 would arise if "lumpy" or discrete capital goods were incorporated into the infinite optimization, though to date this does not appear to have been done.

The objective (criterion, utility, payoff) function. In mathematical optimization alternatives are compared by means of their real value as given by some real valued function. This function defines a preference ordering on the alternatives in the choice space. Objective functions may be classified according to their mathematical properties: smoothness or continuity properties, concavity or convexity properties, separability or interdependence properties, and special forms. Thus we have the following outline which gives some of the relevant distinctions.

Function Characteristics

1. Continuity properties
    1.1 Semicontinuous, upper or lower (allows for step functions)
    1.2 Continuous functions
    1.3 Differentiable functions
    1.4 Twice-differentiable functions
    Etc.
2. Concavity properties
    2.1 Concave (convex)
    2.2 Strictly concave (convex)
    2.3 Pseudo concave (convex)
    2.4 Quasi concave (convex)
    2.5 Strictly quasi concave (convex)
    Etc.
3. Separability properties
    3.1 Partially separable
    3.2 Completely separable
4. Special functional forms
    4.1 Linear
    4.2 Quadratic
    4.3 Power
    Etc.
5. Monotonicity properties
    5.1 Nondecreasing (increasing)
    5.2 Strictly increasing (decreasing)

In discrete or mixed optimization problems the objective function is usually defined on the continuous space within which the choice space is imbedded. The preference ordering is then defined for all continuous choices even though only discrete ones are allowed.

The feasible region. If the choice is unrestricted in the choice space, the optimization model is called "unconstrained." In this case the feasible region is the entire choice space. Otherwise, when the feasible region is a proper subset of the choice space, it is called "constrained." Feasible regions are classified according to various criteria: closedness (containing limit points), boundedness, or more generally by their compactness or noncompactness; convexity properties; and special functional forms. If the feasible region is defined by an equation, or a set of equations, then we have an "equality-constrained optimization model." If it is defined by inequalities, it is called an "inequality-constrained problem." Because an equation can be expressed by two inequalities, the latter contains the former as a special case. Nonetheless, because mathematical techniques employed in each differ markedly, equality and inequality cases should be regarded as separate categories. In either event it is necessary to define constraint functions. For each type of constraint function we get a specific type of optimization problem. Thus the classes of functions enumerated above are relevant from this point of view too. The following outline summarizes the most important criteria for determining types of feasible regions.

Feasible Region Characteristics

1. Unconstrained optimization: The feasible region is the entire space.
2. Equality-constrained optimization: The feasible region is defined by equations. See the table of function characteristics above.
3. Inequality-constrained optimization
    3.1 Compactness or noncompactness
    3.2 Geometric properties
        (1) nonconvexity
        (2) convexity
        (3) strictly convexity
        (4) polyhedral form (as in linear programming)
    3.3 Constraint function types. See the table of function characteristics given earlier.

The basic questions of optimization theory must be posed for each optimization model or class of models: (1) Do solutions exist? (2) How many are there? (3) How can solutions be characterized? (4) How can solutions be found? The answers and the methods used to obtain them depend of course on the characteristics of each model type. The neoclassical economists rarely concerned themselves with the possibility of multiple optima, indeed, they used the calculus of smooth functions to structure models which possessed unique solutions although they were characteristically vague about, or even ignored, the exact model characteristics to justify their results. The implications of these mathematical issues for economic theory are of greater importance than is usually recognized. Indeed, with the appreciation of function characteristics in optimization theory (especially convexity properties) has come the significant realization that what was once assumed to be true of all private or public ownership economies could in fact be proven true only for economies with very special and not too realistic constraint and preference structures.

Modern optimization theory addresses itself very often to situations in which many "best" solutions exist such as in linear programming. In this example the set of solutions forms a simplex, a "polyhedral face" generated by its extreme points. The location of such extreme points was found by Dantzig to involve sequences of straightforward algebraic calculations. This shows how theoretical characteristics yield insights leading to answers to the question: How can solutions be found? Another example, brilliantly expounded in Samuelson's classic "Market Mechanisms and Maximization" [1949] shows how the duality properties of constrained optimization can be used to guide a sequence of relatively simple adjustments to the constrained optimum thus, in effect, mimicking the market process. We shall return to these issues later. However, at this point we illustrate a few of the most important optimization models in a way that brings out some of their distinctive features.

In figure 1 the isoquants of an objective function are illustrated by more or less concentric, somewhat irregular curves. The arrows normal to these isoquants indicate the direction of locally steepest ascent of the objective function. Point A is the optimizer of the unconstrained problem. The curve in the

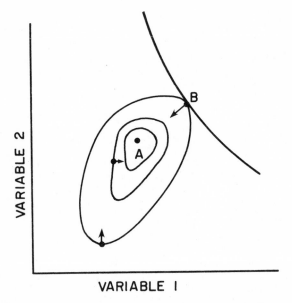

VARIABLE I

Figure 1. Unconstrained and equation-constrained optima

upper right part of the diagram illustrates an equation constraint to which the choice would be confined for an equality-constrained problem, in which case the optimizer is the point B, as point A is no longer feasible. Figure 2 shows how the mathematical programming model varies in its structure according to changes in the choice space and in the type of objective and constraint func-

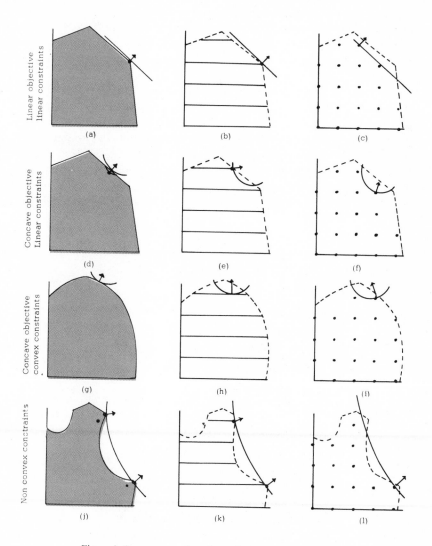

Figure 2. Some types of mathematical programming models

tion. Diagram (a) is the linear programming model, (b) the mixed integer, and (c) the integer linear programming model. In the first column the choice variables can vary continuously; the feasible region is the shaded area on the diagram. In the middle column variable 2 must be an integer while variable 1 can be continuous; the feasible region consists of the parallel lines. In the last column only integer variables are allowed; the feasible region is represented by the dots. The rows show how problems in these three categories change as objective functions and/or constraint functions change from linear to concave or convex or to nonconcave or nonconvex functions. Diagram (l), for example, illustrates integer programming with quasi concave objectives and nonconvex constraints.

Representing choices as integer variables introduces mathematical difficulties of a most formidable nature. There is some intellectual irony in this fact for in the pure integer case the number of feasible alternatives, if the feasible region is bounded, is finite; an exhaustive search is possible. In the continuous case the number of contenders for choice is nondenumerably infinite, even in a problem with only one dimension, and exhaustive search is impossible. Yet it is usually easier to solve continuous models at least approximately than it is to solve discrete ones. In the linear programming model where objective and constraint functions are linear, an unfortunate consequence of this fact is

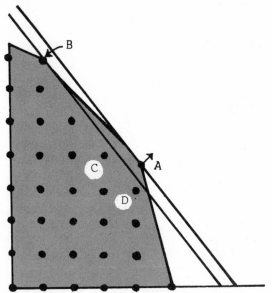

Figure 3. Continuous (A) and integer (B) solutions;
suboptimal integer solutions (C, D)

easily illustrated. Figure 3 shows the true feasible region consisting of integer valued variables (dots) inside the shaded convex feasible region where the variables are assumed to be continuous. The continuous variable optimum is A, a point very far removed from the ("true") integer optimum B. If we round the continuous solution A to its nearest integer value, we get C or D, points also far removed from the optimum.

Infinite-dimensional programming. Optimizing over an infinite horizon arises in economic theories of capital and growth. When formalized, these theories lead to programming models in which the choice space is infinite-dimensional. (We shall take up this class of models later.) What is scarcely appreciated by economists, though fundamental in mathematics, is the extremely close relationship between infinite-dimensional and finite, continuous problems. We touch on this point next because it affords an opportunity to show how concepts from mathematical optimization theory can be exploited to reveal the underlying unity of various schools of economic thought to which we referred in the first section of this chapter.

Let us consider the purely competitive optizimizing problem of the price-taking firm that produces an output in amount y, using an input in amount x according to a production function illustrated by the smooth curve in figure 4. If the profit isoquants are parallel to the straight line marked $\pi = P_y - Q_x$, then the optimum is point E. If instead of the smooth neoclassical curve f(x) we used the linear approximation OBD, we would obtain an approximation to the neoclassical problem which we could represent using linear programming. The solution of this problem is point B in figure 4. By choosing a better linear approximation of the production function—say, OABCD—point A, which is closer to the neoclassical solution, is chosen. By making finer and finer linear approximations we could in this way come as close to the smooth optimum solution E as we pleased, just as a circle can be approximated as closely as we like by a polygon. As we do so, the dimension of the approximating linear programming problem increases, going in the limit to infinity where the approximation is perfect. In this way we see a type of duality between infinite-dimensional linear programming and finite-dimensional non-linear programming.

The mathematical duality just illustrated is analogously reflected in the history of economic thought. It is well known (we recall our earlier references to Samuelson) that the classical theory of production, most clearly expounded by Ricardo in his exegesis of the Malthus-West theory of rent, involves a linear programming problem like that illustrated by the piece-wise linear production function in which the input variable is interpreted to be the amount of land with different qualities and in which the yield declines as more land is brought into cultivation. By increasing the number of qualities of land we see

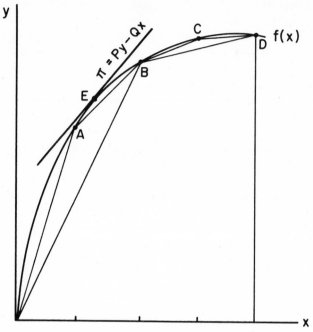

Figure 4. Linear programming as an approximation
of neoclassical optimizing

the convergences of the classical linear programming to the neoclassical smooth production function point of view developed many decades later.

The logical duality of the classical-neoclassical points of view should now alert us to a need for care in how we interpret the term "approximation." Whether we regard the classical linear programming model as an approximation of the neoclassical smooth optimization model or vice versa is a matter not of logic but of relevance, convenience, or interpretation in a particular application. Either may be used as an approximation to some real optimization problem, and one may be preferred to the other on empirical or computational grounds, depending on the nature of the problem at hand. A few economists still seem to think that neoclassical economics is *economics* whereas other forms of optimization theory are methods of operations research of no intrinsic economic interest and useful only in computation settings. Nothing could be further from the truth, as the above exercise demonstrates. Indeed, the neoclassical framework is of no more or less interest or relevance than its classical predecessor, and the very much more general formulation of modern optimization theory encompasses both and establishes their underlying unity.

It is also important to distinguish between model and problem optima. For example, we often use models involving continuous variables when, clearly, many economic variables are discrete in nature (machines, factories, farm buildings). Actual choice situations therefore must often distinguish among "lumpy" alternatives. The continuous optimization *model* must then be thought of as an approximation to an underlying discrete optimization *problem*. That the approximation may not be close is a possibility we have already illustrated in figure 3.

The interested reader should become acquainted with the following texts, which among them cover all of the major optimization model types. We list them in (roughly) ascending order of difficulty: Heady and Candler [1958], Hadley [1962], and Gale [1960] cover linear programming; Hu [1969] is concerned with integer and mixed-integer models; Hadley [1964], Intriligator [1971], Mangasarian [1969], and Karlin [1959] among them cover nonlinear programming, dynamic programming, and optimal control; Canon, Cullum, and Polak [1970] and Leuenberger [1969] give a unified treatment of programming, programming in infinite spaces, and optimal control. Aubin [n.d.] provides an advanced synthesis of optimization and game theory emphasizing duality relationships. There are also several excellent expository pieces by Dorfman [1953] on linear programming, Dorfman [1969] on optimal control, and Baumol [1958].

Parametric Programming and Comparative Static Analysis

In both theoretical and applied economics the study of how optima change in response to changes in the situation of the decision maker is of extreme interest. In optimization theory this study is called parametric programming or perturbation analysis. In economic theory it is called comparative statics. By means of it economists have constructed special theories of consumer demand, of producer supply, and of derived producer demand. Moreover, the careful mathematical study of optimizing behavior plays a central role in modern general equilibrium theory. This is because the theoretical analysis of the existence and properties of general equilibria depend on how well-behaved or smooth optimal sets are in their response to market situations.

In neoclassical models in which unconstrained or equality-constrained optimizations are specified, functions are assumed to be sufficiently smooth to make possible application of ordinary calculus. Equations are defined by setting the gradient of the objective function, or of the Lagrangian (in the equality-constrained case), equal to zero. Any optimum must satisfy these equations. These so-called first-order conditions are then interpreted as implicit functions which can be solved to give the decision variables as functions of the parameters and exogenous variables of the problem. Even if this explicit functional dependence cannot be derived practically, it is often possible to infer its qualitative character such as "an increase in price will cause a fall in demand" and so forth. Econometricians are especially interested in those models for which the equations can be solved, for then the parameters of the optimization model may be estimated in reduced form.

As we have already noted, the classical models did not have sufficient regularity to make possible the application of calculus, and no doubt largely for that reason interest in them waned until the modern era, when the tools for inequality-constrained optimizations were perfected. Efficient algorithms for parametric programming made possible a reconsideration of step supply and demand functions and the kinked total cost functions of the classical production theory. They also made it possible to conduct traditional comparative static analysis for a vastly expanded range of economic problems.

The achievement was not without cost, however, for the neoclassical equilibrium and welfare theory completed by Hicks, Lange, and Samuelson did not cover the more general optimizations used in practical decision making. The methods for studying the modern optimization models in the general equilibrium setting, however, were not long in coming. Arrow and Debreu [1954] and McKenzie [1955] showed how topological methods and convex analysis could be used to extend the results on existence and efficiency of competitive equilibria to an economy made of modern (and classical) mathematical programmers.

The supply and demand functions that emerge from the modern point of view include, in addition to the traditional smooth neoclassical variety of Marshall's principles as shown in figure 5 (b), the classical step functions and the modern multivalued mappings or correspondences of the kind illustrated in figure 5 (a), (b), and (c). In (a) we find several prices at which the underlying optimizing behavior can take on any one of several possible supplies or demands. In (c) this indeterminance is continuous. In (d) optimizing behavior of a consumer also becomes indeterminant after some *income* level is reached. Any quantity within a given range inside the shaded area might be picked. The incorporation of the integer and mixed integer cases into the main stream of economic theory was given an impressive beginning by Charles Frank [1969]. But a complete comparative static treatment of it as needed for general equilibrium theory remains a task for future contributors. The kinky step function and correspondences that derive from modern parametric programming often have more complex qualitative appearances than their neoclassical counterparts and can indeed seldom be expressed in mathematically closed form. Instead they must be derived computationally and except for

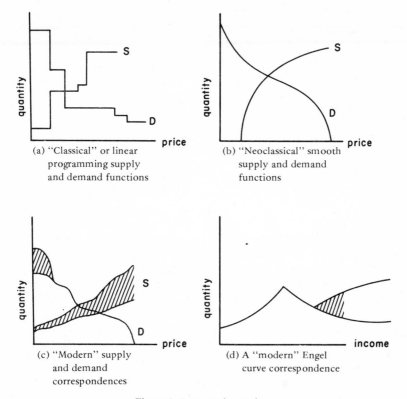

(a) "Classical" or linear
    programming supply
    and demand functions

(b) "Neoclassical" smooth
    supply and demand
    functions

(c) "Modern" supply
    and demand
    correspondences

(d) A "modern" Engel
    curve correspondence

Figure 5. Comparative statics

the smallest problems computers must be used. The trouble and expense of these computations and the corresponding lack of hard, general results in such situations no doubt explain in part the continued vitality of the simpler, better behaved, and less realistic neoclassical models.

The classical work on comparative statics is Samuelson's *Foundations of Economic Analysis* [1948]. He gave the definitive form of the neoclassical parametric optimization and, through the copious exploration of discrete (not infinitesimal) changes and inequalities, anticipated much of the qualitative character of the modern economic structures. Early treatments of parametric linear programming are presented by Simon [1951], Hildreth [1957], and Manne [1956]. Much less has been done in comparative statics for nonlinear and infinite programming, although the very recent work of Araujo, Chichilnisky, and Kalman [1973] promises to provide a breakthrough in this area.

Duality

Our classical predecessors emphasized the fact that use-value was a necessary but not sufficient property for a thing to possess value in exchange. It had also to be scarce or costly to acquire. The neoclassical economists began to unravel the logical mysteries connected with this simple insight. But they failed to unravel them all. It was not until the Kuhn-Tucker theorem for nonlinear programming and the duality theory of linear programming appeared that the essential classical insights on value theory were fully mathematized. The full duality of optimization became evident: as values determine choice, so choice imputes values. Moreover, a resource has economic value only when more of it would allow preferred choices to be made, or when less of it would force acceptance of less preferred alternatives.

In the latter form we see an application of perturbation or comparative static analysis, for one way in which to formalize the duality concepts of value is to study how the value of the best choices varies when one resource at a time is varied slightly. One arrives in this way at the generalized marginal values, shadow prices, Lagrangian or dual variables of general optimization theory, and various versions of the Kuhn-Tucker theorem. Figure 6 (a) illustrates this comparative static view. When constraint one (denoted C1) is perturbed so that the feasible region expands, the best choice shifts from A to B with an increase in the value of the program. Hence, C1 has an imputed value which

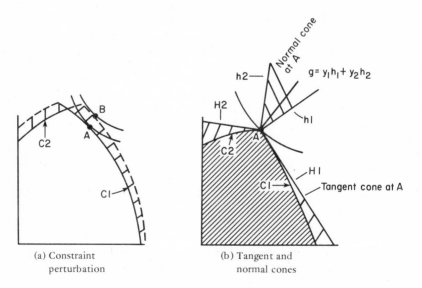

(a) Constraint   (b) Tangent and
    perturbation   normal cones

Figure 6. Two views of duality

is roughly the increment of value divided by the increment by which the constraint is augmented. In contrast, when C2 is shifted, the optimum does not change. Hence, no value is imputed to constraint C2. These imputed values, either positive or zero as the case may be, are, roughly speaking, the partial derivative of the optimal value of the paragram with respect to changes in the limitations or "right-hand-side" coefficients.

An alternative, essentially geometric view of duality is illustrated in figure 6 (b). Here we show an optimum A at which *both* constraints are binding. At this point each constraint possesses a plane of support which is the tangent plane at the optimum point A. The two planes of support are denoted H1 and H2 and are determined by the normal vectors h_1 and h_2. These in turn determine a supporting cone called the tangent cone. It is the intersection of all the half spaces determined by the planes of support containing the feasible region. The gradient g of the objective function, which points in the direction of steepest ascent, can be expressed as a linear combination of the normal vectors that define the supporting cone with weights, say, y_1 and y_2. That is $g = y_1 h_1 + y_2 h_2$. These y's are the dual variables or economic imputations implied by the optimum choice at A.

This geometric point of view brings out in stark relief the relationship between imputed values and the convex shape of the constraints and objective functions of the optimizing problem. Indeed imputed value is difficult to determine or even to interpret in some of the less regular optimization models. In these latter cases little can be said about the possibility or efficacy of decentralized market mechanisms. On the other hand the computation of optima is likewise difficult so that central planning may still be difficult or impossible to carry out in such cases. Procedures more or less the same as trial and error must be invoked.

The references given at the end of the section on optimization models all have good discussions of duality. Much of the contemporary work in duality theory stems from Rockafellar's *Convex Analysis* [1970]. Balinsky and Baumol [1968] supply an elaborate economic exegesis of duality in nonlinear programming, and Leuenberger [1969] gives a good advanced treatment. Aubin [n.d.] provides an extremely general abstract development.

Algorithms

It is often said that modern optimization concepts were given their great impetus by the electronic computer and George Dantzig's simplex method, for it is one thing to know that an optimum exists and quite another to know how to find one economically. The simplex method for linear programming was extended to various quadratic programming models, to mixed integer programming, and to other examples. Very quickly thereafter various gradient methods appeared for nonlinear programming when the functions were convex or concave. Gradient methods (or methods of steepest ascent) of various kinds were suggested, some of which were built directly on the Kuhn-Tucker theorem and some of which were geometrically motivated.

Implicit in every optimization model whose numerical solution is sought, is the question, "What is the optimum way to find the optimum?" That is, "How can the cost of using a given optimizing model be minimized?" One of the very early discoveries connected with the new simplex algorithm was its astonishing efficiency for general classes of problems. Yet, no one has ever shown it to be the best algorithm for general linear programming problems. Indeed, new modifications and improvements continue to appear, and better ways of finding optima for special types of linear programming models are found in a seemingly unending progression.

The technical issues involved can be illustrated by a smooth, unconstrained minimization model that has a geometric analog, the finding of a lowest point, A, in a valley. Now imagine that the diagrams in figure 7 are the contour maps of this valley. A ball could be released at point 0. If it were propelled solely by gravity, it would presumably follow the path of most rapid descent, a smooth curve as shown emanating from the initial point and minimizing its elapsed time of arrival to the optimum point A. This would be an optimum way of finding the minimum if we evaluate cost as time elapsed. But this path involves a continuous adjustment to the local gradient as the latter varies continuously. And it assumes away inertia. Because of the latter the ball would wander off the optimum path, then veer back and forth across it as shown by the dotted line. The ball would not in fact follow the path of steepest descent but a more or less suboptimal one. Practical numerical methods are somewhat similar to the latter kind of path. Indeed, computation algorithms must be blind to the situation as a whole. They proceed for a time in a given direction generally downward, mistakenly move up, then correct the error and determine a new locally best (but globally suboptimal) direction of descent. The path for such an algorithm is illustrated in figure 7 (b).

It can be stated categorically that optimal algorithms are rare and experience must be used to infer how good a given procedure is and under what conditions a given algorithm works well. This is partly because algorithms for digital computers always involve sequences of relatively simple computations based on purely local information. They begin at some initial, perhaps arbitrary starting point, compute some purely local information that indicates a direction in which a new guess may be chosen to improve on the initial guess, and calculate how far to go in that direction. A new guess is chosen and new local information about neighboring alternatives is computed and the

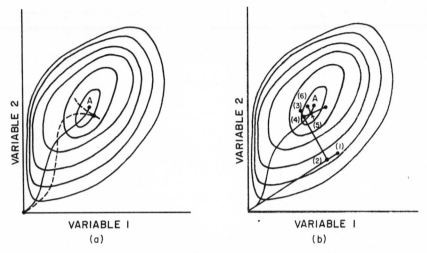

Figure 7. (a) The "optimal" path to A in the absence of friction and
inertia is indicated by the solid line, with inertia it is indicated by the dashed
line; (b) the path of a typical computer or learning algorithm

process continues. In this way a sequence of suboptimizations is generated
which under favorable conditions converges to a final best solution. The reader familiar with the behavioral economics of Simon [1957] and Cyert and
March [1963] should note here the striking similarity between optimizing algorithms and behavioral economics.

Early computational experience with Dantzig's simplex method [1949] is
discussed in an interesting manner by Orchard-Hays [1956]. The concept of
an optimum algorithm and many examples involving unconstrained problems
with one or only a few variables will be found in Wilde [1968]. The sequences
of suboptimizations involved in most algorithms would appear to be analogous to the behavior of decision makers in complex organizations and in market economies. This suggests that the study of such algorithms should have
considerable interest for economists. The formal mathematical study of algorithms was initiated by Zangwill [1969]. A recent contribution is by Fiacco
[1974]. The relationship between otpimizing algorithms and behavioral economics was pointed out in Day [1964] and developed in the context of the
theory of the firm in Day and Tinney [1968]. Related articles were prepared
by Baumol and Quandt [1964] and Alchian [1950]. The reader interested in
computational algorithms for various of the optimization models should find
the following references of interest. A complete exegesis of the simplex method is given in Orchard-Hays [1961]. Important early nonlinear programming

algorithms are those of Frank and Wolfe [1956] for the quadratic programming case, the "methods of feasible directions" in Zoutendijk [1960], and Rosen's gradient projection methods [1960, 1961] for convex (concave) programming. Algorithms based on differential equations that converge to the Kuhn-Tucker conditions and mimic the market process stem from Samuelson [1949] and include Arrow and Hurwicz [1960] and articles in Arrow, Hurwicz, and Uzawa [1958].

Efficiency and Games

The classical notion that many agents simultaneously pursue their several individual advantages in an economy and that the outcome for each depends on the actions of all possessed formidable analytical difficulties that were not fully resolved until Von Neumann's theory of games was developed into a fundamental working tool for economists by Von Neumann and Morgenstern [1944] in their famous book and applied by Debreu [1952] in his paper.

In this theory not just one but many utility or objective functions guide choices so that the optimizing theory as we have reviewed it so far is inadequate. Indeed, the notion of "optimum" must be expanded. This has been done in various ways, but the one central to most work in economics rests on Pareto's concept of an "efficient" or "Pareto optimal" set of actions in which no one agent can choose a preferred action without forcing another player in the game to choose a less preferred alternative.

The theory of games made possible a deeper understanding of many forms of market competition, as developed, for example, in Shubik's *Strategy and Market Competition* [1959]. It also became a basic tool in studying the theory of risky decisions. Games against nature were constructed to formalize the problem facing a single agent when he could only guess what state his environment might take. The application to statistical inference, the scientific counterpart of this theory, was developed very early by Wald [1945].

But in spite of the extension of optimizing concepts involved in the theory of games, the close relationship to conventional optimizing theory became increasingly evident. For example, it was seen that every two-person, zero-sum game was equivalent to a linear programming model. Kuhn and Tucker [1951] showed that Pareto optimal solutions to a class of multiobjective optimization problems could be characterized by the optimum of a linear combination of those objectives. This quite general duality is at the heart of welfare economics which shows the efficiency properties of competitive equilibria.

The basic idea in this relationship between Pareto optima and conventional optimization is captured in the diagram shown in figure 8 (a) already familiar

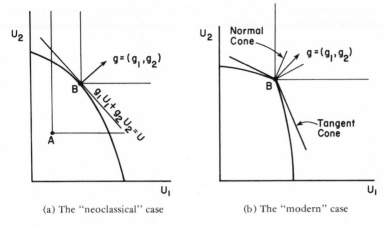

(a) The "neoclassical" case   (b) The "modern" case

Figure 8. Efficient choices

to generations of economists. If more of U_1 or U_2 is better than less, then all vectors in the cone emanating from the point A are "Pareto better" or more efficient than the point A itself. But no point in the cone emanating from the point B is feasible except B. Hence B is a Pareto optimum or efficient point with respect to the variables U_1 and U_2.

The set of attainable utility combinations is supported at B by the plane H represented by the vector $g = (g_1, g_2)$. Hence B optimizes a linear combination $g_1 U_1 + g_2 U_2$. Now if U_1 and U_2 are considered to be the satisfaction levels for agents one and two, respectively, then we see how the Pareto optimum B is represented or "supported" by an ordinary optimum. One may also interpret g as the gradient of a social welfare function $\varphi (U_1, U_2)$, which is optimized at point B.

In figure 8 (b) the situation is shown where the set of attainable (U_1, U_2) combinations is convex as in (a) but not smooth. This "modern" case is analogous with the duality diagram for nonlinear programming shown in figure 6 (b). Here the normal cone at point B gives a set of weights (g_1, g_2) so that maximizing $g_1 U_1 + g_2 U_2$ will give back point B as a solution to the implied convex programming problem.

A good discussion of modern optimization and welfare economics is offered in Dorfman, Samuelson, and Solow [1958, chapter 14]. They bring out the point suggested in figure 8 that the efficient or Pareto optimal solutions to the "game" or multioptimization problem can be obtained by means of parametric programming. An early application of this technique is Manne's study [1956] of the United States petroleum refining industry. The concept of efficient production used by Manne, so closely related to that of the Pareto optimal solutions of a game, was developed by Koopmans [1951]. Standard works on the theory of games in addition to Von Neumann and Morgenstern's classic are the studies by Blackwell and Girshick [1954], Savage [1954], and Karlin [1959]. Elementary expositions are contained in Hurwicz [1945] and Marschak [1946].

Decomposition and Coordination

In the theory of the market economy the relationship between group and individual optima is brought out by showing that a price system exists in such a way that when all agents optimize independently with respect to it then the resulting actions are Pareto optimal and compatible with those prices, i.e., the markets are cleared and all firms and households survive. Koopmans [1957, part I] provides a classic modern nontechnical discussion. The problem of finding the "best" social choice might then be viewed as finding a price adjustment process that will guide a sequence of suboptimizations to an efficient or Pareto optimal point. Such adjustment processes are called tâtonnement processes and represent one general means by which the problem of decomposition of social choice and coordination of individual choices is studied. To be compatible with the requirement of leading to Pareto better solutions, such a process would have to lead to a choice lying in the cone emanating from the initial starting point. Arrow and Hahn [1971] discuss tâtonnement-type models of market processes and Arrow and Hahn [1971] cite earlier work in bibliographical notes.

A second setting in which the relationship between group and individual optima is studied is illustrated by Robinson Crusoe, subject of the most famous parable of the centrally planned economy. A Robinson (or a socialist state) is decomposable into Robinson the consumer and Robinson the producer by means of a price system so that Robinson the consumer can achieve the highest feasible utility at minimum cost and Robinson the producer can maximize his profit of production. This analogy, fully developed by Koopmans [1957], shows that with sufficiently convex technology and preference both the competitive market economy and the socialist economy share the same social equilibria. From this point of view the market is seen to be a device for decomposing the economy's overwhelmingly complex problem of resource allocation into a host of relatively simple, individual suboptimizations which are coordinated by the price system to achieve allocations that are efficient. The idea that marketlike computational procedures could be developed for carrying out central planning was developed by Arrow and Hurwicz [1960].

With this background it is hardly surprising that some of the computer algorithms for solving large-scale complex optimization problems have characteristics similar to those of market tâtonnement or socialist planning processes. In these algorithms the master problem is decomposed into a set of much simpler optimization submodels, one of which plays the role of the coordinator, helmsman, planning bureau, or whatever. Each is solved and the solutions are passed back and forth between them. On the basis of the new information the submodels are reoptimized, and so a sequence of suboptimizations with feedback is generated which, when well conceived, will converge to the solution of the master problem. An early example of such a decomposition procedure was proposed by Dantzig and Wolfe [1961] and applied by Kornai and Liptak [1965]. Kornai [1967] discussed it thoroughly in the national planning setting. Malinvaud [1967] prepared an excellent general discussion of several alternative planning procedures. Lasdon [1970] developed a quite comprehensive text from the computational point of view.

Two fundamental problems complicate the theory and impede progress in its development. One is the formalization of data processing, decision making, and administrative costs and the determination thereby of the optimal level of decentralization. The second is the problem of incentives. Decentralized procedures must be coordinated by an appropriate system of incentives and/ or constraints to bring about a compatibility between decentralized optima and the central optimum. Some progress in the former has been made by the developers of team theory, J. Marschak and Radner [1972], who exploit concepts from decision and game theory to formalize the problem of determining optimal decisions and information networks in organizations. This work stems from Marschak's early concern with developing an economic organization theory. Attention to some of the dynamic aspects of such theory is found in T. Marschak [1959, 1968]. The incentive problem has been tackled by Groves [1973].

Multiple Goals

Increasing attention is being paid to the decision problem in which many goals or objectives are pursued. Formally, the problem is much like the n-person game theory in which many objective functions are simultaneously optimized. Not unexpectedly, then, one way of approaching the problem is by means of the efficiency or Pareto optimality concept with which we have already been concerned in several different settings. In particular, the Kuhn-Tucker efficiency theorem mentioned in the section on efficiency and games serves as the basis for an interactive planning procedure involving a planner who has several measurable goals. In this procedure, developed by Geoffrion, Dyer, and Feinberg [1972], a decision maker is asked to specify an initial set of "weights" g_1 and g_2. An efficient point is found if his goal functions are concave. He is then asked to choose new weights and a new efficient point is found. If the decision maker has a sufficiently regular utility function combining the separate goals or objective functions into a single overall goal, then this iterative sequence will lead to the optimal fulfillment of all the goals. If not, he is left with a number of efficient or Pareto optimal possibilities.

Another approach, suggested by Georgescu-Roegen [1954], is that of lexicographic orderings in which the several goals or objective functions are arranged in a hierarchy. Each is maximized or satiated one after the other until no further scope remains for choice. The relationship of such a procedure to rational choice axioms was investigated by Chipman [1960]. Encarnacion proposed various applications (for example, see Encarnacion [1964]). Day and Robinson [1973] established sufficient conditions for such choice models to be compatible with the requirements of general equilibrium theory. A comprehensive collection involving these and other approaches was assembled by Cochrane and Zeleny [1973].

Risk and Uncertainty

Although the formal study of risk began during the classical era of economics with Bernoulli and Laplace, and though its importance was recognized and accounted for in the neoclassical period by Marshall and Walras and later by Knight [1921] and Hart [1942], its formal treatment by means of optimization theory is of modern origin, at least so far as economic theory is concerned. Early attempts to study the problem mathematically in an economic setting were made by Makower and J. Marschak [1938] and by Tintner [1941]. But it is in Von Neumann and Morgenstern's seminal game theory book and in Savage's fundamental work on decision theory [1954] that the decision-theoretic foundations were definitively established. The Von Neumann-Morgenstern approach is that of *expected utility* and makes it possible to study the "best choice" which accounts for risk using conventional optimization theory.

In brief, probabilities (assumed usually to be subjective in nature) are assigned to states of the world. The utility is then conceived to be a random variable whose expected value is to be maximized by choosing an appropriate act or decision, subject to the constraints of the problem. Risk-averting, risk-preferring, and risk-neutral individuals can be represented in this way and the propensity to hedge, to carry portfolios, or to gamble can be explained. Application in economics are by now widespread and, depending on the specific form of the underlying spaces, the risky decision problem is converted into a linear, quadratic, or more general nonlinear optimization problem. Arrow

[1951] prepared a very comprehensive early survey, and Van Moeseke [1965] published an excellent discussion using modern nonlinear programming theory. Markowitz [1958] took as his subject the analysis of "portfolio" type behavior using quadratic programming. Dillon [1971] wrote a comprehensive review of various approaches.

Bayesian decision theory represents an extension of the Von Neumann-Morgenstern approach to the dynamic setting in which the decision maker faces a sequence of choices. At each stage he may modify his subjective probabilities on the basis of current information. An optimal choice can then be made. This approach represents a true formalization of Knight's concept of uncertainty as opposed to risk, for it explicitly treats the probabilities as unknown. The dynamic nature of the Bayesian point of view is brought out lucidly in J. Marschak's "On Adaptive Programming" [1963]. Various applications to problems in econometrics are developed in Zellner [1971]. Cyert and De Groot [1975] examine its application to the theory of the household.

So far the approaches summarized involve properly accounting for the possibility of doing better or worse than one expects by incorporating into the objective function terms that account for risk and uncertainty. A different component that deserves equal attention is the feasible region, for one outcome of a risky or uncertain decision is the impossibility of carrying out the desired choice. At worst this situation spells disaster, at best it forces a new choice. Again, the specific ways in which this problem has been formalized are numerous, but one must mention all of the "safety-first" and risk-programming procedures—for example, those developed by Charnes and Cooper [1959] and Roy [1952] and reviewed by Sengupta [1969]. Day, Aigner, and Smith [1971] provided an exposition of this approach in the setting of the elementary theory of the firm; in their paper three variants of the approach are discussed—one which minimizes the probability of disaster or maximizes the safety margin (safety), one which maximizes expected utility given a fixed probability of disaster (safety-fixed), and one which maximizes expected utility given that a minimum level of safety (probability of survival) has been reached (safety first). The last approach leads to a lexicographic ordering of survival probabilities and expected utility.

Another approach to the study of decision making under uncertainty is that of game theory where the agent is characterized by a game against nature or where two or more agents, represented by two or more persons in the game, account for the most damaging strategy against them. This approach, founded by Von Neumann [1928], was developed by Von Neumann and Morgenstern [1944]. More recent texts include those by Blackwell and Girshick [1954], Savage [1954], and Karlin [1959]. Elementary expositions are provided by Hurwicz [1945] and J. Marschak [1946].

In all of the above approaches probabilities are explicitly involved. A general principle that need not make explicit use of probability is the "principle of cautious optimizing" outlined elsewhere by Day [1970]. In this approach the decision maker being modeled optimizes in the usual way except that he limits his choices to alternatives "close enough" to a safety zone. The region of "safe enough" solutions can be based directly on a safety metric or "danger distance" instead of a probability of disaster. It therefore generalizes and places on a behavioral footing the idea of safety-first decision making. An alternative but closely related way of modifying the feasible region to account for uncertainty is Shackle's idea of focus loss [1949]. In the form developed by Boussard and Petit [1967] for a firm with a linear programming choice structure, the agent has a focus on loss or disaster level associated with each activity. In addition, the firm has an allowable level of loss usually associated with some minimal survival income. Each activity has an allowable proportion of the total allowable loss, and each activity adds to the allowable loss by increasing the total expected income.

Dynamic Optimization

The role of foresight in decision making can be illustrated by means of a diagram which incorporates several of the fundamental ingredients of dynamic optimization theory. This is done in figure 9. "States of the world" are represented by axis s and acts or decisions (we do not distinguish between the two here) are represented by axis a. Associated with each state is a feasible interval of choices. The interval is determined by a correspondence (see figure 5) in the upper right quadrant. For example, the set of feasible choices associated with the initial state s_0 is that part of the vertical line through the point s_0 that lies in the shaded graph representing the feasibility correspondence. To each act on the upper vertical axis is associated a payoff or outcome as determined by the concave payoff function in the upper left quadrant. For example, π_0 is the payoff associated with the act a_0. The environmental transition is represented in the lower left quadrant and shows how the state changes in response to each act. Thus, if the agent chooses a_0, the succeeding state will be s_1. By measuring the act on the same scale as the payoff we can project the act chosen onto the left horizontal axis, in this way generating a dynamic process.

Now suppose we begin with a rational but myopic decision maker. He knows the feasible region given the state s, and he knows the payoff function. But suppose that he does not know or try to estimate the environmental transition function. Given that he does the best he can in the given situation beginning at s_0, he chooses a_0, which leads to s_1, at which point he picks a_1.

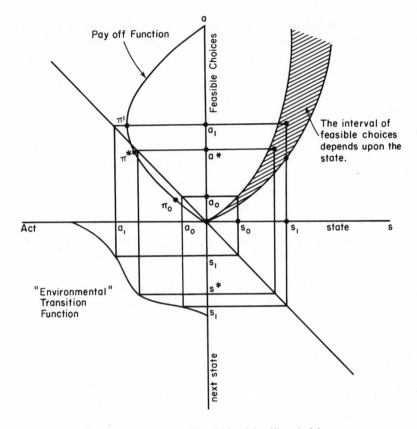

Figure 9. "Short-sighted" and "far-sighted" optimizing

This leads (coincidentally!) back to s_0 and to choice a_0 again. Subsequently an oscillation between a_0 and a_1 occurs. The sequence of payoffs is $[\pi_0, \pi_1, \pi_0, \pi_1, \pi_0, \ldots]$.

Now consider a not-so-myopic individual who knows and takes account of the environmental impact of his actions. Beginning at s_0 he chooses a_0 as before but instead of a_1 at s_1 he picks a^*, realizing that if he picks a_1 as his myopic counterpart did, he will be prevented, because of the environmental feedback, from achieving such a good gain in the next period. His "far-sighted" choice yields a payoff level π^* that can be maintained in perpetuity. Because π^* lies above the chord connecting π_0 and π_1 the average payoff yielded by this far-sighted strategy is better than the myopic strategy.

Of course intertemporal optimization theory encompasses much more complicated situations than the simple one illustrated, but the basic idea is the same: by taking account of the future consequences of present acts one is led to make choices which, though possibly sacrificing some present payoff, will lead to a preferred sequence of events. To complete the basic ingredients of the theory, a utility function or preference ordering must be specified which will rank feasible alternative time paths such as the two alternative paths just illustrated and determine how much present payoff should be sacrificed for the sake of future enjoyment.

The importance of foresight in economic decisions was noted by our classical predecessors, but widespread application of it by the common man was a possibility about which Smith, Malthus, and Ricardo were hardly sanguine. Later economists, however, realized that the concept of foresight was essential for obtaining a deeper understanding of capital accumulation than they had inherited in classical doctrine. An early breakthrough was Böhm-Bawerk's analysis of time preference [1884], a concept formalized by Fisher [1906] using the newly forged neoclassical theory of preference and utility. The redevelopment of these concepts using modern control theory—for example, as exposited by Arrow [1968] —has led to a huge literature on optimal economic growth, a product of the last two decades. At its basis is an intertemporal utility function of a very restricted nature, the existence of which has been investigated by Koopmans [1960] and Koopmans, Diamond, and Williamson [1964].

When this point of view is extended to the multioptimization problem inherent in general equilibrium theory, one must look for the existence of intertemporally efficient (Pareto optimal) choices and the existence of prices that would permit individual intertemporal optimizations, using these prices to achieve the efficient solutions. The role of such intertemporal efficiency prices has been investigated by Malinvaud [1953]. The neoclassical version of general equilibrium theory from the point of view of intertemporally optimizing firms and households was worked out by Hicks [1939], but his focus was that of temporary rather than dynamic equilibrium. A contemporary line of development that extends the optimal control point of view to the game situation is the work on differential games. A recent collection of studies of this kind (Kuhn and Szegö [1971]) includes papers by Berkovitz, Blaquiere, Friedman, Rockafellar, and Varaiya. An example is by Simaan and Takayama [1974].

The utility aspects of decision making are omitted altogether in on important line of optimal growth theory, namely, the line emanating from Von Neumann's general equilibrium model [1945]. In this theory only the technology of the economy is specified. No time preferences enter the argument. Instead, a technologically maximal rate of growth is defined and its existence is determined. The existence of "prices" that would support such a rate of growth by profit-maximizing individuals is also established so that a behavioral analog exists in part. Indeed, the possibility that a real economy could follow such an optimal balanced growth path has been investigated by Tsukui [1968]. Dorfman, Samuelson, and Solow [1958] and Koopmans [1964] provide an excellent exegesis of this theory.

Much contemporary work has concentrated on generalizing the individual optimization model to account for information costs, uncertainty and the joint estimation, and control or dual control problems. This line of work had led to a fusion of Bayesian statistical decision theory as developed, for example, by Zellner [1971] and stochastic control theory as described by Aoki [1967]. An influential control theoretic study dealing with the dual control problem of simultaneously deciding and obtaining improved information is Fel'dbaum [1965]. The Bayesian approach involves dynamic programming techniques as developed by Karlin [1955], Bellman [1957], Bellman and Dreyfus [1962], and Blackwell [1967]. A good review of control theory, dynamic programming, and the closely related calculus of variations is given by Intriligator [1971].

Recursive Optimization

The existence of optimal intertemporal strategies and the implications on individuals or economies whose behavior satisfies the conditions of intertemporal optimality have been the focus of most dynamic optimization theory applied to economics in recent years. The question of whether or not individuals of less than heroic stature could in their daily enterprise discover such behavior has only recently begun to receive attention. One way to approach the problem is to break the complex intertemporal optimization problem down into a sequence of much simpler, possibly myopic or relatively short-sighted suboptimizations with feedback. The decision maker does not know the environmental transition equations but merely approximates them, or more simply he forecasts relevant information on the basis of past observations without trying to estimate the structure of the system as a whole. Then, protecting himself from blunders of short-run overcommitment by rules of caution or uncertainty or risky decision making, he optimizes the current situation. When new observations are available, he reestimates and forecasts the relevant information variables and optimizes anew. Thus a sequence of optimizations with feedback is generated which explains actual behavior and which, if the true environment is well behaved, may converge to a path that is intertemporally optimal in some sense, just as a sequence of tâtonnementlike adjustments may lead to a general equilibrium that is efficient or Pareto optimal.

On the other hand, such a convergence may not occur, as in the example with which we introduced the idea of dynamic optimization in the preceding section. It is probably not hard to convince oneself that such convergence does not always occur and perhaps only rarely occurs in the real world.

Sequences of optimizations with feedback are called recursive programs. We have seen that such systems arise not only in the attempt to develop a formal theory of adaptive behavior as just outlined but also in a variety of seemingly quite different settings. We have, for example, observed that mathematical programming algorithms have this structure. We have observed that tâtonnement and decentralized decision processes have this character also. The explicit mathematical representation of economic behavior using recursive optimization originated with Cournot, who used it to investigate the behavior of competing duopolies. Later variants of duopoly theory that preceded the theory of games and Chamberlin's monopolistic competition theory [1948] used an essentially similar type of model. A growth model based on such a principle was stated by Leontief [1958], and a general class of recursive programs was developed by Day and Kennedy [1970] and Day [1970]. Various applications to quantitative modeling of industrial sectors and agricultural regions have been undertaken by Day and others, some of which have been collected in Takayama and Judge [1973] and a number of others in Day and Cigno [in preparation]. Applications to general equilibrium theory are supplied by Cigno [in preparation] and Allingham [1974]. These applications are based on the premise that economic agents' decisions are best characterized by local suboptimizations of partial models of the economy as a whole which are updated and re-solved period after period in response to new information about what other agents have done and what the economy as a whole has done. Like their counterparts in the field of optimization algorithms the recursive optimization models usually cannot be shown to be the best way for the agents to suboptimize. However, some progress has been made in showing that recursive programs based on plausible behavioral hypotheses may converge to the results obtained from the optimal control point of view.

A special and very limited class of recursive programs arises when an optimal strategy can be derived from the dynamic programming point of view which shows how, on the basis of current information and past choices, the next decision can be decided on in the best way. A special group of models falling in this category that have been widely applied in econometrics is the linear decision rules of Holt, Modigliani, Muth, and Simon [1960] and Theil [1964].

On the Normative Content of Optimizing

In reviewing the theory and application of optimization concepts one is struck by the contrasting interpretations given to mathematical programming and game theory models. On the one hand, an optimization model is formulated to find the "best" solution of some problem. On the other hand, it may be used to characterize the behavior of a real world decision maker. The fallibility of the latter, however, is all too evident to each of us. Moreover, what is "best" clearly rests on a subjective basis—namely, what the agent thinks he likes and wants and what he thinks he can do at the time. These subjective constituents of optimal choice may change whenever something new is learned. How to learn in the optimal way is a problem shrouded in mystery, despite progress in decision theory. What is true of the agents in an economy in general is also true of the model builder and theorist in particular: a solution to an optimizing model is contingent on the structure of the model, something that ultimately rests on the subjective perceptions of mind and on current scientific theories and models which must always be approximations to the real world itself. We thus come to the conclusion that optimality is essentially a logical property of model solutions. Any normative content attributed to optimal solutions must be subjective in character.

Indeed, if one takes into account one's mortal existence and the problem of accommodating the unknown and unknowable preferences of generations yet unborn, one wonders what meaning, if any, the notion of intertemporal optimality has. As the problems associated with global economic development become better known, and as the very-long-run implications of present industrial activity receive increasing attention, this question too is bound to receive more and more attention.

Concluding Remarks

If we were to model our world system microeconomically using optimization theory, we should have to conceive of a game with some three or four billion players, a number growing at a rate of some five thousand per hour. Moreover, the collection of players and its organization into groups of various kinds such as families and firms are variables determined in a complex way by the evolution of the process as a whole. We know also that nature—man's environment—consisting of our nonhuman neighbors, who likewise are evolving in complex living systems, and the physical world must be considered as a player in this game. But what a player! With an uncountable number of strategies at his disposal.

The fact is that none of us takes into account the actions of very many players in this ultimate game. Even if we should like not to do so, we ignore, because we must, all but a few chosen friends and enemies and acquaintances about whom we care or become aware. We account for tiny facets of the universe in our specialized thoughts. And when we turn inward to explore our preferences, we find opening up before us a mystery as infinitely varied and as unfathomable as interstellar space. We make simplified models of ourselves, solve them, and act. But we throw these models away and start over, or we modify them over and over again. If we fail to do so, our humanity withers and we become like automata in our consistency.

Thus, optimization theories can never yield a complete theory of being or becoming. The man who finds his only poetry in mathematical programs, games, and marginal calculations, who fails to listen to his hunches and feel his senses to the full, who ignores the pleadings of the spirit as it cries out from the works of poets and prophets and painters and from dreams, is less a man.

Still optimization models help us in our battle to create order. The simple clarity of their insights is poetry! Possibly even, their concepts belong to the a priori properties of mind by which, according to Kant, thought's content is defined, by which thought's possibilities and limits are demarcated like fiery poles fixing emblazoned zones in the night. In this case it would be futile for some new doctrine of economy to try to get along without them, just as it would be futile for man to try to get along without science and art in general.

References

Alchian, A. [1950]. "Uncertainty, Evolution and Economic Theory." *J. Pol. Econ.* 58: 211-221.

Allingham, M. G. [1974]. "Equilibrium and Stability." *Econometrica* 42:705-716.

Aoki, M. [1967]. *Optimization of Stochastic Systems*. New York, Academic Press.

Araujo, A., G. Chichilnisky, and P. Kalman [1973]. "Comparative Dynamics for Multisectoral Models of Optimal Growth: An Application of Calculus of Banach Spaces." Paper presented at the Econometric Society, New York.

Arrow, K. J. [1951]. "Alternative Approaches to the Theory of Choice in Risk-Taking Situations." *Econometrica* 19:404-437.

―――― [1968]. "Applications of Control Theory to Economic Growth." In *Lectures in Applied Mathematics*, vol. 12 (Mathematics of Decision Sciences, part 2). Providence: American Mathematical Society.

Arrow, K. J., and G. Debreu [1954]. "Existence of an Equilibrium for a Competitive Economy." *Econometrica* 22:265-290.

Arrow, K. J., and F. H. Hahn [1971]. *General Competitive Analysis*. San Francisco: Holden-Day.

Arrow, K. J., and L. Hurwicz [1960]. "Decentralization and Computation in Resource Allocation." In *Essays in Economics and Econometrics*, R. Pfouts, ed. Chapel Hill: University of North Carolina Press.

Arrow, K. J., L. Hurwicz, and H. Uzawa [1958]. *Studies in Linear and Non-linear Programming*. Stanford: Stanford University Press.

Aubin, J. P. [n.d.]. *Mathematical Models of Game and Economic Theory*. Paris: Centre Recherche de Mathematiques de la Décision, Université Paris IX Dauphine.

Balinsky, M. L., and W. J. Baumol [1968]. "The Dual in Nonlinear Programming and Its Economic Interpretation." *Rev. Econ. Studies* 35:237-256.

Baumol, W. J. [1958] . "Activity Analysis in One Lesson." *Am. Econ. Rev.* 48:837-873.
—— [1972]. *Economic Theory and Operations Analysis.* Third ed. Englewood Cliffs, N.J.: Prentice-Hall.
Baumol, W. J., and R. Quandt [1964] . "Rules of Thumb and Optimally Imperfect Decisions." *Am. Econ. Rev.* 54:23-46.
Bellman, R. [1957] . *Dynamic Programming.* Princeton: Princeton University Press.
Bellman, R. E., and S. E. Dreyfus [1962] . *Applied Dynamic Programming.* Princeton: Princeton University Press.
Blackwell, D. [1967] . "Positive Dynamic Programming." In *Proceedings of Fifth Berkeley Symposium on Mathematical Statistics and Probability,* vol. 1, *Theory of Statistics,* L. Le Cam and J. Neyman, eds. Berkeley: University of California Press. Pp. 415-418.
Blackwell, D., and M. A. Girshick [1954] . *Theory of Games and Statistical Decisions.* New York: Wiley.
Böhm-Bawerk, E. von [1889] . *Positive Theory of Capital.* South Holland, Ill.: Libertarian Press, 1959.
Boussard, J. M., and M. Petit [1967] . "Representation of Farmers' Behavior under Uncertainty with a Focus Loss Constraint." *J. Farm Econ.* 49:869-880.
Canon, M. D., C. D. Cullum, and E. Polak [1970] . *Theory of Optimal Control and Mathematical Programming.* New York: McGraw-Hill.
Chamberlin, E. H. [1948] . *The Theory of Monopolistic Competition.* Cambridge: Harvard University Press, Eighth ed., 1962.
Charnes, A., and W. W. Cooper [1959] . "Chance-Constrained Programming." *Management Science* 6:73-79.
Chipman, J. S. [1960] . "The Foundations of Utility." *Econometrica* 28:193-224.
Cigno, A. [1971] . "Production and Investment Response to Changing Market Conditions, Technical Know-How and Government Policies: A Vintage Model of the Agricultural Sector." *Rev. Econ. Studies* 38:63-94.
—— [in preparation] . "Capital Accumulation and General Equilibrium." In *Modelling Economic Change: The Recursive Programming Approach,* R. H. Day and A. Cigno, eds. Amsterdam: North-Holland.
Cochrane, J. L., and M. Zeleny, eds. [1973] . *Multiple Criteria Decision Making.* Columbia: University of South Carolina Press.
Cournot, A. [1838] . *Researches into the Mathematical Principles of the Theory of Wealth.* Translation by N. T. Bacon (1897). Reprinted with Irving Fisher's notes in the Irwin Paperback Classics in Economics. Homewood, Ill.: Richard D. Irwin.
Cyert, R. M., and M. De Groot [1970] . "Multiperiod Decision Models with Alternating Choice as a Solution to the Duopoly Problem." *Quart. J. Econ.* 84:410-429.
—— [1975] . "Adaptive Utility." In *Adaptive Economic Models,* R. Day and T. Groves, eds. New York: Academic Press.
Cyert, R. M., and J. G. March [1963] . *A Behavioral Theory of the Firm.* Englewood Cliffs, N.J.: Prentice-Hall.
Dantzig, G. B. [1949] . "Programming of Interdependent Activities: II, Mathematical Model." *Econometrica* 17:200-211.
Dantzig, G. B., J. Folkman, and N. Shapiro [1967] . "On the Continuity of the Minimum Set of a Continuous Function." *Journal of Mathematical Analysis and Applications* 17:519-548.
Dantzig, G. B., and P. Wolfe [1961] . "A Decomposition Algorithm for Linear Programs." *Econometrica* 29:767-778.

Day, R. H. [1964]. Review of Cyert and March's *A Behavioral Theory of the Firm*. *Econometrica* 32:461-465.

——— [1967]. "Profits, Learning and the Convergence of Satisficing to Marginalism." *Quart. J. Econ.* 81:302-311.

——— [1970]. "Rational Choice and Economic Behavior." *Theory and Decision* 1:229-251.

Day, R. H., D. Aigner, and K. Smith [1971]. "Safety Margins and Profit Maximization in the Theory of the Firm." *J. Pol. Econ.* 79:1293-1301.

Day, R. H., and A. Cigno, eds. [in preparation]. *Modelling Economic Change: The Recursive Programming Approach*. Amsterdam: North-Holland.

Day, R. H., and P. E. Kennedy [1970]. "Recursive Decision Systems: An Existence Analysis." *Econometrica* 38:666-681.

Day, R. H., and S. Robinson [1973]. "Economic Decisions with L** Utility." In *Multiple Criteria Decision Making*, J. L. Cochrane and M. Zeleny, eds. Columbia: University of South Carolina Press.

Day, R. H., and E. H. Tinney [1968]. "How to Co-operate in Business without Really Trying: A Learning Model of Decentralized Decision Making." *J. Pol. Econ.* 76: 583-600.

Debreu, G. [1952]. "A Social Equilibrium Existence Theorem." *Proceedings of the National Academy of Sciences* 38:886-893.

Dillon, J. [1971]. "An Expository Review of Bernoullian Decision Theory in Agriculture." *Rev. Marketing Agr. Econ.* 39:3-80.

Dorfman, R. [1953]. "Mathematical or Linear Programming: A Non-mathematical Exposition." *Am. Econ. Rev.* 43:797-825.

——— [1969]. "An Economic Interpretation of Optimal Control Theory." *Am. Econ. Rev.* 59:817-832.

Dorfman, R., P. A. Samuelson, and R. Solow [1958]. *Linear Programming and Economic Analysis*. New York: McGraw-Hill.

Encarnacion, J. [1964]. "Constraints and the Firm's Utility Function." *Econometrica* 32:215-217.

Fel'dbaum, A. A. [1965]. *Optimal Control Systems*. New York: Academic Press.

Fiacco, A. V. [1974]. "Convergence Properties of Local Solutions of Sequences of Mathematical Programming Problems in General Space." *Journal of Optimization Theory and Applications* 13:1-12.

Fisher, I. [1906]. *The Nature of Capital and Income*. New York: A. M. Kelley. Reprint, 1965.

Frank, C. [1969]. *Production Theory and Invisible Commodities*. Princeton: Princeton University Press.

Frank, M., and P. Wolfe [1956]. "An Algorithm for Quadratic Programming." *Naval Logistics Quarterly* 3:95-110.

Gale, D. [1960]. *The Theory of Linear Economic Models*. New York: McGraw-Hill.

Gale, D., H. W. Kuhn, and A. W. Tucker [1951]. "Linear Programming and the Theory of Games." In *Activity Analysis of Production and Allocation*, T. Koopmans, ed. New York: Wiley. Pp. 317-329.

Geoffrion, A., J. Dyer, and A. Feinberg [1972]. "An Interactive Approach for Multicriterion Optimization with an Application to the Operation of an Academic Department." *Management Science* 19:357-368.

Georgescu-Roegen, N. [1954]. "Choice, Expectations, and Measurability." *Quart. J. Econ.* 68:503-504.

Groves, T. [1973]. "Incentives in Teams." *Econometrica* 41:617-632.

Hadley, G. [1962]. *Linear Programming.* Reading, Mass.: Addison-Wesley.

———— [1964]. *Nonlinear and Dynamic Programming.* Reading, Mass. Addison-Wesley.

Hart, A. G. [1942]. "Anticipations, Uncertainty, and Dynamic Planning." *Studies in Business Administration.* Chicago: University of Chicago Press.

Heady, E. O., and W. V. Candler [1958]. *Linear Programming Methods.* Ames: Iowa State University Press.

Hicks, J. R. [1939]. *Value and Capital.* London: Oxford University Press. Second ed., 1946.

Hildreth, C. [1957]. "Some Problems and Possibilities of Farm Programming." In *Fertilizer Innovations and Resource Use*, E. L. Baum, E. O. Heady, and C. G. Hildreth, eds. Ames: Iowa State University Press.

Holt, C. C., F. Modigliani, J. F. Muth, and H. A. Simon [1960]. *Planning Production Inventories and Work Force.* Englewood Cliffs, N.J.: Prentice-Hall.

Hu, T. C. [1969]. *Integer Programming and Network Flows.* Reading, Mass.: Addison-Wesley.

Hurwicz, L. [1945]. "The Theory of Economic Behavior." *Am. Econ. Rev.* 46:474-479.

Intriligator, M. D. [1971]. *Mathematical Optimization and Economic Theory.* Englewood Cliffs, N.J.: Prentice-Hall.

Jevons, W. S. [1871]. *The Theory of Political Economy.* New York: Macmillan.

Karlin, S. [1955]. "The Structure of Dynamic Programming Models." *Naval Logistics Research Quarterly* 2:285-294.

———— [1959]. *Mathematical Methods in Programming, Games and Economics.* Reading, Mass.: Addison-Wesley.

Knight, F. H. [1921]. *Risk, Uncertainty, and Profit.* Reprinted by London School of Economics, 1931.

Koopmans, T., ed. [1951]. *Activity Analysis of Production and Allocation.* New York: Wiley.

———— [1957]. *Three Essays on the State of Economic Silence.* New York: McGraw-Hill.

———— [1960]. "Stationary Ordinal Utility and Impatience." *Econometrica* 28:287-309.

Koopmans, T. C. [1964]. "Economic Growth at a Maximal Rate." *Quart. J. Econ.* 78: 355-394.

Koopmans, T. C., P. A. Diamond, and R. E. Williamson [1964]. "Stationary Utility and Time Perspective." *Econometrica* 32:82-100.

Kornai, J. [1967]. *Mathematical Planning of Structural Decisions.* Amsterdam: North-Holland.

Kornai, J., and T. Liptak [1965]. "Two-Level Planning." *Econometrica* 33:141-169.

Kuhn, H. W., and G. P. Szegö [1971]. *Differential Games and Related Topics.* Amsterdam: North-Holland.

Kuhn, H. W., and A. W. Tucker [1951]. "Nonlinear Programming." In *Proceedings of the Second Berkeley Symposium on Mathematical Statstics and Probability*, Jerry Neyman, ed. Berkeley: University of California Press. Pp. 481-492.

Lasdon, L. S. [1970]. *Optimization Theory for Large Systems.* New York: Macmillan.

Leontief, W. W. [1928]. "Die Wirtschaft als Kreislauf." *Archiv für Sozialwissenschaft und Sozialpolitik* 60:577-623.

———— [1936]. "Quantitative Input-Output Relations in the Economic System of the United States." *Rev. Econ. Studies* 18:105-125.

—— [1958]. "Theoretical Note on Time-Preference Productivity of Capital, Stagnation and Economic Growth." *Am. Econ. Rev.* 48:105-110.

—— [1960]. "The Decline and Rise of Soviet Economic Science." *Foreign Affairs* 38: 261-272.

Leuenberger, D. G. [1969]. *Optimization by Vector Space Methods*. New York: Wiley.

Makower, H., and J. Marschak [1938]. "Assets, Prices and Monetary Theory." *Economica* (new series) 5:261-88.

Malinvaud, E. [1953]. "Capital Accumulation and Efficient Allocation of Resources." *Econometrica* 21:233-68.

—— [1967]. "Decentralized Procedures for Planning." In *Activity Analysis in the Theory of Growth and Planning*, E. Malinvaud and M. O. L. Bacharach, eds. New York: St. Martin's Press.

Mangasarian, O. L. [1969]. *Nonlinear Programming*. New York: McGraw-Hill.

Manne, A. S. [1956]. *Scheduling of Petroleum Refinery Operations*. Cambridge: Harvard University Press.

Markowitz, H. M. [1958]. *Portfolio Selection*. New York: Wiley.

Marschak, J. [1946]. "Neumann and Morgenstern's New Approach to Static Economics." *J. Pol. Econ.* 54:97-115.

—— [1954]. "Towards an Economic Theory of Organization and Information." In *Decision Processes*, P. M. Thrall, C. H. Coombs, and R. L. Davis, eds. New York: Wiley.

—— [1963]. "On Adaptive Programming." *Management Science* 9:517-526.

Marschak, J., and R. Radner [1972]. *Economic Theory of Teams*. New Haven: Yale University Press.

Marschak, T. A. [1959]. "Centralization and Decentralization in Economics Organization." *Econometrica* 9:137-74.

—— [1968]. "Computation in Organizations: Comparison of Price Mechanisms and Other Adjustment Processes." In *Risk and Uncertainty*, K. Borch and J. Mossin, eds. New York: St. Martin's Press.

Marshall, A. [1890]. *Principles of Economics*. New York: Macmillan. Eighth ed., 1920.

McKenzie, L. W. [1955]. "Competitive Equilibrium with Dependent Consumer Preferences." In *Proceedings of the Second Symposium in Linear Programming*, H. A. Antosiewicz, ed. Washington: National Bureau of Standards. Pp. 277-294.

Mesarovic, M. [1970]. *Theory of Hierarchical Multi-level Systems*. New York: Academic Press.

Moeseke, P. Van [1965]. "Stochastic Linear Programming." *Yale Economic Essays* 5, 1:197-253.

Neumann, J. Von [1928]. "Zur Theorie der Gesellschaftsspiele." *Mathematische Annalen* 100:295-320.

—— [1937]. "Uber ein ökonomisches Gleichungssystem und eine Verallgemeinerung des Browerschen Fixpunktsatzes." *Ergebnisse eines Mathematischen Kolloquiums* 8:73-83.

—— [1945]. "A Model of General Economic Equilibrium." *Rev. Econ. Studies* 13:1-9.

Neumann, J. Von, and O. Morgenstern [1944]. *Theory of Games and Economic Behavior*. Princeton: Princeton University Press. Second ed., 1947.

Orchard-Hays, W. [1956]. "Evolution of Computer Codes for Linear Programming." The Rand Corporation, Santa Monica.

———— [1961]. *Matrices, Elimination and the Simplex Method*. Arlington, Va.: CIER, Inc.

Rockafellar, R. T. [1970]. *Convex Analysis*. Princeton: Princeton University Press.

Rosen, J. B. [1960]. "The Gradient Projection Method for Nonlinear Programming. Part I, Linear Constraints." *Journal of the Society of Industrial and Applied Mathematics* 8:181-217.

———— [1961]. "The Gradient Projection Method for Nonlinear Programming. Part II, Nonlinear Constraints." *Journal of the Society of Industrial and Applied Mathematics* 9:514-532.

Roy, A. D. [1952]. "Safety First and the Holding of Assets." *Econometrica* 20:431-449.

Samuelson, P. A. [1948]. *Foundations of Economic Analysis*. Cambridge: Harvard University Press.

———— [1949]. "Market Mechanisms and Maximization." The Rand Corporation, Santa Monica. Reprinted in *Collected Scientific Papers of Paul Samuelson*, vol. 1. Cambridge: M.I.T. Press (1966).

———— [1959a]. "A Modern Treatment of the Ricardian Economy: I, The Pricing of Goods and Land Services." *Quart. J. Econ.* 73:1-35.

———— [1959b]. "A Modern Treatment of the Ricardian Economy: II, Capital and Interest Aspects of the Pricing Process." *Quart. J. Econ.* 73:217-231.

Savage, L. J. [1954]. *The Foundations of Statistics*. New York: Wiley.

Sengupta, J. K. [1969]. "Safety-First Rules under Change-Constrained Linear Programming." *Operations Research* 17:112-132.

Shackle, G. L. S. [1949]. *Expectations in Economics*. Cambridge: At the University Press.

Shubik, M. [1959]. *Strategy and Market Structure: Competition, Oligopoly and the Theory of Games*. New York: Wiley.

Simaan, M., and T. Takayama [1974]. "Dynamic Duopoly Game: Differential Game Theoretic Approach." Faculty Working Paper #155, College of Commerce, University of Illinois, Urbana-Champaign.

Simon, H. A. [1951]. "The Effects of Technological Change in a Linear Model." *Activity Analysis of Production and Allocation*, T. C. Koopmans, ed. New York: Wiley.

———— [1957]. *Administrative Behavior*. New York: Free Press. Second ed.

Takayama, T., and G. G. Judge [1973]. *Studies in Economic Planning over Space and Time*. Amsterdam: North-Holland.

Theil, H. [1964]. *Optimal Decision Rules for Government and Industry*. Amsterdam: North-Holland.

Tintner, G. [1941]. "The Pure Theory of Production under Technological Risk and Uncertainty." *Econometrica* 9:305-312.

Tsukui, J. [1968]. "Application of a Turnpike Theorem to Planning for Efficient Accumulation: An Example for Japan." *Econometrica* 36:172-186.

Wald, A. [1936]. "Über einige Gleichungssysteme der mathematischen Okonomie." *Zeitschrift für Nationalökonomie* 7:637-670.

———— [1945]. "Statistical Decision Functions Which Minimize Maximum Risk." *Annals of Mathematics* 46:265-280.

———— [1951]. "On Some Systems of Equations of Mathematical Economics." *Econometrica* 19:368-403.

Walras, L. [1874]. *Elements of Pure Economics*. Translated by W. Jaffe. Homewood, Ill.: Richard D. Irwin, 1954.

Wilde, D. J. [1968]. *Optimum Seeking Methods*. Englewood Cliffs, N.J.: Prentice-Hall.
Zangwill, W. I. [1969]. *Nonlinear Programming: A Unified Approach*. Englewood Cliffs, N.J.: Prentice-Hall.
Zellner, A. [1971]. *An Introduction to Bayesian Inference in Econometrics*. New York: Wiley.
Zoutendijk, G. [1960]. *Methods of Feasible Directions*. Amsterdam: Elsevier.

Optimization Models in Agricultural and Resource Economics

Richard H. Day
Professor of Economics
University of Southern California, Los Angeles
Edward Sparling
Professor of Economics
Colorado State University, Fort Collins

The application of optimization concepts to the economics of agriculture and resource use has a history as long as mathematical economics itself. It was in the context of agriculture in an "isolated state" that von Thünen [1966] in 1826 developed his own concept of gain and loss at the "margin" and used it to develop a theory of relative economic value and spatial diversity in the use of land, labor, and capital. Indeed, we have it on the good authority of Marshall [1890] that von Thünen, the first agricultural economist among economists, along with Cournot, provided the initial inspiration for marginalist economics.

On the other hand, von Thünen and his classical predecessors Smith, Malthus, and Ricardo were also employing concepts that are most effectively represented by the use of linear programming theory. It was not until the modern era that the full unity underlying these different classical and neoclassical optimization approaches could be brought out by means of a single mathematical structure which incorporated both points of view as special cases— namely, the Kuhn-Tucker theorem (Kuhn and Tucker [1951]).

The balanced blend of analytical reasoning and careful empirical observation that characterized von Thünen's work was evident in the work of later economists who specialized in agriculture. An important example is provid-

Note: Work on this paper was sponsored in part by the National Science Foundation under grant number GS-35049 and in part by the United States Army under contract number DA-31-124-ARO-D-462.

ed by "budgeting." Its development and widespread application in agricultural economics occurred in the first quarter of this century. Not only was it an
extension of von Thünen's early studies, but it played a central role in the
education of a generation of agricultural economists, thereby helping to prepare the discipline for the rapid adoption of modern optimization methods.
Indeed, in the hands of its best practitioners, budgeting was more than a trivi-
al special case of mathematical programming. It was an explicit arithmetic
procedure for obtaining approximate optima of simple constrained optimization problems and for exploring the broader implications at the regional and
national levels of economic behavior in response to changing economic conditions and policy controls.

The budgeting era may be said to have reached its culmination in 1951, for
in that year Mighell and Black's masterly exercise in budgeting, *Interregional
Competition in Agriculture*, was published. It is something of an irony that
the modern optimization methods introduced in the same year effectively
rendered obsolete that splendid monument to good economic thinking and
patient arithmetic. While no one would think of doing it that way any more,
it is clear that the modern approach has formalized economic optimization
and has eased the computational burdens of using it but has added few if any
insights into the nature of the problem not already fully appreciated in the
economic literature.

The first specific application of modern optimization to agricultural economics was by Hildreth and Reiter in 1951, and the application to the spatial
problems that had dominated much of von Thünen's original work came with
Fox's study [1953] of the feed-livestock economy. But the rapid adoption
and widespread application of modern optimization methods to the economic
analysis of agriculture and resource use may have been largely the result of
the extensive and varied examples produced by Earl Heady and his associates
in the 1950s. From that period on the application of optimization concepts
to the formulation and solution of substantive problems in agriculture and resource economics has led to a literature so vast that a comprehensive survey is
impossible. Consequently, this survey is restricted to selected contributions
(primarily from the American literature) that are of seminal importance from
a historical point of view, that are representative of an important research
area, or that are of contemporary interest. The references cited in the text are
supplemented in the bibliography by a few key survey papers on research that
could not be covered in this paper.

Modern optimization methods and their application in agriculture and resource management are of interest to specialists in many fields, and as a result
articles published in the professional journals for general economics, engineering, operations research, and so on are relevant. Moreover, economists must

be aware of the bulletins emanating from various federal agencies, state experiment stations, world organizations such as the United Nations, and the International Bank for Reconstruction and Development, as well as journals published in other countries. With these observations in mind perhaps the reader may find it possible to forgive the authors for any oversights that occur in this paper and for the somewhat arbitrary nature of the selected references.

The literature reviewed is divided into categories of food and diet, farm and agribusiness management, farm firm development, production response, interregional and spatial economics, natural resources, and agricultural development problems. For convenience in researching the literature table 1, which follows the text of this chapter, classifies the references according to these categories.

Throughout the discussion "neoclassical optimizing" refers to maximizing smooth, unconstrained, or equation-constrained functions using the basic tools of marginal analysis, i.e., traditional calculus. "Classical optimizing" is used here to include the linear programming problem that underlies the classical rent and trade theories and the budgeting arithmetic of von Thünen and later economists. "Modern optimizing" refers to the maximization of objective functions constrained by inequalities or equalities, requiring generalized Lagrange techniques and including the classical and neoclassical approaches as special cases.

Food and Diet

The diet problem seems an appropriate subject with which to begin a review of the literature on applications of modern optimization theory in agriculture and resource economics. Obviously, the efficient use of food resources is a goal of growing importance in our finite world with its rapidly growing, often ill-fed population. The diet problem is that of determining the least cost combination of foods that will meet dietary standards. According to Dorfman, Samuelson, and Solow [1958], Jerome Cornfield was the first to formulate this problem in an unpublished memorandum in 1941. Stigler presents a careful statement and discussion of the problem in "The Cost of Subsistence" [1945]. It is interesting to note that his solution of the problem was not cast explicitly in the modern mathematical programming framework, but instead involved a careful application of the arithmetic budgeting procedures known in agricultural economics for decades.

A thorough and illuminating explicit linear programming treatment of the problem (which cites an unpublished 1947 paper by Dantzig and Laderman) is given by Dorfman, Samuelson, and Solow [1958]. An elaborate empirical study developed for the interesting and important problem of protein supply in a developing economy is found in the work of V. E. Smith [1974].

The economic dietary (food-mix) problem for animal production is logically the same as the one for humans, and Waugh [1951] was the first to exploit linear programming in its explication. The budgeting framework was effectively and independently applied to the same problem at about the same time by Christenson and Mighell [1951]. By way of contrast to the linear programming work, a neoclassical optimizing approach was the basis of Heady's analysis of least cost dairy cow rations [1951] and hog rations (Heady et al. [1953]). An ingenious by-product was the "pork costulator" that allowed farmers to take advantage, without great computational effort, of the marginalism that economic theorists had long supposed to be descriptive of farmers' behavior. Briefly, Heady and his collaborators statistically estimated production functions for animals using experimental data, solved the least cost feed-mix problem for various input-output price combinations, and in this way located points on the derived economic demand function for various feed inputs. The input demand schedule was then represented by means of an inexpensive plastic circular slide rule.

Farm and Agribusiness Management

In 1951 a simplified version of the optimal crop rotation problem using modern optimization methods was published. This was Hildreth and Reiter's contribution [1951] in the famous Koopmans volume. There appears to have been a lag between this seminal application and the widespread adoption of linear programming as a standard working tool in the profession, but the lag was short. With characteristic pragmatism and innovation agricultural economists were quick to see the utility in the new approach. A flood of effective studies in farm management appeared in the mid-fifties. Very early studies were made by King and Freund [1953] and King [1953], Swanson and Fox [1954], and Bowlen and Heady [1955]. Quick to follow were studies by Bishop [1956], Heady, McAlexander, and Schrader [1956], Swanson [1956], and Coutu [1957]. In 1958 Heady and Candler published one of the first comprehensive texts on applied linear programming. Comparative static analyses using parametric linear programming algorithms also appeared at this time (for example, McPherson and Faris [1958] and the elegant piece by Hildreth [1957b]). Somewhat more recent applications are discussed by Krenz, Baumann, and Heady [1962] and Bolton [1964]. This early work is still of interest, and indeed it is worth serious reconsideration for much of it deals with the economics of soil conservation practices which have not been in vogue for some time but which are receiving renewed attention.

The relationship between classical economic (budgeting) thinking and modern optimization theory is reflected in pieces by Mighell [1955] and Kottke [1961] that point out the similarity or equivalence between the budgeting and linear programming approaches. Edwards [1966] gives a lucid exposition of this relationship, and Swanson [1961] notes that linear programming logic has had a profound impact on budgeting procedures. It is also worthwhile to point out that workers in agriculture were quick to find the intellectual intrigue in simplex and parametric programming algorithms and contributed expository pieces as well as methodological wrinkles of considerable ingenuity. Heady's economic interpretation of the simplex algorithm [1954] is a prime example, as are the studies by Hildreth [1957b], Puterbaugh, Kehrberg, and Dunbar [1957], and Candler [1956, 1957, 1960].

The potential usefulness of integer and mixed integer programming in farm management has been recognized for some time. Edwards [1963] suggested a number of possible applications of the techniques to farm problems using Gomory's integer programming algorithm [1958]. There are several integer and mixed integer programming algorithms available, some of which were surveyed in Maruyama and Fuller [1964]. The most current and complete survey of integer programming algorithms is by Geoffrion and Marsten [1972]. Maruyama and Fuller [1964] proposed an "RHS" ("right-hand-side") method, which was essentially a computerized complete enumeration method. Candler and Manning [1961] and Musgrave [1962] used parametric linear programming to deal with decreasing costs and increasing returns. Giaever and Seagraves [1960] and Yaron and Heady [1961] used integer, mixed integer, and nonlinear programming to investigate decisions involving economies of scale.

Marketing analysis of agricultural commodities naturally involves transportation costs and spatial efficiency, aspects of optimization to be considered later in this paper. Several studies, however, may appropriately be mentioned here. Stollsteimer [1963] developed a linear programming model which determines the number, size, and location of plants processing a fixed amount of a single raw material into a single output. Economies of scale were dealt with through the use of parametric programming. King and Logan [1964] attacked the same problem and added an iterative, partly heuristic method to handle economies of scale. Candler, Snyder, and Faught [1972] dealt with a more general problem involving several raw materials and multiple outputs using a concave programming algorithm. The algorithm, a mechanized version of the King-Logan algorithm, is equipped to solve multiple local optima problems. Bressler and Hammerberg [1942] and Hammerberg, Parker, and Bressler [1942] used budgeting to specify optimal route organization and truck sizes. Bressler [1952] applied the same methods to develop an efficient system of city milk distribution in Connecticut.

By the late 1950s rapidly developing computer technology was expanding the scope for sophisticated programming techniques. Bellman's dynamic programming [1957] was one approach which accordingly found increased application to management decisions in various industries; agriculture was no exception. The earliest agricultural applications of Bellman's approach were to optimal replacement problems, as described by White [1959], Faris [1960], and Halter and White [1962]. Burt and Allison [1963] applied the method to a Markov process in choosing wheat rotations, Minden [1968] proposed the use of dynamic programming as a tool for farm investment decisions, and Hinrichs [1972] discussed a recent application in West German agriculture. One of the most attractive features of dynamic programming is the facility with which stochastic parameters may be incorporated (for example, Burt [1965]). After a first flash of excitement induced by the flexibility and potential of Bellman's approach as typified by Throsby [1964], applications have been limited to rather simple subsystems of total farm systems. The explanation (Throsby [1968]) lies partly in the formidable computational requirements of dynamic programming. This is particularly true of allocation problems such as multiperiod farm investment. When both inputs and outputs are multiple, dynamic programming is beset by the "curse of dimensionality," because computational burdens increase exponentially with the number of outputs or inputs considered.

The significance of risk and uncertainty in the farm environment is underscored by the numerous efforts of agricultural economists to embody these concepts in decision models. Freund [1956] made the first application of active stochastic programming to a farm management problem. This technique is essentially the same as that of Markowitz's portfolio selection technique [1952]; the resultant problem is a quadratic program. Examples of applications of active stochastic programming are provided by McFarquhar [1961], Merrill [1965], and S. R. Johnson, Tefertiller, and Moore [1967]. Compared with linear programming, quadratic programming algorithms make heavy computational demands. Hazell [1971a] develops a technique leading to a linear programming problem which incorporates the mean absolute deviation of the objective function parameters, and Thomson and Hazell [1972] report a Monte Carlo study which indicates that Hazell's method gives results which are quite close to quadratic programming results. Chen's remarks [1971] and Hazell's reply should be read with Hazell [1971a]. A separable programming approach which also approximates Markowitz's E,V method was employed by Thomas et al. [1972]. A particularly important method for incorporating uncertainty is the focus-loss approach introduced into agricultural economics by Boussard and Petit [1967]. Boussard [1969] later showed that the descriptive power of the model was at least as good as that of alternative models. In 1955 Dantzig offered a model of sequential programming under uncertainty which combined the merits of linear programming and sequential analysis; Cocks [1968], Rae [1971a, 1971b], and Yaron and Horowitz [1972] have applied this model and its extensions to problems of farm management.

Dillon's expository article [1971] reviews thoroughly the application of subjective probability theory to agriculture. This includes as special cases many of the approaches, mentioned above, including E,V analysis.

Early application of game theory to farm management were restricted to "games against nature." Probably the first example was Schickele's [1950] application to climatic uncertainty. Later, Swanson [1957] suggested application of game theoretic frameworks to the same problem. In a series of analyses Dillon and Heady [1961] applied the Wald, Laplace, and Savage criteria to farmers' choices of enterprises and found a poor descriptive fit. In an extensive application to weather uncertainty, Walker et al. [1960] showed how the various criteria suited different financial situations and attitudes toward risk. In 1962 Dillon wrote his excellent survey article of game theory applied to agriculture, detailing both suggested and actual applications. His conclusion that the use of game theory had nearly run its course was premised on the continued use of ordinary games against nature. More recently, however, McInerney [1967] suggested the use of constrained games against nature. Several theoretical works have followed, notably McInerney [1969], Hazell [1970], Maruyama [1972], and Kawaguchi and Maruyama [1972], and it appears that practical applications of constrained games may be in sight. In private correspondence Professor Maruyama informed the authors of this paper that constrained games were applied in Japanese agricultural economics literature as early as 1966 (see, for example, Imamura [1966]).

Interesting work involving modern techniques of farm management is not always reported in the professional literature, or it may appear in relatively obscure outlets, working memoranda, and so on. An example is the computer-aided real-time farm management advisory service under the direction of John Schmidt of Wisconsin. Similar systems are operating at Purdue and Michigan State. Candler, Boehlje, and Saathoff [1970] outlined the problems of development and implementation of the top farmer program at Purdue. Nonetheless operational developments attest to the practical relevance of what might otherwise be thought of as elegant toys for mathematicians and economic theorists.

The above references only scratch the surface of a vast body of literature, but we hope they provide a sample adequate for illustrating the variety of uses to which modern optimization methods have been put in the study of optimal farm management. Before proceeding to other major areas of application, it would be in the spirit of the present undertaking to comment briefly on the role of the more traditional neoclassical marginal analysis in the farm management setting. The tradition goes back to von Thünen; its definitive modern statement is in Black's *Introduction to Production Economics* [1926] and Heady's *Economics of Agricultural Production and Resource Use* [1952]. Modern developments in statistics have made possible the quantitative exploitation of the neoclassical point of view. The early examples not surprisingly came from the Ames School with a focus on crop-nutrient response (for example, Tintner [1944], Heady [1946], and Heady, Pesek, and Brown [1955]). Some of Glenn Johnson's work at Kentucky and at Michigan State in the 1950s, described in Bradford and Johnson [1953], Haffnar and Johnson [1966], and Johnson and Quance [1972], was also based on this model. Of course, the optimal feed-mix and feed-ration problems solved in either the linear programming way or the neoclassical way are also an important aspect of farm management. (Early work of this kind was mentioned in the section on food and diet.)

Farm Firm Development

Economic development in agriculture (in the absence of a geographical frontier) usually involves the growth of some farm firms and the decline or abandonment of others. From the managerial point of view, in which firm policies to enhance growth are sought, and also from the production response point of view, in which aggregate implications of development and agricultural policy are the focus, farm growth and decline are of interest. Studies of farm development have much in common with the farm management studies already reviewed, and it is not always possible to categorize a model into one class or another unambiguously. For example, the early multiperiodic linear programming studies of farm growth and investment such as Swanson [1955] or Loftsgard and Heady [1959] had managerial, production response, and farm growth aspects. However, this field of application is important enough to consider separately, as is indicated by Irwin's review of various methods for farm growth modeling [1968].

   Irwin and Baker [1962] marked the beginning of a noteworthy series of farm growth models which have emphasized financial aspects of farm firm growth. Martin and Plaxico [1967] report on a polyperiod model of farm growth with investment, capital markets, and consumption all considered in some detail. Johnson, Tefertiller, and Moore [1967] apply Monte Carlo techniques to a firm growth model with stochastic crop yields. White [1959] expands the Martin-Plaxico and Johnson-Tefertiller-Moore models by incorpo-

rating investment, credit, production, and consumption matrices. In two articles [1968a, 1968b] Baker extended and generalized the Irwin-Baker model.
The work of Baker and his protégés is of particular interest as a behavioral approach to modeling firm growth. These studies focus on financial constraints
or rules of thumb. Barry and Baker [1971], for example, use reservation
prices on credit to infer attitudes toward uncertainty.

One problem common to multiperiod linear programming models of farm
growth has been matrix size. Given a single period submatrix of any detail,
the multiperiod model presents formidable problems in construction and in
computation of solutions. J. M. Boussard has made significant strides on both
of these problems: his matrix generating program GEMAGRI (Boussard
[1972]) automatically generates a multiperiod linear program on punched
cards from standard farm records, and his clever application of a turnpike
theorem to the multiperiod linear programming model of farm growth derives
a practical method for finding the "optimal" horizon for such a model (Boussard [1971]).

Heidhues [1966] focuses the recursive programming approach on the study
of farm growth and decline in an analysis of West German farms. His study incorporates considerable technological and financial detail. It was followed by
Steiger's study [1968], summarized in de Haen and Heidhues [1973 and
forthcoming], which developed individual recursive programming models for
all farms in two villages of an area where examples of growth and decay were
evident. A recently completed study by Ahn and Singh [1972] uses a similar
approach to study the differential effect of development policies on farms of
different sizes in a developing agriculture.

A line of work closely related to that of farm growth has long been pursued at the United States Department of Agriculture—namely, the analysis of
resource requirements for achieving various income levels in various farm situations. The work of John Brewster [1957] and others must be mentioned
in this context.

Production Response

One can interpret the solution of an optimizing model as being a long run
equilibrium toward which the economy is tending and/or toward which it
might be encouraged by various incentives and controls. If reality can be described in this way, then optimizing becomes a powerful tool for policy analysis. This idea lies behind many important applications of optimization methods in agricultural economics. Many of the regional budgeting studies that
originated in the 1920s were oriented to such production response purposes.
With the advent of linear programming many joint USDA and state experi-

ment station studies were converted to the new approach. The effects of price supports, income controls, and varying technological, marketing, and pricing situations were investigated using linear programming and parametric programming techniques.

The production response work was generally conducted under the title of "adjustment," and many important examples were sponsored by the USDA. Thus we had one program of research involving the cotton states of the South, one focusing on wheat production in the West, one involving livestock and feedgrains in the Corn Belt, and two more concentrating on dairying in the Lake States and in New England. Only a small proportion of this work has ever been published, but no doubt a significant number of active agricultural economists gained their early training in part through participation in these undertakings. The work was described in general terms in Sundquist et al. [1963], Colyer and Irwin [1967], and the Northeast Dairy Adjustments Study Committee [1963].

A concern that emerged in the course of this work was the aggregation problem involving the question of how much estimates of regional responses were distorted by the use of linear programming models of whole regions or representative farms as opposed to "adding up" individual farm models. As the latter was uneconomic, the issue was one of great importance. The first analysis of the problem using the duality theory of linear programming was by Day [1963]. Further consideration was given by Miller [1966] and Lee [1966]. Buckwell and Hazell [1972] applied a clustering technique to identify groups of farms which could be legitimately aggregated according to an extension of Day's criteria. Empirical work addressing the same issues was reported by Sheehy and McAlexander [1965], Barker and Stanton [1965], and Frick and Andrews [1965].

Another problem encountered in the application of representative firm models was representation of investment and disinvestment. Glenn Johnson's fixed asset theory [1958] was an important step toward solution of this problem.

Parametric programming techniques were applied to the problem of inferring supply functions and resource allocation responses from both aggregative and representative firm models. Kottke [1967] summarizes work in this field.

A quite different point of view was taken by the developers of recursive programming. Their view, as initially applied in agriculture by Henderson [1959], was to use programming models augmented by behavioral constraints of the kind already used by Wood [1951], to estimate short-run behavior of farmers at the regional level in a disequilibrium situation. Henderson's original model was used to make a one-year forecast of the allocation of land to various crops for a hundred United States farming regions. The dynamic implications of Henderson's model were brought out by Day [1963], who then stated the general class of recursive linear programming models to which Henderson's model belonged as a special case. Day's study also gave the first example of how recursive linear programming could be used to trace out the evolution of an industry over time. Applications by Schaller and Dean [1965], Muto [1965], and Cigno [1971] followed. Nontechnical discussions of the general methodology were also contributed by Day [1961, 1962]. An ambitious application of the recursive programming approach was the national model which originated with Glen T. Barton's production response group at the USDA in 1958. Day's 1963 study was the prototype study for this undertaking, and after the follow-up test by Schaller and Dean [1965] a national model was planned and implemented. Sharples and Schaller [1968] described the project during its construction phase. The model is currently being used as an experimental working tool and is being replaced by a more complex general simulation model. An even more ambitious undertaking is Thoss's multisector, multiregional recursive programming model for short-run national planning in Germany [1970]. Henrichsmeyer and de Haen [1972] describe a "next-generation" effort that is currently in the planning stage.

Interregional and Spatial Economics

Of extreme importance in agriculture and in resource economics generally is the study of interregional or spatial efficiency and development. Going all the way back to von Thünen for its conceptual foundation, the application of modern techniques came with the development of the Hitchcock-Koopmans transportation model, a special case of linear programming for which efficient computer algorithms were developed in the early 1950s. Early applications of this model to distribution and pricing are discussed by Judge [1956], Henry and Bishop [1957], Farris and King [1961], Snodgrass and French [1958], and Stemberger [1959].

Beckmann and Marschak [1961] used the more general activity analysis framework of Koopmans and Reiter [1951] to extend the spatial distribution model to include production. Building on this work, Lefeber [1958] specified a linear programming model to determine efficient allocation and shadow prices, given the regional prices of final products and the regional endowment of primary factors. Orden's transshipment problem [1956] is a special case of the Beckmann-Marschak model which King and Logan [1964] applied to determine the optimum location, number, and size of processing plants and factor and final product flows. Judge, Havlicek, and Rizek [1965] studied the optimum location of livestock slaughter and geographical flows of live animals and meat. In Snodgrass and French [1958] an aggregate model is used to determine the optimum interregional flows of whole milk and the corresponding equilibrium prices for 1953. This general model is also applied individually to fluid milk, butter, cheese, evaporated milk, and nonfat dry milk solids. A second model minimizes transportation and processing costs in determining the location of processing plants, and a third model adds production costs to these and specifies optimal production location. In a series of well-known papers Egbert and Heady focus on the best location for producing a fixed final national bill of wheat and feed grains (Heady and Egbert [1959], Egbert and Heady [1961, 1963]). Buchholz and Judge [1966] focus on livestock using the same approach. The Egbert-Heady models were forerunners of a family of works relating to the national allocation of agricultural resources: Heady and Skold [1965], Heady and Whittlesey [1965], Eyvindson, Heady and Srivastava [1975], and Brokken and Heady [1968]. Birowo and Renborg [1965] supply an application to Swedish agriculture.

Characteristics of all of the above work were the exclusion of explicit demand functions and the treatment of prices as exogenous. Building on the theoretical work of Enke [1951] and Samuelson [1952], who showed how trade theory could be formulated in mathematical programming terms, Fox [1953] shows how interregional supply-demand equilibrium could be modeled and solved computationally. The initial model focused on livestock feed. The United States was divided into ten regions and the demand for feed was estimated for each. Using the 1949-50 figures for regional production of feed, numbers and prices of livestock, and their demand equations, Fox derives equilibrium consumption, price, and shipments of feed for each region. In a later article Fox and Taeuber [1955] extend the 1953 model to include livestock. Regional demand and supply functions for livestock are added to the previous model, and a joint equilibrium solution is derived for both feed and livestock.

Dunn [1954] broadens and applies von Thünen's theory of location to the agricultural segment of the economy. An equilibrium system which includes space is formalized and is designed to solve problems on an aggregated or industrial level. Dunn's framework takes multiple products and technological interrelationships into account. Judge [1956] uses the Enke-Samuelson formulation as a basis for determining the spatial equilibrium prices for eggs when the regional supplies of eggs are taken as fixed and the demand functions are explicitly included. He then uses the linear programming transportation model to determine the optimum geographical flows of the commodity. Judge and Wallace [1958] propose an iterative parametric solution procedure to solve for prices, consumption, supplies, and flows when regional demands are represented by functional relations and supplies are predetermined. Judge and Wallace [1959, 1960] develop an equilibrium model for beef and pork, a model which incorporates given regional supplies, transport costs, and demand equations for twenty-one regions of the United States.

Tramel and Seale [1959] develop a reactive programming procedure for determining the competitive prices and flows for the Enke-Samuelson problem. This procedure was applied by Maruyama and Yoshida [1960] in Japan and then was developed into two interrelated sets of interregional quadratic programming models by Takayama and Judge [1964a, 1964b] and Maruyama and Fuller [1964, 1965]. The framework for the quadratic version of the modified Beckmann-Marschak interregional activity analysis model is contained in two 1964 articles by Takayama and Judge. Subsequent articles by Plessner and Heady [1965], Yaron, Plessner, and Heady [1965], and Plessner [1972] contributed to the development of the quadratic programming model and investigated approaches to the problem when market demand functions fail to satisfy the integrability condition. Applications of the Takayama and Judge model include an interregional analysis by Buchholz and Judge [1966] of the United States feed-livestock economy and a spatial equilibrium analysis by Hall, Heady, and Plessner [1968] of the field crop sector of United States agriculture. Applications to other areas: Louwes, Boot, and Wage [1963] apply quadratic programming to the solution of the problem of optimal use of milk in the Netherlands when there are monopolistic tendencies in the market; Bawden [1966] shows how multicommodity international trade problems may be solved by exploiting the quadratic programming model of Takayama and Judge [1964a, 1964b]; Plessner [1967] carries out purely theoretical work designed to show how these operational spatial models fit into the general equilibrium theory. There have been a number of large-scale applications of the Maruyama-Fuller model in the Japanese literature. For example, the studies by Maruyama [1967] and Muto [1965] both had direct impact on Japanese government policy. Dynamic interregional equilibrium using concepts of intertemporal optimality and multihorizon programming has been treated formally by Judge and Takayama [1973], although empirical applications have yet to be achieved.

Interregional economics with a focus on disequilibrium and comparative dynamics instead of equilibrium and comparative statics is proposed by Day [1967] and is given theoretical treatment by Day and Kennedy [1970]. Bawden's spatial model [1966] constitutes an interesting example of this recursive programming approach to the interregional equilibrium problem. He represents regional production by econometric equations that depend on prices which are determined by a transportation model that optimizes short-run trade patterns. It may be regarded as a complex type of cobweb approach to supply-demand interactions as opposed to the equilibrium theory following the Samuelson-Enke formulation. A more recent study by Schmitz and Bawden [1973] applies this methodology to the world wheat market. Quite similar to Bawden's approach is Kottke's application [1970] of a recursive version of the Takayama-Judge model to an imperfectly competitive dairy industry. We have already mentioned the related work by Thoss [1970] and by Henrichsmeyer and de Haen [1972].

There are at least two good survey articles on spatial equilibrium models: Bawden [1964], and Weinschenck, Henrichsmeyer, and Aldinger [1969]. In addition, Takayama and Judge [1971] and Judge and Takayama [1973] furnish extensive bibliographies, exposition of theory and methodology, and examples of applications of spatial and temporal price allocation models.

Natural Resources

Recent applications of quantitative optimization techniques to allocation of natural resources have been numerous, and in particular Bellman's dynamic programming principle has been extensively applied. Underlying this recent work is the general economics of extractive resources. Hotelling's [1931] pioneering application of the calculus of variations to the theory of nonreplenishable resources was perhaps the earliest contribution to this theory. Subsequently, numerous works by S. V. Ciriacy-Wantrup and others laid further theoretical groundwork for the application of sophisticated optimization techniques during the 1960s.

Economic models of commercial fishing have played an important role in developing an approach to replenishable resources. Two seminal works are provided by H. S. Gordon [1954] and Scott [1955]. These neoclassical models were applied by Crutchfield and Zellner [1962] and Quirk and Smith [1969]. Optimal control was used to good effect by Clark [1973]. In 1968 V. L. Smith proposed a general economic model of production from natural resources, and in 1970 Burt and Cummings utilized Bellman's dynamic programming framework to state an even more general theory of production and investment for natural resources. Most of the applied work has been focused on water resources. We shall first review contributions here and then briefly consider pollution studies.

Moore [1961] was one of the first to identify the problems of allocation of water over time. An important subset of the water conservation (temporal allocation) problem is the use of groundwater. In a series of works Burt [1964a, 1964b, 1966, 1967a, 1967b, 1970b] developed an approach to the groundwater problem using dynamic programming and employing stochastic state variables to represent stochastic elements in the supply of groundwater. Closely related to the groundwater problem is the allocation of irrigation water. Burt [1964b] and de Lucia [1969] both treat the case of conjunctive use of groundwater and surface water, and Biere and Lee [1972] treat the case of reservoir water used to recharge groundwater in dynamic programming frameworks, but most of the studies of irrigation water are related to the management of reservoirs for water used directly in irrigation. The decision environment of the reservoir managers includes several elements of uncertainty including the weather and the demand for water. The authors of several articles (R. L. Anderson [1968], R. L. Anderson and Maass [1971], Butcher [1971], and W. A. Hall, Butcher, and Esogbue [1968]) apply stochastic dynamic programming, assuming the supply of water to be stochastic and the demand determinant; Burt and Stauber [1971] assume a given inflow and a stochastic demand; de Lucia [1969], Dudley, Howell, and Musgrave [1971a, 1971b, 1972], Dudley [1970, 1972], and Dudley and Burt [1973] assume both stochastic supply and stochastic demand. The series of articles by Dudley alone and in collaboration with others culminates in the 1973 article by Dudley and Burt, which outlines a general stochastic dynamic programming model to determine optimal levels of intertemporal water application rates, intraseason irrigated acreage, and preseason acreage to be planted.

There have been other approaches to the problem of optimum reservoir management. One is the application of chance-constrained programming to single-purpose reservoirs by Eisel [1970, 1972], Loucks [1970], Joeres, Leibman, and Revelle [1971], and Nayak and Arora [1971]. Guise and Flinn [1970] employ a Takayama-Judge spatial equilibrium model to derive optimal prices for a water system. In an early application of stochastic linear programming Manne [1962] employed Markov process optimization to management of a multipurpose reservoir. Young [1967] was perhaps the first to apply linear decision rules to reservoir management.

Several studies have concentrated on selection, sequencing, and timing of investments in water resource projects. Jacoby and Loucks [1972] have described a technique combining simulation models of river basins and optimization routines to select and assess possible patterns of investment. Cummings and Winkelmann [1970] and Regev and Schwartz [1973] apply the dynamic programming framework of Burt and Cummings [1970] to the problem of interregional investment and allocation of water. Regev and Schwartz are also concerned with economies of scale and therefore apply mixed-integer programming. Young and Pisano [1970] apply nonlinear programming to minimize investment costs in water projects; Butcher, Haimes, and Hall [1969] and Morin and Esogbue [1971] propose special dynamic programming algorithms for sequencing and scheduling of water supply projects; and Erlenkotter [1973] formulates a dynamic programming model to minimize costs of developing a given hydroelectric capacity in a river basin. R. A. Young and Bredenhoft [1972] use a two-stage optimization model to simulate reactions of economic decision makers in a river basin. A current study being conducted under the auspices of Heady at Iowa State is concerned with the allocation of water resources between regions in the United States and the environmental effects of these allocations. A part of this study is reflected in the recent application of the Heady-Egbert regional adjustment model by Heady et al. [1973].

One "natural resource" that is currently in the public eye is the capacity of the environment to absorb society's pollution residuals. An imaginative approach to this problem is illustrated by d'Arge [1971] in his use of a parable of an astronaut irretrievably lost in space. To determine the astronaut's optimal pattern of consumption over time, d'Arge uses optimal control theory. On a more mundane level engineers and economists are developing models which will help to determine "optimal" levels of pollution. At the University of Illinois Earl Swanson and his colleagues have been conducting interdisciplinary work to determine the sedimentation effects of various cropping systems using linear programming models. Narayanan and Swanson [1972] report the results of a parametric linear programming study of the trade-offs between sedimentation and farm income. A similar work was undertaken by Seay [1970]. Graves, Hatfield, and Whinston [1972] outline an approach which employs nonlinear programming to determine optimal methods of water quality control for the Delaware River Estuary. Davidson and Bradshaw [1970] employ Pontriyagin's minimum principle to the treatment of polluted streams, and Hass [1970] proposed the Dantzig-Wolfe decomposition algorithm as a basis for a decentralized method of arriving at optimal water pollution taxes. It is certain that many more such applications will follow as the quality of data and the understanding of environmental systems improves.

Agricultural Development Problems

National planning has been the predominant setting in which optimization techniques have been applied to problems in economic development. For computational reasons these studies have until quite recently been limited to linear programming methods. One of the earliest (and best-known) examples of such a model is that of Sandee [1960]. Some of the more frequently cited works in this field are those by Manne [1966], Manne and Weiskopf [1969], Eckaus and Parikh [1968], Chenery and MacEwan [1966], and Bruno [1967]. Many of these focus on the optimal resource allocation between agriculture and other sectors when such national goals as foreign exchange maximization are pursued. Often they build on and incorporate previous Leontief-style input-output models of the economy in question. This underlying input-output work is summarized in a series of conference proceedings beginning in 1951, and continuing through Barna [1963], Carter and Brody [1972a, 1972b], and Brody and Carter [1973]. An illuminating example focusing on agriculture is the study by Fox, Sengupta, and Thorbecke [1966], who proposed imbedding an input-output model in a more general multisector analysis.

More recent planning models reflect advances in computer technology both in their increased attention to detail and in their use of more difficult optimizing techniques such as mixed-integer programming and decomposition. A number of important examples by such authors as Barraza, Bossoco, Duloy, Norton, Kutcher, Winkelmann, and others will be found in Goreux and Manne [1973]. Dynamic programming and mixed-integer programming techniques have begun to find application in sectoral or single-industry planning models; for example, Manne [1967] applies both techniques to several industries of the Indian economy, and Westphal [1971a] applies mixed-integer programming to the economy of South Korea.

Application of optimization techniques to farm management in less developed countries to date has been limited. McFarquhar and Evans [1957] provide an early application of linear programming to combinations of enterprises in tropical agriculture. More recently Heyer [1971] has applied linear programming to the problem of allocating peasant resources in a small rural area of Kenya. In a second work Heyer [1972] extends her original model to account for uncertainty through the use of a game theoretic framework. Spencer [1973] has applied linear programming to a study of the allocation of labor resources to rice production in Sierra Leone. His study was based on farm management survey data, and its objective was to improve interregional allocation of labor resources. Baker [1973] employs linear programming in an analysis of the role of credit in smallholder farming. Probably nowhere will one find a greater output of useful optimization studies to problems of less developed agriculture than at the Punjab Agricultural University in Ludhiana. Most of these studies are by S. S. Johl and A. S. Kahlon (for example, Johl and Kahlon [1967]) and various of their students. This demonstrates the need for scholars to research local journals and experiment station reports for applied studies relevant to their special problems.

General systems simulation models such as those described by Halter, Hayenga, and Manetsch [1970] are of growing importance in less developed countries. The reason is that they make possible the systematic study of a model economy when data are inadequate, or when goal specification is difficult, or when the economy is simply too complex to optimize with existing algorithms and computers. They also are useful when, as a prelude to systematic planning, one wants to understand how the economy works and how it is likely to respond to policy controls.

General systems simulation includes, as a special category, models in which given components are represented by optimizing submodels. This category also belongs to the class of recursive programming systems of Day and Kennedy [1970]. Examples of the recursive programming approach to the problem of tracking a developing agricultural economy include Singh [1969, 1971], and Ahn and Singh [1972]. Thoss [1970] focuses on multisector development using this technique.

Table 1. Categorization of Survey References into Eight
Branches of Agricultural Economics Research

Citations preceded by an asterisk (*) indicate survey
articles or substantial bibliographical sources.

1. *Introduction.* Day [1977]; Fox [1953]; Hildreth and Reiter [1951]; Kuhn and Tucker [1951]; Marshall [1890]; Mighell and Black [1951]; and von Thünen [1966].

2. *Food and Diet.* Christenson and Mighell [1951]; Heady [1951]; Heady, Woodworth, et al. [1953]; V. E. Smith [1974]; Stigler [1945]; and Waugh [1951].

3. *Farm and Agribusiness Management.* Agrawal and Heady [1968]; *Agrawal and Heady [1972]; J. R. Anderson and Hardaker [1972]; Babbar [1955]; Bellman [1957]; Bishop [1956]; Black [1926]; Bowlen and Heady [1955]; Bradford and Johnson [1953]; Bressler [1952]; Bressler and Hammerberg [1942]; Brewster [1957]; Burt [1965]; Burt and Allison [1963]; Byerlee and Anderson [1969]; Candler [1956]; Candler [1957]; Candler [1960]; Candler [1972]; Candler, Boehlje, and Saathoff [1970]; Candler and Manning [1961]; Candler, Snyder, and Faught [1972]; Charnes [1953]; Charnes and Cooper [1959]; Chen [1971]; Cocks [1968]; Conner, Freund, and Godwin [1972]; Coutu [1957]; Dantzig [1951]; Dantzig [1955]; Dantzig and Wolfe [1960]; *Dillon [1962]; *Dillon [1971]; Dillon and Heady [1961]; Doll [1972]; Dorfman, Samuelson, and Solow [1958]; Edwards [1963]; Edwards [1966]; Faris [1960]; Freund [1956]; Geoffrion and Marsten [1972]; Giaever and Seagraves [1960]; Halter and Dean [1971]; Halter and White [1962]; Hammerberg, Parker, and Bressler [1942]; Hazell [1970]; Hazell [1971a]; Hazell [1971b]; Heady [1946]; Heady [1951]; Heady [1952]; Heady [1954]; Heady [1971]; Heady and Candler [1958], Heady and Egbert [1964]; Heady, McAlexander, and Schrader [1956]; Heady and Pesek [1954]; Heady, Pesek, and Brown [1955]; Heady, Woodworth, et al. [1953]; Hildreth [1957a]; Hildreth [1957b]; Hildreth and Reiter [1951]; Hinrichs [1972]; Hitchcock [1941]; Hutton [1963]; *Hutton [1965]; Imamura [1966]; G. L. Johnson [1952a]; G. L. Johnson [1952b]; G. L. Johnson [1955]; G. L. Johnson and Haver [1953]; G. L. Johnson and Quance [1972]; Kawaguchi and Maruyama [1972]; G. A. King and Logan [1964]; R. A. King [1953]; R. A. King and Freund [1953]; Kottke [1961]; Langham [1963]; Loftsgard and Heady [1959]; McFarquhar [1961]; McInerney [1967]; McInerney [1969]; McPherson and Faris [1958]; Markowitz [1952]; Markowitz [1959]; Maruyama [1972]; Maruyama and Fuller [1964]; Maruyama and Yoshida [1960]; Merrill [1965]; Mighell [1955]; Minden [1968]; Musgrave [1962]; Officer and Halter [1968]; Peterson [1955]; Puterbaugh, Kehrberg, and Dunbar [1957]; Rae [1971a]; Rae [1971b]; Roy [1952];

Table 1. Categorization of Survey References into Eight
Branches of Agricultural Economics Research (Cont.)

Citations preceded by an asterisk (*) indicate survey
articles or substantial bibliographical sources.

Schickele [1950] ; B. J. Smith [1973] ; Stollsteimer [1963] ; Swanson [1955] ; Swanson [1956] ; Swanson [1957] ; Swanson [1961] ; Swanson [1966] ; Swanson and Fox [1954] ; Thomas et al. [1972] ; Thomson and Hazell [1972] ; Throsby [1964] ; *Throsby [1968] ; Tintner [1944] ; Tintner [1955] ; Walker et al. [1960] ; Waugh [1951] ; *Weinschenck, Henrichsmeyer, and Aldinger [1969] ; White [1959] ; Yaron and Heady [1961] ; Yaron and Horowitz [1972].

4. *Farm Firm Development.* Baker [1968a] ; Baker [1968b] ; Baker [1973] ; Barry and Baker [1971] ; Boehlje [1967] ; Boehlje and White [1969] ; Bolton [1964] ; Boussard [1969] ; Boussard [1971] ; Boussard [1972] ; Boussard and Petit [1967] ; Day and Cigno [forthcoming] ; de Haen and Heidhues [1973] ; de Haen and Heidhues [forthcoming] ; *Irwin [1968] ; Irwin and Baker [1962] ; S. R. Johnson, Tefertiller, and Moore [1967] ; J. R. Martin and Plaxico [1967] ; *Renborg [1970] ; Steiger [1968] ; Yaron and Horowitz [1972].

5. *Production Response.* Barker and Stanton [1965] ; Barry and Baker [1971] ; Bolton [1964] ; Boussard [1969] ; Boussard [1971] ; Boussard [1972] ; Boussard and Petit [1967] ; Brokken and Heady [1968] ; Buchholz and Judge [1966] ; Buckwell and Hazell [1972] ; Cigno [1971] ; Colyer and Irwin [1967] ; Cowling and Baker [1963] ; Day [1961] ; Day [1962] ; Day [1963] ; Day [1967] ; Day and Kennedy [1970] ; de Haen [1973] ; Egbert and Heady [1963] ; Eyvindson, Heady and Srivastava [1975] ; Frick and Andrews [1965] ; Heady and Skold [1965] ; Heady and Whittlesey [1965] ; Heidhues [1966] ; Henderson [1959] ; Henrichsmeyer and de Haen [1972] ; G. L. Johnson [1955] ; G. L. Johnson [1958] ; G. L. Johnson and Haver [1953] ; Kottke [1967] ; Kottke [1970] ; Krenz, Baumann, and Heady [1962] ; Lee [1966] ; Maruyama and Fuller [1965] ; Miller [1966] ; Miller [1972] ; Muto [1965] ; Northeast Dairy Adjustments Study Committee [1963] ; Plessner and Heady [1965] ; Schaller [1968] ; Schaller and Dean [1965] ; Schmitz and Bawden [1973] ; Sharples and Schaller [1968] ; Sheehy and McAlexander [1965] ; Sundquist et al. [1963] ; Thoss [1970] ; Wood [1951].

6. *Inter-regional and Spatial Economics.* *Bawden [1964] ; Bawden [1966] ; Bawden, Carter, and Dean [1966] ; Beckmann and Marschak [1961] ; Birowo and Renborg [1965] ; Bressler [1952] ; Bressler and Hammerberg [1942] ; Brokken and Heady [1968] ; Buchholz and Judge [1966] ; Candler, Snyder, and Faught [1972] ; Day [1962] ; Dunn [1954] ; Egbert and Heady [1961] ; Egbert and Heady [1963] ; Enke [1951] ; Eyvindson, Heady, and Srivastava [1975] ; Farris and King [1961] ; Fox [1953] ; Fox and Taeuber [1955] ; Guise and Flinn [1970] ; Haffnar and Johnson [1966] ; Hall, Heady, and Plessner [1968] ; Heady and Egbert [1959] ; Heady and Skold [1965] ; Heady and Whittlesey [1965] ; Heidhues [1966] ; Henrichsmeyer and de Haen [1972] ; Henry and Bishop [1957] ; Hitchcock [1941] ; Judge [1956] ; Judge, Havlicek, and Rizek [1965] ; Judge and Takayama [1973] ; Judge and Wallace [1958] ; Judge and Wallace [1959] ; Judge and Wallace [1960] ; G. A. King and Logan [1964] ; Koopmans [1949] ; Koopmans and Reiter [1951] ; Kottke [1970] ; Lefeber [1958] ; *Leuthold and Bawden [1966] ; Louwes, Boot, and Wage [1963] ; Maruyama [1967] ;

Table 1. Categorization of Survey References into Eight
Branches of Agricultural Economics Research (Cont.)

Citations preceded by an asterisk (*) indicate survey
articles or substantial bibliographical sources.

Orden [1956]; Schmitz and Bawden [1973]; Takayama and Judge [1964a]; Takayama and Judge [1964b]; Takayama and Judge [1964c]; Takayama and Judge [1971]; *Weinschenck, Henrichsmeyer, and Aldinger [1969]; Yaron, Plessner, and Heady [1965].

7. *Natural Resources.* R. L. Anderson [1968]; R. L. Anderson and Maass [1971]; Biere and Lee [1972]; Burt [1964a]; Burt [1964b]; Burt [1966]; Burt [1967a]; Burt [1967b]; Burt [1970a]; Burt [1970b]; Burt and Cummings [1970]; Burt and Stauber [1971]; Butcher [1971]; Butcher, Haimes, and Hall [1969]; Ciriacy-Wantrup [1952]; Clark [1973]; Crutchfield and Zellner [1962]; Cummings and Winkelmann [1970], d'Arge [1971]; Davidson and Bradshaw [1970]; de Lucia [1969]; Dudley [1970]; Dudley [1972]; Dudley and Burt [1973]; Dudley, Howell, and Musgrave [1971a]; Dudley, Howell, and Musgrave [1971b]; Dudley, Musgrave, and Howell [1972]; Eisel [1970]; Eisel [1972]; Erlenkotter [1973]; H. S. Gordon [1954]; R. L. Gordon [1967]; Graves, Hatfield, and Whinston [1969]; Graves, Hatfield, and Whinston [1972]; Guise and Flinn [1970]; Hall, Butcher, and Esogbue [1968]; Hass [1970]; Heady, Madsen, et al. [1973]; Hotelling [1931]; Jacoby and Loucks [1972]; Joeres, Leibman, and Revelle [1971]; Keckler and Larson [1968]; Loucks [1970]; Manne [1962]; Meier and Beightler [1967]; Moore [1961]; Morin and Esogbue [1971]; Narayanan and Swanson [1972]; Nayak and Arora [1971]; Quirk and Smith [1969], Regev and Schwartz [1973]; Revelle, Loucks, and Lyn [1968]; Riordan [1971]; Scott [1955]; Seay [1970]; V. L. Smith [1968]; Tolley and Hastings [1960]; G. K. Young, Jr. [1967]; G. K. Young, Jr., and Pisano [1970]; R. A. Young and Bredehoft [1972].

8. *Agricultural Development Problems.* Adelman [1966]; Ahn and Singh [1972]; Baker [1973]; *Barna [1963]; Brody and Carter [1972]; Bruno [1967]; *A. P. Carter and Brody [1972a]; A. P. Carter and Brody [1972b]; Chakravarty and Lefeber [1965]; Chenery and MacEwan [1966]; Duloy and Norton [1971]; Eckaus and Parikh [1968]; Fox, Sengupta, and Thorbecke [1966]; Goreux and Manne [1973]; Halter, Hayenga, and Manetsch [1970]; Heyer [1971]; Heyer [1972]; Johl and Kahlon [1967]; Mac-Ewan [1971]; McFarquhar and Evans [1957]; Manne [1966]; Manne [1967]; Manne [1973]; Manne and Weiskopf [1969]; Mudahar [1972]; Sandee [1960]; Singh [1969]; Singh [1971]; Spencer [1973]; Westphal [1971a]; Westphal [1971b].

References

Citations preceded by an asterisk (*) indicate survey articles or substantial bibliographical sources.

Adelman, I. [1966]. "A Linear Programming Model of Educational Planning: A Case Study of Argentina." In *The Theory and Design of Economic Development*, I. Adelman and E. Thorbecke, eds. Baltimore: Johns Hopkins Press. Pp. 385-417.

Agrawal, R. C., and E. O. Heady [1968]. "Applications of Game Theory Models in Agriculture." *J. Agr. Econ.* 19:207-218.

*——— [1972]. *Operations Research Methods for Agricultural Decisions.* Ames: Iowa State University Press.

Ahn, C., and I. J. Singh [1972]. "A Dynamic Model of the Agricultural Sector in Southern Brazil: Some Policy Simulations." Paper presented at an ADC conference, Application of Recursive Decision Systems in Agricultural Sector Analysis, Washington, D.C.

Anderson, J. R., and J. B. Hardaker [1972]. "An Appreciation of Decision Analysis in Management." *Rev. Marketing Agr. Econ.* 40:170-184.

Anderson, R. L. [1968]. "A Simulation Program to Establish Optimum Crop Patterns on Irrigated Farms Based on Preseason Estimates of Water Supply." *Am. J. Agr. Econ.* 50:1586-1590.

Anderson, R. L., and A. Maass [1971]. *A Simulation of Irrigation Systems: The Effect of Water Supply and Operating Rules on Production and Income on Irrigated Farms.* USDA Technical Bulletin 1431.

Babbar, M. M. [1955]. "Distributions of Solutions of a Set of Linear Equations (with an Application to Linear Programming)." *J. Am. Stat. Assoc.* 50:854-869.

Baker, C. B. [1968a]. "Credit in the Production Organization of the Firm." *Am. J. Agr. Econ.* 50:507-520.

——— [1968b]. "Financial Organization and Production Choices." *Am. J. Agr. Econ.* 50:1566-1577.

——— [1973]. "Role of Credit in the Economic Development of Small Farm Agriculture." *Small Farmer Credit Analytical Papers.* AID Spring Review of Small Farmer Credit, 19:41-70.

Barker, R., and B. F. Stanton [1965]. "Estimation and Aggregation of Farm Supply Functions." *J. Farm Econ.* 47:701-712.

*Barna, T. [1963]. *Structural Interdependence and Economic Development: Proceedings of an International Conference on Input-Output Techniques, Geneva, Switzerland, 1961.* New York: Macmillan.

Barry, P. J., and C. B. Baker [1971]. "Reservation Prices on Credit Use: A Measure of Response to Uncertainty." *Am. J. Agr. Econ.* 53:222-234.

*Bawden, D. L. [1964]. "An Evaluation of Alternative Spatial Models." *J. Farm Econ.* 46:1372-1379.

——— [1966]. "A Spatial Price Equilibrium Model of International Trade." *J. Farm Econ.* 48:862-874.

Bawden, D. L., H. O. Carter, and G. W. Dean [1966]. "Interregional Competition in the U.S. Turkey Industry." *Hilgardia* 37:437-531.

Beckmann, M., and T. Marschak [1961]. "An Activity Analysis Approach to Location Theory." *Proceedings of the Second Symposium in Linear Programming.* United States Air Force and National Bureau of Standards 1:331-379.

Bellman, R. [1957]. *Dynamic Programming.* Princeton: Princeton University Press.

Biere, A. W., and I. M. Lee [1972]. "A Model for Managing Reservoir Water Releases." *Am. J. Agr. Econ.* 54:411-421.

Birowo, A. T., and U. Renborg [1965]. "Inter-Regional Planning for Agricultural Production in Sweden." OECD Directorate for Agriculture and Food, Inter-Regional Competition in Agriculture, Problems of Methodology, Paris.

Bishop, C. E. [1956]. "Programming Farm-Nonfarm Allocation of Farm Family Resources." *J. Farm Econ.* 38:396-407.

Black, J. D. [1926]. *Introduction to Production Economics*. New York: Henry Holt.

Boehlje, M. D. [1967]. "An Analysis of the Impact of Selected Factors on the Process of Farm Firm Growth." Unpublished M.S. thesis, Purdue University.

Boehlje, M. D., and T. K. White [1969]. "A Production-Investment Decision Model of Farm Firm Growth." *Am. J. Agr. Econ.* 51:546-563.

Bolton, B. [1964]. "Variable Resource Programming for Appraising Farm Adjustment Opportunities." *Agr. Econ. Res.* 16:12-22.

Boussard, J. M. [1969]. "The Introduction of Risk into a Programming Model: Different Criteria and Actual Behavior of Farmers." *European Econ. Rev.* 1:92-121.

——— [1971]. "Time Horizon, Objective Function, and Uncertainty in a Multiperiod Model of Firm Growth." *Am. J. Agr. Econ.* 53:467-477.

——— [1972]. *GEMAGRI: General Description of the Program — User's Manual.* Institut National de la Recherche Agronomique, Paris.

Boussard, J. M., and M. Petit [1967]. "Representation of Farmer's Behavior under Uncertainty with a Focus Loss Constraint." *J. Farm Econ.* 49:869-880.

Bowlen, B., and E. O. Heady [1955]. *Optimum Combinations of Competitive Crops at Particular Locations.* Iowa Agricultural Experiment Station Research Bulletin 426.

Bradford, L. A., and G. L. Johnson [1953]. *Farm Management Analysis.* New York: Wiley.

Bressler, R. G., Jr. [1952]. *City Milk Distribution.* Cambridge: Harvard University Press.

Bressler, R. G., Jr., and D. O. Hammerberg [1942]. *Efficiency of Milk Marketing in Connecticut: Three Economics of the Assembly of Milk.* Connecticut Agricultural Experiment Station Bulletin 239.

Brewster, J. M. [1957]. *Farm Resources Needed for Specified Income Levels.* USDA Agricultural Information Bulletin 180.

Brito, D. L. [1973]. "The Stability of an Optimal Resource Mass." Unpublished manuscript.

Brody, A., and A. P. Carter, eds. [1972]. *Input-Output Techniques.* New York: American Elsevier.

Brokken, R. F., and E. O. Heady [1968]. *Interregional Adjustments in Crop and Livestock Production: A Linear Programming Analysis.* USDA Technical Bulletin 1396.

Bruno, M. [1967]. "Optimal Patterns of Trade and Development." *Rev. Econ. and Stat.* 49:545-554.

Buchholz, H. E., and G. G. Judge [1966]. "Ein Standortmodell der tierischen Produktion der Vereinigton Staaten von Amerika." *Berichte über Landwirtschaft* 44:392-431.

Buckwell, A. E., and P. B. R. Hazell [1972]. "Implications of Aggregation Bias for the Construction of Static and Dynamic Linear Programming Supply Models." *J. Agr. Econ.* 23:119-134.

Burt, O. R. [1964a]. "Optimal Resource Use Over Time with an Application to Ground Water." *Management Science* 11:80-93.

——— [1964b]. "The Economics of Conjunctive Use of Ground and Surface Water." *Hilgardia* 36:31-111.

——— [1965]. "Optimal Replacement under Risk." *J. Farm Econ.* 47:324-346.

——— [1966]. "Economic Control of Groundwater Reserves." *J. Farm Econ.* 48:632-647.

——— [1967a]. "Temporal Allocation of Ground Water." *Water Resources Research* 3:45-56.

——— [1967b]. "Groundwater Management under Quadratic Criterion Functions." *Water Resources Research* 3:673-682.

——— [1970a]. "On Optimization Methods for Branching Multistage Water Resource Systems." *Water Resources Research* 6:345-346.

——— [1970b]. "Groundwater Storage Control under Institutional Restrictions." *Water Resources Research* 6:1540-1548.

Burt, O. R., and J. R. Allison [1963]. "Farm Management Decisions with Dynamic Programming." *J. Farm Econ.* 45:121-136.

Burt, O. R., and R. G. Cummings [1970]. "Production and Investment in Natural Resource Industries." *Am. Econ. Rev.* 60:576-590.

Burt, O. R., and M. S. Stauber [1971]. "Economic Analysis of Irrigation in a Subhumid Climate." *Am. J. Agr. Econ.* 53:33-46.

Butcher, W. S. [1971]. "Stochastic Dynamic Programming for Optimum Reservoir Operation." *Water Resources Bulletin* 7:115-123.

Butcher, W. S., Y. Y. Haimes, and W. A. Hall [1969]. "Dynamic Programming for the Optimal Sequencing of Water Supply Projects." *Water Resources Research* 5: 1196-1204.

Byerlee, D., and J. R. Anderson [1969]. "Value of Predictors of Uncontrolled Factors in Response Functions." *Australian J. Agr. Econ.* 13:118-127.

Candler, W. [1956]. "A Modified Simplex Solution for Linear Programming with Variable Capital Restrictions." *J. Farm Econ.* 38:940-955.

——— [1957]. "A Modified Simplex Solution for Linear Programming with Variable Prices." *J. Farm Econ.* 39:409-428.

——— [1960]. "A 'Short-Cut' Method for the Complete Solution of Game Theory and Feed-Mix Problems." *Econometrica* 28:618-634.

——— [1972]. "Review of Halter and Dean [1971]. *Am. J. Agr. Econ.* 54:149.

Candler, W., M. Boehlje, and R. Saathoff [1970]. "Computer Software for Farm Management Extension." *Am. J. Agr. Econ.* 52:71-80.

Candler, W., and R. Manning [1961]. "A Modified Simplex Procedure for Problems with Decreasing Average Cost." *J. Farm Econ.* 43:859-875.

Candler, W., J. C. Snyder, and W. Faught [1972]. "Concave Programming Applied to Rice Mill Location." *Am. J. Agr. Econ.* 54:126-130.

*Carter, A. P., and A. Brody, eds. [1972a, 1972b]. *Applications of Input-Output Analysis*. Vols. I and II. Amsterdam: North-Holland.

Chakravarty, S., and L. Lefeber [1965]. "An Optimizing Planning Model." *Economic Weekly* 17:237-252.

Charnes, A. [1953]. "Constrained Games and Linear Programming." *Proceedings of the National Academy of Science* 39:639-641.

Charnes, A., and W. W. Cooper [1959]. "Chance-Constrained Programming." *Management Science* 6:73-79.

Chen, J. [1971]. "A Linear Alternative to Quadratic and Semivariance Programming for Farm Planning under Uncertainty: Comment." *Am. J. Agr. Econ.* 53:662-664; P. B. R. Hazell, "Reply," pp. 664-665.

Chenery, H. B., and A. MacEwan [1966]. "Optimal Patterns of Growth and Aid: The Case of Pakistan." *The Theory and Design of Economic Development*, I. Adelman and E. Thorbecke, eds. Baltimore: Johns Hopkins Press. Pp. 149-180.

Christenson, R. P., and R. L. Mighell [1951]. "Food Production Strategy and the Protein-Feed Balance." *J. Farm Econ.* 33:183-191.

Cigno, A. [1971]. "Production and Investment Response to Changing Market Conditions, Technical Know-How, and Government Policies: A Vintage Model of the Agricultural Sector." *Rev. Econ. Studies* 38:63-94.

Ciriacy-Wantrup, S. V. [1952]. *Resource Conservation—Economics and Policies*. Berkeley: University of California Press.

Clark, C. W. [1973]. "The Economics of Overexploitation." *Science* 181:630-634.

Cocks, K. D. [1968]. "Discrete Stochastic Programming." *Management Science* (Theory Series) 15:72-79.

Colyer, D., and G. D. Irwin [1967]. *Beef, Pork and Feed Grains in the Cornbelt: Supply Response and Resource Adjustments*. Missouri Agricultural Experiment Station Research Bulletin 921.

Conner, J. R., R. J. Freund, and M. R. Godwin [1972]. "Risk Programming: An Aid in Planning Reservoir-Irrigation Systems." *Am. J. Agr. Econ.* 54:249-254.

Coutu, A. J. [1957]. "Planning of Total Resource Use on Low-Income and Part-Time Farms." *J. Farm Econ.* 39:1350-1359.

Cowling, K. G., and C. B. Baker [1963]. "A Polyperiod Model for Estimating the Supply of Milk." *Agr. Econ. Res.* 15:15-23.

Crutchfield, J., and A. Zellner [1962]. *Economic Aspects of the Pacific Halibut Industry*. Fishery Industrial Research 1. United States Department of the Interior, Washington, D.C.

Cummings, R. G., and D. L. Winkelmann [1970]. "Water Resource Management in Arid Environs." *Water Resources Research* 6:1559-1568.

Dantzig, G. B. [1951]. "Maximization of a Linear Function of Variables Subject to Linear Inequalities." *Activity Analysis of Production and Allocation*, T. C. Koopmans, ed. New York: Wiley. Pp. 339-347.

—— [1955]. "Linear Programming under Uncertainty." *Management Science* 1:196-207.

Dantzig, G. B., and D. Wolfe [1960]. "The Decomposition Algorithm for Linear Programming." *Operations Research* 8:101-111.

D'Arge, R. C. [1971]. "Essay on Economic Growth and Environmental Quality." *Swedish Journal of Economics* 73:25-41.

Davidson, B., and R. W. Bradshaw [1970]. "A Steady State Optimal Design of Artificial Induced Aeration in Polluted Streams by the Use of Pontryagin's Minimum Principle." *Water Resources Research* 6:383-397.

Day, R. H. [1961]. "Recursive Programming and Supply Prediction." *Agricultural Supply Functions—Estimating Techniques and Interpretation*, E. O. Heady, C. B. Baker, H. G. Diesslin, E. Kehrberg, and S. Staniforth, eds. Ames: Iowa State University Press. Pp. 108-127.

—— [1962]. "An Approach to Production Response." *Agr. Econ. Res.* 14:134-148.

—— [1963]. *Recursive Programming and Production Response*. Amsterdam: North-Holland.

—— [1967]. "A Microeconomic Model of Business Growth, Decay, and Cycles." *Unternehmensforschung* 11:1-20.

—— [1977]. "On Economic Optimization: A Nontechnical Survey." (See the table of contents in this volume.)

Day, R. H., and A. Cigno, eds. [forthcoming]. *Modelling Economic Change: The Recursive Programming Approach*.

Day, R. H., and P. Kennedy [1970]. "Recursive Decision Systems: An Existence Analysis." *Econometrica* 38:666-681.

De Haen, H. [1973]. "Dynamisches Regionalmodell der Produktion und Investition in der Landwirtschaft." *Agrarwirtschaft*, SH 52, Hannover (Göttingen Ph.D. dissertation).

De Haen, H., and T. Heidhues [1973]. "Recursive Programming Models to Simulate Agricultural Development—Applications in West Germany." Institute for Agricultural Economics, Working Paper 18, Göttingen.

——— [forthcoming]. "Farm Growth and Inter-regional Competition." In *Modelling Economic Change: The Recursive Programming Approach*, R. H. Day and A. Cigno, eds.

De Lucia, R. J. [1969]. "Operating Policies for Irrigation Systems under Stochastic Regimes." Ph.D. dissertation, Harvard University.

*Dillon, J. L. [1962]. "Applications of Game Theory in Agricultural Economics: Review and Requiem." *Australian J. Agr. Econ.* 6:20-35.

*Dillon, J. L. [1971]. "An Expository Review of Bernoullian Decision Theory in Agriculture: Is Utility Futility?" *Rev. Marketing Agr. Econ.* 39:3-80.

Dillon, J. L., and E. O. Heady [1961]. "Free Competition, Uncertainty and Farmer Decisions." *J. Farm Econ.* 43:643-651.

Doll, J. P. [1972]. "A Comparison of Annual versus Average Optima for Fertilizer Experiments." *Am. J. Agr. Econ.* 54:226-233.

Dorfman, R., P. A. Samuelson, and R. M. Solow [1958]. *Linear Programming and Economic Analysis*. New York: McGraw-Hill.

Dudley, N. J. [1970]. "A Simulation and Dynamic Programming Approach to Irrigation Decision-Making in a Variable Environment." Ph.D. dissertation, University of New England (Australia).

——— [1972]. "Irrigation Planning: 4. Optimal Interseasonal Water Allocation." *Water Resources Review* 8:586-594.

Dudley, N. J., and O. R. Burt [1973]. "Stochastic Reservoir Management and System Design for Irrigation." *Water Resources Research* 9:507-522.

Dudley, N. J., D. T. Howell, and W. F. Musgrave [1971a]. "Optimal Intraseasonal Irrigation Water Allocation." *Water Resources Research* 7:770-788.

——— [1971b]. "Irrigation Planning: 2. Choosing Optimal Acreages within a Season." *Water Resources Research* 7:1051-1063.

Dudley, N. J., W. F. Musgrave, and D. T. Howell [1972]. "Irrigation Planning: 3. The Best Size of Irrigation Area for a Reservoir." *Water Resources Research* 8:7-17.

Duloy, J., and R. Norton [1971]. "A Programming Model of Mexican Agriculture." Paper presented at an ADC conference, Agricultural Sector Analysis and Planning, Ames, Iowa.

Dunn, E. S., Jr. [1954]. *The Location of Agricultural Production*. Gainesville: University of Florida Press.

Eckaus, R. S., and K. S. Parikh [1968]. *Planning for Growth: Multisectoral Intertemporal Models Applied to India*. Cambridge: Massachusetts Institute of Technology.

Edwards, C. [1963]. "Using Discrete Programming." *Agr. Econ. Res.* 15:49-60.

——— [1966]. "Budgeting and Programming in Economic Research." *Methods for Land Economics Research*. W. L. Gibson, R. L. Hildreth, and G. Wunderlich, eds. Lincoln: University of Nebraska Press. Pp. 165-189.

Egbert, A. C., and E. O. Heady [1961]. *Regional Adjustments in Grain Production: A Linear Programming Analysis*. USDA Technical Bulletin 1241.

——— [1963]. *Regional Analysis of Production Adjustments in the Major Field Crops: Historical and Prospective*. USDA Technical Bulletin 1294.

Eisel, L. M. [1970]. "Comments on 'The Linear Decision Rule in Reservoir Management and Design' by C. Revelle, E. Joeres, and W. Kirby." *Water Resources Research* 6:1239-1241.

―――― [1972]. "Chance Constrained Reservoir Model." *Water Resources Research* 8: 339-347.

Enke, S. [1951]. "Equilibrium among Spatially Separated Markets: Solution by Electric Analogue." *Econometrica* 19:40-47.

Erlenkotter, D. [1973]. "Sequencing of Interdependent Hydroelectric Projects." *Water Resources Research* 9:21-26.

Eyvindson, R. K., E. O. Heady, and U. K. Srivastava [1975]. "A Model Incorporating Farm Sizes and Land Classes." In *Spatial Sector Programming Models in Agriculture*, E. O. Heady and U. K. Srivastava, eds. Ames: Iowa State University Press.

Faris, J. E. [1960]. "Analytical Techniques Used in Determining the Optimum Replacement Pattern." *J. Farm Econ.* 42:755-766.

Farris, D. E., and R. A. King [1961]. *Interregional Competition in Marketing Green Peppers*. North Carolina Agricultural Experiment Station, A.E. Information Series 87.

Fox, K. A. [1953]. "A Spatial Equilibrium Model of Livestock-Feed Economy in the United States." *Econometrica* 21:547-566.

Fox, K. A., J. K. Sengupta, and E. Thorbecke [1966]. *The Theory of Quantitative Economic Policy with Applications to Economic Growth and Stabilization*. Amsterdam: North-Holland. (See especially ch. 12 "Stabilization Policy, Regional Growth and Planning," pp. 344-389.)

Fox, K. A., and R. C. Taeuber [1955]. "Spatial Equilibrium Models of the Livestock-Feed Economy." *Am. Econ. Rev.* 45:584-608.

Freund, R. J. [1956]. "The Introduction of Risk into a Programming Model." *Econometrica* 24:253-263.

Frick, G. E., and R. A. Andrews [1965]. "Aggregation Bias and Four Methods of Summing Farm Supply Functions." *J. Farm Econ.* 47:696-700.

Geoffrion, A. M., and R. E. Marsten [1972]. "Integer Programming Algorithm: A Framework and State-of-the-Art Survey." *Management Science* 18:465-491.

Giaever, H., and J. Seagraves [1960]. "Linear Programming and Economies of Size." *J. Farm Econ.* 42:103-117.

Gomory, R. E. [1958]. "Outline of an Algorithm for Integer Solutions to Linear Programs." *Bulletin of the American Mathematical Society* 64:275-278.

―――― [1963]. "An Algorithm for Integer Solutions to Linear Programs." In *Recent Advances in Mathematical Programming*, R. L. Graves and P. Wolfe, eds. New York: McGraw-Hill. Pp. 269-302.

Gordon, H. S. [1954]. "The Economic Theory of a Common Property Resource: The Fishery." *J. Pol. Econ.* 62:124-142.

Gordon, R. L. [1967]. "A Reinterpretation of the Pure Theory of Exhaustion." *J. Pol. Econ.* 75:274-286.

Goreux, L., and A. S. Manne, eds. [1973]. *Multi-Level Planning: Case Studies in Mexico*. Amsterdam: North-Holland.

Graves, G. W., G. B. Hatfield, and A. B. Whinston [1969]. "Water Pollution Control Using By-Pass Piping." *Water Resources Research* 5:13-47.

―――― [1972]. "Mathematical Programming for Regional Water Quality Management." *Water Resources Research* 8:273-290.

Guise, J. W. B., and J. B. Flinn [1970]. "The Allocation and Pricing of Water in a River Basin." *Am. J. Agr. Econ.* 52:411-421.

Haffnar, B., and G. L. Johnson [1966]. *Cooperative Agronomic-Economic Experiments at Michigan State University.* Michigan State Experiment Station Research Bulletin 11.

Hall, H. H., E. O. Heady, and Y. Plessner [1968]. "Quadratic Programming Solution of Competitive Equilibrium for U.S. Agriculture." *J. Farm Econ.* 50:536-555.

Hall, W. A., W. S. Butcher, and A. Esogbue [1968]. "Optimization of the Operation of a Multiple Purpose Reservoir by Dynamic Programming." *Water Resources Research* 4:471-477.

Halter, A. N., and G. W. Dean [1971]. *Decisions under Uncertainty with Research Applications.* Cincinnati: South-West Publishing.

Halter, A. N., M. L. Hayenga, and T. J. Manetsch [1970]. "Simulating a Developing Agricultural Economy: Methodology and Planning Capability." *Am. J. Agr. Econ.* 52:272-290.

Halter, A. N., and W. C. White [1962]. *A Replacement Decision Process (an Application to a Caged Layer Enterprise).* Kentucky Agricultural Experiment Station Bulletin 677.

Hammerberg, D. O., L. W. Parker, and R. G. Bressler, Jr. [1942]. *Efficiency of Milk Marketing in Connecticut: 1. Supply and Price Relationships for Fluid Milk Markets.* Connecticut Agricultural Experiment Station Bulletin 237.

Hass, J. E. [1970]. "Optimal Taxing for the Abatement of Water Pollution." *Water Resources Research* 6:353-365.

Hazell, P. B. R. [1970]. "Game Theory — An Extension of Its Application to Farm Planning under Uncertainty." *J. Agr. Econ.* 21:239-252.

――― [1971a]. "A Linear Alternative to Quadratic and Semivariance Programming for Farm Planning under Uncertainty." *Am. J. Agr. Econ.* 53:53-62.

――― [1971b]. "A Linear Alternative to Quadratic and Semivariance Programming for Farm Planning under Uncertainty: Reply." *Am. J. Agr. Econ.* 54:644-655.

Heady, E. O. [1946]. "Production Functions from a Random Sample of Farms." *J. Farm Econ.* 28:989-1004.

――― [1951]. "A Production Function and Marginal Rates of Substitution in the Utilization of Feed Resources by Dairy Cows." *J. Farm Econ.* 33:485-498.

――― [1952]. *Economics of Agricultural Production and Resource Use.* Englewood Cliffs, N.J.: Prentice-Hall.

――― [1954]. "Simplified Presentation and Logical Aspects of Linear Programming Techniques." *J. Farm Econ.* 36:1035-1048.

――― , ed. [1971]. *Economic Models and Quantitative Methods for Decisions and Planning in Agriculture.* Ames: Iowa State University Press.

Heady, E. O., and W. Candler [1958]. *Linear Programming Methods.* Ames: Iowa State University Press.

Heady, E. O., and A. C. Egbert [1959]. "Programming Regional Adjustments in Grain Production to Eliminate Surpluses." *J. Farm Econ.* 41:718-733.

――― [1964]. "Regional Programming of Efficient Agricultural Production Patterns." *Econometrica* 32:374-386.

Heady, E. O., R. McAlexander, and W. D. Schrader [1956]. *Combinations of Rotations and Fertilization to Maximize Crop Profit on Farms in North-Central Iowa.* Iowa State College Agricultural Experiment Station Bulletin 439.

Heady, E. O., H. C. Madsen, K. J. Nicol, and S. H. Hargrove [1973]. "National and Interregional Models of Water Demand, Land Use, and Agricultural Policies." *Water Resources Research* 9:777-791.

Heady, E. O., and J. T. Pesek [1954]. "A Fertilizer Production Surface with Specification of Economic Optima for Corn Growth on Calcareous Ida Silt Loam." *J. Farm Econ.* 36:466-482.

Heady, E. O., J. T. Pesek, and W. G. Brown [1955]. *Crop Response Surfaces and Economic Optima in Fertilizer Use.* Iowa State College Agricultural Experiment Station Bulletin 424.

Heady, E. O., and M. Skold [1965]. *Projections of U.S. Agricultural Capacity and Interregional Adjustments in Production and Land Use with Spatial Programming Models.* Iowa Agricultural and Home Economics Experiment Station Research Bulletin 539.

Heady, E. O., and N. K. Whittlesey [1965]. *A Programming Analysis of Interregional Competition and Surplus Capacity of American Agriculture.* Iowa Agricultural and Home Economics Experiment Station Research Bulletin 538.

Heady, E. O., R. C. Woodworth, D. Catron, and G. C. Ashton [1953]. "An Experiment to Derive Productivity and Substitution Coefficients in Pork Output." *J. Farm Econ.* 35:341-354.

Heidhues, T. [1966]. "A Recursive Programming Model of Farm Growth in Northern Germany." *J. Farm Econ.* 48:668-684.

Henderson, J. M. [1959]. "The Utilization of Agricultural Land: A Theoretical and Empirical Inquiry." *Rev. Econ. and Stat.* 41:242-259.

Henrichsmeyer, W., and H. de Haen [1972]. "Zur Konzeption des Schwerpunktprogrammes der deutschen Forschungsgemeinschaft 'Konkurrenzverleich landwirtschaftlicher Standorte.'" *Agrarwirtschaft* 21:141-151.

Henry, W. R., and C. E. Bishop [1957]. *North Carolina Broilers in Interregional Competition.* North Carolina Agricultural Experiment Station, A.E. Information Series 56.

Heyer, J. [1971]. "A Linear Programming Analysis of Constraints on Peasant Farms in Kenya." *Food Research Institute Studies in Agricultural Economics, Trade, and Development* 10:55-67. Stanford: Stanford University Food Research Institute.

——— [1972]. "An Analysis of Peasant Farm Production under Conditions of Uncertainty." *J. Agr. Econ.* 23:135-146.

Hildreth, C. [1957a]. "Problems of Uncertainty in Farm Planning." *J. Farm Econ.* 39: 1430-1441.

——— [1957b]. "Some Problems and Possibilities of Farm Programming." *Fertilizer Innovations and Resource Use,* E. L. Baum, E. O. Heady, J. T. Pesek, and C. G. Hildreth, eds. Ames: Iowa State College Press. Pp. 243-260.

Hildreth, C., and S. Reiter [1951]. "On the Choice of a Crop Rotation Plan." In *Activity Analysis of Production and Allocation,* T. C. Koopmans, ed. Cowles Commission Monograph 13, New York: Wiley. Pp. 177-188.

Hinrichs, P. [1972]. "Sequentielle Entscheidungsmodelle für die Lösung landwirtschaftlicher Planungsprobleme mit Hilfe der dynamischen Programmierung." Ph.D. dissertatin, University of Göttingen.

Hitchcock, F. L. [1941]. "Distribution of a Product from Several Sources to Numerous Localities." *J. Math. Physics* 20:224-230.

Hotelling, H. [1931]. "The Economics of Exhaustible Resources." *J. Pol. Econ.* 39:137-175.

Hutton, R. F. [1963]. *An Introduction to Quadratic Programming.* Pennsylvania State University, Department of Agricultural Economics.

*——— [1965]. "Operations Research Techniques in Farm Management: Survey and Appraisal." *J. Farm Econ.* 46:1400-1414.

Imamura, Y. [1966]. "Farm Planning by Means of the Game Theoretic Programming." (Text in Japanese.) *National Research Institute of Agricultural Sciences*, Bulletin Series H, No. 36.

*Irwin, G. D. [1968]. "A Comparative Review of Some Firm Growth Models." *Agr. Econ. Res.* 20:82-100.

Irwin, G. D., and C. B. Baker [1962]. *Effects of Lender Decisions on Farm Financial Planning*. Illinois Agricultural Experiment Station Bulletin 688.

Jacoby, H. D., and D. P. Loucks [1972]. "Combined Use of Optimization and Simulation Models in River Basin Planning." *Water Resources Research* 8:1401-1414.

Joeres, E. F., J. C. Leibman, and C. S. Revelle [1971]. "Operating Rules for Joint Operation of Raw Water Sources." *Water Resources Research* 7:225-235.

Johl, S. S., and A. S. Kahlon [1967]. *Application of Programming Techniques to Indian Farming Conditions*. Punjab Agricultural University.

Johnson, G. L. [1952a]. *Sources of Income on Upland McCracken County Farms, 1951*. Kentucky Agricultural Experiment Station (Lexington), Progress Report 2.

—— [1952b]. *The Earning Power of Inputs and Investments on Upland Calloway County Farms, 1951*. Kentucky Agricultural Experiment Station (Lexington), Progress Report 2.

—— [1955]. "Results from Production Economic Analysis." *J. Farm Econ.* 37:206-222.

—— [1958]. "Supply Function—Some Facts and Notions." *Agricultural Adjustment Problems in a Growing Economy*, E. O. Heady, H. G. Diesslin, H. R. Jensen, and G. L. Johnson, eds. Ames: Iowa State University Press.

Johnson, G. L., and C. B. Haver [1953]. *Decision-Making Principles in Farm Management*. Kentucky Agricultural Experiment Station Bulletin 593.

Johnson, G. L., and C. L. Quance [1972]. *The Overproduction Trap in U.S. Agriculture*. Baltimore: Johns Hopkins Press.

Johnson, S. R., K. R. Tefertiller, and D. S. Moore [1967]. "Stochastic Linear Programming and Feasibility Problems in Farm Growth Analysis." *J. Farm Econ.* 49:908-919.

Judge, G. G. [1956]. *Competitive Position of the Connecticut Poultry Industry: 7. A Spatial Equilibrium Model for Eggs*. Connecticut Agricultural Experiment Station Bulletin 318.

Judge, G. G., J. Havlicek, and R. L. Rizek [1965]. "An Interregional Model: Its Formulation and Application to the Livestock Industry." *Agr. Econ. Res.* 17:1-9.

Judge, G. G., and T. Takayama [1973]. *Studies in Economic Planning over Space and Time*. Amsterdam: North-Holland.

Judge, G. G., and T. D. Wallace [1958]. "Estimation of Spatial Price Equilibrium Models." *J. Farm Econ.* 40:801-820.

—— [1959]. *Spatial Price Equilibrium Analyses of the Livestock Economy: 1. Methodological Development and Annual Spatial Analyses of the Beef Marketing Sector*. Oklahoma Agricultural Experimental Station Technical Bulletin TB-78.

—— [1960]. *Spatial Price Equilibrium Analyses of the Livestock Economy: 3. Spatial Price Equilibrium Models of the Pork Marketing System*. Oklahoma Agricultural Experimental Station Technical Bulletin T-81.

Kawaguchi, T., and Y. Maruyama [1972]. "Generalized Constrained Games in Farm Planning." *Am. J. Agr. Econ.* 54:591-602.

Keckler, W. G., and R. E. Larson [1968]. "Dynamic Programming Applications to Water Resource System Operation and Planning." *J. Math. Analysis and Applications* 24:80-109.

King, G. A., and S. H. Logan [1964]. "Optimal Location, Number and Size of Processing Plants with Raw Product and Final Product Shipments." *J. Farm Econ.* 46: 94-108.

King, R. A. [1953]. "Some Applications of Activity Analysis in Agricultural Economics." *J. Farm Econ.* 35:823-834.

King, R. A., and R. J. Freund [1953]. "A Procedure for Solving a Linear Programming Problem." North Carolina Agricultural Experiment Station, Journal Paper 563.

Koopmans, T. C. [1949]. "Optimum Utilization of the Transportation System." *Econometrica* (Supplement) 17:136-146.

Koopmans, T. C., and S. Reiter [1951]. "A Model of Transportation." In *Activity Analysis of Production and Allocation*, T. C. Koopmans, ed. New York: Wiley. Pp. 222-259.

Kottke, M. W. [1961]. "Budgeting and Linear Programming Can Give Identical Solutions." *J. Farm Econ.* 43:307-314.

—— [1967]. "The Anatomy of a Step Supply Function." *J. Farm Econ.* 49:107-118.

—— [1970]. "Spatial, Temporal, and Product-Use Allocation of Milk in an Imperfectly Competitive Dairy Industry." *Am. J. Agr. Econ.* 52:33-40.

Krenz, R. D., R. V. Baumann, and E. O. Heady [1962]. "Normative Supply Functions by Linear Programming Procedures." *Agr. Econ. Res.* 14:13-18.

Kuhn, H. W., and A. W. Tucker [1951]. "Nonlinear Programming." In *Proceedings of the Second Berkeley Symposium on Mathematical Statistics and Probability*, Jerzy Neyman, ed. Berkeley: University of California Press. Pp. 481-492.

Langham, M. R. [1963]. "Game Theory Applied to a Policy Problem of Rice Farmers." *J. Farm Econ.* 45:151-162.

Lee, J. E., Jr. [1966]. "Exact Aggregation—A Discussion of Miller's Theorem." *Agr. Econ. Res.* 18:58-61.

Lefeber, L. [1958]. *Allocation in Space: Production, Transport and Industrial Location*. Amsterdam: North-Holland.

*Leuthold, R. M., and D. L. Bawden [1966]. *An Annotated Bibliography of Spatial Studies*. University of Wisconsin Agricultural Experiment Station Research Report 25.

Loftsgard, L. D., and E. O. Heady [1959]. "Application of Dynamic Programming Models for Optimum Farm and Home Plans." *J. Farm Econ.* 41:51-67.

Loucks, D. P. [1970]. "Some Comments on Linear Decision Rules and Chance Constraints." *Water Resources Research* 6:668-671.

Louwes, S. L., J. C. G. Boot, and S. Wage [1963]. "A Quadratic-Programming Approach to the Problem of the Optimal Use of Milk in the Netherlands." *J. Farm Econ.* 45:309-317.

MacEwan, A. [1971]. *Development Alternatives in Pakistan: A Multisectoral and Regional Analysis of Planning Problems*. Harvard Economic Studies 134. Cambridge: Harvard University Press.

McFarquhar, A. M. M. [1961]. "Rational Decision Making and Risk in Farm Planning—An Application of Quadratic Programming in British Arable Farming." *J. Agr. Econ.* 14:552-563.

McFarquhar, A. M. M., and A. Evans [1957]. "Linear Programming and the Combination of Enterprises in Tropical Agriculture." *J. Agr. Econ.* 12:474-497.

McInerney, J. P. [1967]. "Maximin Programming—An Approach to Farm Planning under Uncertainty." *J. Agr. Econ.* 18:279-289.

McInerney, J. P. [1969]. "Linear Programming and Game Theory Models—Some Extensions." *J. Agr. Econ.* 20:269-278.

McPherson, W. W., and J. E. Faris [1958]. " 'Price Mapping' of Optimum Changes in Enterprises." *J. Farm Econ.* 40:821-834.

Manne, A. S. [1962]. "Product-Mix Alternatives: Flood Control, Electric Power, and Irrigation." *Int. Econ. Rev.* 3:30-59.

———— [1966]. "Key Sectors of the Mexican Economy, 1962-1972." *The Theory and Design of Economic Development*, I. Adelman and E. Thorbecke, eds. Baltimore: Johns Hopkins Press. Pp. 263-289.

———— [1973]. *Multi-Sector Models for Development Planning: A Survey*. Stanford Institute for Mathematical Studies in the Social Sciences Technical Report 91.

————, ed. [1967]. *Investments for Capacity Expansion: Size, Location, and Time Phasing*. Cambridge: M.I.T. Press.

Manne, A. S., and T. E. Weiskopf [1969]. "A Dynamic Multisectoral Model for India, 1967-75." *Applications of Input-Output Analysis*, vol. 2, A. P. Carter and A. Brody, eds. Amsterdam: North-Holland. Pp. 70-102.

Markowitz, H. [1952]. "Portfolio Selection." *J. Finance* 7:77-91.

———— [1959]. *Portfolio Selection: Efficient Diversification of Investments*. New York: Wiley.

Marshall, A. [1890]. *Principles of Economics*. London: Macmillan. Eighth edition, 1920.

Martin, J. R., and J. S. Plaxico [1967]. *Polyperiod Analysis of Growth and Capital Accumulation of Farms in the Rolling Plains of Oklahoma and Texas*. USDA Technical Bulletin 1381.

Maruyama, Y. [1967]. "Prediction, Uncertainty and Production Planning—A Combined Use of Statistical Techniques and Nonlinear Programming." *J. Rural Econ.* 39:1-12.

———— [1972]. "A Truncated Maximin Approach to Farm Planning under Uncertainty with Discrete Probability Distributions." *Am. J. Agr. Econ.* 54:192-200.

Maruyama, Y., and E. I. Fuller [1964]. "Alternative Solution Procedures for Mixed Integer Programming Problems." *J. Farm Econ.* 46:1213-1218.

———— [1965]. *An Interregional Quadratic Programming Model for Varying Degrees of Competition*. Massachusetts Agricultural Experimental Station Bulletin 555.

Maruyama, Y., and S. Yoshida [1960]. "Interregional Competition in Fresh Potatoes and Their Optimal Shipment Programs." *Studies in the Structure of Farm Product Markets*, T. Yajuma, ed. Sapporo, Japan: Hokkaido University.

Meier, W. L., and C. S. Beightler [1967]. "An Optimization Method for Branching Multi-Stage Water Resource Systems." *Water Resources Research* 3:645-652.

Merrill, W. C. [1965]. "Alternative Programming Models Involving Uncertainty." *J. Farm Econ.* 47:595-610.

Mighell, R. L. [1955]. "Alternative Methods of Programming." *Agr. Econ. Res.* 7:63-69.

Mighell, R. L., and J. D. Black [1951]. *Interregional Competition in Agriculture*. Cambridge: Harvard University Press.

Miller, T. A. [1966]. "Sufficient Conditions for Exact Aggregation in Linear Programming Models." *Agr. Econ. Res.* 18:52-57.

———— [1972]. "Evaluation of Alternative Flexibility Restraint Procedures for Recursive Programming Models Used for Prediction." *Am. J. Agr. Econ.* 54:68-76.

Minden, A. J. [1968]. "Dynamic Programming: A Tool for Farm Firm Growth Research." *Canadian J. Agr. Econ.* 16:38-45.

Moore, C. V. [1961]. "A General Analytical Framework for Estimating the Production Function for Crops Using Irrigation Water." *J. Farm Econ.* 43:876-888.

Morin, T. L., and A. M. Esogbue [1971]. "Some Efficient Dynamic Programming Algorithms for the Optimal Sequencing and Scheduling of Water Supply Projects." *Water Resources Research* 7:479-484.

Mudahar, M. [1972]. "Recursive Programming Models of the Farm Sector with an Emphasis on Linkages with Nonfarm Sectors: The Punjab, India." Ph.D. dissertation, University of Wisconsin.

Musgrave, W. F. [1962]. "A Note on Integer Programming and the Problem of Increasing Returns." *J. Farm Econ.* 44:1068-1076.

Muto, K. [1965]. *Predicting the Acreage of Major Crops in New York State Using Recursive Programming.* National Research Institute of Agricultural Sciences Bulletin 33.

Narayanan, A. V. S., and E. R. Swanson [1972]. "Estimating Trade-Offs between Sedimentation and Farm Income." *J. Soil and Water Conservation* 27:262-264.

Nayak, S. C., and S. R. Arora [1971]. "Optimal Capacities for a Multireservoir System Using a Linear Decision Rule." *Water Resources Research* 7:485-498.

Northeast Dairy Adjustments Study Committee [1963]. *Dairy Adjustments in the Northeast.* University of New Hampshire Experiment Station Technical Bulletin 498.

Officer, R. R., and A. N. Halter [1968]. "Utility Analysis in a Practical Setting." *Am. J. Agr. Econ.* 50:257-277.

Orden, A. [1956]. "The Trans-shipment Problem." *Management Science* 2:277-285.

Peterson, G. A. [1955]. "Selection of Maximum Profit Combinations of Livestock Enterprises and Crop Rotations." *J. Farm Econ.* 37:546-554.

Plessner, Y. [1967]. "Activity Analysis, Quadratic Programming and General Equilibrium." *Int. Econ. Rev.* 8:168-179.

———— [1971]. "Computing Equilibrium Solutions for Imperfectly Competitive Markets." *J. Farm Econ.* 53:191-196.

Plessner, Y., and E. O. Heady [1965]. "Competitive Equilibrium Solutions with Quadratic Programming." *Metroeconomica* 17:117-130.

Puterbaugh, H. L., E. W. Kehrberg, and J. O. Dunbar [1957]. "Analyzing the Solution Tableau of a Simplex Linear Programming Problem in Farm Organization." *J. Farm Econ.* 39:478-489.

Quirk, T., and V. L. Smith [1969]. "Dynamic Economic Models of Fishing." In *Proceedings of the H. R. McMillan Fisheries Economics Symposium*, A. Scott, ed. Vancouver: University of British Columbia.

Rae, A. N. [1971a]. "Stochastic Programming, Utility, and Sequential Decision Problems in Farm Management." *Am. J. Agr. Econ.* 53:448-460.

———— [1971b]. "An Empirical Application and Evaluation of Discrete Stochastic Programming in Farm Management." *Am. J. Agr. Econ.* 53:625-638.

Regev, U., and A. Schwartz [1973]. "Optimal Path of Interregional Investment and Allocation of Water." *Water Resources Research* 9:251-262.

*Renborg, U. [1970]. "Growth of the Agricultural Firm: Problems and Theories." *Rev. Marketing Agr. Econ.* 38:51-101.

Revelle, C. S., D. P. Loucks, and W. R. Lyn [1968]. "Linear Programming Applied to Water Quality Management." *Water Resources Research* 4:1-9.

Riordan, C. [1971]. "General Multistage Marginal Cost Dynamic Programming Model for the Optimization of a Class of Investment-Pricing Decisions." *Water Resources Research* 7:245-253.

Roy, A. D. [1952]. "Safety First and the Holding of Assets." *Econometrica* 20:431-449.

Samuelson, P. A. [1952]. "Spatial Price Equilibrium and Linear Programming." *Am. Econ. Rev.* 42:283-303.

Sandee, J. [1960]. *A Demonstration Planning Model for India.* Bombay: Asia Publishing House.

Schaller, W. N. [1968]. "A National Model of Agricultural Production Response." *Agr. Econ. Res.* 20:33-46.

Schaller, W. N., and G. W. Dean [1965]. *Predicting Regional Crop Production.* USDA Technical Bulletin 1329.

Schickele, R. [1950]. "Farmers' Adaptations to Income Uncertainty." *J. Farm Econ.* 32:356-374.

Schmitz, A., and D. L. Bawden [1973]. *The World Wheat Economy: An Empirical Analysis.* University of California, Giannini Foundation Monograph 32.

Scott, A. [1955]. "The Fishery: The Objectives of Sole Ownership." *J. Pol. Econ.* 63: 116-124.

Seay, E. E., Jr. [1970]. "Minimizing Abatement Costs of Water Pollutants from Agriculture: A Parametric Linear Programming Approach." Ph.D. dissertation, Iowa State University.

Sharples, J. A., and W. N. Schaller [1968]. "Predicting Short-Run Aggregate Adjustment to Policy Alternatives." *Am. J. Agr. Econ.* 50:1523-1536.

Sheehy, S. J., and R. H. McAlexander [1965]. "Selection of Representative Benchmark Farms for Supply Estimation." *J. Farm Econ.* 47:681-695.

Singh, I. J. [1969]. "The Consumption Behavior of Peasant Households: A Case Study of Punjab, India." (Mimeo.) Ohio State University Department of Economics.

―――― [1971]. "The Transformation of Traditional Agriculture: A Case Study of Punjab, India." *J. Farm Econ.* 53:275-284.

Smith, B. J. [1973]. "Dynamic Programming of the Dairy Cow Replacement Problem." *Am. J. Agr. Econ.* 55:100-104.

Smith, V. E. [1974]. "A Diet Model with Protein Quality Variable." *Management Science* 20:971-980.

Smith, V. L. [1968]. "Economics of Production from Natural Resources." *Am. Econ. Rev.* 59:409-431.

Snodgrass, M. M., and C. E. French [1958]. *Linear Programming Approach in the Study of Interregional Competition in Dairying.* Purdue Agricultural Experiment Station Bulletin 637.

Spencer, D. C. S. [1973]. *The Efficient Use of Resources in the Production of Rice in Sierra Leone: A Linear Programming Study.* Unpublished Ph.D. dissertation, University of Illinois.

Steiger, H. U. [1968]. "Analyse des Strukterwandels in der Landwirtschaft mit einem dynamischen mikrooekonomischen Produktionsmodell." *Agrarwirtschaft,* Special Issue No. 30, Hannover.

Stemberger, A. P. [1959]. "Evaluating the Competitive Position of North Carolina Eggs by Use of the Transportation Model." *J. Farm Econ.* 41:790-798.

Stigler, G. J. [1945]. "The Cost of Subsistence." *J. Farm Econ.* 27:303-314.

Stollsteimer, J. F. [1963]. "A Working Model for Plant Numbers and Locations." *J. Farm Econ.* 45:631-645.

Sundquist, W. B., J. T. Bonnen, D. E. McKee, C. B. Baker, and L. M. Day [1963]. *Equilibrium Analysis of Income-Improving Adjustments on Farms in the Lake States*

Dairy Region. University of Minnesota Agricultural Experiment Station Technical Bulletin 246.

Swanson, E. R. [1955]. "Integrating Crop and Livestock Activities in Farm Management Activity Analysis." *J. Farm Econ.* 37:1249-1258.

—— [1956]. "Application of Programming Analysis to Corn Belt Farms." *J. Farm Econ.* 38:408-419.

—— [1957]. "Problems of Applying Experimental Results to Commercial Practice." *J. Farm Econ.* 39:382-389.

—— [1961]. "Programmed Solutions to Practical Farm Problems." *J. Farm Econ.* 43: 386-392.

*—— [1966]. "Operations Research Techniques." In *Methods for Land Economic Research*, W. L. Gibson, Jr., R. J. Hildreth, and G. Wunderlich, eds. Lincoln: University of Nebraska Press. Pp. 191-222.

Swanson, E. R., and K. Fox [1954]. "The Selection of Livestock Enterprises by Activity Analysis." *J. Farm Econ.* 36:78-86.

Takayama, T., and G. G. Judge [1964a]. "Spatial Equilibrium and Quadratic Programming." *J. Farm Econ.* 46:67-93.

—— [1964b]. "An Interregional Activity Analysis Model for the Agricultural Sector." *J. Farm Econ.* 46:349-365.

—— [1964c]. "An Intertemporal Price Equilibrium Model." *J. Farm Econ.* 46:477-484.

—— [1971]. *Spatial and Temporal Price and Allocation Models*. Amsterdam: North-Holland.

Thomas, W., L. Blakeslee, L. Rogers, and N. Whittlesey [1972]. "Separable Programming for Considering Risk in Farm Planning." *Am. J. Agr. Econ.* 54:260-266.

Thomson, K. J., and P. B. R. Hazell [1972]. "Reliability of Using the Mean Absolute Deviation to Derive Efficient, E,V Farm Plans." *Am. J. Agr. Econ.* 54:503-506.

Thoss, R. [1970]. "A Dynamic Model for Regional and Sectoral Planning in the Federal Republic of Germany." *Economics of Planning* 10:89-132.

*Throsby, C. D. [1964]. "Some Dynamic Programming Models for Farm Management Research." *J. Agr. Econ.* 16:98-110.

—— [1968]. "Dynamic Programming Activity Analysis and the Theory of the Firm." *Rev. Marketing Agr. Econ.* 36:20-27.

Tintner, G. [1944]. "A Note on the Derivation of Production Functions from Farm Records." *Econometrica* 12:26-34.

—— [1955]. "Stochastic Linear Programming with Applications to Agricultural Economics." In *Proceedings of Second Symposium on Linear Programming*, vol. 1, pp. 197-228, United States Air Force and National Bureau of Standards.

Tolley, G. S., and V. S. Hastings [1960]. "Optimal Water Allocation: The North Platte River." *Quart. J. Econ.* 74:279-295.

Tramel, T. E., and A. D. Seale, Jr. [1959]. "Reactive Programming of Supply and Demand Relations—Applications to Fresh Vegetables." *J. Farm Econ.* 41:1012-1022.

Von Thünen, J. H. [1966]. *Von Thünen's Isolated State*. Translated by C. M. Wartenberg. Oxford, Pergamon Press.

Walker, O. L., E. O. Heady, L. G. Tweeten, and J. T. Pesek [1960]. *Applications of Game Theory Models to Decisions on Farm Practices and Resource Use*. Iowa State University Agricultural Experiment Station Bulletin 488.

Waugh, F. V. [1951]. "The Minimum-Cost Dairy Feed." *J. Farm Econ.* 33:299-305.

*Weinschenck, G., W. Henrichsmeyer, and F. Aldinger [1969]. "The Theory of Spatial Equilibrium and Optimal Location in Agriculture: A Survey." *Rev. Marketing Agr. Econ.* 37:3-70.

Westphal, L. E. [1971a]. *Planning Investments with Economies of Scale.* Amsterdam: North-Holland.

—— [1971b]. "An Intertemporal Planning Model Featuring Economies of Scale." In *Studies in Development Planning,* H. B. Chenery, ed. Cambridge: Harvard University Press.

White, W. C. [1959]. "The Determination of an Optimal Replacement Policy for a Continually Operating Egg Production Enterprise." *J. Farm Econ.* 41:1535-1542.

Wood, M. K. [1951]. "Representation in a Linear Model of Nonlinear Growth Curves in the Aircraft Industry." In *Activity Analysis of Production and Allocation,* T. C. Koopmans, eds. New York: Wiley. Pp. 216-221.

Yaron, D., and E. O. Heady [1961]. "Approximate and Exact Solution to Nonlinear Programming Problems with Separable Objective Function." *J. Farm Econ.* 43: 57-70.

Yaron, D., and U. Horowitz [1972]. "A Sequential Programming Model of Growth and Capital Accumulation of a Farm under Uncertainty." *Am. J. Agr. Econ.* 54:441-451.

Yaron, D., Y. Plessner, and E. O. Heady [1965]. "Competitive Equilibrium — Application of Mathematical Programming." *Canadian J. Agr. Econ.* 13:65-79.

Young, G. K., Jr. [1967]. "Finding Reservoir Operating Rules." *Journal of the Hydraulics Division,* ASCE, vol. 93, no. HY6, Proceedings Paper 5600, pp. 297-321.

Young, G. K., Jr., and M. A. Pisano [1970]. "Nonlinear Programming Applied to Regional Water Resource Planning." *Water Resources Research* 6:32-42.

Young, R. A., and J. D. Bredehoft [1972]. "Digital Computer Simulation for Solving Management Problems of Conjunctive Groundwater and Surface Water Systems." *Water Resources Research* 8:533-556.

Agricultural Production
Function Studies

Roger C. Woodworth
Agricultural Economist
Agricultural Resource Branch
Tennessee Valley Authority

Following World War II, agricultural economists made a sustained effort to improve methodology and develop applications in quantifying agricultural production relationships mathematically and in using this knowledge to determine economic attributes of the production process. These studies involved calculus and incorporated such recent developments in statistics as more efficient design of experiments, multiple regression, and tests of significance. Perhaps more important from the standpoint of applied economics, the work used production principles based on marginal analysis and equilibrium conditions.

In 1939 Sune Carlson in his classic book, *A Study on the Pure Theory of Production*, defined the production function as the relationship between the variable productive services and the output under the assumption that the plant or fixed services remained constant. He said that this relationship could be most conveniently expressed in mathematical form, writing the amount of output as a function of the different variable services. He also defined marginal productivity, the production surface, isoquants, isoclines, ridge lines, the expansion path, isocosts, and other properties with economic implications derived from the production function.

Several contributions to agricultural economics literature synthesized the advances of Carlson [1939], Hicks [1946], and others, relating the theory of the firm to the applied field of agricultural production economics. The well-known text by Black and his associates [1947], *Farm Management*, and

Heady's "Elementary Models in Farm Production Economics Research" [1948] were important contributions in the immediate postwar period. Later, Heady's *Economics of Agricultural Production and Resource Use* [1952a] and Bradford and Johnson's *Farm Management Analysis* [1953] became the basic references for the new orientation in agricultural production economics. During this same period Allen's *Mathematical Analysis for Economists* [1953] and Tintner's *Econometrics* [1952] were widely used texts for mathematical and econometric models and methods.

Earlier work in quantifying production relationships sometimes involved a continuous relationship with or without a mathematical expression of the relationship between input and output. Mitscherlich was perhaps the first to suggest a nonlinear production function relating fertilizer use to crop output [1928]. Spillman [1933] also utilized an exponential yield curve with similar characteristics.

The USDA Technical Bulletin 1277, *Input as Related to Output in Farm Organization and Cost of Production Studies*, by Tolley, Black, and Ezekiel [1924] stimulated much interest in production function analyses of farm enterprises from farm data. Examples of production relationships include a tabular production surface of daily gain for steers as related to daily corn and hay consumption and output of pork showing diminishing marginal feed productivity.

During the World War II period three USDA studies, stimulated by John D. Black of Harvard, were published. They related output of milk, pork, and beef to total feed consumed (Jensen et al. [1942], Atkinson and Klein [1945], and Nelson [1945]).

A variety of applications has been made involving the production function approach with and without reference to agriculture. Of special interest to agricultural economists are those concerning the farming and agribusiness industries, groups of farms, production of specific crops or livestock, and other rural applications. This review primarily relates to production functions of agricultural crop and livestock enterprises from experimentally derived input-output data. Prior to this main area of concentration, however, a brief discussion of other applications of the production function approach in agriculture is presented.

The pre-World War II industry studies (Douglas [1934], Douglas and Gunn [1942]) using cross-section or time series data, provided some of the methodology for more recent work including use of the exponential function generally known as the Cobb-Douglas. Logarithmic transformations have been widely used because of their convenience in interpreting elasticities of production, minimal requirements for degrees of freedom, and its simplicity of computation.

Aggregate Production Functions

A series of whole-farm production function studies have been conducted in which different farms were used to get different levels and combinations of inputs, and farm income was used as the dependent variable. The best-known early applications in the United States are those presented by Tintner and Brownlee [1944] and Heady [1946].

Bradford and Johnson [1953] analyzed TVA test-demonstration farm records in Marshall County, Kentucky. Marginal value productivities were derived for acres of land, months of labor, investment in forage and livestock, and current expense. They concluded that a larger investment in livestock and forage, a lower machinery investment, and a reduced relative labor input would be needed to equate marginal value productivities with costs. Studies by Heady and Shaw [1954] and Heady and Baker [1954] were concerned with productivity in four farming areas in Montana, Alabama, and northern and southern Iowa. Heady [1955] compared resource productivity and imputed shares between landlord and tenant for a sample of rented farms. Heady and Swanson [1952] compared marginal productivities of farm resources for five areas of Iowa. In 1956 Heady, Johnson, and Hardin edited *Resource Productivity, Returns to Scale, and Farm Size*, a collection of studies concerned with a variety of concepts, procedures, and problems of production function analysis using cross-sectional farm data.

Hildebrand [1960] reported results from Kansas using farm record data for different years and with variations in the model used. An important finding of his research was the wide variability of results from year to year and from model to model in spite of the fact that nearly all of the correlation coefficients were significant at the one-percent probability level.

These and later studies note important implications for the allocation and productivity of resources in agriculture. Their major limitations relate to the great heterogeneity of conditions from farm to farm, the complete or relative absence of control or measurement of variables not included in the function, and the real possibility of multicollinearity among variables. The literature in economics journals contains many articles on the limitations and possible sources of bias in production function research with cross-section or time series data. Plaxico [1955] warned against use of this research for making adjustments on individual farms. Griliches [1957] showed how lack of specification of a management variable could bias the productivity estimates for capital upward and returns to scale downward. Similarly, lack of quantification of the quality of labor could increase the elasticity of capital and decrease the elasticity of labor. (See also Bronfenbrenner [1944], Mundlak [1961], and Reder [1943].)

Other studies have used time series or cross-sectional data in a Cobb-

Douglas analysis of various policy issues for the United States. Two examples are D. G. Johnson's analysis [1960] of output implications of a declining farm labor force and Griliches's study [1957] of the sources of productivity growth using sixty-eight regions as observations and including levels of education as an input.

In the latter part of the 1950s researchers began to utilize linear programming as a way of synthesizing production relationships without having to rely on time series or cross-sectional data from existing farms. Early work includes that of McPherson and Faris [1958] to derive milk output as a function of the price of milk. Martin, Coutu, and Singh [1960] analyzed levels of capital and management on small farms. O'Neal [1959] studied resource productivity in north Georgia using data from linear programming to obtain income estimates for different levels and combinations of resources. Several regional projects, such as the Southern Farm Management Research Committee S-42 work, were conducted to determine the effects of alternative prices and programs on farm adjustments and output.

Applications of functional analysis in the agricultural processing and marketing industries developed in the 1940s were also important forerunners to the crop and livestock production function work which followed. Bressler's approach [1945] in synthesizing cost curves for milk plants using budgeting and industrial engineering techniques resulted in great interest within the profession. Nicholls [1948] used weekly time series data from fourteen departments of a midwestern meat packing firm to predict the number of hogs processed as a function of total man-hours and labor per person per week.

Few production function studies are reported relating to rural development. Undoubtedly the difficulty of specifying outputs has inhibited research in this and related fields. While water supply, sewage treatment, and refuse removal can be quantified relatively easily, many other services have no physical unit of measure. One recent example deals with functions for student achievement in rural high schools by Bieker and Anschel [1974a, 1974b]. For a review of applications in the field of public finance, see Shoup [1969] and Hirsch [1970].

The literature in recent years contains numerous articles on alternative or modifying forms for the Cobb-Douglas production equation to change the assumptions on the elasticity of substitution, marginal products, and returns to scale. Examples include Zellner and Revankar [1969], and Dobell [1968]. Halter, Carter, and Hocking [1957] showed how modifications could allow for all three phases of the production relationship.

Production Functions for Crop Production

In about 1950 production economists, inclined toward the new emphasis on production economics research, started investigations in the economics of fertilizer use. Interest among professional workers developed rapidly, and investigations and assessments were under way at agricultural experiment stations and by the regional farm management research committees, the USDA, the TVA, and private industry.

In assessing the present state of knowledge researchers pointed out that recommendations to farmers traditionally had been the responsibility of physical scientists (Dorner [1954], Hutton [1955]). As a result, criteria of physical response rather than economic response was generally used. Also, experiments were relatively inefficient for quantifying the economic range of the production surface. Examination of agronomic data revealed that rates of application were generally not at high enough levels to permit identification of the economic optimum. The reliance on testing for significant differences in yield for different levels of a fertilizer nutrient typically resulted in research designs where nutrient levels were spaced geometrically, whereas characterization of response as a continuous relationship with treatment levels evenly spaced is more efficient for estimating functional relationships. Reporting only averages of locations and years obscured or concealed economically important variables. Physical and economic interrelationships among nutrients and other important variables were unknown or of uncertain validity. Questions were raised about what effect optimizing N, P, and K simultaneously would have on economic optima compared with determining optimum levels of each nutrient separately with the others at a constant level.

During 1954 formal multidisciplinary studies involving agronomists, economists, and statisticians were under way in several states including Iowa, Kentucky, Michigan, North Carolina, Virginia, Idaho, Indiana, Texas, and Vermont and also at the USDA (National Academy of Sciences [1961]). The fertilizer industry was providing substantial support for projects on the economics of fertilizer use. The TVA was supporting projects and held the first of several annual seminars bringing together production economists, agronomists, and statisticians.

The extent and magnitude of multidisciplinary cooperation which developed was remarkable. Glenn L. Johnson [1957] stated that these "evidences of cooperation on the part of agronomists make it inappropriate to continue the protestations long made by economists, that the design of agronomic experiments does not permit economic interpretation of experimental results."

Ibach and Mendum [1953] wrote a USDA report showing procedures for calculating the most profitable combinations of N, P, and K using the exponential yield curve. At Iowa State Heady and Shrader [1953] delved into the interrelationships of agronomy and economics in research and in making recommendations to farmers. The multifactor experiments at Iowa conducted by Heady and his associates were reported in a series of journal articles and station bulletins. The initial work on corn in 1952 involved a 9 by 9 incomplete N-P factorial replicated twice in a completely randomized design. This type of design was used to include a wide range of nutrient inputs without making the experiment too large. The wide range of nutrient applications was selected to ensure that the most profitable rates derived from marginal analysis would fall within the limits of the experiment and for efficiency in estimating the production surface.

Data presented by Heady, Pesek, and Brown [1955] include several types of regression equations estimated by least squares regression procedures including the Cobb-Douglas, the quadratic cross-product, and the quadratic square root equations. Isoquants were calculated to estimate combinations of nutrients to produce given yields, and the marginal properties were derived to obtain the least cost combinations of nutrients to produce a given yield and the combinations and levels of nutrients to maximize profits per acre for given sets of prices. A series of experiments followed for different crops and sections of the state and involved other variables such as rotations, initial levels of nutrients, and seeding rates. (See Heady, Doll, and Pesek [1958], Heady, Pesek, and McCarthy [1963], and Heady, Pesek and Rao [1966].)

Several important contributions during this period resulted from projects at North Carolina State University. Initially, work involved alternative procedures for analyzing existing data. These included analysis of alternative continuous functions, use of a price map to simplify presentation of optimum rates for alternative prices, and the development of a discrete model less restrictive than the traditional continuous function but still subject to a diminishing returns restriction. The involvement of statisticians Richard L. Anderson and D. D. Mason resulted in methodological developments over the years. (See P. R. Johnson [1953], Stemberger [1957], and C. G. Hildreth [1954].)

Nine years of cooperative agronomic-economic research in Michigan, conducted by Glenn L. Johnson and his associates, were summarized in Hoffman and Johnson [1966]. This report traces the attempts of researchers to characterize the response from fertilizer use under conditions where response is often obscured by other factors. When experiments involving complete rotations and "conventional" small-plot techniques began in 1954, the results generally showed a high unexplained within-treatment variation. Researchers became increasingly concerned about the universe for which the results would apply. These two problems became the central focus of experimentation.

A system was developed for using large plots on randomly selected farm fields that met selective soil and management conditions. These "controlled survey" experiments had a common check plot on each field so that between-farm differences could be accounted for, and the number of plots on any one farm was reduced to four, including the check plot. Comparable data were obtained from a farmer survey and from small-plot experiments. The authors concluded that the "controlled survey" technique was a more reliable way of getting input-output data than past efforts and that future investigators should be encouraged to define explicitly the population about which they hoped to make inferences. The authors indicated a belief that this technique should be considered as an approach in developing countries in attempting to get maximum research and extension information from a given outlay of funds.

The work and cost required for multifactor experiments caused research workers to develop and try new designs. A composite design developed by Box [1954] for industrial research was used at North Carolina (Hurst and Mason [1957], Mason [1956, 1957]). This design required a minimum of 15 treatment combinations per replication compared with 125 for the 5^3 complete factorial. Tramel [1957a] developed a modification called the triple cube design, requiring 31 treatment combinations, and C. G. Hildreth [1957] proposed an interlaced factorial design. The designs were compared by B. P. Havlicek, Smith, and J. Havlicek [1962] in a greenhouse experiment using a 5^3 factorial as a standard of comparison. The authors concluded that the composite designs are useful when successfully centered on the point of maximum yield but that miscentering resulted in biased production functions. In agricultural crop studies the location of the maximum varies with moisture conditions and other factors, often resulting in an observed maximum different from a generalized predicted one.

Interest by statisticians in improving methodology has continued. Recently Anderson and Nelson [1975] explored techniques using intersecting straight lines as an alternative to conventional curvilinear forms of curve fitting. Other important contributions are also being made by statisticians overseas (Gomes [1970], Yates [1967]).

Several studies have incorporated water from irrigation as a variable. Moore [1961] dealt with a general analytical framework. Hexem, Heady, and Caglar [1974] derived production functions relating water and nitrogen to yield for corn, wheat, cotton, and sugar beets from seventy experiments in five western and southwestern states.

A significant number of research reports have dealt with the variations of yield curves over time. Involved are variations in weather, an important factor over which farmers have little or no control, and the accumulation or depletion of nutrients in the soil. Economists have used several approaches to this problem. Brown and Oveson [1958] discussed year-to-year variations in the response of spring wheat to nitrogen applications for ten years. Orazem and Herring [1958] analyzed the effects of soil moisture at seeding time and rainfall during the growing season as related to nitrogen response by grain sorghum in Kansas. Knetsch and Smallshaw [1958] calculated a response relationship to nitrogen and drought on millet for a Tennessee location. Smith and Parks [1967] extended this analysis by simulating results over many years with a computer simulation technique and long-term weather records. They calculated a probability distribution of different outcomes from using alternative levels of nitrogen.

Swanson, Taylor, and Welch [1973] used three decision models for analyzing the year-to-year variation in corn response to nitrogen for eight locations and for five seasons in Illinois: (1) to maximize the average return, (2) to maximize the minimum return, and (3) to minimize the maximum regret or loss from not choosing the correct rate given the season.

Researchers have given attention to the importance of varying fertilizer use with changing crop-fertilizer price ratios. Hutton and Thorne [1955] pointed out that for the 1953 Iowa corn experiment it would take a substantial change in the ratio to make a difference of $4 in per-acre income and that the difference would be less than $1 based on the historical annual price ratios of the 1951-54 period. They also pointed out that using N and P_2O_5 in a one-to-one ratio instead of the optimum ratio would decrease income $0.11 to $0.33 per acre for 1951-54 annual prices.

Using North Carolina data, J. Havlicek and Seagraves [1962] found similar net income consequences for corn. The highest cost of a wrong decision with corn prices varying between $0.75 and $1.75 and nitrogen at $0.11 per pound was $2.90 per acre. Similarly, Knetsch [1961], using Tennessee data for corn, found that nitrogen rates could be varied by fifty or sixty pounds in either direction from the optimum with very small profit losses. Swanson, Taylor, and Welch [1973] came to similar conclusions for corn from nitrogen fertilizer studies at eight locations in Illinois. Taking one location as an example, they concluded that a drop in the corn-nitrogen price ratio from thirty to ten would require less than a twenty-pound decrease per acre in the economically optimum level of nitrogen application.

Other studies have shown a higher economic consequence for use of non-optimum rates. For example, a Georgia study by Woodworth et al. [1957] for Coastal Bermuda hay in an unfavorable season shows a loss of $7 per acre if the hay value is $30 per ton when using an optimum rate for $20 hay. For a favorable season, the loss is $21 per acre. High economic consequences were also found for Bahiagrass hay (Beaty et al. [1961]).

The problems of determining the population to which a given response function would be applicable and relating results from agricultural experiment stations to given populations of farmers have been especially troublesome to economists concerned with crop production. Ibach, of the USDA

Economic Research Service, developed a generalized response concept and used it to make estimates of responses to fertilizer for major crops by states. The specific estimates were made by researchers in the state experiment stations and published as USDA Agricultural Handbook 68 [1954]. These basic data were used by Ibach and others for examining the outcomes of alternative policy proposals. Ibach [1957] developed estimates of land and fertilizer combinations to produce the United States corn crop. The generalized relationships were revised and published by Ibach and Adams [1968] as USDA Statistical Bulletin 431. The revised publication contains estimates for the agricultural subregions of each state. They represent an interpretation of experimental evidence, farmers' experiences, and also the distribution of the crop by soil type, cropping patterns, and levels of management.

Taylor and Swanson [1974], dealing with the economic effects of imposing per-acre restrictions on nitrogen fertilizer in Illinois, compared results from research on experiment stations with the Ibach-Adams [1968] generalized response functions and with farmers' yields for eight subregions of the state. They concluded that while the Ibach-Adams response functions do not agree exactly with actual average yield, they seem much closer than experimental functions.

Some of the more interesting applications of production function research relate to specialty crops. Eidman, Lingle, and Carter [1963], working with cantaloupe production in California, identified the relationship between fertilizer use as a function of time of ripening and total yield. Nitrogen delayed maturity while phosphate tended to hasten maturity. They developed a procedure for handling multiharvest periods. Many publications have combined production function analyses with budgeting or other techniques. A useful example is the Woolf, Sullivan, and Phillips [1967] study of cotton production, which includes production functions relating to irrigation, fertilizer, and plant population per acre. By budgeting costs, they compared irrigated and nonirrigated net returns.

Several publications summarize aspects of production function research in crop production. Heady and Dillon [1961] present the Iowa research and include a chapter from other countries. Dillon [1968] contains chapters on concepts, procedures, and applications from the United States and other countries.

Publication 918 of the National Academy of Sciences [1961] summarizes basic economic, design, and statistical analysis concepts, with sections on historical development, examples of practical application, and an extensive bibliography.

In two books resulting from TVA-sponsored seminars Baum, Heady, and Blackmore [1956] and Baum, Heady, Pesek, and C. G. Hildreth [1957] document the principal developments in methodology and application in articles by authors from economics, agronomy, and statistics. They are useful in describing research needs and problems as seen by the authors at that time. A journal article by Munson and Doll [1959] gives an excellent overview of concepts and research experiences from a number of states. For practical applications of economic principles in fertilizer use based on research analysis, see North Central Regional Publication 54 (North Central Farm Management Research Committee [1954]) and Southern Farm Management Extension Publication Number 10 (North Carolina Agricultural Extension Service [1962]).

Production Functions for Animal and Poultry Production

Production functions for animal and poultry production date back to USDA technical bulletins by Jensen et al. [1942], A. G. Nelson [1945], and Atkinson and Klein [1945]. These studies carried out by the USDA and several agricultural experiment stations in collaboration have been widely quoted and stand as landmarks in the field of production economics and farm management. They were concerned primarily with optimum marketing rates rather than the estimation of marginal rates of substitution between feeds, and succeeded in developing interdisciplinary cooperation and data appropriate for some aspects of marginal analysis.

In the early 1950s Heady and Olson [1951, 1952] and (independently) Redman [1952] at Kentucky published exploratory studies estimating isoproduct and marginal rate of substitution relationships for grain-forage feed for milk production. Heady and Olson used selected treatment from the Jensen study, and Redman also used existing data.

Each set of authors indicated that a basic purpose in conducting the research was to contribute to the national goals of soil conservation and the interests of many in agriculture to conserve grain and use more forage. Each was concerned with developing appropriate methodology for delineating new knowledge and exploring the interrelationships between the physical and economic implications of grain-forage feeding relationships in milk production.

Redman, in relating his research to the field of feeding standards, concluded: "It was undoubtedly necessary in the earlier stage of development to make such simplifying assumptions as perfect substitutability of feeds and constant returns of milk per unit of feed input in order to derive more useful knowledge about feeding for milk production. However, the time has now arrived for relaxing these assumptions of linear relationships and for incorporating the concept of changing marginal rates of substitution implied by the law of diminishing returns."

These studies were exploratory and uncertainties still remained about the true nature of the response surfaces and substitution rates. Opposing views were expressed in the *Journal of Farm Economics* (Mighell [1953a, 1953b], Heady and Olson [1953]). See H. R. Jensen [1977] for further comment.

In May 1957 a symposium on the nutritional and economic aspects of feed utilization was held at Michigan State University. It was sponsored by that university, the North Central Dairy and Farm Management Research Committees, the Farm Foundation, and the USDA. This meeting brought together research and extension workers in dairy nutrition, production economics, animal breeding, statistics, and agronomy to focus attention on interdisciplinary opportunities for improving knowledge concerning feed utilization by dairy cattle. The proceedings were published as a book edited by Hoglund et al. [1958].

Starting in 1956, a series of research reports document interdisciplinary research at Iowa involving experiments specifically designed to estimate the production surface for milk output. These experiments used four levels of hay-to-concentrate ratios and three levels of intensity of feeding. In the analysis of these data logarithmic, quadratic, and square root functions were derived by least squares regression as alternative means of specifying the production function. Heady, Jacobson, et al. [1964] include an analysis incorporating other variables such as different characteristics of cows (maturity, ability, inbreeding, and weight) and environmental conditions so that optimum feeding ratios and level of milk production can be estimated for more specific conditions of production. Also, point estimates are supplemented by confidence regions.

The existence of diminishing marginal rates of substitution in feeding has been confirmed by other researchers. Coffey and Toussaint [1963] pointed out that from analysis of the Iowa experiments the most profitable rations lie near the stomach capacity limit for most historical prices of hay, grain, and milk and that returns do not vary much over a fairly wide range of feeding levels. Dean [1960] reported on a California experiment in which rations for some treatments were changed after each twenty-eight-day period to measure carry-over effects. Hoover et al. [1967] used Kansas experiments carried out from 1956 to 1961 and concluded that the resulting production surfaces were similar to the Iowa study and that the general forms of the equations of best fit were similar. Paris et al. [1970] reported on dairy production functions where yield was alternatively measured as whole milk, fat, 4-percent milk, and skim milk.

Feeding trials to determine concentrate roughage production relationships in beef feeding have been conducted in Oklahoma (Plaxico and Pope [1959]) and in Iowa (Heady, Carter, and Culbertson [1964]). Plaxico and his associates concluded that comparisons of the Oklahoma beef study with the Iowa dairy results imply a greater curvature of the isoproduct contours for feedlot beef animals compared with milk production and that the economic incentive to adjust rations to price ratios may be greater. Also, under certain price relationships substantial savings might be made by feeding steers and heifers different rations.

Studies of corn-soybean meal feed substitution relationships for hogs in drylot feeding were reported from Iowa (Heady, Woodworth, et al. [1953, 1954]). The experimental trials included three experiments with treatments ranging from 10-percent to 20-percent protein. The data derived were used to specify: (1) least cost rations for different price relationships; (2) rations to get hogs to market weight in minimum time; (3) maximum profit rations based on historical prices for two weaning dates; and (4) optimum marketing weights. Methodological aspects included alternative equations and the use of three weight intervals as well as the whole-weight range to allow greater flexibility in substitution rates. Least cost rations resulted in a higher net return per pig compared with least time rations in fifteen years of a sixteen-year period for a November 1 weaning date and when marketed at 225 pounds. The difference was $1.00 or more per pig in five of the years and $5.82 in one year. A second publication in this series (Heady, Catron, et al. [1958]) reported results from feeding hogs corn and soybean meal for hogs produced on pasture instead of drylot.

A number of studies have been concerned with feed-weight of bird relationships in broiler production. Fellows and Judge [1952] were concerned in a Connecticut bulletin with marginal costs and returns from feeding broilers to different weights. Budgeting was used to relate this to total costs, total returns, and net returns. A special "slide rule" device made it possible for the producer to find maximum profit marketing weights for various prices. In a Washington State University study Baum and Walkup [1953] analyzed the feed-weight of bird relationships for high energy feeds compared with other rations. Heady, Balloun, and McAlexander [1956] analyzed the results of an experiment in which chicks were fed protein levels varying from 16 percent to 26 percent. Data are presented to determine least cost and least time rations as well as optimum marketing weights for specified protein levels. Heady, Balloun, and Dean [1956] published similar data for turkeys.

Assessments

Accomplishments. A wide range of experiments to characterize farm production relationships and to derive economic implications has been conducted since 1950. More studies have been concerned with crop than animal production owing in part to higher costs of large-scale animal experiments. These experiments have provided a test of the practical application and importance of principles of production economics and of plant and animal science. The literature contains evidence of a considerable advance in methodology as well as many practical applications. The results serve as a reminder to agricultural workers and farmers that most inputs are not combined in fixed proportions as point recommendations imply, but that combinations and levels can be changed as prices and other conditions warrant. They serve as a conceptual guide for making recommendations to farmers. In one state a single-level recommendation for fertilizer was changed to three levels for alternative management situations based on production function studies. Most states that had agronomic-economic studies in the 1950s and early 1960s changed recommendations as a result of the work. Generally, the change was to increase the level of application.

These studies were a useful source of input-output data for farm adjustment studies, either directly or as a basis for making judgments from all available data, of the most appropriate alternative levels of inputs and associated production. The methodology, or at least the less complex aspects, had a very important application for guiding research and development in increasing food production in developing countries. In this case, the higher costs of inputs such as fertilizer, restrictions in foreign exchange, supply restrictions, and a pressing need for increased food supply multiply the importance of efficient use of scarce resources.

A climate has evolved from this research that demonstrates the potential accomplishments of interdisciplinary approaches to problem solving. Undoubtedly, it has been a crucial factor in developing the awareness on the part of production specialists and administrators that production economists can make important contributions in planning and analysis of production experiments. Physical scientists have become more aware of the need to design experiments using the production function approach, involving design and analysis of experiments for continuous relationships as opposed to discrete responses. In recent years increasing numbers of plant and animal scientists have been conducting their own experiments on this basis—a healthy trend which helps to provide production economists with useful input-output data and at the same time allows more effort in economic analysis compared with time spent in obtaining physical data.

Limitations. Greater difficulties are experienced in quantifying biological response relationships than would be encountered in most industrial processes. Soil variability, weather, insects, diseases, residual fertilizer in the soil, nutrients in the soil, and previous crop history frequently conspire to confound researchers with unpredictable results. Response to applied P and K has been particularly uneven because of the accumulation from previous fertilization. In multivariate crop experiments in several states responses to these nutrients have not been statistically significant, reducing economic analysis to responses to applied N only. Perhaps these results should reinforce the view that precision crop production is a long way in the future. A second view would be that advances in plant science knowledge in terms of response prediction are needed before full utilization can be made of marginal relationships in crop production.

In the past decade many production economists have expressed the opinion that production function research from controlled experiments was of limited consequence, pointing to the very modest differences in net income associated with a fairly wide range of application rates for selected production functions or along certain isoproduct curves. At the same time interest waned because of continuing crop surpluses and relatively low prices for feedgrain, protein, and fertilizer. Researchers went on to new problems and approaches.

There appears to be adequate evidence that for corn and similar crops the profit consequences of not adjusting fertilizer rates optimally for normal year-to-year changes in prices are small or inconsequential. A finding that the nature of some or many response relationships does not make it worthwhile to change the levels or combinations of inputs from year to year for usual variations in price ratios is important knowledge. Finding the conditions and commodities for which it is worthwhile is also important knowledge. Discussions in the literature on this issue are based on only a few experiments, mostly for corn, and for the price variations arising in the 1950s and early 1960s.

In justifying, planning, and conducting projects economists frequently have overemphasized the importance of economic optima. The factor-product equilibrium is an appropriate guide for economic decision making but cannot be applied with the precision implied by the theoretical model. Discovery of a precise optimum may not in itself be valuable knowledge if a wide range of application rates makes little difference in net income. Rauchenstein [1953] observed that choice of forage production systems and how they fit into the whole-farm business were far more important than feed substitution possibilities to the economic health of dairy farms. (See also Coffey and Toussaint [1963].)

Many of the multinutrient fertilizer experiments were designed without sufficient basic knowledge of yield response patterns. For some of these, no meaningful economic analyses were possible because of nonsignificant or erratic responses. Where meaningful responses were obtained, they varied greatly from year to year because of weather differences. Clearly much more needs to be known about factors which affect response to P and K before elaborate

3-factor experiments to obtain economic optima can be routinely justified. The longer range aspects of N and P buildup in the soil have economic implications for farmers and for society, yet these have received scant attention in the literature on production functions and on the economics of fertilization. The general assumption of a variable resource (fertilizer) applied to a fixed resource (land) does not have universal application. Other models should be considered—for example, when land is not fixed for the individual farmer and idle or rented land can be substituted for fertilizer to produce a given level of output, when risk is an important factor, or when it is appropriate to consider an animal as the fixed plant rather than land.

Future Outlook and Research Needs

The desirability of quantifying production relationships in agriculture will continue in the future. While linear programming has become the dominant methodology for obtaining the most profitable farming systems, partial analyses based on production function studies have merit in analyzing numerous policy and farm-level decisions when interrelationships with other aspects of the farm organization are of secondary importance. In addition to that, the results of production function studies are useful in selecting data for linear programming studies.

Recent events should remind us not only that price ratios do not remain indefinitely within prescribed limits but that restrictions in the supply of fertilizer or feed can occur. Farmers and farm magazines have again raised questions about how much fertilizer to use or how to minimize feed costs. Important policy issues have again been raised about how threatened shortages and higher costs of fertilizer and energy could affect total production and how fertilizer and energy could be used more efficiently to minimize increases in the costs of food to consumers. Production function studies provide useful insights into these and such other national goals as reducing energy requirements and minimizing detrimental effects on the environment.

Additional assessment is needed of the conditions under which it could be desirable to change the rates and levels of inputs as price ratios change. This should be done systematically for a variety of crops. Similarly, additional assessments are needed of the production and income implications of restrictions in the use of inputs which may be scarce or subject to environmental controls.

In the future production function research will be needed to update existing information on production relationships as new technology and other conditions change and to provide new information in several priority areas. Much of the production function research now available in the literature was conducted a decade or more ago and is probably out of date. One area of needed research involves alternative processes in beef production utilizing forages. There is a general lack of knowledge concerning production relationships needed in selecting a forage system from the many possible combinations, the selection of fertilizer rates, and the effect of these variables on quality of beef and on net income. The rising relative cost of water along with the fact that water costs are being more closely associated with the level of water use in irrigated farming areas will increase the benefits from pinpointing optimum water application rates.

For farmer decision making improvements are needed in specifying the population for which the relationships apply. In crop production this means more research carried out on farms rather than on experiment stations. Also, a variety of economic models and research techniques should be used to provide more useful information and to duplicate better the decision making models most appropriate for farmers in different circumstances.

The production function approach needs to be an integral part of the training of physical scientists with more of the needed projects designed and carried out by physical scientists themselves. At the present time many experiments are being carried out by physical scientists with objectives that suggest the production function approach as the most efficient but that utilize more traditional, less efficient procedures. If the production function approach were used by these researchers in the future, much more data on production processes would be available for economic analysis.

In many developing countries production function studies have a higher value than in the United States economy. Typically, there is a critical need to increase food production, but foreign exchange may be required for the importation of fertilizer and the cost of the fertilizer to farmers may be high. Policy issues involve the provision of adequate incentives for using fertilizer efficiently. In a controlled economy this may require setting the prices of fertilizer and product so that the desired production can be accomplished with a minimum of foreign exchange. If the use of fertilizer is a relatively new technology in the country, neither farmers nor agricultural workers have the historical experience to determine the best rates of use except by costly trial and error. Economic studies to determine optimum rates of fertilizer use can make a major contribution under these circumstances.

Many advances in methodology will probably be made by physical scientists and statisticians or will involve them in some way. In crop production there is a great need for a greater understanding of response relationships and of nontreatment variation. Advances in this direction could lead to improved criteria for selection of functional relations and to the development of new models with the desired characteristics. Advances in knowledge which result in increased statistical efficiency, lower cost, and greater reliability for decision making could result in much greater utilization in partial or complete farm decision making models and in models for the analysis of related policy issues.

References

Allen, R. G. D. [1953]. *Mathematical Analysis for Economists*. London: Macmillan.

Anderson, R. L., and L. A. Nelson [1975]. "A Family of Models Involving Intersecting Straight Lines and Concomitant Experimental Designs Useful in Evaluating Response to Fertilizer Nutrients." *Biometrics* 31:303-318.

Atkinson, L. J., and J. W. Klein [1945]. *Feed Consumption and Marketing Weight of Hogs*. USDA Technical Bulletin 894.

Baum, E. L., E. O. Heady, and J. Blackmore, eds. [1956]. *Methodological Procedures in the Economic Analysis of Fertilizer Use Data*. Ames: Iowa State University Press.

Baum, E. L., E. O. Heady, J. T. Pesek, and C. G. Hildreth, eds. [1957]. *Economic and Technical Analysis of Fertilizer Innovations and Resource Use*. Ames: Iowa State University Press.

Baum, E. L., and H. G. Walkup [1953]. "Some Economic Implications of Input-Output Relationships in Fryer Production." *J. Farm Econ.* 35:223-235.

Beaty, E. R., R. C. Woodworth, G. A. Slappey, and J. Powell [1961]. *Response of Pensacola Bahiagrass to Nitrogen*. Georgia Agricultural Experiment Station Bulletin NS 85.

Beringer, C. [1956]. "Estimating Enterprise Production Functions from Input-Output Data on Multiple Enterprise Farms." *J. Farm Econ.* 38:923-930.

Berry, R. L. [1956]. *Most Profitable Use of Fertilizer on Corn, Oats, and Wheat in South Dakota*. South Dakota Agricultural Experiment Station, Agricultural Economics Pamphlet 69.

Bieker, R. F., and K. R. Anschel [1974a]. "Estimating Educational Production Functions for Rural High Schools: Some Findings." *Am. J. Agr. Econ.* 56:515-519.

———— [1974b]. "Estimating Educational Production Functions for Rural High Schools: Reply." *Am. J. Agr. Econ.* 56:835-36.

Black, J. D., M. Clawson, C. R. Sayre, and W. W. Wilcox [1947]. *Farm Management*. New York: Macmillan.

Box, G. E. P. [1954]. "The Exploration and Exploitation of Response Surfaces: Some General Considerations and Examples." *Biometrics* 10:16-60.

Bradford, L. A., and G. L. Johnson [1953]. *Farm Management Analysis*. New York: Wiley.

Bradley, M. [1974]. "Estimating Educational Production Functions for Rural High Schools: Comment." *Am. J. Agr. Econ.* 56:833-834.

Bressler, R. G., Jr. [1945]. "Research Determination of Economies of Scale." *J. Farm Econ.* 27:526-539.

Bronfenbrenner, M. [1944]. "Production Functions: Cobb-Douglas, Interfirm, Intrafirm." *Econometrica* 12:35-44.

Brown, W. G. [1956]. "Free Choice versus Least-Cost Mixed Rations for Hogs." *J. Farm Econ.* 38:863-868.

Brown, W. G., and G. H. Arscott [1958]. "A Method for Dealing with Time in Determining Optimum Factor Inputs." *J. Farm Econ.* 40:666-673.

—— [1960]. "Animal Production Functions and Optimum Ration Specifications." *J. Farm Econ.* 42:69-78.

Brown, W. G., T. L. Jackson, and R. G. Petersen [1962]. "A Method for Incorporating Soil Test Measurement into Fertilizer Response Functions." *Agron. J.* 54:152-154.

Brown, W. G., and M. M. Oveson [1958]. "Production Functions from Data over a Series of Years." *J. Farm Econ.* 40:451-457.

Carlson, S. [1939]. *A Study on the Pure Theory of Production.* London: P. S. King and Son.

Carter, H. O., and H. O. Hartley [1958]. "A Variance Formula for Marginal Productivity Estimates Using the Cobb-Douglas Function." *Econometrica* 26:306-313.

Chucka, J. A., A. Hawkins, and B. E. Brown [1943]. *Potato Fertilizer-Rotation Studies on Aroostook Farms—1927-1941.* Maine Agricultural Experiment Station Bulletin 414.

Coffey, J. D., and W. D. Toussaint [1963]. "Some Economic Aspects of Free-Choice Feeding of Dairy Cows." *J. Farm Econ.* 45:1213-1218.

Dean, G. W. [1960]. "Consideration of Time and Carryover Effects in Milk Production Functions." *J. Farm Econ.* 42:1512-1514.

De Janvry, A. [1972]. "Optimal Levels of Fertilization under Risk—the Potential for Corn and Wheat Fertilization under Alternative Price Policies in Argentina." *Am. J. Agr. Econ.* 54:1-10.

Dillon, J. L. [1968]. *The Analysis of Response in Crop and Livestock Production.* New York: Pergamon Press.

Dobell, R. [1968]. "A Symposium on CES Production Functions: Extensions and Comments—Introductory Remarks." *Rev. Econ. and Stat.* 50:443-445.

Doll, J. P. [1958a]. "Evaluation of Alternative Algebraic Forms for Production Functions." Ph.D. dissertation, Iowa State University.

—— [1958b]. "A Method of Deriving Fertilizer Nutrient Combinations for Limited Capital Situations." Unpublished paper, Tennessee Valley Authority.

—— [1972]. "A Comparison of Annual versus Average Optima for Fertilizer Experiments." *Am. J. Agr. Econ.* 54:226-233.

—— [1974]. "On Exact Multicollinearity and the Estimation of the Cobb-Douglas Production Function." *Am. J. Agr. Econ.* 56:556-563.

Doll, J. P., E. H. Jebe, and R. D. Munson [1960]. "Computation of Variance Estimates for Marginal Physical Products and Marginal Rates of Substitution." *J. Farm Econ.* 42:596-607.

Dorner, P. [1954]. "Economic Interpretation of Agronomic Data Relating to Fertilizer Usage." Tennessee Agricultural Experiment Station.

Douglas, P. H. [1934]. *The Theory of Wages.* New York: Macmillan.

Douglas, P. H., and G. T. Gunn [1942]. "The Production Function for American Manufacturing for 1914." *J. Pol. Econ.* 50:595-602.

Eidman, V. R., J. C. Lingle, and H. O. Carter [1963]. "Optimum Fertilization Rates for Crops with Multi-Harvest Periods." *J. Farm Econ.* 45:823-830.

Engelstad, O. P., and W. L. Parks [1971]. "Variability in Optimum N Rates for Corn." *Agron. J.* 63:21-23.

Engelstad, O. P., and G. L. Terman [1966]. "Fertilizer Nitrogen: Its Role in Determining Crop Yield Levels." *Agron. J.* 58:536-539.

Faris, J. E. [1960]. *Economics of Replacing Cling Peach Trees.* California Agricultural Experiment Station, Giannini Foundation Report 232.

Fellows, I. F. [1952]. "The Economics of Grassland Farming in the Northeast." *J. Farm Econ.* 34:759-764.

Fellows, I. F., and G. G. Judge [1952]. *Economic Decision Making for Broilers.* Connecticut Agricultural Experiment Station Bulletin 302.

Foreman, W. J., and O. Steanson [1956]. *A Method of Determining Profitable Rates of Fertilizer Use: Nitrogen on Coastal Bermuda for Hay.* Georgia Agricultural Experiment Station NS 22.

French, B. L. [1956]. "Functional Relationships for Irrigated Corn Response to Nitrogen." *J. Farm Econ.* 38:736-747.

Fuller, W. A. [1965]. "Stochastic Fertilizer Production Functions for Continuous Corn." *J. Farm Econ.* 47:105-119.

Gomes, F. P. [1970]. "Use of Polynomial Response Surfaces in the Study of Experiments with Fertilizers." *Proceedings, International Biometrics Conference.* Hannover, Germany.

Griliches, Z. [1957]. "Specification Bias in Estimating Production Functions." *J. Farm Econ.* 39:8-20.

——— [1963]. "Estimates of the Aggregate Agricultural Production Function from Cross-Sectional Data." *J. Farm Econ.* 45:419-428.

Halter, A., H. O. Carter, and J. Hocking [1957]. "A Note on the Transcendental Production Function." *J. Farm Econ.* 39:966-974.

Hansen, P. L. [1949]. "Input-Output Relationships in Egg Production." *J. Farm Econ.* 31:687-697.

Hansen, P. L., and R. L. Mighell [1956]. *Economic Choices in Broiler Production.* USDA Technical Bulletin 1154.

Havlicek, B. P., W. G. Smith, and J. Havlicek, Jr. [1962]. "On the Choice of Designs for the Estimation of Production Functions." Purdue University Production Economics Paper 6210.

Havlicek, J., Jr., and J. A. Seagraves [1962]. "The Cost of the Wrong Decision as a Guide in Production Research." *J. Farm Econ.* 44:157-167.

Heady, E. O. [1946]. "Production Functions from a Random Sample of Farms." *J. Farm Econ.* 28:989-1004.

——— [1948]. "Elementary Models in Farm Production Economic Research." *J. Farm Econ.* 30:201-225.

——— [1951]. "A Production Function and Marginal Rates of Substitution in the Utilization of Feed Resources by Dairy Cows." *J. Farm Econ.* 33:485-498.

——— [1952a]. *Economics of Agricultural Production and Resource Use.* New York: Prentice-Hall.

——— [1952b]. "Use and Estimation of Input-Output Relationships or Productivity Coefficients." *J. Farm Econ.* 34:775-786.

——— [1954a]. *Resource Productivity and Returns on 160-Acre Farms in North Central Iowa.* Iowa Agricultural Experiment Station Research Bulletin 412.

——— [1954b]. "Choice of Functions in Estimating Input-Output Relationships." *Proceedings of the Southern Agricultural Workers Association, 51st annual meeting, Agricultural Economics and Sociology Section.*

——— [1955]. "Marginal Resource Productivity and Imputation of Shares for a Sample of Rented Farms." *J. Pol. Econ.* 43:500-511.

——— [1957]. "An Econometric Investigation of the Technology of Agricultural Production Functions." *Econometrica* 25:249-268.

—— [1963]. "Marginal Rates of Substitution between Technology, Land and Labor."
  J. Farm Econ. 45:137-145.

Heady, E. O., and C. B. Baker [1954]. "Resource Adjustments to Equate Productivities
  in Agriculture." *Southern Econ. J.* 21:36-52.

Heady, E. O., S. Balloun, and G. W. Dean [1956]. *Least-Cost Rations and Optimum
  Marketing Weights for Turkeys.* Iowa Agricultural Experiment Station Research
  Bulletin 443.

Heady, E. O., S. Balloun and R. McAlexander [1956]. *Least-Cost Rations and Optimum
  Marketing Weights for Broilers.* Iowa Agricultural Experiment Station Research
  Bulletin 442.

Heady, E. O., W. G. Brown, J. T. Pesek, and J. Stritzel [1956]. *Production Functions,
  Isoquants, Isoclines and Economic Optima in Corn Fertilization for Experiments
  with Two and Three Variable Nutrients.* Iowa Agricultural Experiment Station
  Research Bulletin 441.

Heady, E. O., H. O. Carter, and C. C. Culbertson [1964]. "Production Functions and
  Substitution Coefficients for Beef." *Agricultural Production Functions,* E. O.
  Heady and J. L. Dillon, eds. Ames: Iowa State University Press. Pp. 452-474.

Heady, E. O., D. V. Catron, D. E. McKee, G. Ashton, and V. Speer [1958]. *New Procedures in Estimating Feed Substitution Rates and in Determining Economic Efficiency in Pork Production. II, Replacement Rates for Growing-Fattening Swine
  on Pasture.* Iowa Agricultural Experiment Station Research Bulletin 462.

Heady, E. O., and J. L. Dillon [1961]. *Agricultural Production Functions.* Ames: Iowa
  State University Press.

Heady, E. O., J. P. Doll, and J. T. Pesek [1958]. *Fertilizer Production Functions for
  Corn and Oats, Including Analysis of Irrigated and Residual Return.* Iowa Agricultural Experiment Station Research Bulletin 463.

Heady, E. O., N. L. Jacobson, J. P. Madden, and A. E. Freeman [1964]. *Milk Production
  Functions in Relation to Feed Inputs, Cow Characteristics and Environmental
  Conditions.* Iowa Agricultural Experiment Station Research Bulletin 529.

Heady, E. O., G. L. Johnson, and L. S. Hardin, eds. [1956]. *Resource Productivity, Returns to Scale, and Farm Size.* Ames: Iowa State University Press.

Heady, E. O., J. P. Madden, N. L. Jacobson, and A. E. Freeman [1964]. "Milk Production Functions Incorporating Variables for Cow Characteristics and Environment." *J. Farm Econ.* 46:1-19.

Heady, E. O., and R. O. Olson [1951]. "Marginal Rates of Substitution and Uncertainty
  in the Utilization of Feed Resources with Particular Emphasis on Forage Crops."
  Iowa State J. Science 26:49-70.

—— [1952]. *Substitution Relationships, Resource Requirements and Income Variability in the Utilization of Forage Crops.* Iowa Agricultural Experiment Station
  Research Bulletin 390.

—— [1953]. "Mighell on Methodology." *J. Farm Econ.* 35:269-276.

Heady, E. O., and J. T. Pesek [1954]. "A Fertilizer Production Surface with Specification of Economic Optima for Corn Grown on Calcareous Ida Silt Loam." *J. Farm
  Econ.* 36:466-482.

Heady, E. O., J. T. Pesek, and W. G. Brown [1955]. *Crop Response Surfaces and Economic Optima in Fertilizer Use.* Iowa Agricultural Experiment Station Research
  Bulletin 424.

Heady, E. O., J. T. Pesek, and W. O. McCarthy [1963]. *Production Functions and Meth-*

ods of Specifying Optimum Fertilizer Use under Various Uncertainty Conditions for Hay. Iowa Agricultural Experiment Station Research Bulletin 518.

Heady, E. O., J. T. Pesek, and V. Y. Rao [1966]. *Fertilizer Production Functions from Experimental Data with Associated Supply and Demand Relationships*. Iowa Agricultural Experiment Station Research Bulletin 543.

Heady, E. O., J. Schnittker, S. Bloom, and N. L. Jacobson [1956]. "Isoquants, Isoclines, and Economic Predictions in Dairy Production." *J. Farm Econ.* 38:763-779.

Heady, E. O., J. Schnittker, N. L. Jacobson, and S. Bloom [1956]. *Milk Production Functions, Hay/Grain Substitution Rates and Economic Optima in Dairy Cow Rations*. Iowa Agricultural Experiment Station Research Bulletin 444.

Heady, E. O., and R. Shaw [1954]. *Resource Return and Productivity Coefficients of Selected Farming Areas in Iowa, Alabama, and Montana*. Iowa Agricultural Research Bulletin 427.

Heady, E. O., and W. D. Shrader [1953]. "The Interrelationships of Agronomy and Economics in Research and Recommendations to Farmers." *Agron. J.* 45:496-502.

Heady, E. O., and E. R. Swanson [1952]. *Resource Productivity in Iowa Farming*. Agricultural Experiment Station Bulletin 388.

Heady, E. O., R. C. Woodworth, D. Catron, and G. C. Ashton [1953]. "An Experiment to Derive Productivity and Substitution Coefficients in Pork Output." *J. Farm Econ.* 35:341-355.

—— [1954]. *New Procedures in Estimating Feed Substitution Rates in Determining Economic Efficiency in Pork Production. I, Replacement Rates of Corn and Soybean Oilmeal in Fortified Rations for Growing-Fattening Swine*. Iowa Agricultural Experiment Station Research Bulletin 409.

Hexem, R. W., E. O. Heady, and M. Caglar [1974]. *A Compendium of Experimental Data for Corn, Wheat, Cotton and Sugar Beets Grown at Selected Sites in the Western United States*. Center for Agricultural and Rural Development, Iowa State University Special Research Report.

Hicks, J. R. [1946]. *Value and Capital*. London: Oxford University Press.

Hildebrand, J. R. [1960]. "Some Difficulties with Empirical Results from Whole-Farm Cobb-Douglas-Type Production Functions." *J. Farm Econ.* 42:897-904.

Hildreth, C. G. [1954]. "Point Estimates of Ordinates of Concave Functions." *J. Am. Stat. Assoc.* 49:598-619.

—— [1955]. "Economic Implications of Some Cotton Fertilizer Experiments." *Econometrica* 23:88-98.

—— [1957]. "Possible Models for Agronomic-Economic Research." In *Economic and Technical Analysis of Fertilizer Innovations and Resource Use*, E. L. Baum, E. O. Heady, J. T. Pesek, and C. G. Hildreth, eds. Ames: Iowa State University Press. Pp. 176-186.

Hildreth, R. J. [1957]. "Influence of Rainfall on Fertilizer Profits." *J. Farm Econ.* 39: 522-524.

Hildreth, R. J., F. L. Fisher, and A. G. Caldwell [1955]. *An Economic Evaluation of Experimental Response to Coastal Bermuda Grass to Nitrogen under Irrigation*. Texas Agricultural Experiment Station Miscellaneous Publication 128.

—— [1956]. *Influence of Rainfall on Profits from Fertilizer Applications to East Texas Forage*. Texas Agricultural Experiment Station Miscellaneous Publication 184.

Hirsch, W. Z. [1970]. *The Economics of State and Local Governments*. New York: McGraw-Hill. Pp. 147-165.

Hoffman, B. R., and G. L. Johnson [1966]. *Summary and Evaluation of the Cooperative*

Agronomic-Economic Experimentations at Michigan State University — 1955-1963. Michigan Agricultural Experiment Station Research Bulletin 11.

Hoglund, C. R., G. L. Johnson, C. A. Lassiter, and L. D. McGilliard, eds. [1958]. *Nutritional and Economic Aspects of Feed Utilization by Dairy Cows.* Ames: Iowa State University Press.

Hoover, L. M., P. L. Kelley, G. M. Ward, A. M. Feyerherm, and R. Chaddha [1967]. "Economic Relationships of Hay and Concentrate Consumption to Milk Production." *J. Farm Econ.* 49:64-78.

Hurst, D. C., and D. D. Mason [1957]. "Some Statistical Aspects of the TVA-North Carolina Cooperative Project on Determination of Yield Response Surfaces for Corn." In *Economic and Technical Analysis of Fertilizer Innovations and Resource Use*, E. L. Baum, E. O. Heady, J. T. Pesek, and C. G. Hildreth, eds. Ames: Iowa State University Press. Pp. 207-216.

Hutton, R. F. [1955]. *An Appraisal of Research on the Economics of Fertilizer Use.* Tennessee Valley Authority, Agricultural Economics Report T 55-1.

Hutton, R. F., and D. W. Thorne [1955]. "Review Notes on the Heady-Pesek Fertilizer Production Surface." *J. Farm Econ.* 37:117-119.

Ibach, D. B. [1953]. "Use of Production Functions in Farm Management Research." *J. Farm Econ.* 35:938-956.

——— [1957]. *Substituting Fertilizer for Land in Growing Corn.* USDA Agricultural Research Service, ARS 43-63.

Ibach, D. B., and J. R. Adams [1968]. *Crop Yield Response to Fertilizer in the United States.* USDA Statistical Bulletin 431.

Ibach, D. B., and S. W. Mendum [1953]. *Determining Profitable Use of Fertilizer.* USDA, Bureau of Agricultural Economics, FM 105.

Jacobson, N. L. [1959]. "Problems in Designing Feeding Experiments from a Nutritional Standpoint." In *Nutritional and Economic Aspects of Feed Utilization by Dairy Cows*, C. R. Hoglund, G. L. Johnson, C. A. Lassiter, and L. D. McGilliard, eds. Ames: Iowa State University Press. Pp. 206-212.

Jensen, E. [1940]. "Determining Input-Output Relationships in Milk Production." *J. Farm Econ.* 22:249-258.

Jensen, E., J. Klein, E. Rauchenstein, T. E. Woodward, and R. H. Smith [1942]. *Input-Output Relationships in Milk Production.* USDA Technical Bulletin 815.

Jensen, H. R. [1977]. "Farm Management and Production Economics, 1946-1970." In *A Survey of Agricultural Economics Literature: Volume 1, Traditional Fields of Agricultural Economics, 1940s to 1970s*, Lee R. Martin, ed. Minneapolis: University of Minnesota Press.

Johnson, D. G. [1960]. "Output and Income Effects of Reducing the Farm Labor Force." *J. Farm Econ.* 42:779-796.

Johnson, G. L. [1955]. "Results from Production Economic Analysis." *J. Farm Econ.* 37:206-222.

——— [1956a]. "A Critical Evaluation of Fertilization Research." In *Farm Management in the West — Problems in Resource Use*. Proceedings of the Western Agricultural Economics Research Council, Farm Management Research Committee. Report 1, pp. 33-40.

——— [1956b]. "Interdisciplinary Considerations in Designing Experiments to Study the Profitability of Fertilizer Use." In *Methodological Procedures in the Economic Analysis of Fertilizer Use Data*, E. L. Baum, E. O. Heady, and J. Blackmore, eds. Ames: Iowa State University Press. Pp. 22-36.

—— [1957]. "Planning Agronomic-Economic Research in View of Results to Date, and the Role of Management in Planning Farms for Optimum Fertilizer Use. In *Economic and Technical Analysis of Fertilizer Innovations and Resource Use*, E. L. Baum, E. O. Heady, J. T. Pesek, and C. G. Hildreth, eds. Ames: Iowa State University Press. Pp. 217-225, 261-270.

—— [1963]. "Stress on Production Economics." *Australian J. Agr. Econ.* 7:12-26.

Johnson, P. R. [1953]. "Alternative Functions for Analyzing a Fertilizer-Yield Relationship." *J. Farm Econ.* 35:519-529.

Judge, G. G., J. S. Plaxico, D. L. Brooks, W. L. McCaslan, R. H. Thayer, G. W. Newell, and K. E. Dunkelgod [1959]. *The Economics and Technical Impact of Floor Space per Bird and Temperature in Broiler Production.* Oklahoma Agricultural Experiment Station Processed Series P-318.

Knetsch, J. L. [1956]. "Methodological Procedures and Applications for Incorporating Economic Considerations into Fertilizer Recommendations." M.S. thesis, Michigan State University.

—— [1959]. "Moisture Uncertainties and Fertility Response Studies." *J. Farm Econ.* 41:70-76.

—— [1961]. "Some Possible Implications of Fertilizer Response Studies Conducted over Time." Unpublished manuscript.

Knetsch, J. L., and W. L. Parks [1958]. *Interpreting Results of Irrigation Experiments— A Progress Report.* Tennessee Valley Authority, Agricultural Economics Report T 59-1.

Knetsch, J. L., L. S. Robertson, Jr., and W. B. Sundquist [1956]. "Economic Considerations in Soil Fertility Research." *Michigan Agricultural Experiment Station Quarterly* 39:10-16.

Knetsch, J. L., and J. Smallshaw [1958]. *The Occurrence of Drought in the Tennessee Valley.* Tennessee Valley Authority, Report T58-2 AE.

Krantz, B. A., and W. V. Chandler [1954]. *Fertilize Corn for Higher Yields.* North Carolina Agricultural Experiment Station Bulletin 366.

Lorenz, O. A., J. C. Bishop, B. J. Hoyle, M. P. Zobel, P. A. Minges, L. D. Doreen, and A. Ulrich [1954]. *Potato Fertilizer Experiments in California.* California Agricultural Experiment Station Bulletin 744.

McAlexander, R., and R. Hutton [1957]. "Determining Least-Cost Combinations." *J. Farm Econ.* 39:936-941.

McPherson, W. W. [1955]. *Some Algebraic Expressions Used in Estimating Input-Output Relationships.* Southern Farm Management Research Committee.

McPherson, W. W., and J. E. Faris [1958]. "Price Mapping of Optimum Changes in Enterprises." *J. Farm Econ.* 40:821-834.

Martin, L. R., A. J. Coutu, and H. S. Singh [1960]. "The Effects of Different Levels of Management and Capital on the Incomes of Small Farmers in the South." *J. Farm Econ.* 42:90-102.

Mason, D. D. [1956]. "Functional Models and Experimental Designs for Characterizing Response Curves and Surfaces." In *Methodological Procedures in the Economic Analysis of Fertilizer Use Data*, E. L. Baum, E. O. Heady, and J. Blackmore, eds. Ames: Iowa State University Press. Pp. 76-98.

—— [1957]. "Statistical Problems of Joint Research." *J. Farm Econ* 39:370-381.

Mighell, R. L. [1953a]. "What Is the Place of the Equal-Product Function?" *J. Farm Econ.* 35:29-43.

———— [1953b]. "A Further Note on the Equal-Product Function." *J. Farm Econ.* 35: 276-280.

Mitscherlich, E. A. [1928]. "Das Gesetz des Minimums und das Gesetz des abnehmenden Bodenertrages." *Landwirtschaft Jahrbuch* 38:537-552.

Moore, C. V. [1961]. "A General Analytical Framework for Estimating the Production Function for Crops Using Irrigation Water." *J. Farm Econ.* 43:876-888.

Mundlak, Y. [1961]. "Empirical Production Function Free of Management Bias." *J. Farm Econ.* 43:44-56.

Munson, R. D. [1958]. *Some Considerations in the Future Development of Agronomic-Economic Research.* Unpublished paper, Tennessee Valley Authority.

Munson, R. D., and J. P. Doll [1959]. "The Economics of Fertilizer Use in Crop Production." *Advances in Agronomy* 11:133-169.

National Academy of Sciences [1961]. *Status and Methods of Research in Economic and Agronomic Aspects of Fertilizer Response and Use.* National Research Council Publication 918.

Nelder, J. A. [1966]. "Inverse Polynomials, a Useful Group of Multi-Factor Response Functions." *Biometrics* 22:128-141.

Nelson, A. G. [1945]. *Relation of Feed Consumed to Food Products Produced by Fattening Cattle.* USDA Technical Bulletin 900.

Nelson, M., E. N. Castle, and W. G. Brown [1957]. "Use of the Production Function and Linear Programming in Valuation of Intermediate Products." *Land Economics* 33:257-261.

Nicholls, W. H. [1948]. *Labor Productivity Functions in Meat Packing.* Chicago: University of Chicago Press.

North Carolina Agricultural Extension Service [1962]. *The Economics of Fertilizer Use in the South.* Southern Farm Management Extension Publication 10.

North Central Farm Management Research Committee [1954]. *Profitable Use of Fertilizer in the Midwest.* Wisconsin Agricultural Experiment Station Bulletin 508 (North Central Regional Publication 54).

O'Neal, W. G. [1959]. "Effects of Different Farm Resource Combinations on the Marginal Value Productivity of Resources on General Commercial Farms in the Limestone Valley Area of Georgia." M.S. thesis, University of Georgia.

Orazem, F., and R. B. Herring [1958]. "Economic Aspects of the Effects of Fertilizers, Soil Moisture and Rainfall on the Yields of Grain Sorghum in the (Sandy Lands) of Southwest Kansas." *J. Farm Econ.* 40:697-708.

Oury, B. [1965]. "Allowing for Weather in Crop Production Model Building." *J. Farm Econ.* 47:270-283.

Paris, Q., F. Malossini, A. Pilla, and A. Romita [1970]. "A Note on Milk Production Functions." *Am. J. Agr. Econ.* 52:594-598.

Parks, W. L., and J. L. Knetsch [1959]. "Corn Yields as Influenced by Nitrogen Level and Drought Intensity." *Agron. J.* 51:363-364.

Paschal, J. L. [1953]. *Economic Analysis of Alfalfa Yield Response to Phosphate Fertilizer at Three Locations in the West.* USDA, Bureau of Agricultural Economics, FM 104.

Paschal, J. L., and B. L. French [1956]. *A Method of Economic Analysis Applied to Nitrogen Fertilizer Rate Experiments on Irrigated Corn.* USDA Technical Bulletin 1141.

Pesek, J. T., and E. O. Heady [1958]. "Derivation and Application of a Method for Determining Minimum Recommended Rates of Fertilization." *Soil Science Society of America Proceedings* 22:419-423.

Pesek, J. T., Jr., E. O. Heady, and E. Venezian [1967]. *Fertilizer Production Functions in Relation to Weather, Location, Soil and Crop Variables.* Iowa Agricultural Experiment Station Research Bulletin 554.

Plaxico, J. S. [1955]. "Problems of Factor-Product Aggregation in Cobb-Douglas Value Productivity Analysis." *J. Farm Econ.* 37:664-675.

Plaxico, J. S., P. Andrilenas, and E. S. Pope [1959]. *Economic Analysis of a Concentrate—Roughage Ratio Experiment.* Oklahoma Agricultural Experiment Station Bulletin P310.

Rauchenstein, E. [1953]. "Forage-Grain Substitution: Its Importance in the Economics of Milk Production." *J. Farm Econ.* 35:562-571.

Reder, M. W. [1943]. "An Alternative Interpretation of the Cobb-Douglas Function." *Econometrica* 11:259-264.

Redman, J. C. [1952]. "Economic Aspects of Feeding for Milk Production." *J. Farm Econ.* 34:333-345.

Redman, J. C., and S. Q. Allen [1954]. "Some Interrelationships of Economic and Agronomic Concepts." *J. Farm Econ.* 36:453-465.

Robertson, L. S., G. L. Johnson, and J. F. Davis [1957]. "Problems Involved in the Integration of Agronomic and Economic Methodologies in Economic Optima Experiments." In *Economic and Technical Analysis of Fertilizer Innovations and Resource Use*, E. L. Baum, E. O. Heady, J. T. Pesek, and C. G. Hildreth, eds. Ames: Iowa State University Press. Pp. 226-240.

Robinson, J. [1955]. "The Production Function." *Econ. J.* 65:67-71.

Schechter, M., and E. O. Heady [1970]. "Response Surface Analysis and Simulation Models in Policy Choices." *Am. J. Agr. Econ.* 52:41-50.

Schultz, T. W. [1958]. "Output-Input Relationships Revisited." *J. Farm Econ.* 40:924-932.

Shaw, R. H. [1956]. "The Fertilizer Problem: Resource-Enterprise and Tenure Relationships and Criteria for Optima." In *Farm Management in the West—Problems in Resource Use*. Proceedings of the Western Agricultural Economics Research Council, Farm Management Research Committee. Report 1, pp. 9-22.

Shephard, R. W. [1953]. *Cost and Production Functions.* Princeton: Princeton University Press.

Shoup, C. S. [1969]. *Public Finance.* Chicago: Aldine.

Smith, W. G., and W. L. Parks [1967]. "A Method for Incorporating Probability into Fertilizer Recommendations." *J. Farm Econ.* 49:1511-1515.

Spillman, W. J. [1933]. *Use of the Exponential Yield Curve in Fertilizer Experiments.* USDA Technical Bulletin 348.

Stauber, S., and F. Miller [1963]. *Corn Yield Response to Nitrogen and Irrigation in Southeast Missouri.* Missouri Agricultural Experiment Station Special Report 39.

Stemberger, A. P. [1957]. *Economic Implications of Using Alternative Production Functions for Expressing Corn-Nitrogen Production Relationships.* North Carolina Agricultural Experiment Station Technical Bulletin 126.

Stritzel, J. A. [1958]. "Agronomic and Economic Evaluation of Direct and Residual Fertilizer Nutrients." Ph.D. dissertation, Iowa State University.

Sullivan, G. D. [1964]. *Profitable Levels of Forage Fertilization.* Louisiana Agricultural Experiment Station, DAE, Research Report 334.

Sundquist, W. B., and L. S. Robertson [1959]. *An Economic Analysis of Some Con-*

trolled Fertilizer Input-Output Experiments in Michigan. Michigan State University Agricultural Experiment Station Technical Bulletin 269.

Swanson, E. R. [1956]. "Determining Optimum Size of Business from Production Functions." In *Resource Productivity, Returns to Scale, and Farm Size,* E. O. Heady, G. L. Johnson, and L. S. Hardin, eds. Ames: Iowa State University Press. Pp. 133-143.

Swanson, E. R., C. R. Taylor, and L. F. Welch [1973]. "Economically Optimal Levels of Nitrogen Fertilizer for Corn — An Analysis Based on Experimental Data, 1966-71." *Ill. Agr. Econ.* 13:16-25.

Swanson, E. R., and F. H. Tyner [1965]. "Influence of Moisture Regime on Optimum Nitrogen and Plant Population for Corn." *Agron. J.* 57:361-364.

Taylor, C. R., and E. R. Swanson [1973]. "Experimental Nitrogen Response Functions, Actual Farm Experience and Policy Analysis." *Ill. Agr. Econ.* 13:26-32.

———— [1974]. "Economic Impact of Imposing per Acre Restrictions on Use of Nitrogen Fertilizer in Illinois." *Ill. Agr. Econ.* 14:1-5.

Tintner, G. [1944a]. "A Note on the Derivation of Production Functions from Farm Records." *Econometrica* 12:26-34.

———— [1944b]. "An Application of the Variate Difference Method to Multiple Regression." *Econometrica* 12:97-113.

———— [1952]. *Econometrics.* New York: Wiley.

Tintner, G., and O. H. Brownlee [1944]. "Production Functions Derived from Farm Records." *J. Farm Econ.* 26:566-571.

Tolley, H. R., J. D. Black, and M. J. B. Ezekiel [1924]. *Input as Related to Output in Farm Organization and Cost of Production Studies.* USDA Technical Bulletin 1277.

Tramel, T. E. [1957a]. "Suggested Procedure for Agronomic-Economic Fertilizer Experiments." In *Economic and Technical Analysis of Fertilizer Experiments,* E. L. Baum, E. O. Heady, J. T. Pesek, and C. G. Hildreth, eds. Ames: Iowa State University Press. Pp. 168-175.

Tramel, T. E. [1957b]. "Alternative Methods of Using Production Functions for Making Recommendations." *J. Farm Econ.* 39:790-793.

Ulveling, E., and L. Fletcher [1970]. "A Cobb-Douglas Production Function with Variable Returns to Scale." *Am. J. Agr. Econ.* 52:322-326.

United States Department of Agriculture [1954]. *Fertilizer Use and Crop Yields in the United States.* USDA Agr. Handbook 68.

Walker, O., S. Wiggans, and T. Pogue [1962]. *An Economic Analysis of Fertilizer and Seeding Rates for Spinach Production in Eastern Oklahoma.* Oklahoma Agricultural Experiment Station Bulletin 596.

Woodworth, R. C. [1956]. "Organizing Fertilizer Input-Output Data in Farm Planning." In *Methodological Procedures in the Economic Analysis of Fertilizer Use Data,* E. L. Baum, E. O. Heady, and J. Blackmore, eds. Ames: Iowa State University Press. Pp. 158-170.

Woodworth, R. C., R. E. Proctor, G. W. Burton, and A. B. Mackie [1957]. *Profitable Use of Fertilizer in the Production of Coastal Bermuda in the Coastal Plain Area of Georgia.* Georgia Agricultural Experiment Station Technical Bulletin 13.

Woolf, Willard F., G. D. Sullivan, and S. A. Phillips [1967]. *An Economic Analysis of Irrigation, Fertilization, and Seeding Rates for Cotton in the Macon Ridge Area of Louisiana.* Louisiana Agriucltural Experiment Station Bulletin 620.

Yates, F. [1967]. "A Fresh Look at the Basic Principles of the Design and Analysis of

Experiments." In *Proceedings of the Fifth Berkeley Symposium,* vol. IV, *Biology and Problems of Health Sciences,* L. M. Le Cam and Jerzy Neyman, eds. Berkeley: University of California Press. Pp. 777-790.

Zellner, A., and N. S. Revankar [1969]. "Generalized Production Functions." *Rev. Econ. Studies* 36:241-250.

Zulberti, C. A., J. T. Reid, and G. L. Casler [1973]. *The Use of the Daily Production Function to Select the Feeding Program for Growing and Fattening Cattle.* Cornell University, Department of Agricultural Economics, AE Res. 73-14.

Part III. Systems Analysis and Simulation
in Agricultural and Resource Economics

The initial draft of this paper was prepared at the University of California, Davis, for presentation at the annual AAEA meeting held in Gainesville, Florida, in 1972. The final draft was prepared in December 1974. In the interim the authors received support from the University of Missouri (Columbia) and Iowa State University. Perhaps the only advantage of permitting the drafting of this paper to continue so long was the opportunity that it provided for obtaining useful reviews. The original version of the paper and the survey chapters on econometrics and optimization, presented at the Florida AAEA meeting, were reviewed by Oscar Burt, Verner Hurt, and Richard Foote. Their comments were very useful in helping us to become more fully aware of some of the literature in agricultural economics. The reviewers appointed by the Literature Review Committee were Thomas Naylor, Ludwig Eisgruber, and Albert Halter. The comments by these individuals, particularly by Eisgruber, were helpful in forcing us to come to grips with the special features of systems analysis and simulation and the issues we have raised with respect to control. Our initial partners in crime, Richard Day and George Judge, should also be acknowledged for their helpful comments and suggestions. John Doll and Lee Martin, members of the Literature Review Committee, provided valuable comments on an earlier draft and at times not-so-gentle prodding concerning the final draft of the paper. Finally, a number of our colleagues were kind enough to comment on the manuscript (although their kindness did not always carry over into their review and comments), which also helped us to improve the final draft: Ben French, Gerald Dean, Bruce Dixon, John Freebairn, J. C. Headley, and Sam Logan. Errors of omission and commission are of course our own responsibility.

S. R. J.
G. C. R.

Systems Analysis and Simulation:
A Survey of Applications in Agricultural
and Resource Economics

S. R. Johnson
Professor of Economics and Agricultural Economics
University of Missouri, Columbia

Gordon C. Rausser
Visiting Professor of Business Administration and Economics
Graduate School of Business Administration
Harvard University

Systems analysis and simulation have had a recent but marked influence on teaching and research in agricultural economics. See, for example, the surveys by J. R. Anderson [1974a], Armstrong and Hepp [1970], and Charlton and Thompson [1970] and the expository treatments by Babb and French [1963], Dent and Anderson [1971], Eidman [1971], Eisgruber and Nielson [1963], Hesselbach and Eisgruber [1967], B. Johnson and Eisgruber [1969], Shruben [1968], Snyder and Swackhamer [1966], Suttor and Crom [1964], and Tyner and Tweeten [1968]. Surveys, expository treatments, and bibliographies on the subject outside of agricultural economics are numerous. Useful examples may be found in American Management Association Report 55 [1961], Harling [1958], Kotler and Schultz [1970], Malcolm [1960], Mihram [1972], Naylor [1969a, 1969b], Orcutt et al. [1961], and Vichnevetsky [1969]. Although most of the more formal concepts have been developed externally, the approach has found wide application in the profession.

The factors identified as accounting for the assimilation of systems concepts and simulation in agricultural economics and in other applied subject areas are of course about as numerous as the individuals who have commented on the subject (Cohen and Cyert [1965], Conway and Maxwell [1959], Hoggatt and Balderston [1963], Kornai [1971], Kotler and Schultz [1970], Kuehn [1962], McMillan and Gonzalez [1965], Martin [1968], Mesarovic, Macko, and Takahara [1970], Mize and Cox [1968], Naylor, Balintfy, et al. [1966], Optner [1960], Schmidt and Taylor [1970], Tocher [1963]). Three factors particularly applicable to agricultural economics are the pragmatic orientation of the research, the increasingly eclectic nature of the problems studied, and the concern with the extension of knowledge and the related need for powerful pedagogical devices (Leontief [1971], Porter et al. [1966]).

Research efforts are usually designed to bring available information to bear on particular types of problems which arise in public and private sectors. The accepted mission of the profession is not so much to investigate theoretical or institutional subtleties as to provide a basis for informed decisions. If this admittedly oversimplified conception of the research efforts of agricultural economists is appropriate, then the problematic focus is useful in explaining the extent to which systems concepts and simulation techniques have been employed. It is in this situation that systems concepts and related techniques for analysis are most appealing.

Second, as problems for the agricultural sector of the economy have been redefined to include natural resources, community and economic development, more complex firm and market decision situations, and policy questions at regional and national levels, there has been an increase in the use of systems concepts and simulation. Models employed in studying these problems typically reveal unresolved theoretical questions. Moreover, the more ambitious of these models frequently cut across the boundaries of traditional disciplines. In such circumstances tractable models are likely to involve theoretical components in nonprimitive forms and even internal tests of alternative behavioral assumptions.[1] To complicate matters further, these models do not usually lend themselves to a closed form solution. Results obtained through numerical and other analogs are therefore attractive alternatives.

Finally, there is the concern with transmitting research results to students, governmental officials, and agents in the industry serviced. Simulation methods have turned out to be an efficient means for communicating complex ideas and empirical results. This was noted and exploited rather quickly by agricultural economists (Babb [1964], Babb and Eisgruber [1966], Longworth [1969]). The advantages of the approach result from the comparative ease with which models, highly specialized to applied situations, can be described and from the possibility of allowing interactions between individuals and the models.

Historical Perspective

The history of research, teaching, and extension activities reveals a gravitation toward simulation methods and systems concepts. Historical observations of this type are useful since they give perspective to claims of novelty and a sense of proportion regarding results to be obtained from the "new" approaches. In viewing the development of that portion of agricultural economics which can be identified with model building, three periods are noted. Early efforts were empirical. Studies of farm management and industry organization were largely descriptive (Taylor [1929]). Hypotheses and models were suggested by observation and formed with few preconceptions suggested by deductive theory. Among the more frequently mentioned examples of this work are the studies by Black [1924], Bean [1929], and Moore [1914]. G. L. Johnson [1970] has referred to some of the methods involved in these studies as "pencil and paper" projections. Once formulated, these models were subjected to additional empirical information for evaluation and further refinement.

A second period of interest began in the late 1930s, and it was strongly influenced by parallel developments in economic and statistical theory. The neoclassical theory of consumer and firm behavior together with the theory of markets gave rise to a number of interesting and productive hypotheses and/or models for application in agriculture. The important departure brought on by these models was an increased preoccupation with the deductive basis for the hypotheses advanced. A chronicle of this sequence of events as it relates to applications of statistical method has been compiled by Judge [1968]. More attention was given to the process of model formulation. Specialization of the models for particular situations required statistical methods which explicitly recognized theoretical restrictions and problems posed by passively or nonexperimentally generated data. Finally, the importance of primitive behavioral assumptions in adding generality to hypotheses for statistical analysis was also recognized. Applications of models based upon these theoretical foundations seemed to represent the primary focus of the profession in the period following World War II.

More recently, interests have shifted to areas requiring models which depart from the rigidities of the neoclassical theories of firms, individuals, and markets. Related studies have raised perplexing methodological issues. The theoretical underpinnings of hypotheses (or restrictions) provided by the neoclassical theory have tended to become either unavailable or quite demanding in terms of deductive rigor. Choices open to the applied researcher are either to limit the scope of the investigations until more adequate theoretical results are forthcoming or to construct more descriptive models—incorporating the accumulated knowledge from economics and perhaps related disciplines where appropriate. In this sense the latter approach represents a combination of the early empirical methods and the more recent deductive methods (for example, Bonini [1963, 1964], Cohen and Cyert [1961], and Cyert and March [1963]).

Our introductory and historical comments have implied that simulation and systems concepts have substantial potential for application in agricultural economics. The appeal of the approach is that it permits the investigator or teacher to view problems as they exist rather than as some predefined analytical structure admits. Implicit in this observation is the idea that flexibility is the major attribute of the systems approach. That is, the methods associated with the systems approach are commonly viewed as unconfining (Manetsch, Hayenga, et al. [1971]). We shall attempt to substantiate this claim in the review of past applied work. We shall also show that this flexibility comes at some sacrifice, apparently not fully recognized in agricultural economic studies. In fact, concern about these limitations is increasing. A general discussion of the limitations which may arise in connection with policy implications of agricultural sectoral models is presented by Rausser and Johnson [1975]. Similar criticisms have been advanced by the Department of Defense [1970] and more generally by Ansoff and Slevin [1968]. These shortcomings of the approach are suggested not to deter the use of systems concepts and simulation, but to provide a balanced survey. Alternative methods or approaches to applied problems can be viewed as incurring opportunity costs for the usefulness of anticipated results. It is our intention to develop the survey so that these alternatives are apparent.

Our objective is to provide a heuristic survey of the postwar developments in simulation and systems analysis within agricultural economics. In this context it is important not only to summarize applications but also to provide a systematic basis for evaluating these efforts. The first portion of this chapter is devoted to providing the systematic basis. Following this, applications of systems concepts are examined by functional categories.

These include gaming, process models, firm models, market models, aggregate models, economic development, and natural resource models. Although the classification is arbitrary it provides a convenient framework for comparing and evaluating the studies reviewed. The survey concludes with a critical appraisal of agricultural economics work involving systems and simulation. This critique includes an assessment of noteworthy findings, promising developments, and conceptual issues which have been raised by the application of systems and simulation methods.

Since the evaluation of empirical results presented in the reviewed studies is the subject of other survey papers commissioned by the American Agricultural Economics Association, our comments on these aspects are limited. Instead our principal concern is with model characteristics and with the application of simulation methods.

Nomenclature

A number of terms common to systems concepts and simulation have specialized meanings. It is important therefore to identify these terms before the discussion of the approach and/or methods. Many of these definitions are consistent with treatments existing in literature but are included for completeness. Where possible, consistencies and departures from definitional frameworks usually found in the literature are indicated.

A "system" is a collection of interrelated components or elements with a purpose. More elaborate definitions of systems featuring specifications of the number of elements, the types of relationships between elements, and purposes or goals are common (Ackoff [1971], Mihram [1972]).[2] These features will be explicitly recognized in the section on the classifications of systems types. For the present it is noted that an interesting discussion of model purpose and type as related to agricultural economics has been provided by Drynan [1973].

A "model" is a synthetic representation of a system. Models of systems may take a variety of forms. Four of these which have common usage in systems studies are discussed by Ackoff [1971], Churchman [1971], A. M. Lee [1970], and Mihram [1972] : symbolic models (those which require mathematical or logical operations and which can be used to formulate a solution to the problem at hand); iconic models (those which pictorially or visually represent certain aspects of a system); analog models (those which employ one set of properties to represent another set of properties of the system); and physical models (those which involve material objects in representing systems). For the purposes at hand attention is confined to symbolic and analog models. The bulk of modeling in agricultural economics has involved symbolic representations of systems, and digital or electric analogs of such symbolic models or systems. That is, because of the predisposition of agricultural economists toward abstraction, studies of systems normally proceed with the development of a symbolic model. Symbolic models are then typically converted to digital or electric analogs for purposes of investigation.

Constructing a model of a system may be viewed as a development process. Activities occurring in this developmental process have been identified as analysis, synthesis, and design. "Systems analysis" is the purposeful study of systems. "Systems synthesis" is the act of characterizing a system, including the identification, classification, and specification of components or elements and the relationships giving the model a cohesive structure. "Systems design" is the process of investigating and selecting modes for studying systems (that is, selecting the framework within which regulatory, structural, and institutional changes of systems are to be examined). Alternatively, design can be viewed as the process of choosing a format for combining the synthesized system components and relationships to meet modeling objectives.

Analysis, synthesis, and, for most problems, design may be viewed collectively as steps in the process of developing a sufficient understanding of a system for the construction of a model. Hence, these activities may be interpreted as steps essential to scientific inquiry. Isolating primitive elements and concepts or relationships and weaving them into a representation of the system which is consistent with its perceived purposeful functioning and the research objectives is the essence of these modeling activities.

"Experimentation" is the purposeful perturbation of the system or model representation and observation of the results. In our use of this term we are obviously after a very general concept of the process associated with the manipulation of systems or models and observing consequences. The generality of the definition is useful since it permits the consideration of simulation, Monte Carlo methods, and gaming as special types of experiments. In addition to providing a framework for considering the alternative process of experimentation, the approach is convenient for the subsequent discussion of experimental design.

"Simulation" is a process of experimenting with models or systems. It is important to note that this definition implies a view of simulation as a method and not as a substitute for a model (Naylor [1971]). Building a representation or model of a system could be viewed as constructing an image or simulation of the system. According to the definitional structure adopted for the survey, this process is termed "model construction" and experimentation with it is termed "simulation." There may be some confusion in this choice of terminology since simulation is used with both meanings in the systems literature. For our purposes, a simulation is an experiment with a model of a system, not the model itself. Given this definition, there are three useful but not necessarily exclusive distinctions which can be made for types of experiments with systems models. (For a more detailed discussion of these alternatives for analysis of systems models, see Rausser and Johnson [1975]. The more refined classification used in the paper cited includes analytical closed-form representations, analytical simulation, and ad hoc simulation.)

"Simulation algorithms" are techniques for characterizing the operations of systems models through related constructs. "Analytical simulation" is a method of experiment based on systematized rules of search and design. "Exploratory simulation" is a process of monitoring outcomes with systems which are not algorithms and which do not involve systematized rules of search and design.

For purposes of the survey we confine our attention to analytical simulation and exploratory simulation. Simulation algorithms were included simply for completeness and to give some substance to the earlier conjecture that many of our so-called modern concepts in the study of systems can be viewed as outgrowths or extensions of ideas which have long been familiar in problem solving. This observation is more fully developed by Day and Sparling [1977]. Iterative procedures incorporated in algorithms of the type used in solving optimization problems may be viewed as sequences of simulations of the digital counterpart of an algebraic model (Dorfman [1963], Meier [1967]).

Much is made of the distinction between analytical and exploratory (or ad hoc) simulation methods. Analytical simulations as indicated by Dorfman [1965] have distinct advantages in studying characteristics of more tightly defined systems models. Exploratory simulations are, however, quite useful in certain phases in model construction and evaluation.

The relationship between computer simulation, Monte Carlo methods, and gaming is illustrated by the following definitions: A "computer simulation" is an experiment with a digital or electric analog of a systems model. The "Monte Carlo method" is a branch of mathematics which is concerned with experiments on sequences of random numbers (Hammersley and Handscomb [1964]). This definition of Monte Carlo methods is somewhat more restrictive than modern usage of the term might suggest (J. R. Anderson [1974a], Donaldson and Webster [1968], A. M. Lee [1970]). Broader definitions of the Monte Carlo method encompass most numerical techniques, whether employed in stochastic or nonstochastic models. The essential element in most definitions seems to be that the Monte Carlo method refers to experiments with algebraic models which involve a stochastic structure. If this definition is adopted, then Monte Carlo methods are most closely related to simulations as employed with closed form stochastic models (J. R. Anderson [1974a]). In fact, given our definitional structure, Monte Carlo methods are a proper subset of simulation methods. This follows because Monte Carlo methods refer to experiments with special types of systems models. However, the term is useful even in the discussion of systems and simulation since by convention it refers to a substantial body of numerical work in statistics and mathematics.[3]

"Gaming" is the process of experimenting with models of systems which involve a human response as a strategic component. As the definition implies, games as models of systems are partially physical.[4] They are models involving controlled human interactions. Experiments with such models are usually termed "gaming." These experiments are often highly structured in terms of participant options and possible interactions (Evans, Wallace, and Sutherland [1967]). As with the Monte Carlo methods, gaming methods are therefore special types of simulations, again with the specialty coming from the types of models and/or systems involved in the experiments.

Systems Concepts

In addition to the fundamental definitions in the preceding section, the systems literature includes a number of concepts which must be clearly identified if the survey of applications is to be internally consistent. The informal nature of the models used in applications of systems and simulation in agricultural economics makes the commonality provided by this discussion of concepts important as a basis for cataloguing applied studies and thus providing systematic content.

Types of Systems

There are numerous approaches to the classification of systems (Ackoff [1971], McMillan and Gonzalez [1965]). As might be expected, the existing approaches including the one employed for the purposes of this survey are based on types of components, relations, and system purposes. More refined and specialized classifications based on economic considerations have also been advanced (Naylor [1971]). System and model types identified here, however, are confined to those required in structuring the survey.

Stochastic/nonstochastic systems. Stochastic systems include random components or relations. The converse is true for nonstochastic systems. A similar partitioning is useful in distinguishing between systems models. The distinction implies that it is not necessary for the stochastic characteristics of the model to correspond to those of the system. Stochastic models of nonstochastic systems are, for example, quite consistent with the Bayesian view of probability theory (Jeffreys [1961]). From a pragmatic standpoint the relationship between models and systems can be rationalized on the basis of model purpose. For example, useful models for decision purposes are generally simplified representations of systems; as such, the more intricate aspects of the systems outcomes may be characterized using error terms with prescribed probabilistic characteristics.

Static/dynamic models. The distinction refers of course to the time dimension of the system or model. Static models abstract from time while dynamic models are ones in which time enters in an integral way (Frisch [1935-36], Samuelson [1947]). Again, a correspondence between model and system with respect to this characteristic is not necessary. To illustrate the point we simply note that many agricultural economists for a number of years have been busily applying static neoclassical theory to intrinsically dynamic systems.

Dynamic systems and their representations often incorporate a concept termed "feedback." The term, although used in a number of contexts, refers to information flows between time periods in dynamic models. In fact, it is essential to models which are truly sequential in nature. For this reason, attempts to develop provisions for feedback in models of systems have attracted substantial attention (Forrester [1961], Nance [1971]). In the context of model construction, feedback is most naturally viewed in terms of control.

Open/closed systems and models. Closed systems and models are bounded in terms of their relationship to the environment. If environmental factors modify the system or model in a relevant way, then the system or model is said to be unbounded or open (Mihram [1972]). Clearly the closedness or openness of a system or model is related to the boundedness of the elements. Obviously, boundedness is dependent upon model and system purpose. Most models surveyed, because of the economists' concern for analytical content, are bounded. However, in the sense that such models are used in evolving an understanding of the system and, accordingly, modifying the structure, they are open.

Historical/nonhistorical distinctions. These terms are used with two meanings in the systems and simulation literature. In the early writings models were constructed with the objective of reproducing historical sequences of events (Forrester [1961]). Examples of these historical models may be found in early behavioral studies of the firm (Cohen and Cyert [1965]), Shubik [1960]). The distinction between historical and nonhistorical models in this early literature was with respect to whether or not recorded values of environmental elements were characterized by estimated probability distributions or as observed sequences (Churchman [1960]). More recently the terms have been used to distinguish between concepts of systems and systems models which are temporally related and those which are not.

Decomposability. The concept of decomposability has been widely employed in agricultural economics applications. Decompositions of aggregate models into sectors (Manetsch, Hayenga, et al. [1971]) and firms by function (Babb [1964]) are examples of situations in which the concept has been applied. An important advantage of this view of systems and models is that it permits the development of research projects in manageable parts (French [1974]). When systems and models are decomposed, the feedback concept again assumes importance. In this instance it refers to flows of information between the decomposed parts of the system or model.

Interaction. Systems concepts can embrace entities which are extremely complex. In such situations researchers may begin with highly simplified models and develop them on the basis of interactions with the system. That is, the modeling process is one in which information on the system, obtained by viewing it in the context of a model, is used in refining provisional specifications. For example, models of complex systems may be initially specified using functional components, with the interconnections represented in a highly simplistic form. Information obtained by simulating the model may then be used to develop more realistic relationships between the components and, in fact, to specialize component specifications. This information may result from comparing the outcomes of the simulations to the observed system or from more implicit comparisons of outcomes with preconceived ideas about the working of the system.

Models which explicitly recognize this process and structure the relationship between researcher and system may be termed interactive. The consequences of these characteristics are far-reaching and involve the so-called "uncertainty principle of modeling" (J. R. Anderson [1974a]) and, more generally, adaptive systems models and various learning hypotheses. With each of the alternatives the modeling of systems is viewed as an exploratory process. We begin with a modeling objective but substantial uncertainty about the structure and functioning of the system. A trial and error approach is used to isolate the important elements of the system and their implications for the model formulation. Whether this evolutionary process is itself modeled as an adaptive or dual control problem or proceeds in a more ad hoc manner, the end result is most likely a model characterizing more accurately those system aspects that are critical to the purpose of the modeling exercise.

System purpose. This characteristic of systems and models can be tied directly to the more traditional concepts in agricultural economics. Our characterization of systems by purpose will permit classifications for the applications survey along established lines of inquiry. That is, economic aspects of agricultural sectors may be viewed as having general purposeful functions in terms of production, distribution, and valuation, depending upon the paradigm through which the system is perceived. Refinements associated with identifying more operational concepts of purpose have to some extent led to a compartmentalization of the systems research. That is, we find studies of the processing system, firm growth, and development each referring to a purposeful function of the system. The identification of systems functions and modeling objectives is thus crucial to the evaluation of the systems research surveyed and more generally to the evaluation of the systems approach.

Modeling Objectives

Models are constructed to provide information about systems. Hence, they may be used for a number of purposes not necessarily corresponding to the purposeful functioning of the system. Depending upon research objectives, the investigator may use descriptive, explanatory, predictive, or decision models.

Descriptive models. Most descriptive models are exploratory in nature. The researcher observes a system and constructs a model which is designed to describe the functioning of the system. That is, "a descriptive model simply sets forth a set of relationships which have 'bound together' different variables in situations in which they have been previously observed." (Strotz and Wold

[1960]). Information developed from the model is then used in attempts to understand the functioning of the system and to support inferences under alternative assumptions about conditioning by the environmental factors.

Descriptive models have been widely employed in systems studies. Clarkson and Simon [1960], Cohen and Cyert [1965], Forrester [1961], Goldberg [1968], Orcutt [1960], and Shubik [1960] are among those who have advocated and developed descriptive modeling techniques. As the cited works suggest, the emergence and prominence of descriptive modeling is closely tied to behavioral theories in the social sciences. More recent descriptive models attracting substantial attention were employed by Forrester [1971] and Meadows et al. [1972] in investigating implications of a long-term continuation of assumed relationships between population, resource consumption, and the societal and economic structure.

Explanatory models. Models of this type are constructed with objectives which are in a number of respects similar to those for the descriptive case. The principal distinction is that explanatory models are causal. This is of course a "loaded" term and hence may require elaboration. In this context we are using the definition of Strotz and Wold [1960]. That is, in the statistical sense "z is a cause of y if, by hypothesis, it is or 'would be' possible by controlling z indirectly to control y, at least stochastically."

The relationships specified involve assumptions about the direction of influence of variables. Hence, in explanatory models the chief concern is with the isolation and refinement of causal relationships and tests of associated implications vis-à-vis the observed system and a priori theories. Internal consistency and tests of competing hypotheses on the behavioral mechanism driving the system are the objectives emphasized in these modeling endeavors.

Prediction. Forecasting and prediction are important functions of modeling efforts in agricultural economics and other policy sciences. Predictions of price movements, changes in location, mobility of factors, and the like have an important role in many policy questions. In these models there can be less concern with internal workings than with forecasting accurately. This is particularly true of situations in which the dynamic models are constructed to deal with short-run forecasting problems (Gross and Ray [1965]). From a philosophical standpoint these models are often advanced in a positive economics tradition. As will be apparent from the subsequent discussion, the predictive objective of the modeling activities admits some different procedures for model construction and simulation.

Decision problems. In economic systems these problems have a generally accepted set of components. As usually conceived, they involve controllable and environmental variables, objective functions, and structures which relate the controlled and environmental variables to output variables (Fox, Sengupta, and Thorbecke [1966]). The model specified as an optimizing problem is used as a basis for policy prescriptions for the system. As a consequence research efforts are concerned with both the implications of the optimizing solutions and the accuracy with which the model portrays the system. When expressed in a dynamic context, these two problems can be productively viewed in adaptive or dual control theory frameworks (Rausser and Freebairn [1974a], Tse [1974]).

Decision problems may be usefully grouped into two major types—regulatory and institutional. Regulatory decision models are developed for policy questions given a particular institutional and environmental structure (Haitovsky and Wallace [1972]). For institutional decision models, the structure itself is allowed to vary and thus the larger questions on the organization of the general system within which the subsystems operate are considered. Such decision problems are of course most difficult, since by convention the subsystems of study have usually been examined within the context of dominant paradigms. The systems approach to construction of symbolic and digital models has made a substantial contribution by creating an awareness of the limitations of research results based entirely on regulatory models of systems.

Paradigms. Since the publication of Kuhn's work [1970] concerning scientific revolutions, our perspective on the modeling of systems and the implications drawn from related research results has changed. The major point made by Kuhn was his observation on the importance of the paradigm concept to the results of scientific investigations. Roughly put, paradigms are to scientific inquiry as maintained hypotheses are to the standard types of statistical investigations (Rausser [1973]). In other words, the philosophical structure within which we operate contains a number of propositions or primitive concepts which are not, in principle, testable. While this is somewhat disquieting for the more traditional philosophical framework (Black [1953], Popper [1959]), recognition of the existence of paradigms has substantial implications for the analysis of systems. The departure from standard neoclassical models represented by systems research efforts, if generously interpreted, may be viewed as the beginnings of a professional movement to paradigms more appropriate for current policy questions. In fact, a chronicle of the evolution of the ideas on models and systems as viewed in terms of a departure from the neoclassic economic theories since the early 1960s might be appropriately titled "paradigm lost."

Systems Analysis

As suggested earlier, systems analysis is the process by which an investigator with a specific objective initiates modeling or research. The system in question is observed and the investigator's perception of the problem under investigation is sharpened. It is conventional to view this process as one in which the elements and components of the systems are identified and the relationships between them are specified. Decisions made in this phase of the research process relate to the size and scope of the model, the level of abstraction appropriate for question under study, and the sources of information and data. Most of the systems studies by agricultural economists have (1) a body of relevant theoretical and applied (disciplinary) literature (2) operating data on some or all of the variables or elements identified as possible components, and (3) a stock of informal knowledge distilled by individuals closely connected or involved with the operation of the system.

Systems analysis is the process of accumulating this information along with the observed behavior of the system and coming to an initial decision as to research strategy (Deutsch [1969]). The diversity and specialty of methods and models available in the systems literature make the process more involved than if traditional economics paradigms were employed. The preliminary difficulty in the selection of an appropriate approach at least admits the advantage of not operating with an overly confining model or paradigm. For this reason the systems analysts may find their efforts more innovative in nature than those of researchers following a structured approach or existing paradigm to the problem under investigation.

Systems Synthesis

After studying the system and accumulating the associated data and results as well as decisions on a research strategy, the investigator is confronted with the problem of developing an analytically tractable characterization of the processes to be investigated. Activities of identifying and classifying elements and components by function, specifying the environmental consideration and alternative institutional frameworks, and distilling the behavioral hypotheses are all involved in systems synthesis. This is the juncture at which the investigator's perception of system and modeling objectives must be formalized.

A major advantage of identifying this stage of the systems approach is that it permits attention to be focused on the process of distilling accumulated knowledge into a manageable set of perceptions. The comparatively unconfining approach to synthesis which is typical in systems work gives rise to the possibility of developing models which are more specialized than those which result from more structured approaches. An advantage of these specialized models for the accumulation of scientific knowledge is their potential as sources of behavioral hypotheses which can be refined and studied in more simplified constructs.

The concern with firm growth represents a particularly interesting example of systems synthesis in agricultural economics research. As growth phenomena began to attract attention among researchers, systems models were synthesized as a basis for refining the problem and the hypotheses to be investigated. Results of this work have subsequently been incorporated in more formalized analytical models of dynamic firm behavior. That is, the evolution from highly personalized and specialized models to ones which involve more analytically tractable structures and results of less specific applicability is easily traced in this area of inquiry.

The systems literature contains numerous suggestions on mechanical aids for the synthesis process. Event graphs, tree diagrams, and flow charts are among the aids mentioned as possibilities for structuring systems synthesis. Whatever the symbolic approach, it is important to recognize that at this stage the major components of the systems model emerge and are linked to the modeling objectives and the system in question.

Systems Design

Designs of the systems and, in fact, of the models themselves are important since they determine the nature of questions to be asked in the inquiry. At this point research objectives and the elements of the model are structured for the analysis of regulatory decision alternatives. That is, the institutional framework within which the model is to be studied is set forth and incorporated in the structure. If viewed from a more general vantage point, the systems design problem is one of selecting hypotheses associated with the system which will have a maintained status in the study of the model. These decisions, of course, depend on the purpose of the system and model, since they set the framework within which the regulatory questions concerning the system are to be posed. Appropriate designs are thus crucial in positioning the model to produce information on the system which is consistent with the objectives of the investigator.

Depending on the objectives of the model, the design may be a hypothesis on the working of the system, the structure of a decision model or a particular forecasting mechanism. In this regard it is important to distinguish between the more utilitarian design problems within the model (regulatory questions) and those which involve maintained hypotheses on the function of the system (institutional questions). The latter are in a real sense investigator control variables in the implicit optimization problems associated with developing suitable descriptive, explanatory, and forecasting models. As decisions taken in regard to design determine an institutional framework, they also constrain regulatory results obtained from systems models.

Model Representation

Models of systems tend to take highly variable forms or structures, even when the purposeful functioning of the system and the modeling objectives are the same. Nevertheless, modeling processes and the considerations influencing them are fairly standard. In this section these processes and considerations are reviewed, emphasizing their adaptive and sequential nature.

Classes of Models

The earlier discussion of systems types applies as well to models. That is, models are themselves systems. The nonstochastic/stochastic classification is most important in regard to the development of model representations. Following an approach suggested by Bellman [1961] and independently by Fel'dbaum [1965], we can distinguish three types of models in relation to this characteristic: deterministic, stochastic, and adaptive.

Deterministic models are those with all components and relationships assumed known with probability one. Stochastic models are those with some random components and relationships but with the distributions of the associated random variables assumed to be known. Adaptive models are those with components and relationships about which there is initially some uncertainty (for example, the parameters of the relevant probability distributions may be unknown). The uncertainty on the structure and components changes by learning as the process evolves. Clearly, then, the first two model types are special cases of adaptive models.

Adaptive modeling can incorporate learning processes which are passive or active. Passive learning processes are those in which information is accumulated about the system or model strictly as a by-product of operating or controlling it. Active learning processes are those in which the learning and the operation of the system are treated as joint products; this feature may be referred to as dual or adaptive control. Active learning processes, although not formalized or structured, are obviously common in systems modeling. That is, provisional models are constructed and then probed or simulated as a basis for improving the representation as well as for obtaining the information to satisfy the modeling objectives.

The structure of the problem associated with developing model representations which best meet the research objectives and thereby provide the most accurate representation of the system (given restrictions on resources and model purpose) is one of adaptive control. To be sure, strategies for developing adaptive models may be viewed as solution sequences for control problems. This aspect of the model construction process is emphasized in the subsequent discussion since it represents a unifying concept for connecting the various tasks involved in developing representations of systems. Much of the perceived flexibility of systems modeling and simulation as approaches to agricultural economics research problems derives from the use of an unstructured adaptive modeling process. By emphasizing the features of the adaptive control process involved in model construction our comments will illustrate the price of this flexibility in terms of inefficient model development.

Construction of Models

Model construction can be viewed as involving five principal steps. These steps are model specification, parameter estimation, verification, validation, and revision. At each of the steps the researcher must make decisions which are crucial to the success of the modeling endeavor. Although steps taken in the process of constructing models are reversible, it is important to recognize their opportunity costs for inefficient strategies with respect to these five steps along with implicit time and resource budgets.

Specification. After the system has been analyzed and a model has been synthesized and designed, the investigator is confronted with the specific problems of model specification. For digital and symbolic models this specification, whether provisional or final, must include an algebraic structure and an operating model. Such specifications, of course, involve compromises.

If the models are specified on the basis of primitive and generally accepted normative and physical concepts, the results have wider acceptability. Structures deduced upon accepted normative propositions and established technical relationships have greater generality, given that the paradigm governing the modeling process is appropriate. Models of this type are more easily tested and usually are less complex structurally. Alternatively, there are highly specialized models based largely on ad hoc propositions. In contrast to the primitive alternatives these are more easily specified because the process is one of simply observing the system and formulating (in abstract form) the behavioral and other structural relations. The difficulty with these models relates to the information content of the results. If the behavioral and structural hypotheses are not refined, then empirical tests are reduced in importance by virtue of the large number of competing hypotheses. There are obviously trade-offs; primitive models are less complex structurally and allow formal tests to be developed but are difficult to specify without artificially restricting the investigator's perception of the system. The converse holds for specialized models.

The process of model formulation for investigating economic systems therefore imposes some fairly artistic demands upon the researcher. Often we find model specification proceeding in the aforementioned adaptive fashion— typically tending toward some middle ground. Models with high empirical content are refined so as to adapt them to larger classes of systems. Alternatively, models more influenced by theory tend to move toward greater realistic content, becoming specialized to particular situations.

Parameter estimation. Parameters may be estimated using a number of methods. These range from econometric methods applied to linear simultaneous equation systems (Hood and Koopmans [1953]) to those which tend to disregard sample or past observations on the systems (Forrester [1961]). In the former situation a maintained hypothesis is specified and sample information is utilized to obtain estimates of the structural parameters and sampling distributions. In the latter approach Forrester rejects available sample data as containing little or incorrect information about the structure. Parameter estimates are introduced on a subjective basis or are calculated using technical and engineering types of relationships (Marsden, Pingry, and Whinston [1974]). Hence, systems models may rely heavily upon statistical method or may reject the use of available historical data (1) because it is inappropriate (Forrester [1968]), (2) because it involves substantial error (due to the sampling process), or (3) because structural change is suspected.

In addition to differences due to assumed sources of useful information, parameter estimation methods are frequently sequential or iterative in nature (Wallace and Ashar [1972]). It is also common for the estimation process to involve considerable pretesting of the structure. Formal statistical procedures have been developed for such problems. They are reviewed by Judge [1977] (in particular see his discussion of preliminary test estimators).

Thus, parameter estimates are obtained using sample or prior information and then modified based on performance of the model representation for the system. Because of the diversity of estimation methods both in terms of information sources and the iterative procedures involved, a rather general framework is needed for evaluating applications of the systems concepts and simulation in agriculture. Such a framework is available and, although impractical for many applications, it does give some perspective for the work to date. This perspective can provide a basis for assessing the advantages and limitations of the past work and can furnish some insight on possible future developments.

A framework for considering estimation in systems models must of course reconcile the use of alternative data sources. Appropriate approaches include Bayesian (Zellner [1971], Zellner and Chetty [1965]) or classical mixed estimation methods (Aitchison and Silvey [1958], Judge and Yancey [1969], Theil [1971]). In both instances sample data and extraneous information on parameter distributions are systematically applied to obtain estimates of the structure. Recent advances in mixed and Bayesian estimation techniques also admit evolving structures with nonstationary parameters (Eldor and Koppel

[1971], Freebairn and Rausser [1974]). In each of these approaches data and nondata oriented processes are essentially the same with the difference being a matter of the relative certainty with which the extraneous estimates of the parameters are held.

In addition to their appeal for the data source problem, the Bayesian and mixed estimation approaches are sufficiently general to provide for the incorporation of iterative procedures frequently used in obtaining parameters of systems models. Given the selection of a particular model or representation on the basis of available data or information, classical inference procedures are violated if the same information is reused to estimate the parameters and investigate their reliability. In many applied situations such inconsistencies are either not recognized or are justified on grounds of simplicity, avoidance of complications, and the substantial uncertainty associated with selecting the proper maintained hypothesis or model specification—the last typically a result of the model specification alternatives mentioned earlier (Rausser and Johnson [1975]).

In the context of these difficulties the Bayesian approach at present seems to be the most viable one for selecting among alternative model specifications. The difficulty in making applications of it concerns the problem of isolating a structure sufficiently general that choices of alternative forms can be considered as nested hypotheses. In fact, Dhrymes et al. [1972] have recently suggested that, given the availability of informative prior distributions, the Bayesian approach to the model selection problem offers a far handier solution than the classical approach. Leamer [1970] has explored the implications of alternative weighting functions in this context, and Zellner [1971] has provided a general outline of Bayesian procedures for comparing and choosing among models. A useful summary and comparison of Bayesian and classical procedures for discriminating among alternative specifications of single-equation models has been presented by Gaver and Geisel [1974]. This treatment includes some promising classical developments as alternatives to the currently more popular Bayesian views on the discrimination problem.

Parameter estimation is also influenced if models are adaptive. Many times while systems models are being constructed, estimated, and simulated additional data on the structure becomes available or is actively sought. Although systematized procedures for handling the estimation problem in such models currently involve mathematical difficulties, applied systems modeling appears to be gravitating in this direction. Results which may be of some use in grasping these ideas are contained in Aoki [1975], Chow [1975], Prescott [1972], Rausser and Freebairn [1974a], Tse [1974], and Zellner [1971].

Verification. This is the process by which the investigator determines whether or not the model performs in accordance with the intended purpose.

For example, in algebraic models, verification is concerned with completeness, the existence of solutions, internal functioning, and the like. The most common use of the term, however, appears in conjunction with digital computer models or analogs. In this context the term relates to establishment of desired isomorphic relationships between system, model, and digital analog.

Validation. This represents the process of corroborating the model with the system. In the construction process validation is employed to evaluate the ability of the model to duplicate the required characteristics of the system and in fulfilling the modeling objectives. The process is clearly a judgmental question and as such presents a number of problems (Naylor and Finger [1967]). First, if the requirement is a close corroboration with the system, how should the data on the functioning of the system be summarized and compared to outputs of the model for tests of consistency? Second, how important is prior information relative to the data on the system and how should these two types of information be combined in corroborating the model?

At a more philosophical level, what framework should be employed to determine which hypotheses on the system are to be tested and which are to be maintained? The paradigm within which we operate also renders a number of questions unanswerable. Simulation and analytical methods are to an extent competing alternatives in the process. The basis for a choice between these alternatives is examined later.

Revision. The four preceding steps may be considered to be either a final process or a provisional process. In a provisional process the fifth or revision step is concerned with an assessment of whether or not the model should be altered to make it more suitable for the intended objectives. Information on which this decision is based may come from observing the system, on the basis of the implications of model outputs, a refinement of modeling objectives, or a refinement in the model.

Whatever revisions are made, it is important to specify systematically the sources of information and the process by which the information is to be used to revise the model. Such conditions are as much a part of the prior information used to construct the model as the more frequently employed theoretical underpinnings and data sources. If such specifications are not included, then the modeling process becomes identified with the investigator or the team involved in its construction. Its value for other research efforts or general scientific purposes is therefore severely limited. In short, by structuring this process we are narrowing the artistic or personal content of the models.

Applied work in systems modeling and simulation has been particularly weak regarding this aspect of model construction. That is, models presented in the literature usually evolve from provisional specifications. In fact, the flexibility of this evolutionary process is sometimes mentioned as an advantage of the approach and the resulting models. The unfortunate result of this approach, however, is that the scientific community interested in the research must often accept or reject the model on faith alone. While this may be acceptable from a functional and positive view, it makes the accumulation of knowledge on the system in question an inefficient process.

Adaptive Models

The preceding discussion concluded that iterative procedures by which systems models are typically constructed might be productively viewed within the context of an adaptive control framework. Choices of optimal decisions with respect to model specification and revision when viewed in an adaptive control framework are concerned with the dual effects of the improvement in the objective function which occurs as an indirect result of more reliable structure estimates and the more usual direct effects of setting the controls. Attractive features of this approach for economic decision problems are discussed in Aoki [1974], Chow [1975], Prescott [1967, 1971, 1972], Rausser and Freebairn [1974a, 1974b], Tse [1974], and Zellner [1971]. After a review of the essentials of the adaptive control formulation of sequential decision problems in the following section, the framework is shown to apply also to decision problems arising in model construction.

Decision and economic policy problems. The adaptive control framework in the context of economic decision problems involves a number of components: (1) Specification of the relevant decision maker(s) and the control or instrument variables available for manipulation. Decision points and procedures for revision of policy decisions, in the light of new information, should also be noted. (2) Specification of an objective function ranking the desirability of different states of the system. Arguments in this function are certain key performance variables, including endogenous and control variables, thought by the policy or decision makers to have significant implications for the problem under study. (3) Specification of constraints or a policy possibility set which includes (a) state transformation functions relating the internally determined variables in each period to the policy variables, other exogenous variables, and lagged variables describing the beginning state of the system, (b) initial conditions for the system, and (c) other constraints delineating the feasible control variable and endogenous variable spaces. (4) Specification of the processes of information generation, together with prescriptions for the analysis of data by policy makers as the decision sequence proceeds. The fourth component embraces mathematical learning processes whereby the additional information may be used to lessen initial uncertainties about objectives, the constraint functions, and states of the system.

In short, adaptive control methods are dynamic optimizing procedures (applied to multiperiod decision problems) in which imperfect knowledge is a key characteristic. A discrete period, sequential decision making process is assumed. In each decision period a policy is selected from a set of feasible actions so as to maximize the objective function. The constraint functions delineate the feasible policy space and specify the endogenous variables included in the objective function in terms of the instrument environmental or conditioning variables and the initial state of the system.

Operationally, uncertainty arises principally with respect to the effects of alternative policy actions on various performance variables, i.e., the constraint or transformation functions. Typically, the constraint functions are based on an approximated model of the system under consideration. A common (simplifying) procedure has been to estimate the model first (using the term in the general sense suggested earlier) and then to derive the "optimal" policy assuming the provisional parameter estimates are equal to their "true" values, where possible recognizing uncertainty of future exogenous variables and additive random disturbances which enter the model. Procedures for solving problems of this type involve the concept of certainty equivalence (Chow [1972], Holt [1962], Simon [1956], Theil [1964]). Treating the parameters as known with certainty, however, is obviously unsatisfactory. They are in general only approximations of the true but unknown, or perhaps even random, parameters.

The imperfect knowledge of the relationships comprising the constraints which specify effects of alternative policy decisions may be viewed as resulting from four major sources: (1) approximations, including omitted variables, simplifying mathematical functions, and various forms of aggregation which lead to the inclusion of stochastic rather than deterministic relationships; (2) data limitations (small samples); (3) structural changes; and (4) the future environment (uncertainty about future values of the noncontrollable or environmental variables).

Adaptive control methods explicitly recognize that as a system progresses through the sequence of periods data become available which can be used to update or revise the decision maker's perception of the policy possibility set. These revisions, in general, should not be regarded as separate from the derivation of an optimal policy. Alternative decisions may reveal more or less information about the actual system via different sets of the resulting data obtained. The inherent benefits of the additional information depend upon whether or not an "improved" representation of the structure results in superior future control. The incurred costs of such information emanate, in part, from the choice of a current policy which is less than optimal from a pure control point of view. In short, the optimal policy may involve decisions which are of a dual nature, particularly if losses associated with current decisions can be recovered in subsequent periods by utilizing improved information on the structure.

As previously noted, the adaptive control approach to decision and economic policy problems corresponds to Bellman's approach [1961, pp. 198-209] as well as Fel'dbaum's third class of control systems [1965, pp. 24-31]. In effect, optimal adaptive controls require a simultaneous solution to combined control and sequential experimental design problems and thus are dual in nature. This dual nature is characterized by three elements.

The first element concerns the direct effect of decisions on the criterion function. The total effects may include these direct effects of the decision variables themselves and, through the transformation functions relating the system at different states, their indirect effects on current and future values of the state or endogenous variables.

The second element is concerned with the learning process. Closed-loop control policies for each period, presuming the existence of a set of sufficient statistics, are conditioned on information related to the current state of the system and on the most recent estimate of the probability distribution function for the unknown elements of the decision problem. With respect to the unknown elements, as we proceed into the future additional sample information becomes available. These data additions allow learning to take place regarding, for example, unknown coefficients of the constraint functions. Formal procedures for utilizing sample additions to update probability distribution specifications include Bayesian methods, least squares revision methods, Kalman-type filters, as well as others. (For a discussion of Kalman-type filters, see Kalman [1960]; for an exposition of least squares revision methods, see Albert and Sittler [1965] and Freebairn and Rausser [1974]).

The third element concerns experimental design. Adaptive control strategies are conditional functions depending in part on the moments of the probability distribution functions for the unknown components of the decision problem. Normally, the expected value of the criterion function resulting from these strategies is improved, the more concentrated the probability function is about its expected value. Note also that the properties of the revised probability distribution functions (on which future decisions are based) depend on available sample information. Current decisions can influence the sample information which is generated and thus becomes available over future control periods. Since this information has a direct bearing on future estimates of the probability distribution functions and these in turn influence the efficiency of future decisions, an experimental dimension is involved in current actions.

The above considerations and implied models have been notably lacking in applications of systems and simulation to the various empirical problems in agricultural economics (Burt [1969]). Illustrative applications of these considerations are available in Rausser and Freebairn [1974a] and Rausser [1974a]. A more heuristic application, numerically exploring alternative policies, has been developed by Boehlje and Eisgruber [1972]. Engineers have also examined the applicability of these concepts to economic problems. Examples of these applications include the work of Buchanan and Norton [1971], Murphy [1968], and Perkins, Cruz, and Sundararajan [1972]. Formulations of adaptive control models have also been employed in mathematical and engineering fields, at least, in a theoretical context (Aoki [1967], Anstrom and Wittenmark [1971], Bar-Shalom and Sivan [1969], Bellman and Kalaba [1959], Curry [1970], Early and Early [1972], Gunckel and Franklin [1963], Kogan [1966], Tarn [1971], and Tse and Athans [1970, 1972]). From the viewpoint of economic policy the adaptive control formulation represents an extension of the pioneering models advanced by Tinbergen [1952] .

Formally the adaptive control problem may be specified in this way: Find the sequence of conditional policy strategies u_t^* (P^{t-1}, y_{t-1}), $t = 1, 2, \ldots, T$, to maximize

$$(1) \qquad J = E\ [W(y_1, u_1, y_2, u_2, \ldots, y_T, u_T)]$$

subject to

$$(2) \qquad y_t = \Phi_t\ (y_{t-1}, u_t, x_t, e_t) = \Phi_t\ (Z_t, e_t)$$

where $Z_t = [y_{t-1}, u_t, x_t]$

$$(3) \qquad P^t(\Phi_t^T, e_t^T, X_t^T) = I_t\ [P^{t-1}\ (\Phi_{t-1}^T, x_{t-1}^T), y_t, z_t)]$$

where $\Phi_t^T = (\Phi_t, \Phi_{t+1}, \ldots, \Phi_T)$ $e_t^T = (e_t, e_{t+1}, \ldots, e_T)$ $x_t^T =$ $(x_t, x_{t+1}, \ldots, x_T)$

$$(4) \qquad y_t \,\epsilon Y_t,\ u_t\ \epsilon U_t,$$

$$(5) \qquad y_0 = y(0),\ \text{and}$$

$$(6) \qquad P^0\ (\Phi_0^T, e_0^T, x_0^T = P\ (0)$$

In the preceding formulation W is the objective function, E is the expectation operator, y_t is an n x 1 vector of endogenous or state variables, u_t is an m x 1 vextor of control variables, x_t is an ℓ x 1 vector of noncontrollable exogenous variables, and e_t is an n x 1 vector of disturbance terms. The function P^t (.) denotes the joint probability distribution or its set of sufficient statistics conceived at time t. The sets Y_t and U_t represent n- and m-dimensional Euclidean vector spaces and are referred to as the admissible set of state and control variables, respectively. The n-dimensional vextor, y(o), denotes the initial prior probability distribution function.

The above specification assumes that the unknown components of the problem, Φ, e, and x, are concerned only with transformation functions (2). The objective or preference function, the planning horizon (T), and the initial conditions are presumed known. Furthermore, the state vectors y_t are assumed to be measured accurately (that is, the state of the system is completely accessible in each of the t periods). Note that the probability distribution functions (3) are sufficiently general to allow for the case in which distributions of the stochastic elements are known as well as the case in which these distributions are unknown. For the latter case, moments of the probability distributions are assumed to be stochastic and some a priori probability density for these moments is presumed to be available. Usually the disturbance terms e_t, are assumed to have zero expectation and to be intertemporally independent and identically distributed. This assumption can be relaxed, but at an increase in the cost of computations. Also multiple lag systems and measurement errors and delays in observing state or noncontrollable exogenous variables can be explicitly incorporated by operating with appropriately augmented constraint functions (2), or state vectors (Aoki [1967]). For constraint structures involving multiple lags, a state-space representation may be easily derived (Rausser [1974b]). Note also that three properties must be satisfied before the adaptive control or any other dynamic model representation can be given a meaningful interpretation. These properties are stability, controllability, and observability. Economists are familiar with stability analysis but are less familiar with the other two properties. The controllability property is concerned with reconstructability — that is, it is possible to uncover or recover unobservable system data. For a discussion of these properties and their importance in constructing systems models, see Aoki [1975].

Adaptive model construction. The adaptive control framework just described can be utilized to provide a basis for structuring the model revision process. As previously noted ad hoc revision processes can be viewed as involving inefficient use of the information gained from provisional specifications and as resulting in highly personalized final models. The attractive feature of the adaptive control framework in this context is not so much that it presents a basis for deriving a unique optimal path for the development of research models but that it provides a unifying set of activities for model construction and a norm against which the personalized strategies can be compared.

As noted later in the survey of applications, systems models applied to descriptive, behavioral, forecasting, and decision problems in agricultural economics are typically highly specialized to particular situations. Researchers begin with some concepts from theory, results of other applied work, perhaps some personal views, and historical data on the system to develop a provisional specification. Given constraints which exist with respect to resources available for the research project and the time frame within which the research is planned, the analyst proceeds from one provisional specification to another until a version of the model is available which, given the constraints, satisfies the objectives of the research endeavor. For institutional reasons, owing to the existence of experiment station projects, the objectives of the research process are usually stated in rather precise terms. Research budgets, available time, and other constraints are also known with a fair degree of certainty. As with the conventional adaptive control problem, one important issue is the uncertainty with respect to the effect of actions taken by the researcher on the ultimate modeling objective. By recognizing the process of proceeding from one provisional structure to another as a transition between states in the implicit control problem and by making more explicit the policy or strategy governing the evolution to the final version of the model, research involving systems models can be placed on a sound scientific footing. The availability of such information on model construction and the formalization of the implicit control problem provide a firm basis for critical appraisal of the resulting formulation and at the same time establish the foundation for a more systematic process of knowledge accumulation.

Model types. Special cases associated with the application of adaptive control concepts in developing model representations of systems may be viewed in terms of the various model types. For descriptive models the objective function would be stated incorporating the reliability with which the parameters describing the relations or systems in question can be obtained. Constraints would involve the untestable hypotheses governing the basic structure, assumptions about the probabilistic nature of the structure being estimated, and research budget restrictions. Given this situation, the researcher is in a position to view alternative strategies for developing the descriptive model as competing policies for the solution of the implicit control problem. Formalizing and structuring the associated learning processes may contribute to the ability to assess competing descriptive models and may provide a basis for contemplated extensions.

For behavioral and forecasting models the approach suggested by the adaptive framework is essentially the same. The major difference is of course in the formulation of the objective function. Different model purposes imply the inclusion of different arguments in the objective function used to evaluate the performance of the model construction process (Cooper [1972]). In the case of behavioral models emphasis is typically placed upon the reliability of specified causal relations. For forecasting models the objective would involve the properties of the forecast values vis-à-vis preconceptions about the operation of the system being studied and/or the observed outcomes for system variables.

In decision problems the adaptive control approach may be applied directly. The effectiveness of decision models is contingent upon the accuracy with which the system to be regulated has been characterized. Hence, development of an adequate model representation is just a component of the more general problem motivating the formulation of the decision model. The only differences occur when the development of the decision model takes place apart from the solution to the decision problem. It has been shown elsewhere (Fisher [1962]) that this approach to the solution of decision problems generally results in policies inferior to those which obtain when estimation is an integral part of the problem.

Tractability

The framework proposed for adaptive model construction is obviously demanding. In fact, solutions to the associated adaptive control problems of the type encountered in model construction are as yet limited to highly simplified structures. Even for the case of a quadratic objective function and linear constraints, it is presently impossible to express the optimal adaptive control explicitly in analytic form (Aoki [1967]). Furthermore, numerical solution procedures rapidly encounter the "curse of dimensionality" for even modest control problems. The simple and pedagogic models found in Marschak [1963] and Ying [1967] illustrate this computational burden.

Approximations to solutions are possible, however, and, although not currently viewed as such, they are the object of most simulations of systems models. From this perspective the tractability problem of model construction becomes somewhat different. Recognizing that a closed-form solution to the model construction process as posed in the previous discussion is possible only in highly restrictive cases (Tse and Bar-Shalom [1973], Tse, Bar-Shalom, and Meier [1973]), various feasible, near-optimal solutions may be applied routinely in the construction and operation of systems models.

The complexity this observation adds to the process of systems analysis is related to choices of models and tractability. On one hand, a model might be designed which could be specialized for a particular system by a rather routine application of the adaptive control framework. More complicated models, on the other hand, may prohibit such an application and thus become more highly personalized than the researcher might wish.

System versus model approximations. Models, in general, involve approximations of the system being studied—approximations in the sense that they are abstractions necessary to achieve useful research results. These approximations are a function of available knowledge of the system along with specifications required to serve the purpose(s) for which the model is constructed.

Since models are themselves systems, similar observations apply to approximations of models. This relationship is particularly important for the tractability problem. It suggests that researchers might find it worthwhile to use approximations of their models. Solutions to the control problem as formulated for the more simplified models could then be used in developing research strategies for the more complex model representations. If such simplifications can be made on systematic mathematical grounds (for example, Taylor's series approximations, stochastic structure, and so on), then the observations derived from these research strategies and subsequently applied to similar but more elaborate models may have greater generality. The previously noted value of the adaptive control framework would suggest that this approach, although not novel, could prove quite productive.

Analytical versus ad hoc simulation. Information gained at the various stages in the systems modeling process frequently occurs as a result of simulating provisional structures. The previous discussion has indicated that there is a choice about how such simulations or experiments might be conducted. If conducted on an ad hoc basis, they may contain less information than if systematically (analytically) structured. Given such a framework, design of the experiments can be viewed as an approximating procedure. Advantages of such optimum seeking procedures over ad hoc methods are widely accepted in economics. Hence, there is yet another reason for seriously considering the tractability problem in the design of systems models. More will be said later about the use of experimental designs. It suffices for now to indicate that recognition of this choice provides the basis for a useful link between the literature on systems and simulation and some rich results relating to optimal designs and evolutionary experimental procedures.

Simulation

Simulation is the method by which experimental information about systems or models of systems is generated. It is used in formulating, evaluating, and applying models of systems. These methods range from ad hoc trials to highly structured procedures used for numerical approximations (Naylor, Wertz, and Wonnacott [1967, 1968]). In this section we discuss major types of simulation and systems modeling.

Analogs

Most applications of systems concepts begin with the construction of a symbolic model. These symbolic models may incorporate flow charts, algebraic statements, and various types of physical items. Although such formulations may be useful in aiding the conceptualization of the system being studied, they do not necessarily lend themselves to experimental processes. The exception is of course when the statement of the model is itself a computer program.

To simulate a model, it is frequently necessary to convert it into a form more convenient for the intended trials. These alternative constructs are typically physical or digital analogs. When they are isomorphic to the algebraic statement of the model, results of the experiments conducted using them can be more effectively employed as a basis for studying the function of the model or system.

Physical analogs are most commonly used in gaming, teaching, and behavioral types of activities. Gaming models are always at least partially physical in nature. Models used in teaching and in extension activities also tend to be physical since they are set in an interactive operative mode. Finally, many behavioral experiments are physical analogs. Consumer panels used in determining attitudes and preferences are illustrative of the physical analogs used in behavioral investigations.

Physical models or analogs have been less important in agricultural economics than in other applied sciences. The extensive use of prototypes and analog computers in engineering, for example, finds few counterparts in agricultural economics. However, the behavioral option, particularly in the context of "experimental economics" has the most potential for further application (Naylor [1972], V. L. Smith [1962]).

Digital analogs are used in computer simulations. It is in this area that the impact of the current computer technology on systems studies is most evident. Such analogs can be constructed using any of a number of programming languages currently available. In fact, the concern with programming efficiency led early investigators to develop special purpose computer languages.

There are several levels of communication which correspond directly to machine functions. At a higher level, assembly languages are mnemonic symbols which are defined in terms of, and can be translated into, basic machine language. A compiler is a program which accepts statements written in complex and high-level languages and converts them to basic machine language. Most compilers are problem oriented and different from machine and assembly languages. They are composed of language symbols and operations required by a special type of problem. COBAL, for instance, is a problem oriented language applicable to problems involved in the data handling aspects of accounting. Finally, simulation programming languages are just special types of problem oriented languages. In fact, it is worth noting that these special-purpose languages have developed in an evolutionary manner usually in association with large and extended investigations involving the simulation of various systems models (Kiviat [1967], Krasnow and Merikallio [1964]).

As these languages are designed to facilitate experiments with particular types of models, it is natural to conclude that their principal objectives are (1) to provide data representations that permit straightforward and efficient modeling, (2) to permit the facile portrayal and reproduction of dynamics within modeling systems, and (3) to facilitate the study of stochastic systems (that is, they contain procedures for the generation and analysis of random variables) and time series.

Aside from these common objectives, even the more general simulation programming languages are problem focused. For example, SIMSCRIPT II is an event-oriented language and therefore is useful in simulating systems which can be viewed as sequences of events with particular types of attributes. Various types of management and behavioral problems lend themselves to simulations with this special programming language (Kiviat, Villaneuva, and Markowitz [1968]). DYNAMO is a special-purpose language used to study closed systems of continuous variables in which the broad characteristics of information feedback within the system are important attributes in determining dynamic performance. This language was developed in connection with the industrial dynamics advanced by Forrester [1961]. SIMULATE, developed by Holt et al. [1965] is concerned with capturing those parameters and decision variables critical in the determination of model stability.

CSL is an activity-oriented language (IBM [1966a]) useful for simulating models based upon systems involving queues, waiting lines, sequencing of events in an efficient manner, and the like. GPSS is a transaction language (IBM [1966b]) which can be used to simulate problems involving efficient processing of individuals, ships, and cars.

In summary, these special-purpose computer languages facilitate simulation of various types of systems models. They are somewhat more removed from the basic languages than the common scientific computer languages such as FORTRAN and require more elaborate compilers. However, they tend to facilitate the processing of particular types of statements or commands in a very efficient manner. Current trends are for these special language characteristics to be integrated into more versatile computer programming languages (Naylor [1971]). Unless substantial amounts of simulation of a particular type are anticipated or the simulation problems require very specialized language features, investments in such languages for applied researchers do not appear to be economical.

Verification

Uses of simulation in verification are commonplace in the agricultural economics applications, especially when the models and analogs are digital. As most applications of systems methods incorporate digital models or analogs, we confine examination of verification to its use in the context of computer simulation. As noted previously, this process is mechanical and is intended to determine whether the digital analog operates in accord with the model specification.

Digital models of systems are often large and complex both in terms of program logic and stochastic structure. Moreover, the models are generally of dynamic systems. The first step in the process should therefore include checks for syntax and other possible specification and programming errors. Secondly, the output variables may require checking (say, with the sample data) to appraise the ability of the program to reproduce the data on which it is based.

In these verification processes the logic of the model is appraised numerically. In this sense, acceptable results are not always reassuring for the possibility of obtaining unacceptable ones, especially if the model is stochastic. Another difficulty arises from comparisons of outputs with data. This might be done, for example, to see whether the summarizations of the observed data (say, for some type of multivariate distribution or stochastic process) are appropriate. Since these models frequently include statistics which are not sufficient and prior information which has not been efficiently combined with the observed data, the comparisons may be inconclusive for verification.

Validation

The appropriateness of a particular model of a system can be viewed from two standpoints. First, as is commonly done, the performance of the structure can be investigated for its ability to reproduce or predict the variables in the system which are internally determined. When these investigations can be performed on a sampling basis, useful statistical results are available for evaluating and choosing between possible structural models (Rausser and Johnson [1975]). Second, models of large and complex systems are likely to employ specifications implied by normative propositions. As much of the structural specification may follow from these propositions, it is natural to assess their generality in corroborating the model with the system. This of course takes us away from the positivistic approach to validation and into some more general philosophical questions (G. L. Johnson and Zerby [1973], Kuhn [1970]).

PHILOSOPHICAL ISSUES

Application of Kuhn's [1970] notion of a paradigm to economics is becoming increasingly fashionable. In the present context it is useful to note that a paradigm typically defines a large set of possible hypotheses and makes no claims for the validity of any particular member of that set. Paradigms, unlike the hypotheses to which they give rise, cannot be validated by experimental or statistical methods. For example, the purely competitive model is not a hypothesis but a paradigm; although a specific hypothesis embodying some version of the competitive model can, in principle, be tested, the competitive model cannot. This does not suggest that the competitive model ought to be abandoned. On the contrary, since abstractions from details are essential, usable models must be misspecifications of the system to which they refer. The only option is to construct models which fall short of a complete specification of the system under examination. In this sense all model representations are partially reduced forms (owing to omission of variables, distortion of relationships, aggregation) even though frequently identified as structural models. It is always possible to imagine a more fundamental explanation of the phenomenon under examination involving more equations and thus internally determined variables. Hence it appears reasonable to suggest (1) that models cannot be solely judged by the resemblance between their specification and the systems which they are designed to represent and (2) that the choice of different model specifications of the same system by different investigators implies no presumption that one of them must be in error. For these reasons, it is safer to investigate "sufficiency" (the adequacy of the constructed model for the purposes designed) than "realism."

THE CLASSICAL SITUATION

When considered in connection with alternative structural specifications (and methods of estimating parameters), the classical concept of validation becomes rather vague. Classical statistical techniques of validating estimated relationships are in principle straightforward (Ramsey [1969], Ramsey and Zarembka [1971]). Data required for an assumed structure are obtained through sampling the population, and parameters are estimated and inferences are made on the basis of sampling distributions of the statistics. Under sufficiently strong distributional assumptions the process of establishing the validity of the model is a matter of examining its predictive power as well as agreement of the estimated parameters with qualitative restrictions implied by the underlying theory. Acceptable parameter values and accurate predictions are also standards by which the validity of more general types of systems models may be evaluated. Methods for examining properties of these structural models are, however, far from standard (Rausser and Johnson [1975]).

ALTERNATIVE STRUCTURAL SPECIFICATIONS

The first point of departure from the classical situation is the possibility of alternative structural specifications. As the theoretical basis for systems

Evaluation Criteria for Investigating the Explanatory and Predictive Power of Systems Models

	Explanatory	Predictive[d]

Point Criteria	1. Coefficient of multiple determination[a]
	2. Durbin-Watson statistic[b]
	
	3. Graphical analysis of residuals
	
	4. t statistic[b]
		1. Mean forecast error[c] (changes and levels)
		2. Mean absolute forecast error[c] (changes and levels)
		3. Mean squared forecast error[c] (changes and levels)
		4. Any of the above relative to[c]
		  a. the level or variability of the predicted variable
		  b. a measure of "acceptable" forecast error for alternative forecasting needs and horizons

	5. Chi-square or F statistics[b]
	6. Aitchison-Silvey test [1958] of a priori restrictions
	7. Ramsey specifications error tests [1969] [b]
	  a. omitted variable test
	  b. functional form test
	  c. simultaneous equation test
	  d. heteroscedasticity test
	  e. chi-square "goodness-of-fit" test for normality
	8. Sample mean squared error[c] (changes and levels)
	9. Information inaccuracy statistics for sample data
		5. t statistic[b]
		6. Chi-square or F statistics[b]
		
		7. Theil's inequality coefficient[e]
		
		8. Information inaccuracy statistics for nonsample data

Tracking Criteria	1. Number of sample turning points missed 2. Number of turning points falsely explained 3. Number of sample under or over estimations	1. Number of nonsample turning points missed 2. Number of turning points falsely predicted 3. Number of nonsample under or over prediction

	Explanatory	Predictive[d]
	4. Rank correlation of $\Delta\hat{y}_t$ and Δy_t[f]	4. Rank correlation of $\Delta\hat{y}_n$ and Δy_n[f]
	5. Test of randomness for directional explanations	5. Test of randomness for directional predictions
	6. Test of randomness for explained turning points	6. Test of randomness for predicted turning points
	7. Information theory statistics for sample data[g]	7. Information theory statistics for nonsample data[g]
Error Criteria	1. Bias and variance of explained error	1. Bias and variance of forecast error
	2. Errors in start-up position versus errors in explained changes ($\Delta\hat{y}_t$)	2. Errors in start-up position versus errors in predicted changes ($\Delta\hat{y}_t$)
	3. Comparison with various "naive" explanations	3. Comparison with various "naive" forecasts
	4. Comparison with indicator qualitative errors	4. Comparison with "judgmental," "consensus," or other noneconometric forecasts
Spectral Criteria	1. Comparison of power spectra for estimated and sample data series	1. Comparison of power for predicted and nonsample data series
	2. Spectral serial correlation test of structural or reduced form sample disturbances	2. Spectral serial correlation test of structural or reduced form nonsample disturbances
	3. Cross-spectral statistics of relationships between estimated and actual sample values	3. Cross-spectral statistics of relationships between predicted and actual nonsample values

[a]This measure, like a number of the other measures presented, is strictly applicable only to single-equation models. Some multiple-equation counterparts of this measure are discussed in Dhrymes et al. [1972].

[b]These criteria represent only approximate small-sample tests if the assumptions of the classical model are not fulfilled (Ramsey [1969]).

[c]Classical hypothesis testing procedures cannot be employed for these statistics since their small-sample properties are generally unknown.

[d]This column is adapted from Dhrymes et al. [1972].

[e]For a critical appraisal of this predictive criterion, see Jorgenson et al. [1970].

[f]$\hat{y}_t$ denotes values of endogenous variables obtained from the model, y_t is the corresponding observation, $t = 1, \ldots, T$. For the prediction of nonsample observation period, $n = T + 1, \ldots, T + m$, a similar designation.

[g]These statistics are descriptive measures of observed (explained and unexplained), model (correct and incorrect), and joint (corresponding and noncorresponding) information.

analysis is far from complete, this is the usual situation (Heady [1971], H. G. Johnson [1951], Thorbecke [1971]). At issue is the comparative validity of the two or more structural models.[5] A host of alternative evaluation criteria can be utilized in assessing the validity of alternative systems models. As some authors have suggested, these various criteria should be examined in the context of a "Sherlock Holmes inference" approach—that is, a process of data analysis involving Sherlock the analyst assembling bits of evidence to produce a plausible story (Dhrymes et al. [1972]). This evaluation may involve attempts to determine both explanatory and predictive powers of the systems models.

Criteria advanced to examine the explanatory (nonpredictive) power of systems models are associated with comparisons of estimated and sample values of internally determined variables. Specifically, conventional measures of "goodness of fit" complemented by "change of direction" tests or tracking criteria assume importance in this context. A number of tests that might be employed to evaluate the explanatory power of systems models are indicated in the accompanying list. They are most meaningful when parameters of the models have been systematically estimated without recourse to artificial conditioning variables (for example, time counters in time series data). In systems models with substantial numbers of dummy shift variables and time counters these internal consistency tests lose much of their value. Little is revealed about the validity of the model from consistency tests in such instances since the model becomes simply a mechanism for reproducing the sample data.

Comparing alternative models on the basis of their explanatory power rests on the idea that the model which explains the sample data best is most valid. Comparisons of this type are difficult since some model representations may perform well on the basis of one or more criteria but poorly on the basis of others. Thus a weighting scheme of some sort is required. Generally, the degree of model validity increases with the number of positive results registered.

These explanatory comparisons are frequently based either on analysis of variance and results of test statistics widely used in statistical inference or on direct comparisons of the estimated values of the jointly determined variables with sample data. In the former case comparisons can be made by testing differences in explanatory powers of reduced forms (Dhrymes et al. [1972]). In the latter case a number of alternatives are available for evaluating the "goodness of fit" of the simulated series and sample data. These tests range from classical chi-square analysis to more sophisticated comparisons involving the use of spectral analysis (Fishman and Kiviat [1967], Howrey [1971], Rausser and Johnson [1975]). Comparison of simulated and actual series seems to be a natural alternative for evaluating validity, although (as noted below) it has distinct limitations.

With nonsample data available alternative models can be compared on the basis of their ability to forecast or predict values of the endogenous or internally determined variables. An evaluation of the predictive power of alternatives systems models represents a more formidable examination than the evaluation of the explanatory power of such models. Typically, a wide variety of alternative models or theories presents approximately equivalent degrees of validity on the basis of explanatory or "goodness of fit" criteria. As a consequence, more stringent predictive performance criteria are usually sought. A number of these are included in the list of evaluation criteria. Each involves an assessment of the homogeneity of predictions for alternative models with nonsample data.

Model comparisons based on predictive criteria appear to be made better on an ex post rather than an ex ante basis. With ex post predictions observed values of the exogenous or conditioning variables can be utilized. All errors then result from the structural specification and parameter estimates. No impurities are created by errors in forecasting the values of the exogenous variables. There are few special situations (involving linear systems models and well-behaved error terms) in which forecasting performance procedures yield classical statistical tests (Jorgenson, Hunter, and Nadiri [1970], Dhrymes et al. [1972]). In the more general situations, however, no statistical tests appear to be available at this time. This simply reflects the fact that statisticians have not yet succeeded in developing techniques for evaluating sequences of dynamically generated forecasts for a set of jointly determined variables.

For systems models one departure from the classical situation which frequently arises is data availability. Current experience reveals that sufficient data are not available for the larger systems models (Dudley and Burt [1973], Fletcher, Graber, Merrill, and Thorbecke [1970], Halter, Hayenga, and Manetsch [1970], Manetsch, Hayenga, et al. [1971], Thorbecke [1971]). As indicated, the only alternative is to supply missing or nonestimable parameter values from prior knowledge, based either on experience with similar relationships from corresponding situations or on educated guesses. The adaptive estimation procedures required in the case of insufficient data leave little to salvage in terms of classical validation methods (Van Horn [1971]). Predictive tests based on sample data have less meaning owing to the sequential or adaptive estimation procedures. Tests of estimates of individual parameters are also of limited value for the same reasons. Finally, it is highly unlikely that scarce data will be reserved for testing the model. When data limitation problems are considered along with problems of alternative structural representations, it is clear that conventional approaches to validation are largely uninformative. The inconclusiveness of these approaches has led researchers to use internal consistency to examine large-scale and nonlinear systems models.

INTERNAL CONSISTENCY

Suppose a model describing a system has been estimated and tested where possible with classical statistical procedures. If the results of this first validation procedure are not convincing, further information on the validity of the structural model may be sought. One source of such information is an investigation of the dynamic implications of the system representation. If these dynamic implications corroborate the established theory on the functioning of the system, then the investigation yields results which support the validity of the model. On the other hand, if the dynamic implications do not corroborate the theory and institutional knowledge, the validity of the model may be questioned.

There are well-established methods for investigating the dynamic implications of both linear and nonlinear structural models (Adelman and Adelman [1959], Evans [1969], Fishman and Kiviat [1967], Howrey [1971], Howrey and Kelejian [1971], Howrey and Klein [1972], Rausser and Johnson [1975]). These methods are based upon the fact that lagged relationships in systems models can be viewed as difference or differential equations. Aside from straightforward impact multiplier analyses based directly on the reduced forms, other types of multipliers (for example, interim, cumulated, and equilibrium multipliers) based on final forms or solutions of difference equations can be used for examinations of stability and convergence. Applications of methods for examining internal consistency typically proceed by using the estimated reduced form. The procedure is to insert the partially tested estimates of the structural parameters, obtain the reduced form, and determine its dynamic properties. Other forms of the model can also be employed to ascertain the dynamic properties of the structural model. For further details, see Rausser [1974a].

Both analytical and simulation methods can be used to examine the properties of systems of the type usually encountered (Fishman [1967], Fishman and Kiviat [1967], Howrey and Kelejian [1969], Naylor [1970], Rausser and Johnson [1975]). Although there is currently some disagreement about the circumstances under which one general method is preferred to another, the following guidelines seem reasonable (Howrey and Kelejian [1969], Naylor [1970]). For nonstochastic and comparatively simple linear and nonlinear models analytical methods offer advantages to ad hoc simulations (Howrey and Kelejian [1969], Rausser and Johnson [1975]). As the models become large and sampling or prior distributions of the parameter estimates as well as the stochastic disturbances entering the system are recognized, simulation methods seem to be more tractable means of obtaining information about the dynamic behavior of the system (Nagar [1969]). Although simulation methods have the advantage of being applied to the structural form of the model, the general implications of the simulated series are in many cases unclear. Hence, ad hoc simulation as a means of obtaining dynamic properties is recommended only when analytical methods or analytical simulation methods are not feasible (Rausser and Johnson [1975]).

NORMATIVE CONSIDERATIONS

Models of economic systems are typically behavioral in nature. The behavioral expressions incorporated in the structures of such models may be distilled from previous empirical and theoretical investigations or may be descriptive as in the case of firm or process systems models. The behaviorialist view is that these relationships are descriptive and do not require inquiries about their normative underpinnings. The positive view would assert that the implicit normative assumptions contained in the behavioral specifications are unimportant. If the model containing these behavioral conditions lacks predictive power, then its use is rejected. Neither of these approaches, however, represents a very comfortable position for applied models of economic systems (G. L. Johnson and Zerby [1973]). It is well known that specifications of individual supply and demand functions involve normative considerations. In the purely competitive theory we are tightly confined by a paradigm. Departures tend to include implicit value judgments about the advisability of concentration in industries, land reforms, income redistributions, and so on. It is pleasant to contemplate generating such statements or relations from primitive and widely acceptable normative assumptions and thus capturing a detailed specification of the paradigm governing the model. However, economic theory is not rich enough to provide such a structure for models of complex economic systems. We are left, therefore, with models including behavioral relationships which involve nonprimitive and possibly conflicting normative assumptions.

Experimentation

Two observations have been made regarding simulation. First, it is a method of experimenting with models of systems. Second, given the purposeful intent of simulation whether used in model construction or application, it is beneficial to systematize choices of design points. The second observation follows naturally if simulation processes are viewed within a control framework. Methods of systematizing experiments with systems models as they relate to experimental design are considered in this section.

SENSITIVITY ANALYSIS

Sensitivity analysis is simply the process of gathering information with which to evaluate the robustness of decisions taken in constructing and applying models (Maffei [1958]). In model construction, for example, the internally determined variables may be examined for their sensitivity to choices in parameters, structure, or environmental conditioning variables. The corresponding sensitivity or variation would of course be evaluated using an implicit or explicit criterion function. Applications, whether for descriptive, behavioral, forecasting, or decision models, can be subjected to similar types of evaluations.

In sensitivity analysis interest is directed to areas where doubt, uncertainty, and ignorance are greatest. A model which is very sensitive to changes in assumptions about which there is substantial uncertainty will warrant skepticism. A useful distinction to keep in mind in this regard is the difference between local and global sensitivity (Zellner and Peck [1973]). In a local sense many models may be insensitive to changes in exogenous factors, parameters, and so on, but very sensitive to such changes in a global sense. For these situations, the investigator should report the "range" of the constructed model's robustness.

The important aspect of sensitivity analysis, in general, is its experimental nature. Hence, in selecting the trials or experiments to be conducted in a sensitivity examination, the researcher can choose between ad hoc and formal experimental design settings. The literature relating to the advantages and disadvantages of such choices is extensive. (See Burdick and Naylor [1966], Fishman [1971a, 1971b], From [1969], Friedman [1971], Gordon [1970], and Kleijnen [1974, 1975].) The advantage of making experimental design choices is of course associated with the increase in information which results from a systematic selection of the experiments (Hufschmidt [1962], Hunter and Naylor [1970]).

Application of experimental designs methods to problems of model sensitivity have received increased attention in the literature. Ignall [1972], Naylor [1970], Naylor, Burdick, and Sasser [1967], and Zellner and Peck [1973] illustrate the use of these methods and the types of results that can be obtained. Methods employed in designing simulation experiments have been rather routine. Complete factorial experiments are by far the most common. It is clear, however, that as familiarity with experimental methods increases more sophisticated designs will be employed (Kleijnen [1974]). Such designs are particularly valuable when specialized types of information are sought or when the number of factors and levels make a complete factorial experiment infeasible (Kleijnen [1975]). The advantage of the more specialized techniques is that trade-offs for the designs are known in advance (Handscomb [1969]). That is, the researcher using such a design would know which hypotheses are maintained and which are testable given the choices on factors, factor levels, design points, spread, and center. Extensive reviews and expositional treatments of complete factorial, incomplete block, composite, and other more common types of experimental designs useful in systems work are contained in John [1971], Mendenhall [1968], and Kleijnen [1974, 1975].

RESPONSE SURFACES

Response surfaces are simply functional relationships between parameters, environmental variables, structural choices, and, perhaps, criterion functions and internally determined variables (Naylor, Burdick, and Sasser [1967]). Such surfaces may be used in evaluating dynamic properties of models, corroborating them with information from the system, determing internal properties or consistency, and verification. As with sensitivity analysis it is important to recognize that when such relationships cannot be obtained as closed-form solutions, numerical approximation procedures must be employed which are in fact experiments. Again, the investigator is faced with the problem of systematic versus ad hoc choices of the factors selected for examination.

The literature on response surfaces is rich and contains well-developed procedures which have substantial potential for systems studies. The first applications in an agricultural context, though not to systems models as such, were made by Finney [1945]. More recent work on the study of response surfaces, however, dates from important papers by Box [1954] and Box and Wilson [1951]. These papers contain clear statements of the philosophical basis for response surface examination and sequential experimental designs. The latter problem amounts to a multistage exploratory investigation of response surfaces.

In relating the statistical literature to systems studies we should first indicate an important point of distinction. The development of the response surface literature occurred largely in association with the study of industrial processes (John [1971]). For this type of study the intent was not so much to explore the entire surface as it was to capture some efficient level of the process surface. The contrast between uses of the technique may be important for descriptive, behavioral, and forecasting models. In these cases it may be necessary to have knowledge of an entire region of the surface and not just a configuration created by a sequence of smaller evolutionary experiments. With such qualifications in mind, the expository results contained in the collection of works edited by Davies [1954] and in the review paper by Hill and Hunter [1966] are recommended as useful references on response surfaces.

Aspects of response surface investigations from the standpoint of sequential analysis and optimal design are developed in a technical but comprehensive review by Chernoff [1972]. As stated earlier, the analytical problems associated with optimal choices of sequential designs are basically problems in control theory. Note that although analytical solutions are practical only for small problems, the framework should still prove useful. In particular, simulation of systems models using this framework provides for viewing the process as simply an approximation to the solution of a complex analytical problem. The framework allows research investigators to focus on useful principles which can be used in simulating systems models, whatever the purpose. This assertion assumes added importance in the context of model tractability and the possibility of developing research strategies using models of models.

EXPERIMENTAL DESIGNS

Numerous choices exist with respect to experimental design. Such choices are of course made in the context of the system purpose, the nature of the experimental problem, and the resources available to the researcher. Given decisions on the factors and factor levels, the assumption on the nature of the response surface and characteristics of interest determine the design (Hill and Hunter [1966]).

First-order experimental designs are used to generate information necessary to fit first-degree (linear) equations. Once the sample information is obtained, such equations may be estimated by standard statistical techniques. That is, by ordinary least squares techniques. These techniques yield parameter estimates with desirable sampling characteristics if estimation problems are assumed to be independent of decision criteria and the experiments are not sequential. Aside from matters concerned with scaling of factors, designs for obtaining the required data are quite easily constructed. This simple design problem follows from the lack of complexity of the assumed response function. Optimal designs are defined as those which for arbitrary residual variances give a minimum value for the trace of the variance-covariance matrix of the estimated coefficients. Examples of optimal designs are 2 n-p factorials and the Plackett-Burman designs (John [1971]).

Second-order experimental designs are used to generate sample information required to fit second-order polynomial surfaces. As it can be argued that such surfaces approximate more complex ones via Taylor series expansions, higher-order designs are usually not employed. Additional reasons for confining attention to second-order designs are complications introduced by the generation of data necessary to fit higher-order polynomials.

Most designs used in fitting second-order polynomials are symmetric and are scaled to prevent problems associated with units of measure. Examples of such designs are central composites, incomplete factorials, and complete factorials. The applicability of the designs for particular problems is determined by the number of coefficients in the polynomial to be estimated, reliability requirements, and available resources for the experiments (John [1971], Naylor, Burdick, and Sasser [1967], Shechter and Heady [1970]).

"Sequential" experimental designs are simply procedures for conducting sequences of experiments. More ad hoc types of procedures are available in Box [1957] and Box and Hunter [1959]. These designs explore response surfaces by first estimating them for restricted regions and then moving on to estimate other regions on the basis of the information obtained. As J. R. Anderson [1974a] points out, "it is possible to program the automatic location of successive experiments (according to some steepest ascent procedure) and the automatic switching to the intensive search which may be accomplished by simply supplementing the last factorial or triangle design into a composite or hexagonal second-order design, respectively." Gradient and steepest ascent methods are used when such sequences are seeking stationary points in the response surface.

"Policy improvement" experimental designs make use of a number of available policy improvement or optimizing techniques (Emshoff and Sisson [1970]). These techniques often involve sequential designs which begin with an extensive search via simple exploratory experiments arranged so as to converge toward some peak (or valley) of the surface and subsequently to switch to intensive search methods as the optimum is approached. The intensive methods are typically based on second-order response functions while the extensive searches are based on two-level complete factorials (Cochran and Cox [1957]) and "equilateral triangle" designs (Mihram [1972]). For surfaces characterized by irregularities and discontinuities, of course, an exhaustive search will be required (Conlisk and Watts [1969]).

More formal optimizing designs may be based upon methods of optimal control. Dynamic programming solutions appear to be a practical option for designs in smaller problems. For larger problems associated with selecting among various designs at different stages in the decision process, complex error structures, and numerous factors and levels, the only alternative is some type of approximation (Chernoff [1972]).

SIMULATION AND PREPOSTERIOR ANALYSIS

Agricultural economics as an applied discipline is concerned with problems of estimating response functions (usually technical) for use in resource allocation problems. But attempts to obtain more reliable estimates of parameters in themselves present resource allocation problems. As with the more general sequential experiments discussed above, the process of estimating response functions can be viewed as a type of control problem.

The criterion in such problems is implicitly a functional involving within-period gains resulting from the experiment. The structure is given by the nature of the function to be estimated. Control variables are defined for alternative designs, design characteristics, and the extent of experimentation. One difficulty with this framework for response surface estimation involving physical experiments is that the additional information provided by the experimentation is not known until the trials are conducted. If the process is perceived in a Bayesian context (with posterior parameter distributions at one point in time becoming prior distributions in the next), then the revised parameter estimates cannot be known until the posterior distributions are calculated. A promising approach to this problem has been applied by Anderson and Dillon [1968]. They suggest that simulations of a systems model—incorporating what is known of the population and sampling characteristics of the error sources—be employed in numerically examining the problem of optimally allocating resources in response surface research. This process is referred to as preposterior analysis.

Simulations of systems models constructed for this purpose can be useful in providing information on the potential of additional nonsynthetic experimental information. This is especially evident in traditional response surface estimation problems. The concept is also of value in giving guidelines for the design of experiments to estimate the information content of additional sample data. These methods would seem to be applicable to situations in which exploratory research is being conducted for the purpose of developing useful descriptive or behavioral structural models of economic systems, especially where additional data may be required.

Possibilities exist for applications of preposterior analysis in the estimation of response surfaces and the construction of some behavioral and descriptive economic models. However, for research on the structure of economic models, the process may be somewhat more complicated. Complications arise in interpreting simulated data when multiple responses are present (the usual situation) and in establishing the connection between exploratory developments and the underlying theory. Although the problems just mentioned limit its operational value at present, the appeal of the method for systematically utilizing synthetically generated data commends it as an alternative in the application of systems and simulation analysis to agricultural economics research.

Artificial Intelligence and Heuristic Methods

A promising application of simulation concepts is in the development of artificial intelligence. Models utilizing this concept attempt to recreate decision makers' thought and discovery processes, rules of thumb applied to complex real-world systems, intelligent behavior, and effective problem-solving or search methods. They embrace a philosophy for approaching problems heuristically rather than with an organized and definable set of techniques. For many problems not solvable by classic mathematical and statistical models, these methods may be useful. They involve attempts to move toward optimum-seeking solution procedures rather than optimal solutions (Kuehn and Hamburger [1963]).

Artificial intelligence is characterized by Meier, Newell, and Pazer [1969] as "efficient use of the computer to obtain apparently intelligent behavior rather than to attempt to reproduce the step-by-step thought process of a human decision maker." It is concerned with computer oriented heuristics designed to accomplish such items as search, pattern recognition, and organization planning (Chen [1971], Hare [1967], G. E. Lee [1974]). In a more sophisticated setting it may also include learning and inductive inference.

Although systems models, simulation, and allied techniques were suggested early as means for generating information about economic systems (Clarkson and Simon [1960], Shubik [1960], Simon and Newell [1958]), related heuristic programming and learning constructs have received little attention by agricultural economists. The process of constructing and simulating any model of a system can be viewed loosely as one of developing artificial intelligence. Hence, the observed lack of associated applications is based mainly on the absence of formal consideration of these processes.

The connection of these processes with the theory of learning (Bush and Estes [1959]) is apparent. Heuristic programming and learning theory have been most popular in the study of games (Shubik [1960]). However, they have wide potential applicability in exploratory research associated with the eclectic models employed in agricultural economics. From an economic point of view and in relation to decision models, learning theory is an allocation problem. Hence, applications of heuristic programming and the generation of artificial intelligence fit nicely with the overall adaptive control theory framework. These and the previous comments on the use of synthetically generated data and preposterior analysis present a formal basis on which learning about economic structures and technical response surfaces can proceed. In a more decision oriented context dual control provides a framework within which exploratory models and policies can be developed.

In addition to the areas already mentioned or implied, there are other avenues for possible application of heuristic methods. One is experimental economics (Castro and Weingarten [1970], MacCrimmon and Tota [1969], Naylor [1972], V. L. Smith [1962, 1964], Watts [1969]). Most of these studies are closely connected with the gaming models in which learning and heuristic programming methods found initial application. Few propositions of the traditional economic theories of individual behavior have been tested in controlled experiments; the few tests available refer mostly to the equilibrating process of simple competitive markets (Kagel et al. [1975]). In comparison with other social sciences where theoretical foundations are not as unified, this is a striking statement. Applications of systems methods in obtaining information about how agents learn and operate within various economic systems would appear to have substantial potential. Simulation methods could be applied advantageously to generate artificial intelligence about the behavior of these economic agents. Some initial efforts in this direction are mentioned in the discussion of gaming literature.

Interpretation

Interpreting results of the simulation of systems models presents substantial problems. More specifically, the amount of data or output generated from simulating large-scale stochastic systems models often gives rise to difficulties. Aside from providing a boon to the paper industry, ill-considered objectives of the research analysis result in the investigator being overwhelmed by a mass of computer output. To be useful the output must be in summarized form (Kleijnen [1972]). Such summaries, however, are likely to be conditioned on the basis of the type of model, the nature of the system, and the purpose of the modeling exercise. As these summaries contain different types of information, it is important that choices of such vehicles be made on an informed basis.

For stochastic and dynamic model representations summary measures of probability distributions over time are frequently required. In this context the "multiple response problem" is often encountered. An outcome may be treated as one of many experiments, each with a single response, or all responses may be combined into a single response. The latter procedure, of course, involves the explicit formulation of a utility or criterion function.

In general, summary measures based on preference function specifications reflect several goals and thus multidimensional structures are relevant. Two general cases of multidimensional preference functions may be distinguished: (1) a scalar valued function providing a single overall utility index may be specified if the various dimensions of utility can be amalgamated in some way; and (2) where amalgamation is not possible (that is, where it is not possible to convert various objectives or goals into a common rubric), but where it is possible to rank goals in order of preference or priority, a lexicographically ordered preference or vector valued function may be specified.[6] In addition, some combination of these two specifications might be employed. Amalgamation procedures require specifying barter terms or trade-offs among different goals. To be sure, for most models a scalar valued preference function simplifies the computation and presentation of the numerical results. When the goals or arguments are not comparable, or when they cannot be expressed on a quantitative scale, or when the marginal rate of substitution between them is zero (lexicographic orderings), the investigator may resort to a vector valued function for his specification.

Other problems associated with summary measures based on preference functions emanate from their temporal dimensions. In particular, questions related to time preference rates and discount factors are raised. These complications of course are in no way unique to interpretations of simulation results.

DESCRIPTIVE MODELS

Output from simulations of descriptive models may be used to make decisions on further refinements of the model or advanced as an addition to the scientific knowledge on the system being studied. If such outputs are used to revise the descriptive model, then they are best interpreted using some type of objective function governing the revision process. If such an index, amalgamating the various performance measures which might be desired in the descriptive model, can be formed, then the simulations can be systematically viewed. Under these conditions, appropriate summary statistics and relationships to be reported are suggested by the objective or criterion function, model structure, and system.

The presentation of results for evaluating the descriptive models is a more difficult problem. The reason is that any summary of results involves an assumption about how the model is to be used. Ad hoc simulations are the most difficult to summarize and interpret in this regard. Analytical simulations, based on implicit or explicit objectives regarding the potential use of the descriptive model, produce data which are more easily interpreted.

EXPLANATORY MODELS

Explanatory models or behavioral models produce outputs similar to those of descriptive models. Moreover, with the exception of the causality, the problems of interpreting and summarizing simulated output are identical. As with the descriptive models, a clear interpretation of output requires an explicitly stated objective of the modeling exercise. Concern with causality may lead to closer scrutiny of structural coefficients and possible alternatives for structural form. On balance, however, the more ad hoc the simulation process, the more difficult it is to interpret and summarize the outputs.

PREDICTION AND FORECASTING MODELS

Some fairly definite options are available for summarizing and interpreting output from simulations of forecasting models. First, the fact that the models are being experimented with suggests that more direct statistical procedures are not applicable—probably because of model or system complexity. In this situation results of the simulations should be summarized using the response surface generated by the experimental process. Approximating such a surface with a quadratic expression and designing experiments accordingly gives rise to results which allow more meaningful interpretations than those obtained from ad hoc simulations.

For multiperiod forecasts characteristics of simulated series can be summarized using spectral analysis. Moreover, for some model representations the spectral form can be analytically derived. This includes characterizing the stochastic response of the analytical solution to a system of difference equations by the use of spectral (frequency domain) analysis and indirectly the derivation of the covariance matrix of the internally determined variables (time domain) (Granger and Hatanaka [1964], Naylor, Wertz, and Wonnacott [1969]). In essence, the spectral methods provide a compact description of the second-moment properties for a stochastic version of the model. One of the principal advantages of the spectral analytical approach is that its results are more easily interpreted. As Howrey [1971] points out, "using this method it is possible to derive the stochastic properties directly from the model rather than performing a simulation and then analyzing the results of the simulation." Furthermore, replications of the stochastic model solutions (as in the case of simulation) are not required and the analytical approach provides a relatively simple means of examining alternative functional forms and parameter estimates. Such characterizations give results which for most model purposes are more informative than collections of ad hoc trials.

DECISION MODELS

Simulations of decision models concerned with regulatory issues are best viewed as policy strategies for the associated control problems. Explicit statements of the criterion functions in such models permit at least numerical approximations of optimal solutions. Results obtained thus have a natural interpretation and can be summarized according to the explicitly defined criterion functions.

For institutional types of decision models the problem of interpreting results is generally more complex. Institutional changes which leave the objective unaltered but involve deletions or additions of constraints can be investigated in a sensitivity analysis framework. Other types of changes contemplated may involve wholesale reorganizations of the system. In these situations objective functions for evaluating institutional designs are less easily identified. As a consequence, the interpretation of results must be cautious. Exploratory simulations proceeding in an ad hoc or evolutionary manner are frequently the only option in such circumstances.

Applications of Systems Analysis and Simulation

Since their introduction in engineering and military science, systems analysis and simulation have been widely applied to problems arising in many disciplines. In disciplines related to agricultural economics such as management science (Hare [1967]), operations research (Hollingdale [1967]), computer science [Fine and McIsaac [1966]), social planning [Ingram, Kain, and Ginn [1973]), politics (Coplin [1968]), forestry (Kourtz and O'Reagan [1968]), ecology (Patten [1971], Watt [1966]), and geology (Harbaugh and Bonham-Carter [1970]), the use of these methods has been growing rapidly. It is of course beyond the scope of the present survey to review all of the systems analysis and simulation literature. Only selected applications of systems models and simulation methods in agricultural economcis are catalogued and discussed.

At the outset it should be noted that our intention is not to present and discuss a complete list of the published systems work in agricultural economics since World War II. Those interested in a "who's who" or "who done it first" treatment will have to await a survey with different objectives. Our intention in compiling the studies has been to examine a sufficient number of applications to be indicative of common characteristics and future trends. In assembling these studies we have naturally tended to concentrate on those with the widest circulation in the profession. The reader wishing to review systems work in agricultural economics further should consult surveys by J. R. Anderson [1974a] and LaDue and Vincent [1974] for a different perspective on some of the studies we include and for reference to works not incorporated into this discussion.

With the exception of games (which are treated separately because of their extensive use in pedagogical contexts), the applications are grouped and discussed by subject area. Included are models of firms and processes, markets, aggregate systems, and development and natural resource problems. The arrangement of the survey along these lines is designed to serve as a basis for comments on the comparative development of systems methods in the various fields and to provide a reasonably homogenous setting for evaluating modeling attempts. Evaluative comments are closely identified with the earlier general observations on systems and systems analysis. Since reviews of research results in each of the listed subject areas are presented in volumes 1 and 3 of *A Survey of Agricultural Economics Literature*, our comments are confined to methods. The results facilitated by the use of systems and simulation concepts and inventive applications of associated research methods will be stressed. The general references are summarized in table 1. (Full bibliographical information on these sources is given in the References section at the end of this chapter.)

Games and Gaming

Games as a class of systems models have had an important impact on teaching and extension methods. Whether computerized or not, the wide use of games in these educational activities suggests that useful economic and managerial concepts can be efficiently communicated through participation in a structured decision process (Shubik [1972]). Data resulting from actions of participants in games can in turn be used to form and test various behavioral hypotheses.

HISTORY

Games as related to systems and simulation owe their beginnings to the development of similar constructs for investigating various war strategies. The historical basis for the more modern developments with gaming has been nicely documented by Longworth [1970]). War games apparently attracted the attention of business people in about 1956 when the American Management Association sponsored a group to develop a management game called "Monopologs" (Longworth [1970], Bellman, Clark, et al. [1957]). These efforts generated substantial interest in the use of management games as teaching or learning devices during the late 1950s and early 1960s (Greenlaw, Herron, and Rawdon [1962]).

Management games have been described (Longworth [1970]) as falling into three rather broadly defined categories—the total enterprise games, which include the early management games as well as their much more complex descendants; the specialized or industry games, which relate to a specific industry; and the functional games.

The early interests of agricultural economists in games are typically identified with the names of Babb [1964], Eisgruber [1964], and Hutton [1966]. As these initial efforts were strongly influenced by the business management games, it is not surprising that they were concerned with farm management. In fact, as Garoian [1967] points out, nonagricultural business management games were utilized in some agricultural economic classes before the development of agricultural games. An earlier application, but with a slightly different orientation, involved production control in a cheese plant (Glickstein et al. [1962]). Subsequent efforts have addressed the more complex problems encountered in group interactions of participants as well as more comprehensive enterprise models. An extensive survey of these efforts is contained in Longworth [1970]. A less detailed recent discussion of games and simulation can be found in LaDue and Vincent [1974].

DISTINGUISHING CHARACTERISTICS

Models concerned with games and gaming fit within our conceptual framework. From the standpoint of participants, games are decision problems. Participants are typically provided with some information, perhaps incomplete, about the game and are asked to play by making decisions according to some specified criterion. Playing the game then requires participants to operate within a prescribed decision framework. The flexibility of the decision framework and the facility for allowing participants to refine their perception of the decision problem through structured or unstructured learning processes determines the complexity of the game.

If games are utilized as a pedagogical device, then it is assumed that playing will result in increased proficiency. The increase in proficiency may, of course, come about as a consequence of an increase in the participant's modeling skills and analytical ability or through the accumulation of factual information about the structure of the system (Cohen and Rehnman [1961]). If games are utilized as a research tool, then records of individual play are utilized as a basis for examining the behavioral hypotheses or the outcome of the game itself. In the first case the means by which various types of economic agents make decisions may be investigated. The second case involves the types of studies typically identified with the subject of experimental economics (Castro and Weingarten [1970], Frahm and Schrader [1970], Frazier, Narrie, and Rodgers [1970], Naylor [1972], V. L. Smith [1964], Whan and Richardson [1969]).

ILLUSTRATIVE FORM

Structures of models used for games are standard. The models include a mechanism for presenting the participant with options. The characteristics associated with the options include a payoff, restrictions on future choices, and in some cases implications for the participant's relationship to other players. As previously indicated, information available to players on the characteristics of the options and even the number of options usually includes a degree of uncertainty. Players make a sequence of choices under prescribed rules of play. The outcomes of these choice sequences are then evaluated in terms of some criteria specified either relative to the player's behavior or a standard identified with an optimal strategy given some general behavioral objective.

SURVEY

The characteristics of twenty-five gaming models are summarized in table 2. Reviewing the table permits some general conclusions on the focus of research in this area. Fourteen of the games involve farm management problems, four are concerned with the management of retail and processing functions, five are marketing models which include participant interaction, and two are vehicles for generating data to be used in behavioral research. If the surveyed works are representative, then it would seem safe to conclude that most applications of gaming concepts include individual decision makers and microeconomic units. Aggregate models and group decision making—except in some marketing applications—have not been the subject of gaming applications.

The first computerized farm management game, developed by Eisgruber [1965], was based on a model of a central Indiana mixed enterprise firm. This game was employed as a prototype for the development of a farm management game and a poultry farm management game (Fuller [1968], Fuller, Ruggles, and Yergatian [1968]). Four other farm management games are those developed by Faris, Wildermuth, and Pratt [1966], Hutton [1966], Kay [1973], and Vincent [1970b]. The Hutton game has been widely employed in teaching farm business analysis to high school and adult students (Curtis [1968]).

The characteristics of the remaining models vary widely. The recent models, with the exception of those used entirely for behavioral research, are computerized. Computerization of games simply makes them more manageable and thus permits more complex structures and elaborate stochastic components. As the discussion of the prototype indicates, most are multistage processes and thus involve a time component in the selection of strategies. In general, the games used are akin to those developed in management or, more generally, in the business disciplines.

Other noteworthy references for games and gaming models are Bentz and Williams [1965], Hutton and Hinman [1968], LaDue and Vincent [1974], Longworth [1969], F. J. Smith and Miles [1967], Von Neumann and Morgenstern [1944], Walker and Halbrook [1965], and Wehrly [1969].

SUMMARY AND EVALUATION

Applications of gaming concepts in agricultural economics have been generally successful. Over the past ten years they have assumed a prominent role in undergraduate and extension teaching activities. Babb and French [1963] were apparently the first to recognize the potential value of management games for these activities. Intuitively, important benefits are anticipated if firm decision makers are allowed to experiment with a simulation model rather than with its real-world counterpart.

There are some limitations of the existing models or (to take the positive view) some promising options for further model development in comparatively unexplored areas of application. First, regarding the development of gaming models, there is limited evidence of efforts to corroborate the games with the decision situations for which the participants are being trained. Although considerable efforts have been made to construct realistic games (that is, to make the model valid for the system studied), little formal information is available which might be utilized to corroborate them with the underlying systems. Advances in this direction would involve more systematic procedures for structure specification and parameter estimation.

With regard to simulation or play, gaming exercises could become more useful as learning tools if more attention were given to the processes by which participants arrive at strategies. Many of the games appear to do little more than force participants to formulate objectives for play. The exercise could be enhanced if more careful consideration were given to the processes by which optimal strategies are determined. One such game has been introduced by Eisgruber [1965]. A related area of unexploited potential involves the possibility for integrating this facet of games with the Von Neumann and Morgenstern [1944] results on utility maximization and decision making under uncertainty. Ideas which might be developed in this context have been suggested by Shubik [1960] and Wagner [1958].

Second, little attention has been devoted to problems of determining the educational value of games. Except for the works by Babb [1964], Babb and Eisgruber [1966], Curtis [1968], Hammond, Strain, and Baumel [1966], and McKenney [1962], all of which are rather surprising in the inconclusiveness of their findings, formal results on this subject are unavailable. In general, the studies indicate that games or gaming exercises are productive; however, there is little economic analysis of the costs and benefits of games in the different types of teaching and extension activities (Dolbear, Attiyeh, and Brainerd [1968]). If games are to be used as teaching devices, then more careful evaluations of their effectiveness in different teaching and extension contexts would be useful in the design of new games and in promoting more informed use of existing games. Interesting attempts to evaluate the educational value of games in classroom situations are currently finding an outlet in the *Journal of Economic Education*. A particularly desirable feature of these results is that they are based on data gathered under explicit experimental controls (Weidenaar [1972]).

Finally, it seems that the potential of games as a tool in behavioral research could be more fully exploited (Babb, Leslie, and Slyke [1966]). The studies by V. L. Smith [1964] and Frahm and Schrader [1970] are indicative of models which can be developed for these purposes. Experimental tests of propositions from the theory and specific ideas on the firm and market operation appear quite useful. Examples of the latter include tests of competing hypotheses concerning the behavior of cooperative managers and members, operators in farm growth models, market actions, and the degree of uncertainty as to actions of competitors.

Firm and Process

Systems models of firms and processes are of the decision type. Typically they are concerned with the problem of providing information to be utilized for improved resource allocation within the decision units modeled. The majority of these models involve firm decision situations and are designed to produce results for dealing with problems of uncertainty, growth and adjustment, and adaptation. These problems present substantial conceptual and computational difficulties for the more traditional neoclassical and activity analysis models of the firm. Application of the systems approach has given rise to a number of ambitious modeling efforts in this area.

HISTORY

Many of the early firm and process model applications outside of agricultural economics may be found in such journals as *Management Science, Operations Research, Behavioral Science,* and the *Journal of the Association of Computing Machinery.* Engineering applications of process models are frequently found in *Simulation,* and business applications have appeared in *Simulation and Games.* Within economics, systems analysis and simulation assumed increased importance with the introduction of the behavioral theory of the firm paradigm (Cyert and Marsh [1963]). This paradigm appears to be particularly useful when restricted to the analysis of firm behavior; it was developed, in part, by the use of simulation. Moreover, it often involves a number of disciplines in addition to economics. For example, Bonini [1964] has introduced accounting, organization theory, and behavioral science into a model representation of firm behavior. Similarly, Cyert and March [1963] have employed behavioral science, psychology, sociology, and organization theory along with economics. In a process model context such multidisciplinary approaches have been most frequently applied to the design of communication and data handling systems (Beged-Dov [1967], Vazsonyi [1965]).

The interests of agricultural economists in firm and process models are obviously longstanding. Applications of systems concepts and simulation methods in this context, however, are of recent origin.[7] In fact, the earliest of the studies surveyed was published in 1962 (Glickstein et al. [1962]). Hence, the literature on applications of systems concepts and simulation methods to firm and process models involves more recent studies. Because of this, and, as we mentioned earlier, because subject area surveys have been commissioned in these fields by the American Agricultural Economics Association, we shall not dwell on the history of firm and process models prior to the development of systems applications.

DISTINGUISHING CHARACTERISTICS

Firm and process models are typically stochastic and dynamic and involve some nonlinearities. The stochastic aspects of these models are a particularly important feature and usually emanate from exogenous weather conditions or prices. In a management context the resulting risk and uncertainty are dealt with nicely by simulation. These methods do not require that the forecast density function of the decision parameters satisfy any particular shape or mathematical equation, and thus they allow the researcher to employ the complete range of data pertaining for each parameter (Clarke [1968]). This analytical complexity is introduced as a result of attempts to model the intricacies of the firm or process. As a consequence of such complexity, direct solution methods—even for the simpler objective functions—are usually not feasible. Hence, models are simulated for policy choices, for sensitivity to parametric and structural change, and the like. Results of the simulations are evaluated using objective functions or are simply presented as outcomes from selected courses of action.

ILLUSTRATIVE FORM

As noted earlier, firm models are studied largely for decision purposes. It will be clear from the survey that applications have been mainly concerned with regulatory decisions. Though facilitating studies of more elaborate problems, systems and simulation concepts have not changed the context of the research questions in these models.

In the case of process models a typical form would address the design and analysis of a facility layout. The principal advantage of simulation in evaluating facility layouts is that the actual cost of the physical facility is avoided. Examples of these forms include warehouse locations for large-scale multiplant firms (Kuehn [1962]) and iterative models for determining the optimal location of a firm's facilities (Armour and Buffa [1963]). Other typical forms of process models include job-shop sequencing and such farm processes as harvesting and storage.

SURVEY

Although not mutually exclusive, the studies listed in table 2 can be classified according to whether they are process models, management and farm planning models, or growth models.

Process models involve specific types of producing and marketing activities or plants over which a firm has control. These studies are typified by models of the sort developed by Brooks [1962], Cloud, Frick, and Andrews [1968], Doster [1970], Glickstein et al. [1962], Smith and Parks [1967], Sorensen and Gilheany [1970], and Wright and Dent [1969]. Of these, the work by Glickstein et al. [1962] is noteworthy because it preceded many of the others and influenced subsequent investigations. Recent models are more elaborate in their complexity and in their sources of uncertainty. This uncertainty often emanates from stochastic weather conditions. Most farm process models have addressed the operation of the soil-plant-water system (Nelson and Schuck [1974]). Subcomponents of this system have been incorporated in models of dryland cropping (Blackie and Schneeberger [1971], Dumsday [1971]), grazing (Goodall [1971], Jones and Brockington [1971], Wright [1970]), and irrigated cropping (Phillips [1969]). Harvesting and storage processes have also been examined. For the former, efforts have been concentrated on the efficient selection of machinery (Cloud, Frick, and Andrews [1968], Donaldson and Webster [1968], Jose, Christensen, and Fuller [1971], Sorensen and Gilheany [1970], van Kampen [1971]). In the case of storage processes inventory analysis has been employed to determine efficient quantities of fodder to harvest or purchase (Morley and Graham [1971]). The models employed in these studies have comparatively simple objectives, which include minimizing costs, maximizing returns over costs, and mean variance types of efficiency criteria.

The growth models may be thought of as extensions of budgeting studies applied in farm planning. Perhaps because of the preoccupation with farm management and planning in traditional agricultural economics departments, these models are numerous. Studies of this type include those by R. L. Anderson [1968], Donaldson and Webster [1968], Eidman, Dean, and Carter [1967], Halter and Dean [1965], Hinman and Hutton [1970], Hutton [1966], Vincent [1970a, 1970b], and Zusman and Amiad [1965]. These and other studies include examination of crop farming (Dumsday [1971], Flinn [1971], van Kampen [1971], Zusman and Amiad [1965]), mixed farming (Hutton and Hinman [1968]), beef (Halter and Dean [1965], Trebeck [1971]), sheep (J. R. Anderson [1971], Hughes [1973], Johnston [1973], Wright [1970], Wright and Dent [1969]), pigs (Dent [1971]), dairy (Hutton [1966]), and turkeys (Eidman, Dean, and Carter [1967]). Roughly one-half of these investigations focused on the choice of production methods. The remaining one-half are concerned not only with the choice of production level but also with marketing and investment strategies. The analytical purposes of these studies might be characterized as investigating the temporal aspects of product sales (Eidman, Dean, and Carter [1967]), input management rules (Dent [1971]), economics of soil conservation (Dumsday [1971]), economics of amalgamation (Johnston [1973]), and spatial diversification (Trebeck [1971]). In most of these applications we find examples of individual firms planning in dynamic and stochastic environments. The advantage of the systems approach for stochastic planning problems lies in its flexibility. Numerous production activities can be considered along with many types of strategies for combining them.

Four of the planning models merit special comment. Each represents an innovation which would appear to be promising for future planning work. The first study, by Eidman, Dean, and Carter [1967], combines simulation and Bayesian decision theory to evaluate uncertainty in commercial turkey production contracting. Incorporating a Bayesian formulation of the decision problem provided a way of dealing systematically with decisions encountered in farm planning. The second study, by Halter and Dean [1965], examines management policies under conditions of both weather and price uncertainty. Observed historical data were used to estimate probability distributions, which were in turn sampled for range conditions in the specified range feedlot problem. By using this means of summarizing the characteristics of the historical environmental conditions, the authors were able to evaluate the numerical results from the models within a related probabilistic framework.

The third study, by Zusman and Amiad [1965], is noteworthy for the methods applied in examining the response surface of the firm model and, correspondingly, for the way the model was simulated. Here again, weather uncertainty and cropping patterns were explicitly recognized with respect to the response surface. The methods used preceded the current interest in experimental design and response surface identification (Naylor [1971]). Also, analytical criteria and the method of steepest ascent were used as bases for choosing sequences of policy simulations. That is, choices of policy variables were made using information available on the response surface in the maximizing framework suggested by the decision problem. Choices of policies then amounted to a numerical type of gradient method optimizing procedure.

Finally, important efforts to develop general firm planning models have been made by Hutton and Hinman. In the first model, developed by Hutton [1966], dairy herd characteristics were emphasized. The planning horizon for this model is variable and the model may be simulated stochastically. The principal limitations of this model are its heavy technical input requirements and the exclusion of all enterprises except for the dairy herd. More recently, Hutton and Hinman [1968] developed a model designed to process data for a wide range of farm planning situations. Stochastic price and purchase options, sale of capital items, and input and product price trends are admitted. The specified production functions are linear and independent. All activities in this model are defined by the user, and specific applications are available in Hinman and Hutton [1970, 1971].

Turning to the studies on firm growth, a limited number of references are summarized in table 3 and by Armstrong, Connor, and Strickland [1970], Harle [1968], and Patrick and Eisgruber [1968]. Other firm growth investigations involving the application of simulation methods include Boehlje and Eisgruber [1972], Charlton [1972], Dalton [1971], Eisgruber and Lee [1971], Hinman and Hutton [1971], S. R. Johnson, Tefertiller, and Moore [1967], Lins [1969], and Walker and Martin [1966]. The authors of these studies were among the first to argue for the use of simulation in farm growth research. Much of the subsequent work on simulation and farm growth models has been undertaken by Eisgruber and his associates at Purdue University. In Patrick and Eisgruber [1968] simulation was employed to deal with multiple firm goals; in Eisgruber and Lee [1971], and particularly in Boehlje and Eisgruber [1972], a search routine was constructed to select superior alternatives. The routine, which combined the Monte Carlo method with a "hill climbing" procedure, is based in part upon the earlier work of Thompson [1970]. Decision rules characterizing this routine assign probabilities to various activities which are subsequently revised depending upon the income generated when alternative combinations of activities are chosen. Sequential combinations depend upon the updated probabilities associated with each activity.

The construction of the tabular survey for firm growth models was particularly difficult. As a result of the comprehensive and difficult investment and decision problems involved in the study of firm growth, many of the applied studies in this area could be classified as being based on systems and simulation concepts. Most models are highly specialized and require numerical approaches for solution. Lastly, the study of firm growth in agricultural economics represents an interesting phenomenon in applied work. The firm growth work probably began in response to the increases observed in farm size, and at first it was largely descriptive. As these early efforts were refined, attempts to reconcile them with more conventional theories emerged. This trend is evident in a series of papers from a Great Plains Regional Committee conference held in 1965 (Great Plains Agricultural Council [1967]. Because of its flexibility the systems approach was of considerable value in facilitating applied work and in stimulating theoretical interest in this area.

Other references relating to firm and process models that should be noted are Albach [1967], Burt [1968], Flinn [1971], Great Plains Agricultural Council [1967], and Tanago [1973].

SUMMARY AND EVALUATION

Of the firm and process models surveyed, approximately 75 percent are dynamic, 60 percent are stochastic, 70 percent are nonlinear, almost all involve passive validation, roughly 90 percent have a decision orientation, and, finally, about 50 percent are both stochastic and nonlinear.

In reviewing the studies in table 3 as they relate to the general framework for systems analysis and simulation presented earlier, we find them deficient in a number of respects. Work to validate or corroborate models with systems has been limited. The quality of the results obtained from some modeling efforts suggests that a substantial amount of informal validation work was done. However, there is little mention of the application of the more formal and systematic tests discussed earlier. Since the purpose of these models is the generation of information to be employed in regulating or controlling the related systems, it appears that more explicit and systematic attempts to validate the models would have been advantageous.

A second area of potential for improving models and results is in the design of the simulation experiments. In a number of the planning, process, and growth models the subject of investigation is some type of response surface (perhaps the value of a profit function based on options pertaining to regulatory variables). The models are so complex (in terms of nonlinearities and stochastic components) that the study of response surfaces without considerable attention to experimental design may provide misleading information. As these models become more realistic and complex, the problem of identifying, with a high degree of reliability, the response surfaces of interest is likely to increase in importance.

Our last observation concerns the objective functions implicitly or explicitly employed. Because the models are stochastic, it is necessary to apply various kinds of indexing schemes to accommodate the stochastic arguments. The Bayesian and related expected utility approaches represent a promising development in this regard. The work of Eidman, Dean, and Carter [1967] represents a positive step in this direction. As these ideas are introduced, it will be necessary to take advantage of their full benefits in terms of possibilities for analytical solutions (Burt [1968]). In this connection the analytical simulation methods used by Zusman and Amiad [1965] will also become more commonplace in future work with process and firm models.

Market or Industry Models

Market or industry models typically involve the study of structures governing the movement of commodities from producers to consumers. Many of these studies are of distribution channel systems. Others are concerned with single market systems for particular products. Research objectives are associated with improved understanding of the behavior of such systems and their evolution over time or with improving the decision processes of the components comprising the system. Behavioral market and industry models often involve attempts to improve the understanding of interaction and feedback relationships among various components. Decision model applications are frequently concerned with the evaluation of alternative marketing policies.

HISTORY

Agricultural applications in this area have been strongly influenced by the earlier studies of Cohen [1960] and Balderston and Hoggatt [1962]. Both studies were concerned with distribution systems. The Cohen model, consisting of over sixth equations, involved an attempt to explain the behavior of various elements in the vertical structure of the hide and leather industry.[8] Balderston and Hoggatt examined price and sales determination in the West Coast lumber industry. Major decisions about prices, order levels, and production levels for each of the components (hide dealers, leather tanners, shoe manufacturers, shoe retailers, and final buyers) were included in the Cohen model. The Balderston and Hoggatt model was less concerned with the vertical structure of the lumber industry than with the critical role played by lumber brokers in matching potential sellers (timber growers) and potential buyers (lumber retailers).

Both of these models were highly complex, including large numbers of decision modules and linkages incorporating nonlinear and stochastic features. In this regard the Balderston and Hoggatt model offers an interesting contrast to the work of Cohen. Balderston and Hoggatt began with a set of postulates regarding the economic behavior of different market participants (rather than with a set of historical series) and utilized artificial data to determine how the specified market operated under different conditions. They concentrate on attempting to understand the properties of a hypothetical model. Thus, their simulations are essentially synthetic in nature. The principal features of the model include limited information, varying information costs, preference orderings, and localized search. A very similar approach has been employed by Preston and Collins [1966]. Cohen, however, operated with real-world data, and, since his constructed model was too complex to solve directly, he resorted to a simulation of it over time. Although the results were not particularly favorable, this model nevertheless remains a prototype for many of the subsequent econometric simulation efforts in the area of vertical market structures. A common feature of the Balderston and Hoggatt [1962] and Cohen [1960] studies is the high degree of specialization achieved for the market and industry studied. This feature and the modeling and simulation techniques which evolved for studying systems at this level of abstraction are reflected in a number of agricultural economics applications.

Earlier attempts to model the conceptual apparatus of economic theory and the linkages between individuals and groups (Clarkson and Simon [1960], Orcutt [1960], Orcutt et al. [1961]) have led to much in the way of subsequent applications. These attempts might be regarded as a combination of the sorts of applications found in the firm and process category and those appearing in this section. Orcutt's enterprising approach of aggregating individual consumer and producer behavior is fraught with data and computational difficulties. Simulation of mixed-level models involving both individual and aggregate demand and supply relationships is particularly difficult. As Manderscheid and Nelson [1969] have pointed out, such models include variables which are exogenous at one level and endogenous at another (for example, price at the firm and industry levels). Hence, to achieve consistency between the two levels, feedback effects must be recognized and iterative simulations are usually required. These iterative simulations involve resimulation of the individual or micro units if the aggregate industry level variables are not consistent with the magnitudes of these variables when treated exogenously at the micro level.

Although less comprehensive, the Balderston and Hoggatt work on the lumber industry may be viewed in the same spirit as the Orcutt approach. Other less ambitious investigations have concentrated on only the demand side of particular industries or markets. These include imperfectly competitive market models (Amstutz [1967]) along with a number of advertising and marketing applications (Kotler and Schultz [1970]). Agricultural economics applications have typically concentrated on the supply side. For example, Bender [1966] and Duewer and Maki [1966] have analyzed the meat industrial structure by simulating representative firms, their interactions, and meat product markets.

DISTINGUISHING CHARACTERISTICS

The characteristics of these models peculiar to the study of market processes include (1) the heavy use of separate decision components and the related decomposability for studying particular aspects of the systems, (2) the variation in theoretical, empirical, and intuitive content, and (3) the high degree of complexity resulting from provisions for the interaction of components and the low level of abstraction. Effective utilization of these models requires substantial familiarity with the intricacies of the market or process being studied. Model forms generally evolve from provisional structures through interaction with industry personnel and internal comparisons of decomposed decision unit performance. This is the reason an institutional knowledge of the industry is important as a prerequisite for model construction and evaluation of simulations. This observation is not surprising since existing economic theories of market organization are sufficient only to give useful guidelines for studies which represent minimal abstractions from the true systems.

ILLUSTRATIVE FORM

The major components of market or industry models are usually associated with one or more of the following sectors: consumer, retailer, wholesaler, transportation, producer, inventory, and foreign trade. The structural composition of these models is often specified so that interactions between components can be treated recursively. This characteristic typically is rationalized on the basis of information flow within the industry and is important in making the problem analytically tractable. Representations of these components include lagged effects and interacting variables as well as nonlinear relationships. Departures from linearity, however, are not substantial. Although most of the constructed models contain stochastic elements, only seven of the twenty-four studies surveyed recognize stochastic components when simulation experiments are performed. The majority of the models were investigated only in a deterministic or expected value form.

The observed model complexities are generally consistent with the typical behavioral orientation of such studies. As previously noted, the objective of such modeling exercises is to distill information on the causal characteristics of the system. It is therefore quite consistent for researchers to use the uncertainty principle or, more formally, the adaptive control framework in coming to a selected form which meets the objectives of the investigation and satisfies the constraints imposed by the resources available for the study. Owing to the prominence of these evolutionary methods, an illustrative form of the model is difficult to isolate. The research decision process by which these models evolve often has a definite structure, but the models are as different as the markets or industries studied. In fact, the implication of this observation for problems of generalizing results is also a major concern with firm and process models. We can therefore cite common characteristics but not a general form.

SURVEY

As firm and process models are highly individualistic, our survey is restricted to a discussion of several representative studies. The studies selected for detailed examination include Candler and Cartwright [1969], Crom and Maki [1965a], Naylor, Wallace, and Sasser [1967], Raulerson and Langham [1970], Vernon, Rives, and Naylor [1969]. Each one has interesting features vis-à-vis the market or industry studied and their connection to the earlier works of Cohen and Balderston and Hoggatt.

The Raulerson and Langham study [1970] was concerned with the Florida frozen concentrated orange juice industry. The authors applied Forrester's industrial dynamics approach [1961] along with the associated DYNAMO simulation language. The model used consisted of 137 equations representing features of growers, processors, retailers, and consumers. Parameters entering many of these equations were specified on an a priori or subjective basis. Conscious attempts were made to isolate the information feedback characteristics and the related amplifications and delays presumed to exist in the industrial system being modeled. Validation of the constructed model was accomplished by graphically comparing simulated and actual sample values for selected variables. Tracking and turning points were emphasized as measures of model performance.

A major objective of the Raulerson and Langham model was to examine alternative policies. The policies included (1) free market or no intervention, (2) product allocation to two separate markets, (3) removal of productive trees, (4) curtailment of new tree plantings, and (5) various combinations of options (2) through (4).

The Crom and Maki model [1965a] is perhaps most closely related to Cohen's work [1960]. The authors' purpose was to construct an econometric model to explain behavior in the beef and pork sectors of the United States economy. The model is recursive except for beef and pork prices, which are specified to be jointly determined. The unknown parameters of the model are estimated from historical data. Ad hoc simulations of a nonstochastic version of the model are used as a basis for behavioral conclusions. The procedures employed are bothersome in terms of our earlier comments on validation. More specifically, Crom and Maki [1965a] revised equational specifications (changing length of time lags, coefficients, and limiting values) after examining historical comparisons of sample and simulated values. Many of these changes were conditioned upon particular values of endogenous variables determined by such graphical comparisons. In other words, behavioral relations were modified until a representation was achieved which could reproduce the historical (sample) period with sufficient accuracy. Unfortunately, the conditional changes were introduced ex post and only on the basis of the graphical comparisons—no other justification or explanation is provided. This approach is an obvious violation of classical statistical methods, Bayesian methods, and other inference procedures. The reported R^2's and significance tests (not reported) on the estimated coefficients have no real meaning. The chief danger of this approach is that the constructed model will not isolate to an acceptable degree the systematic and enduring characteristics of the system under examination.

The Naylor, Wallace, and Sasser model [1967] and the Vernon, Rives, and Naylor model [1969] are similar to the models by Cohen [1960] and Crom and Maki [1965a]. Both models were constructed around the distributional components of a single industry. Time series data were utilized to estimate unknown parameters of models specified in recursive form. The Vernon, Rives, and Naylor model [1969] recognizes a monopolistic structure on the selling side and an oligopsonistic structure on the buying side of the tobacco leaf market. This model consists of nineteen equations, seven behavioral and twelve identities. Policy variables such as acreage allotments, support prices, and soil bank plans are incorporated as exogenous factors to the model, but no policy or decision examinations are provided. Marketing factors including effects of advertising expenditures on cigarette consumption were excluded from the analysis. Validation was attempted by using Cohen's process simulation approach [1960] and graphical comparisons of the resulting simulated and sample values.

The Naylor, Wallace, and Sasser model [1967] of the textile industry consists of nine behavioral equations. The basic orientation of the model is behavioral. Process simulation analysis is employed over the historical record, no policy alternatives are examined, and experimental design methods are not utilized. A principal aspect of this study involves the application of alternative validation techniques. Three techniques (graphical, spectral, and total variance analysis) are utilized to compare simulation results with observed data. The spectral analysis approach was found to be the most useful. One of the principal advantages of this approach is its compact description of the second-moment properties of stochastic models. In contrast to the spectral simulation approach a spectral analysis approach is also possible. In nonlinear stochastic models this approach may be referred to as the spectral analytical simulation method since approximations to the nonlinearities present in model must be utilized (Rausser and Johnson [1975]).

The Candler and Cartwright study [1969] is substantially different from those just outlined. In terms of response surfaces it is somewhat similar to Zusman and Amiad [1965] except that the objective is to estimate the performance surface throughout the space corresponding to selected ranges of the variables or factors. Relationships are advanced to capture the effects of specific assumptions regarding these variables on the resulting outcomes. The problem was to derive more general and explicit functional relationships between decision variables, structural parameters, and performance statistics. With these functions outcomes or performance measures can be estimated directly without recourse to additional simulations. The study is not one of direct optimization, but rather it focuses on estimation of the objective function components that are associated with particular levels of the decision and exogenous variables. The use of experimental design procedures was emphasized in the simulation of the model. Second order polynomials were utilized to approximate the performance surfaces. The relative weights attached to multiple performance statistics were not specified. Instead, separate functions were estimated for each performance statistic that might enter the ultimate objective function. The suggested procedures were applied to a budgetary study of the potential for increased sheep production in New Zealand.

Finally, the vast amount of work on simulating a number of subsectors within the textile industry and the commodity analysis completed at the Harvard Business School should be at least briefly mentioned. For the textile industry, the computer simulation model developed by Zymelman [1965] serves as the principal illustrative example. The commodity analysis work is basically descriptive; most of these investigations employ a systems taxonomy but do not involve any attempt at quantitative synthesis. This approach might be characterized as a systems analytical description of a commodity or industry (B. C. French [1974]) and involves efforts to identify structural changes and desirable adjustments. Applications of this approach include Goldberg's analysis of wheat, soybeans, and oranges [1968]; Arthur, Houck, and Beckford's analysis of the banana industry [1968]; Marion and Arthur's analysis of the broiler industry [1973]; and Morrissy's work on fruits and vegetables [1974]. Although this descriptive work represents an obvious requisite for the development of analytical models, none of these applications has explicitly addressed the synthesis and design stages of the systems modeling approach.

Among the other important studies using market and industry models are the following: Agarwala [1971], Armbruster et al. [1972], Barnum [1971], Bell, Henderson, and Perkins [1972], Benson [1969], Benson, Bender, and Lofourcade [1972], Crom [1967], Crom and Maki [1965b], Desai [1968],

B. C. French and Matsumoto [1969], Holder, Shaw, and Snyder [1971], Koenig, Hilmersen, and Yuan [1969], Lavington [1970], Manetsch [1974], Nevins [1966], Weymar [1968].

SUMMARY AND EVALUATION

Approximately 80 percent of the models surveyed in this section are dynamic, only 30 percent are simulated stochastically, roughly 75 percent are nonlinear, and about 30 percent are both stochastic and nonlinear; less than 10 percent are actively validated. Most of these applications have a behavioral model purpose. It is also interesting to note that these applications fall into one of two general classes—either the Orcutt mixed-level microaggregate [1960] or the strictly aggregate industry or market-level class. The models by Balderston and Hoggatt [1962] and Duewer and Maki [1966] serve as examples of the former class, and the models by Cohen [1960] and Vernon, Rives, and Naylor [1969] are illustrative examples of the latter class. Most of the strictly aggregate class of market or industry models involve process simulations of econometric representations. Such simulations utilize generated endogenous values of the past periods to determine, in part, the current period simulated values. In other words given the value of lagged endogenous variables for periods t-1, t-2, etc., the model computes values for the internally determined variables for period t.[9] Owing to their highly specialized nature these models are difficult to evaluate. Presumably all worked acceptably for the purposes intended.

A number of things can be learned from reading the accounts of the exercises and the types of results which were obtained. First, it is apparent that response function and associated experimental designs employed by Candler and Cartwright [1969] along with the experimental design techniques discussed here can be used to advantage in testing the behavioral propositions implicit in these models and in the validation exercises. Second, the estimation procedures employed could be more systematized by employing the parameter estimation methods discussed earlier. The combination of prior information, whether subjective or from other studies, with data using these techniques should be useful in improving the reliability of the parameter estimates. Third, it would appear that future studies could benefit from a more explicit recognition of the adaptive decision problem involved in model construction. The adaptive model construction framework suggested here should result in the development of better models and a reduction in their individualistic content.

Aggregate Models

Simulation studies of aggregate systems include those related to national economic levels and to agriculture at a sectoral level. Although a survey of national models is not within the scope of this paper, it would be unfortunate not to mention the large number of models available and the importance of simulation and systems methods in corroborating them with the system and in applying them to forecasting and decision problems. For those interested in becoming acquainted with this work we recommend a survey paper by Fromm and Klein [1973] and a recent collection of simulation studies of the United States economy appearing in a volume edited by Klein and Burmeister [1976] as useful starting points in the literature.

Aggregate models of the agricultural sector tend to have less econometric content than the national models. Because of data limitations, concerns with detailed behavioral relationships and associated interactions, and the incidence of particular policies, these models tend to be complex and accordingly to involve research approaches closely related to those discussed in connection with firm and process models.

HISTORY

Studies of policy questions for various commodity sectors have been of major interest to agricultural economists since the 1930s (Heady and Tweeten [1963]). In general, the development of quantitative methods to analyze problems posed in comparing and evaluating alternative governmental policies applied to the agricultural sector have reflected those used to solve other types of problems. The first attempt to construct a detailed representation of the United States agricultural sector appears to be the model developed by Cromarty [1958]. The principal emphasis in the Cromarty analysis was on construction; the purpose of developing the model was to measure the major relationships within the agricultural sector and between agriculture and the remainder of the economy. The model was not used for forecasting purposes, policy formation, or intercommodity analysis. Similar representations of the United States agricultural sector may be found in Fox [1963] and Evans [1969]. The Evans study, although not frequently referenced in the agricultural economic literature, was one of the first attempts (along with Tyner and Tweeten [1968]) to simulate an econometric representation of the United States agricultural sector. Using ad hoc simulations, Evans examined the sensitivity of his model representation to increases in personal disposal income, consumer nonfood prices, productivity within the beef and hog sectors, and soybean meal exports, and he evaluated such policies as increased acreage restrictions for feedgrain and increased milk and soybean price supports. The approach was much the same as that used in the research efforts devoted to the construction and simulation of macroeconometric models (Fromm and Klein [1973], Fromm and Taubman [1968], Holt [1965]).

In recent years still more aggregated simulations have been performed in attempts to forecast future world population, income, natural resource stocks, and food production (Forrester [1971], Meadows, Meadows, Randers, and Behrens [1972]). These representations are strong departures from the earlier simulations of macro and agricultural econometric sector models. The data base for such futuristic world models is virtually nil, and the assumptions and methods employed are highly questionable. Accordingly this work has encountered energetic and caustic criticism (Cole et al. [1973]).

Turning back to specific aggregate models in agricultural economics, we find a large number of studies on various commodities and agricultural sectors. These studies employ quite different model construction and policy evaluation techniques. Some are more closely linked to systems and simulation concepts, and others emanate from more traditional econometric origins. The studies examined in this section are largely associated with the former group. However, it will be clear from subsequent as well as previous comments that the distinction between these two sets of methods is artificial.

DISTINGUISHING CHARACTERISTICS

Aggregate models are typically constructed for decision and forecasting purposes. For decision problems the object is to evaluate the implications of alternative policies. Although the models have a strong decision orientation, only the study by Shechter and Heady [1970] operated with an explicit criterion function. The criterion function employed by these authors is only partially explicit, expressed in terms of four independent criteria for which neither weights, satisfactory levels, nor orderings were specified. Hence, there was no attempt to resolve conflicts between farm income and, say, government costs; instead, weight or ordering assignments to various goals are reserved by these authors for policy makers.

Other studies have relied on implicit objective functions (reflected by the specified performance variables and the particular policies examined). Most of these aggregate models are dynamic and nonhistorical and incorporate feedback mechanisms in a recursive fashion. The models are generally nonlinear, but not in a way which presents substantial problems for derivation of the reduced forms or the generation of the endogenous variables from the structural form. Although the question of corroboration is discussed in connection with each of the models, few formal tests or descriptive measures are advanced in attempts to validate the representations.

ILLUSTRATIVE FORM

Models in this classification, although diverse, can be reasonably characterized as systems representing one or more components of developed agricultural sectors. They are typically highly aggregative and incorporate many simplifying specifications (for example, Cobb-Douglas aggregate production functions), and almost all of the models refer to the United States agricultural sector. The exception in table 4 is the United Kingdom food and agricultural model constructed by McFarquhar and Evans [1971]. Most are constructed to examine quantitative effects of alternative governmental policies (price supports, governmental inventory purchases, acreage allotments and diversion programs, government payments). The agricultural sector systems examined are usually decomposed into a number of components or subsystems and a building-block approach is employed in model construction. Although the major components of these models differ, they are generally concerned with supply and demand for various products, in some cases with agricultural input or resource levels, and with linkages to the nonagricultural economy. Other aggregate components are often included to generate internally determined factors such as farm income. These are recursive to and derived from the basic components.

SURVEY

The works of Edwards and De Pass [1971], Lin and Heady [1971], McFarquhar and Evans [1971], Ray and Heady [1972], Shechter [1972], and Tyner [1967] are selected for specific discussion. These studies are viewed as representative of the approaches to aggregate systems modeling. The Tyner study [1967] forms the basis for the results reported in Tyner and Tweeten and is similar in nature and scope to the Lin and Heady model [1971]. Both models are recursive, with the equations estimated by means of ordinary or autoregressive least squares. Moreover, both examine via ad hoc simulation experiments effects of the elimination of all governmental programs and alternative assumptions about the rate of technological change. The output or commodity components of the two models are represented by a single aggregate production function, supply (or sales), and a demand set of equations.

The Ray and Heady model [1972] utilizes a categorization of variables similar to the groupings employed by Tyner and Tweeten [1968] but is less aggregative, containing submodels for livestock, feedgrain, wheat, soybeans, cotton, and tobacco. All of these submodels are recursively related, and they include resource use, production, price, final demand, and gross receipt components. The model is passively validated; no attempt is made to recognize the underlying stochastic distributions in the various simulation runs, and the simulations performed are not formally designed. The ad hoc and historical policy simulations examined include the removal of government price and income support programs, increases in input prices, and 10-percent increases in corn and wheat support prices. The apparent deficiencies of the constructed model are the weak linkages between the various commodity submodels and, in turn, their linkages with the national economy.

The model constructed for the United Kingdom by McFarquhar and Evans [1971] is similar to the preceding models, involving far more detail than those by Tyner and Tweeten [1968] and Lin and Heady [1971] and roughly the same level of detail as the model by Ray and Heady [1972]. Three components of the model—final demand, intermediate and primary demands, and supply—are treated recursively and each component is simulated separately. The first component, the final demand, encompasses twenty-seven food products and one nonfood product. All equations giving these quantities are estimated by ordinary least squares. The intermediate primary demand component is composed of thirty-nine agricultural and nonagricultural input products related to products consumed as food. This component is constructed as an input-output model assuming constant technology. The supply component is treated as four subsystems based on commodities: wheat, barley, cattle, and sheep. Most of the equations for these subsystems are dynamic, involving simple adjustment mechanisms or geometric lags, and are estimated by stepwise least squares. The model is employed to examine the potential effects of the entry of the United Kingdom into the European Economic Community (EEC) along with associated price and import policies.

The model by Edwards and De Pass [1971] is different from those just discussed and is quite similar to one reported by Edwards [1970]. The concern is with domestic rural development—that is, with the growth and distribution of population, income, and employment across rural and urban sectors. Accordingly, the model contains rural and urban components. Owing to difficulties of isolating these two major components on an aggregate basis for the United States, four alternative and basically arbitrary delineations were examined. Simulated results for these four delineations were found to be invariant with respect to general conclusions regarding future prospects. Urban and rural, income, employment, and population growth equations are developed on a similar exponential basis. A net migration equation between the two components is also specified. Parameters of the structure were estimated by trial and error, the criterion being the reproduction of 1970 data from the 1960 data for population, income, and employment. Sensitivity analysis was utilized to investigate various parameter changes as well as alternative policies. Various targets for population, income, and employment were specified. Promising policy actions proved to be associated with an expansion of job opportunities. More jobs in rural areas and, to a lesser extent, increased labor productivity appeared to have a greater impact than either reductions in outmigration or rural population birth rate decreases.

One of the more interesting applications of aggregate models is the Shechter study [1972] (for a condensed version of this model, see Shechter and Heady [1970]). In some respects it proceeds along the lines of the investigations found in Candler and Cartwright [1969] and Zusman and Amiad [1965]. The model is based on both micro components (individual farms in northern and southern Iowa) and macro components (aggregate output variables of all farms). A response surface analysis approach to simulation experiments is emphasized. The experimental design is partial factorial, and optimal search procedures take place for univariate responses. For each of the four response variables and associated surfaces relative maximum or minimum points were discovered. An independent examination of each variable revealed that rather large improvements could be made in the design of the system.[10] Validation of the underlying micro and macro components representing the real system involved a simple historical comparison of observed and explained values for a few of the systems outputs.

Other simulation methods which might be classified as aggregate models include the works of Agarwala [1971] and Reutlinger [1970a]. The Agarwala model analyzes various stabilization policies for agricultural markets. Reutlinger's study stands in contrast to the remaining models surveyed in this section. Reutlinger explicitly recognizes stochastic aspects and uncertainty associated with attempts to evaluate buffer stocks of grain programs at national levels.

Other aggregate models that should be noted are those by Blase, MacMillan, and Tung [1973], Chen [1970], Lins [1973], and Schaller [1968].

SUMMARY AND EVALUATION

Most of the models surveyed in this section are dynamic and nonlinear and have decision or policy orientations. However, there are indeed few of these models, perhaps too few, that are stochastically simulated or actively validated. Most of these studies totally neglect uncertainty of the behavioral components modeled; if stochastic components are incorporated in various representations (particularly the econometric specifications), they too are neglected in the simulation of the constructed models. We fully expect that this will be corrected in future efforts to model and examine various policies at sectoral levels.

It should be clear from the comments in connection with the survey that the study by Shechter and Heady [1970] is the most advanced in terms of applications of systems concepts and simulation methods. The recognition of response surface estimation problems and the application of appropriate experimental designs form an important step in the development of useful results from aggregative systems models. As evidence of this assumption we need only compare the other studies with the one by Shechter and Heady.

The final commentary on the studies concerns the use of validation methods. In reflecting on the recent experience with national models, we wish to emphasize our aggrement with Cooper [1972], when he suggests that careful corroborative analysis is extremely important for the policy and forecasting functions of aggregate models.

Future research with regard to the aggregate class of models surveyed in this section will most likely be even more ambitious than those currently available. Given present perceptions of world problems, these simulations will involve such variables as population, incomes, resource stocks, food production, and demand. As J. R. Anderson [1974a] has asserted, "agricultural economists will ultimately become very involved in at least the improved specification of rates of technological change in food and fiber production, off-farm migration rates, income elasticities for farm products, and so on, at world levels."

Development Models

Problems of economic development also lend themselves to the systems analysis approach. They are typically eclectic and highly specialized to the country under examination. These characteristics are presumably due to different institutions, to a wide diversity of agricultural industries, to large differences in the resource bases, and to the exploratory nature of the analyses. The eclectic nature of these systems models is illustrated by the inclusion of demographic and sociological components. The specialization is based not only on the particular traits of the agricultural industry and related institutions but also on the diverse political structures and restrictions with regard to potential policy variables and objectives. The exploratory aspects of these models derive from their strong policy orientation and from an absence of fundamental types of behavioral and technical relationships and data which might be employed to identify them.

HISTORY

Applications of systems concepts and simulation methods to development problems are largely outgrowths of the Nigerian consortium (Manetsch, Hayenga, et al. [1971]). The ambitious Nigerian model developed at Michigan State University had its origins (both data requirements and conceptualization) in early applications of systems concepts by Holland [1962, 1968]. The first of these (the pioneering work) examined problems of economic development and foreign trade policy for Venezuela. This was closely followed by Gillespie and Holland [1963], an exploratory development planning model with special reference to India. In 1967 Kresge constructed a similar general simulation model to be used for policy evaluations in Pakistan. These studies represent initial applications of systems concepts and simulation methods to development planning, although they are nonagricultural, it is clear that they have influenced subsequent efforts in the construction of development models. In addition to the Michigan State work on Nigeria and Korea (Manetsch [1974]), the models include those constructed by Foster and Yost [1969] for Uganda, by Mathis [1969] and Billingsley and Norvell [1971] for the Dominican Republic, Singh and Day [1972] for the Indian Punjab, and Simpson and Billingsley [1973] for Paraguay.

An overview of historical efforts in this field also suggests that development models may be viewed simply as transfers of methods applied to similar problems in developed countries. For example, the work of Halter and Miller [1966] had a marked influence on the models constructed at Michigan State University for Nigeria and Korea. Other applications such as Day and Singh [1971], Singh and Day [1972], and Taylor [1969] provide further support for this claim.

DISTINGUISHING CHARACTERISTICS

Because of the unavailability of data and other problems just mentioned, systems models constructed for development studies have some easily identifiable characteristics. They generally make substantial use of component and decomposition possibilities. Although levels of component autonomy along with levels of aggregation are different among models, both are much in evidence. The value of the components approach in these studies is based upon team research project possibilities, as typified by the Nigerian study (Manetsch, Hayenga, et al. [1971]), and associated advantages for dealing with the problems created by a lack of information.

Another important characteristic of these models relates to their theoretical content. With a few exceptions (notably the models by Day and Singh [1971] and Singh and Day [1972]) the models are aggregative—that is, specified at industry, regional, or sectoral levels. As a consequence, the models are often descriptive, with more emphasis on the structure of particular economies than on established theories. As indicated earlier this characteristic of the models adds substantially to the validation problems. The data are limited in quantity and quality. Aspects of this latter problem are further complicated by the multitude of alternative hypotheses associated with the specified structural models.

ILLUSTRATIVE FORM

The forms of development models are highly variable. Some are aggregate and thus similar to the type discussed in the preceding section. Others are market or industry models and therefore resemble those mentioned in the section on Market or Industry Models. A third class consists of micro models which have very close ties with theories of the firm and individual behavior. Special types of micro models are concerned with the diffusion of new techniques among farmers in traditional sectors. A rural sociological approach to this problem has been advanced by Carroll [1968], and a microeconomic approach that simulates farmers' perceptions and their changes by Bayesian analysis (probabilities are revised as experience accumulates) and then aggregates individual technique switching rates to community adoption rates is presented by O'Mara [1971]. The common aspect of these models is of course that they concentrate on the dynamic features of the less developed economic systems studied.

SURVEY

The sector economy models surveyed are those by Halter, Hayenga, and Manetsch [1970], Manetsch [1974], Manetsch, Hayenga, et al. [1971], and Taylor [1969]. Along with these models we might also have included those by Billingsley and Norvell [1971] and Foster and Yost [1969],[11] which are not sectoral or economy models but which incorporate similar methods of analysis. Both models have demographic components; the Billingsley and Norvell model is concerned with evaluating alternative government fertility policies, and the Foster and Yost model is concerned chiefly with the relationship between growth, education, and income in less developed economies.

Sector models identified with Michigan State University [1973] are by Halter, Hayenga and Manetsch [1970], Manetsch, Hayenga, et al. [1971], and Manetsch [1974]. These studies report on massive systems modeling efforts in Nigeria and Korea. The models employed in the studies are complex and extensive by comparison to others surveyed. Each uses advantageously the components concepts just mentioned. The methods of model formulation, estimation, and simulation employed in the studies are not innovative. Encouraging aspects of the endeavors involve possibilities for adapting the software for work with other economies (Manetsch [1974]) and the fact that the work has generated considerable interest among policy makers. It is also interesting to note that these efforts were developed for clearly defined clients—namely, government planners. The research investigators on this project were able to interact with their clients and to obtain their support in acquiring the information and data to construct the model representation. This effort was, of course, costly; development and operation costs associated with the Nigerian model were approximately $300,000 (Manetsch, Hayenga, et al. [1971]).

In the remaining sectoral model Taylor [1969] presents a departure from the larger and more comprehensive efforts just discussed. It is a systems model tied quite closely to the Domar theory of economic growth for developed countries. It is estimated by standard econometric techniques and is evaluated by means of a highly structured format.

The regional model listed in table 6 is by Day and Singh [1971] (see also Singh and Day [1972]). This development model is noteworthy in two respects. First, it corresponds to a micro firm model and as such has stronger theoretical underpinnings than the other development models. The model is designed to study the change from traditional to commercial agriculture in the Punjab. It is recursive, with a number of feedback alternatives involving changes in the adaptation of technology, market prices, and so on. The incorporation of a lexicographic ordering of objectives seems to represent a very promising possibility for models applied in the development context. A second noteworthy aspect of this study is the set of validation procedures employed. Not only do the authors include a discussion and application of formal validation procedures, but the procedures themselves are novel in the sense that they involve the use of information theoretic concepts (Day and Singh [1971]).

Models for industries include studies by Aldabe and Rijckeghem [1966], Lehker and Manetsch [1971], Manetsch and Lenghner [1971], Manetsch, Ramos, and Lenchner [1968], Miller and Halter [1973], and Roberts and Kresge [1968]. Aside from institutional and information problems which are typical in development studies, these works are similar to the industry studies reported in the market model survey. The models are typically descriptive, without well-defined criterion functions, and are designed for studying or forecasting influences of policy actions on industry output, price, and the like.

Other references using development models include G. L. Johnson [1970], Rausser [1973], and Thorbecke [1971].

SUMMARY AND EVALUATION

Most of the development models have decision or policy purposes and, as expected, all are dynamic. Approximately three-quarters of these models are also nonlinear. However, few of the models were simulated stochastically, and only approximately one-third were actively validated.

With the exception of the model by Day and Singh [1971], the systems studies are themselves underdeveloped with respect to the design of policy experiments and response surface examination. (For a more detailed discussion of the possibilities along these lines, see Rausser and Johnson [1975].) The lack of advancement regarding method can be explained in part by the fact that the studies were highly exploratory and frequently performed under time constraints and with inadequate information bases. It is in these areas that development studies are likely to be improved. The work already done in development modeling suggests a high payoff for refining the methods used in these studies.

Although methodological difficulties confronted in the construction of development models will continue to represent formidable obstacles (Norvell [1972]) and much justified skepticism exists concerning the value of such exercises, it appears that funding sources for such efforts will provide renewed and augmented support. A project under way by Heady and his associates in Thailand, employing a large number of people, is one illustrative example justifying this expectation. It is hoped that such work will result not only in improved policy selections by the governments of developing countries but also in improved methods of data gathering, modeling, and simulation. In particular, this would be an ideal area in which to consider questions of proper data basis and, in fact, what data should be collected by the public sector (Rausser [1973]). Unfortunately, as yet such questions have not been explicitly addressed.

Resource Models

In this area, as with gaming models, the modern applications of systems concepts and simulation methods have much historical significance. However, in contrast to the importance of simulation in the early development of gaming models, the emphasis in the resource literature was initially on the concept of a system. Systems concepts, growing out of the physical aspects of the problems studied and the engineering literaure, found a very natural application in studies of resource problems.

HISTORY

The evolution of modern systems concepts as related to water resource problems has been well documented by Hufschmidt [1963]. Apparently the notion of systems especially in the context of river basin planning has been clearly understood since about 1900. Evidence of the long familiarity of engineers with the concept may be found in still earlier writings (Ellet [1853]). The concept in an operational setting first found extensive application in the integrated program initiated under the Tennessee Valley Authority in 1933. By 1950 it had been employed at operational policy levels in structuring approaches to water resource problems (President's Water Resource Policy Commission [1950]).

Modern treatments of water resource systems based on quantitative models began at about the time that electronic computers emerged as a research tool. As the systems framework was largely in place, the application of simulation tools to resource models came rapidly. Interdisciplinary water resources planning was initiated at Harvard in 1955, and by 1962 the highly influential volume, *Design of Water-Resource Systems*, was published (Maass et al. [1962]). This volume and the studies associated with it have had an important impact not only on water resources research but on applications of modern systems concepts and simulation methods in other fields of economics as well as other areas of the social and physical sciences.

DISTINGUISHING CHARACTERISTICS

Systems and simulation applications to natural resource and regional development problems often involve the public sector. As Kain and Meyer [1968] have noted, simulation is particularly useful when evaluating "public investments characterized by important externalities, broad social objectives and durable installations."[12] When we add to these features the importance of uncertainty, technological change, research and development strategies, and the sequential aspects of natural resource decision making, computer simulation becomes an even more appealing tool (Rausser and Dean [1971a, 1971b]).

In a mechanistic sense models of resource systems are generally dynamic and nonlinear. Some nonlinearities are fairly substantial, including those involving artificial time-counter relationships. Dynamic structures of these models are often characterized by lagged, internally determined, and conditioning variables and are represented by a system of difference equations. Approximately 50 percent of the models are simulated in stochastic form. Most stochastic simulations are limited, however, in the sense that only additive stochastic (disturbance) elements are recognized—that is, only first moments of sampling distributions of the structural parameter estimates are used. They also include a large number of the stochastic simulations developed for the physical models representing hydrologic phenomena.

Simulation experiments for this group of models are more sophisticated than for the models previously surveyed. Various partial and complete factorial designs have been employed to examine response surface questions. Some designs also involve optimum seeking methods. Validation procedures however, are less precise. Only eight of the studies went beyond graphical comparisons of sample or historical and simulated values of selected output variables. The predictive properties of the models were typically neglected in corroborating them with the systems in question.

ILLUSTRATIVE FORM

Table 7 contains a tabular survey of applications of simulation methods to agriculturally related resource problems. It is by no means an exhaustive list, but simply one intended to be representative of the available works involving natural resource and regional economic systems. Most of this work has focused on river basin systems or watershed systems. Hence, the major components of the models frequently include information on the various flood, demographic, transportation and use sectors, reservoirs for irrigated crop production, and the like. These components are often treated recursively and there is typically a substantial amount of temporal interaction and feedback among them.

Benefit-cost criteria usually provide the basis for evaluating alternative policy decisions in these systems. Decision models comprise about one-half of studies surveyed. Most of the others are behavioral models and are largely descriptive. The behavioral models are principally concerned with the development of physical relationships such as those involving natural hydrologic phenomena (Maass et al. [1962]).

SURVEY

The models specified in Halter and Miller [1966], Hufschmidt and Fiering [1966], Hamilton et al. [1969], Rausser, Willis, and Frick [1972], Rausser and Willis [1976], Jacoby [1967], Dudley and Burt [1973], and V. T. Chow and Kareliotis [1970] are viewed as representative of this group and selected for further discussion. The first three models concern river basin systems. The Halter and Miller model represents an early application of industrial dynamics to water resource development projects. The proposed projects of the Halter and Miller model were dam construction and channel improvements in the Calapooia River Basin. The benefits of dam construction and channel improvements included irrigation, flood control, fishing, and drainage. A particularly interesting aspect of this model was the treatment of the temporal distribution for hydrologic flows. These flows were generated internally in the model by a random number generator process. Considerable care was taken in attempts to assure that the simulated hydrologic data conformed to historical flows. The experimental design used for the decision problem was reasonably simple with no indication of how the combination of project size and operating rules was selected and evaluated.

The Hufschmidt and Fiering model [1966] is more general than the one advanced by Halter and Miller. The Hufschmidt and Fiering study presents the steps and procedures for a simulation program including aspects related to collecting and organizing hydrologic and economic data. These procedures were applied to the Delaware River basin and to its subsystem, the Lehigh River basin. An interesting development for synthesizing hydrologic events is provided. Pollution is considered along with abatement costs. Three criteria were employed to validate the models. For decision applications, economic consequences (benefit and costs) associated with design variables and outputs were evaluated under several assumed interest rates, static and dynamic investment patterns, and discounting methods. An explicit criterion function was specified—namely, the present value of expected net benefits along with the variance of these benefits. A few basic plans were investigated and, from the knowledge accumulated, improvements were made upon the basic plans and the search continued. However, no specific search procedure was developed.

The third river basin study conducted by Hamilton et al. [1969] is of a more regional nature than either of the other two. As a case study of systems simulation applied to regional economic and river systems modeling, it should prove of value for some years to come. A useful aspect of this study is the inclusion of an appendix containing a short discourse on the management of a multidisciplinary research project. The principal objective of the work was to advance the state of the systems simulation art for regional analysis, particularly where social and technological factors form an integral part of the system under examination. The illustrative model (Susquehanna River basin) is composed of three major components that describe the demographic, employment, and water supply characteristics of nine subregions comprising the river basin.

Important features of the Hamilton systems model are (1) the inclusion of demographic and economic components in a single model; (2) the explicit application of economic and engineering concepts to regional water resource problems; (3) dynamic aspects in the form of feedbacks and lagged variables within the various components as well as between components; and (4) the ability of the model to facilitate sensitivity analysis. One of the interesting results of the simulation analysis was the indication that water shortages emanate not from scarcity of the water resource itself but from current water treatment, storage, and distribution systems.

Turning from the river basin models, we must note the recent studies by Rausser, Willis, and Frick [1972] and Rausser and Willis [1976], which were advanced in an attempt to determine the proper level of public subsidies for water desalting plants, the investment levels and sequencing of various water source developments, and the allocation of water across different use sectors. The bases for the public subsidies are the external benefits which result from "learning"—in this case, the accumulation of knowledge on desalting techniques. Experience gained in the construction and operation of a particular desalting plant is presumed to lead to more efficient production for future plants. In a dynamic context costs depend not only upon the current level of production but also upon cumulative experience.

A "learning by doing" model provides the basis for the nonlinear and dynamic learning functions (Rausser, Willis, and Frick [1972] estimated by classical *and* Bayesian methods. For the Bayesian estimates, two alternative families of prior probability density functions were utilized. The first was based on the learning experience of nondesalting industries and the second on sample desalting costs of foreign plants. Based in part upon these estimates, a joint probability distribution including external learning benefits was specified. Since it was not possible to derive the marginal density function for benefits analytically, computer simulation experiments were employed. Given the approximated external benefit distributions, appropriate levels of public (state and federal) subsidies under alternative assumptions were derived. The computed subsidies enter a multiple source decision framework comprised of two major components, one for sequencing investments in water supply facilities and the other for allocating water supplied under uncertainty across regions and use sectors. Since the "curse of dimensionality" precluded an analytical solution, these two components along with the subsidy component were solved separately, and iterative simulation was employed to achieve consistency among the three components (Rausser and Willis [1976]).[13]

The model developed by Jacoby [1967] emphasizes alternative investment and operating decisions for electric power plants in West Pakistan. The potential investments in generation facilities for each of several electric power markets are analyzed. Each plan was constrained to satisfy predetermined power demands, and the associated temporal patterns of operating costs were specified. The computer simulation model generates outputs of various plants, ranges of fuel prices, transmission constraints for each year, the distribution of foreign exchange rates, and the distribution of opportunity costs of capital. The latter information is particularly important given the multi-purpose nature of hydroelectric and irrigation developments in the regions investigated. Experimental designs employed in this simulation analysis involved both multistage techniques and partial factorial designs. On the basis of a single basic demand projection several plans were tested, some of which were eliminated from further analysis. This initial analysis provided a new set of combinations to be investigated. Unfortunately, no real attempt was made to validate the constructed model.

The Dudley and Burt [1973] model was intended to determine the "best" area size for irrigation in conjunction with a reservoir of given capacity. The specified criterion function involves a twenty-year planning horizon, net revenue derived from irrigated cropland, net revenue derived from dryland crops, and fixed costs of capital items. The actual effects of varying acreages were determined by simulating over a twenty-year period for both stochastic demand and supply. The acreage for which the largest value of the criterion function was obtained was regarded as optimal for irrigation development.

Sensitivity analysis was employed in an attempt to determine how the selected acreage should be altered under varying opportunity costs. Opportunity costs were allowed to vary from 50 to 150 percent of original estimates. Quadratic functions (for each level of opportunity costs) relating net revenue to irrigable acreages were also estimated, and penalties for employing suboptimal acreages were computed. No attempt to verify the constructed model is advanced, and the experimental design is simple.

A number of models related to the above efforts have been constructed to analyze rural and regional development problems. An illustrative example of a rural development model is the work of Doeksen and Schreiner [1972], which was utilized to analyze state investments in agricultural processing. Following the model developed by Hamilton et al. [1969], Fullerton and Prescott [1975] constructed a regional development planning model for Iowa. This model provides a formal basis for achieving spatial and temporal consistency between the state economy and its smaller components (counties and cities). Systems concepts and simulation have also been applied to natural wildlife resources. For example, several interesting simulation experiments conducted to improve the management of a deer herd are discussed by F. M. Anderson et al. [1971].

Recent applications which follow an earlier suggestion by Dorfman [1965] to combine the use of analytical optimization and simulation methods are the models developed by Jacoby and Loucks [1972] and Dudley and Burt [1973]. The first study involves construction of a river basin planning model in which the number of available development opportunities is extremely large. To analyze the resulting framework in a tractable fashion, Jacoby and Loucks employ analytical optimization models to screen the set of possible plans and select a smaller number for detailed simulation analysis. The stochastic aspects of the problem are explicitly recognized in this study and in the Dudley and Burt model. The latter model, following the earlier work of Dudley [1972], uses a simulation model to compute state variable transition probabilities, which in turn are utilized in a stochastic dynamic programming model to determine (1) the optimal intertemporal water application rates, (2) the optimal abandonment of irrigated acreage for the remainder of the season, and (3) the optimal acreage to plant for potential irrigation at the beginning of the season.

As previously indicated, several of the studies represented in table 7 refer to physical models concerned with hydrologic phenomena. The model by V. T. Chow and Kareliotis [1970] is representative of these studies. This hydrologic model was formulated in the context of a watershed system and was applied to the upper Sangamon River basin. The model input is rainfall and the output is runoff and evapotranspiration. Runoff is composed of three stochastic components—groundwater storage, total rinfall, and total losses. Three alternative models for these processes are compared and evaluated. These models are basically a moving average, a sum of harmonics, and an autoregressive specification. In selecting among models the non-nested nature of the hypotheses (or the disparate families of hypotheses) represented by the alternative model representations was not recognized. Instead the selection was based upon correlogram and spectral analysis. All three runoff components were found to exhibit correlograms oscillating without any indication of dampening. Along with the power spectrum of the sample data revealing significant peaks for six-month and annual periods, this resulted in the selection of a combined sum of harmonics and autoregressive time series model representation. No explicit attempt was made to validate this mode, feedback effects were notably lacking, and experimental designs were not utilized in simulating runoff processes.

Other useful references on resource models include R. L. Anderson and Maass [1974]; Askew, Yeh, and Hall [1971]; Chen [1971]; Ellis [1966]; Howitt et al. [1974]; Huggins and Monke [1968]; Leistritz [1970]; McMahon and Miller [1971]; Masch and Associates [1971]; Miernyk [1969]; Pisano [1968]; Rodriguez-Iturbe, Dawdy, and Garcia [1971]; Shih and Dracup [1961]; Stillson [1969].

SUMMARY AND EVALUATION

The resource systems models are generally more advanced relative to the other survey application areas, particularly in terms of their detail and the methods employed in using simulation for decision analysis. However, they might be characterized as deficient in terms of model validation and theoretical foundations. Owing to their complexity, this is not an unexpected result. In general, the early and substantive work done with systems in connection with water resources research and the sustained record of incorporating new developments are reflected in the quality of the models and the promising results obtained.

A trend of recent vintage and one that we hope will continue and experience further growth is explicit recognition of risk and uncertainty. In addition to the studies surveyed here various models have been advanced to explore the impact of risk by stochastically simulating alternative project performance. Illustrative applications of these efforts may be found in the occasional staff paper series of the World Bank (for example, Pouliquen [1970] and Reutlinger [1970b]). Applications of these methods along with other approaches to uncertainty in a water resource context are treated in Rausser and Dean [1971a, 1971b].

Critique and Appraisal

In the previous sections we have discussed and documented the value of systems concepts and simulation in agricultural economics. The impact of the modern development of systems analysis and simulation techniques, however, is apparent. New and more ambitious approaches to problems posed in the context of existing paradigms and exploratory work with less confined constructs have been stimulated by the development of systems and simulation methods. In fact, the vitality associated with the renaissance in research and teaching processes which has occurred as a result of the incorporation of these methods may represent their most important contribution. Grappling with the difficulties presented by applications of this highly flexible approach and attempting to refine it should continue to provide the profession with a basis for a stream of useful results.

Our survey of both methods and empirical applications indicates that the value of systems analysis and simulation can be more fully exploited if the two processes are themselves more systematically employed. Moreover, the appropriate framework to be utilized as a basis for systematizing the processes of model construction and use involves concepts of adaptive control. Given the usual stated objectives of model construction and the dynamic, searching processes implied by the use of systems concepts and simulation, adaptive control procedures present a natural framework for systematizing the sequences of decisions required to implement the approach. The fact that the most useful applications and the most promising developments of method can be shown to embody these concepts should suffice to underscore their current and potential importance for the processes of systems analysis and simulation.

One of the much emphasized attributes of systems and simulation methods relates to the use of the approach as a substitute for more expensive or larger-scale physical experiments. Within the adaptive control framework problems resulting from attempts to formulate and investigate such models have a natural criterion function — that is, the criterion function is to maximize the information content of the results less the costs of complexity, given physical, institutional, time, and budget constraints. Policy or control variables for problems formulated in this context, however, are less apparent. At present they would seem to be discrete types of choices such as methods of parameter estimation, complexity of the model, scale of prototype, choices of paradigm, verification procedures, and the like. Choices of control variables would of course vary with the problem being studied and the purpose of the modeling exercise.

An interesting method for handling problems of this type is the preposterior analysis suggested by J. R. Anderson and Dillon [1968]. For crop response function estimation, this approach provides the researcher with a means of effectively positioning actual physical experiments. As a consequence, model complexity and the cost of the physical experimentation can be reduced. In this exercise the control variables relate to the extent of preposterior analysis and the choices of physical experiments based on such information. Although not fully exploiting the sequential nature of such problems, the structured approach advanced by these authors has a wide area of potential application. Surfaces generated by criterion functions in decision models, predictive performance functions, and measures of appropriate behavior characterization can obviously be viewed in a response framework. Accordingly, the associated response functions can be explored, at least conceptually, using methods of preposterior analysis.

Model construction is an obvious activity in which an adaptive framework can be advantageously applied. Currently, a major limitation associated with the flexibility of systems analysis and simulation, particularly in the context of exploratory modeling, is the close identity of the model with the researcher. Adaptive control procedures employed in moving sequentially from provisional to final models of systems can be quite helpful in depersonalizing research results. In this manner the adaptive modeling approach can aid in making research results verifiable by other investigators. Concerns associated with this aspect of systems models and results of simulations (Department of Defense [1972], Rausser and Johnson [1975]) are likely to provide strong incentives for developing models on the basis of more structured processes.

A related development concerns the process of verifying models. Our discussion of the applications indicates that with some notable exceptions (for example, Singh and Day [1972]) agricultural economists have been somewhat lax in corroborating systems models. Methods of accomplishing this task are rapidly being developed (Rausser and Johnson [1975]). As these advances represent an additional means of evaluating comparative models, they should find wider application as systems analysis and simulation become more commonly applied in agricultural economics research. Alternative model verification procedures are of course choices in the context of the adaptive model construction problem.

These advances in verification techniques have in large part been made possible by the advancement of structured rationalizations for the process of estimating or specializing systems models for particular situations. In this regard, the debate surrounding the Forrester contention [1961] that sample data or past data on the system are not useful in constructing models has been grossly unproductive. Instead of searching for an estimation method sufficiently general to incorporate the Forrester argument, many researchers have apparently chosen instead to reject statistical and econometric approaches to model construction. The unfortunate result was and is that the associated models have little generality. If one cannot establish that the parameters of a systems model are at least partially estimated on a sampling basis, then the foundations for generalizing the results and verifying the model simply are not present. In view of these problems, the mixed estimation methods (Theil [1971]), the Bayesian methods (Zellner [1971]), and the associated generalizations to the sequential processes involved in model construction (Leamer [1970]) represent most promising developments.

Applications of the systems models are also likely to benefit from more highly systematized simulations. The shopworn and increasingly suspect argument that systems analysis presents a method for analyzing problems without a criterion function will soon lose its acceptance. If viewed with sufficient abstraction, it is clear that all models (since they are readily admitted to be purposeful) involve some type of criterion function (Rausser and Freebairn [1974a, 1974b]). This being the case, experiments with systems models can be much improved. Recognition and incorporation of the criterion function can provide a basis for conducting experiments with the systems models which are considerably more informative. In this regard, the works of Zusman and Amiad [1965], Shechter and Heady [1970], and Jacoby and Loucks [1972] represent examples of methods of model application which are likely to prevail in future work.

The same observations apply of course to behavioral and predictive models. That is, given a criterion for the research exercise, experimental designs can be advantageously applied to enhance the value of simulated results. Again, the emphasis is on a more structured approach to the application of the models. Applications of these methods are likely to produce results of the type developed by Candler and Cartwright [1969]. Incentives for explicitly identifying criterion functions are also likely to occur as a result of difficulties arising in summarizing and presenting outcomes of simulations. Without some method of summarizing these experiments the output from model simulations can quickly become unmanageable. Summarizing, however, if it is to be useful and to represent the outcomes of the experiments accurately, requires the specification of a criterion function. Hence, full exploitation of systems models conditioned upon the various time and budget constraints and the presentation of results in the most meaningful fashion are among the compelling arguments in favor of complete specification of the model including the criterion function.

Given the preceding comments concerning the structuring of model development and applications, one might counter by suggesting that past applications of the systems approach were justified in proceeding in an unsys-tematized manner because they were heuristic. Here again, however, there are well-established arguments for structuring research efforts more carefully. In fact, the major points associated with the gathering of artificial intelligence and heuristic modeling (Kuehn and Hamburger [1963], Meier, Newell, and Pater [1969]) are themselves based on systematized search techniques. Their implications for learning about systems through systems analysis and simula-tion are therefore consistent with the methods which have identified the adaptive control framework with promising developments.

What are we to infer from these observations on promising developments and their identification with adaptive control processes? Obviously, they do not imply that everyone should rush out and purchase a copy of the latest text on adaptive control. Research and teaching activities based on systems concepts and simulation, although effectively viewed within the control framework, present problems which are not currently mathematically trac-table. Hence, it is principally the conceptual basis of control rather than actual solutions to adaptive control problems which is advanced here as pro-viding a basis on which systems analysis and simulation can be systematized.

If the argued relationships between modern control theory and systems analysis are correct, then we may anticipate substantial adjustments in both our research and teaching efforts. Contrary to rather widely held opinions, the advent of systems and simulation concepts has not freed us from our pre-vious preoccupation with economic theory and quantitative methods. That is, instead of allowing researchers to circumvent some more traditional areas of training in quantitative methods and theory, the more advanced aspects of systems and simulation analysis require even stronger backgrounds in these areas. It is becoming increasingly clear that a knowledge of computer pro-gramming or some special simulation language is not a license for conducting effective research in agricultural economics. Statistical and theoretical ques-tions raised by the application of systems models are of such magnitude that research produced by mechanical applications of the approach is likely to be of little general interest.

The implications of the foregoing observations for the training of graduate and undergraduate students and for our extension tasks are reasonably clear. The flexibility of the systems method has suggested applications which take us away from the familiar confines of neoclassical theory, classical statistical methods, and some of our closely held methodological paradigms. As applica-tions of systems models become more systematized, it seems inevitable that additional study of optimization theory (in dynamic and stochastic contexts) and Bayesian and sequential statistical methods will become more common-place. Moreover, our conceptions of the process of learning and generating new knowledge are quite likely to be severed from the positive doctrines which dominated thinking along these lines in the 1950s and 1960s.

The advent of the predicted changes should be most encouraging. It fore-tells the eventual merger of our theories of individual behavior with data or empirical evidence and methods of estimation. It would be unfortunate not to acknowledge the debt of such advancements to the concepts of systems and systems analysis. The questions raised by the development and applica-tion of systems concepts and simulation methods have had a substantial im-pact in stimulating interest in refining techniques of estimation and in extend-ing the theory. At the same time our discussion has indicated that systems analysis of economic problems as currently applied in the discipline is itself in for some rather substantial alterations.

Tables of General References and Surveys

Table 1 contains a list of the general references on systems simulation analysis and simulation cited in the text. In the remaining six tables the references on the various kinds of applications are summarized: table 2, gaming and related models; table 3, firm and process models; table 4, market and industry mod-els; table 5, aggregate models; table 6, economic development models; table 7, natural resource models. In these tables the studies are identified by the names of the authors and the year of publication, and the modeled situation, the objectives, and the decision variables are described briefly. The reported characteristics in table 2 include the time dimension and whether or not the model is multistage, competitive, open or closed, computerized, or stochastic. The reported characteristics in tables 3-7 include type of model, type of simu-lation, computer language, validation procedures, and information on wheth-er the model is dynamic, stochastic, or nonlinear.

Most of the characteristics listed in tables 2-7 are self-explanatory. The three characteristics which may require elaboration are validation, type of simulation, and the competitive versus noncompetitive classification for the gaming models. The terms used to describe the validation process are active and passive. All researchers are of course concerned with corroborating model representations with systems and, in fact, are probably implicitly doing so at all stages of the construction process. Such implicit corroborative activities are described in the tables as passive validation. Corroboration processes that are more systematic and that involve the results of tests and associated pro-cedures are classified as active validation processes.

The simulations of the models are classified as historical, ad hoc, and de-signed. Historical simulations refer to experiments with models in which the conditioning variables are entered as historical data series. Ad hoc simulations refer to experiments in which the design points (values for conditioning variables, parameters, and so on) have been chosen in an intuitive or nonsystematic fashion. Designed simulations are those in which the experiments with the models have been developed using an experimental design. This implies the inclusion of an implicit or explicit response or objective function and the choice of a method of selecting design points which will produce the information required to identify the associated relationship.

Competitive games are defined as those in which the actions of one player or team do not affect the outcomes for other players or teams. In contrast, for noncompetitive games the outcomes are dependent upon player or team interactions.

Along with the above clarifications it should be noted that in the decision variable columns of tables 3-7 we report for *behavioral* and *forecasting* models the endogenous variables which refer to actions taken by the behavioral units, whereas for *decision* models we report those exogenous variables which refer to policy actions that might be taken by public or private decision makers. Second, the procedures for classifying models as linear or nonlinear are arbitrary; some models in which only weak departures from linearity exist are classified as linear models. Third, we classify as stochastic those models which are simulated stochastically (not constructed models which incorporate stochastic elements). Last, in the case of simulation models for which the computer language is unknown (for instance, because it was not reported and could not be inferred), Fortran is listed.

Table 1. General References on Systems Simulation Analysis and Simulation

Ackoff [1971]	Bean [1929]
Adelman and Adelman [1959]	Bellman [1961]
Aigner [1972]	Bellman, Clark, et al. [1957]
Aitchison and Silvey [1958]	Bellman and Kalaba [1959]
Albert and Sittler [1965]	Black [1924, 1953]
American Management Association [1961]	Boehlje and Eisgruber [1972]
J. R. Anderson [1974a, 1974b]	Bonini [1963, 1964]
J. R. Anderson and Dillon [1968]	G. E. P. Box [1954, 1957]
Ansoff and Slevin [1968]	G. E. P. Box and Hunter [1959]
Aoki [1967, 1974, 1975]	G. E. P. Box and Wilson [1951]
Armstrong and Hepp [1970]	M. J. Box and Draper [1972]
Astrom and Wittenmark [1971]	Buchanan and Norton [1971]
Atkinson [1970]	Burdick and Naylor [1966, 1969]
Babb [1964]	Burt [1969]
Babb and Eisgruber [1966]	Bush and Estes [1959]
Babb and French [1963]	Castro and Weingarten [1970]
Bar-Shalom and Sivan [1969]	Chan [1971]
	Charlton and Thompson [1970]

Table 1. General References on Systems Simulation Analysis and Simulation (Cont.)

Chernoff [1972]
Chorafas [1965]
Chow [1972, 1973, 1975]
Churchman [1960, 1968, 1971]
Clarkson and Simon [1960]
Cochran and Cox [1957]
Cohen and Cyert [1961, 1965]
Conlisk and Watts [1969]
Conway and Maxwell [1959]
Cooper [1972]
Coplin [1968]
Cox [1961, 1962]
Curry [1970]
Cyert and March [1963]
Davies [1954]
Day [1971]
Day and Sparling [1977]
Dent and Anderson [1971]
Department of Defense [1970]
Deutsch [1969]
Dhrymes et al. [1972]
Donaldson and Webster [1968]
Dorfman [1963, 1965]
Drynan [1973]
Early and Early [1972]
Eidman [1971]
Eisgruber and Nielson [1963]
Eldor and Koppel [1971]
Emery [1969]
Emshoff and Sisson [1970]
M. Evans [1969]
Fel'dbaum [1965]
Fine and McIsaac [1966]
Finney [1945]
Fisher [1962]
Fishman [1967, 1968, 1971a]
Fishman and Kiviat [1967]
Fletcher et al. [1970]
Forrester [1961, 1968]
Fox, Sengupta, and Thorbecke [1966]
Freebairn and Rausser [1974]
C. E. French [1974]
Friedman [1971]
Frisch [1935-36]
Fromm [1969]
Fromm and Taubman [1968]
Gaver and Geisel [1974]

Geisel [1970]
Goldberg [1968]
Gordon [1970]
Granger and Hatanaka [1964]
Gross and Ray [1965]
Gunckel and Franklin [1963]
Haitovsky and Wallace [1972]
Halter, Hayenga, and Manetsch [1970]
Hammersley and Handscomb [1964]
Handscomb [1969]
Hare [1967]
Harbaugh and Bonham-Carter [1970]
Harling [1958]
Heady [1971]
Hesselbach and Eisgruber [1967]
Hill and Hunter [1966]
Hinman and Hutton [1970]
Hoggatt and Balderston [1963]
Hollingdale [1967]
Holt [1962]
Holt et al. [1964]
Hood and Koopmans [1953]
Howrey [1971]
Howrey and Kelejian [1969, 1971]
Howrey and Klein [1972]
Hufschmidt [1962]
Hunter and Naylor [1970]
IBM [1966a, 1966b]
Ignall [1972]
Ingram, Kain, and Ginn [1973]
Jeffreys [1961]
John [1971]
B. Johnson and Eisgruber [1969]
G. L. Johnson [1970]
G. L. Johnson and Zerby [1973]
H. G. Johnson [1951]
S. R. Johnson, Tefertiller, and Moore
    [1967]
Jorgenson, Hunter, and Nadiri [1970]
Judge [1968, 1977]
Judge and Yancey [1969]
Kagel et al. [1975]
Kalman [1960]
Kiviat [1967]
Kiviat, Villanueva, and Markowitz
    [1968]
Kleijnen [1972, 1974, 1975]

Table 1. General References on Systems Simulation Analysis and Simulation (Cont.)

Klein and Burmeister [1976]
Kogan [1966]
Kornai [1971]
Kotler and Schultz [1970]
Kourtz and O'Reagan [1968]
Krasnow and Merikallio [1964]
Kuehn [1962]
Kuehn and Hamburger [1963]
Kuhn [1970]
LaDue and Vincent [1974]
Lavington [1970]
Leamer [1970]
A. M. Lee [1970]
G. E. Lee [1974]
Leontief [1971]
MacCrimmon and Tota [1969]
Maffei [1958]
Malcolm [1960]
Manetsch, Hayenga, et al. [1971]
Marschak [1963]
Marsden, Pingry, and Whinston [1974]
Martin [1968]
Meadows et al. [1972]
Mehra [1974]
Meier [1967]
Meier, Newell, and Pazer [1969]
Mendenhall [1968]
Mesarovic, Macko, and Takahara
    [1970]
Mihram [1972]
Mize and Cox [1968]
Moore [1914]
Murphy [1968]
Nagar [1969]
Nance [1971]
Naylor [1969a, 1969b, 1970, 1971,
    1972]
Naylor, Burdick, and Sasser [1967]
Naylor and Finger [1967]
Naylor, Wertz, and Wonnacott [1967,
    1969]
Nijkamp [1970]
Optner [1960]
Orcutt [1960]
Orcutt et al. [1961]

Patten [1971]
Perkins, Cruz, and Sundararajan [1972]
Popper [1959]
Porter et al. [1966]
Prescott [1967, 1971, 1972]
Ramsey [1969]
Ramsey and Zarembka [1971]
Rausser [1973, 1974a, 1974b]
Rausser and Freebairn [1974a, 1974b,
    1976]
Rausser and Johnson [1975]
Rothenberg [1961]
Samuelson [1947]
Schechter and Heady [1970]
Schlaifer [1959]
Schmidt and Taylor [1970]
Schruben [1968]
Shubik [1960]
Simon [1956]
Simon and Newell [1958]
V. K. Smith [1973]
V. L. Smith [1962, 1964]
Snyder and Swackhamer [1966]
Strotz and Wold [1960]
Suttor and Crom [1964]
Tarn [1971]
H. C. Taylor [1929]
Theil [1964, 1971]
Thorbecke [1971]
Tinbergen [1952]
Tocher [1963]
Tse [1974]
Tse and Athans [1970, 1972]
Tse and Bar-Shalom [1973]
Tse, Bar-Shalom, and Meier [1973]
Tyner and Tweeten [1968]
Van Horn [1971]
Vichnevetsky [1969]
Wallace and Ashar [1972]
Watt [1966]
Watts [1969]
Ying [1967]
Zellner [1971]
Zellner and Chetty [1965]
Zellner and Peck [1973]

Table 2. Gaming Models in Agricultural Economics

References	Situation	Objectives	Time Unit[a]	Multi-stage	Compe-titive	Open-Closed	Decision Variables	Comput-erized	Sto-chastic
Babb and Eisgruber [1966]	Each team manages a farm supply store that has been deteriorating financially	To learn about management in a competitive environment	U	Yes	No	Open	Price, inventory, credit, employment, storage capacity, truck expenditures, investments	Yes	Yes
Babb and Eisgruber [1966]	As many as four dairies compete in a local market	To stress importance of financial planning and to understand the nature of competition and strategy formulation	Month	Yes	No	Open	Price, advertising practices, commission rates	Yes	No
Babb and Eisgruber [1966]	Operating a farm in pure competition	To stress farm management and illustrate choice of product combination	Year	Yes	No	Open	Production levels, method of production, land purchase, sale, and/or purchase of breeding stock	Yes	Yes
Babb and Eisgruber [1966]	Firms selling four types of products in an urban market	To learn about marketing management	U	Yes	Yes	Open	Margins, specials, advertising, orders, stamps, personnel, loans	Yes	No

243

Table 2. Gaming Models in Agricultural Economics (Cont.)

References	Situation	Objectives	Time Unit[a]	Multi-stage	Compe-titive	Open-Closed	Decision Variables	Comput-erized	Sto-chastic
Bellman, Clark, et al. [1957]	Firms competing for a known consumer market	To provide a means of executive training using simulation techniques in a multiperson business game, stressing long-run policy decisions	U	Yes	Yes	Open	Price, production rate, marketing budget, research and development, budget, investment	Yes	No
Bentz and Williams [1965]	Teams operate four egg-handling plants in Illinois	To examine relationship between a firm and its environment	Month	Yes	No	Closed	Input purchases, capital investments, prices paid	Yes	Yes
Curtis [1968]	Managing a single farm	To evaluate the effectiveness of business simulation models for teaching farm business analysis and record keeping for high school and adult students (the simulation technique is compared with more traditional methods)	Year	Yes	No	Closed	Basic inputs, debt servicing, borrowing	Yes	No

Eisgruber [1965]	Operating a single farm	To examine the effects of limited capital, uncertainty, price cycles, specialization vs. diversification, etc., in management	Year	Yes	Yes	Closed	Crop levels, fertilizer (amounts and types), livestock, land, breeding stock purchased or sold	Yes	Yes
Faris, Wildermuth, and Pratt [1966]	Operating a San Joaquin Valley farm	To stress farm operating decisions	Year	Yes	Yes	Closed	Production levels, land purchsed, machinery combinations	Yes	Yes
Frahm and Schrader [1970]	English (ascending bid) and Dutch (descending bid) auction markets compared with respect to (1) price variation, (2) speed of convergence, (3) average prices, and (4) observed equilibrium prices	To test hypotheses under a given situation	U	Yes	Yes	Open	Assigned selling price and marginal processing cost	No	No
Frazier, Narrie, and Rodgers [1970]	Livestock auction market	To determine the inherent inefficiencies of a given size and scale of auction markets and to evaluate systems simulations as a research and/or management tool	U	Yes	Yes	Closed	Utilization of facilities, storage capacity, length of entry and exit queues; volume of livestock	Yes	Yes

Table 2. Gaming Models in Agricultural Economics (Cont.)

References	Situation	Objectives	Time Unit[a]	Multi-stage	Compe-titive	Open-Closed	Decision Variables	Comput-erized	Sto-chastic
Fuller [1968]	Connecticut Valley cash crop and dairy farm	To relate managerial principles to decision making	Year	Yes	Yes	Open	Production levels of crops and dairy	Yes	Yes
Fuller, Ruggles, and Yergatian [1968]	New England brown egg poultry farm	To stress impact of trade-off between income and security	Year	Yes	Yes	Closed	Selection of marketing system, capital investments, production levels	Yes	Yes
Greenlaw, Herron, and Rawdon [1962]	Firm selling single (unnamed) product in two regional markets; demand fluctuations present	To provide a dynamic experience in marketing decision making. To emphasize competitive interaction in marketing decision making and difficulties of internal organization	U	Yes	Yes	Open	Price, expenditure for sales force, national and local advertising; of less importance are production and transportation	No	No
Greenlaw, Herron, and Rawdon [1962]	Physical production and distribution of goods; producer-wholesaler-retailer links emphasized	To examine order and inventory policies in a dynamic marketing situation	U	Yes	No	Open	Price, orders, inventory	No	No
Hutton and Hinman [1968]	Farm planning exercise; user specifies situation and parameters that pertain to his concern	To evaluate alternative farm plans	Year	No	Yes	Open	Inputs, level of capital, financing, sales, technical coefficients, production levels	Yes	Yes

Kay [1973]	Market, crops, livestock	To provide an aid in teaching farm and ranch decision making	Month	Yes	Yes	Open	Crop acreage, fertilizer levels, acreage for purchase or rent, type of livestock operation	Yes	Yes
Longworth [1970]	Australian dryland grazing and cropping farm	To weigh short-run tactical decisions vs. long-run strategy	Year	Yes	Yes	Open	When to buy and sell, levels of output, capital, investments	Yes	Yes
McKenney [1962]	Firms selling three (similar) products	To provide production planning experience and to demonstrate interdependency of functional decisions within a firm; stress is on time dimension	U	Yes	Yes	Open	Price, advertising expenditure, design and styling expense, production levels, investment in plant capacity and/or securities	Yes	No
F. J. Smith and Miles [1967]	Managing a 640-acre farm	To relate economic principles and farm management	Month	Yes	Yes	Closed	Levels of production, land and machinery purchase	Yes	No
V. L. Smith [1964]	Sellers make offers, buyers accept or reject; sellers and buyers both active in the market process; buyers make bids, sellers accept or reject	To test hypothesis concerning the price equilibrium and adjustment behavior of markets under three market organization conditions	U	Yes	Yes	Open	Trading session prices along with price limits	Yes	No
Vincent [1970b]	Farm construction and operation	To familiarize participants with problems faced in farm development	Year	Yes	Yes	Open	Production levels, land purchases, capital allocation	Yes	Yes

Table 2. Gaming Models in Agricultural Economics (Cont.)

References	Situation	Objectives	Time Unit[a]	Multi-stage	Compe-titive	Open-Closed	Decision Variables	Comput-erized	Sto-chastic
Walker and Halbrook [1965]	A 200-acre corn farm in the Great Plains area	To understand problems of growth under uncertainty	U	Yes	Yes	Closed	Livestock inventory and capital investment	No	Yes
Wehrly [1967]	Managing a farm on the southern plains of Texas	To demonstrate how plans made under perfect knowledge work out under "average" conditions	Year	Yes	Yes	Closed	Crop production levels	No	Yes
Whan and Richardson [1969]	Statistical model of auction market with application to Australian wool	To develop a simulation model of an auction market demonstrating the relationship between variation in valuation, price variation, and the number of independent bidders	U	Yes	Yes	Open	Product quality, price limits, number of bidders, size of lots	Yes	Yes

[a]U indicates an unspecified time dimension or one which was other than monthly or yearly.

Table 3. Firm and Process Simulation Models in Agricultural Economics

References	Objectives	Components	Decision Variables	Model Characteristics — Dynamic	Stochastic	Non-linear	Validation	Model Function	Simulation	Computer Language
Albach [1967]	To formulate model of unstable firm growth	Sales, research, firm growth	Actual sales, planning time for new products	Yes	Yes	Yes	Passive	Decision	Ad hoc	FORTRAN
R. L. Anderson [1968]	To establish optimum crop patterns on irrigated farms based on preseason water supply estimates	Moisture conditions, water supply	Water allocation, acreage restrictions	No	No	Yes	Passive	Decision	Historical	FORTRAN
J. R. Anderson [1971]	To analyze effects of spatial diversification of wool growers in Australia on the economic profitability of the firm	Weather, state of pasture, emergency pasture plan, prices, financial situation	Feeding and selling—transfer strategies	Yes	Yes	Yes	Passive	Decision	Ad hoc	FORTRAN
Armstrong, Connor, and Strickland [1970]	To combine simulation and linear programming to study farm firm growth	Farm simulator for short term tactical decisions, an ex post linear programming routine	Choice of enterprise, production methods, production levels	Yes	No	No	Passive	Decision	Historical	FORTRAN

Table 3. Firm and Process Simulation Models in Agricultural Economics (Cont.)

References	Objectives	Components	Decision Variables	Model Characteristics				Vali-dation	Model Function	Simulation	Computer Language
				Dy-namic	Sto-chastic	Non-linear					
Brooks [1962]	To model the C&H sugar refinery at Crockett	Input, output, processing stations, demand, capacity	Production levels, input levels	Yes	No	No	Passive	Decision	Ad hoc	FORTRAN
Cloud, Frick, and Andrews [1968]	To determine the optimal date for hay harvesting	Output, machinery, weather	Scheduling of activities, selection of production mode, inputs	No	No	Yes	Passive	Decision	Designed	FORTRAN
Dent [1971]	To construct a model for a typical pig enterprise to investigate the impact of operational policies on the return to capital investment	Breeding, fattening, capital investing	Type of investment, management practices	Yes	Yes	Yes	Passive	Decision	Designed	DYNAMO
Donaldson and Webster [1968]	To utilize simulation to assist in selecting farm plans with highest gross margins	Production, resource revenue	Production preferences, input levels	No	Yes	No	Passive	Decision	Ad hoc	FORTRAN
Doster [1970]	To use a simulator to help in formulating plans for a corn farm	Harvesting, hauling, handling, storage, marketing	Planting schedule, form and time of sale, harvest schedules, equipment utilization	No	No	No	Passive	Decision	Ad hoc	FORTRAN

Eidman, Dean, and Carter [1967]	To demonstrate Bayesian decision theory for management decisions under uncertainty using commercial turkey production as an example	Capital stock, production, mortality, net returns	Marketing strategy (contract or independent)	Yes	Yes	Yes	Passive	Decision	Designed	FORTRAN
Eisgruber and Lee [1971]	To specify a growth model of a farm firm within the context of the systems approach	Corn production, pig production	Corn and pig production plans, resource and purchase policies	Yes	Yes	Yes	Passive	Decision	Designed	FORTRAN
Glickstein et al. [1962]	To apply simulation to a cheese manufacturing plant to analyze production under varying conditions	Plant and equipment, supplies and services, labor	Purchasing policy, process scheduling	Yes	Yes	Yes	Passive	Decision	Ad hoc	FORTRAN
Goodall [1971]	To develop a model that describes the sheep-grazing activities of inland Australia	Production activities, initial inventories, managerial, weather	Production levels, managerial decision	Yes	Yes	Yes	Passive	Decision	Historical	FORTRAN
Halter and Dean [1965]	To use simulation in evaluating management policies under uncertainty using a large ranch as an example	Rangeland, feedlot, and weather environment	Purchasing, scheduling, and selling	Yes	Yes	Yes	Passive	Decision	Ad hoc	DYNAMO

Table 3. Firm and Process Simulation Models in Agricultural Economics (Cont.)

References	Objectives	Components	Decision Variables	Model Characteristics Dy-namic	Sto-chastic	Non-linear	Vali-dation	Model Function	Simulation	Computer Language
Harle [1968]	To use simulation in farm planning by concentrating on data production rather than data manipulation	Capital, production, risk	Method of production, production levels	Yes	Yes	Yes	Passive	Decision	Ad hoc	Not known
Hinman and Hutton [1970]	To incorporate a generally accepted theory of the firm into a simulator to handle many different farm situations	Production, resources, inventory, input, financial	Debt level, marketing strategy, investment, input levels, insurance	Yes	Yes	No	Passive	Behavioral	Ad hoc	FORTRAN
Hutton [1966]	To use a simulation model of a dairy herd in the selection of a herd replacement policy	Inputs, outputs, capital, financial	Replacement and input levels	Yes	Yes	Yes	Passive	Decision	Designed	FORTRAN
Patrick and Eisgruber [1968]	To measure the influence of managerial ability and capital market structure on the rate of farm firm growth	Managerial, resource, financial, expectations	Credit availability and terms, investment	Yes	No	Yes	Passive	Fore-casting	Designed	FORTRAN

Author	Objective	Components	Decision variables							Language
Smith and Parks [1967]	To predict, on a probability basis, optimum levels of fertilizer application when drought is considered to be a random variable	Input, output, environment	Level of fertilizer to apply	No	Yes	Yes	Passive	Decision	Historical	FORTRAN
Sorensen and Gilheany [1970]	To evaluate different harvesting strategies on a sugar plantation	Harvest, cane hauling, milling, weather	Labor allocation and level, harvest scheduling, machinery assignment	Yes	Yes	Yes	Passive	Decision	Designed	GPSS
Tanago [1973]	To construct a simulation model of a farm, using different decision theoretic approaches for analyzing the output generated	Production, market, capital	Hay machinery investment, crop area, hours worked per week	Yes	Yes	Yes	Passive	Decision	Historical	FORTRAN
Van Kampen [1971]	To provide a simulation model that may be used to minimize total harvest cost over a number of years allowing for the influence of weather	Weather, crop activities, harvest costs	Number of combines, techniques of operating the combines, drying capacity, storage capacity	Yes	Yes	Yes	Passive	Decision	Designed	ALGOL

Table 3. Firm and Process Simulation Models in Agricultural Economics (Cont.)

References	Objectives	Components	Decision Variables	Model Characteristics Dy-namic	Model Characteristics Sto-chastic	Model Characteristics Non-linear	Vali-dation	Model Function	Simulation	Computer Language
Vincent [1970a]	To construct a model to explain the future state of poultry producers	Feed production, egg production, financial, capital	Investment levels, production levels, marketing strategy	Yes	Yes	Yes	Passive	Decision	Designed	FORTRAN
Vincent [1970b]	To explain the use of a farm simulator that can be adapted to many different farm firms	Capital and credit, livestock and crops, machinery	Farm acquisition, type and quantity of capital stock, production levels	Yes	Yes	Yes	Passive	Decision	Designed	FORTRAN
Wright and Dent [1969]	To measure the effect of withdrawing land from grazing to cropping for part of the year	Biological environment, market structure, input and output	Land allocation	Yes	No	Yes	Passive	Decision	Designed	FORTRAN
Zusman and Amiad [1965]	To determine optimal farm plans under weather uncertainty.	Weather, market, livestock, inventory, crop, seasonal	Production levels, livestock herd size, inventory levels, sales, purchases	Yes	Yes	Yes	Passive	Decision	Designed	FORTRAN

254

Table 4. Market and Industry Simulation Models in Agricultural Economics

References	Objectives	Components	Decision Variables	Model Characteristics			Vali-dation	Model Function	Simulation	Computer Language
				Dy-namic	Sto-chastic	Non-linear				
Armbruster et al. [1972]	To evaluate farm marketing boards as a means of increasing farm bargaining power: test case western late potato system	Production, marketing, bargaining	Negotiated price; production quotas, acreage, marketing allocation	Yes	Yes	Yes	Passive	Decision	Designed	FORTRAN
Balderston and Hoggatt [1962]	To examine the dynamics of a market viewed as a complex system of behavior in which information is limited and costly	Timber growers, retailers, broker transactions	Price, output, financing	Yes	Yes	Yes	N.A.	Behavioral	Designed	FORTRAN
Barnum [1971]	To measure the effect of the introduction of stochastic terms on the reliability of deterministic conclusions obtained from simulation of the foodgrains market in India	Price, production, income, imports	Government purchases, importation of P.L. 480 surplus foodgrains	Yes	Yes	No	Passive	Decision	Designed	FORTRAN

255

Table 4. Market and Industry Simulation Models in Agricultural Economics (Cont.)

References	Objectives	Components	Decision Variables	Model Characteristics			Validation	Model Function	Simulation	Computer Language
				Dynamic	Stochastic	Nonlinear				
Bell, Henderson, and Perkins [1972]	To analyze the fertilizer industry with respect to sources of raw materials, interrelationship between supply and demand	Production, storage handling, transportation, processing, sales, pollution	Input prices, fertilizer purchases, output levels	No	No	No	Passive	Decision	Ad hoc	FORTRAN
Bender [1966]	To provide a basis for determining in what season of the year promotional activities should be concentrated and the effects of change in feedgrain prices on the broiler industry	Costs, capacity, seasonal demand	Production levels, input levels, investment, purchases	No	No	Yes	Passive	Behavioral	Ad hoc	FORTRAN
Benson [1969]	To develop a computer simulation model for interregional competition in the broiler industry that can answer questions at the firm, region, and industry levels	Firm, capacity, supply, demand, region	Production levels, feed purchased, production schedules, spatial allocations	No	No	Yes	Passive	Behavioral	Ad hoc	FORTRAN

Citation	Purpose	Sectors/Variables	Decision variables							
Benson, Bender, and Lofourcade [1972]	To develop a simulation model of the broiler industry to estimate the intensity of interregional competition and its sensitivity to changes in decision variables	Demand, supply, capacity, producing regions, spatial markets	Spatial allocations, price premiums, feed prices	No	No	No	Passive	Forecasting	Designed	FORTRAN
Candler and Cartwright [1969]	To illustrate the use of experimental design and regression analysis in the estimation of functional relationships as a basis for deriving "performance statistics"	Financial, output prices, input prices	Choice of weights entering the performance function	No	No	Yes	Passive	Decision	Designed	FORTRAN
Cohen [1960]	To examine detailed aspects of business behavior and dynamic interaction among firms using the shoe-leather-hide sequence as an example	Consumers, retailers, manufacturers, tanners, hide dealers	Prices, production levels, orders, inventory levels, consumer expenditures	Yes	No	Yes	Passive	Behavioral	Historical	FORTRAN

Table 4. Market and Industry Simulation Models in Agricultural Economics (Cont.)

References	Objectives	Components	Decision Variables	Model Characteristics			Vali-dation	Model Function	Simulation	Computer Language
				Dy-namic	Sto-chastic	Non-linear				
Crom [1967]	To indicate the trading pattern changes and the potential for re-adjustment be-tween alternative market organiza-tions in 1975 under alternative assump-tions	Transportation capacity, labor, beef, pork, re-gional	Regional produc-tion, regional con-sumption, regional allocation	No	No	No	Passive	Fore-casting	Ad hoc	FORTRAN
Crom and Maki [1965b]	To develop a means of studying historical and pro-jected changes in the livestock-meat economy's market organization and structure	Pork, beef, in-ventory, produc-tion, foreign trade, demand, margins	Slaughter produc-tion levels, inven-tory levels, breeding, culling	Yes	No	Yes	Passive	Behavioral	Historical	FORTRAN
Desai [1968]	To evaluate the operation of the milk stabilization program in Cali-fornia and to indi-cate the direction and magnitude of possible changes	Producers, proces-sors, market share, demand, cost	Production, prices, advertising, govern-ment price regula-tion	Yes	Yes	Yes	Passive	Behavioral	Designed	FORTRAN

Study	Objective	Components	Variables						
Duewer and Maki [1966]	To investigate the interrelationships and interactions among the various parts of the livestock-meat industry from a systems analysis standpoint	Producers, market slaughterers, processors, wholesalers, retailers, households	Purchases, sales, production levels, entry, exit, transaction partner selection	Yes	No	No	Passive	Behavioral	Ad hoc	FORTRAN
B. C. French and Matsumoto [1969]	To develop economic information which may aid various groups of the brussels sprouts industry in decision making	Production, freezer, fresh, inventory	Marketing policy, sprout size, product allocations, inventory levels	Yes	No	Yes	Passive	Forecasting	Ad hoc	FORTRAN
Koenig, Hilmersen, and Yuan [1969]	To demonstrate how systems theory can be employed in the analysis and control of semiclosed biological processes of the type encountered in the agricultural industry	Feed, labor, plants (broiler, pullet, egg), markets	Sales, feed and labor inputs, government purchases	Yes	No	No	Passive	Decision	Ad hoc	FORTRAN

Table 4. Market and Industry Simulation Models in Agricultural Economics (Cont.)

| References | Objectives | Components | Decision Variables | Model Characteristics | | | Vali-dation | Model Function | Simulation | Computer Language |
				Dy-namic	Sto-chastic	Non-linear				
Krebs, Hayenga, and Lehker [1972]	To evaluate and compare various support and supply control policies for navy beans in the U.S. by means of simulation	Domestic supply and demand, foreign supply and demand	Government prices, support levels, marketing control, acreage control, supply allocation	Yes	No	Yes	Passive	Decision	Ad hoc	FORTRAN
Lavington [1970]	To construct a model applicable to markets for frequently purchased goods	Market, individual, consumer	Distribution, retail price, advertising policies	Yes	Yes	Yes	Passive	Decision	N.A.	FORTRAN
Manetsch [1974]	To describe work in progress on the development of a computer simulation model for the softwood plywood industry	Integrated producers, independent producers, integrated jobbers and office wholesalers, independent office wholesalers, less than carload retailers, less than carload markets, carload markets	Production levels, sales, inventory levels, prices	Yes	No	No	Passive	Behavioral	Ad hoc	FORTRAN

260

Author [Year]	Objective	Endogenous Variables	Exogenous/Decision Variables							Language
Naylor, Wallace, and Sasser [1967]	To simulate the textile industry and to present three alternative validation tests	Supply, demand, employment, profit, prices, investment, earnings	Advertising, inventory levels, investment purchases	Yes	Yes	No	Active	Behavioral	Historical	FORTRAN
Raulerson and Langham [1970]	To investigate the problems of fluctuating orange supplies and grower profits in the frozen concentrate orange juice sector of the Florida citrus industry	Growers, processors, retailers, consumers	Tree planting, tree removal, supply control, market allocations	Yes	No	No	Passive	Decision	Ad hoc	DYNAMO
Vernon, Rives, and Naylor [1969]	To explain the behavior of the tobacco industry and to evaluate the impact of the efforts of alternative governmental and managerial policies	Leaf production, price, cigarettes	Production levels, pricing, purchases, inventory levels	Yes	No	No	Passive	Behavioral	Historical	SIMULATE
Weymar [1968]	To describe and explain the nature of the dynamic response of the world cocoa industry to annual fluctuations in world cocoa production	World consumption, price, expectations, inventory	Inventory levels, consumer purchases, price and inventory levels	Yes	Yes	Yes	Active	Behavioral	Designed	FORTRAN

Table 4. Market and Industry Simulation Models in Agricultural Economics (Cont.)

| References | Objectives | Components | Decision Variables | Model Characteristics | | | Vali-dation | Model Function | Simulation | Computer Language |
				Dy-namic	Sto-chastic	Non-linear				
Zymelman [1965]	To develop an analog computer solution for the stabilization of employment, prices, and profits in the cotton textile gray goods industry	Demand, production, price, inventory	Production levels, inventory levels, orders	Yes	No	Yes	Passive	Decision	Ad hoc	ALGOL

Table 5. Aggregate Simulation Models in Agricultural Economics

References	Objectives	Components	Decision Variables	Model Characteristics			Validation	Model Function	Simulation	Computer Language
				Dynamic	Stochastic	Nonlinear				
Blase, MacMillan, and Tung [1973]	To design a computer model to facilitate public decision making concerning local government revenues and expenditures	Expenditures, revenues, budgets	Tax rates, borrowings, expenditure levels	Yes	No	Yes	Passive	Decision	Ad hoc	FORTRAN
Chen [1970]	To develop an agricultural sub-model for the U.S. economy as a market sector simulator for forecasting sales of a major farm equipment manufacturer	Supply and demand for ten commodity classes (simultaneous), supply response of crops (recursive), corporate forecasting system	Production levels, marketings, inventory control, financial planning	Yes	No	Yes	Passive	Decision	Historical	FORTRAN
Edwards [1970]	To present a simple simulation model which generates alternative time paths of population, income, and employment in a two-region model for the U.S.	Two regions, each having employment, income, and population growth components	Migration levels, population growth, worker productivity levels	Yes	No	Yes	Passive	Forecasting	Ad hoc	FORTRAN

263

Table 5. Aggregate Simulation Models in Agricultural Economics (Cont.)

References	Objectives	Components	Decision Variables	Model Characteristics			Validation	Model Function	Simulation	Computer Language
				Dynamic	Stochastic	Non-linear				
Edwards and De Pass [1971]	To use a simulation model to project rural-urban population, income, and employment for the U.S. through 2020	Urban, rural	Policies designed to increase job opportunities and labor productivity, reduce natural rate of population growth, limit out-migration	Yes	No	Yes	Passive	Decision	Ad hoc	FORTRAN
Lin and Heady [1971]	To investigate whether slower technical change or more reliance on free markets would have lessened overcapacity and raised income for U.S. farms	Commodity markets, resource markets, production, income	Government farm programs on prices, income, resource employment technology	Yes	No	No	Active	Decision	Ad hoc	FORTRAN
Lins [1973]	To construct a simulation model of farm sector which can be used to evaluate policies concerning the financial structure of the farm sector	Farm and non-farm income, real estate, capital consumption, financed assets, inventories	Financial debt, capital investments, land purchases	Yes	No	No	Passive	Decision	Ad hoc	FORTRAN

Reference	Objective									
McFarquhar and Evans [1971]	To project changes in production and consumption of food and agricultural products in the U.K. between 1968 and 1975	Consumption, agricultural supply, input-output model, wheat, barley, cattle, sheep	Production levels, sales and purchases, E.E.C. participation of U.K.	Yes	Yes	No	Passive	Forecasting	Ad hoc	FORTRAN
Schaller [1968]	To outline the research on a national economic model of production response developed by the Farm Production Economics Division, Economic Research Service	Production response, input-output equilibrium	Production levels, diversion program, allotments	Yes	No	No	Passive	Decision	Historical	FORTRAN
Shechter and Heady [1970]	To apply simulation models in deriving response surfaces for policy analysis in the feed-livestock sector	Micro level (individual firm units), macro level (aggregate output variables of all firms)	Minimum acreage diversion, national price support, payment and loan rates, diversion payment rate	No	Yes	Yes	Passive	Decision	Designed	FORTRAN

Table 5. Aggregate Simulation Models in Agricultural Economics (Cont.)

| References | Objectives | Components | Decision Variables | Model Characteristics | | | Vali-dation | Model Function | Simulation | Computer Language |
				Dy-namic	Sto-chastic	Non-linear				
Tyner [1967]	To investigate the productivity of aggregate farm inputs and to develop a model to predict the impact of changes in government diversions, payments to farmers, acreage controls, price supports	Input, output, market, farm financial, nonfarm sector	Government programs as listed under "objectives"	Yes	No	Yes	Passive	Decision	Ad hoc	FORTRAN
Tyner and Tweeten [1968]	To present a methodology that can be used to study issues of farm-nonfarm interaction	Input, output, market, farm financial, nonfarm sector	Government payments to farmers, diversions of cropland	Yes	No	Yes	Passive	Decision	Ad hoc	FORTRAN

Table 6. Economic Development Simulation Models in Agricultural Economics

References	Objectives	Components	Decision Variables	Model Characteristics			Validation	Model Function	Simulation	Computer Language
				Dynamic	Stochastic	Nonlinear				
Aldabe and van Rijckeghem [1966]	To use simulation for quarterly forecasting of the Argentina cattle stock and its main components	Slaughter, herd death and birth rates	Mortality rates, fertility coefficients, stock levels	Yes	No	No	Passive	Behavioral	Designed	FORTRAN
Billingsley and Norvell [1971]	To build an economic demographic simulation model to project the economic effects of changing the population growth rate of the Dominican Republic	Fertility, population, gross national product, mortality and birth rates	Government supported fertility control, labor force participation	Yes	No	Yes	Active	Decision	Ad hoc	FORTRAN
Day and Singh [1971], Singh and Day [1972]	To explain the transition from subsistence or traditional agriculture to commercialized modern agricultural in the Indian Punjab through accounting for strategic details	Farm activities and decision variables within regions, annual objective function, technology matrix, technical constraints representing regional resource limitations, behavioral relations	Technology adaptation, crop mix, resource use	Yes	Yes	No	Active	Behavioral	Designed	FORTRAN

Table 6. Economic Development Simulation Models in Agricultural Economics (Cont.)

References	Objectives	Components	Decision Variables	Model Characteristics				Model Function	Simulation	Computer Language
				Dynamic	Stochastic	Non-linear	Validation			
	of technology, farm decision making, and market environment	including adaptive mechanisms, feedback functions, exogenously given prices and supplies of variable production factors								
Foster and Yost [1969]	To study and clarify the relationship between population growth, expenditures on education, and economic development in an underdeveloped rural economy	Demographic, educational, income	Resource allocation, schooling, birth, education expenditures	Yes	Yes	No	Passive	Behavioral	Designed	FORTRAN
Gillespie and Holland [1963]	To report on some exploratory experiments in economic dynamics performed on a simulated underdeveloped economy	Supply, demand, production sectors, capital and investment, import-export	Investment allocation, foreign trade policies, anti-inflation policies, exchange rates and tariff levels	Yes	No	Yes	Passive	Decision	Designed	DYNAMO

Reference	Objective	Sectors/Variables	Policy Variables							Language
Hayenga, Manetsch, and Halter [1968], Halter and Manetsch [1970]	To illustrate the application of simulation as a problem-solving approach to the development of the Nigerian agricultural economy	Regional (southern tree and root crops and northern annual crops and livestock) inputs, production, marketing, consumers, trade, population	Marketing board prices, production research and extension expenditures, taxes and subsidies, intrastructure investments	Yes	No	Yes	Passive	Decision	Designed	FORDYN
Holland [1962]	To examine the problems of economic development and foreign trade policy for an underdeveloped country	Production, export, consumer, capital	Public service, investment allocations and levels	Yes	No	Yes	Passive	Decision	Designed	DYNAMO
Kresge [1967]	To present a general simulation model to be used for policy evaluations by developing countries with Pakistan as an example	Final demand, industrial production, income, regions	Level of investment and import substitution developments	Yes	No	No	Passive	Decision	Ad hoc	FORTRAN
Lehker and Manetsch [1971]	To examine the feasibility of using simulation to analyze the planning of beef production in Northeast Brazil	Nutritional cash crops, herd management, credit	Land use, production levels, sales policies, herd management modernization	Yes	No	Yes	Active	Decision	Designed	FORTRAN

Table 6. Economic Development Simulation Models in Agricultural Economics (Cont.)

References	Objectives	Components	Decision Variables	Model Characteristics Dynamic	Stochastic	Nonlinear	Validation	Model Function	Simulation	Computer Language
Manetsch [1974]	To describe the role of simulation models in the study of Korean rural development	Agricultural production, regional sectors, urban and rural consumption, population, prices	Policy alternatives: 1) increase food self-sufficiency and growth of rural income; 2) budget reallocation for rural development; 3) move agricultural sector to reliance on competitive markets	Yes	No	Yes	Passive	Decision	Ad hoc	FORDYN
Manetsch, Hayenga, et al. [1971]	To develop a general system simulation approach for examining agricultural development which is operational	Regional agricultural sectors (northern annual crop-beef model and southern perennial annual crop model), nonfarm sectors	Land allocations, level of modernization, marketing board and export tax policies, investment allocation and levels	Yes	Yes	Yes	Active	Decision	Designed	FORDYN
Manetsch, Ramos, and Lenchner [1968]	To develop a computer simulation program for modernizing cotton production in northeast Brazil	Production, credit, transportation, processing, marketing, consumption	Research and extension expenditures	Yes	Yes	Yes	Passive	Decision	Designed	FORTRAN

Model	Objective	Components	Decisions							
Manetsch and Lenchner [1971]	To develop a simulation model to compute the consequences of alternative development strategies for the Brazilian textile industry	Regions, production cloth type, inputs	Allocation of investment by region and production mode, adoption of technology	Yes	No	Yes	Passive	Decision	Historical	FORTRAN
Mathis [1969]	To develop an economic model of the cocoa industry for the Dominican Republic which will be useful in evaluating the influence of investments and other policy decisions in an economic development program	Traditional farms, modern farms, extension, research, disease and pest control, credit, income, marketing and transportation, export and domestic consumption	Development loans, government expenditures, investment	Yes	No	Yes	Active	Decision	Designed	DYNAMO
MSU Agricultural Sector Simulation Team [1973]	To illustrate application of simulation techniques to problems of planning and policy making for the Nigerian agricultural sector	Regional inputs, production, marketing, consumption, trade, services, national accounts	Production levels, marketing decisions, technology introduction	Yes	No	Yes	Passive	Behavioral	Designed	FORDYN

Table 6. Economic Development Simulation Models in Agricultural Economics (Cont.)

References	Objectives	Components	Decision Variables	Model Characteristics Dy-namic	Model Characteristics Sto-chastic	Model Characteristics Non-linear	Vali-dation	Model Function	Simulation	Computer Language
Miller and Halter [1973]	To illustrate the consequences through time of a set of policies estimated to shift the Venezuelan cattle industry from traditional to modern production	Traditional and modern beef pro-duction, crop sec-tor, consumption	Price policies, land development, extension expen-ditures	Yes	No	Yes	Passive	Decision	Designed	FORTRAN
Roberts and Kresge [1968]	To explore the interface between the economy of an underdeveloped nation and its transportation system using Co-lombia as an ex-ample	Final demand, in-dustrial production income, interregion-al commodity flows, regional output, transportation costs	Choice of trans-port mode, trans-portation system expansion, output levels	Yes	No	Yes	Passive	Behavioral	Ad hoc	FORTRAN
L. J. Taylor [1969]	To examine struc-tural change in sectoral output levels during the course of econom-ic growth and to examine the forces underlying these patterns	Input, output, trade, consumption, indus-try production, pri-mary production, services	Import substitu-tion, government expenditures	Yes	No	Yes	Passive	Behavioral	Designed	FORTRAN

Table 7. Natural Resource Simulation Models in Agricultural Economics

References	Objectives	Components	Decision Variables	Model Characteristics			Validation	Model Function	Simulation	Computer Language
				Dynamic	Stochastic	Nonlinear				
R. L. Anderson and Maass [1974]	To develop and test procedures by which operators and builders of irrigation systems can compare and evaluate alternative methods of distributing water among farmers	Production benefits, water allocation, water supply	Crop levels, water sequencing, operating procedure to deliver water, selection of crops to be irrigated	Yes	No	Yes	Passive	Decision	Designed	FORTRAN
Askew, Yeh, and Hall [1971]	To simulate critical periods of drought to assist in the planning and construction of reservoirs and to compare generating techniques	Rivers, stream flow	Maximum permissible extraction rate, duration of low stream flow and the accumulated deficiency relative to the mean flow	Yes	Yes	Yes	Active	Behavioral	Designed	FORTRAN
Chen [1971]	To develop a costing procedure which will be a practical and useful tool in planning cottage resorts	Investment, cost	Type of accommodations, secondary business facilities, outdoor recreational facilities, length of season	No	Yes	No	Active	Behavioral	Designed	FORTRAN

Table 7. Natural Resource Simulation Models in Agricultural Economics (Cont.)

References	Objectives	Components	Decision Variables	Model Characteristics Dynamic	Sto-chastic	Non-linear	Vali-dation	Model Function	Simulation	Computer Language
Chow and Kareliotis [1970]	To formulate a mathematical model of a stochastic hydrologic system	Precipitation, runoff, storage	Conceptual watershed storage, stream flow	Yes	Yes	Yes	Passive	Behavioral	Historical	FORTRAN
Dudley and Burt [1973]	To estimate the long-run optimal area to develop for irrigation, given the size of a reservoir	Water supply, water demand, crops, moisture, costs	Acreage to be developed for irrigation	Yes	Yes	Yes	Passive	Decision	Ad hoc	FORTRAN
Ellis [1966]	To present a systems model of recreational activity in Michigan that can be utilized to predict the outcome of proposed changes or innovations	Population centers, transportation, destination	Activity by type of recreation and location	No	No	Yes	Passive	Decision	Ad hoc	FORTRAN
Halter and Miller [1966]	To test the applicability of simulation in evaluating water resource de-	Hydrologic flows, upstream and downstream flows, costs, benefits, drainage	Size of proposed reservoir and channel capacity, channel improvements	Yes	Yes	Yes	Passive	Decision	Designed	DYNAMO

274

Study	Objective								
	velopment projects and to test alternate resource management policies for an actual river basin								
Hamilton et al. [1969]	To apply systems simulation to regional analysis, specifically the Susquehanna River basin	Demographic, employment, water (quantity and quality), spatial	Wage levels, migration levels, workers' productivity, population levels	Yes	No	Yes	Active	Forecasting	Designed	DYNAMO
Howitt et al. [1974]	To project the impact of changing water quality in the Salton Sea of California on the recreational use and the investment climate for recreational facilities	Water quality, recreational activities and facilities	Fishing and non-fishing participation, investment in recreational facilities	Yes	No	Yes	Passive	Decision	Ad hoc	FORTRAN
Hufschmidt [1963]	To find an optimal design for a given river basin system	Reservoirs, hydropower plants, irrigation system, flood damage system	Reservoir storage capacity, active and inactive storage capacity, installed capacity at alternative power plant sites, output levels for irrigation water	Yes	Yes	Yes	Passive	Decision	Designed	FORTRAN

Table 7. Natural Resource Simulation Models in Agricultural Economics (Cont.)

References	Objectives	Components	Decision Variables	Model Characteristics			Vali-dation	Model Function	Simulation	Computer Language
				Dy-namic	Sto-chastic	Non-linear				
Hufschmidt and Fiering [1966]	To outline a procedure for water resource simulation with an application to the Lehigh River basin	Supply of water, demand for water-derived products and services, flood, energy, temporal, benefits	Hydrologic conditions, dam and reservoir capacities, type of irrigation works, size of power plants, levels of flood damage alleviation	Yes	Yes	Yes	Passive	Decision	Designed	FORTRAN
Huggins and Monke [1968]	To develop a model to simulate the surface runoff from watersheds by delineating the model to a grid of small independent elements	Rainfall, runoff	Rainfall interception, infiltration	No	No	Yes	Active	Behavioral	Historical	FORTRAN
Jacoby [1967]	To develop a model to evaluate major investment and operating decisions for electric power planning using West Pakistan as an example	Costs, agricultural sector, irrigation water, electrical power, foreign exchange rates, power demand, spatial markets	Size and location of multipurpose hydroelectric and irrigation development, operating rules, type of plant	Yes	No	Yes	Passive	Decision	Designed	FORTRAN

276

	Purpose									
Leistritz [1970]	To determine forces that have major influence on the farm real estate market	Supply, demand, farm size	Land purchases, land prices, land rented, rental rates	Yes	No	Yes	Passive	Behavioral	Designed	FORTRAN
McMahon and Miller [1971]	To demonstrate the proper use of a first-order nonseasonal Markov model with skewed data in the synthetic generation of stream flows	Hydrologic flows	Not available	Yes	Yes	Yes	Active	Behavioral	Historical	FORTRAN
Masch and Associates [1971]	To develop a set of interrelated water-quality models capable of routing water quality parameters through a stream subsystem	Thermal behavior, waste assimilation, routing of conservative minerals, spatial, water quality, runoff	Location of waste loadings and withdrawals	Yes	No	Yes	Active	Behavioral	Designed	FORTRAN
Miernyk [1969]	To develop a model as a basis for long-range projections of economic activity in the Colorado River basin with water quality and quantity constraints	Water supply, water demand, spatial, production, agricultural, commercial, industrial, municipal sectors	Crop production levels, water purchases, water treatment (purification)	No	No	No	Passive	Forecasting	Designed	FORTRAN

Table 7. Natural Resource Simulation Models in Agricultural Economics (Cont.)

References	Objectives	Components	Decision Variables	Model Characteristics Dynamic	Sto-chastic	Non-linear	Vali-dation	Model Function	Simulation	Computer Language
Pisano [1968]	To provide a set of options to be used in river basin planning for water quality management	Water quality, stream flows, reservoir levels, pollutant concentrations	Various combinations of reservoir sizes, reservoir releases and waste input schedules, water quality standards	Yes	Yes	Yes	Active	Behavioral	Designed	FORTRAN
Rausser, Willis, and Frick [1972]; Rausser and Willis [1976]	To determine the probability distribution of the external learning benefits emanating from the construction of a water desalting plant, and how subsidy measures based upon these benefits influence capital investments and water allocations	Learning, desalting plants, costs, external benefits, fresh water transport, reservoirs, use sectors and their demand for water	Public subsidies, investment sequencing of alternative water source developments, water allocation	Yes	Yes	Yes	Passive	Decision	Designed	FORTRAN
Rodriguez-Iturbe,	To compare various Markovian	Stream flows	Seasonal structure, periodicity,	Yes	Yes	Yes	Active	Behavioral	Designed	FORTRAN

278

Reference	Objective									
Dawdy, and Garcia [1971]	models with respect to their adequacy in the preservation of the required reservoir storage characteristics of the historical record	cyclic variation, random filters								
Shih and Dracup [1961]	To use a hybrid computer simulation model to solve the three-dimensional non-uniform diffusion equations for determining evaporation from finite areas of water	Wind, temperature, humidity, atmospheric pressure	Not available	No	No	Yes	Passive	Behavioral	Historical	FORTRAN
Stillson [1969]	To outline a regional trade model to determine the economic impact of proposed pollution abatement programs for the western basin of Lake Erie	Tradable commodities, untradable commodities, transportation system, costs, prices, final demand, spatial	Type of abatement program (size and technology), taxes	No	No	No	Passive	Decision	Historical	FORTRAN

Notes

1. The term "nonprimitive" is used to indicate the theoretical content of these models. As the level of abstraction increases, the behavioral notions on which the model is based become more primitive. Most systems models are based on intuitive or ad hoc specification and thus are often highly specialized.

2. The more frequently quoted definitions may be found in Chorafas [1965], Churchman [1960, 1968], Emery [1969], and Orcutt [1960]. In a more recent examination Churchman [1971] suggests nine necessary conditions for the existence of a system. A system (1) must be goal seeking, (2) must involve a measure of performance, (3) must have a client whose interests are served by the system, (4) must have components which are goal seeking and which jointly influence the measure of system performance, (5) must have an environment which also influences the measure of performance, (6) must involve a decision maker who can influence the measure of system performance, and (7) must involve a designer who conceptualizes the nature of the system; furthermore, (8) the designer's intention must be to change the system so as to maximize its value to the client, and (9) the designer's intention must be ultimately realizable.

3. The literature on this subject is extensive. For example, Monte Carlo methods have been used to study sampling properties of parameter estimators in econometric models (V. K. Smith [1973]). This connection between Monte Carlo and simulation methods suggests a number of avenues the survey might take. The more traditional Monte Carlo applications, particularly for examining properties of estimates, are quite interesting but are outside the purview of this survey.

4. J. R. Anderson [1974a] and LaDue and Vincent [1974] have suggested that the identification of certain types of simulations as gaming is not a useful distinction. We would concur. The delineation is useful, however, for purposes of the present survey, since gaming applications have developed in some very distinctive directions.

5. This discussion and the subsequent one for the most part do not consider the actual complexity of selecting among alternative model specifications (Geisel [1969]). Classical techniques are largely silent in the case of non-nested hypotheses or the disparate families of hypotheses represented by alternative model representations. Cox [1961, 1962] and Atkinson [1970] have examined such techniques in the context of non-nested hypotheses. Unfortunately, the tests developed by these authors cannot be performed in any routine manner and are rather costly. This is because the developed test statistic depends on the nature of the hypotheses to be tested.

6. For the use of a range of arbitrary algebraic specifications of multidimensional utility functions to summarize simulations results, see Fromm and Taubman [1968]. More general discussions of performance function specification and estimation are presented by Rausser and Johnson [1975] and Rothenberg [1961]. Of all the approaches considered, the implicit performance function estimation proposed by Nijkamp [1970] is perhaps the most practical.

7. It would be easy to review some of the process model studies conducted—for example, in California during the 1950s—and to conclude that, although not recognized as such, the research methods employed were closely akin to what is now termed systems analysis.

8. The Cohen study is the original reference to the validation procedure of regressing simulated endogenous values on actual endogenous values (or vice versa) and testing the null hypothesis that the intercept coefficient of this regression equals zero and the as-

associated slope coefficient equals unity. As shown in Aigner [1972] and Rausser and Johnson [1975], this procedure is incorrect in the context of stochastic simulation.

9. Process simulation was first characterized by Cohen [1960], who differentiated this concept from one-period change models. The latter models utilized actual historical data to generate simulated values and were unfortunately characterized by Cohen [1960] as being coincidental with econometric models. This has caused some confusion in the literature (LaDue and Vincent [1974]); econometric models can obviously be simulated on either a one-period basis or a process basis. The dichotomy is, in fact, equivalent to the distinction between ex post and ex ante generated values of endogenous variables in a forecasting context.

10. Specifically, it was found "possible to cut cost by 67 percent and reduce surplus accumulation by 46 percent below the lowest corresponding benchmark values of these responses. Similarly average income was raised by about 10 percent. However, only a slight improvement, 3 percent, was achieved in participant income" (Shechter and Heady [1970]).

11. For detailed comparisons of alternative sectoral models with specific reference to their uses in planning and program design, see Thorbecke [1971].

12. Kain and Meyer [1968] also cite a number of computer simulation applications to regional and urban problems, metropolitan growth, and community renewal.

13. The "curse of dimensionality" refers to the fact that when control variables and time periods are increased the solution space for dynamic programming problems becomes large and quite complex (Bellman [1961]).

References

Ackoff, R. L. [1971]. "Toward a System of Systems Concepts." *Management Science* 17:661-671.

Adelman, I., and F. Adelman [1959]. "The Dynamic Properties of the Klein-Goldberger Models." *Econometrica* 27:596-625.

Agarwala, R. [1971]. "A Simulation Approach to the Analysis of Stabilisation Policies in Agricultural Markets: A Case Study." *J. Agr. Econ.* 22:13-28.

Aigner, D. J. [1972]. "A Note on Verification of Computer Simulation Models." *Management Science* 18:615-619.

Aitchison, J., and S. D. Silvey [1958]. "Maximum-Likelihood Estimation of Parameters Subject to Restraints." *Annals of Math. Stat.* 29:813-828.

Albach, H. [1967]. "Simulation Models of Firm Growth." *German Economic Review* 5: 1-26.

Albert, A., and R. W. Sittler [1965]. "A Method of Computing Least Squares Estimators That Keep Up with the Data." *J. SIAM Control* 3:384-417.

Aldabe, H., and W. van Rijckeghem [1966]. *The Use of Simulation for Forecasting Changes in the Argentine Cattle Stock*. Paper presented to Development Advisory Service Conference, Bellagio, Italy.

American Management Association [1961]. *Simulation and Gaming: A Symposium*. Management Report 55. New York.

Amstutz, A. E. [1967]. *Computer Simulation of Competitive Market Response*. Cambridge: M.I.T. Press.

Anderson, F. M., A. N. Halter, G. E. Connolly, and W. M. Longhurst [1971]. *Simulation*

Experiments with a Biomanagement Model of a Deer Herd. Oregon Agricultural Experiment Station Technical Paper 3124.

Anderson, J. R. [1971]. "Spatial Diversification of High-Risk Sheep Farms." In *Systems Analysis in Agricultural Management*, J. B. Dent and J. R. Anderson, eds. Sydney: Wiley. Pp. 239-266.

Anderson, J. R. [1974a]. "Simulation: Methodology and Applications in Agricultural Economics." *Rev. Marketing Agr. Econ.* 43:3-55.

——— [1974b]. *Systems Simulation in Agricultural Management*. University of New England, Armidale, New South Wales, Australia. Mimeo.

Anderson, J. R., and J. L. Dillon [1968]. "Economic Considerations in Response Research." *Am. J. Agr. Econ.* 50:130-142.

Anderson, R. L. [1968]. "A Simulation Program to Establish Optimum Crop Patterns on Irrigated Farms Based on Preseason Estimates of Water Supply." *Am. J. Agr. Econ.* 50:1586-1590.

Anderson, R. L., and A. Maass [1974]. *A Simulation of Irrigation Systems*. USDA, ERS Bulletin 1431.

Ansoff, H. I., and D. P. Slevin [1968]. "An Appreciation of Industrial Dynamics." *Management Science* 14:383-397.

Aoki, M. [1967]. *Optimization of Stochastic Systems—Topics in Discrete-Time Systems*. New York: Academic Press.

——— [1974]. "On Some Price Adjustment Schemes." *Annals of Econ. and Social Measurement* 3:95-115.

——— [1975]. *Optimal Control and System Theory in Dynamic Economic Analysis; A System-Theoretic Approach*. New York: American Elsevier.

Armbruster, W. J., L. Garoian, A. N. Halter, and J. G. Youde [1972]. *Simulation of Farm Bargaining Board Policies in the Western Late Potato System*. Oregon State University Agricultural Experiment Station Technical Bulletin 119.

Armour, G. C., and E. S. Buffa [1963]. "A Heuristic Algorithm and Simulation Approach to Relative Location of Facilities." *Management Science* 9:924-309.

Armstrong, D. L., L. J. Connor, and R. P. Strickland [1970]. "Combining Simulation and Linear Programming in Studying Farm Firm Growth." In *Simulation Uses in Agricultural Economics*, D. L. Armstrong and R. E. Hepp, eds. Michigan State University, Agricultural Economics Report 157.

Armstrong, D. L., and R. E. Hepp, eds. [1970]. *Simulation Uses in Agricultural Economics*. Michigan State University, Agricultural Economics Report 157.

Arthur, H. B., J. P. Houck, and G. L. Beckford [1968]. *Tropical Agribusiness Structure and Adjustments—Bananas*. Harvard University, Division of Research, Graduate School of Business Administration.

Askew, A. J., W. W. Yeh, and W. A. Hall [1971]. "A Comparative Study of Critical Drought Simulation." *Water Resources Research* 7:52-62.

Astrom, K. J., and B. Wittenmark [1971]. "Problems of Identification and Control." *J. Math. Analysis and Applications* 34:90-113.

Atkinson, A. C. [1970]. "A Method of Discriminating between Models." *J. Royal Stat. Soc.* (Series B) 32:323-353.

Babb, E. M. [1964]. "Business Games as a Marketing Extension Tool." *J. Farm Econ.* 46:1024-1028.

Babb, E. M., and L. M. Eisgruber [1966]. *Management Games for Teaching and Research*. Chicago: Educational Methods.

Babb, E. M., and C. E. French [1963]. "Use of Simulation Procedures." *J. Farm Econ.* 48:876-877.

Babb, E. M., M. A. Leslie, and M. D. Slyke [1966]. "The Potential of Business-Gaming Methods in Research." *J. Business* 39:465-472.

Balderston, F. E., and A. C. Hoggatt [1962]. *Simulation of Market Processes*. University of California (Berkeley), Institute of Business and Economic Research.

Barnum, H. [1971]. "Simulation of the Market for Foodgrains in India." *Am. J. Agr. Econ.* 53:269-274.

Bar-Shalom, Y., and R. Sivan [1969]. "On the Optimal Control of Discrete-Time Linear Systems with Random Parameters." *IEEE Transactions on Automatic Control*, AC-14:3-8.

Bean, L. H. [1929]. "The Farmers' Response to Price." *J. Farm Econ.* 11:368-385.

Beged-Dov, A. G. [1967]. "An Overview of Management Science and Information Systems." *Management Science* 13(12):817-831.

Bell, D. M., D. R. Henderson, and G. R. Perkins [1972]. *A Simulation of Fertilizer Industry in the U.S.: With Special Emphasis on Fertilizer Distribution in Michigan*. Michigan State University, Agricultural Economic Report 189.

Bellman, R. [1961]. *Adaptive Control Processes: A Guided Tour*. Princeton: Princeton University Press.

Bellman, R., C. E. Clark, D. G. Malcolm, C. J. Craft, and F. M. Ricciardi [1957]. "On the Construction of a Multi-Stage, Multi-Person Business Game." *Operations Research* 5:469-503.

Bellman, R., and R. Kalaba [1959]. "A Mathematical Theory of Adaptive Control Processes." *Proc. Nat. Acad. Sci.* 45:1288-1290.

Bender, F. E. [1966]. "Performance of the Broiler Industry — A Simulative Approach." *J. Farm Econ.* 48:1467-1476.

Benson, V. W. [1969]. "Interregional Competition in the Broiler Industry: A Computer Simulation Model." Unpublished Ph.D. dissertation, University of Maryland.

Benson, V. W., F. E. Bender, and O. Lofourcade [1972]. *Interregional Competition in the Broiler Industry: A Computer Simulation Model*. Vols. 1 and 2. University of Maryland Agricultural Experiment Station Miscellaneous Publications 782 and 793.

Bentz, R. P., and R. J. Williams [1965]. *Illinois Egg-Handler Simulation*. University of Illinois (Urbana), Department of Agricultural Economics. Mimeo.

Billingsley, R., and D. Norvell [1971]. *ECO-POP: A Macro Economic-Demographic Simulation Model*. Texas A & M University, Department of Agricultural Economics and Rural Sociology, Departmental Program and Model Documentation 71-6.

Black, J. D. [1924]. "Elasticity of Supply of Farm Products." *J. Farm Econ.* 6:145-155.
——— [1953]. "Should Economists Make Value Judgments?" *Quart. J. Econ.* 67:286-297.

Blackie, M. J., and K. C. Schneeberger [1971]. "Simulation of the Growth Response of Dryland and Irrigated Corn." *Canadian J. Agr. Econ.* 19(3):108-112.

Blase, N. A., J. A. MacMillan, and F. Tung [1973]. *Simulation of Local Government Performance, Revenue and Expenditure Alternatives*. University of Manitoba, Department of Agricultural Economics and Farm Management, Research Bulletin 73-1.

Boehlje, M. D., and L. M. Eisgruber [1972]. "Strategies for the Creation and Transfer of the Farm Estate." *Am. J. Agr. Econ.* 54:461-472.

Bonini, C. P. [1963]. *Simulation of Information and Decision Systems*. Englewood Cliffs, N.J.: Prentice-Hall.

——— [1964]. "Simulation of Organizational Behavior." In *Management Controls: New Directions in Basic Research*, C. P. Bonini, R. K. Jaedicke, and H. M. Wagner, eds. New York: McGraw-Hill. Pp. 91-101.

Box, G. E. P. [1954]. "The Exploration and Exploitation of Response Surfaces: Some General Considerations and Examples." *Biometrics* 10:16-60.

——— [1957]. "Evolutionary Operation: A Method for Increasing Industrial Productivity." *Applied Statistics* 6:81-101.

Box, G. E. P., and J. S. Hunter [1959]. "Condensed Calculations for Evolutionary Operation Programs." *Technometrics* 1:77-95.

Box, G. E. P., and K. B. Wilson [1951]. "On the Experimental Attainment of Optimum Conditions." *J. Royal Stat. Soc.* (Series B) 13:1-45.

Box, M. J., and N. R. Draper [1972]. "Estimation and Design Criteria for Multi-Response Nonlinear Models with Nonhomogeneous Variance." *Applied Statistics* 21:13-24.

Brooks, R. M. [1962]. "A Sugar Refinery Simulation Model." *Management Technology* 2:117-127.

Buchanan, L. F., and F. E. Norton [1971]. "Optimal Control Applications in Economic Systems." In *Control and Dynamic Systems: Advances in Theory and Applications*, vol. 9, C. T. Leondes, ed. New York: Academic Press. Pp. 141-187.

Burdick, D. S., and T. H. Naylor [1966]. "The Design of Computer Simulation Experiments for Industrial Systems." *Communications of the ACM* 9:329-339.

——— [1969]. "Response Surface Methods in Economics." *Rev. Int. Stat. Institute* 37:18-35.

Burt, O. R. [1968]. "An Application of Statistical Decision Theory to Commerical Turkey Production: Comment." *Am. J. Agr. Econ.* 50:756-758.

——— [1969]. "Control Theory for Agricultural Policy: Methods and Problems in Operational Models." *Am. J. Agr. Econ.* 51:394-403.

Bush, R. R., and W. K. Estes, eds. [1959]. *Studies in Mathematical Learning Theory*. Stanford: Stanford University Press.

Candler, W., and W. Cartwright [1969]. "The Estimation of Performance Functions for Budgeting and Simulation Studies." *Am. J. Agr. Econ.* 51:159-169.

Carroll, T. W. [1968]. "Simulation of the Diffusion of Agricultural Innovations in Rural Communities of Transitional Societies." Unpublished Ph.D. dissertation, Massachusetts Institute of Technology.

Castro, B., and K. Weingarten [1970]. "Toward Experimental Economics." *J. Pol. Econ.* 78:598-607.

Chan, M. M. W. [1971]. "System Simulation and Maximum Entropy." *Operations Research* 19:1751-1753.

Charlton, P. J. [1972]. "Financing Farm Business Growth." *Farm Management* 2:60-70.

Charlton, P. J., and S. C. Thompson [1970]. "Simulation of Agricultural Systems." *J. Agr. Econ.* 21:373-384.

Chen, D. T. [1970]. "A Macro-Simulation Model for Forecasting Farm Equipment Sales." In *Corporate Simulation Models*, A. N. Schrieber, ed. Seattle: University of Washington Press. Pp. 163-207.

Chen, D. Y. [1971]. "A Simulated Economic Cost Model for Wisconsin Cottage Resorts." Unpublished Ph.D. dissertation, University of Wisconsin, Madison.

Chernoff, H. [1972]. *Sequential Analysis and Optimal Design*. Philadelphia: SIAM.

Chorafas, D. N. [1965]. *Systems and Simulation*. New York: Academic Press.

Chow, G. C. [1972]. "Optimal Control of Linear Econometric Systems with Finite Time Horizon." *Int. Econ. Rev.* 13:16-25.

———— [1973]. "Problems of Economic Policy from the Viewpoint of Optimal Control." *Am. Econ. Rev.* 63:825-837.

———— [1975]. "Introduction to Stochastic Control Applications." *Annals of Econ. and Social Measurement* 4:207-214.

Chow, V. T., and S. J. Kareliotis [1970]. "Analysis of Stochastic Hydrologic Systems." *Water Resources Research* 6:1569-1582.

Churchman, C. W. [1960]. "Sampling and Persuasion." *Operations Research* 8:254-259.

———— [1968]. *The Systems Approach*. New York: Delta.

———— [1971]. *The Design of Inquiring Systems: Basic Concepts of Systems and Organization*. New York: Basic Books.

Clarke, L. J. [1968]. "Simulation in Capital Investment Decisions." *J. Industrial Engineering* 10:495-498.

Clarkson, G. P. E., and H. A. Simon [1960]. "Simulation of Individual and Group Behavior." *Am. Econ. Rev.* 50:920-932.

Cloud, C. C., G. E. Frick, and R. A. Andrews [1968]. *An Economic Analysis of Hay Harvesting and Utilization Using a Simulation Model*. University of New Hampshire Agricultural Experiment Station Bulletin 495.

Cochran, W. G., and G. M. Cox [1957]. *Experimental Designs*. Second edition. New York: Wiley.

Cohen, K. J. [1960]. *Computer Models of the Shoe, Leather, Hide Sequence*. Englewood Cliffs, N.J.: Prentice-Hall.

Cohen, K. J., and R. M. Cyert [1961]. "Computer Models in Dynamic Economics." *Quart. J. Econ.* 75:112-127.

———— [1965]. *Theory of the Firm: Resource Allocation in a Market Economy*. Englewood Cliffs, N.J.: Prentice-Hall.

Cohen, K. J., and E. Rhenman [1961]. "The Role of Management Games in Education and Research." *Management Science* 7:131-166.

Cole, H. S. D., C. Freeman, M. Jahoda, and K. L. R. Pavitt [1973]. *Models of Doom: A Critique of "The Limits to Growth."* New York: Universe.

Conlisk, J., and H. Watts [1969]. "A Model for Optimizing Experimental Designs for Estimating Response Surfaces." *Am. Stat. Assoc., Proc. Social Stat. Section* 64: 150-156.

Conway, R. W., and W. L. Maxwell [1959]. "Some Problems of Digital Systems Simulation." *Management Science* 6:92-110.

Cooper, R. L. [1972]. "The Predictive Performance of Quarterly Econometric Models of the United States." In *Econometric Models of Cyclical Behavior*, vol. 2, B. G. Hickman, ed. New York: Columbia University Press. Pp. 813-926.

Coplin, W. D., ed. [1968]. *Simulation in the Study of Politics*. Chicago: Markham.

Cox, D. R. [1961]. "Tests of Separate Families of Hypotheses." *Proceedings of Fourth Berkeley Symposium on Mathematical Statistics and Probability*, vol. 1, *Contributions to the Theory of Statistics*, J. Neyman, ed. Berkeley: University of California Press. Pp. 105-123.

———— [1962]. "Further Results on Tests of Separate Families of Hypotheses." *J. Royal Stat. Soc.* (Series B) 24:406-424.

Crom, R. J. [1967]. *Simulated Interregional Models of the Livestock-Meat Economy*. USDA, ERS Agricultural Economics Report 117.

Crom, R. J., and W. R. Maki [1965a]. "A Dynamic Model of a Simulated Livestock-Meat Economy." *Agr. Econ. Res.* 17:73-83.

———— [1965b]. "Adjusting Dynamic Models to Improve Their Predictive Ability." *J. Farm Econ.* 47:963-972.

Cromarty, W. A. [1958]. "Changing Relationships between Agriculture and the National Economy." *J. Farm Econ.* 40:1568-1578.

Curry, R. E. [1970]. *Estimation and Control with Quantized Measurements.* Cambridge: M.I.T. Press.

Curtis, S. M. [1968]. "The Use of a Business Game: An Evaluation of Simulation for Teaching Farm Business Analysis to High School and Adult Students." *Am. J. Agr. Econ.* 50:1025-1034.

Cyert, R. M., and J. G. March [1963]. *A Behavioral Theory of the Firm.* Englewood Cliffs, N.J.: Prentice-Hall.

Dalton, G. E. [1971]. "Simulation Models for the Specification of Farm Investment Plans." *J. Agr. Econ.* 22:131-141.

Davies, O. L., ed [1954]. *The Design and Analysis of Industrial Experiments.* London: Oliver and Boyd.

Day, R. H. [1971]. "Comments on the Two Above Papers." In *Frontiers of Quantitative Economics*, M. C. Intriligator, ed. Amsterdam: North-Holland. Pp. 259-268.

Day, R. H., and I. Singh [1971]. "A Microeconometric Study of Agricultural Development." University of Wisconsin, Social Systems Research Institute 7120.

Day, R. H., and E. Sparling [1977]. "Optimization Models in Agricultural and Resource Economics." (See the table of contents in this volume.)

Dent, J. B. [1971]. "Livestock Performance and Capital Investment in Farm Enterprises." In *Systems Analysis in Agricultural Management*, J. B. Dent and J. R. Anderson, eds. Sydney: Wiley. Pp. 267-294.

Dent, J. B., and J. R. Anderson, eds. [1971]. *Systems Analysis in Agricultural Management.* Sydney: Wiley.

Department of Defense [1970]. "Advantages and Limitations of Computer Simulation in Decision Making." O.S.D. Case 3568.

Desai, M. J. [1968]. *The Computer Simulation of the California Dairy Industry.* Giannini Foundation Special Report.

Deutsch, R. [1969]. *System Analysis Techniques.* Englewood Cliffs, N.J.: Prentice-Hall.

Dhrymes, P. J., E. P. Howrey, S. H. Hymans, J. Kmenta, E. E. Leamer, R. E. Quandt, J. B. Ramsey, H. T. Shapiro, and V. Zarnowitz [1972]. "Criteria for Evaluation of Econometric Models." *Annals of Econ. and Social Measurement* 1:291-324.

Doeksen, G. A., and D. F. Schreiner [1972]. "Investments in Agricultural Processing for Rural Development in Oklahoma." *Am. J. Agr. Econ.* 54:513-519.

Dolbear, F. T., Jr., R. Attiyeh, and W. C. Brainerd [1968]. "A Simulation Policy Game for Teaching Macroeconomics." *Am. Econ. Rev.* 58:458-468.

Donaldson, G. F., and J. P. G Webster [1968]. *An Operating Procedure for Simulating Farm Planning—Monte Carlo Method.* Wye College (Ashford, Kent), Department of Economics.

Dorfman, R. [1963]. "Steepest Ascent under Constraint." In *Symposium on Simulation Models: Methodology and Application to the Behavioral Sciences*, A. C. Hoggatt and F. E. Balderston, eds. Cincinnati: South-Western Publishing. Pp. 237-244.

Dorfman, R. [1965]. "Formal Models in the Design of Water Resource Systems." *Water Resources Research* 1:329-336.

Doster, D. H. [1970]. "Extension Uses of Simulation in Evaluating Corn Harvesting Systems." Purdue University, Department of Agricultural Economics.

Drynan, R. G. [1973]. "On Models in Agricultural Economics." Unpublished paper, University of New England, Armidale, New South Wales, Australia.

Dudley, N. J. [1972]. "Irrigation Planning: 3, The Best Size of Irrigation Area for a Reservoir." *Water Resources Research* 9:306-324.

Dudley, N. J., and O. R. Burt [1973]. "Stochastic Reservoir Management and System Design for Irrigation." *Water Resources Research* 9:507-522.

Duewer, L. A., and W. R. Maki [1966]. "A Study of the Meat Products Industry through Systems Analysis and Simulation of Decision Units." *Agr. Econ. Res.* 18:79-83.

Dumsday, R. G. [1971]. "Evaluation of Soil Conservation Policies by Systems Analysis." In *Systems Analysis in Agricultural Management*, J. B. Dent and J. R. Anderson eds. Sydney: Wiley. Pp. 152-172.

Early, R. H., and B. N. Early [1972]. "On the Relative Performance of the Optimal Control System with M Measurements." *IEEE Transactions on Automatic Control* AC-17:555-557.

Edwards, C. [1970]. "A Simple, Two-Region Simulation of Population, Income, and Employment." *Agr. Econ. Res.* 22:29-36.

Edwards, C., and R. De Pass [1971]. *Rural-Urban Population, Income, and Employment: A Simulation of Alternative Futures*. USDA, ERS Agricultural Economic Report 218.

Eidman, V. R., ed [1971]. *Agricultural Production Systems Simulation*. Southern Farm Management Research Committee, Stillwater, Oklahoma.

Eidman, V. R., G. W. Dean, and H. O. Carter [1967]. "An Application of Statistical Decision Theory to Commercial Turkey Production." *J. Farm Econ.* 49:852-868.

Eisgruber, L. M. [1964]. "Operational Games and Simulators in Farm Management." *Proceedings of the North Central Farm Management Workshop*, University of Illinois, Urbana, pp. 53-65.

——— [1965]. *Farm Operation Simulator and Farm Management Decision Exercise*. Purdue University Agricultural Experiment Station Progress Report 162.

Eisgruber, L. M., and G. E. Lee [1971]. "A Systems Approach to Studying the Growth of the Farm Firm." *Systems Analysis in Agricultural Management*, J. B. Dent and J. R. Anderson, eds. Sydney: Wiley. Pp. 330-347.

Eisgruber, L. M., and J. Nielson [1963]. "Decision-Making Models in Farm Management." *Canadian J. Agr. Econ.* 11(1)60-70.

Eldor, H., and L. B. Koppel [1971]. "A Generalized Approach to the Method of Steepest Ascent." *Operations Research* 19:1613-1618.

Ellet, C. [1853]. *The Mississippi and Ohio Rivers, 1853: Containing Plans for the Protection of the Delta from Inundation; and Investigation of the Practicability and Cost of Improving the Navigation of the Ohio and Other Rivers by Means of Reservoirs with an Appendix on the Bars at the Mouth of the Mississippi*. Philadelphia: Lippincott, Grambo.

Ellis, J. B. [1966]. *Part I: A Manual for "Program RECSYS."* Recreation Resource Planning Division Michigan Department of Conservation, Technical Report 1.

Emery, F. E., ed [1969]. *Systems Thinking*. New York: Viking-Penguin Books.

Emshoff, J. R., and R. L. Sisson [1970]. *Design and Use of Computer Simulation Models*, London: Macmillan.

Evans, G. W., II, G. F. Wallace, and G. L. Sutherland [1967]. *Simulation Using Digital Computers*. Englewood Cliffs, N.J.: Prentice-Hall.

Evans, M. [1969]. "Non-linear Econometric Models." In *The Design of Computer Simulation Experiments*, T. H. Naylor, ed. Durham: Duke University Press. Pp. 369-392.

Faris, J. E., and J. Wildermuth [1966]. *The California Farm Management Game*. University of California Agricultural Experiment Station and Giannini Foundation of Agricultural Economics.

Fel'dbaum, A. A. [1965]. *Optimal Control Systems*. New York: Academic Press.

Fine, G. H., and P. V. McIsaac [1966]. "Simulation of a Time-Sharing System." *Management Science* 12:B180-B194.

Finney, D. J. [1945]. "The Fractional Replication of Factorial Arrangements." *Annals of Eugenics* 12:291-301.

Fisher, W. D. [1962]. "Estimation in the Linear Decision Model." *Int. Econ. Rev.* 3:1-29.

Fishman, G. S. [1967]. "Problems in the Statistical Analysis of Simulation Experiments: The Comparison of Means and the Length of Sample Records." *Communications of the ACM* 10:94-99.

——— [1968]. "The Allocation of Computer Time in Comparing Simulation Experiments." *Operations Research* 16:280-295.

——— [1971]. "Estimating Sample Size in Computing Simulation Experiments." *Management Science* 18:21-38.

Fishman, G. S., and P. J. Kiviat [1967]. "The Analysis of Simulation-Generated Time Series." *Management Science* 13:525-557.

Fletcher, L. B., E. Graber, W. C. Merrill, and E. Thorbecke [1970]. *Guatemala's Economic Development: The Role of Agriculture*. Ames: Iowa State University Press.

Flinn, J. C. [1971]. "The Simulation of Crop-Irrigation Systems." In *Systems Analysis in Agricultural Management*, J. B. Dent and J. R. Anderson, eds. Sydney: Wiley. Pp. 123-151.

Forrester, J. W. [1961]. *Industrial Dynamics*. Cambridge: M.I.T. Press.

——— [1968]. "Industrial Dynamics—After the First Decade." *Management Science* 14:398 415.

——— [1971]. *World Dynamics*. Cambridge, Mass.: Wright-Allen.

Foster, P., and L. Yost [1969]. "A Simulation Study of Population, Education and Income Growth in Uganda." *Am. J. Agr. Econ.* 51:576-591.

Fox, K. A. [1963]. *A Submodel of the Agricultural Sector*. Paper prepared as a contribution to the Brookings-SSRC econometric model of the United States.

Fox, K. A., J. K. Sengupta, and E. Thorbecke [1966]. *The Theory of Quantitative Economic Policy with Applications to Economic Growth and Stabilization Policy*. Chicago: Rand McNally.

Frahm, D. G., and L. F. Schrader [1970]. "An Experimental Comparison of Pricing in Two Auction Systems." *Am. J. Agr. Econ.* 52:528-534.

Frazier, T. L. D. B. Narrie, and T. F. Rodgers [1970]. *Simulation Procedures for Livestock Auction Markets*. University of Georgia Agricultural Experiment Station Research Bulletin 74.

Freebairn, J. W., and G. C. Rausser [1974]. "Updating Parameter Estimates: A Least Squares Approach with an Application to the Inventory of Beef Cows." *Rev. Marketing Agr. Econ.* 42:83-99.

French, B. C. [1974]. "The Subsector as a Conceptual Framework for Guiding and Conducting Research." *Am. J. Agr. Econ.* 56:1014-1022.

French, B. C., and M. Matsumoto [1969]. *An Analysis of Price and Supply Relation-*

ships in the U.S. Brussels Sprouts Industry. Giannini Foundation Research Report 308.

French, C. E. "Selected Alternative Programs for Bringing the Real World to the Undergraduate Classroom." *Am. J. Agr. Econ.* 56:1163-1175.

Friedman, B. M. [1971]. "Econometric Simulation Difficulties: An Illustration." *Rev. Econ. and Stat.* 53:381-384.

Frisch, R. [1935-36]. "On the Notion of Equilibrium and Disequilibrium." *Rev. Econ. Studies* 3:100-105.

Fromm, G. [1969]. "The Evaluation of Economic Policies." *The Design of Computer Simulation Experiments*, T. H. Naylor, ed. Durham: Duke University Press. Pp. 335-368.

Fromm, G., and L. R. Klein [1973]. "A Comparison of Eleven Econometric Models of the United States." *Am. Econ. Rev.* 63:385-393.

Fromm, G., and P. Taubman [1968]. *Policy Simulations with an Econometric Model.* Washington, D.C.: Brookings.

Fuller, E. I. [1968]. *The Use of the Northeast Farm Management Game in Massachusetts.* University of Massachusetts, Department-of Food and Agricultural Economics. Mimeo.

Fuller, E. I., L. Ruggles, and C. Yergatian [1968]. *Massachusetts Poultry Farm Management Game, Players Information, Year 1 and Year 2.* University of Massachusetts, Department of Food and Agricultural Economics.

Fullerton, H. H., and J. R. Prescott [1975]. *An Economic Simulation Model for Regional Development Planning.* Ann Arbor: Science Publishers.

Garoian, L. [1967]. "Review of 'Management Games for Teaching and Research' by E. M. Babb and L. M. Eisgruber." *J. Farm Econ.* 44:765-766.

Gaver, K. M., and M. S. Geisel [1974]. "Discrimination among Alternative Models: Bayesian and Non-Bayesian Methods." In *Frontiers in Econometrics*, P. Zarembka, ed. New York: Academic Press.

Geisel, M. S. [1969]. "Comparing and Choosing among Parametric Statistical Models: A Bayesian Analysis with Macroeconomic Applications." Unpublished Ph.D. dissertation, University of Chicago.

Gillespie, R. W., and P. Holland [1963]. *Experiments on a Simulated Underdeveloped Economy: Development Plans and Balance-of-Payments Policies.* Cambridge: M.I.T. Press.

Glickstein, A., E. M. Babb, C. E. French, and J. H. Greene [1962]. *Simulation Procedures for Production Control in an Indiana Cheese Plant.* Purdue University Agricultural Experiment Station Research Bulletin 757.

Goldberg, R. A. [1968]. *Agribusiness Coordination: A Systems Approach to the Wheat, Soybean and Florida Orange Economies.* Harvard University, Graduate School of Business Administration.

Goodall, D. W. [1971]. "Extensive Grazing Systems." In *Systems Analysis in Agricultural Management*, J. B. Dent and J. R. Anderson, eds. Sydney: Wiley. Pp. 173-187.

Gordon, R. J. [1970]. "Short and Long Term Simulations with the Brookings Model: A Comment." University of Chicago, Center for Mathematical Studies in Business and Economics, Report 7019.

Granger, C. W. J., and M. Hatanaka [1964]. *Spectral Analysis of Economic Term Series.* Princeton: Princeton University Press.

Great Plains Agricultural Council [1967]. *Economics of Firm Growth.* South Dakota State University Agricultural Experiment Station Bulletin 541.

Greenlaw, P. S., L. W. Herron, and R. H. Rawdon [1962]. *Business Simulation in Industrial and University Education*. Englewood Cliffs, N.J.: Prentice-Hall.

Gross, D., and J. L. Ray [1965]. "A General Purpose Forecast Simulator." *Management Science* 11:B119-B135.

Gunckel, T. L., and G. F. Franklin [1963]. "A General Solution for Linear Sampled-Data Control." *J. Basic Engineering* (Series D) 85:197-203.

Haitovsky, Y., and N. Wallace [1972]. "A Study of Discretionary and Nondiscretionary Monetary and Fiscal Policies in the Context of Stochastic Macroeconometric Models." In *The Business Cycle Today*, V. Zarnowitz, ed. New York: National Bureau of Economic Research. Pp. 261-309.

Halter, A. N., and G. W. Dean [1965]. "Use of Simulation in Evaluating Management Policies under Uncertainty: Application to a Large Scale Ranch." *J. Farm Econ.* 47:557-573.

Halter, A. N., M. L. Hayenga, and T. J. Manetsch [1970]. "Simulating a Developing Agricultural Economy: Methodology and Planning Capability." *Am. J. Agr. Econ.* 52:272-284.

Halter, A. N., and S. F. Miller [1966]. *River Basin Planning—A Simulation Approach*. Oregon State University Agricultural Experiment Station Special Report 224.

Hamilton, H. R., S. E. Goldstone, J. W. Milliman, A. L. Pugh, III, E. B. Roberts, and A. Zellner [1969]. *Systems Simulation for Regional Analysis: An Application to River-Basin Planning*. Cambridge: M.I.T. Press.

Hammersley, J. M., and D. C. Handscomb [1964]. *Monte Carlo Methods*. London: Methuen.

Hammond, D. H., J. R. Strain, and C. P. Baumel [1966]. "Simplifying Management Games for Extension Programs." *J. Farm Econ.* 48:1026-1028.

Handscomb, D. C. [1969]. "Monte Carlo Techniques: Theoretical." In *The Design of Computer Simulation Experiments*, T. H. Baylor, ed. Durham: Duke University Press. Pp. 252-262.

Harbaugh, J. W., and G. Bonham-Carter [1970]. *Computer Simulation in Geology*. New York: Wiley.

Hare, V. C., Jr. [1967]. *Systems Analysis: A Diagnostic Approach*. New York: Harcourt, Brace, and World.

Harle, J. T. [1968]. "Towards a More Dynamic Approach to Farm Planning." *J. Agr. Econ.* 19:339-345.

Harling, J. [1958]. "Simulation Techniques in Operating Research—A Review." *Operations Research* 6:307-319.

Hayenga, M. L., T. J. Manetsch, and A. N. Halter [1968]. "Computer Simulation as a Planning Tool in Developing Economies." *Am. J. Agr. Econ.* 50:1755-1759.

Heady, E. O., ed. [1971]. *Economic Models and Quantitative Methods for Decisions and Planning in Agriculture*. Ames: Iowa State University Press.

Heady, E. O., and L. G. Tweeten [1963]. *Resource Demand and Structure of the Agricultural Industry*. Ames: Iowa State University Press.

Hesselbach, J., and L. M. Eisgruber [1967]. *Betriebliche Entscheidungen Mittels Simulation*. Hamburg and Berlin: Paul Parey.

Hill, W. J., and W. G. Hunter [1966]. "A Review of Response Surface Methodology: A Literature Survey." *Technometrics* 8:571-590.

Hinman, H. R., and R. F. Hutton [1970]. "A General Simulation Model for Farm Firms." *Agr. Econ. Res.* 22:69-77.

———— [1971]. "Returns and Risks of Expanding Pennsylvania Dairy Farms with Different Levels of Equity." *Am. J. Agr. Econ.* 53:608-611.

Hoggatt, A. C., and R. E. Balderston [1963]. *Symposium on Simulation Models: Methodology and Applications to the Behavioral Sciences.* Cincinnati: South-Western Publishing.

Holder, S. H., Jr., D. L. Shaw, and J. C. Snyder [1971]. *A Systems Model of the U.S. Rice Industry.* USDA, ERS Technical Bulletin 1453.

Holland, E. P. [1962]. "Simulation of an Economy with Development and Trade Problems." *Am. Econ. Rev.* 52:408-430.

———— [1968]. *Simulating the Dynamics of Economic Development.* World Bank Economics Department Working Paper 90, Washington.

Hollingdale, S. H., ed [1967]. *Digital Simulation in Operational Research.* London: English Universities Press.

Holt, C. C. [1962]. "Linear Decision Rules for Economic Stabilization and Growth." *Quart. J. Econ.* 76:20-45.

———— [1965]. "Validation and Application of Macroeconomic Models Using Computer Simulation." *The Brookings Quarterly Econometric Model of the United States,* J. S. Duesenberry, G. Fromm, L. R. Klein, and E. Kuh, eds. Chicago: Rand McNally. Pp. 637-650.

Holt, C. C., R. W. Shirey, D. V. Steward, J. L. Midler, and A. Stroud [1964]. "Program SIMULATE; A User's and Programmer's Manual." University of Wisconsin, Social Systems Research Institute. Mimeo.

Hood, W. C., and T. C. Koopmans, eds. [1953]. *Studies in Econometric Method.* New York: Wiley.

Howitt, R. E., S. F. Moore, C. V. Moore, and J. H. Snyder [1974]. "A Simulation Approach to Recreation Planning (a Case of Changing Quality)." *Annals of Regional Science* 8:35-50.

Howrey, E. P. [1971]. "Stochastic Properties of the Klein-Goldberger Model." *Econometrica* 39:73-87.

Howrey, E. P., and H. H. Kelejian [1969]. "Simulation *versus* Analytical Solutions." In *The Design of Computer Simulation Experiments,* T. H. Naylor, ed. Durham: Duke University Press. Pp. 207-231.

———— [1971]. "Simulation *versus* Analytical Solutions." In *Computer Simulation Experiments with Models of Economic Systems,* T. H. Naylor, ed. New York: Wiley. Pp. 299-319.

Howrey, E. P., and L. R. Klein [1972]. "Dynamic Properties of Nonlinear Econometric Models." *Int. Econ. Rev.* 13:599-618.

Hufschmidt, M. M. [1962]. "Analysis by Simulation: Examination of Response Surface." In *Design of Water Resource Systems,* A. Maass, M. M. Hufschmidt, R. Dorfman, H. A. Thomas, Jr., S. A. Marglin, and G. M. Fair, eds. Cambridge: Harvard University Press. Pp. 391-442.

———— [1963]. "Simulating the Behavior of a Multi-Unit, Multi-Purpose Water-Resource System." In *Symposium on Simulation Models: Methodology and Applications to the Behavioral Sciences,* A. C. Hoggatt and F. E. Balderston, eds. Cincinnati: South-Western Publishing. Pp. 203-220.

Hufschmidt, M. M., and M. B. Fiering [1966]. *Simulation Techniques for Design of Water-Resource Systems.* Cambridge: Harvard University Press.

Huggins, L. F., and E. J. Monke [1968]. "A Mathematical Model for Simulating Hydrologic Response of a Watershed." *Water Resources Research* 4:529-539.

Hughes, N. H. B. [1973]. *Viability and Survival of the Wool-Producing Farm Firm*. University of New England (Armidale, New South Wales), Agricultural Economics and Business Management Bulletin 16.

Hunter, J. S., and T. H. Naylor [1970]. "Experimental Designs for Computer Simulation Experiments." *Management Science* 16:422-434.

Hutton, R. F. [1966]. *A Simulation Technique for Making Management Decisions in Dairy Farming: Narrative Flow Chart and Computer Code Description*. USDA, ERS Agricultural Economic Report 87.

Hutton, R. F., and H. R. Hinman [1968]. *A General Agricultural Firm Simulator*. Pennsylvania State University, Department of Agricultural Economics and Rural Sociology, Report 72.

IBM, United Kingdom Limited Data Centre [1966a]. *Control and Simulation Language Manual*. London.

―――― [1966b]. *General Purpose Simulation/360: Application Description*. H20-0186-1, GH20-4035.

Ignall, E. J. [1972]. "On Experimental Designs for Computer Simulation Experiments." *Management Science* 18:384-388.

Ingram, G. K., J. F. Kain, and J. R. Ginn [1973]. *The Detroit Prototype of the NBER Urban Simulation Model*. New York: National Bureau of Economic Research.

Jacoby, H. D. [1967]. *The Use of Digital Simulation in Electric Power Planning*. Harvard University, Development Advisory Service.

―――― [1971]. "An Electric Power System Planning Model for West Pakistan." In *Development Policy II ― The Pakistan Experience*, W. P. Falcon and G. F. Papanek, eds. Cambridge: Harvard University Press.

Jacoby, H. D., and D. P. Loucks [1972]. "Combined Use of Optimization and Simulation Models in River Basin Planning." *Water Resources Research* 9:1401-1414.

Jeffreys, H. [1961]. *Theory of Probability*. Third edition. Oxford: Clarendon Press.

John, P. W. M. [1971]. *Statistical Design and Analysis of Experiments*. New York: Macmillan.

Johnson, B., and L. M. Eisgruber [1969]. *Annotated Bibliography on Simulation in Business Management*. Purdue University, Department of Agricultural Economics.

Johnson, G. L. [1970]. *The Role of the University and Its Economists in Economic Development*. University of Guelph, Department of Agricultural Economics. Pub. AE70/2.

Johnson, G. L., and L. K. Zerby [1973]. *What Economists Do about Values ― Case Studies of Their Answers to Questions They Don't Dare Ask*. East Lansing: Michigan State University Press.

Johnson, H. G. [1951]. "The Taxonomic Approach to the Study of Economic Policy." *Econ. J.* 61:812-832.

Johnson, S. R., K. R. Tefertiller, and D. S. Moore [1967]. "Stochastic Linear Programming and Feasibility Problems in Farm Growth Analysis." *J. Farm Econ.* 49:908-919.

Johnston, B. G. [1973]. *A Simulation Study of the Economics of Amalgamation in the Arid Pastoral Zone of N.S.W.* University of New England (Armidale, New South Wales), Agricultural Economics and Business Management Bulletin 18.

Jones, J. G. W., and N. R. Brockington [1971]. "Intensive Grazing Systems." In *Systems Analysis in Agricultural Management*, J. B. Dent and J. R. Anderson, eds. Sydney: Wiley. Pp. 188-211.

Jorgenson, D. W., J. Hunter, and M. I. Nadiri [1970]. "The Predictive Performance of

Econometric Models of Quarterly Investment Behavior." *Econometrica* 38:213-224.

Jose, H. D., R. L. Christensen, and E. I. Fuller [1971]. "Consideration of Weather Risk in Forage Machinery Selection." *Canadian J. Agr. Econ.* 19(1):98-109.

Judge, G. G. [1968]. "The Search for Quantitative Economic Knowledge." *Am. J. Agr. Econ.* 50:1703-1717.

―――― [1977]. "On Estimating the Parameters of Economic Relations." (See the table of contents in this volume.)

Judge, G. G., and Yancey, T. A. [1969]. "The Use of Prior Information in Estimating the Parameters of Economic Relationships." *Metroeconomica* 21:97-140.

Kagel, J. H., R. C. Battalio, H. Rachlin, L. Green, R. L. Basmann, and W. R. Klemm [1975]. "Experimental Studies of Consumer Demand Behavior Using Laboratory Animals." *Economic Inquiry* 13:22-38.

Kain, J. F., and J. R. Meyer [1968]. "Computer Simulations, Physio-Economic Systems, and Intraregional Models." *Am. Econ. Rev.* 58:171-181.

Kalman, R. E. [1960]. "A New Approach to Linear Filtering and Prediction Problems." *Journal of Basic Engineering* (Series D) 82:35-45.

Kay, R. D. [1973]. *Texas A & M Farm and Ranch Management Game.* Texas A & M University, Department of Agricultural Economics and Rural Sociology, Departmental Program and Model Documentation 73-1.

Kiviat, P. J. [1967]. "Development of Discrete Digital Simulation Languages." *Simulation* 8:65-74.

Kiviat, P. J., R. Villanueva, and H. M. Markowitz [1968]. *The SIMSCRIPT II Programming Language.* Englewood Cliffs, N.J.: Prentice-Hall.

Kleijnen, J. P. C. [1972]. "The Statistical Design and Analysis of Digital Simulation: A Survey." *Management Informatics* 1:57-76.

―――― [1974]. *Statistical Techniques in Simulation, Part 1.* New York: Marcel Dekker.

―――― [1975]. *Statistical Techniques in Simulation, Part 2.* New York: Marcel Dekker.

Klein, L. R., and E. Burmeister [1976]. *Econometric Model Performance: Comparative Simulation Studies of the U.S. Economy.* Philadelphia: University of Pennsylvania Press.

Koenig, H. E., A. Hilmersen, and L. Yuan [1969]. "Modern System Theory in the Agricultural Industry: An Example." *Transactions ASAE* 12:190-194.

Kogan, Y. A. [1966]. "Comparison of Non-optimal and Optimal Strategies in Dual Control Problems." *Automation and Remote Control* 27:590-600.

Kornai, J. [1971]. *Anti-Equilibrium: On Economic Systems Theory and the Tasks of Research.* Amsterdam: North-Holland.

Kotler, P., and R. L. Schultz [1970]. "Marketing Simulations: Review and Prospects." *J. Business* 43:237-295.

Kourtz, P. H., and W. G. O'Reagan [1968]. "A Cost-Effectiveness Analysis of Simulated Forest Fire Detection Systems." *Hilgardia* 39:341-366.

Krasnow, H. S., and R. A. Merikallio [1964]. "The Past, Present and Future of Simulation Languages." *Management Science* 11:236-267.

Krebs, E. H., M. L. Hayenga, and J. M. Lehker [1972]. *Various Price and Supply Cost Programs for Navy Beans―Simulation Analysis.* Michigan State University, Agricultural Economics Paper 212.

Kresge, D. T. [1967]. *A Simulation Model for Economic Planning: A Pakistan Example.* Harvard University, Development Advisory Service, Economic Development Report 81. Mimeo.

Kuehn, A. A. [1962]. "Complex Interactive Models." In *Quantitative Techniques in Marketing Analysis*, R. E. Frank, A. A. Kuehn, and W. F. Massy, eds. Homewood, Ill.: Irwin. Pp. 106-123.

Kuehn, A. A., and M. J. Hamburger [1963]. "A Heuristic Program for Locating Warehouses." *Management Science* 9:643-666.

Kuhn, T. S. [1970]. *The Structure of Scientific Revolutions*. Second edition. Chicago: University of Chicago Press.

LaDue, E. L., and W. H. Vincent [1974]. *Systems Theory and Simulation: A Critique of Literature*. Michigan State University, Agricultural Economics Report 261.

Lavington, M. R. [1970]. "A Practical Microsimulation Model for Consumer Marketing." *Operations Research Quarterly* 21:25-46.

Leamer, E. E. [1970]. "Model Selection Searches: A Bayesian View." Harvard Institute of Economic Research, Discussion Paper 151.

Lee, A. M. [1970]. *Systems Analysis Frameworks*. New York: Wiley.

Lee, G. E. [1974]. "Artificial Intelligence in the Pre-Decision Process of Business Planning." Unpublished Ph.D. dissertation, Purdue University.

Lehker, J. N., and T. J. Manetsch [1971]. *Systems Analysis of Development in Northeast Brazil: The Feasibility of Using Simulation to Evaluate Alternative Systems of Beef Production in Northeast Brazil*. Michigan State University, Divison of Engineering Research Technical Report 613A.

Leistritz, F. L. [1970]. "Simulation Analysis of the Farm Real Estate Market and Farm Enlargement in Southwest Nebraska." Unpublished Ph.D. dissertation, University of Nebraska.

Leontief, W. [1971]. "Theoretical Assumptions and Nonobserved Facts." *Am. Econ. Rev.* 61:1-7.

Lin, S. A. Y., and E. O. Heady [1971]. "Simulated Markets, Farm Structure, and Agricultural Policies." *Canadian J. Agr. Econ.* 19(1):55-65.

Lins, D. A. [1969]. "An Empirical Comparison of Simulation and Recursive Linear Programming Firm Growth Models." *Agr. Econ. Res.* 21:7-12.

――― [1973]. *A Simulation Model of Farm Sector Social Accounts*. USDA, ERS Technical Bulletin 1486.

Longworth, J. W. [1969]. "Management Games and the Teaching of Farm Management." *Australian J. Agr. Econ.* 13:58-67.

――― [1970]. "From War-Chess to Farm Management Games." *Canadian J. Agr. Econ.* 18(2):1-11.

Maass, A., M. M. Hufschmidt, R. Dorfman, H. A. Thomas, Jr., S. A. Marglin, and G. M. Fair [1962]. *Design of Water-Resource Systems*. Cambridge: Harvard University Press.

MacCrimmon, K. R., and M. Tota [1969]. "The Experimental Determination of Indifference Curves." *Rev. Econ. Studies* 36:443-451.

McFarquhar, A. M. M., and M. C. Evans [1971]. "Projection Models for U.K. Food and Agriculture." *J. Agr. Econ.* 22:321-345.

McKenney, J. L. [1962]. "An Evaluation of a Business Game in an MBA Curriculum." *J. Business* 35:278-286.

McMahon, T. A., and A. J. Miller [1971]. "Application of the Thomas and Fiering Model to Skewed Hydrologic Data." *Water Resources Research* 7:1338-1340.

McMillan, C., and R. F. Gonzalez [1965]. *Systems Analysis: A Computer Approach to Decision Models*. Homewood, Ill.: Irwin.

Maffei, R. B. [1958]. "Simulation, Sensitivity, and Management Decision Rules." *J. Business* 31:177-186.

Malcolm, D. G. [1960]. "Bibliography on the Use of Simulation in Management Analysis." *Operations Research* 8:169-177.

Manderscheid, L. V., and G. L. Nelson [1969]. "A Framework for Viewing Simulation." *Canadian J. Agr. Econ.* 17:(1)33-41.

Manetsch, T. J. [1967]. "The U.S. Plywood Industry – Systems Study." *IEEE Transactions on Systems Science and Cybernetics* 55C:3.

——— [1974]. "Basic Systems Theory and Concepts Underlying Construction of the Korean Simulation Model with Implications for Further Work." United States AID Conference for the Evaluation of the Korean Sector Simulation Model, Airlie House, Virginia.

Manetsch, T. J., M. L. Hayenga, A. N. Halter, T. W. Carroll, M. H. Abkin, D. R. Byerlee, K-Y. Chong, G. Page, E. Kellogg, and G. L. Johnson [1971]. *A Generalized Simulation Approach to Agricultural Sector Analysis with Special Reference to Nigeria.* East Lansing: Michigan State University.

Manetsch, T. J., and S. C. Lenchner [1971]. *Systems Analysis of Development in Northeast Brazil: The Feasibility of Using Simulation to Evaluate Alternative Policies for Development of the Brazilian Textile Industry,* Michigan State University, Division of Engineering Research, Technical Report G-13B.

Manetsch, T. J., F. A. Ramos, and S. C. Lenchner [1968]. *Computer Simulation of a Program for Modernizing Cotton Production in Northeast Brazil.* Michigan State University, Systems Science Program, Working Paper 3.

Marion, B. W., and H. B. Arthur [1973]. *Dynamic Factors in Vertical Commodity Systems: A Case Study of the Broiler System.* Ohio Agricultural Research and Development Center Research Bulletin 1065.

Markowitz, H. H., B. Hausner, and H. W. Karr [1963]. *SIMSCRIPT: A Simulation Programming Language.* Englewood Cliffs, N.J.: Prentice-Hall.

Marschak, J. [1963]. "The Payoff-Relevant Description of States and Acts." *Econometrica* 31:719-726.

Marsden, J., D. Pingry, and A. Whinston [1974]. "Engineering Foundations of Production Functions." *J. Econ. Theory* 9:124-140.

Martin, F. F. [1968]. *Computer Modeling and Simulation.* New York: Wiley.

Masch, F. D., and Associates [1971]. *Simulation of Water Quality in Streams and Canals.* Texas Water Development Board Report 128.

Mathis, W. K. [1969]. *An Economic Simulation Model of the Cacao Industry of the Dominican Republic.* Texas A & M University, International Programs Information Report 69.2.

Meadows, D. H., D. L. Meadows, J. Randers, and W. W. Behrens, III [1972]. *The Limits to Growth.* New York: Universe.

Mehra, R. K. [1974]. "Identification in Control and Econometrics: Similarities and Differences." *Annals of Econ. and Social Measurement* 3:21-47.

Meier, R. C. [1967]. "The Application of Optimum-Seeking Techniques to Simulation Studies: A Preliminary Evaluation." *J. Financial and Quantitative Analysis* 2:30-51.

Meier, R. C., W. T. Newell, and H. L. Pazer [1969]. *Simulation in Business and Economics.* Englewood Cliffs, N.J.: Prentice-Hall.

Mendenhall, W. [1968]. *Introduction to Linear Models and the Design and Analysis of Experiments.* Belmont, Cal.: Wadsworth.

Mesarovic, M. D., D. Macko, and Y. Takahara [1970]. *Theory of Hierarchical, Multi-Level Systems*. New York: Academic Press.

Michigan State University, Agricultural Sector Simulation Team [1973]. "System Simulation of Agricultural Development: Some Nigerian Policy Comparisons." *Am. J. Agr. Econ.* 55:404-419.

Miernyk, W. H. [1969]. "An Interindustry Forecasting Model with Water Quantity and Quality Restraints." In *Systems Analysis for Great Lakes Water Resources*. Proceedings of Fourth Symposium on Water Research, Ohio State University, 1969.

Mihram, G. A. [1972]. *Simulation: Statistical Foundations and Methodology*. New York: Academic Press.

Miller, S. F., and A. N. Halter [1973]. "Systems-Simulation in a Practical Policy-Making Setting: The Venezuelan Cattle Industry." *Am. J. Agr. Econ.* 55:420-433.

Mize, J. H., and J. G. Cox [1968]. *Essentials of Simulation*. Englewood Cliffs, N.J.: Prentice-Hall.

Moore, H. L. [1914]. *Economic Business Cycles: Their Law and Causes*. New York: Macmillan. Reprinted in 1967 by A. M. Kelley.

Moreley, F. H. W., and G. Y. Graham [1971]. "Fodder Conservation for Drought." In *Systems Analysis in Agricultural Management*, J. B. Dent and J. R. Anderson, eds. Sydney: Wiley. Pp. 212-236.

Morrissy, J. D. [1974]. *Agricultural Modernization through Production Contracting*. New York: Praeger.

Murphy, M. C. [1968]. "A Stochastic Approach to Investment Appraisal." *Farm Economist* 11:304-318.

Nagar, A. L. [1969]. "Stochastic Simulations of the Brookings Model." In *The Brookings Model: Some Further Results*, J. S. Duesenberry, G. Fromm, L. R. Klein, and E. Kuh, eds. Chicago: Rand McNally. Pp. 423-456.

Nance, R. E. [1971]. "On Time Flow Mechanisms for Discrete System Simulation." *Management Science* 18:59-73.

Naylor, T. H. [1969a]. "Simulation and Gaming, Bibliography 19." *Computing Reviews* 10:61-69.

———, ed. [1969b]. *The Design of Computer Simulation Experiments*. Durham: Duke University Press.

——— [1970]. "Policy Simulation Experiments with Macroeconometric Models: The State of the Art." *Am. J. Agr. Econ.* 52:263-271.

———, ed. [1971]. *Computer Simulation Experiments with Models of Economic Systems*. New York: Wiley.

——— [1972]. "Experimental Economics Revisited." *J. Pol. Econ.* 80:347-352.

Naylor, T. H., J. L. Balintfy, D. S. Burdick, and K. Chu [1966]. *Computer Simulation Techniques*. New York: Wiley.

Naylor, T. H., D. S. Burdick, and W. E. Sasser [1967]. "Computer Simulation Experiments with Economic Systems: The Problem of Experimental Design." *J. Am. Stat. Assoc.* 62:1315-1337.

Naylor, T. H., and J. M. Finer [1967]. "Verification of Computer Simulation Models." *Management Science* 14:92-101.

Naylor, T. H., W. H. Wallace, and W. E. Sasser [1967]. "A Computer Simulation Model of the Textile Industry." *J. Am. Stat. Assoc.* 62:1338-1364.

Naylor, T. H., K. Wertz, and T. H. Wonnacott [1967]. "Methods of Analyzing Data from Computer Simulation Experiments." *Communications of the ACM* 10:703-10.

—— [1968]. "Some Methods for Evaluating the Effects of Economic Policies Using Simulation Experiments." *Rev. Int. Stat. Institute* 36:184-200.

—— [1969]. "Spectral Analysis of Data Generated by Simulated Experiments with Econometric Models." *Econometrica* 37:333-352.

Nelson, M., and S. K. Schuck [1974]. *Agricultural Development with Unlimited Supplies of Land: The Peruvian Case*. Washington, D.C.: Resources for the Future.

Nevins, A. J. [1966]. "Some Effects of Uncertainty: Simulation of a Model of Price." *Quart. J. Econ.* 80:73-87.

Nijkamp, P. [1970]. "Determination of Implicit Social Preference Functions." Unpublished manuscript, Netherlands School of Economics, Econometric Institute.

Norvell, D. G. [1972]. "A Simulation Study of Population, Education, and Income Growth in Uganda: Comment." *Am. J. Agr. Econ.* 54:524-526.

O'Mara, G. T. [1971]. "A Decision-Theoretic View of the Microeconomics of Techniques Diffusion in a Developing Country." Unpublished Ph.D. dissertation, Stanford University.

Optner, S. L. [1960]. *Systems Analysis for Business Management*. Second edition. Englewood Cliffs, N.J.: Prentice-Hall.

Orcutt, G. H. [1960]. "Simulation of Economic Systems." *Am. Econ. Rev.* 50:893-907.

Orcutt, G. H., M. Greenberger, J. Korbel, and A. M. Rivlin [1961]. *Microanalysis of Socioeconomic Systems: A Simulation Study*. New York: Harper and Row.

Patrick, G. F., and L. M. Eisgruber [1968]. "The Impact of Managerial Ability and Capital Structure on Growth of the Farm Firm." *Am. J. Agr. Econ.* 50:491-506.

Patten, B. C., ed. [1971]. *Systems Analysis and Simulation in Ecology*. Vol. 1. New York: Academic Press.

Perkins, W. R., J. B. Cruz, Jr., and N. Sundararajan [1972]. "Feedback Control of a Macroeconomic System Using an Observer." *IEEE Transactions on Systems, Man, and Cybernetics* SMC-2:275-278.

Phillips, B. J. [1969]. "Rainfall Distributions and Simulation Models [1969]." In *Proceedings, 41st ANZAAS Congress, Section 8, Mathematical Sciences, Adelaide.*

Pisano, W. C. [1969]. *River Basin Simulation Program*. United States Department of the Interior, Division of Technical Control, Federal Water Pollution Control Administration.

Popper, K. R. [1959]. *The Logic of Scientific Discovery*. New York: Basic Books.

Porter, J. C., M. W. Sasieni, E. S. Marks, and R. L. Ackoff [1966]. "The Use of Simulation as a Pedagogical Device." *Management Science* 12:B170-B179.

Pouliquen, L. Y. [1970]. *Risk Analysis in Project Appraisal*. World Bank Staff Occasional Paper 11. Baltimore: Johns Hopkins Press.

Prescott, E. C. [1967]. "Adaptive Decision Rules for Macro Economic Planning." Unpublished Ph.D. dissertation, Graduate School of Industrial Administration, Carnegie-Mellon University.

—— [1971]. "Adaptive Decision Rules for Macroeconomic Planning." *Western Econ. J.* 9:369-378.

—— [1972]. "The Multi-Period Control Problem under Uncertainty." *Econometrica* 40:1043-1058.

President's Water Resource Policy Commission [1950]. *A Water Policy for the American People*. Government Printing Office.

Preston, L. E., and N. R. Collins [1966]. *Studies in a Simulated Market*. Berkeley: IBER Publications.

Ramsey, J. B. [1969]. "Tests for Specification Errors in Classical Linear Least-Squares Regression Analysis." *J. Royal Stat. Soc.* (Series B) 31:350-371.

Ramsey, J. B., and P. Zarembka [1971]. "Specification Error Tests and Alternative Functional Forms of the Aggregate Production Function." *J. Am. Stat. Assoc.* 66:471-477.

Raulerson, R. C., and M. R. Langham [1970]. "Evaluating Supply Control Policies for Frozen Concentrated Orange Juice with an Industrial Dynamics Model." *Am. J. Agr. Econ.* 52:197-208.

Rausser, G. C. [1973]. "The Validity and Verification of Complex System Models: Discussion." *Am. J. Agr. Econ.* 55:273-279.

——— [1974a]. "Structural Change, Value of Estimating and Adaptive Control." University of Chicago, Department of Economics (working paper).

——— [1974b]. "Alternative Econometric Model Forms, Forecasting and Naive Comparison." Iowa State University, Department of Economics. Mimeo.

Rausser, G. C., and G. W. Dean [1971a]. "Uncertainty and Decision-Making in Water Resources." In *California Water: A Study in Resource Management*, D. Seckler, ed. Berkeley: University of California Press. Pp. 233-250.

——— [1971b]. "An Appendix on Water Resource Decision Making under Conditions of Uncertainty." In *California Water: A Study in Resource Management*, D. Seckler, ed. Berkeley: University of California Press. Pp. 310-344.

Rausser, G. C., and J. W. Freebairn [1974a]. "Approximate Adaptive Control Solutions to U.S. Beef Trade Policy." *Annals of Econ. and Social Measurement* 3:177-203.

——— [1974b]. "Estimation of Policy Preference Functions: An Application to U.S. Beef Import Quotas." *Rev. Econ. and Stat.* 56:437-449.

——— [1977]. "Structural Changes and Updating Econometric Model Coefficient Estimates." Harvard Business School (working paper).

Rausser, G. C., and S. R. Johnson [1975]. "On the Limitations of Simulation in Model Evaluation and Decision Analysis." *Simulation and Games* 6:115-150.

Rausser, G. C., and C. E. Willis [1976]. "Investment Sequencing, Allocation and Learning in the Design of Water Resource Systems: An Empirical Application." *Water Resources Research* 12:317-330.

Rausser, G. C., C. Willis, and P. Frick [1972]. "Learning, External Benefits, and Subsidies in Water Desalination." *Water Resources Research* 8:1385-1400.

Ray, D. E., and E. O. Heady [1972]. "Government Farm Programs and Commodity Interaction: A Simulation Analysis." *Am. J. Agr. Econ.* 54:578-590.

Reutlinger, S. [1970a]. "A Simulation Model by Evaluating National Buffer Stock Programs." Paper presented at the second world congress of the Econometrics Society, Cambridge.

——— [1970b]. *Techniques for Project Appraisal under Uncertainty*, World Bank Staff Occasional Paper 10. Baltimore: Johns Hopkins Press.

Roberts, P. O., and D. T. Kresge [1968]. "Simulation of Transport Policy Alternatives for Colombia." *Am. Econ. Rev.* 58:341-359.

Rodriguez-Iturbe, I., D. R. Dawdy, and L. E. Garcia [1971]. "Adequacy of Markovian Models with Cyclic Components for Stochastic Streamflow Simulation." *Water Resources Research* 7:1127-1143.

Rothenberg, J. [1961]. *The Measurement of Social Welfare*. Englewood Cliffs, N.J.: Prentice-Hall.

Samuelson, P. A. [1947]. *Foundations of Economic Analysis*. Cambridge: Harvard University Press.

Schaller, W. N. [1968]. "A National Model of Agricultural Production Response." *Agr. Econ. Res.* 20:33-46.

Schlaifer, R. [1959]. *Probability and Statistics for Business Decisions*. New York: McGraw-Hill.

Schmidt, J. W., and R. E. Taylor [1970]. *Simulation and Analysis of Industrial Systems*. Homewood, Ill.: Irwin.

Schruben, L. W. [1968]. "Systems Approach to Marketing Efficiency Research." *Am. J. Agr. Econ.* 50:1454-1468.

Shechter, M. [1972]. "A Simulation Model for Agricultural Policy." In *Future Farm Programs: Comparative Costs and Consequences*, E. O. Heady, L. V. Mayer, and H. C. Madsen, eds. Ames: Iowa State University Press. Pp. 275-325.

Shechter, M., and E. O. Heady [1970]. "Response Surface Analysis and Simulaton Models in Policy Choices." *Am. J. Agr. Econ.* 52:41-50.

Shih, C., and J. A. Dracup [1961]. "Simulation of Evaporation from Constant Source with Finite Areas." *Water Resources Research* 5:281-90.

Shubik, M. [1960]. "Simulation of the Industry and the Firm." *Am. Econ. Rev.* 50:908-919.

—— [1972]. "On the Scope of Gaming." *Management Science* 18 (part 2) P20-P36.

Simon, H. A. [1956]. "Dynamic Programming under Uncertainty with a Quadratic Criterion Function." *Econometrica* 24:74-81.

Simon, H. A., and A. Newell [1958]. "Heuristic Problem Solving: The Next Advance in Operations Research." *Operations Research* 6:1-10.

Simpson, J. R., and R. V. Billingsley [1973]. "Application of a Macroeconomic Demographic Simulation Model to Planning in Paraguay." Paper contributed to the Fifteenth International Congress of Agricultural Economists, Sao Paulo, Brazil.

Singh, I., and R. H. Day [1972]. "A Microeconomic Chronicle of the Green Revolution." Ohio State University, Department of Agricultural Economics (discussion paper).

Smith, F. J., and S. Miles [1967]. *Oregon Farm Management Simulation*. Oregon State University, Cooperative Extension Service and Agricultural Economics Department.

Smith, V. K. [1973]. *Monte Carlo Methods: Their Role for Econometrics*. Lexington, Mass.: Lexington Books.

Smith, V. L. [1962]. "An Experimental Study of Competitive Market Behavior." *J. Pol. Econ.* 70:111-137.

—— [1964]. "Effect of Market Organization on Competitive Equilibrium." *Quart. J. Econ.* 77:181-201.

Smith, W. G., and W. L. Parks [1967]. "A Method for Incorporating Probability into Fertilizer Recommendations." *J. Farm Econ.* 49:1511-1515.

Snyder, J. C., and G. L. Swackhamer [1966]. *Management Planning and Control Systems*. Purdue Agricultural Experiment Station Research Bulletin 809.

Sorensen, E. E., and J. F. Gilheany [1970]. "A Simulation Model for Harvest Operations under Stochastic Conditions." *Management Science* 16:B549-B565.

Stillson, R. T. [1969]. "Regional Trade and Structure Model for Pollution Abatement Study." *Systems Analysis for Great Lakes Water Resources*. Proceedings of Fourth Symposium on Water Research, Ohio State University, 1969.

Strotz, R. A., and H. O. A. Wold [1960]. "Recursive vs. Nonrecursive Systems: An Attempt at Synthesis." *Econometrica* 28:417-427.

Suttor, R. E., and R. J. Crom [1964]. "Computer Models and Simulation." *J. Farm Econ.* 46:1341-1350.

Tanago, A. G. [1973]. *Hay-Making Machinery Selection under Risk: A Simulation Approach.* University of New England (Armidale, New South Wales) Farm Management Bulletin 17.

Tarn, T. J. [1971]. "Extended Separation Theorem and Exact Analytical Solution of Stochastic Control." *Automatica* 7:343-350.

Taylor, H. C. [1929]. "The New Farm Economics." *J. Farm Econ.* 11:357-367.

Taylor, L. J. [1969]. "Development Patterns: A Simulation Study." *Quart. J. Econ.* 83: 220-241.

Theil, H. [1964]. *Optimal Decision Rules for Government and Industry.* Amsterdam: North-Holland.

——— [1971]. *Principles of Econometrics.* New York: Wiley.

Thompson, S. C. [1970]. *A User's Manual for Monte Carlo Programming.* University of Reading, Department of Agricultural Economics, Study 9.

Thorbecke, E. [1971]. "Preparing Sector Programs for Agriculture: Sector Analysis, Models and Practice." Paper presented at the Conference on Strategies for Agricultural Development in the 1970s, Stanford University.

Tinbergen, J. [1952]. *On the Theory of Economic Policy.* Amsterdam: North-Holland.

Tocher, K. D. [1963]. *The Art of Simulation.* Princeton: Van Nostrand.

Trebeck, D. B. [1971]. "Spatial Diversification by Beef Producers in the Clarence Region." *Rev. Marketing Agr. Econ.* 39(3):15-25.

Tse, E. [1974]. "Adaptive Dual Control Methods." *Annals of Econ. and Social Measurement* 3:65-83.

Tse, E., and M. Athans [1970]. "Optimal Minimal-Order Observer-Estimators for Discrete Linear Time-Varying System." *IEEE Transactions on Automatic Control* AC-15:416-426.

——— [1972]. "Adaptive Stochastic Control for a Class of Linear Systems." *IEEE Transactions on Automatic Control* AC-17:38-52.

Tse, E., Y. Bar-Shalom, and L. Meier, III [1973]. "Wide-Sense Adaptive Dual Control for Nonlinear Stochastic Systems." *IEEE Transactions on Automatic Control* AC-18:109-117.

Tyner, F. H., Jr. [1967]. *A Simulation Analysis of the Economic Structure of U.S. Agriculture.* Unpublished Ph.D. dissertation, Oklahoma State University.

Tyner, F. H., and L. G. Tweeten [1968]. "Simulation as a Method of Appraising Farm Programs." *Am. J. Agr. Econ.* 50:66-81.

Van Horn, R. L. [1971]. "Validation of Simulation Results." *Management Science* 17: 247-258.

Van Kampen, J. H. [1971]. "Farm Machinery Selection and Weather Uncertainty." In *Systems Analysis in Agricultural Management*, J. B. Dent and J. R. Anderson, eds. Sydney: Wiley. Pp. 295-329.

Vazsonyi, A. [1965]. "Automated Information Systems in Planning, Control and Command." *Management Science* 11:B2-B41.

Vernon, J. M., N. W. Rives, Jr., and T. H. Naylor [1969]. "An Econometric Model of the Tobacco Industry." *Rev. Econ. and Stat.* 51:149-158.

Vichnevetsky, R. [1969]. *Simulation in Research and Development.* American Management Association Management Bulletin 125.

Vincent, W. H. [1970a]. "Simulation for Problem-Solving in the Poultry Industry." In

Simulation Uses in Agricultural Economics, D. L. Armstrong and R. E. Hepp, eds. Michigan State University, Agricultural Economics Report 157.

Vincent, W. H. [1970b]. *Simfarm 1: A Farm Business Simulator and Farm Management Game*. Michigan State University, Agricultural Economics Report 164.

Von Neumann, J., and O. Morgenstern [1944]. *Theory of Games and Economic Behavior*. Princeton: Princeton University Press.

Wagner, H. M. [1958]. "Advances in Game Theory: A Review Article." *Am. Econ. Rev.* 48:368-387.

Walker, O. L., and W. A. Halbrook [1965]. *Operational Gaming and Simulation as Research and Educational Tools in the Great Plains*. Oklahoma State University, Department of Agricultural Economics Paper 659. Mimeo.

Walker, O. L., and J. R. Martin [1966]. "Firm Growth Research Opportunities and Techniques." *J. Farm Econ.* 48:1522-1531.

Wallace, T. D., and V. G. Ashar [1972]. "Sequential Methods in Model Construction." *Rev. Econ. and Stat.* 54:172-178.

Watt, K. E. F., ed. [1966]. *Systems Analysis in Ecology*. New York: Academic Press.

Watts, H. W. [1969]. "Graduated Work Incentive: An Experiment in Negative Taxation." *Am. Econ. Rev.* 59:463-472.

Wehrly, J. S. [1969]. *Farm Organization and Investment Game*. Texas A & M University.

Weidenaar, D. J. [1972]. "A Classroom Experiment Demonstrating the Generation of a Market Demand Function and the Determination of Equilibrium Price." *J. Econ. Education* 3:94-100.

Weymar, F. H. [1968]. *The Dynamics of the World Cocoa Market*. Cambridge: M.I.T. Press.

Whan, R. B., and R. A. Richardson [1969]. "A Simulated Study of an Auction Market." *Australian J. Agr. Econ.* 13:91-100.

Wright, A. [1970]. *Systems Research and Grazing Systems: Management-Oriented Simulation*. University of New England (Armidale, New South Wales) Farm Management Bulletin 4.

Wright, A., and J. B. Dent [1969]. "The Application of the Simulation Techniques to the Study of Grazing Systems." *Australian J. Agr. Econ.* 13:144-153.

Ying, C. C. [1967]. "Learning by Doing—An Adaptive Approach to Multiperiod Decisions." *Operations Research* 15:797-812.

Zellner, A. [1971]. *An Introduction to Bayesian Inference in Econometrics*. New York: Wiley.

Zellner, A., and V. K. Chetty [1965]. "Prediction and Decision Problems in Regression Models from the Bayesian Point of View." *J. Am. Stat. Assoc.* 60:608-616.

Zellner, A., and Peck, S. C. [1973]. "Simulation Experiments with a Quarterly Macroeconometric Model of the U.S. Economy." In *Econometric Studies of Macro and Monetary Relations*, A. A. Powell and R. A. Williams, eds. Amsterdam: North-Holland. Pp. 149-168.

Zusman, P., and A. Amiad [1965]. "Simulation: A Tool for Farm Planning under Conditions of Weather Uncertainty." *J. Farm Econ.* 47:574-594.

Zymelman, M. [1965]. "A Stabilization Policy for the Cotton Textile Cycle." *Management Science* 11:572-580.

Part IV. Agricultural Economic
Information Systems

This survey includes the work of many people. It was originally organized and partly drafted by Harry C. Trelogan and Earl E. Houseman. The contributors included J. Richard Grant, John W. Kirkbride, Will Simmons, Christian A. Stokstad, Charlene Olsson, Mardy Myers, David E. Cummins, Gerald E. Schluter, Wayne V. Dexter, Donald D. Durost, Orville E. Krause, Joel Frisch, George A. Pavelis, Robert C. Otte, Henry W. Dill, Jr., Theodore R. Eichers, John B. Penson, Jr., Earle E. Gavett, John F. Gale, Earl F. Hodges, George C. Allen, Harry H. Harp, Hazen F. Gale, Paul E. Nelson, Lawrence A. Jones, Bernal L. Green, Thomas F. Hady, Ronald Bird, Max F. Jordan, Robert C. McElroy, Gaylord E. Worden, C. Kyle Randall, and Leroy C. Quance. Early drafts of the survey benefited from reviews by Nathan M. Koffsky, Karl A. Fox, James T. Bonnen and James P. Cavin.

M. L. U.

Developments in Agricultural Economic Data

M. L. Upchurch
Professor, Food and Resource Economics
University of Florida

The Setting for Agricultural Data

Data are the raw materials of economic analysis. They lend substance to description. Properly ordered, they reveal problems and solutions to problems. It would be hard to imagine the subject of agricultural economics without data. Indeed, agricultural economists pioneered the use of quantitative analysis in the social sciences. Despite the variety and quantity of data readily available to every agricultural economist, probably no economist ever had all the data he wanted, in exactly the form or at the time that he desired.

Much of the development of present systems of agricultural economic data occurred before World War II. Beginning with the Census of 1839, and especially after the creation of the United States Department of Agriculture (USDA) in 1862, steady improvements were made in the coverage, accuracy, and scope of agricultural data. Substantial improvements were made in the 1920s and 1930s with the creation of the Bureau of Agricultural Economics. Preoccupied with the deep-seated economic problems of that period, agricultural economists everywhere demanded better data.

Given this early development, post-World War II economists and decision makers turned their attention and their pens mostly to topics other than data as such. The early postwar literature has few references dealing specifically with problems of data, as Arnold and Barlowe [1954] point out. Yet substan-

Note: M. L. Upchurch formerly served as Administrator of the Economic Research Service of the United States Department of Agriculture, Washington, D.C.

tial improvements in the quality and coverage of some kinds of data have been made; these will be discussed later. Only recently have a few agricultural economists and statisticians raised serious questions about data.

Not long ago the agricultural statistician and the economist were frequently the same person. With increased specialization in statistical sampling, data collection, processing, and analysis, the institutional and intellectual separation of data collection and economic analysis has widened, especially since the early 1950s. This has reduced the economist's and the statistician's sense of interdependence for the design of data systems.

Specialization in farming, the increasing role of farm-related business in agriculture, and the changing role of government have altered demands for economic data. Also, integration of farming with off-farm firms providing a higher proportion of factors of production and marketing services has accentuated the difficulties of statistical estimation. The development of these interrelated trends, evident before World War II, accelerated in the postwar period and seems likely to continue.

In modern agriculture demands for data that measure economic and social phenomena associated with farming and rural living have proliferated. Most regularly reported statistics are provided by public services, including federal and state censuses, current agricultural statistical services, and market news services. Research analysts frequently acquire additional data through special surveys, often obtained under contract, for profile or cross-sectional analysis. Marketing economists depend heavily upon private survey firms for data to facilitate distribution, advertising, and sales decisions.

For decades statistical reports have provided some data on all commodities of economic significance. Demands for new or additional data pertaining to farm supplies and prices in crop and livestock estimating are usually for more detail about individual commodities involving every conceivable dimension— time, space, and, most frequently, quality.

The specialization of farm functions, accompanied by the shift of more and more functions to off-farm businesses, has engendered demands for data on factors of production. Data on fertilizer, pesticides, and custom services have consequently assumed much greater importance, especially to agribusiness. Modern technology throughout agriculture also creates demands for greater accuracy and timeliness of data. Farms and associated service businesses now require large amounts of capital and depend heavily on borrowed funds. These conditions call for more stringent controls that begin with data for planning and operating decisions.

Statistical technology has, in general, developed methods to meet these demands, but they are costly. For example, with the greater specialization of farms the design and acquisition of representative samples, plus the strict requirements for obtaining data according to specifications, make data acquisition much more expensive and difficult. The additional resources needed often are not available. To conserve funds smaller samples are used, but this makes it more difficult to control measurement errors and raises costs for training personnel and quality control.

Objective methods are replacing subjective approaches to agricultural crop and livestock estimating. These too are expensive. Until well after World War II almost total reliance for crop estimating was placed upon the mail questionnaire for collecting data from farmers. Its great virtue was its low cost. The method was feasible because from early times the United States had literate farmers who were willing to give information to their government and had a dependable, inexpensive mail service. The system was founded on the assumption that a large response from farmers all over the country would adequately reflect year-to-year change. Changes indicated by crop reporters were tied to census and marketing data to derive estimates of totals.

Statisticians thoroughly familiar with the agriculture of their states could be relied upon to avoid gross errors and make proper allowance for unusual occurrences. Cumulative errors in nonprobability sampling estimates, projected one year after another, could be trued up every five years when an agricultural census gave a full count. Regression and other techniques were adapted for the removal of bias. The resulting agricultural estimates became the envy of the world.

This approach seemed adequate until about the beginning of World War II when changes in farm practices and structures began to accelerate. More precise and more reliable estimates were needed. Probability samples were required for estimating counts of such units as farms, acres, trees, and head of livestock. Objective measurements that fit into mathematical models were required for quantitative indications of yields previously reported in qualitative terms. These features have been introduced into crop and livestock estimates.

Specifically planned surveys based on probability samples call for greater discipline from the statistician and his respondents. Since virtually all agricultural estimates are derived from information voluntarily given, cooperation is essential. Development and maintenance of sampling frames, personal contacts to ensure response from individuals drawn in a sample, and field measurements made by trained enumerators are major elements in increasing costs because they are tasks for professional statisticians.

Farm and rural social statistics have been derived in part as products of such regular economic surveys as the agricultural census. These surveys are being devoted increasingly to the purposes of commercial agriculture. Other rural social data have been derived from the population census and from episodic surveys. Demands for social or demographic data, however, have risen sharply in the past decade and are becoming more insistent.

The electronic computer facilitates mass data handling, statistical computations, and report preparation and dissemination. Advanced statistical techniques enhance the quality of output. Availability of the standard error computed from the sample data to indicate the degree of reliability of a probability sample is an excellent case in point. The adaptation of computer services to keep farm records and accounts illustrates the degree to which automatic data processing can assist agricultural management.

The preoccupation of economists with model building since World War II has led to some confusion regarding the relative importance of models and data. The eagerness of economists to employ models has sometimes led to questionable applications of data, and conclusions drawn from tenuous data are also tenuous, regardless of the sophistication of the model.

There is no good substitute for care in planning the acquisition of the specific data needed for an anticipated decision. The efficiency of collection can be increased by combining data needs into fewer surveys, but this is limited by the frequency and length of surveys that can be made without encountering respondent fatigue. Another limitation is the degree to which social survey questions can be integrated with established economic surveys without compromising the activity. Most economic data from individuals are now given voluntarily, through great effort is often necessary to obtain cooperation. Social data often are given very reluctantly. If respondents balk on social data questions, the economic survey suffers.

Increasing costs for acquisition of data, increasing needs for accuracy of results, and strong competition for the funding required for statistical programs present a continuing challenge to those responsible for providing agricultural economic statistics.

The World War II period brought a new demand for agricultural statistics. Special surveys by the USDA obtained the information needed to plan agricultural production and to deal with food, machinery, and manpower requirements. This work was carried out by the Bureau of Agricultural Economics (BAE), which had the responsibility for collecting basic agricultural data and for carrying out statistical analyses and economic research.

Cooperative federal-state arrangements for collection of crop and livestock data, which had been initiated in some states after World War I, were given new impetus with the passage of the Agricultural Marketing Act of 1946. A variety of agricultural data projects were initiated with matched federal-state funds under provisions of the act. The intent was to initiate marketing data services, not to support them indefinitely. An example of important statistical work that was started under such arrangements and later continued under regular appropriations was the *Pig Crop Report* for the Corn Belt states (USDA, SRS [quarterly]).

Today, cooperative federal-state agreements cover the collection of agricultural statistics in forty-seven states—with forty-one state departments of agriculture and six state agricultural colleges, universities, or experiment stations. Additional cooperative agreements cover dairy manufacturing statistics in thirty states. Market news services are also administered under federal-state sponsorship with cooperative agreements in effect in forty-three states. This joint endeavor avoids duplication of efforts, reduces reporting burdens on farmers, and provides both federal and state governments with better data covering a broader range of subjects than either could provide independently. For the fiscal year 1974, obligations for the principal agricultural statistics programs of the USDA total approximately $27.5 million. Cooperating states contribute an additional $4 million for state programs.

Demands for more accurate, more timely, and more detailed agricultural data have grown sharply over the past three decades. These three dimensions compete with each other for the resources used to produce data and, unfortunately, the support for them has been unbalanced. Occasionally there has been strong support for public funds to obtain additional data on specific items or commodities, but much less general support for the research and program modifications needed to improve accuracy or even to maintain acceptable levels of accuracy. A significant exception grew out of the experience in forecasting cotton production in 1951, described later in this chapter, which attracted the attention of Congress and the public to shortcomings in agricultural estimating techniques. This resulted in an appropriation for research on methods and led to the development of a long-range plan for shifting to probability sampling in farm surveys and to objective techniques for measurement of crop yields.

Needed improvements in agricultural data programs have had to compete for public funds with other demands on the public purse, including needed statistical improvements in other sectors. A common complaint over the years has been that more concern has been devoted to improving data about hogs than about rural people and their general welfare. There is a recognized need for more and better data about rural people, but funds for these purposes are limited. Competition for the statistical dollar has been especially keen in recent years, as the Office of Management and Budget (OMB) has exercised considerable restraint on government expenditures generally and budgets for statistical purposes in particular. However, industry groups and trade associations with specific commodity interests, often have been effective in gaining support for their data needs.

The American farmer provided the original demand for a system of current agricultural statistics as he looked to his government to provide unbiased information about crop and livestock supplies, marketing conditions, and prices. Even today, the system remains heavily oriented toward farmers' needs. Farmers are the primary respondents for much of the data provided voluntarily. They, as well as the organizations representing them, must feel that they receive something of value in return for their cooperation. It must be recognized, however, that people in agribusiness and in government use statistical data at least as much as farmers do. Altogether, it is beyond the means of any statistical system to satisfy completely the total data needs expressed by users (Simpson [1967]).

Over time, data systems for crop and livestock estimates and for market news have become largely separate from data systems relevant to economic organization and efficiency in agriculture. It has been easier to meet the needs of users of commodity statistics than to keep pace with the changing requirements for economic analyses resulting from major changes in the structure of the agricultural economy. These difficulties were succinctly summarized in a report by the American Agricultural Economic Association (AAEA) Committee on Economic Statistics (AAEA [1972]). The problem is essentially one of using outdated concepts that no longer match a greatly transformed industry.

The Census of Agriculture

For more than a century the Census of Agriculture has been a basic source of economic data about agriculture and farm people. The Census, taken every five years, has been the only nation-wide source of county data. Although some states have a local census and tax roll data, the Census has long been the authoritative source of information about crops, livestock, farms, and farm people. Most other sources of data are based on samples of varying types that provide reliable estimates only on a state, regional, or national basis. The Census itself has changed over the years in content, coverage, techniques of enumeration, and methods of summarization and publication. It is not the purpose here to dwell on these changes in detail, but a few highlights are worthy of note.

From time to time the Census definition of a farm has been changed. This has prompted questions about the comparability of data from one census period to the next. The literature of agricultural economics is sprinkled with articles by authors struggling with the reconciliation of data over time. The questions become critical when one realizes that the number of farms is used in many ways for the allocation of federal funds among states and for estimating farm income, a vital item in policy considerations.

Some agricultural economists argue that the Census defines as farms large numbers of rural places that are not farms at all but rural residences with a bit of farming incidental to other occupations or sources of income. They contend that the number of farms and farm people is inflated for political or other reasons. On the other hand, some economists support the definition of a farm as any rural residence that is the site of agricultural enterprise, no matter how small the output. They reason that although many rural residences account for little in the way of agricultural production they contribute to the total number of people living on farms.

Arguments over the definition of a farm have become much sharper in recent years, owing in part to the changing structure of the farming sector, in part to the increasing costs of census enumeration, and in part to the changing character of the rural population. Because of increasing specialization in farming and the movement of many functions off the farm, modern farms increasingly fail to fit the traditional definitions. This is especially true in the highly specialized producing areas of California and Florida and in sectors like broiler production, beef feeding, and nursery and ornamental crops.

Traditionally, the Census of Agriculture was a full enumeration of all places or establishments that met the accepted definition. In 1945 the Census began to use sampling to obtain certain items of data. The chief motive seemed to be to reduce the cost of enumeration. But sampling raised questions of reliability of local data, and some sampled items could be reported only for large areas (to avoid disclosing information about individual farms or firms). Nevertheless, sampling continues to be used for selected items and for special surveys.

Other changes to reduce the cost of enumeration have been tried. In the 1964 Census respondents were mailed a questionnaire and were asked to fill it out before the enumerator arrived. This saved some time for the enumerator, but it introduced the possibility of greater respondent bias and increased the editing task. In 1969 and in 1974 the Census relied almost completely on mail response, using an abridged questionnaire for smaller farms. This reliance on mail response has in fact made the 1969 and 1974 censuses a sample—a sample without full knowledge of the population of farms it is supposed to represent.

Since the 1920s the Census of Agriculture has been a special source of data about farm people. This information supplemented and complemented demographic data obtained in the decennial Census of Population. While the Census of Agriculture still serves this purpose to some extent, its usefulness has been seriously eroded. Farm people are not the unique group they once were in the United States. Instead it is found that some farmers do not live on farms, some people who live on farms are not farmers, and fewer and fewer rural families depend on farming for a livelihood. Economic and welfare policies and programs focus less on farm people as such and more on rural people as a group. Thus the sociological data from the Census of Agriculture fails to provide the information needed for many public and private decisions.

It has long been argued that the Census of Agriculture should obtain additional kinds of data. Farm machinery makers want more detail about the kind, age, and number of machines on farms; feed dealers want more information on livestock and feed supplies; government personnel want to know more about the broad characteristics of farms, the resources used, and dozens of other items. Obviously the Census cannot supply everything for everybody. The scope of the Census is limited by the amount of funds available for enumeration, summarizing, and publication and by the tolerance of respondents. Furthermore, the issue of privacy is another factor conditioning the kind and amount of information that can be gathered.

In recent years some agricultural economists have questioned the efficacy of the Census for supplying data needed by those concerned with all segments of the agricultural industry and by those interested in the welfare of rural people. For instance, the Census has been chiefly a census of "farms," not a census of "agriculture," and it has not been coordinated with other economic censuses. Thus, no consistent body of data is available for the agricultural industry. The information about farm people traditionally included in the Census is also far from adequate to serve the needs of those concerned with rural welfare and rural development. The increasing dissatisfaction among agricultural economists with the Census portends substantial change for the future.

Survey Methods

Developments in Theory

Although much mathematical theory of probability had been developed before 1900, it attracted very little interest outside the academic world before World War I. The application of probability theory required randomization and replication. Hence, experimental researchers and survey data collectors were confronted with fundamentally new techniques for acquiring and analyzing data. This resulted in inconvenience and in some cases caused additional work and cost. Resistance was encountered, especially from established investigators who had confidence in their ability to judge the representativeness of experiments or samples. Was the return from putting probability theory into practice worth the effort or cost? Many issues about the virtues of probability sampling and statistical inference were debated during the 1930s and 1940s.

A paper published by Neyman [1934] on random versus nonrandom methods encouraged general acceptance of probability sampling for surveys. Many other papers on the subject appeared before 1950. By then the principles of sample design, founded in probability theory, had begun to appear in books on sample surveys. One of the first books on sample survey methods contained a good discussion of general principles and criteria (Hansen, Hurwitz, and Madow [1953]).

By 1950 workers in all disciplines using sample surveys were beginning to recognize that errors associated with causes other than sampling were often more important than sampling error. Hence, an increasing amount of research was directed toward measurement of nonsampling error and finding the means of reducing or controlling it.

The new questions which began to be asked of data in the 1930s pointed up the need for new approaches to survey sampling and estimation. An adequate means of evaluating the accuracy of one-time surveys using nonprobability methods did not exist. Also, new statistical series based on nonprobability methods could not be introduced with adequate confidence in their accuracy. The established data series based on nonprobability methods also were questioned because of the acceleration of changes in the agricultural economy. "Nonprobability methods" as used here refers mainly to the nationwide system of crop reporters who responded voluntarily to mail questionnaires.

By 1940 some researchers on survey methods felt the potential for improving nonprobability methods was too limited to be worth pursuing. They had become convinced that in the long run probability sampling should replace nonrandom methods. The prospect of greater accuracy and the advantage of having a statistical practice supported by relevant theory argued for their view.

At the same time, however, many persons expressed strong preferences for trying to find convenient and low-cost ways to improve the farm crop reporter system, the system that had been used for many years and that had served informational needs very well. Kramer and Shaffer [1954] studied the question of bias in the mail survey and concluded that mail surveys should remain as a major source of farm data.

Unfortunately, cost comparisons of various survey methods often left much to be desired. Most were simple tabulations of the cost per questionnaire or the total cost of doing a survey of a given size without regard for the scope and accuracy of the information. One principle of probability sampling was to design samples so as to minimize the sampling error per dollar of cost, but comparison of probability and nonprobability sampling under that criterion was inadequate. The issue was not easily resolved because major changes in the method of sampling required larger appropriations.

Research projects for sample surveys in agriculture, with emphasis on the development and application of sampling theory, were established by 1940. One part of this research program dealt with methods of forecasting and estimating crop yields and another with sampling methods for farm surveys generally.

Changes in Sampling Methods

Area sampling. Complete up-to-date lists of all farms have never been available. Lists of producers of specific crops like peanuts or tobacco are sometimes available from public records; these often are useful for special surveys, but they do not serve for more general surveys of the farming sector. Prospects for obtaining reasonably complete lists, especially of large farms, have gradually improved. In the absence of a complete list frame, area sampling has been the leading approach to probability sampling. In recent years the use of multiple frame sampling, which makes joint use of area and list frames, has been increasing.

Early experience with area sampling (Jessen [1942]) led to a project for developing a master sample of agriculture (King and Jessen [1945]). The most significant output of the project was an area sampling frame that provided a convenient basis for selecting area samples; the first major use of the master sample was in the 1945 Census of Agriculture. Farmers in the sample areas were asked supplemental questions not on the regular census questionnaire.

After 1945 the area sampling frame was also used for numerous small, one-time farm surveys for agricultural economics research. Two factors favored rapid adoption of area sampling in surveys of this type: (1) the researchers generally were interested in sampling that would assure reliable results; (2) flexibility in the use of research funds permitted researchers to choose their methods of data collection. Although the cost of data was important, it was not a critical factor that limited the methods of sampling.

Agricultural economists became interested in establishing a current periodic survey of agriculture that would fill a variety of data needs outside the scope of current crop and livestock estimates. The first significant effort was the "Quarterly Survey of Agriculture in 1945," which made use of two-stage probability area sampling. After four or five quarters it failed because the sample was too small and the funds were insufficient to expand and sustain the survey. However, strong interest in an annual survey of agriculture for economic data has persisted. The needs have been only partially met by supplementary sample surveys conducted as part of the quinquennial Census of Agriculture or in conjunction with it.

For established statistical series the situation was entirely different. There was a commitment to continue the existing series, thus preventing the allocation of funds for use in conjunction with the more expensive probability methods. The additional funds that were made available in this way were not sufficient to accomplish major changes in methods. Furthermore, many agricultural statisticians favored continuing and improving the convenient inexpensive methods of collecting data by mail from voluntary reporters.

A congressional investigation into the reasons for a large error in a 1951 forecast of cotton production probably was the event of most significance in helping to unify forces and to gain support for improving current agricultural statistics. The investigation led to a small appropriation in 1953 for research and development, and thereafter much progress was made. In 1957 a four-part plan for long-range improvements was presented to Congress by Newell (U.S. Congress [1957]). The highest priority was given to the first part of the plan, which was devoted to the development of better survey methods to improve accuracy, to provide a technically better foundation for present and future statistics, and to develop a more flexible system for keeping pace with the rapidly changing structure of agriculture. The second part of the plan dealt with the strengthening of price statistics. The third part focused on measures to reduce the time between data collection and the release of reports and to make possible more frequent reports during critical periods. The fourth part covered the needs for additional data and services.

Probability area sampling for crop and livestock estimates was introduced on a pilot or research basis in 1954. By 1967 the initial goal of two fully operational nationwide area surveys, one in June and one in December, had been attained. These applications of area sampling were summarized by Houseman and Trelogan [1967]. Fortunately, this period of growth in probability sampling coincided with rapid technological development in automatic data processing. Computers provided statisticians with a tool that facilitated sophisticated sample designs and made possible timely summarization and analysis of survey data.

Multiple frame sampling. With increased specialization in agriculture, and with the increase in the size of some producing units, the statistical efficiency of area sampling for many purposes has been decreasing. Since updated lists of farms with adequate control information on size and type are not available, the area frame continues to be the only complete sampling frame available. However, multiple frame sampling offers many of the advantages of both area and list sampling. The use of multiple frame sampling has been increasing since about 1965. Beginning in about 1970 a major effort has been made to utilize multiple frame sampling for livestock surveys. This was a direct result of widespread dissatisfaction among livestock producers over a 1.9 percent revision in cattle numbers following the 1964 Census of Agriculture. The need for sampling errors of 1 percent or less was apparent and the multiple frame sample was found to be the most economical approach. The basic concepts of multiple frame sampling are quite simple, but the operating problems are difficult to master.

Methods of Crop Forecasting

The three primary sources of information for making forecasts are (1) farmers' appraisals of crop conditions, (2) measurements of environmental factors, and (3) biological or plant measurements. To forecast crop yields a forecasting model is necessary. It must be derived from past data and studies of the relationships between yields and the factors correlated with yields. The updating of the parameters in the models presents a problem because of the increasing tempo of change in cultural practices and the introduction of new crop varieties and new chemicals. Farmers' appraisals have been used since 1912 to forecast yields. The techniques are described in the "Scope and Methods" bulletin of the Statistical Reporting Service (USDA, SRS [1964, 1975]). Although this source of information is still utilized, there is increasing reliance on biological or plant measurements, particularly for certain commodities.

Much of the research on crop forecasting before 1945 focused on weather-yield relationships. This did not result in the most useful forecasting models because the spatial and temporal representation of environmental data was inadequate and because measurements over a period of years for some environmental characteristics were unavailable. Furthermore, it became increasingly clear that the relationship of yield to environment was extremely complex, involving nonlinear relationships and many interactions. This type of research was abandoned during World War II, but there has been renewed interest in it in recent years because much more complete measurements of crop environments can be obtained through the use of remote sensing technology.

Biological or plant measurements have played an increasingly important role in forecasting yield and production of a growing list of crops. In these "objective yield surveys" trained enumerators regularly visit selected fields and orchards. These are chosen on a probability basis. Enumerators make actual counts and measurements of plants and fruiting characteristics during the growing season. Observations are used to forecast yields assuming normal weather for the remainder of the growing season and to estimate production following harvest.

Current Commodity Statistics

Crop and Livestock Statistics Reports

The changes in the structure of agriculture during the past three decades would seem to call for a reexamination of the data on products, prices, supplies, and labor to ensure that the data are compatible and consistent with the concepts, models, and analytical tools utilized in agriculture today (Trelogan [1968a, 1968b]). Data users from the agricultural industry do not appear to have involved themselves in such an evaluation, however, and changes in statistical reports derive largely from in-depth analyses prepared by data suppliers.

The great demand for data on commodity inventories and supplies continues, and in specialized areas there is pressure for additional detail and greater frequency. For example, in the area of livestock production the reports have been expanded to provide quarterly data for hogs and pigs and quarterly or even monthly surveys of cattle on feed. Meanwhile, there is surprisingly little call for new kinds of data except from a few professional agricultural economists or a few specialized interest groups who want data on such commodities as popcorn, mink, cut flowers, mushrooms, and white corn. Data relating to new commodities generally get into the reporting system only when specialized interest groups help obtain additional congressional appropriations for that purpose.

Although in content the crop and livestock statistics reports closely resemble those of three decades ago, the quality has been much improved. Survey methodology and procedures have moved steadily in the direction of greater accuracy. Analytical procedures have been redirected to utilize the gains offered by such methodology. For major crop and livestock items production estimates are first established at the national level (taking advantage of the fact that the sampling errors in the national figures are much lower than those in the figures for individual states) and then are modified as necessary to establish state estimates that conform to the national total and that are consistent with a thorough evaluation of state survey data.

Current survey methodology also provides a means for evaluating the original survey results. Quality check surveys bring into focus the adequacy of each major survey, thus providing a more sophisticated means of evaluating survey results as well as giving emphasis to procedures that need to be strengthened.

Several changes applicable to broad groupings of commodities have been made in the post-World War II period. One measure has been to limit the frequency of crop forecasts or estimates for states which account for not more than 1 percent of the national total. This concept is applied to forecasts of production for all field crops, fruits, and nuts. The goal is to provide current data only for those states that collectively account for approximately 95 percent of the national total. The number of states included in the limited group varies by commodity. Since World War II, for example, the August 1 forecast of corn production for twenty-one states is now carried forward until the end of the season in January. Hay statistics have been limited to three categories— alfalfa and alfalfa mixtures, all other hay, and total hay. The initial forecast of production for most spring planted crops is made on August 1. The April winter wheat production forecast has been discontinued. Cotton statistics are no longer published separately and instead are included in the *Monthly Crop Production Report*. Rice statistics have been refined to show acreage, yield, production, and stocks by length of grain.

Vegetable statistics have undergone major change and production forecasts have been eliminated. The statistics for most vegetables are broken down into four seasonal groups, each of which includes the intended acreage to be planted, the acreage planted, and end-of-season production.

The limited estimate concept also has been applied to livestock statistics. Inventory numbers are now shown for all states only for hogs on December 1 and for cattle and sheep on January 1. July 1 inventory data were introduced for cattle. Inventory estimates at other times provide data only for those states meeting the limited estimate criterion as outlined above. Other changes in livestock statistics include the elimination of data on the length of time cattle are on feed and the addition of inventory data by weight groups. The classification by age and sex in the cattle inventory has been discontinued, but weight groupings by sex are shown. Market hog inventories are shown by weight groups rather than by age.

The limited estimate concept is also utilized for data on monthly milk and egg production, layer numbers, milk cows, turkey breeder hens and turkeys raised. Estimates for milk and egg production are now provided only quarterly for all states.

Statistical series for farm labor are being shifted from a monthly to a quarterly basis, with survey data for both farm labor numbers and wage rates relating to the twelfth day of the quarterly month. Wage rate statistics will provide greater detail with data on piece rate wages as well as wages by kind of work performed.

In 1973 a new series of weekly statistics on the export sales of selected agricultural commodities was initiated. The series identifies the export sales volume of wheat and flour, feedgrains, rice, soybeans, and cotton and their products outstanding at the close of each week to selected geographic areas of the world.

Further improvements in the coverage and frequency of crop and livestock estimates may be expected as changes in the agricultural industry occur which require changes in data, as the needs for data in industry and government change, and as the resources and technology for data collection and reporting suggest further improvement.

Commodity Supply and Utilization Data

Most annual supply and utilization series for commodities were initiated before World War II. Subsequently, agricultural economists have modified or extrapolated from these basic series to reflect the changing data needs of government, industry, and producers. Some of these refinements are discussed below.

Dairy data. While sales of whole milk and cream declined in recent years, sales of low-fat and skim milk rose substantially. Since milk equivalent sales data did not reflect these changes, Mathis [1968] developed a series showing product weight of total fluid sales and sales of individual fluid items (whole milk, cream, and low-fat milk). Data on commercial disappearance (sales) of all milk, butter, American cheese, other cheese, nonfat dry milk, canned milk, and frozen desserts were developed to represent better the commercial market for milk and dairy products.

As dairy imports expanded sharply in the late 1960s, there was considerable pressure to extend import quotas to additional dairy products. To meet the needs of the dairy industry and the government agencies making policy decisions in this area, Mathis developed a monthly report summarizing imports of individual dairy products and of all dairy products on a milk equivalent basis. These data are used by the dairy industry, the USDA, the Tariff Commission, and other government agencies and are now published regularly in *Dairy Situation*, import data are also published in *Dairy Market News Report*.

When cheese consumption began to expand rapidly in recent years, consumption data for separate cheese varieties and for natural and processed cheese were needed. To fill this void, data were developed to show per-capita consumption of many individual cheese varieties, natural and processed cheese, and processed cheese foods and spreads (R. R. Miller [1972]).

Whey, a by-product of cheese making, pollutes water supplies when it is dumped in streams or sewer systems. With the current emphasis on solving pollution problems, more uses are being found for whey. To meet the needs of the dairy industry and government agencies for whey statistics, data on the production and utilization of whey have been developed (Mathis [1970]).

Poultry data. When poultry inspection became mandatory in 1959 for all slaughtered poultry moving in interstate commerce, information became available which permitted development of quarterly estimates of supply and disappearance, data published in *Poultry and Egg Situation*. The supply and utilization data for broilers and turkeys were expanded in 1960. These series have been widely used in demand and price analyses as well as in short-term forecasting.

Livestock data. Supply and utilization data for edible offal have been compiled by the Economic Research Service (ERS) and its predecessor agencies since 1949 in response to industry interest. These data, published annually in *Livestock and Meat Situation*, supplement supply and utilization data for beef, veal, pork, and lamb and mutton, helping to determine both total and average consumption of high protein foods. Since offal production is not reported directly, estimates are based on research showing the average yield of edible offal per hundred pounds of dressed weight.

Foodgrain data. In the early 1960s Askew [1969] developed a historical series of privately held stocks of wheat, rice, and rye, outside government ownership or control and therefore available to the commercial market. In response to questions about returns and costs to millers, a series of relations between wheat and flour prices in Minneapolis and Kansas City was developed. This series shows changes in millers' basic costs and returns.

The USDA ceased publication of buckwheat data after a long-term decline in supply and demand. When the demand for buckwheat picked up again in the early 1970s, a series of data on buckwheat prices, supplies, and demand again became a part of *Wheat Situation* (Gomme [1972]).

When government price supports in the form of supplemental payments to farmers were in effect, new data were needed on the average prices received by farmers, the prices to program participants including the value of the marketing certificates, and the blend prices, showing the average return per bushel of wheat sold with government payments added to the value of sales (Askew [1969]). Because of a change in the method of making certificate payments to program participants, the ERS in 1971 developed a program participant price series now published in *Wheat Situation*.

A lower price support in 1964 made wheat competitive with feedgrains. To illustrate the relative competitive position of wheat and feedgrains in different regions, the ERS developed a wheat and feedgrain price series, showing the relative price levels for grain regionally, including an adjustment for feeding value (Jennings [1958]).

Methodology for estimating domestic use directly by wheat class rather than as a residual was developed (Bitting and Rogers [1963]), resulting in a comprehensive series on the utilization of wheat for food. Export inspection by class made possible an even more complete breakdown of supply and distribution for each class of wheat; this was first published in the early 1960s.

Tobacco data. A series on annual retail expenditures on tobacco products was developed in the mid-1950s from Department of Commerce data on consumer expenditures and published semiannually in *Tobacco Situation*. It provided a breakdown for cigarettes, cigars, and other products, thus becoming a reference point for industry comparisons and margins analysis.

A series of data on tobacco used in cigarettes was begun in about 1950, published annually in *Tobacco Situation*. A similar series on a marketing year basis is published in *Annual Report on Tobacco Statistics* by the Agricultural Marketing Service (AMS). These series also include tobacco used per cigarette and show critical shifts in tobacco utilization since the early 1950s.

An output series for the production of smoking tobacco, chewing tobacco, and snuff has been issued quarterly by AMS, since 1966, following the repeal of the federal excise tax on those products. Quarterly data are summarized in *Tobacco Situation* and in industry statistical compilations.

Statistics on unmanufactured tobacco exports under government-financed or assisted programs have been compiled from program records and published in *Tobacco Situation* for calendar and fiscal years since the inception of Public Law 480 in the mid-1950s. This series summarizes export assistance programs and allows comparisons with other commodities.

United States cigarette production by length of cigarette and type (filter or nonfilter tip) was first compiled in the mid-1950s from annual surveys of leading manufacturers, with industry totals published annually in *Tobacco Situation*. This series provides a reference both on changing industry structure and on shifts in tobacco requirements.

Tobacco leaf represented in tobacco sheet stocks has been reported quarterly since 1958 by the AMS and published in *Tobacco Stocks Report*. This series offers data for each kind of tobacco and a measure of changes in the requirements for manufacturing cigars and cigarettes. Such data provided a key factor variable in explaining the sharp drop in flue-cured tobacco usage in the mid-1960s, as discussed in R. H. Miller's [1968] analysis for the 1950-66 crop years.

Oilseed data. Data series for several oilseed crops and products were developed under Kromer's leadership in the late 1950s and 1960s for price support programs and Commodity Credit Corporation activities. These provided detailed information on stocks and supplies and permitted a breakdown between government controlled and free stocks. Supply and utilization data were developed for soybeans, soybean meal, soybean oil, and soybean oil products (Kromer [1970]). These data measured the postwar growth of the industry and were valuable for making short-term and long-term forecasts of soybean supply and disposition.

Feedgrain data. Originally developed in the late 1930s, the grain-consuming animal unit (GCAU) series has been updated several times with the revision by Allen and Devers [1973] reflecting more modern feeding rates of farm animals. A GCAU is simply one milk cow equivalent in terms of feed consumption based on average feeding rates during 1959-61; each class of livestock and poultry is converted into GCAU's by using the ratio of its feed consumption to the feed consumption of a milk cow. With good information on animal reproduction cycles and farmer response to change in livestock prices, animal numbers can be forecast accurately even before most feed crops are planted. As a result, the animal unit series provides the first solid basis for projecting short-run feed requirements. It is published regularly in *Feed Situation.*

Fiber data. James Donald developed several major data series related to fiber utilization and trade, including domestic fiber use (mill use adjusted for raw fiber equivalent of textile manufactures) in actual and cotton equivalent pounds. Because of sizable net imports these series presented a much more accurate picture of actual fiber use in the United States than was available earlier. They are published regularly in *Cotton Situation* and *Wool Situation.*

Price Statistics and Indexes

Price statistics of the USDA since World War II have been designed largely to satisfy the legal requirements of the Agricultural Adjustment Acts of 1948 and 1949. These required indexes of prices received and prices paid by farmers (Parity Index) on a 1910-14 base to be used in computing parity prices for farm products as the basis for a price support program.

Both indexes were revised in January 1950 (Stauber, Koffsky, and Randall [1950]). The prices paid index was revised to add 160 commodities for a total of 335 with a base weight period of 1935-39. Consumer expenditure studies in 1935-36 and again in 1941-42 provided the basis for individual commodity and group weights. Based on trial indexes using varying numbers of commodity items, those commodities which accounted for 0.5 percent or more of the group expenditure were to be represented in the group index. The increased number of commodities required under this criterion had been provided by an expansion in the collection of prices paid by farmers from about 200 commodities in 1935 to nearly 500 in 1949.

The index of prices received by farmers was revised in 1944 to add 5 commodities, bringing the total to 48, and to include 12 subgroup index numbers using marketings for 1935-39 as quantity weights. Only minor changes were made in 1950.

Although the need for periodic surveys to obtain information on changes in the pattern of farm expenditures was generally recognized, such a survey was not made until early 1956. Data from this survey were incorporated into a revision of the Parity Index in 1959 (Stauber [1956], Stauber, Hale, and Peterson [1959]). The revised indexes were of the same general form as those that emerged from the 1950 revision, with the weighting pattern representing the average of all farms. The same major and minor commodity groups and subgroups indexes were retained. The base weight period for prices paid was 1955, the year of record for the expenditure survey. The prices received base weight period was 1953-57, thus centering on the year of the prices paid base weights. The deficiencies in coverage for prices received were relatively minor; the price series included about 93 percent of receipts from sales of farm products. For prices paid about 8.5 percent of production expenditures were not represented because of lack of price information on machine hire and custom work, marketing expenses for crops and livestock, cash rent, irrigation, and insurance. For family living about 12 percent of the expenditures remained uncovered in the Parity Index with medical, dental, and hospital expenses accounting for 7.4 percent and personal insurance and recreation accounting for the remainder. The omission of medical and dental expenditures accounts for a large portion of the difference in trend since 1959 between the Family Living Index and the Consumer Price Index of the Bureau of Labor Statistics (Houck and Soliman [1971]). The details of the series of prices received and prices paid by farmers are described in volume 1 of Agriculture Handbook 365 (USDA [1957, 1970]).

The data for the prices received and the prices paid series are based on mail surveys using nonprobability samples, which has subjected this price series to criticism. Research undertaken to establish feasibility and cost factors in collecting data by personal enumeration from a probability sample indicated significant differences between average prices as reported on the mail inquiry and from the enumerated probability sample in an Ohio study (Stauber [1964]).

The price data series of the USDA were reviewed by the National Bureau of Economic Research in 1973 and recommendations were made to the Congress (U.S. Congress [1974]). In general the Bureau found the program to be well designed and well executed and recommended only minor changes.

Market News

The Federal-State Market News Service, administered by the AMS in cooperation with state agencies, collects and disseminates market information to aid producers and marketing agencies in their daily marketing and production decisions. The procedures for gathering daily data on prices, supplies, and market conditions have changed since World War II in response to changes in marketing practices. Market news reporting has become more difficult because markets have become more decentralized, with a decline in trading at

324   M. L. UPCHURCH

terminal markets and an increase in direct sales from producers or packers to wholesale buyers. Wholesale buying organizations have grown larger, and their numbers have decreased. Some of these changes are described in the June 1966 reports of the National Commission on Food Marketing [1966a, 1966g] and other sources.

Other marketing changes include increased foreign sales of grain; integration of the broiler industry, with the turkey industry following a similar pattern; formula pricing of poultry and eggs; increased sales from producing areas of fruits and vegetables packaged in consumer packs; and more shipments of products by truck than by rail. Also, changes in government price support programs released more cotton, wheat, and feedgrain for free market trading, thereby requiring greater market news coverage.

The AMS has attempted to respond to these changes by establishing reporting to provide greater coverage of producing areas, collecting price and supply information at livestock auction markets and on direct sales, providing information on the relationship of carcass prices to live cattle prices, reporting on export prices of grain, and reporting prices on ready-to-cook broilers— the first point of sale—rather than on live poultry. In the fruit and vegetable market news the AMS has reported prices on consumer packages and has also attempted to collect information on the volume of supplies moving by truck.

The relocation of livestock yards and packing and processing plants from urban to rural areas meant that market news reporters had to cover more locations. In many cases the frequency of reporting is now less than daily. Special weekly reports covering national or regional markets have been introduced to provide information on market trends. New reports have been added for ornamental crops and for prices of imported produce when such data are available.

Some of the market news problems have been intensified by changes in marketing practices. One persistent problem is the difficulty of obtaining sufficient prices to report an average price when buying is concentrated in a few hands, when only a small proportion of the commodity moves through the market under observation, and when sale of a large percentage of a crop such as cotton or grain is contracted before harvest. Increased exports and containerized shipments of grain, packaging of eggs in consumer cartons at producing points, and the increased movement of agricultural supplies by truck also present challenges in obtaining accurate data on prices and supplies. Gaps remain in the data available on prices and supplies of raw fruits and vegetables used for processing.

Farm Data

Farm Income and Expenditures

Procedures for estimating farm income have not undergone radical change since World War II. In addition to basic data on gross farm income, farm production expenses, and the residual net farm income, work in this area includes outlook and situation reports and near-term forecasting. State estimates of production expenses were developed during the early 1950s, and these led to a viable series on net farm income by states.

One of the major new sources of data on farm production expense data was the 1955 Farm Expenditure Survey (USDA, AMS, and Bureau of the Census [1958]). Although this was carried down to the state level, it provided many new benchmarks for the numerous accounts making up total farm production expenses. In the early 1960s the basis for estimating the income of the farm population was changed from national income to personal income. This allowed direct comparisons of the income of farm people with the income of nonfarm people on a per-capita disposable personal income basis.

Another major undertaking since World War II has been an attempt to develop methods for estimating income parity for farmers as distinct from price parity for commodities. This work was prompted in part by the provision in the Agricultural Adjustment Act of 1938 to provide farmers with parity of income, a provision that was never put into effect because no one knew quite how to do it. Some of the outstanding work in this area was initiated by Masucci [1962], whose article broke new ground. Further work was carried out under the direction of Kyle Randall and an important study was released in 1967 (U.S. Congress [1967a]).

Another area in which considerable progress has been made is the development and annual publication of estimates of United States farm numbers by sales classes of farms, including estimates of income and expenses, and later government payments by sales classes (Grove [1939]). Koffsky provided much of the overall leadership in the postwar work on farm income estimates.

The present national data system on farm output, input, and cost was essentially established before national income accounts were developed. A move is under way to shift the conceptual emphasis in agricultural income data toward the rationale of national income and product accounts. Exploratory work on alternative additional frameworks has been provided by Weeks [1970, 1971a] and by a special task force on farm income data appointed by the ERS administrator.

Calls have been made for major changes in farm income estimates because of the feeling that the data did not reflect the rapid postwar changes in the structure of agriculture. Some agricultural economists contend that farm income estimates do not reflect accurately the present income position. Efforts to restructure farm income data are concentrated in the ERS; little is being done in the land grant colleges.

One major deficiency in the farm income estimates is believed to be the understatement of farm production expenses and the failure to distinguish between current expenses and capital stock. Statisticians and agricultural economists have pointed repeatedly to the shortage of basic data on depreciation, repairs and operations, and hired farm labor. In addition, expense accounts do not include custom work and machine hire purchased by farmers. The 1971 Production Expenditure Survey of the Statistical Reporting Service (SRS) is being used to provide new benchmarks for farm production expenses. An annual survey of production expenses should now do much to make up deficiencies in the expense accounts and contribute to a better measure of net farm income.

Farm income and expense estimates are important to policy makers and to the farm community, providing as they do the only comprehensive measure of the combined effects of changing prices, production, sales, and production costs on farm operators.

Enterprise Budgets

One basic source of data for economic analysis from the dawn of the agricultural economics profession is in enterprise budgets. Renewed interest in enterprise budgets was stimulated by legislation that provided for price supports based on costs of production, first in the 1960s for cotton and more recently for other crops. A large number of crop and livestock enterprise budgets have been prepared by the ERS and its predecessors since World War II, generally for a single period, and have been published by state experiment stations.

Enterprise budgets for major crops grown in each of six production regions have been published under the overall title of *Selected U.S. Crop Budgets, Yields, Inputs and Variable Costs* (USDA, ERS [1973b]). The budgets reflect arithmetic averages for production areas or resource situations within production areas, using expected yields for 1970. Family labor was included with hired labor, but machinery depreciation was excluded. Preharvest and harvest costs were shown separately. Many of the data for these budgets were taken from the studies of production adjustments, but data from other sources were used to update coefficients and prices when available.

A budget generator has been developed by Walker to computerize budget preparations. The computer program consists of a routine including the title, footnote, identification number, and input-output coefficients of the budget. Subroutines include necessary internal computations for creating a budget. This program was designed with flexibility to allow users to apply additional subroutines. This computer program is now in use at several state universities.

Farm Costs and Returns Data Series

Annual time series data on farm organization, costs, and income for a number of farm types were initiated in the BAE before World War II under the direction of S. E. Johnson and W. D. Goodsell. These data were published in Statistical Bulletin 197, Agricultural Information Bulletins 158, 176, and 230, and in ERS reports 446, 478, and 480 (Goodsell [1956], Goodsell et al. [1956], USDA, ARS [1958], USDA, ARS [1960], USDA, ERS [1962-72], USDA, ERS [1970], Evans and Hughes [1971], and Weisgerber [1971]). These data provided useful illustrative material for judging the effects of policy changes on particular types of farms. The development of better procedures in recent years led to discontinuation of the series.

Agricultural Sectors of National Input-Output Models

Four national input-output models have been constructed since World War II. The Bureau of Labor Statistics (BLS) constructed the first for the 1947 economy and the Department of Commerce Office of Business Economics (OBE) published tables for 1958, 1963, and 1967.

Construction of the agricultural sector accounts in the 1947 BLS study was directed by Ritz [1955]. The basic data work was done under contract in the BAE by a group under the leadership of Fox and Norcross. The group defined agricultural sectors on a "product" basis rather than the more usual "establishment" basis, owing to the nature of the available data. Accounts for seventeen commodity sectors and one agricultural services sector were constructed. The use of a product definition for agriculture precluded the inclusion of the outputs of various activities often associated with farming, such as farm rentals and custom work for other farmers.

The second major contribution in the area was a study published in 1959 by Masucci [1959]. Based on detailed analysis of information from the 1954 Census of Agriculture and Manufactures and from the 1955 Survey of Farmers' Expenditures, this study presented estimates on the dollar volume of transactions between and among the agricultural and nonagricultural sectors. The BLS classification scheme of seventeen commodity sectors and a service sector, all classified on a product basis, was maintained. Although basically following the 1947 framework, Masucci treated by-products and waste products more explicitly.

The earlier classification scheme was further changed from a strict "product" classification to include secondary outputs of the agricultural sectors. Among these were gross rental value of farm operators' dwellings, gross rents paid to farm landlords, and custom work done for other farmers. The ERS also developed the estimates of agricultural sector accounts for the 1963 and 1967 tables published by the Office of Business Economics (U.S. Department of Commerce [1969, 1974]).

Modifications since the 1959 study of the input-output accounts for agriculture have been restricted to conceptual changes. Some of the data problems are unresolved. For example, input-output table construction requires estimates of total agricultural production gross of such internal transactions as home-grown feed and seed and intrastate livestock shipments, and this estimate is not regularly made. Farm income production expenditures accounts have historically omitted custom hire, because these inputs were treated as interfarmer transfers and miscellaneous business expenses; these inputs should be included in the accounts. To the extent that custom work done by nonfarmers and miscellaneous business expenses are significant, inputs to agriculture are understated because the official "gross national product originating in farming" did not include these inputs.

No surveys of farm production expenditures were made from 1955 to 1971. Information from the 1971 and later farm production expenditure surveys is being incorporated into the official farm income production expense accounts. This will correct in subsequent tables the sources of known distortions in the input structure. Commodity sector distributions of input categories must be estimated indirectly because most input data are calculated on an establishment basis. Data on trade and transportation margins for agricultural commodities are limited.

Agricultural economists have made extensive use of the national input-output tables as descriptive tools. Earl Heady and his colleagues conducted a series of studies classifying the national agricultural sectors into regional sectors while utilizing the 1947 BLS study as a resource for nonagricultural sector structures (G. A. Peterson and Heady [1955], Schnittker and Heady [1957], and Carter and Heady [1959]). Elrod and LaFerney [1970] used an updated version of the 1958 OBE table to estimate income and employment multipliers. Weeks [1970] utilized an aggregated version of the 1963 OBE table as a basis for discussing the size, structure, and pervasiveness of American agriculture. Schluter [1972] utilized the 1963 OBE table to trace out the effects of income generated in agriculture from final demand in terms of the components of the national income and product accounts. An example of the efforts made to expand the role of national input-output tables beyond that of a descriptive tool is Weeks's version of the 1963 OBE table, which has been maintained by the ERS as a policy impact analysis model (Weeks [1970]).

Farm Output, Input, and Productivity

During World War II farmers were encouraged to produce at full capacity to meet wartime demands. After World War II there was a general concern for what might happen to the farm and nonfarm economies in the shift from wartime to peacetime.

Analysis of past changes was needed as a basis for a rational response to the peacetime problems in agriculture. The only measures of total agricultural (crop and livestock) production were the production for sale and home consumption index series. Production of individual commodities and a total crop production index were published by the Crop Reporting Board. The production for sale and home consumption series measured production volumes moving into the marketing system or used for home consumption. These measures were more closely related to changes in farm income than to changes in farm resources used in a particular year.

Barton and Cooper [1945] developed and published a farm output and gross farm production index series in the mid-1940s. Both series measured production in the year produced, even though some of the output might be sold or consumed in succeeding years. Farm output measured the volume of farm production available for eventual human use, and the gross farm production series included farm produced power. Index numbers were constructed for each of the nine census geographic regions beginning in 1919 and for the United States beginning in 1910.

Indexes for net livestock and total crops were constructed as major subgroups in the development of the output index. Thus, there were two index series within the USDA measuring total crop production—the Crop Reporting Board with a reference period of 1923-32 = 100 and this new crop index with 1935-39 = 100. Both series tend to have the same annual movement.

In 1953 a statistical review committee headed by O. C. Stine suggested that only the farm output series be published annually to avoid confusion with the gross farm production series, with the gross farm production series made available for research purposes. Only one crop production series was to be published, the Crop Reporting Board index would be published in the current year and the Barton-Cooper series would be used for the historical series. Weights were revised to make the series comparable. In 1954 the two production series were reweighted using 1947-49 for the weights and reference period. The livestock indexes were changed from net to gross indexes.

Concern was also expressed on whether data by census regions were misleading chiefly because the Corn Belt was in two census regions (East North Central and West North Central). In 1959 the farm output and related series were shifted for the first time to a basis of ten farm production regions and calculated back to 1937 (Durost [1960]).

Cooper, Barton, and Brodell [1947], Jennings [1958], and others developed a series of input measures in the mid-1940s. These measures included farm workers, manhours, cropland used for crops, animal units of breeding livestock, power and machinery including and excluding horses and mules, and total inputs. These input series measured the inputs used to produce each year's production.

Partial and overall measures of input productivity were obtained by dividing the appropriate production index by the appropriate input series. These input and productivity series were published in the late 1940s (Barton and Cooper [1948], Cooper, Barton, and Brodell [1947]). Data for the power and machinery series and the total input series were not maintained after these publications appeared. Data on the animal units of breeding livestock and livestock production per breeding unit were also discontinued in 1966.

Loomis and Barton [1961] later redeveloped the total input series. This series, like the previous one, included all farm labor, real estate, and all other inputs committed to agricultural production. An overall productivity series was computed by dividing the index of farm output by the index of total inputs. They used two weighting periods, 1935-39 and 1947-49, for the period after 1950. The series was computed only by decades from 1870 to 1900 and annually beginning in 1910. This input series was further revised, and the annual data were published in *Changes in Farm Production and Efficiency* (USDA [annual]), beginning with the 1971 issue. Lambert developed the new series by building up from the ten farm production regions, using 1947-49 weights from 1939 to 1954 and 1957-59 weights from 1955 to date. His regional data start in 1939, as does the farm output series; he also developed overall productivity data for each of the farm regions.

Farm Population

The USDA began publication of annual estimates of the farm population in 1923, following the introduction of farm residence as a basis of classification in the 1920 Census of Population. Annual estimates were based on farmer responses to mail questionnaires. Historical estimates for the 1910-20 period were developed in the 1930s to provide data for parity income estimates required by legislation (Grove [1939]).

With the publication of these historical estimates a continuous series of data on farm population from 1910 has been used by the ERS and its predecessor agencies. Revisions required by changes in the definition of the farm population (Banks, Beale, and Bowles [1963]) have been published from time to time (Banks and Beale [1973]). These estimates relate to the rural population living on farms, regardless of occupation. Before 1960 the farm population was determined by the respondents' answers to the survey question, "Is this house on a farm (or ranch)?" In the 1960 and 1970 censuses the farm population consisted of all those who lived in rural territory on places of ten or more acres if as much as $50 worth of agricultural products were sold from the place in the reporting year and those living on places under ten acres with at least $250 worth of agricultural products sold. The farm population series was expanded in 1944 to include such characteristics as age, sex, and labor force status. Quarterly estimates were made for 1944-49 and annual estimates were made from 1950 to date.

The ERS farm population estimates are now based on the current population surveys of the Bureau of the Census, an annual ERS survey, the decennial population census, and related data. The annual ERS report covers the farm population and components of annual change (births, deaths, and migration) by geographic regions. The ERS and the Bureau of the Census cooperatively release estimates of the farm population by age, sex, color, labor force status, and related data. The sampling error for the farm population is relatively high—about 2 percent. No measure of sampling error is available for the estimates for geographical areas.

In addition to sampling problems the farm population estimates are also subject to conceptual difficulties. Many farm operators and workers do not live on farms, and many people living on farms are employed elsewhere. The "farm population" has become less meaningful than formerly as an economic indicator of the farming sector and as a guide to the welfare of rural people.

Production Resources and Costs

Finance

Agricultural economists have been involved for many years in securing data related to farm finance. Since World War II this work has focused mainly on the financial and equity position of farmers, financing the growth of farm firms, the changing financial structure of agriculture, and future financing needs.

The main source of data has been the ERS and its predecessor agencies; the farm debt series goes back to 1910. Concern in 1944 over postwar financial adjustments in agriculture led the ERS to develop an annual series on the balance sheet of United States farms showing assets and liabilities by major categories (Tostlebe et al. [1945]). Although largely based on existing data, estimating procedures for several additional debt and asset items were developed.

In large part the methodology for the annual balance sheet series continues as developed originally. The items most subject to error and incompleteness are noncommercial bank financial assets and debt owed to noninstitutional lenders. The underlying concepts of the series have been questioned from time to time, however, and Burroughs [1949], one of the original authors, and Irwin [1968] have discussed the concepts and the interpretation and use of the series.

The basic series on farm debt and other balance sheet items have been useful in analyzing economic growth and the changing capital structure of farming. It was found that more details were needed on flows of funds during the year and on debt and debt-asset-income relationships for different segments of the farm sector. Many agricultural economists attempted to meet these needs from surveys conducted by the Census. The 1960 Census sample survey was the first effort to obtain data both on real estate debt and on non-real estate debt, including debt to merchants, dealers, and other noninstitutional lenders. This survey also provided data on debts and assets by age of operator, income, and type and size of farm. Garlock and Allen [1964] were leaders in initiating the 1960 Census survey; Melichar (U.S. Federal Reserve System [1964]) supervised summarization of the data. The 1964 Census survey provided much the same data on debt.

The 1970 Census sample survey was broadened to include data on specific capital purchases financed by internal as opposed to external sources of funds. Data were also obtained on the off-farm and other income earned by farm operators and their families. A number of economists from the Farm Credit Administration, the Federal Reserve System, and the Bureau of the Census assisted ERS economists in designing the questionnaire and in developing and compiling the data from the 1970 survey. Many economists see a need for even more complete data to permit description and analysis of the system through which funds flow into and out of the farm sector (Penson, Lins, and Irwin [1971], Heady and Tweeten [1963], and Penson [1972]).

The rapid capitalization of agriculture during the past several decades has generated concern over the adequacy of capital. Pioneering work was done in this area by Tostlebe [1957]. More recent projections of future financing needs of the farm sector have been made in several studies by Heady and Tweeten [1963], Melichar and Doll [1969], and Melichar (U.S. Federal Reserve System [1964]).

Credit Institutions

Statistics of credit institutions and noninstitutional lenders have been used to reveal the characteristics of debt owed by farmers and the volume, adequacy, and cost of credit used by farmers. Data from credit institutions that have been used include information on loans outstanding, loans made, interest rates, loan maturities, delinquencies, and foreclosures, shown by type of lender, by area, and whether secured by farm real estate.

Many agricultural economists involved themselves in developing or improving statistics on institutional and noninstitutional creditors relating to data series or one-time studies. Much of this work was started before World War II in the former Agricultural Finance Branch of the ERS and its predecessors. Publication of the *Balance Sheet of Agriculture, 1945* was the beginning of a series of basic data on asset values and farm debt as a whole. Annual data have become an important measure of farmers' financial condition. Norman Wall and Fred Garlock guided the development of the annual *Agricultural Finance Outlook*, *Agricultural Finance Review*, and the statistical supplement to the *Review*. Data dealing specifically with farm mortgage debt have been distributed in two publications, *Farm Mortgage Debt* and *Farm Mortgage Lending*. Another publication, *Index of Deposits in Country Banks*, was developed as an important measure of the ability of rural banks to meet farm loan demands.

Much of the statistical work done on farm finance in the Federal Reserve System was developed by R. J. Doll and E. Melichar. Some of their efforts are represented in *Farm Debt, Data from the 1960 Sample Survey of Agriculture*; *Merchant and Dealer Credit in Agriculture, Data from the 1960 Sample Survey of Agriculture*; and in "Capital and Credit Requirements of Agriculture and Proposals to Increase Availability of Bank Credit" (Melichar and Doll [1969]).

The Farm Credit Administration (FCA) has been active in providing farm credit data with particular emphasis on Federal Land Bank and Production Credit Association (PCA) loans. Planting was responsible for many of the series, including reports of the sample surveys of PCA loans at five-year intervals. The annual report of the FCA contains data on its operations by states.

Several data series on farm credit extended by commercial banks and other lenders were sponsored by the American Bankers' Association (ABA) under the direction of Savage and Derr (ABA [monthly]). Regular publications such as *Agricultural Credit and Related Data* and *Agricultural Banking Developments* were the vehicles for distributing much of the data.

University and other institutional research staffs have done little in the way of compiling and distributing farm credit statistics. Rather, they have emphasized analysis of the existing farm finance procedures and programs, often recommending changes to improve the extension and use of farm credit and anticipating future farm credit needs. Numerous journal articles, circulars, and college textbooks have been produced by these institutional researchers.

Farm Real Estate

Farm real estate data have focused mostly on the prices of farm land and on the participants in farm real estate markets. Data on financing real estate transfers and on the distribution of loans for real estate purchases by type of lender were added as the percentage of sales financed at higher debt-to-value ratios increased. Although basic collection procedures remained unchanged, the type of data collected has evolved as needs have changed. Semiannual summaries of farm real estate market activity have been published in *Farm Real Estate Market Developments* by the ERS. Brief summaries also have appeared in *Balance Sheet of the Farm Sector*, *Farm Cost Situation*, and *Agricultural Finance Outlook*.

The basic challenge in real estate data collection is to sample changing real estate transfers adequately through a static group of reporters. Several attempts have been made to collect transfer data from courthouse records, but the process was too costly and the data were not sufficiently reliable. Many transfers were not recorded until years after the initial agreement, the records did not always reflect the full price or other considerations in a sale, and sampling was inadequate.

As the farm and nonfarm sectors become more and more interdependent, the impact of nonfarm factors on farm real estate values becomes increasingly important, adequate measures of this relationship have not been developed. The further separation of farming as defined by the Census of Agriculture into commercial and noncommercial sectors hampers accurate measurement of asset earnings in the commercial sector because a growing volume of farm assets contributes little to commercial production.

Research on farm real estate has historically been divided between state market studies and analyses of aggregate data for the United States. Some analysis has been done on the impact of specific institutional factors such as farm commodity programs or highway construction.

The state studies have usually attempted to determine the actual level of land values within the state, the variation in values among areas, the characteristics of the participants in the real estate market, and the influence of the various factors on real estate prices (Anderson, Loftsgard, and Erickson

[1962], Crosswhite and Vaughn [1962], Crowley [1972], Davis and Miller [1959], Dovring and Scofield [1963], Fischer, Burkholder, and Muehlbeier [1960], Gibson and Chambliss [1966], Hurlburt [1950], Murray and Reinsel [1965], and Pine and Scofield [1961]). Despite many attempts to quantify the impact of specific factors on real estate values, the data remain inadequate because of the great variation in sales prices, the small number of observations available, and the probability that the sales which occur are not representative of all rural real estate.

At the national level much of the research in the last decade has developed around an observation that land values and net farm income are not changing proportionately (Boyne [1964], Chryst [1965], Herdt and Cochrane [1966], Hurlburt [1959], Renshaw [1957], Tweeten and Martin [1966], and Tweeten and Nelson [1970]). These studies generally have assumed a national farm real estate market and have attempted to explain the observed divergence of trends in net income and land values with aggregate data. Several econometric models that predict the national average value of farmland have been developed.

A model developed by Tweeten and Martin [1966] is typical of recent national studies. A unique study by Boyne [1964] examined the impact of changes in the value of all assets, including real estate, on the wealth position of farm operators. In general, research at the national level illustrates the differences of opinion that exist among economists about the cause of the upward trend in land values.

Most commodity studies have focused on the effect of price support and production control programs on the value of land used for specific crops. These studies have shown that allotments do have a capitalized value and that the long-term average capitalization rate is in the neighborhood of 15 percent. In general, the commodity studies indicate that farm program benefits have been capitalized into land values and that the implied capitalization rates are considerably higher than the market rate of interest.

Machinery and Equipment

A national inventory of principal machines on farms is published annually in *Changes in Farm Production and Efficiency* (USDA, ERS [1972a]). Tractors, trucks, and automobiles were enumerated by the Census in 1920. The annual series based on census counts, shipments by manufacturers of machines for farm use, survey data, trends in census data, and estimated annual discard rates began in about 1939.

The early data included mainly counts of major machines on farms and trends from year to year. Initially, the machines were small, and those on farms were relatively new; the discards were low and the numbers increased at a rapid rate. As mechanization progressed, additional data on age, size, and annual use of machines were collected. Annual collections of data were largely confined to the inventory of machines on farms. Periodical mail surveys and occasional enumerative surveys were made to assess age, size, and annual use. Data involving inventories of machines were used in series on farmers' purchases of machines, repair costs, and depreciation, and in *Balance Sheet of the Farming Sector.*

A contract study on use, depreciation, and replacement of machines and custom operations was made in 1956 (Parsons, Robinson, and Strickler [1960]). This one-time nationwide survey was a stratified multistage probability sample of 80 county sampling units and 541 segments. Data from this survey made possible the first calculations of the average age and the average service life of machines. Later data involving sales of principal machines to farmers have been useful in computations of discard rates, tractor horsepower, average age, average useful life, and other relationships.

More information is needed on work-related farm accidents and pollution to serve as a base from which to assess progress in muffling sound, equipping machines with roll-over protection, educating drivers to operate and maintain machines in a safe manner, and minimizing emissions. Further information is needed on long-range purchase patterns for major machines.

Fertilizer

A boom in the production of synthetic anhydrous ammonia came out of World War II. Used for munitions during the war, ammonia is the basic stock for virtually all nitrogen fertilizers. Ammonia producers sought an outlet for their product by wooing farmers in the Midwest as prospective users of fertilizers. This helped to shift the center of fertilizer consumption from the cotton and tobacco production areas in the Southeast to the Corn Belt.

Much of the post-World War II economic research into the use of commercial fertilizer was inaugurated by Ibach and Adams. Donald Ibach and others who worked with him in the ERS and in the ARS. Although their work was largely agronomic, it provided a foundation for the study of the economics of fertilizer use. One major contribution was the development of a method for estimating crop response to various levels of application of primary plant nutrients. Ibach devised a method for estimating the use of fertilizer by crops and by states, based upon data obtained from the agricultural censuses.

From 1969 to 1973 the fertilizer industry underwent a reversal from excess production capacity and low prices to tight supply and record high prices for primary plant nutrients. Because the domestic economy and agriculture depend heavily on the fertilizer industry—about a third of domestic crop production is attributed to fertilizer—the USDA has expanded its research into the structure of the industry. The ERS monitors the supply and demand situation annually in *Fertilizer Situation*. Other departmental publications about fertilizer are the SRS *Fertilizer Consumption Report* and the Agricultural Stabilization and Conservation Service *Fertilizer Supply*, each published yearly. Nevertheless, gaps remain in the fertilizer data, especially in the areas of nonfarm use of fertilizer, fertilizer production and consumption in foreign countries, transportation of fertilizers from producing points to farms, and production and use of secondary nutrients and micronutrients—growing segments of the fertilizer industry.

Feed

Principal changes in feed-livestock data have come from intensive efforts to make indexes of relationships more useful. Current index series make use of basic nutritional standards developed by the National Academy of Science, Council of Animal Nutrition. Daily minimum nutrient requirements with allowance for waste and shrinkage by type and kind of livestock are used to develop feeding rates for a specific base period. All feedstuffs are measured in feed units which facilitate measurement by nutrient source such as concentrates, harvested roughage, and pasture. Index series are now available by state and by specific type and class of livestock and poultry. These include (1) grain-consuming animal units, (2) roughage-consuming animal units, (3) grain-and-roughage-consuming animal units, (4) livestock production units based on concentrates, and (5) livestock production units based on all feeds. In response to the need for a measure of feedgrain use by states, an annual balance showing feedgrain surplus and deficit was developed for each state, using grain-consuming animal units and SRS feedgrain crop estimates.

In addition to the five index series mentioned above, a high-protein animal unit series at the national level is maintained to identify end-use by individual livestock species. For the 1973-74 feeding year, estimates of nonagriculturally produced feedstuff fed to livestock and poultry were initiated. The three major items added were urea, salt, and mineral mixtures.

Two one-time surveys were completed, one in 1966 on consumption of urea as a feed ingredient for cattle (Allen and Mighell [1969]) and the second in 1970 on the formula feed industry. Each covered an area for which adequate data were lacking. Before 1965 the source of urea data was the Tariff Commission, which indentified the share of urea used for feed. The 1966 survey showed much more urea being fed to cattle than was reported to be manufactured under the 42 percent label. Apparently a considerable quantity of fertilizer urea containing 46 percent nitrogen was being mixed in feeds. As far as livestock feeding is concerned, the two kinds of urea are almost perfect substitutes.

In addition to the conventional uses for which they were designed, feed-livestock index data have been used by business firms to determine the market potential and the possibilities of market penetration. In a landmark case involving freight rates of the Southern Railway, the grain-consuming animal unit series was used by the U.S. Interstate Commerce Commission [1963] to estimate the consumption of feed grains in the nine southeastern states. The case was appealed through the federal court system to the Supreme Court, which held that the methodology and the results were logical and acceptable.

Major gaps still exist in the livestock-feed data with respect to (1) the movements of feed ingredients from production to consumption, in both the quantity moved and the method of transportation, to determine impacts on regional production patterns, (2) the quantities used and the characteristics of recently developed commercial byproduct feeds, (3) the kind and amount of microingredient feed additives fed to different kinds of livestock and poultry, (4) determination and evaluation of the net gain obtained by additions of microingredients to livestock and poultry feeds, and (5) the kind and amount of feed going to nonfarm livestock.

Pesticides

At the end of World War II most of the pesticides in general use were inorganic materials. With the development of the new synthetic organic pesticides it became economically feasible to control many pests more effectively. By the early 1960s more than 10,000 commercial pesticide formulations were available. They have helped to make possible increased specialization and more intensive farming. The demand for pesticides increased sharply during the postwar years, but so did public concern over the use of pesticides and their side effects.

In 1964 Congress authorized an expanded program of research on the agricultural use of pesticides. The Agricultural Appropriations Act of 1965 provided funds to the USDA to undertake an intensified program of research, education, and regulation, recognizing that pest control is an economic problem as well as a biological and physical problem. The data available at the time were inadequate to evaluate the economic implications of pesticide use. The ERS with the help of the SRS was authorized to conduct nationwide enumerative farm surveys to collect and analyze the needed data. Three nationwide enumerative surveys were conducted to get detailed data on farm use of pesticides for 1964, 1966, and 1971 (Andrelenas, Eichers, and Fox [1967], Fox et al. [1968], Andrelenas [1974]). These surveys provided the basis for at least twenty publications and numerous staff and administrative reports showing quantities of pesticides, expenditures for pesticides, and types and forms of pesticides used by farmers on specified crops and livestock.

The data obtained in these surveys were also used to estimate the effects of pesticides on productivity and the consequences of restricting or prohibiting the use of certain pesticides. Such economic impact studies represent an important application of the data in recent years, and they have been used in Environmental Protection Agency (EPA) advisory hearings and pesticide registration reviews and in public hearings on proposed pesticide restrictions. Other studies based on data from the surveys were prepared for the Congress, the President's Office of Science and Technology, the Council on Environmental Quality, and the EPA. In addition, government agencies, researchers at various agricultural experiment stations and universities, and many others have used the data. Entomologists, weed scientists, and other researchers have contributed technical information to the economic evaluations.

The 1971 survey filled gaps in earlier data and provided more recent information. In addition to recording types, quantities, and costs of pesticides used, this survey collected information on the pesticide containers used and their disposal, the hazards to human beings from the use of pesticides, the methods of pesticide application on row crops, and the reasons for using specific pesticides and their effectiveness against major pests. These data helped appraise the potential for using alternative methods of pest control and for making adjustments in agriculture to reduce the need for chemical pesticides.

Farm Labor

National statistics on farm labor are obtained from continuing household and establishment surveys and from special surveys. The major household surveys are the decennial Census of Population and the monthly Current Population Survey. The reports appearing in *Occupation by Industry* PC(2)-7C are prepared from the decennial census. Both *Employment and Earnings*, a BLS monthly bulletin, and *Hired Farm Working Force*, an ERS annual series with ancillary reports, are derived from the Current Population Survey.

The major establishment surveys include the Census of Agriculture, which is taken every five years, and the quarterly Agricultural Labor Survey by the USDA, SRS. The Census of Agriculture reports for each state and the nation as a whole are published from the five-year survey although they contain little data on farm labor. Additional data obtained in conjunction with the quarterly Agricultural Labor Survey have been published by the Department of Labor in reports transmitted to Congress. These reports, entitled *Hired Farm Workers*, present data relative to the effects of minimum wage legislation on the supply and demand for hired farm workers.

Estimates of agricultural employment are issued quarterly by SRS and are published in *Farm Labor*. Data are included on family workers, hired workers, total workers, and hours worked, covering the United States, all standard federal regions, and all contiguous states except those in Region 1.

Since January 1974 estimates have been based on a probability survey using the multiple frame concept. Before January 1974 monthly estimates were based on a nonprobability mail survey. The necessity for the change to probability sampling became apparent as farms grew more specialized and the mail survey lists no longer represented the large or seasonal labor users. The sample survey covers the week of the twelfth day of January, April, July, and October and records the actual payrolls of about 18,000 scientifically selected farms for these weeks—timing that matches the week specified in employment and wage series constructed by other government agencies. The current survey requires that workers must have been employed on the farm during the survey week. They may be counted as farm workers more than once if they worked that week on two or more farms in the sample; the number of hours worked and the wages earned are not counted twice.

Wage rates are obtained for different types of work and methods of pay. Wages by method of pay include wages per hour for piece rate, wages other than piece rate, wages per hour only (perquisites also received), cash wages only (any method of pay but no perquisites received), and cash wages per hour only (no perquisites). Wages by type of work include wages per hour for field and livestock work, packinghouse work, machine operation, maintenance and bookkeeping, supervision, and other agricultural work. Although some workers do more than one job, the respondent classifies the worker according to what he did most of the time during the survey week.

The results of a special survey of farm enterprises, conducted by the Census of Agriculture in 1972 on 1971 farming operations, were published in nine parts as volume 5, Special Reports. A large volume of labor data for the nine major farm enterprises was obtained. A supplementary census of agricultural services was conducted in 1969 and published as volume 3 in 1972. It presents numbers of employees and payrolls for businesses serving agriculture as defined in the population of the survey.

Since World War II the need for farm labor statistics has increased in part because of more urgent policy issues affecting labor (minimum wage, unemployment insurance, safety, and others), in part because of the increased cost of labor, in part because of growing concern over the welfare of hired workers, and for other reasons. This prompted the SRS to drop the mail survey and turn to the enumerated multiple frame approach worked out by Stokstad and Garrett (Small [1975]).

Labor statistics are used by the ERS to construct a series on man-hours of labor used in farming. Estimates are developed for individual farm enterprises by applying average man-hour labor requirements to the official estimates of acreage and yield reported in SRS *Crop Production* reports. With data from the agricultural censuses benchmark estimates of man-hours per acre are developed for farm enterprises in each state. *Trends in Output Per Man-Hour in the Private Economy, 1909-58* (U.S. Department of Labor, BLS [1954]) and subsequent BLS releases present indexes of production per man-hour, but only for all of agriculture.

Some labor information gaps were filled by data collected in the 1964 and 1966 "ERS Pesticide Surveys" (Andrelenas, Eichers, and Fox [1967], Fox et al. [1968]). These surveys obtained data on labor input, the value of perquisites furnished workers, and pay levels of workers by job classification. Other noncontinuing surveys such as the cotton cost survey, cling peach survey, and the flue-cured tobacco survey by governmental, academic, and other organizations have also helped to fill voids in labor data. More detail on the number and kind of workers in the farm labor force, the types of jobs they perform, and the skill requirements of those farm jobs are needed on a national basis.

Insurance

Crop insurance coverage, premiums, and indemnities have been included in an annual data series prepared by the ERS and its predecessors since before World War II. Originally data were collected from insurance companies, but now they are obtained mainly from several insurance statistical associations. Data on crop losses and the cost of insurance protection are important in the financial management of farms, in the operations of concerns supplying capital to agriculture, in planning and operation of the USDA crop insurance program, and for other purposes.

An earlier series on farm property insurance premiums and indemnities of farm mutual insurance companies was discontinued because of the nonfarm trend in the business of mutual insurance companies. A series of indemnities and premiums more representative of farms has been expanding since 1960. A one-time study of this development was made by W. R. Bailey and Jones [1970], with data furnished by insurance company statistical associations. Insurance data are regularly published in the ERS *Agricultural Finance Review*.

Marketing

Agricultural marketing research was expanded with enactment of the Research and Marketing Act of 1946. Since then, researchers in the USDA and in the state experiment stations have added greatly to the knowledge and understanding of agricultural marketing. Bibliographies of USDA reports from 1950 through 1969 list over a thousand publications for marketing economics research.

Marketing research studies over the past twenty-five years have dealt with a variety of subjects including market development, merchandising and promotion, transportation, food distribution, costs and margins, and public programs. Some examples are the effect of the pilot food stamp program on retail food store sales (Frye [1962]), the food service industry (Van Dress [1971]), the agricultural exemption in interstate trucking (Miklius [1969]), the comparative cost to consumers of convenience foods and home-prepared foods (Harp and Dunham [1963]) and potato flakes (Dwoskin and Jacobs [1957]). These analyses were one-time studies based largely on primary data. These and hundreds of other marketing studies carried out in the land-grant universities and other state and federal institutions developed a great volume of data on marketing functions and the marketing of special commodities.

A comprehensive report, *Agricultural Markets in Change* (USDA, ERS [1966]), summarized past and prospective changes in markets and marketing functions for agricultural products, with chapters on innovations, market development, transportation, and commodity marketing systems. Also in 1966 the ERS prepared several studies for the National Commission on Food Marketing [1966b-1966g] including a special analysis of cost and profit components of farm-retail spreads for farm-originated foods.

In addition to one-time marketing studies, agricultural economists of the USDA have developed several major data series on agricultural marketing costs and charges. Two major series are now maintained by the ERS to meet current and continuing needs for information on food marketing costs and the farmer's share of the consumer's food dollar; these are "market basket" and "marketing bill" statistics and appear regularly in *Marketing and Transportation Situation* and other situation reports.

Development of these statistical series was prompted by the widespread belief that marketing costs too much. Consumers felt that marketing costs were pushing retail food prices up, and farmers felt that they were holding commodity prices down. Periodically the ERS evaluates and revises the procedures used to estimate the market basket and marketing bill data. Procedures and methods are also regularly reviewed by the USDA Statistical Review Board.

Market Basket Statistics

Waugh and Been originated the farm-food market basket statistics in 1936 in response to a widespread interest in farm-retail price spreads. Data sources and methods have been refined and improved many times since 1936. Market basket data show changes in the marketing charges for domestic farm-originated foods. They also show the relation between changes in prices paid by consumers and returns to farmers. This series has been published in *Marketing and Transportation Situation* since May 1942; a monthly supplement, *Price Spreads for Farm Food*, has been published since May 1971.

The market basket represents the average quantities of sixty-five domestic farm-originated foods purchased annually per household in retail stores in 1960-61 by families of urban wage earners and clerical workers and by single persons living alone. It does not include foods consumed away from home, imported foods, seafoods, or other foods not of domestic farm origin. Quantities are held constant so that changes in the value of the market basket will give accurate estimates of price changes. Prices of these sixty-five foods are used to estimate the market basket retail cost, the returns received by farmers, and the farm-retail spread, with data published for forty-six individual foods.

The primary sources of price data for the market basket series are the retail prices reported by the BLS and the prices received by farmers reported by the SRS. Market basket quantity weights are obtained from BLS expenditure studies at approximately ten-year intervals in order to obtain weights for the Consumer Price Index.

Marketing Bill Data

The other major USDA series on marketing costs is the "marketing bill," first published in 1945. This series reports total charges made by marketing firms for transporting, processing, and distributing domestic farm-originated foods purchased by civilian consumers in this country. It is the difference between civilian expenditures for these foods and farm value, which is an estimate of gross returns to farmers for products equivalent to those purchased by consumers.

Civilian expenditures for farm foods include expenditures for food bought in retail stores, restaurants, and other away-from-home eating establishments and directly from farmers, processors, and wholesalers. Expenditures for imported foods, fish, and other foods not originating on domestic farms are excluded.

The early development of marketing bill data was done by Been et al. [1945]. Initial estimates were based on the assumption that all food was sold through retail stores. Separate estimates of labor costs for marketing, of inter-city rail and truck transportation costs, and of marketing firm profits were introduced in the mid-1950s. In 1957 the procedures were revised to include the additional cost incurred on food purchased in eating places and to exclude the cost of food sold at less than retail prices (Hiemstra [1968]).

In 1967 the marketing bill statistics were reestimated by Scott, Gale, and Findlay, using the commodity flow method which had been recommended by Waldorf (Gale [1967]). For census years benchmark estimates are made of the commodity volumes flowing through the different marketing agencies (assemblers, processors, wholesalers, retailers) and the marketing charges added at each stage in the process. These estimates are based on data from the censuses of manufactures and of business and on published data from the USDA, the Office of Business Economics of the Department of Commerce, the Interstate Commerce Commission, the Internal Revenue Service, trade publications, and other sources. Annual estimates derived from less extensive data are used to interpolate between census years and extrapolate beyond the last benchmark.

The commodity flow method used for census years is conceptually superior because it incorporates the effects of changes in marketing channels, in gross margins for specific agencies, and in services offered and allows the introduction of new products. The price-quantity method provides an alternative estimate in benchmark years and an interpolating series for other years.

Several major cost components have been estimated since 1959. The procedures for making these estimates from Internal Revenue Service data were developed by Wesson, who established series for advertising, rent, depreciation, interest, taxes, business, and other cost components. Estimates of the cost of container packing materials were added by Eley [1971]. By 1972 about 90 percent of the total marketing bill was allocated to specific cost components. The rest of the bill was unallocated among fuel and power, intracity transportation, institutional costs, and miscellaneous items.

Recently, Crawford [1974] made several refinements in the marketing bill data, including separate estimates for foods consumed at home and in public eating places, hospitals, and in-plant food service establishments from 1963 on. The refinement of the marketing bill data was facilitated by the availability of benchmark data from an ERS survey of eating establishments (Van Dress [1971]). Estimates were also made for noncensus years for agency components (wholesaler, processor, retailer, public eating places). These estimates showed the labor costs and profits separately. Additional work is under way to disaggregate the marketing bill further.

Related Statistical Series

The ERS publishes several statistical series that are useful in analyzing changes in the marketing bill and market basket statistics. These include

(1) Indexes of Labor Costs per Hour and per Unit of Product Marketed, (2) Output per Man-Hour in Factories Processing Farm Foods, (3) Prices of Intermediate Goods and Services, and (4) Indexes of Railroad Freight Rates for Farm Products. A description of most of these series is given in the eleven-volume *Major Statistical Series of the U.S. Department of Agriculture: How They Are Constructed and Used* (USDA [1957-72]).

Data on Farm-Related Business

As nonfarm businesses have become increasingly important in the agricultural industry, economists have sought data beyond the traditional USDA and Census of Agriculture sources. The Census of Manufactures and the Census of Business have become useful sources of data, particularly with revisions in the standard industrial classification that permit identification of farm-related businesses.

The USDA has been represented on committees responsible for periodically reviewing and improving the *Standard Industrial Classification Manual* (U.S. Office of Management and Budget [1974]). As industry-related information is aggregated and published according to "SIC" codes, they implicitly limit the economic interpretations that can be made from the series. Over the years numerous changes have been made in the codes and, consequently, in the data, making them more useful to agricultural economists. In 1972 one of several improvements was to exclude garden tractors and implements from the farm machinery and equipment category, making that category represent more accurately the establishments producing machinery and implements for commercial farming operations. A separate category was created for garden tractors and implements. New categories also have been developed for establishments which provide soil preparation services, crop services and protection, crop harvesting and preparation for market, as well as for establishments primarily engaged in furnishing complete farm management services.

Since World War II major changes in farm-related business data include (1) the transfer of fats and oils from the chemical sector to the foods sector, (2) the transfer of fluid milk processing from wholesale trade to manufacturing, (3) the development of the *Annual Survey of Manufactures*, which annually presents many of the data provided by the Census, (4) periodic computation and publication of concentration ratios by all four-digit industries (as listed in the SIC Manual) for the largest four, eight, and twenty firms, composed of establishments of same four-digit classification aggregated to their parent firm but including only establishments for that industry alone, (5) the computation of specialization, coverage, and other ratios (for example, value added per man-hour of production worker, value added per employee, and cost of materials and payroll per dollar of shipments), and (6) the development of enterprise statistics which aggregate on a company basis rather than an establishment basis.

Although the economic censuses provide a statistical image of the food and kindred product industries in terms of numbers, size, location of establishments, and some efficiency measures, they do not include such data as profits, advertising expenditures, and fringe benefits, which are relevant to analyses of conduct and performance of the industry. Such data are provided in *Internal Revenue Service Source Book* and *Statistics of Income*, publications issued eighteen months or more after data collection, and are not compatible with economic census data.

Data relating to public storage facilities are reported by the Census of Business, under SIC "Farm Product Warehousing and Storage" and "Refrigerated Warehousing." Some warehousing is included for wholesale establishments which primarily sell cotton and grain; some uncertainty exists about the completeness of coverage of "captive" warehouses owned and operated by some of the largest processors.

The USDA conducts periodic cost analyses of grain and cotton storage, with projections for two to three years between studies. It also maintains a data file of public warehouse facilities in operation; these data include measures of capacity.

In addition to the sources just mentioned, *Current Industrial Reports* from the Bureau of the Census regularly provide product sales for numerous lines of agricultural inputs both by quantity and value, such as tractors specified by horsepower of units purchased and feeds by kind.

The USDA also has maintained up-to-date information on marketing and supply service cooperatives since World War II. These series report the number, size, location, activities, and tabulations by types of product, largely in *Statistics of Farmer Cooperatives*. Some data are also reported in other USDA series such as *Agricultural Statistics* and *Balance Sheet of Agriculture* and in cooperative firm house organs. The Farmer Cooperative Service (FCS) prepares technical reports which are released intermittently. These focus on such issues as vertical and horizontal integration and on particular kinds of cooperatives such as dairy herd improvement or rural electrification.

Food Consumption and Nutrition

Food Consumption and Related Data

The development of food consumption data has a long and complicated history involving several USDA and other federal agencies and the work of scores of individuals. Only a few highlights can be mentioned here.

Inadequate consumption by many families during the Great Depression brought proposals for raising nutritional levels and expanding the demand for food. About one-third of the 1939 Yearbook of Agriculture, *Food and Life* (USDA [1939]) dealt with human nutrition and food consumption. Other subjects were farm legislation and programs. Although the initial focus of the Agricultural Adjustment Act of 1933 and later legislation was to improve the incomes of farmers, there was an immediate need to supply food to hungry people.

Specific efforts were made to increase the consumption of surplus foods under the Food Stamp Plan of 1939. The idea was to increase the demand for food by what amounted to stratified pricing, an idea developed by Fred Waugh and promoted by Milo Perkins. In that same year came the School Lunch Program, followed by the School Milk Program in 1940. Each of these programs was temporarily suspended during World War II.

The war required a marked sharp expansion of American farm output accompanied by allocation of available supplies, not only to the military forces and the civilian population but also to the United Kingdom, the Soviet Union, France, and other Allied nations. This decreased domestic civilian supplies of a number of commodities well below the levels of market demand and brought on consumer rationing. The rationing program made evident the need for more information on the price and income elasticities of food demand and on the nutritive content of food.

The food supply continued to be a problem in the postwar years, owing to the need for food relief abroad and the renewed interest in the Food Stamp Plan and related programs. Finally, the need for better planning in food and agricultural programs stimulated long-range projections of desirable consumption levels and production goals. Meanwhile the need for better data on food consumption and demand, nutritional objectives, and production potentials continued to increase.

One of the earliest statistical estimates of domestic food consumption was O. E. Baker's "Changes in Production and Consumption of Farm Products and the Trend in Population," published in 1925 (Baker [1929]). Some years later, although the BAE did not regularly publish estimates of domestic food consumption, it collected and compiled a considerable amount of consumption data and published a series of special reports on the effects of the droughts of 1934 and 1936 on consumption. In the meantime a comprehensive set of per-capita food consumption estimates was developed in the Program Planning Division of the Agricultural Adjustment Administration by Wells, Nelson, Cavin, and Elliott, utilizing much of the data already available in the BAE. This set of estimates was used by Stiebeling and Coons [1939] in the 1939 Yearbook of Agriculture and for other purposes (Stillman [1949]).

In anticipation of wartime needs the BAE issued in March 1941 an appraisal of the current food situation entitled "Consumption of Agricultural Products" (Anderson [1941]). At about this time the program planning group of the Agricultural Adjustment Agency was transferred to the BAE, where the consumption series was completed. These efforts were merged with other BAE work in this field, all of which was placed under the direction of O. C. Stine, who established a food consumption section within the Division of Statistical and Historical Research.

The gifted young statistician Meyer Girshick was brought into the division to improve the statistical competence of that group and the statistical work throughout the BAE. Although he had to devote considerable time to work on certain critical wartime problems with the Statistical Research Group at Columbia University, he and his small staff succeeded in improving and coordinating the food consumption activities within the department. Beginning in 1942 consumption estimates for the major foods were regularly issued in a new publication, *The National Food Situation*, together with an evaluation of the supply-price outlook and reports of significant actions taken by the War Food Administration.

Among the other accomplishments were coordination and standardization of major food series on a calendar-year basis and the development of adequate waste and loss factors which made it possible to express per-capita consumption in comparable retail weight equivalents. These advances also made possible the construction of a meaningful price-weighted index of per-capita consumption of all foods and provided the Bureau of Human Nutrition and Home Economics with a much improved basis for determining the nutritive value of annual food supplies. One notable addition to the consumption series was the inclusion of the data on fish consumption which had been compiled in the course of a very extensive research effort (Sherr, Power, and Kahn [1948]).

For more than a decade after World War II Marguerite Burk [1956] was the primary force in the development of food consumption and related data. The data and methodology are contained in *Consumption of Food in the United States, 1909-48*, which was revised and brought up to date in 1953 (USDA, BAE [1949, 1953]). In addition, Burk's reports contained detailed descriptions of the structure of the data system, the data sources, and the major limitations of the estimates. All this was further supplemented by valuable material on such topics as income, prices, and expenditures related to food consumption.

The 1953 report also contained an innovative set of estimates designated as "Supply-Distribution Indexes" (largely compiled by Marguerite Burk and Martin Gerra) and designed to provide a comprehensive view of the national food sector. Essentially they were a series of index numbers which for any given year indicated the proportion of United States food supplies derived from domestic production, stock changes, and imports; they also indicated the proportions of these supplies distributed for civilian and military consumption, nonfood uses, commercial exports, USDA deliveries for such purposes as lend-lease and relief, and year-end stock changes. In addition, the series permitted simultaneous analysis of changes over time among the various sources of supply and the channels of utilization. Eventually the quantities being used for domestic feed and seed were eliminated.

Hiemstra succeeded Burk as head of the Food Consumption Section for the period 1963-69, during which two additional handbooks were published, *U.S. Food Consumption in 1965* (USDA, ERS [1965]) and *Food—Consumption, Prices and Expenditures* (Hiemstra [1968]). These publications extended and improved the work of Burk and her associates and also made important additions. Quarterly consumption estimates were published for meats, poultry, eggs, and fats and oils. Estimates for Alaska and Hawaii were incorporated into the national totals. Food donated by the USDA was reported as a separate component of civilian consumption, four separate measures of per-capita food consumption were calculated and compared, and a substantial volume of significant new material on food prices and expenditures was added.

Although many specialized research projects and their authors cannot be included in this general survey, the contributions of a number of the commodity specialists with responsibilities in the consumption field are mentioned in the section on Commodity Supply and Utilization Data. Special mention should be made of the work of Frederick V. Waugh. Though his research covered an extremely wide range of topics, he devoted a considerable amount of attention to the demand for food. This is especially evident in his outstanding bulletin, *Demand and Price Analysis* (Waugh [1964]), which was selected for the Publication of Enduring Quality Award in 1974 by the AAEA.

Near the end of World War II economists began to speculate on the nature and possibilities of full employment under peacetime conditions. Many economists developed long-range projections to provide perspective on the structure of the economy under alternative assumptions with respect to population, employment, productivity, income, and related factors. Between May and December 1945 the USDA published four interbureau reports under the title *What Peace Can Mean to American Farmers* (USDA, Interbureau Coordinating Committee on Postwar Planning [1945a-1945d]). The long-term USDA series on per-capita food consumption, together with related information on price and income elasticities, were important elements in making these projections realistic and useful. Later projections were published in "Prospective Demands for Food and Fiber" (Daly [1957]) and "Potential Demand for Farm Products over the Next Quarter Century" (Koffsky [1960]), which had been presented to a seminar group at Iowa State University.

Though most of the work on food consumption has been in terms of national aggregates, there has been great interest in and need for more detailed breakdowns. In 1959 Burk and Lavell compiled per-capita food consumption indexes for households by region, urbanization, and household income based on the 1955 USDA Household Food Consumption Survey (Lavell [1959]). A study by Price [1967], also based on these data, indicated that variations in household consumption were due to the age and sex composition of its members. Regional studies have been of special interest to groups such as marketing firms. Perhaps the most intensive effort in this direction has been that of Raunikar, Purcell, and Elrod [1969], who compiled regional, state, and market area data for a number of commodities.

Despite the impressive accomplishments in the compilation of data on food consumption, much important work remains. At present the principal requirements are for (1) more data on food used by restaurants and institutions, (2) more accurate estimates of waste and losses in marketing, (3) estimates of waste in the home, (4) more data on the distribution of consumption among household members, and (5) food consumption by major subgroups of the population both within and among households. Consumption data for bakery products and other highly processed products, more adequate data for estimating quarterly consumption, more frequent and smaller cross-sectional surveys between the traditional larger surveys, and continuing information on methods and data from other countries are also needed.

The Index of Supply and Utilization

The development of supply-utilization balance sheets for individual commodities and groups of commodities was a major accomplishment in understanding the structure of supply and demand for agricultural products, inadequate as they were for analysis of the agricultural sector. The index of supply and utilization was developed, primarily by Burk and Gerra, to fill this gap (USDA, AMS [1955]). The development of this series permits simultaneous analysis of changes over time and among utilization channels and supply sources. The categories of utilization are food, feed, seed, other nonfood, and exports. Commodities and channels can be combined or disaggregated at will by the investigator. The scarcity of literature using this data system suggests that the profession has failed to exploit it fully (Egbert [1969]).

The supply-utilization index is based on value aggregates with constant farm prices and annual quantities of farm commodities. Gross production and utilization were published at first, but the indexes were later changed to a net concept to eliminate the double counting of feed used for livestock production and seed used for producing new crops. Indexes for all commodities, food commodities, livestock commodities, and crop commodities are published regularly in ERS *Situation* reports. In addition, the component value aggregates by major commodity group are available from the ERS.

The long-term goal is to integrate this system with other agricultural and nonagricultural sector accounts. Such integration would make possible more accurate estimation of the structural supply-demand relationships at various stages in the food and fiber production, supply, and marketing systems. Data on farm receipts and expenses, consumer expenditures, value added in marketing, value of exports and imports of agricultural commodities, and others would be involved.

The Nutritive Value of Diets in the United States

During World War II administrators with responsibilities for production and distribution of food needed basic information on family food consumption. Inadequate data stimulated two lines of research — namely, the calculation of the nutritive value of food available annually for consumption by the domestic civilian population and a national survey of household food consumption which included calculation of the nutritive value of the household food supplies by urbanization and income level. A national survey of urban families was made in 1948 (USDA, Bureau of Human Nutrition and Home Economics [1949]), and of all urban and rural families by region in 1955 (USDA, ARS [1957a]); data for four seasons were collected in 1965-66 (USDA, ARS [1972]). Numerous smaller surveys of selected groups of households were made by the USDA between the large national surveys of 1955 and 1965. The survey data have also been compared over time (LeBovit et al. [1961], USDA, ARS [1957a, 1969]).

Annual estimates of the nutritive value of the food supply can be used to assess the national availability of nutrients and to estimate changes in availability over time. The estimates are derived by applying nutrients per unit to per-capita consumption of various commodities (USDA, ERS [1968]).

Most household surveys do not measure the nutritive values of diets of individual household members. Surveys of individual diets were undertaken in a series of studies from 1947 through 1958 at state agricultural experiment stations in cooperation with the USDA and several state departments of public health. The first nationwide survey of individual diets was made in spring 1965 in connection with the 1965-66 household survey (USDA, ARS [1972]).

One of the problems in estimating nutrition levels is assigning nutritive value factors to reported food quantities. It is often difficult for survey respondents to describe accurately the foods used. The proliferation of processed foods makes it more difficult to determine the basic food ingredients and the nutrient content of each. In the annual time series on food supply it is almost impossible to allow for shifts within product groupings—from leaner to fatter beef or from stewing or roasting chicken to fryers. To supplement the basic food composition factors, several surveys of manufacturers of vitamin and mineral preparations were undertaken to obtain information on the contribution of enrichment and fortification of foods for inclusion in the time series data (Friend [1963]).

Another problem is the estimation of waste and losses of food in homes, institutions, and public eating places and the destruction of nutrients in cooking and preparation. Some estimates of the value of the vitamins lost in cooking have been incorporated into survey calculations for 1955 and later years. Very little is known about the amount of food wasted in the home and other eating places.

A major problem in interpreting the nutritive value of diets is the lack of a suitable standard for adequacy. The usual yardstick is the Recommended Dietary Allowances of the Food and Nutrition Board of the National Research Council. These are the allowances recommended to provide for the nutritional health of the majority of the population with the margin over the minimal requirements varying widely among nutrients. Diets containing less than the recommended allowances of nutrients are not necessarily deficient. Although the allowances are not a precise tool for rating the diets of individuals or households, they are fairly satisfactory for evaluating the diets of the population as a whole and of major population groupings based on geographic location, age, ethnic origin, and other factors.

Natural Resource Economic Data

Land Use

Data on land use were first shown in land records as a basis for assessment, and surveyors of the public domain recorded descriptions for sales purposes. Questions on land use were first included in the Census of Agriculture in 1840. Over the years questions in the Census gradually increased in detail and were given special attention in the Census of 1925. The closing of the frontier plus World War I demands for farm products resulted in concern about the man-land ratio. In 1920 the USDA prepared its first estimates of the amount of land in various major uses, and the totals were published in the 1923 *Yearbook of Agriculture* (USDA [1924]).

During the next twenty years various agencies, states, counties, and planning and zoning jurisdictions developed land use data and land inventory maps as land use problems arose because of the drought and agricultural depression. By the end of World War II, however, there was still no comprehensive system for collection, analysis, and publication of land use data. Since then, the needs for land use data for problem definition, analysis, and planning have risen sharply because of conflicts in land use resulting from the expanding population and accelerated economic growth.

In 1947 the USDA developed major land use data by states from census data and from records of state and farm agencies. This series has been updated periodically (see, for example, Wooten and Anderson [1957]). Dozens of local, state, and regional studies during the late 1940s and 1950s reported data on land use. Few of these studies developed much new data, however, and none was continued to provide data over time for the same universe.

The SRS has developed an area-segment sampling program for the United States which periodically provides data on land in crop production. At present, land not in crops is not accounted for, but the crop production sample could become the basis for acquiring data on other land uses.

The demand for data on the use of land for recreation has been increasing, but the collection of much data is complicated because much of the land used for recreation is also used for other purposes. Selected outdoor recreation statistics from various sources have been compiled by the United States Department of the Interior, Bureau of Outdoor Recreation [1971], but articulation is a problem because of differences in definition, timing of data collection, and geographical coverage of different sources of data.

The USDA has done several studies by comparative airphoto analysis to show the nature of land use changes in the rural-urban fringe and to develop population and land coefficients. It has also made a comparative airphoto analysis of land reclamation and abandonment by tract with illustrations of "before" and "after" use (Dill [1967], Dill and Otte [1970, 1971]).

Analytical studies of land planning programs are difficult because of differences in detail, timing, definitions, and geographical indexing of the various independent series of data. For many purposes it is necessary to analyze land use changes on the basis of individual tracts and to correlate socioeconomic data with the data on the physical attributes. Data published as county totals do not reveal the land use changes actually occurring on a tract basis, such as cropland reclamation and abandonment or urbanization. Data on specific tracts now must be acquired by specialized field surveys.

A comprehensive unified land data system on a tract basis (CULDATA) has been proposed (Cook and Kennedy [1966]). The initial proposal to automate all legal land records has been extended to include other land use and socioeconomic data. From this basis a standard land use coding manual could be developed which would provide digital equivalents for types of land use in great detail. This program would be a first step toward building a data bank for land use analyses within the total systems concept. Automated data capabilities make such a system feasible. At present, however, land use data remain either on a very generalized basis, such as the work of Wooten and Anderson [1957], or are available piecemeal in specialized studies.

Land Tenure

Throughout most of the nineteenth century the problems and issues of land tenure in the United States revolved around the management and disposal of the public domain. Toward the latter part of the century a few people became concerned about the rising rate of tenancy among farmers and especially with the high incidence of tenancy and sharecropping in the South. When Francis A. Walker was director of the Census of 1880, he initiated a special statistical study of land ownership and tenancy (Walker [1883]). The census of 1890 and each census since then have developed data on the tenure status of farms.

Following some initial work by H. C. Taylor, B. H. Hibbard, and a few others early in this century, several studies of tenancy and tenure were made during the 1920s and 1930s, prompted mostly by concern for the low estate of tenants, especially sharecroppers in the cotton and tobacco regions. Several New Deal programs in the Rural Resettlement Administration and its successor agencies sparked a demand for data on land tenure, tenancy, and related characteristics of the rural economy. Agricultural economists in the BAE and in most of the land-grant colleges responded with studies of both local and national import.

In addition to the detailed Census data on tenure obtained in 1934 and 1939, substantial volumes of data were developed by special studies. Works Progress Administration projects in some states produced very detailed data on tenure, including maps of every tract of land in the state classified by tenure status. This work was discontinued with the approach of World War II and has not been resumed on anything like the scale evident in the 1930s.

After World War II the attention of agricultural economists to questions of tenancy waned considerably. The improved economic situation in agriculture during and after the war, the rapid decline of the cropper system in cotton production, and growing public concern over other problems turned attention to other issues, with a few outstanding exceptions. In the West a group of economists became involved in tenure issues on public lands. In the South the Southwest Land Tenure Research Committee, sponsored by the Farm Foundation and the agricultural experiment stations, remained active and made a number of outstanding studies (Bertrand and Corty [1962]).

The Southern Land Economics Research Committee, which succeeded the old "Tenure" committees, continued to sponsor outstanding work on land problems including tenure. The results of this work appeared, for example, in *Farmland Tenure and Farmland Use in the Tennessee Valley* (Southern Land Economics Research Committee [1970]). Most of the work on land tenure and tenancy since 1960 resulted in little new data. Census data and such public records as tax rolls, the files of the ASCS (USDA), and the work of the Farmers Home Administration provided most of the information for these studies.

Inventory of Conservation Needs

A National Inventory of Soil and Water Conservation Needs (CNI) was first conducted in 1958 under the leadership of the Soil Conservation Service (SCS) with the data updated and expanded in 1967 (USDA, SCS [1958, 1967]). Eight USDA agencies, the Bureau of Indian Affairs, and the Department of the Interior cooperated. In addition, land-grant universities and other federal, state, and local agencies interested in water, forest, range, and wildlife conservation also participated at state and county levels.

Information on land use and treatment needs was obtained for every county from sample areas, with more than 160,000 samples inspected (basic sampling rate, 2 percent; size, 40 to 640 acres). Detailed soil surveys were made of the sample areas to determine the land capability class and subclass before the field inspections. Sample area data were processed and expanded to the inventory acreage in each county. This information was analyzed by county CNI committees and adjusted if it differed substantially from known values. Land use and treatment estimates for forest lands were closely correlated with data supplied by the Forest Service experiment stations. Information was also obtained for some 19,000 small watersheds on the nature and extent of flood prevention and water management problems that could be solved only through project action; this information led to feasibility estimates for project developments. The national inventory has produced the most comprehensive data hitherto available on the nation's land resources.

Soil Surveys

The National Cooperative Soil Survey was initiated in 1899 as a joint effort of several federal and state agencies. The SCS now has the primary responsibility, with the cooperation of the Forest Service, the Bureau of Indian Affairs, the Bureau of Reclamation, and the Bureau of Land Management. The land-grant colleges and universities (departments of soils, natural resources, conservation, or others) and other state agencies also cooperated. The major objectives of the survey were (1) to prepare soil maps, (2) to describe the characteristics of the different kinds of soil, (3) to classify the different kinds of soil into the nationwide classification system, (4) to interpret the soils for alternative uses and treatment, and (5) to publish this information.

About 40 percent of the 1.8 billion acres of land in the United States and the Caribbean area is now mapped. Soil mapping of some 45 million acres is done annually by 1,200 soil scientists in the field with the support of 200 additional scientists. Some 80,000 different kinds of soil are now recognized in the United States, and each has a unique set of physical and chemical properties and other characteristics such as depth, slope, and extent of flooding and erosion.

Soil surveys published at the county level provide soil maps, descriptions, and classifications. The estimated yields of the common agricultural soils are given for specified levels of management. Since 1957 interpretations of each of the mapped soils have been made for use in engineering, community planning, drainage and irrigation projects, and recreation and wildlife conservation programs.

Water

Data on the characteristics and uses of the nation's water resources became available somewhat later than farm and land use data. The first Census of Irrigation in 1890 was designed to provide information on the role of water in the agriculture of the West. Although this produced some information on water uses, little general information was developed on water supplies. Special studies in connection with reclamation project planning occasionally developed data on water supply, but even here the information was often not reliable. The early work of such men as Mead [1926, 1931] and Teele [1927] on the economics of reclamation and irrigation failed to develop either the funds or the capacity for collection of comprehensive data on water. The National Resources Board of the 1930s made a serious effort to inventory the nation's water resources, but much basic information simply did not exist. Even today the information for many areas of the country is far from adequate.

Water resource information was not collected in any consistent way before 1950. Water management and allocation problems were recognized in general land economics studies, but few researchers isolated the water variable. Water management was largely an undefined subset of reclamation, land drainage, flood control, or soil conservation activities. Such water data as existed were likely to be the product of experimental work in agronomy and forest management.

Agricultural economists made little use of this information although they conducted numerous studies related to irrigation, soils and soil conservation, and especially water conservation. Before 1950 both the basic science of hydrology for measuring water movement and use and precise quantitative work in farm management were still evolving. Quantitative analyses in resource economics were not emphasized, perhaps partly because of the heritage of the Commons/Dewey/Veblen school in resource economics (Commons [1924], Dewey [1938], Veblen [1914]).

During the 1950s the science of hydrology advanced considerably and farm management became "production economics" with quantitative firm theory applied to agriculture. Toward the end of the decade natural resource economists were catching up with production economists in quantification. A major turning point in the utilization of specific water data for agricultural economics studies was marked in a report by Beringer [1961], who showed both the conceptual fallacy and the lack of empirical basis for assuming water resources to be an inseparable complement of land.

In the 1960s many econometric water studies were completed that either derived or employed production-function relationships in which water appears as an independent variable or as an analytical proxy, such as a drought-day or an atmosphere of soil moisture stress. More important, a capability was developed for cataloguing the sources and characteristics of basic data that could be used for both farm economic studies and meso and macro area water planning studies. Some pioneering work in this direction was carried out by Gertel [1962a, 1962b]. The United States Water Resources Council produced one national assessment [1968]. Although the Council continues to sponsor work on water resources, the Bureau of the Census and the United States Geological Survey remain the chief producers of current macroinformation on water resources, uses, and supplies.

Forests

The prime compiler of data on forest resources is the Forest Service, which conducts a continuing survey in cooperation with different state agencies and private groups, as authorized by the McSweeney-McNary Forest Research Act of 1928. Its objective is to inventory periodically all forest lands, their extent, condition, and volume of timber and to ascertain rates of growth and depletion. State surveys of timber resources are completed each year for 10 percent of the states, and individual state reports are published as completed. About every ten years a national report is prepared providing estimates of timber resources for all states for one common year. The national reports since World War II are *Timber Resources for America's Future* (USDA, Forest Service [1958]), and *Timber Trends in the United States* (USDA, Forest Service [1965]). A later report uses 1970 as the base year (USDA, Forest Service [1974]). These reports appraise current forest land and timber resources, analyze the demand outlook for timber, and project future supplies. Survey procedures involve a combination of airphoto interpretation and ground measurements on samples of points and plots drawn for each county. Basic inventory data include acreages and volumes of standing timber by class and current rates of utilization, replacement, and growth.

The Forest Service also publishes annual reports on the demand and price situation for forest products. Quarterly reports are published on the production of major forest products, prices employment, and on trade in the forest industries of the Pacific Northwest.

Weather Indexes

For many years agricultural economists have sought ways to improve the reliability of production projections. This led to inquiry into the relationships between weather and crop yields. Historically most weather studies had been done on small plots, but in the 1950s and 1960s concern for improving policy decisions required more aggregate analysis. A number of studies dealt with the relative impact of weather and technology on aggregate crop yields.

Three general approaches were used. The first used regression analysis to relate meteorological variables and a time trend to yields. The technology trend was predetermined by the time trend. The second approach used phenological data from test plots to determine the weather impact. The residual was the technology impact. The third approach used simultaneous equations where the weather and technology variables were included in the model at the same time to determine the impact of each.

In several studies of aggregate wheat, grain sorghum, corn, and soybean yields over 1962-65, Thompson [1962, 1963a, 1963b] initially used a linear time trend to express the effects of technology on yields. Later Thompson [1966] introduced two subjective technology variables for corn, using monthly temperature and rainfall data, separately and in combinations, as weather variables. Together the weather variables explained more variation in yield than did the technology variable, leading Thompson to conclude that recent yield increases were due primarily to good weather. Hence, he expected yields to decline with more normal weather.

Oury [1965] also used a time trend as his technology variable, combining rainfall and temperature data into one weather variable to explain changes in aggregate corn yields from 1890-1927 and 1928-1956.

Phenological weather variables measure weather indirectly by observing its apparent effects on yield. The basic method for constructing the index is to use linear time trends to represent the effects of technological change on small plots (usually experimental check plots or variety tests). The ratio of observed check plot yields to trend check plot yields for a given year is then used as an index of the net impact of weather that year. The technology used on the check plot is held constant, making yield variation due largely to weather. This method was used by G. L. Johnson [1952] in a study of burley tobacco yields, by Hathaway [1955] in a study of the Michigan dry bean industry, and by Stallings [1961] in computing phenological weather indexes by crops of the United States from the early 1900s to the 1950s. Heady and Auer [1966] derived phenological indexes for a large number of field crops in most of the major producing areas. Their indexes were based on data obtained from crop nursery variety tests and hybrid test plots. The aggregated indexes were then used in a regression of state yields, adjusted for the effects of fertilizer application and variety improvement, acreage planted, weather, and time.

Shaw and Durost [1962, 1965] constructed weather indexes for corn crop reporting districts in the Corn Belt from state hybrid test data in each district. These were aggregated to state levels and used to regress the state corn yield on the index with three technological variables. The investigators concluded that most of the recent yield increase could be imputed to technological innovation rather than to generally good weather, in contrast to the conclusions of Thompson.

Perrin [1968] regressed yields simultaneously on a small number of technological variables and on a similar number of meteorological variables. All variables were measured independently. The resulting regression equations allow the imputation of historic yield changes to various weather and technological variables and provides the basis for predicting future yields if normal weather is assumed. Perrin's study included corn in Iowa and Illinois, grain sorghum in Kansas and Nebraska, and spring wheat in North Dakota. The contribution of weather and technological changes was estimated through a procedure involving derivation of aggregate production functions in which grain yield, fertilizer applied, and genetic and cultural practices were the variables for each subregion of each state. The weather variable was a modification of the drought index developed by Palmer [1962]. It is a single variable which incorporates several meteorological variables relevant to moisture stress. His results also suggested that increases in yields came mostly from improved technology, not from good weather.

The SRS has adopted phenological methods for estimating and forecasting yields in its crop estimating program. Bruce Kelly and his associates developed a variety of models to forecast yields for the major grains, potatoes, and a number of tree fruits (USDA, SRS [1964, 1975]).

Airphotos

Progress in the use of airphotos as a source of data in land utilization research has been rapid in recent years. Airphoto analysis has been especially useful in obtaining data for studies of river basins, watersheds, or other natural areas where data collected by political subdivisions may not apply and for studies of changing land use in areas where acreage information is not collected on a regular basis. Three techniques for using airphotos include direct identification, airphoto comparison analysis, and use of small-scale airphotos or airphoto index sheets to study large areas.

In direct interpretation a natural body of land such as a river floodplain is studied to identify and quantify land use by flood frequency zones and by modified frequency zones with control measures (Dill [1955]).

The use of airphoto comparison analysis of recent pictures compared with earlier coverage can provide data on changes that have taken place in land use by clearing and draining forest land, urbanization, or reversion of land to forest (Dill and Otte [1971]). This technique is particularly useful in disclosing land use changes where conflicting trends are not revealed by traditional data.

Data on land use in large areas can be obtained from small-scale airphotos in a relatively short time with a minimum of personnel and expense. A study of the entire Mississippi alluvial basin covering about 24 million acres was made by two people in six months (Frey and Dill [1971]).

The use of airphoto analysis and other sophisticated sensor devices now under development to obtain data for economic analysis is expected to increase in the United States and elsewhere (Dill [1967]). Earth resources satellites now in operation have the capability of collecting data on a wide variety of subjects including land use, plant diseases, temperatures, and pollution. The challenge in exploiting this capability lies mostly in developing techniques for interpretation and for handling the large volume of observations that are potentially possible.

Remote Sensing

As a result of three streams of technology, remote sensing has emerged as a potential source of data for agricultural economics research. First, the space program has developed vehicles to carry sensors and permit frequent or even continuous observation of crop production and land use phenomena. The Earth Resources Technology Satellite, launched by NASA in 1972, covers any given spot on the earth's surface approximately every eighteen days but permits observation only when the site is free from cloud cover. The frequency of coverage can be increased marginally by modification of the orbit and sensor design or infinitely by increasing the number of satellites. An orbit that permits a satellite to hover over a given area of the earth is possible, but the corresponding increase in altitude severely attentuates sensor capability.

The second development is in sensors. Airphoto interpretation has been used to obtain land use, forestry, and crop data of specific types and in limited situations for many years. Improved resolution, specialized narrow-band imagery, and expanded use of the infrared range of the electromagnetic spectrum have made possible many new applications of photo interpretation for data acquisition. For many types of data, use of these sensors provides real savings over acquisition by ground survey or other conventional methods. However, so long as human interpretation is required, time and labor costs will place definite economic limiations on these uses.

The third area of technology useful in remote sensing is the computer. Sensors, particularly those operating continuously from orbiting spacecraft, produce overwhelming quantities of raw observations. Using these observations to develop signatures for specific crops or other target phenomena requires considerable computer capacity. In addition, observations on each small area of the earth's surface must be codified so that it can either be displayed on a map or tabulated by country, river basin, or other desired geographic entity. This involves recording, storage, and retrieval of very large quantities of data which are expensive for the computers operating today.

Automated crop identification and measurement have been achieved experimentally and even applied on a pilot basis. The Laboratory for Applications of Remote Sensing at Purdue has used the output from a multiband spectral sensor to develop and utilize unique signatures for wheat and other selected crops in automated recognition.

Comprehensive programs for obtaining data by remote sensing are probably some years away. All the technology needed has not been developed fully, even at the research level. Beyond that is the need for development of operational programs integrated with, complementing, and supplementing present data-gathering procedures. Selected applications of remote sensing using conventional aircraft have been used for data collection, and further use of these methods seems likely in the near future. The ultimate development of remote sensing with satellites will come when one type of instrument package aboard one or more vehicles can give continuous worldwide coverage to record information for a number of purposes at the same time.

International Data

Agricultural economists elsewhere in the world have the same data interests as those in the United States. Although substantial gaps and deficiencies exist in the domestic data, much greater data gaps occur in most other countries of the world, especially in the so-called developing nations. There data of any kind are scarce, reliable data are even scarcer, and the small number of trained statisticians and economists available to gather and use good data suggests that improvements will be slow and costly.

For many years efforts have been made to gather and publish agricultural economic data for all countries of the world. The old International Institute of Agriculture made its major contribution as a collector and publisher of information about the agricultural economies of the world, but it had neither the authority nor the resources to overcome deficiencies of basic data within participating countries. Economic data relevant to international affairs are foremost among the statistical areas in need of development and refinement. Statistics on trade in agricultural commodities have improved markedly since World War II, but much less progress has been made with other types of data.

International agencies, notably the United Nations Food and Agriculture Organization (FAO), have worked diligently to acquire and improve world agricultural statistics. Symbolic of these efforts has been the decennial World Census of Agriculture.

The World Census of Agriculture

The first concerted effort toward achieving a world census of agriculture was undertaken for 1930 by the International Institute of Agriculture. It was not very successful because many countries lacked the resources and the will to conduct a census. A second attempt to get a world census was completely disrupted by World War II.

The FAO directed its initial work toward a world census of agriculture in 1950. It made a good start toward the resolution of many problems encountered in striving for comparability of data among nations and regions. These problems, which often loom large within a developed country, are even more formidable in an international setting. The preparation of definitions for units of measure and for such commonplace terms as "heifer" and "fowl" that can be understood throughout the world is very difficult. Uniform measures of land and products do not exist. Other characteristics of agriculture such as mechanical power can be quantified only in such classification terms as incidence or nonincidence. In addition, the effectiveness of the programs may be limited by uncooperative national regimes or by the lack of trained personnel in undeveloped nations. Nevertheless, patient and persistent staff work, aided and abetted by foreign aid programs of developed nations, achieved a little progress toward better world censuses in 1960 and 1970 and toward a projected census for 1980.

The FAO staff assistance, devoted to improving the standards of statistical performance in member countries, is supplemented by specialized training schools and conferences. For example, training schools up to nine months in length are regularly conducted in the United States, France, and India to train foreign nationals in census taking and administration.

Annual Country Statistics

In addition to its persistent and continuous efforts to encourage and introduce standardized census data country by country, the FAO endeavors to assist in the development of current data services useful for policy and management decisions. The results, however, have not been uniform, and the data are often not timely enough to meet intranational or international planning needs.

The FAO is not the only agency concerned with worldwide agricultural data. Other international organizations, both private and governmental, strive from time to time to improve the collection and availability of statistics. Individual countries, especially the developed countries, strive to acquire relevant data on food production, food demand, food trade, and such supplementary data as precipitation and temperature indicative of crop prospects. Remote sensing has been hailed as a solution in this regard, but much more research must be done before the potentials of space technology can be realized in statistical data gathering.

The Agency for International Development (AID) training and research programs often include a component for data gathering, analysis and dissemination. These contribute to wider recognition of the usefulness of data, especially if government leaders find that information systems can be included in applications for assistance and that data can be helpful in applications for grants, loans, or emergency assistance.

With the assumption of leadership in managing food stocks and promoting the expansion of production, the United States has had to acquire at least a modicum of a statistical base for decision making. One result of this was the *World Food Budget to 1970* (USDA, ERS [1964]); indigenous secondary data were supplemented with observations obtained through agricultural attachés. The attachés seldom had the opportunity or the resources for systematic collection of data, and their observations were often highly subjective. Nevertheless, their carefully edited data represented one of the most reliable sources of comprehensive data on the world food situation. Subsequent efforts by the ERS to quantify world food production, consumption, and trade have developed much more reliable data on world agriculture.

World Food Data

Trends in population and in food supplies throughout the world since World War II have stimulated the interest of agricultural economists and many others in information about food supplies, food demand, and trade in food commodities. Lester Brown's classic bulletin, *Man, Land and Food* (USDA, ERS [1963]), served to heighten concern over the world food situation and to focus on the relationship between world food needs and agricultural policy in the United States. Many studies and conferences since that time have altered appraisals of the world food problem, but they all served to emphasize the need for more complete and precise information. Concerns about the adequacy of relevant data have never been more urgent.

Several developments point toward much greater attention to the improvement of worldwide information on food supplies. The proliferation of publicly supported financial institutions, private foundations, and national assistance programs directed toward economic growth and the alleviation of poverty and hunger calls for better information on existing conditions. The tightening of margins between food supplies and food needs such as occurred in the mid-1960s and again in the early 1970s plus the growing concern over restraints on international trade in food further emphasize the need for better data. Each of several "world food conferences" demonstrated the need for information.

Studies of the world food situation by international agencies and others number in the hundreds. These sometimes focus on individual countries or areas and sometimes on specific commodities or problems; they sometimes try to be all inclusive and comprehensive. To try to list, summarize, or appraise such work here would be a digression. Suffice it to say that most of such work develops little new data and most suffers from incomplete, inaccurate, or inadequate data.

Rural Area Development

Rural Poverty

Socioeconomic data on the rural population received relatively little attention from agricultural economists until the mid-1950s. The data in the early studies were concerned with low-production farms (Martin [1970]) and low income in agriculture (Hendrix [1955]) with little attention to rural nonfarm data. Later studies in the 1950s and the early 1960s collected some rural nonfarm data on small scattered areas (Southern and Hendrix [1959], Henderson [1960], and Crecink and Hoover [1960]), but there was still a general dearth of data on rural poverty at the time the Economic Opportunity Act of 1964 was passed.

With the availability of the socioeconomic data from the 1960 Census of Population, efforts among agricultural economists to describe rural poverty problems increased considerably. The "poverty threshold" first developed for use by the Council of Economic Advisers had no residence or family-size differentials (A. R. Bird [1964]). The improved thresholds developed by the Social Security Administration provided agricultural economists with an opportunity to make a significant research input into policy decisions. Initially poverty thresholds included a farm differential of 40 percent on the premise that food and other farm amenities were produced on the farm at no cost. The data developed by agricultural economists to show the inequity of the differential were instrumental in the eventual reduction of the differential to 15 percent in 1969 (Bonnen [1966], Hoover and Green [1970], Madden et al. [1968]).

Other recent studies by agricultural economists have continued to add to the expanding rural poverty data bank. These include a series of studies on the typology of rural poverty (McElveen [1969], Crecink and Steptoe [1970], and Hoover and Green [1970]), broader descriptive studies (Clawson [1967], Martin [1970]), and a study of the retraining potential of the rural poor (Konyha [1971]). In addition to these special studies the 1970 Census of Population developed much new data about rural people and their welfare. These data, together with increasing exploitation of such public records as social security, promise to improve the data base for analyses of the income problems of rural people.

Rural Housing

Rural housing has been a fairly recent addition to the research interests of agricultural economists. In recent years, however, agricultural economists have begun to play an important role in pointing out significant differences between rural housing and urban housing, some of the reasons for these differences, and the impact of various housing programs.

An early contributor was G. H. Beyer of Cornell University, who gleaned information from the 1940 and 1950 Census of Housing on the relationships of quality in farm housing to income, age, race, and tenure of occupants (Beyer and Rose [1957]). A more comprehensive analysis of the 1960 data included rural nonfarm housing in addition to farm housing (Beyer [1965]). Another early effort was the study, under the leadership of Joseph H. Yeager at Auburn University, of rural housing conditions and housing finance in parts of the southeastern Cotton Belt, the Corn Belt, and the dry-land wheat areas. Although there were a few projects before 1960, organized housing research by the USDA appears to date from about 1960, when several cooperative studies of housing credit were initiated under the leadership of Lawrence A. Jones (Jones [1966], Hamlin [1970], Sargent, Davidson, and Jones [1964]).

Work on rural housing underwent a major expansion after the Economic

Development Division was organized in the ERS in 1965 and after rural housing loans became a major part of the Farmers Home Administration program in the late 1960s. One major thread of USDA research involved attempts to develop data on the status of rural housing and on the magnitude of the effort required to improve it to acceptable standards. Several USDA bulletins reflected this purpose. In another area of research the factors associated with poor housing were investigated. Studies were made in the Ozarks (Spurlock [1968]), in South Carolina (A. D. Edwards and Jones [1964], Hurst [1969]). Other work involved gathering and analyzing data on housing costs (a major study was done in cooperation with Ohio State University) and on alternatives (such as mobile homes) to conventional housing (Burnham and Jones [1969]).

Health

Agricultural economists have largely neglected health as a subject for analysis. Since 1945 only four articles about health have appeared in the American Journal of Agricultural Economics.

One study (Stillman [1949]) documented the rural health problem by examining available data on health care facilities in rural areas.

The second article (Ball and Wilson [1968]) was focused on the spatial variation in rates of health training and practice and the quality of health service available across the nation. This was a broad consideration of health manpower and related services available in rural areas. Ball and Wilson showed that rural residents with health insurance have less effective coverage because of the relative scarcity of health services in rural areas. They also demonstrated that economics could contribute substantially to insights regarding health and identified several aspects of health in need of economic analyses.

The third article (Brown [1969]) examined the response of consumers to the health hazard resulting from the use of pesticides on cranberries and its possible effect on demand for the commodity. The study dealt rather more with the effect of a health hazard on elasticity of demand than with health as such.

In the fourth article Perkinson [1969] examined the location of hospital beds in Michigan. The author tested the common presumption that the larger cities were better supplied with health facilities than rural areas. He found this to be untrue, using the number of hospital beds per 1,000 population as the unit of measure. Counties with a town of 5,000 population and located beyond convenient traveling distance from a city of 25,000 or more had more hospital beds per 1,000 population than the larger cities. Several factors believed to influence the supply of hospital beds in Michigan were discussed.

Although only four articles on rural health have appeared in the *American*

Journal of Agricultural Economics, economists have devoted substantial attention to the health status of rural people and the availability of health facilities. A number of special studies and local area studies have developed data, but no national study has generated data specifically on rural people.

Local Governments

Agricultural economists have carried on a small but fairly steady volume of research in the field of local government since World War II. These efforts have involved data collection only to the extent that data were needed to test particular hypotheses. Since 1957, however, substantial volumes of data have been available from the Census of Government and various state and local reports.

Probably the largest single focus has been on property taxes. Since the 1920s the ERS and its predecessor agencies have maintained statistical series on farm real estate taxes and on farm personal property taxes (Mathews and Bird [1970], Shapiro [1963], and Stinson, Courtney, and Bird [1969]). Real estate tax data have been based on decennial census data, updated by annual questionnaires mailed to local tax officials. Minor changes were made in methodology after World War II.

Agricultural economists at some of the agricultural experiment stations also were active. Examples include George Aull at Clemson University, who pioneered in assessment ratio studies in South Carolina, Gabbard and Cherry [1948], Heneberry and Barlowe [1962], Loftsgard, Johnson and Ostenson [1963], Pine [1956], Simmons [1949], and C. C. Taylor et al. [1960].

In the 1940s and early 1950s the emphasis was primarily on taxes paid by farmers. Bulletins were published by the USDA and other organizations estimating sales, state and federal income, and other types of tax payments by farmers (R. Bird [1955], Stocker. [1953, 1955, 1956, 1963], Stocker and Ellickson [1959]). Agricultural economists also were active in studying differential assessment laws for farmland (Hady and Stinson [1967], Hady [1970], House [1961, 1967]).

During the late 1950s and early 1960s gradual changes in emphasis occurred under the leadership of Stocker in the ERS and others. The research emphasis shifted to include work on the local government services that the farmer's taxes helped pay for and the organization of the local governments that levied the taxes and supplied the services (Hein [1960], Lutz [1961], Stinson [1967], and Stocker [1957]). Most of this work was not primarily directed at data collection, but it often produced useful data. A joint study by the USDA and Indiana University (Stoner [1967]) produced new information on the extent of cooperation among local governments in the United States. Attention was also given to the costs of providing various governmental services in units of varying sizes—a partial return to an area of active agricultural economics research in the 1930s (Shapiro [1963], Voelker [1969], and Wessel [1963]).

The growth of interest in rural economic development has resulted in a considerable expansion of work on state and local governments, but the major part of this work has not been directed specifically at the exploitation of new data sources.

The Future

Before examining some present problems with agricultural data and speculating about the future, the reader who has waded this far through a tedious manuscript deserves some comments that may place our data systems in a perspective that may not have been obvious from the previous pages. Agricultural economists in the United States during the quarter century following World War II were more fortunate than most of their colleagues elsewhere in the wealth of data at their command. Never before in the history of economics did practitioners have the means to test empirically the basic precepts of their science. Data were available (albeit not always in the exact form or detail desired) to test relationships between supply, demand, price, use of resources, incomes, and dozens of other areas of interest to economists, policy makers, and the agricultural industry). Agricultural economists owe a deep debt to such pioneers as Stine, Waugh, Bean, Ezekiel, Wells, and dozens of others in the USDA and in the land-grant colleges.

When the major body of data was being developed in the 1920s and 1930s, some of the most important questions being asked of the data and of agricultural economists had to do with the performance of farms and the welfare of farm people. The data assembled from the Census of Agriculture and many other sources were designed to help answer these questions. In recent years agricultural economists are finding the traditional systems of data to be obsolete. One reason for this is that the agricultural industry itself has changed. Farms are fewer, larger, and more specialized. Farming is more highly integrated with supply businesses and processing and marketing businesses, which are an increasingly important part of the total agricultural industry. Finally, fewer rural people farm, and fewer farmers live on farms. These trends and others are well known to agricultural economists.

Policy issues of recent years have come to revolve around the performance of the entire agricultural industry and its major sectors, not just farming, and the economic situation of rural people, not just those who farm or live on farms. Thus our traditional data systems have failed to supply the raw material needed to address many of the modern issues of concern to agricultural economists.

Agricultural economists have become concerned about the availability, adequacy, and relevancy of data. Under various titles the need for more and better data has been the subject of at least one session at the annual meetings of the AAEA in the past several years. Some typical session titles were "Adapting Data to New Conditions" (1958), "Statistical Bottlenecks to Econometric Analysis" (1964), and "Improvements Needed in Statistics for Making Policy and Program Decisions" (1966). (See Wells [1958], Schaller [1964], and AAEA [1972].)

Despite this apparent concern over the years, it is interesting that the centerpiece of the statistical session of the 1972 annual meeting was a paper entitled "Our Obsolete Data Systems: New Directions and Opportunities" (AAEA [1972]) the report of the AAEA Committee on Economic Statistics. It provides a view of some major deficiencies in our statistical data systems.

"These agenda items overlap considerably but can be reduced to a general concern about obsolescence in older data systems, and most frequently, to a need for new and better data.

"1. Developing a new theoretical basis for obsolete data systems is an urgent necessity. The most clearly obsolete concepts are our demographic ideas. . . .

"2. Better measures of social well-being are needed whether in health, education, personal safety, housing, income and employment, or leisure and recreation. . . .

"3. Program evaluation is an increasingly strategic need to which our data systems are now poorly prepared to respond. To the traditional program management emphasis on efficiency has been added a growing concern for the equity and general social performance—not only of public programs but also of some of our society's private institutions such as the medical delivery system.

"4. The income and asset distributions of rural society need to be explored. . . .

"8. Regional and local area development data systems should be developed. . . .

"9. We need better statistics on nonfood and fiber sector economic activity in rural areas. . . .

"It is quite clear that the greatest flaws in our data systems arise from our failure to conceptualize social problems in a systematic manner and to match this with equal concern for the design of statistical systems to measure social system phenomena. . . .

"Agricultural economists have a major intellectual obligation to contribute to the development of an adequate data system for social needs. This is a must if the rural areas of the nation are to become viable communities of reasonable growth and if rural people are ever to attain levels of human welfare comparable to the rest of society. The unique characteristics of rural society are not likely to be recognized in the construction of a national system of social statistics unless rural social scientists take an early and active role in the intellectual investments leading to development of those data systems—a process already well under way."

The reader should not conclude from the above quotations that all is both wrong and hopeless. Such is not the case. Our agricultural data systems have served very well in the past; in fact, agricultural economists have been envied by other social scientists for the wealth of data they have at their disposal. But social and economic changes have occurred and will continue to occur, making our traditional systems in truth "obsolete."

As we have noted, the changes include broadening of the questions which we address to ourselves. When our present data systems were developed, most of the questions dealt with the efficiency of farms, the productivity of farms in the aggregate, and the welfare of farmers. Our data served fairly well for these purposes. Now, however, we are increasingly concerned with the performance of the industry. We are concerned with the capacity of this industry to provide the nation's supply of food and fiber at reasonable cost and with the exportable supplies that help pay for our imports. We are concerned with the relationships among segments within the industry and between it and other industries and the national economy. We are concerned with how the industry uses our nation's resouces and how income is divided among participants in the industry. At present out data do not address these questions very well.

Data systems must change over time with the changing structure of economic research. On the demand side, there has been a shift in relative emphasis from microeconomic or "firm" research to macroeconomic or "social" research. We are realizing, as Shaffer [1968] expressed it, that we have been overly concerned about the efficiency of an already fairly efficient peapacking plant when there are more pressing social problems. Emerging social problems such as providing adequate public services, environmental quality, and energy supplies require more aggregative economic analysis of the whole or major sectors of our society.

The changing structure for economic research in agriculture is related to developments in the scientific method, to the increasing costs of research, and to technological developments in automatic data processing. The early emphasis was on farm management and the collection of data in keeping with the inductive scientific philosophy associated with Francis Bacon and later in American agriculture with George Warren and the empiricism of the Cornell school.

Over time, our general research philosophy has sought equal treatment to all substages of research in a cyclical inductive-deductive scientific method. As described by Cohen and Nagel [1934], modern scientific method involves five generally recognized substages of research—recognizing and defining the problem, formulating a hypothesis, designing empirical procedures, assembling and analyzing the data, and interpreting the findings. Completion of one research cycle often leads to new problems and the need for new data. Data requirements are interrelated with other substages of research and are specified more in terms of a preconceived body of theory and applied to a particular research problem in the form of a cause and effect hypothesis. As progressive research cycles have been completed, a model of technical and economic relationships in agriculture has evolved and data needs have become more systematic, additive, and recurring.

Public support for research and development in agriculture is diminishing in relative terms while salary and other costs are increasing (Hathaway [1969]). As the cost structure for research resources and the demand for aggregate social research increase, economizing principles must be applied. Research resources, including data generating activities, will be combined along an expansion path of least cost combination.

Another major development is the advance in automatic data processing and accompanying growth in simulation and systems analysis. This has encouraged the evolution of a more complete scientific method involving research cycling which with each round becomes more complex, more realistic, and increasingly sophisticated with respect to interrelationships between all substages of research. It also points up the need for more research requiring not only net social benefit or macroeconomic analysis but also connecting links to disaggregated levels such as firms, individuals, and households. Large-scale systems analysis enables an additive and integrative approach to these research needs and the simulation of many relevant alternatives with respect to technical and economic uncertainties and policy choices. Advances in automatic data processing technology, involving both hardware and software, constitute a major unrealized positive shift in the supply curve for economic research. Originally computers were used merely to replace routine and costly manual data processing and storage. But as more sophisticated economic systems are translated into machine language and are combined with data systems, the researcher's imagination provides the only real limiting factor to the size and complexity of data and analytical systems.

Some attributes of data systems that proved essential in the past are very likely to continue so in the future. Data are an essential ingredient in decision making, whether the decision is based on barn-door arithmetic or the most sophisticated and computerized analytical system. The value imputed to data per se derives from their use by management in private enterprise, by government policy makers, and by the general public as consumers and voters. The purpose of a data system is to make the desired data accessible to the decision makers.

Technical Developments in Agricultural Estimates Methodology

Harry C. Trelogan, C. E. Caudill,
Harold F. Huddleston, William E. Kibler,
and Emerson Brooks
*Statistical Reporting Service, United
States Department of Agriculture*

History of Methodology for Agricultural Statistics before 1940

It is only in recent years that farm data, although found in ancient records (for example, in Egyptian scrolls), have been developed to represent large areas or nations in quantitative terms. Even in the United States, now in the forefront in applying farm data to economic and political problems, the development of an information system for the collection, processing, dissemination, and interpretation of agricultural statistics has been a slow process. Here we will characterize briefly the period before World War II, noting the progress in crop and livestock estimates that did occur, before dealing more comprehensively with the postwar period when the application of modern statistical technology was accelerated.

The statistical base for an agricultural information system evolved in response to national development needs. Its growth and effective contributions to development were favored by recognition of its value by political leaders, accompanied by scientific progress that facilitated the collection and analysis of the necessary data. Farmer George Washington, with a strong aversion to urban merchants who obtained market advantage by acquiring and holding supply information, left a legacy of beneficial influence. Government support for making market information public began in 1839. Progress came more rapidly during periods of national adversity when the availability of farm products was of crucial importance.

The Civil War created an early opportunity in this direction. Abraham Lincoln sought to persuade the British to stay out of the conflict by calling their attention to the prospective food supplies from the North, which he was confident would compare favorably with the more obvious supply of cotton from the South. Arrangements for crop estimates were made quickly in 1862 in the newly created office of Commissioner of Agriculture. These estimates proved their worth, laying the foundation for a strong farm statistical program that was founded in the tax system with a specific appropriation in 1865. Subsequent crisis periods—panics caused by needs for foreign exchange, business depressions, droughts and floods, and two world wars—created demands for better supply information, based on reliable statistics. Only the highlights of the technological revolution in statistical methods that brought the United States to its present preeminent position in this work can be treated here.

Originally the problems consisted mainly of obtaining nationwide data on the acreage and production of the major grain crops and numbers of livestock. Census data were adequate for the development of supply weights by production areas. Since the farms within a given production area were similar in many respects, an alert observer could develop acceptable production estimates, and the inexpensive and dependable mail service could be used for data collection from both farmers and county agents.

Data were obtained from farms by crop reporters in every county, usually in terms of percentages of the previous year. These data were brought together for state estimates that in turn were combined in Washington to make national estimates. Statistical reporters in each state were expected to be familiar enough with growing areas and conditions to be able to exercise judgment regarding the reasonableness of the resulting estimates. Examination of the data by experienced statisticians led to national estimates that were essentially summarizations of state estimates.

For several decades great dependence was placed on human judgments in arriving at the single best estimate for each item, for each state, for each growing season, and for annual national estimates. Crops and livestock were followed through the markets to export or consumption as a means of verifying each estimate. As more and more evidence was accumulated, year-end estimates were revised. Unless substantial revisions were clearly needed beforehand, the policy was to examine all estimates at the end of the following year for possible revisions so that the annual estimates became the bases for comparisons in the next year. Each item was examined for compatibility with the next Census of Agriculture when those data became available.

The Agricultural Census, which was developed outside the USDA in 1840, was designed to provide a full count of American farms taken at ten-year intervals (later changed to five-year intervals). Even though the completeness of the censuses—which were taken by temporary political employees until 1960—varied greatly, they provided more detailed farm data than any other source, and they were used to true up crop and livestock estimates based on sample data. Experience showed that errors in a low census estimate tended to be compounded in subsequent years because of a cumulative downward bias in the annual estimates. With a ten-year interval between censuses the error could become substantial at times. For example, the 1899 USDA estimate of corn acreage was 82,109,000 acres compared with 94,914,000, or nearly 16 percent more, reported two years later by the census for 1899. The USDA estimate of wheat acreage was 44,055,000, whereas the census figure was 52,589,000 or 19 percent more. Consequently, a corps of special field agents was created at the turn of the century, in part to overcome this known bias of farm crop reporters.

In 1905 the Crop Reporting Board was established, with substantial representation from the field workers, to apply group judgment in making the best estimates from all sources of data. The statistical methods developed out of the experience of men with little formal training during these early decades of crop estimates were generally creditable.

Since 1900 when the Census used electric machines for the first time to tabulate part of the agricultural data, the Census Bureau has held a position of leadership in developing mechanical and electronic data handling capabilities. It played a pioneering role in the development of Hollerith (punch card) machines and eventually electronic computers.

USDA crop estimators combined returns from township reports, county reporters, state agents, and field agents (each covering several states) but changed methods little despite an influx of suggestions during World War I. Many ideas were explored but rejected, including the possibility of expressing condition reports in terms other than percentages of "normal," the recruitment of county agents as reporters, and the use of threshers' returns for grain. Other ideas were adopted, such as the use of round numbers for weights by counties, the development of quantitative estimates as the basis for forecasts, the reporting of intentions to plant and to breed—all of which gradually gained wide acceptance. Two innovations of lasting benefit were the introduction of Civil Service appointments for statisticians in 1914 to assure the availability of qualified staff and state cooperative arrangements in 1917 to reduce confusion and to strengthen the estimates especially in states that had annual state farm censuses. The number of reporters and the number of crops reported both continued to increase, and many special surveys were undertaken during World War I.

In the postwar period expansion of the information system continued with greater stress on prices; a gradual transition from reporting "judgment data" to "individual farm data" for acreage began and was in full use by 1926. In 1924 a Rural Mail Carrier Survey for acreages began, to be taken in September of each year. Data on intentions to plant, collected earlier in each year, were converted into "Prospective Plantings" by the removal of bias.

A movement to give the staff members statistical training which emphasized sampling and correlation took hold. Several types of graphic analyses were developed in the late 1920s, based on ratios of currently reported acreage to the acreage reported for the same farm the previous year, the acreage reported in the census year, and the total acreage in the farm. These analyses revealed different types of bias ocurring for such items as cash crops—biases that needed to be taken into account in forecasting. During the same period several researchers in other parts of the Bureau of Agricultural Economics developed new statistical techniques that proved to be very useful. The multiple curvilinear correlation technique developed by Ezekiel [1924] was one of these. C. R. Sarle simultaneously developed graphic methods to reduce the laborious process for crop estimates, and Bean [1930] commented on the graphic method.

Objective measures for estimating acreages were explored including counting the fields planted to particular crops from train windows along specified stretches of track. The number of telephone poles bordering each field indicated size. In 1923 this approach was adapted by installing meters on automobiles to measure road frontage bordering fields of specified crops. Later yield forecasts were checked by counting plants or cotton bolls to get objective checks on judgment data. Condition reports gave way to forecast yields per acre read from regression charts indicating past relationships. Allowances had to be made for such observed phenomena as potential boll weevil damage in cotton, weather conditions, and acreage abandonment during the growing period. Similar innovations were introduced for fruits and vegetables to respond to needs for quantitative data by specialized areas of production.

Livestock estimation came in for special attention with the postwar price decline. The Rural Mail Carrier Survey, in which the carrier put an inquiry card in the mailboxes of ten growers on his route, was initiated in 1922 for a pig survey. This proved to be a practical means of getting an acceptable sample, and it was extended to other livestock and livestock products (for example, milk produced yesterday) for many years afterward. Historic questions (number this year and last year) and questions on intentions to breed were perfected and widely adopted. Data on livestock movements were gathered from numerous sources, along with births and deaths, enabling estimators to maintain balance sheets by states.

Beginning in 1925 the Census of Agriculture has been taken every five years, thus reducing cumulative error problems in crop estimating. Several decades passed before the advocates of getting at least benchmark data by sampling methods were heard. These demands were heard after mail censuses failed to achieve close enough approximations to full counts and after annual sample-estimate benchmarks had been adopted by the USDA for crop estimates.

Annual prices received for agricultural products in local markets have been reported since 1866. Data on monthly prices for crops were first collected in 1908, on monthly prices for meat animals and livestock in 1910. Needs arising during World War I stimulated the collection of data on prices paid by farmers, first from the farmers but later from suppliers, and also stimulated reports on the supply and demand for farm labor. Later refinements included obtaining local farm product prices from elevators, mills, and dealers, abandoning the mid-month price for milk in favor of averages for the month as a whole, substituting market season averages for December 1 prices for crops, and realigning crop reporting districts to coincide more closely with marketing areas.

Index numbers have been used to express changes in prices for crops, for livestock, and for all farm products. Growth of the parity concept stimulated interest as the concept became embodied in farm policy legislation. Such developments called for close attention to the maintenance of adequate samples and to index number construction with minimum bias. In general, the Laspeyres formula was used.

The twin emergencies of depression and drought during teh 1930s presented many new demands and problems to crop estimators and diverted attention from recognized technical research needs. Nevertheless, the quest for data on weather and weather forecasting with respect to crop forecasting continued. By the late thirties, however, researchers were sensing the futility of weather analysis and recognizing other means of predicting crops. New approaches were sought, but World War II intervened, disrupting their development.

Technical Developments in Agricultural Estimates Methodology, 1940-50

During the 1940s technical developments in the Division of Agricultural Statistics occurred in all aspects of its work—data collection, tabulation, analysis, publication, and dissemination. As American industry expanded its operations to provide the vast quantities of war matériel required by Britain and France, the number of workers available to American farm operators sharply decreased. Consequently Agricultural Estimates services were requested to expand and improve farm employment information. By the fall of 1941 the decision had been made to set up large-scale farm labor enumerative surveys, using a probability sample based on areas of land throughout the country.

The principal technical problem was how to associate farms with selected sample areas. If data were obtained for all farms with *any* land inside the sample segment, large farms would be overrepresented. If only farms with *all* their land inside the segment were enumerated, small farms would be overrepresented. After considerable study it was decided to designate a "headquarters" for each farm with land inside the sample segment; if the headquarters was inside the segment, data for that farm would be used in the analysis. Enumerators were given detailed criteria for determining farm headquarters:

1. With only one occupied or unoccupied dwelling on the farm, the dwelling is the headquarters.

2. With two or more dwellings and the operator living on the farm, the operator's dwelling is the headquarters.

3. With two or more dwellings and the operator living off the farm, the dwelling of greatest value is the headquarters.

4. With no dwelling but with a building on the farm, the building is the headquarters. With two or more buildings, the one of greatest value is the headquarters.

5. With no buildings on the farm, the main entrance is the headquarters. The main entrance is the point where the farm operator usually turns off a public road, private road, trail, or path to the farm he operates. If a farm with no buildings is composed of two or more separate tracts of land, the headquarters for the farm is the main entrance to the tract with the greatest value.

6. With no buildings on the farm and no point regarded as the main entrance, then the farm headquarters is the northwest corner of the tract with the greatest value.

Later, when segments had been delineated in towns and cities, the operator's residence served as the headquarters and the other categories were no longer needed.

As demands increased for additional data on a wider range of subjects, a plan evolved for the creation of a nationwide sample from which subsamples could be drawn for probability area surveys in order to collect data on almost any phase of American agriculture. The result was the establishment in 1944 at Iowa State University of the "Master Sample of Agriculture" as a joint venture with the Division of Agricultural Statistics and the Bureau of the Census. As finally constituted, the Master Sample was a scientifically drawn sample of about 67,000 areas of land, each area having natural boundaries (as far as possible) and each containing on the average the headquarters of five farms, making a total of approximately 300,000 farms or roughly 5 percent of the estimated 6,000,000 farms in the United States at that time. The sample segments varied in size from less than a square mile in Indiana to over a hundred square miles in Nevada. The sample (1/18 of the segments) was drawn in a systematic fashion with a random starting point. Thus, every acre of land in each of the 3,000 counties in the United States had a known chance of being included in the Master Sample, which was subdivided into three major divisions: (1) incorporated towns and cities, (2) unincorporated places, and (3) open country. The sampling rate of 1/18 rather than 1/20 (5%) resulted from an early plan to draw one of each 18 sections or one-half of a township. A 5-percent sample was considered necessary to provide state acreage estimates of major crops with acceptable sampling errors of around 6 percent.

Master Sample segments were used by the Census Bureau in connection with the 1945 Census of Agriculture. Probably the first subsample drawn for actual use was the so-called 101 County General Purpose Sample. The following procedure was used in drawing the sample:

1. All counties in the United States were classified into twenty groups on the basis of major type of farming region (corn, cotton, dairy, general and self-sufficient, range livestock, western specialty wheat, and residual) and major geographic region (Northeast, North Central, South, and West).

2. The result was twenty groups of counties, with each group wholly within one major type of farming region and within one major geographic region.

3. The twenty groups were subdivided into 101 strata (with about 60,000 farms in each stratum) by using component indexes; approximately twelve Census of Population and Census of Agriculture items (such as demographic farm characteristics, farm labor force, county characteristics, and household welfare items) were combined, by using two or three different weighting systems on the twelve variables, into two or three component indexes (Haygood [1945]; Haygood and Bernert [1945]); Hansen, Hurwitz, and Madow [1953, vol. 1, pp. 387-390]).

4. From each of the 101 strata one county was selected by the use of random numbers, so that the probability of a county being chosen was proportional to the number of farms in that county.

The 101 County General Purpose Sample was designed to provide an efficient national sample that would be representative of major type of farming regions. Within these regions it would be representative of certain important socioeconomic variables of the region. It was not designed to be representative of individual states.

For the special farm labor enumerative surveys made in March, May, and September 1945, the 101 County General Purpose Sample was augmented by an additional 57 counties selected by the same procedure. Special segments were developed in the 158 counties for the wage surveys with each containing about five farm headquarters.

In an attempt to provide some of the economic data needed on agriculture in the United States, surveys of agriculture were made in April, July, and October 1945 and in January 1946. Interviews were obtained from about 2,800 farmers each quarter. The 101 County General Purpose Sample was used for these surveys. Although the results were of limited direct use, the surveys clearly represented the type needed to provide answers to the multitude of economic questions facing USDA officials and other decision makers and analysts. Not until the 1970s would there be a definite program of early quarterly surveys to lay the groundwork and to provide answers of sufficient scale to cope with the technical problems involved.

In 1946 the Division of Special Farm Statistics was established in Agricultural Estimates specifically to inaugurate a program of periodic enumerative surveys. The first of these (January, 1947) was an enumerative survey of 15,000 farms associated with a selection of Master Sample segments in 800 counties. This survey initiated the economical practice of using a short questionnaire for basic items and a long questionnaire for data on additional questions. Other innovations were made after careful pretesting in the field. The system of state supervisors, part-time district supervisors, and local enumerators—a system that had been largely developed in the course of farm employment surveys during World War II—was expanded and improved for the January 1947 enumerative survey and other surveys.

The varied techniques and procedures used by Agricultural Estimates developed out of the willingness of the staff to undertake unusual surveys such as the series of enumerative and objective yield surveys made in 1949 and 1950. The governors of Virginia and North Carolina got into a friendly argument over which state had recorded the greatest gains in corn yields in the previous ten years. The Agricultural Estimates offices in Washington and in the two states, in cooperation with their respective state colleges of agriculture, conducted special enumerations and field counts to decide the matter. The results indicated that Virginia was the winner in both years. A probability sample of areas of land in all but a few urban counties in each state resulted in an enumeration of 2,400 of the 173,000 farms in Virginia and 3,300 of the 287,000 farms in North Carolina. This was one of the earliest attempts to make objective counts of corn on farms selected by a probability sample of land areas on a state basis. In the first year the responsibility for field operations in Virginia was divided between two agencies and the results demonstrated the advisability of avoiding such arrangements.

Another survey that added to the accumulating technical skills of Agricultural Estimates was the survey made of farm housing in 1950. Observations, measurements, and interview information were obtained on some 20,000 farms in 382 counties in 45 states. In the South pictures were taken of each house in the sample segments. Because of the "closed season" on field surveys between March 15 and May 15 when the federal Census was being taken in the field, the housing survey was started in the southern tier of states from New Jersey to California on February 20 and in the remaining states on May 15.

Beginning in about 1944 it became necessary to obtain approval of the Division of Statistical Standards of the Bureau of the Budget for the purpose and procedures of any survey made by a federal agency in which nine or more people would be contacted. This regulation forced Agricultural Estimates to give careful consideration to the purpose, subject matter, questionnaire design, sampling plan, field procedures, and analytical methodology for its projects, especially for enumerative and objective yield surveys. Although obtaining clearance from the Bureau of the Budget was often frustrating, the result was an improved product. It also resulted in the upgrading of the technical competence of the staff in survey planning, questionnaire design, sampling techniques, operating procedures, and statistical analysis. In 1946, for the first time, individuals were hired because of their special talents in formulating survey inquiries. The Division of Agricultural Statistics sent out annually about ten million questionnaires, and after 1944 additional attention was given to their construction and use with an undoubted improvement in their effectiveness.

Technical Advances in Agricultural Statistical Methodology, 1950-70

Building primarily on concepts and methodology developed and used for special surveys on an ad hoc basis between 1930 and 1950, the statistical methodology used for crop and livestock estimates underwent dramatic changes during the two decades following 1950. Pressure for these changes came from several sources, among them the congressional investigation of the 1951 cotton estimates and new developments in automatic data processing.

The congressional investigation highlighted the need for updating the methodology used for crop and livestock estimates and led to increased funding to implement new procedures as they were developed. Following the investigation a long-range plan was prepared for the agricultural estimates program of the USDA. The plan had four objectives, commonly referred to as Project A (on acreage, yield, and production and livestock inventories), Project B (on farm prices), Project C (on data handling methods), and Project D (on new or additional types of estimates).

Project A contained the plan for meeting the most fundamental needs of the estimating program, and at the same time it provided the framework for implementing the other projects. Consequently this part of the overall plan received the most attention during the 1950s and 1960s. Project A was most concerned with the implementation of a nationwide probability system of surveys which would provide independent unbiased estimates with known precision. The system was designed to use the Master Sample area frame developed during the 1940s at Iowa State University (King and Jessen [1945]). A probability sample of about 17,000 area sampling units averaging about one square mile in size was designed to strengthen state and national crop and livestock estimates. This sample was fully implemented for the forty-eight contiguous states by 1965. The results of studies conducted during the 1950s were used to modify and improve procedures as the implementation process evolved. These studies revealed serious deficiencies in the available area sampling frame for the western and more urbanized eastern states, leading to the construction of a new land use area frame in these states (Huddleston [1965]). The work was completed by 1965 and provided a major resource for sampling United States agriculture. By 1978 new land use area frames will be operational in each of the forty-eight contiguous states.

Most of the major technical advances in agricultural estimating during the 1950s were directly related to progress on the implementation of probability sampling. The new system provided for (1) the use of area sampling in continuing operational surveys, (2) the combined use of list and area sampling for agricultural surveys, (3) crop yield forecasting based on probability samples of fields, (4) the use of cross-sectional surveys of plant characteristics in developing yield models, and (5) the refinement of "crop cutting" techniques for estimating crop yields.

Area sampling, although used in a limited way before 1950, was viewed by many as being too expensive for a continuing system of surveys. Arnold King, one of the developers of the Master Sample Frame at Iowa State during the 1940s, once stated that he went into private survey work because he could see no possibility that area frame methodology would ever be used in the USDA crop and livestock estimates program. Many improvements and innovations were made in this methodology as it was implemented. We have already mentioned the development of a new frame based on land use strata. Other significant changes included the use of smaller sampling units than those visualized when the Master Sample Frame was constructed. This change, combined with use of the "closed segment" estimator, reduced survey costs with only minimal increases in sampling variance (Hendricks, Searls, and Horvitz [1964]).

Earlier surveys revealed the susceptibility of area sampling to the bias introduced by the "extreme value" or "outlier" problem, particularly for livestock characteristics. This problem was especially troublesome in state estimates because of the relatively large changes in level of estimates it caused from survey to survey (Searls [1963]). Use of "censored" or "truncated" estimators partially solved this problem, but the primary solution came from the use of a list frame in combination with the area sample. The list frame contained the relatively few livestock and poultry operators within each state who were classified as "large." This procedure enabled the sample to cover, with a very small sample of operators, a large part of the population to be estimated, and it stabilized the level of estimates by reducing sample variance at a relatively low cost.

Crop Yield Estimates and Forecasts

The area sample provided for the first time a probability sample of fields for which data could be collected from farmers to generate independent estimates of crop yields (Hendricks [1963]). With the development and introduction of objective yield models for forecasting this sample of fields is now used only for estimates at or after harvest.

Project A plans heavily emphasized the improvement of early season yield forecasts for major crops such as corn, cotton, soybeans, and wheat. The greatest contributions to yield estimating during the two decades following 1950 were the development and operational use of objective forecast models based on actual plant measurements and the use of very small sample plots for preharvest observations and eventual harvest. Objective yield forecast models based on cross-sectional surveys of plant characteristics (number of plants per acre, number, size, and weight of fruit, number of nodes) were developed between 1950 and 1970. Data for running these models are obtained from a probability sample of fields enumerated in the area sample. Within each field small randomly located plots are estimated early in the growing season. These plots are visited once each month to obtain plant counts and measurements until the crop is mature. At this time the plots are harvested and the production is weighed to obtain an estimate of biological yield. To estimate the yield actually harvested by the farmer, a gleaning survey is conducted in the same fields to estimate harvest loss. The net yield is obtained by subtracting the harvest loss from the estimate of biological yield.

The use of very small plots was a major advance in estimating crop yields based on "crop-cutting" techniques. "Crop-cutting" surveys for estimating yields were in use before 1950, but the early surveys usually involved the harvest of entire fields. The procedure was generally applied only in areas where an ample supply of cheap labor was available, which was not the case in the United States. Small plots, on which data collection is relatively inexpensive, can lead to biased estimates unless very precise, well-defined procedures are followed regarding what to include. With wheat plots of about .0001 acres, the inclusion of one additional wheat plant from outside the plot will cause an upward bias of 10,000 in plant population per acre. A major training effort was required to assure that counts and measurements were as precise as possible. In fact, all of the changes in methodology following 1950 have required significant increases in training. Today, approximately one-fourth of the survey budget is devoted to training.

Although most of the early advances in techniques in the United States were associated with the area sample approach which required data collection by personal interviews, some attention was devoted to probability mail surveys, particularly with regard to minimizing bias as a result of nonresponse. Procedures developed for handling this problem are discussed by Hendricks [1949].

Multiple Frame Estimation Theory

Surveys involving more than one sampling frame had been used before 1950, but little theory had been developed for two or more frames in a single survey design. Cooperative agreements between the Statistical Reporting Service and H. O. Hartley led to the development of theory for multiple frame sampling (Hartley [1962]). Beginning with the development of "large operator" lists in the Project A area sample, this methodology based on relatively complete lists of all livestock producers is now used as a second major system of probability surveys for livestock and poultry estimates. Also, quarterly probability surveys to obtain farm labor and wage rate data have replaced the monthly nonprobability surveys that previously served this purpose. These surveys include a list of known employers of agricultural labor in conjunction with an area sample. The area sample estimates that proportion of the population not covered by the list frame. Since the lists used for these surveys are not constructed to contain all farms, extension of this methodology to other surveys has been limited; however, a major effort is currently under way (to be completed by 1978) to build and maintain a list of *all* farm operators. This will enable the use of multiple frame sampling for practically all major surveys included in the agricultural estimates work of the USDA.

Advances in Automatic Data Processing

Paralleling the development in statistical theory and methodology was the rapid change after 1950 in the methods for processing data. All of the changes in agricultural estimating methodology since 1950 are highly dependent on the capabilities of the modern computer for data analysis and reduction. Beginning with a small first-generation computer in 1958, statistical work has employed each new generation of computers as they have evolved. Today, data processing for agricultural estimates involves a network, with each state statistical office and the Washington office tied directly to the same computer. This network enables rapid data transmission between the field and Washington and also provides large-scale computing capabilities to each state statistical office.

Future Possibilities for Technological Advances

Work is now under way in two areas which will have a major impact on agricultural statistical methodology by 1990. One area is the collection of data by satellite (remote sensing). The other area involves the development of techniques for physiological crop modeling, employing environmental as well as plant characteristic variables. Complete details on how the research in these areas will be used are not now available, but it is already clear that these methods are potentially of great value in improving crop acreage and production estimates (Ray and Huddleston [1976], Arkin, Vanderlip, and Ritchie [1976]).

Assessment of the Current Agricultural Data Base: An Information System Approach

James T. Bonnen
Professor of Agricultural Economics
Michigan State University

It is a capital mistake to theorize before one has data.

SIR ARTHUR CONAN DOYLE

The discovery of facts . . . depends at least in part on concepts, assumptions, and inferences which can only be defended with reference to normative presumptions.

MARC J. ROBERTS

If there is no "given" in experience, then there is no difference between deduction and induction.

C. W. CHURCHMAN

In 1969 the American Agricultural Economics Association established the Committee on Economic Statistics to evaluate questions that were being raised about the quality and reliability of certain types of agricultural data. In cooperation with the Statistical Reporting Service (SRS) and the Economic Research Service (ERS) of the Department of Agriculture different elements of the agricultural data base were examined (AAEA [1972], Hildreth [1975], Bonnen [1975], Brandow [1976]). The committee worked with many government, university, business, professional, and foundation groups in contributing to a widening sense of the current deficiencies and future needs of the agricultural data base. Instability and uncertainty in the world food situation since 1973 have made the adequacy of information on food and agriculture an urgent worldwide concern.

Note: This paper has been adapted from two articles by the author, who wishes to express his gratitude to the *American Journal of Agricultural Economics* (Bonnen [1974]) and the Agricultural Development Council (Bonnen [1976]) for permission to reprint substantial portions of those articles. The critical assistance of a number of reviewers is acknowledged in the original articles. The brief discussion of the Census of Agriculture, which has not been published before, was reviewed by the Bureau of Census and by Karl Wright and Eldon Weeks. The author is responsible for any errors or misinterpretations that may remain. The research for this paper was financed by Michigan Agricultural Experiment Station Project 991.

386

The Current State of Our Information Systems

The AAEA Committee on Economic Statistics concluded that in those instances in which early agricultural data series were not performing as well as they had in earlier years, the problem most frequently was a growing obsolescence in the concepts which the data system attempted to measure (AAEA [1972]). Some of these concepts, such as the idea of a farm, are so old and so much a part of our historical tradition that we hardly think of them as concepts at all. But the idea of the "family farm," with all its value and organizational assumptions, constitutes the central concept around which most of our food and fiber statistics are designed and collected. Yet it has become an increasingly obsolete representation of the reality of the food and fiber section. The concept guided the early development of agricultural data systems especially during their greatest period of growth in the 1920s and 1930s. The structure of the food and fiber industry today only vaguely resembles the structure that prevailed at that time. The world has changed and the concept has not.[1]

Conceptual Obsolescence in Agricultural Data

The data systems which constitute the agricultural data base of the United States are among the oldest in the federal statistical establishment. The first Census of Agriculture was taken in 1840. Only the censuses of population and manufactures are older. The Department of Agriculture was established in 1862, and by the last quarter of the nineteenth century it was collecting data for many purposes. The United States agricultural data system was given its modern form during the period of the Great Depression, which in agriculture extended from the 1920s until World War II. It was during this period that the system extended its capability beyond that of simply counting things such as agricultural output and acreage by crop, farm numbers, and farm population. Out of this period came the basic concepts underlying the modern usage in farm income and prices and the social and economic accounting capability of the present agricultural information system. The chief focus at that time was the income or welfare of farmers, and a one-to-one relationship was generally assumed to exist between a farm and a farm family. The modern institutional and organizational form of the federal agencies that operate these agricultural information systems also was created during the 1920s and 1930s. There have been modifications, but the general purposes and administrative structure of the system remain fundamentally the same.

Much of our agricultural data base is far more accurate today than the same type of data in the past. Most of these improved data are based on concepts that are biological or physical and have not changed or have changed little. Examples would be the number of cattle and pigs and the acreage and yields of potatoes or cotton produced. The great improvement in accounting, measurement, and data-processing capability over the last thirty years has combined with conceptual stability to increase the quality of some data. Thus, despite the criticism they receive, modern crop and livestock production estimates, with their biological and physical concept base, tend to be far better statistics than they were fifty or even ten years ago.

Certain statistics based on social science concepts have also retained most of their reliability and in some cases have actually been improved. This tends to be the case for food and fiber statistics in areas where technological and organizational changes have not been rapid. For example, measures of farm production of wheat and most cereals appear to have lost little in conceptual reliability while gaining much in reliability of measurement. Grain prices are another matter. At the other end of the spectrum, where change in the food and fiber sector has been most extreme, statistics for broiler production on farms are weak and broiler prices at the farm level have become nearly impossible to collect or interpret. In poultry and eggs and in many fruit and vegetable products, contracting and vertical integration of both inputs and outputs have undermined, if not destroyed, the traditional concept of the farm which underlies production and marketing statistics. The discovery of beef prices has also grown more difficult and the data ambiguous. Price-spread data present even greater difficulties (Brandow [1976]). Data on other livestock and on cotton, tobacco, peanuts, and other commodities fall between these two extremes.

Conceptual obsolescence in data is of two types. It can occur not only because of changes in the organization and nature of the food and fiber industry, as just described, but also because the agenda of food and fiber policy (public and private) shifts drastically, as it has recently, changing the questions which the information system is expected to answer. When the questions change, it is almost always found that the conceptual base of some data, especially secondary data, is not a fully appropriate representation and also that some data critical to the new questions are not even being collected. When normative or positive change occurs either in the object being represented by data or in the environment of the object, some degree of conceptual obsolescence is almost certain to follow.

Recent major examples of conceptual obsolescence of data arising from changes in the environment of agriculture can be seen in the entirely new questions which agricultural economists are asked to answer today, as a consequence of new values held and new positive knowledge about the environment, the energy economy, and the world food situation. The overall agenda of urgent agricultural policy issues has changed a great deal since the Great

Depression when the better part of our present data system was designed and built. Some older data have been conceptually redesigned to respond to new questions, but by and large we have "made do," fiddling with different definitions of the same concept. Thus, for example, the farm has been periodically redefined in recent agricultural censuses, but the concept itself has slowly become obsolete in so many uses that no matter how sensible the new definition we still measure something that in some major degree no longer exists.

Farm income is an example of both types of conceptual obsolescence. While improvements have been made in the concept and in the accounting rules which make operational the farm income concept, we still fail to net out certain expenses and assets and we miss some income flows entirely (Weeks [1971a], Carlin and Smith [1973], Simunek [1976], Hildreth [1975]). Changing the design and implementing the farm income concept are difficult and are often distorted by the congressional political imperatives of the day. Farm income data are still inconsistent with the current conceptual design of national income accounting (AAEA [1972]).

Farm input and output measures have long exhibited many conceptual deficiencies, even though some improvements have been made periodically. As the American farm became industrialized, specialization spun off many production, processing, and marketing functions from the farm to agricultural business firms. As a consequence, agriculture long ago ceased to be just farms. We still lack an adequate paradigm with which to describe and categorize a modern food and fiber industry and its subsectors and to provide a general conceptual basis for sector statistics. We do not, for example, have an integrated and consistent set of descriptors of the size and productivity of the food sector or its social performance.

The Census of Agriculture

The Census of Agriculture exhibits problems which are a function of its unique role in the United States agricultural data base. The Census has long served as the five-year baseline to which less accurate data are periodically adjusted. The Census collects data not otherwise available: detailed descriptive data on the structure of agriculture by county, state, and national levels; certain farm characteristics by type of farming, economic class, and various other farm classifications, enterprise data on size, physical inputs, outputs, costs, and cash receipts for major crops and livestock, much of it by national, state, and county levels of aggregation; and data on the farm family. Perhaps the most valuable aspect of the Census is that it has been the only reliable, nationally uniform source of time series data at the county level.

The Census shares with other agricultural data systems the serious problems of conceptual obsolescence, especially in its basic unit of observation, the farm, and in the lack of an adequate paradigm to describe the economic activities of the total food sector. There are many problems involved, but the "establishment" concept, which is the basic unit of observation in the economic censuses, is considered by some analysts to be the appropriate starting point in developing a new basic unit of observation for the collection of data from farmers. In any event, the 1974 Census provided, for the first time, some data by the Standard Industrial Classification (SIC) code using a modified establishment concept.

The Census remains essentially a census of farms, although farming, despite its absolute economic growth, has declined to less than 15 percent of the economic activity of the total food sector. Both the Census of Agriculture and the USDA collect data on some activities of nonfarm agricultural firms, but the data, while quite valuable, are not comprehensive and there is no food sector paradigm that allows the data to be meaningfully aggregated into useful sector statistics. The current plan to move the agricultural census into the same time frame as other economic censuses will allow little integration of sector data until a common conceptual base, including an adequate paradigm for the food sector built around a common basic unit of observation, has been developed.

Historically, any census was a complete enumeration. In the agricultural censuses after World War II basic data continued to be obtained through complete enumeration, but sampling was introduced to reduce the cost of obtaining certain additional kinds of data. In the 1969 Census all data for farms with $2,500 or more in sales were collected on a 100 percent basis, but all data for farms with less than $2,500 in sales were collected on a 50 percent sample basis. For the 1974 Census all data were collected on a 100 percent basis. In addition, the 1969 Census and the 1974 Census represented a shift from an area frame to a list frame universe. The latter universe was developed from 1964 Census records augmented primarily by farm addresses maintained for administrative purposes by the Agricultural Stabilization and Conservation Service, the Social Security Administration, and the Internal Revenue Service. This consolidated list of addresses provides a less expensive way of specifying the universe of farms, but it contains many nonfarm names and is currently incomplete and thus introduces error. The USDA has also increased its use of list frames for sampling. At best a list frame is never really complete or up to date, this raises a question about whether a list frame alone can ever provide an adequate base for the collection of complex and detailed data.

After some experimentation in earlier years the Census was shifted almost entirely in 1969 and 1974 from the traditional method of having enumerators interview farmers and fill out the questionnaires to having mail questionnaires filled in by the farmers and sent back to a central location. This change

helped somewhat to control the continual rise in costs, but it substituted respondent variability for the previous enumerator bias and introduced problems of error as a result of incomplete list frame coverage and, especially in
1974, a higher nonresponse rate. Since 1969 the Census of Agriculture has
been a mailed-in report from a list frame universe. This complete transformation in methodology slowed the escalation of costs of the Census but at the
expense of a significant reduction in the timeliness and quality of the data.
This has been especially true of its most valuable feature, county data, some
of which now appear to be quite unreliable and no longer very useful in some
of the most important traditional applications.

The decline in the quality of Census data has been compounded by longer
and longer publication delays. Many data have been published so late as to
be nearly useless except for historical purposes. This has contributed to the
erosion of the Census as a baseline for "truing up" other independently collected data. Indeed, following the 1973 flap over the Secretary of Commerce's intention not to take the 1974 Census, bills were introduced in the
Congress and hearings were held on a proposed transfer of the agriculture census functions to the Department of Agriculture. These bills did not emerge
from committee, but such notions will persist if the quality of agricultural
census data does not improve and if the commitment of the Commerce Department to the Census of Agriculture continues to wane.

Many of the problems of the Census of Agriculture arise out of inadequate
resources and a long-term lack of administrative support in facing the extremely complex problems of a census in a rapidly changing economic sector
of more than two and a half million farmer entrepreneurs. The top political
leadership of the Department of Commerce has too often viewed the Census
of Agriculture as a service activity which is marginal to the mission of the
department and thus a natural candidate for budget cuts and administrative
neglect.

One study of the agricultural data system suggested the uncoupling of agricultural census data collection from its five-year cycle, redesigning it as a
series of annual sample surveys in which sample size can be more closely related to the desired level of statistical reliability (American Agribusiness Associates [1973]). This would reduce the statistical design and organizational
inefficiencies created now by the peak-load problems of the five-year census
cycle. This approach might be implemented for the data now collected in the
agricultural census whether the responsibility is assigned to the Bureau of the
Census or the USDA. Like any other statistical design, this approach would
also have some inherent limitations. If an adequate investment is made by the
Bureau of the Census in developing a satisfactory list frame and in reconcep-
tualizing the food sector paradigm, then there would be a genuine organiza-

tional advantage in keeping these data functions in the Bureau of the Census where they could be conceptually integrated with the other economic census statistics, especially those for nonfarm agricultural firms.

One factor often missed in attempting to understand the data quality problems of the agricultural census is the great increase in the number and complexity of the questions asked in the agricultural census during the period since World War II. This is a reflection of the growing complexity of the food and fiber sector itself under the fragmenting impact of progressively greater industrial specialization. Specialization of production processes invariably leads to greater informational requirements for the coordination of fragmented production and marketing processes. In short, the explosive growth in the need for food and fiber sector information for both private and public decision making appears to have grown beyond the capacity of the Census of Agriculture to sustain as a statistical vehicle. Rising complaints of respondent burden combined with an increase in distrust of government has resulted in congressional pressure on the Bureau of the Census to reduce the respondent burden substantially in planning for the 1978 Census. This leaves the Bureau of the Census with a Hobson's choice of either drastically reducing the number of questions and, therefore, the volume of useful information or greatly reducing the size of the sample, perhaps completely eliminating the capability for producing reliable county-level agricultural data — or some combination of the two alternatives. If the Census ceases to produce county data, its primary rationale for existence as a unique statistical vehicle will have ended.

Statistics for Rural Society

In the case of social and economic statistics for rural society, the overpowering problem, as the AAEA Committee on Economic Statistics [1972] pointed out, is the lack of data. This often is because there has been no demand for the financing of data collection. But even in areas of increasing public concern, as in rural development and natural resource management, and in the various dimensions of human welfare, little coherent data and few well-developed information systems exist. The primary reason is the absence of a satisfactory conceptual or theoretical base for either data collection or analysis. Economists cannot even define adequately what is meant by economic or rural development.

Institutional Obsolescence

Rapid or steady long-term technological, organizational, and associated value changes not only create obsolescence and mismatching in the conceptual base but also in the institutional structure of statistical systems. This is often compounded by the reorganization or development of new administrative structures without adequate care for the integrity or capability of involved data systems. Changes in basic statistical measurement techniques (for example, shifting the agricultural census from complete enumeration of an area frame to list frame surveys) which are unmatched by an implementing organizational adjustment can create another form of institutional obsolescence and inefficiency (American Agribusiness Associates [1973]). As a result of institutional obsolescence or reorganization, current administrative structures often do not bring the necessary information together at the time and places in the structure where it is most needed by decision makers.

Vested Interests in Data

Changing the design of data or its collection and the related information system always involves property rights, some publicly held and others privately held. The redesigning of information output and availability always redistributes those property rights and thus is a difficult feat to achieve in the face of the vested interests in data and information.

Bureaucracies, those who staff them, and various user groups and clientele develop substantial vested interests, not only in specific data output but also in existing concepts and measurement procedures. Thus, they behave as if they had a property right in certain data or analysis systems and often are able to enforce their interest politically. Any change in the design of the system must face this problem as a cost of eliminating or replacing an old statistic with newly designed data. The same observations can be made about any attempt to modify an established analytical process. Arrow [1974] rightly characterizes this as one of human capital made obsolete by change. Information systems are the human capital side of the development process. When human capital becomes obsolete, its replacement or redesign is far more difficult than the replacement of physical capital.

Some data problems arise because many of the property rights vested in information are privately held by firms and interests with considerable economic and thus political influence. As we attempt to redesign or create new data to respond to the public interest in problems of international trade with the Soviet Union or China or in new public policy issues involving the behavior and performance of the food and fiber sector, we find that essential information is often held by a few firms whose immediate interests would not be served by the release of that information. As industrial concentration continues to grow in food and fiber markets, the issue of private ownership of information versus the public's right to know will become more and more critical and heated. Giant firms acquire with their great size not only an impact on markets but also a major responsibility for public information. Where the data on a market are collected from and distributed to firms by a trade association, the tendency to withhold data from the public is even greater (Stigler [1961]).

Empiric Failure in Design and Collection of Data

Another problem is the increasing tendency of economists to propagate endless theories, concepts, and models of unknown value because they fail to design and collect data for an adequate empirical test. In his 1970 presidential address to the American Economic Association Wassily Leontief indicted economists for this failing. Leontief faulted economists for being satisfied with secondary data which do not match and thus cannot adequately test their theoretical concepts. His point was that theory will never be improved without empirical test, and in its absence, economists are playing sterile games.

Variations on Leontief's criticism have been voiced in many such addresses by economists (Bergmann [1974], Blackman [1971], Hahn [1970], Phelps Brown [1972], Maisel [1974], Worswick [1972]). Bergmann argued that the situation is worse than Leontief imagined: "... these days the best economists don't even look at secondhand data; they get them on magnetic tape and let the computer look at them. Economists have voluntarily set for themselves the limits on data collection faced by students of ancient history." Rivlin [1975] has lamented that "disdain for data collection is built into the value and reward structure of our discipline. Ingenious efforts to tease bits of information from unsuitable data are much applauded; designing instruments for collecting more appropriate information is generally considered hack work."

Leontief pays a high compliment to agricultural economists by explicitly exempting agricultural economics from his indictment. He describes the discipline as "an exceptional example of a healthy balance between theoretical and empirical analysis and of the readiness of professional economists to cooperate with experts in the neighboring disciplines ..." However, the AAEA Committee on Economic Statistics argued in 1972 that the honor Leontief accords us "properly belongs to an earlier generation" and that agricultural economists are now falling into the same errors which Leontief ascribes to other branches of the economics profession.

The capacity and reputation of agricultural economics were built around a balanced investment in theoretical and empirical analysis. We have now lost much of our early interest in the design and collection of data and often fail to collect needed data or to respect those who do. There is evidence that we are failing also to update our conceptual base at a pace sufficient to keep up with major changes in agriculture. Conceptual failure directly undermines the deductive process of knowing, and empirical failure directly undermines the inductive process of knowing. Thus, we must contend with two kinds of failure, either of which could prove disastrous if not corrected.

Data, Analysis, and Information: A Paradigm

One of the first problems encountered by the AAEA Committee on Economic Statistics [1972] was a confused but common vocabulary which erroneously equates data with information and fails to differentiate the distinctive steps in the process by which data and information are produced. There also seems to be no clear understanding of how the analytical process or system of inquiry over which the agricultural economist presides relates to data collection and to the information system.

The Nature of Data and Data Systems

Every data system involves an attempt to represent reality by describing empirical phenomena in some system of categories, usually in quantified form. Data are the result of measurement or counting, but when one sets out to quantify anything, the first question that must be answered is, "What is to be counted or measured?"[2] If the configuration of data produced is to be internally consistent and to have some correspondence with reality, the quantified ideas must bear a meaningful relationship to each other and to the reality of the world being described. In other words, there must be some concept of the reality of the world that is to be measured. Reality is nearly infinite in its variation and configuration and must be simplified or categorized if the human mind is to handle it in a systematic way. Thus, in producing accurate data, one either implicitly or explicitly develops a set of concepts which in some significant degree is capable of portraying and reducing the nearly infinite complexity of the real world in a manner that can be grasped by the human mind. Data are a symbolic representation of those concepts. If the concepts are not reasonably accurate reflections of that real world, then no amount of sophisticated statistical technique or dollars invested in data will produce useful numbers. (See figure 1.)

Although data presuppose a concept concepts cannot be measured directly (or, in a strictly logical sense, cannot be measured at all). Rather, we make the concepts operational by establishing (defining) categories of empirical phenomena (variables) which are as highly correlated as possible with the reality of the object of our inquiry.

Thus, there are three distinct steps which must be taken before one can produce data which purport to represent any reality. These are (1) conceptualization, (2) operationalization of concept (definition of empirical variables, and (3) measurement. The failure or deficiency of any one of these

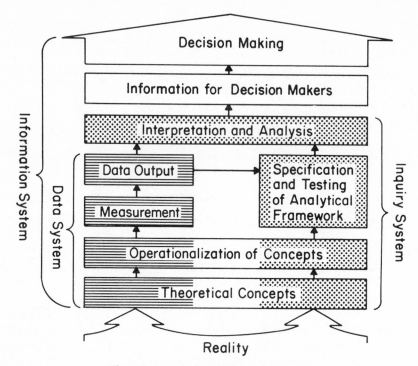

Figure 1. An agricultural information system.

data system components constrains the quality and characteristics of the data produced. An inadequacy at any stage can be offset only to a very limited extent by improvements or manipulations at the other stages. Thus, the great improvements in statistical methodology and data-processing techniques over the last generation cannot offset failures at the conceptual level, for no matter how well one measures and manipulates the numbers one will still be measuring the wrong thing. For example, the parity price concept, no matter how well measured, is a poor representation today of farmer welfare. The "cost of production" concept central to the operation of the Agriculture Act of 1973 is so inadequate as a representation of the complexities of farm cost structures that no amount of genius in making it operational or measuring it can redeem its inadequacy as a concept.

It is worth noting that the term "reliability of data" has three possible meanings in this paradigm: reliability of measurement, which is the meaning the statistician usually attributes to the term; reliability of operationalization; and conceptual reliability.[3]

The Nature of Information

Data are not information (Eisgruber [1967], Dunn [1974]). An information system includes not only the production of data but also analysis and interpretation of these data in some purposeful policy decision or problem solution context. The demand for data is generated by the need to make decisions on problems, but decision makers rarely use raw data. Rather, there are intervening acts of interpretation ranging from statistical and economic analysis through less complex program and political evaluations, and the like which transform data into information by placing them in a specific problem context to give the data meaning and form for a particular decision or decision maker. Data are symbolic artifacts which acquire most of their meaning and value from the context and design of the information system in which they appear. Information, then, is a process which imposes form and gives meaning. Thus, an information system includes a data system, the analytical and other capabilities necessary to interpret data, and, finally, the decision maker.

Analysis as a Function of Information

What does the agricultural economist do when he plays the role of analyst? In our training we all acquired much the same epistemological sense of how to analyze and solve problems; that is, there is a base of theoretical concepts, a body of theory purporting to represent reality which we make operational through the definition of variables, often specified formally in a model which must be matched with data or measured representations of the variables. The model or analytical framework is then tested against the data and conclusions are drawn. Thus, in these three steps in analysis, we find two of the same components observed in a data system—that is, theoretical concepts and operationalization of those concepts.

Thus, in data systems (left side, figure 1) and in analytical systems of inquiry (right side, figure 1), we operate from the same set of theoretical concepts and, ideally, the same set of definitions which make those concepts operational. Unless economic theory and economic statistics meet on common conceptual ground, there can be no mesh between empirical analysis and theory—between the inductive and deductive processes.

Agricultural economists—especially the academic economists—are clearly responsible not only for the design and maintenance of the profession's analytical framework but also for the design of the conceptual base of the data systems which provide the empirical content for analysis. The notion held by some economists that statisticians alone are responsible for the design and production of data represents a gravely distorted view of our professional responsibilities. It reflects an epistemological weakness and also a lack of understanding of the historical development of data systems. From earliest times data systems have been created to solve specific problems, and specialists in the appropriate areas of knowledge have always been involved in the design of the data systems.

An information system is the total process by which knowledge is generated and brought to bear on social decisions—public and private. As social scientists and statisticians, we are concerned with social information processing. The design of the information system establishes the nature of the relationship between the decision maker, the information on which decisions are based, the analytical process which transforms data into information, and the design and collection of data.

The Imperative of Information System Design

It is the conscious design of the information system as a system which must be fully respected if data are to be accurate and if the information upon which decisions are based is to be relevant and reliable—or even available. One of the most fundamental errors which we now make as agricultural professionals is the failure to perceive and design activities as subsets of the information systems which give them their meaning and significance. This is a design failure which takes different forms.

There are many different "ways of knowing," or epistemological positions. The validity of any one depends on its teleological context. Thus, the purpose of the system of inquiry controls or limits the appropriate epistemological basis of any specific information system (Churchman [1971]).

All information systems are problem solving or purposive because they are subsets or components of social systems which are designed for some problem-solving purpose. Thus, data collection and analysis always have a purpose and can only be understood fully in a social system or decision context.

Data collected for societal decision making must have a social theory base. No matter how ad hoc the collection of data may seem, every measurement act is guided consciously or unconsciously by conceptual and value structures which exist prior to the act of measurement. Data and information are never value-free or theory-free. Conversely, all concepts or theories have a prior empiric basis that is explicit or experiential. Theory and data are, thus, epistemologically interdependent.

For this reason any quantitative or statistically based information system exhibits both inductive and deductive epistemological bases. Consequently, in an information system we do not *know* anything until, as a necessary condition, a deductive analytic mode of inquiry is tested against and combined with an inductive empiric model of inquiry. What is known from such a process grows in extent and reliability by a repetition of interaction between the deductive and inductive modes, in which both the analytic content and the empiric content of the process are reformulated and improved on the basis of what is learned from each prior iteration.

An analytical hypothesis or model and the data for its empirical test must have the same conceptual and definitional base. This is perhaps too logical and obvious to mention, yet a failure to appreciate this fact lies at the heart of our apparent inability to understand and deal with the problem of the accuracy of information provided in agricultural economics. It also is related to the progressive deterioration in the sense of professional responsibility on the part of economists (including agricultural economists) for the design of the data they use.

The points made in the last three paragraphs are implicit in Leontief's insistence on the necessity for empirical testing of all theoretical formulations with data which are designed around the proper concepts. They are also implicit in the statement by the AAEA Committee on Economic Statistics [1972] that accurate and useful data can be collected only in a conceptual frame which is an accurate representation of the reality the data are supposed to describe. Data are symbolic of some phenomena which they are designed to represent. The quality of that representation is only as good as the adequacy of the conceptual base or its operationalization or its measurement.

When the phenomenon that is being represented changes rapidly, as it has in the food and fiber industry, the conceptual base of the information system must be redesigned frequently to keep up with the changes in reality and the problems being studied. If the rate of change is high enough, the need for conceptual redesign becomes nearly continuous. This is the fundamental problem in the design of information for agriculture. Failure to keep up with the changes in the policy agenda and in the reality of agriculture leads to significant conceptual obsolescence, and the system begins to lose its capacity as an accurate guide for problem identification and solution or management. This paradigm of the constituent processes of an information system provides a conceptual template with institutional analogues for the design of data and information systems.

The Design and Management of Information Systems

Let us turn now to some of the general information system design and management questions raised by the development or industrialization of agriculture, by economic organization differences, and by the behavior of various information system participants.

Development and Information

Information systems are an essential part of any decision process, public or private. Thus, the social returns on any investment in information are derived from the benefits generated by that information in the decision structure of a social system. Information systems appear to have a unique role in an industrializing or developing society. Without an adequate information system the potential gains in productivity from specialization and new technologies are lost in inadequate coordination and management of the developing industry or economy. As one moves into a developmental mode and begins to set conscious national goals for economic and social development, the need for data and the social value of that data increase greatly. Agricultural information systems have played a strategic role in the growing productivity of this country over the past century. Although it is generally understood that industrialization and development increase the demand for information and the social returns, it is not often recognized that development also brings about a change in the kind of information demanded.

The earliest systems for data collection in any society usually arise out of administrative and management needs. The data required can be described as primarily static and descriptive and as involving clear, relatively fixed goals and simple or low levels of information processing. As a society's economic structure grows more complex and specialized, the demands are not just for more data and greater accuracy in the articulation of detail. Increasingly the demand is for data and information in a "learning or developmental mode" (Dunn [1974]), in which the goals of decision making are not completely specified; and one purpose of the information system is to assist the decision maker in specifying the goals in a progressively more complete form (that is, in redesigning the information system). In a developmental mode goals and problems may continue to change as learning takes place and thus may never be completely or finally specified. It is obvious that one is not well served in this situation by data and information which are basically static.

Note too that in the learning or developmental mode the information system which perceives and acts on data is itself changing in structure and behavior in response to the information it processes. Thus, the information system must be capable of perceiving changes not only in the environment but also in itself, even under conditions in which such changes themselves become goals (Dunn [1974]).

As if this were not demanding enough, in the most industrially and agriculturally advanced countries where the reality of the world (especially in agriculture) continues to change rapidly, the need to redesign the system eventually becomes continuous. It follows that if agricultural information is to be accurate and reliable the capacity for redesign must be a normal internal function of the information system. If the designer does not become a part of the system in this situation, the capacity of the system to produce useful information will deteriorate.

Another significant observation can be made about the design of information systems. Any system designed to solve problems will inevitably combine and use different fields of knowledge. Therefore, the concepts underlying the information system will be derived from different disciplines. Agricultural information systems are an excellent example. If such a system is to produce useful data and, in the process, manage its own continuing redesign, a general "theory of social information processing" or theory of theories, a "meta-theory," is needed. In other words, we must have a means of synthesizing concepts from different bodies of knowledge into a meaningful relationship to each other (Dunn [1974]).

A meta-theory for information system design may well be an impossible practical goal. But the logic of its necessity is valid and has the virtue of keeping in front of the designers of information systems the true complexity of the task. The design of data and information systems is not a job we can assign to any but the best minds. The theory of information from a single discipline such as economics or statistics is not adequate to the task.

Economic Structure and Information

In the design of information systems the configuration of major economic sectors in the society and the degree of concentration of these economic structures make a great deal of difference in public and private sector information needs. As one looks across the entire economy, from the agrarian sector to the most industrialized manufacturing sector, it is evident that differences in concentration or industrial structure have great impact on public and private sector data needs.

In some economic sectors an industry or firm can recapture the gains from data collection and analysis financed by that industrial association or firm. The government has little business collecting this kind of data unless, as is sometimes the case, there is an urgent or overriding public interest in such data. There are other economic sectors where the benefits of private investment in data can never be captured by an individual firm or even an entire industry. The difference is found primarily in the nature of the industrial structure itself.

If an industry is a monopoly involving only one firm, then the benefits of any investment in statistics for that industry will accrue directly to the private gain of the monopoly. Thus it can afford to pay for, and can expect to get, the benefits of any investment in information needed to manage the industry. The more concentrated the industry, the greater the returns to private investments in data. And the more concentrated the industry, the less the justification for public investment in data for private use. Over the same continuum the justification for public investment in data for public use at first declines from significant levels, but as higher levels of industry concentration are approached the need for data and its social rate of return should rise again. This is especially true if the society has policies which constrain or regulate monopolies.

At the other extreme of industrial structure, where an industry may be made up of thousands or even millions of independent firms as in agriculture, the amount of private sector investment in data collection and analysis that can be justified by an individual firm (because it can be recaptured in the firm's balance sheet) would be extremely small, if not zero. In fact, the public returns to private investments in information would probably exceed private returns.

Increasing demands for data are generated by the greater and greater specialization that has resulted from the modernization or industrialization of agriculture. Social returns on the investment in data for improved coordination and management of specialized industrial processes are usually very high. In very competitive unconcentrated industries such as agriculture these gains are only realizable through public investment. The great increases in productivity in United States agriculture over the past century can be traced in substantial part to the contribution of publicly collected data for private management decision making. The improved efficiency in the use of resources has accrued to the society in the form of lower food costs and the release of most of the farm labor force for employment in nonfarm pursuits. Returns to information and coordination in the development process have always been high, particularly in atomistic economic sectors such as agriculture (Hayami and Peterson [1972]).

It is thus no accident that most national governments collect far more detailed statistics on highly competitive industries such as agriculture than on highly concentrated industries such as steel. This is a logical allocation of public resources which follows from the very nature of the industrial structures themselves.

The Dysfunctional Behavior of the Actors:
A System Management Problem

The difficulty with most of the literature on the problems of agricultural data and information systems is that the authors often overlook the forest and see only the trees. There has been a general failure to see any aspect of these problems in their systems context. We need to think more about the nature of the social systems of which information systems are an inherent part. This does not keep us from discussing data as such, but it is well to stand back occasionally and look at the whole as we try to diagnose problems. We are only beginning to do this and no one can claim more than a partial understanding of the difficulties we face.

The initial designers of an information system will usually perceive the whole of the system. They will at least understand the system well beyond the subset they inhabit. In the early stages of the development of an information system there is limited organizational specialization, and often no professional statisticians are available. In fact, it is a rare administrative data system which has a statistician in attendance at its birth.

As the agricultural sector of the United States has developed, its public and private agricultural information systems have exhibited progressively greater specialization in organization and growth of bureaucracy and professional staff. This is an inevitable consequence of growth and creates a situation in which the information system management problem is largely one of managing bureaucracies and highly specialized professionals.

The skills of different types of professionals are necessary for developing sophistication and capacity in any information system. Nevertheless, the attitudes of professionals and various professional groups increasingly seem to affect the design and functioning of agricultural data systems in a deleterious manner. As science and society have become more and more specialized, and as specialized vocations have been transformed into professions, both specialization and professionalism have begun to have an effect on the perception of the nature and role of data systems and analysis.

Once professionalized, the agencies which produce statistics tend to see data as an end in itself—unless the agency is tied very directly to client or user groups. Many statisticians have only a limited grasp of the analytical methods and the information system needs for which specific data sets are inputs. Statisticians as professionals also tend to view their responsibility in the data system as limited to the application of statistical methods to the production of data (in their view, the final product). Thus, to many statisticians the improvement of data means little more than the improvement of the professional quality of statistical agency performance, which is quite important but is not a very large part of the total design problem in data collection. As organization men they also believe in rapidly growing budgets and freedom from interorganizational commitments and restrictions. Such narrow perceptions of professional responsibility get in the way of adequate information system design, coordination, and management. Nevertheless, the statistician's performance must be judged to be better than that of the economist.

Economists have come to be so specialized that their common attitude toward data and data systems is narrowed to a bored yawn—it's someone else's responsibility. Frequently they do not today understand the nature of the relationship between their analysis and the data systems upon which they must draw, particularly as it concerns the quality of data. Few understand the responsibility they have for maintaining the conceptual foundation of that data base. Indeed, judged by how they behave rather than by what they say, economists with depressing frequency fail to perceive that the theoretical structure of their discipline is also simultaneously the conceptual base of the data system which produces the numbers they use. To repeat, economic theory and economic statistics unavoidably meet on a common conceptual ground. If they do not, there can be no mesh between empirical analysis and theory. As this mesh deteriorates, the capacity of the profession for doing accurate analysis also deteriorates in an equal degree (Morgenstern [1973], Nieto-Ostolaza [1973]). Often contempt is openly expressed for economists who spend time on the collection and design of data. There is thus a failure to understand the nature of the data system and the epistemological interdependence of data systems and analysis. This, of course, is an oversimplification—and there are honorable exceptions in all the disciplines—but increasingly the consequence is that few social scientists perceive the information system within which they work and, as a result, almost no one acts to manage, improve, or renew the system.

The attitudes of many political appointees or managers in the federal government, including those who direct the varied elements of national data collection and analysis, also often have a very unfortunate impact on information systems. Information tends to be viewed by politicians as a free good, which because of the scale and complexity of the federal executive and its great capacities, should be forthcoming without cost and on demand, no matter how esoteric or unusual that demand for data may be. In commenting on the quality of the data and information produced in response to the typical political demand for instant data, a colleague once remarked of the political managers of his agency, "When they want it bad, they get it bad!"

There are several other traits that tend to be quite disruptive of a well-designed and well-managed information system. Agencies are repeatedly reorganized with little care for the structure and integrity of the information and data systems involved. After three or four reorganizations one finds that what may once have been a coherent data or information system is now scattered across the agency, and if it is coordinated at all it is by individuals acting informally and not by the structure of the system itself. The older the agency, the greater the validity and frequency with which this observation may be made.

The effective time horizon or planning span of political decision makers rarely goes beyond the next budget or the next election. They will assure you (and rightly so, by their own standard) that anything that exists as a potentiality at any greater distance in time is not a real or urgent problem because the probabilities are high that the problem will not materialize in the form envisioned or that the political decision maker will not be there or will no longer be responsible. The political and budgetary costs of changes in statistical systems must be faced immediately. The benefits are rarely perceptible except in periods of time running well beyond the next budget and the next change in administration. This often severely disturbs the management of agricultural data systems, particularly when the systems are simply subordinate parts of administrative structures and are not organized as formal data systems.

Kings, pharaohs, and khans of ancient times used to behead the bearer of bad tidings. Today political decision makers still have a tendency to sack, demote, or punish those who produce data that are embarrassing or that make them uncomfortable. In a modern bureaucracy this is simply transmitted down through the hierarchy so that ultimately some statistician or economist is made the goat. Farm income is a politically sensitive statistic in domestic agricultural policy. Through administration after administration, various political decision makers have blamed statisticians and economists for all the deficiencies of that statistic. Yet when examined closely, one will find that the statisticians and economists—the technicians—have for decades recommended remedial action, generally with limited results because the political decision maker in that generation refused to assume the costs of making the change, thus transmitting to another political decision maker in a subsequent administration (with luck, of another party) the even greater political costs of failing to reform the system. Perhaps the immediate political decision maker's hands are tied, but they should at least stop blaming statisticians and economists for the failures of politicians.

Conclusion

It is worth reflecting on the impact of progressively greater specialization of society and subsequent organizational fragmentation on information system design. The problems of any society dominate its policy agendas and the information systems which are the basis of society's capacity for problem solving. But when specialization begins seriously to fragment the social organization, the scope for externalities in the society grows and with it the problems of the society. However, the capacity for problem solving tends to decline because the same social organizational fragmentation also shatters the information systems, making it more difficult to maintain a coherent, integrated information design for any problem purpose. Perhaps it is this phenomenon which we are seeing in the dysfunctional behavior of information system actors and in the lack of integration today in many agricultural information systems. In any case, it makes evident the serious need for information system design and management.

No information system has unlimited capability. The act of design is one of progressive elimination of some potentialities in order to sharpen other specific capabilities. The purpose of social system decision processes, which information must serve, provides the primary principle of information design.

There are two distinctive but interdependent parts of the design process. One involves the design of the system, the other the design of information proper. Specification of the system involves elimination of the impossibilities and the potential system subsets that are not relevant, given one's purpose and context. Specification of the system also involves the design of the institutions within which data are to be designed, collected, analyzed, and used in the decision process. Many of these decisions are made without reference to data or analysis, since they are primarily political or social decisions.

The design of information involves decisions on what information to collect and analyze and how to do it. The purpose of the system provides some of the decision criteria, but the dominant element within those limits is found in the economics of information. Thus, the assessment of the cost of a bad or erroneous decision versus the cost of information becomes critical.

My objective here precludes an adequate discussion of the complex and important problems of the economics of information. But it is worth noting that in any social system the greater the level of uncertainty (up to a limit), the higher will be the value of information. Appropriately designed information allows one to reduce uncertainty and to manage its undesired consequences. But uncertainty is inherent in the human condition. While "sufficient expenditure" on information will keep the effects of uncertainty "upon people . . . within tolerable or even comfortable bounds . . . it would be wholly uneconomic to eliminate all its effects" (Stigler [1961]).

World food and feedgrain stocks vanished in 1972-73. The consequent price instability and production fluctuations in subsequent years have dumped every nation's food and agricultural policy into a sea of uncertainty. The value of information has increased many times over, thus exposing more clearly the many weaknesses in our information systems and giving rise to a call for construction of a world food information system (United Nations, World Food Conference [1974], U.S. Congress, Office of Technology Assessment [1976a]). During the past several decades of excess stocks and shelter from market uncertainty, we have undervalued our agricultural information systems so greatly that we have not invested adequately in some systems and we have allowed others to decay seriously.

Information is an expensive commodity as well as a valuable one. Returns to careful decisions about data and information are high. In the search for an effective information system the economic and statistical models, the estimation and optimization procedures, and the corresponding inferences and choices are interdependent links in the information chain. The opportunity decision cost of considering any one of the above ingredients in isolation is very high.

The cost of poor decisions and subsequent lack of appropriate information is extremely high (Bonnen [1973]). The foundation of effective information management for agricultural decisions is careful design of data and information.

Notes

1. Conceptual obsolescence is not limited to agricultural statistics. All of our older social and economic statistics share in this problem. It is also obviously a difficulty that will continue to plague all data systems involving social and economic behavior in a society in which change is rapid.

2. Data, strictly speaking, are not limited to quantified forms, but this discussion is confined to statistical data. Implicit in the question of what is to be measured is also the question of why.

3. This observation was contributed by L. V. Manderscheid.

Rural Economic
and Social Statistics

W. Keith Bryant
Professor of Consumer Research and Public Policy
New York State College of Human Ecology,
Cornell University

Elsewhere in this volume Upchurch [1977] deals with post-World War II developments in the data systems for the food and fiber sector of the economy, and Bonnen [1977] makes an assessment of the data base of the food and fiber sector from the standpoint of its status as a modern information system. In this chapter the state of the economic and social data for rural people and areas is discussed and the causes of the state of the data are pursued somewhat further. Some modest suggestions for improvement arise from the analysis. The bulk of the material used in the preparation of this chapter has been drawn from work done by members of the AAEA Task Force on Social and Economic Statistics.[1] The Task Force was the creation of the AAEA Committee on Economic Statistics under the chairmanship of J. T. Bonnen.

In reporting on the work of the Task Force, Gardner [1975] used an economic framework to analyze the state and long-run future of rural social and economic statistics. He identified the demand for such statistics as deriving from the prior demand for knowledge. The demand for knowledge stems from its consumption value, as an end in itself, and from its value as a tool in public and private planning and in program development, implementation, and evaluation, all of which takes place under conditions of uncertainty. It is the latter segment of the demand that is the driving force behind the total de-

Note: The author wishes to express his gratitude to J. T. Bonnen, L. R. Martin, G. Judge, and L. Tweeten for incisive criticisms of an early draft.

408

mand for statistics. Moreover, he stressed the nature of the demand as a public good and on that ground justified the dominating presence of the federal government on the supply side of the market. The supply side, he noted, is characterized by a centralized system, composed of the federal agencies which gather statistics, and a decentralized system (almost a nonsystem) in which individuals and agencies, typically funded by grants from the federal government, collect small amounts of data for very specific purposes.

Such a framework is useful for making a further analysis of the state of the economic and social statistics for rural areas and people. But what is its state? One indicator is the attention Bonnen and Upchurch gave to social statistics. Bonnen [1977] devoted one paragraph to the subject. In it he identifies the reasons for the lack of such statistics as a lack of demand and "the absence of a satisfactory conceptual or theoretical base for either data collection or analysis." Upchurch [1977] devoted 4 manuscript pages out of a total of 122 pages to statistical developments in the areas of rural poverty, housing, health, and local government. Over one-half of the citations of the literature in this section of his manuscript had to do with local government.

Another indication of the state of the data is the fact that the Census of Population and Housing, the Current Population Survey, the Bureau of Labor Statistics, the Center for Health Statistics, and the Bureau of Economic Analysis all produce a flood of statistics pertaining to the economic and social conditions of people and areas. If the state of such data is poor, it must be because the data produced do not sufficiently refer to rural people and areas, are conceptually irrelevant, or appear too infrequently or because the problems on which the data are used are not well specified.

Each of these indictments is true in some respect, as has been pointed out by others. Vlasin [1973] and Edwards [1973] discussed the lack of agreement over the conceptual base underlying area and regional growth and development. The lack of measurements on program inputs, costs, and intended and unintended outputs are discussed by Daft [1973] and Madden [1973]. Hathaway, Beegle, and Bryant [1968] questioned the continued usefulness of the rural farm, rural nonfarm, and urban classifications used by the Census of Population. Bryant [1973] summarized the implications of new developments in labor supply theory and in the economics of the households and found rural labor market data systems as well as other data on rural people lagging behind the theory. Hathaway [1972] analyzed the characteristics of rural areas and drew conclusions about needed labor market information in rural areas. Gardner [1973] examined the implications of human capital theory for data on rural human resources. Bawden and Kershaw [1973] analyzed available data on the low income population and found little such data for rural areas. In addition, the criticisms of planning and evaluation of rural human and regional programs in the middle and latter parts of intercensal periods are legion.

Statistics are used in the production of knowledge which in turn is used in planning, program implementation, and evaluation. All of these processes take place under uncertainty, and it is the uncertainty that is the sine qua non of the demand for knowledge. The demand for statistics, therefore, is an input demand and as such is influenced by the underlying demand for knowledge, the "price" of statistics, the prices of other inputs, and the underlying technical processes. The price of statistics calls up the supply side of the statistics market. It is instructive to consider each in turn.

The Demand for Economic and Social Statistics

The size and structure of the demand for knowledge about social and economic conditions of rural areas and people stands in marked contrast to the demand for knowledge about commercial agriculture. The national importance of commercial agriculture, the fact that many agricultural markets were national or international rather than local, and its status as an industry made political lobbying easy, and its original overwhelming presence in rural areas combined by the turn of the century to create a great demand for agricultural statistics primarily by the private sector, to have that demand focused at the federal level, and to have one federal agency primarily responsible for data collection, use, and dissemination. The assumption of responsibility for national agricultural price policy in the late 1920s and 1930s by the federal government and the escalating importance of farm price policy in the 1940s and 1950s created an explosive public demand for data on commercial agriculture. These forces coming from the public sector helped to focus the demand at the federal level. The encroachment of public agencies on private agricultural markets resulted in further private demand for information.

Not so with respect to the demand for social and economic statistics about rural people and areas. Such a demand is simply part of the larger demand with respect to all areas and all people, urban and rural. As such it crosses all industries, areas, and people, each with different demands. Hence, no lobby as potent as an industry group could form and focus the demand. Since health, education, and welfare policy are still viewed as individual, local, and at most state concerns by many people and groups, the focusing of the demand for knowledge of social conditions at the federal level has been slow.[2] To the extent that there is any federal focus of the demand for social statistics today, it is within the Department of Health, Education, and Welfare, a department deeply fragmented by its three subject areas, and within the Department of Housing and Urban Development. Most programs of the latter department have to do with housing, both rural and urban. But its focus is upon the major cities, which provide its political support. Since knowledge of economic conditions is demanded by state and local governments, business, and labor (the last two acquiring their own federal departments at an early stage), the demands for economic statistics—although focused at the national level—are fragmented among several federal agencies. The demand for statistics about social and economic conditions of rural people is further fragmented by the sporadic and declining demand from the USDA.

Just as the demand for commercial agricultural statistics derives in part from national agricultural policy, so too the demand for economic and social statistics derives from national policies with respect to health, education, welfare, and regional policies. But the differences between national agricultural policy and the other policies breed great differences in the kind of statistics demanded. Commercial agricultural policy generates a demand for statistics about one industry at either the local or national market level. At the local level the information in demand about agriculture is chiefly information about production whereas at the national level statistics about both sides of farm product markets are in demand. The national policies generating demands for social and economic statistics on rural people and areas can be exemplified by regional economic policy. Take, for instance, the Area Redevelopment Act of 1961, the Appalachian Regional Development Act of 1965, the Public Works and Economic Development Act of 1965, and the more recent Rural Development Act of 1972. These acts essentially disburse federal monies, loans, and loan guarantees to regions, states, and local areas on the presentation and approval of plans for improvement of either economic or social overhead capital. The statistics demanded by such plans as well as the statistics necessary to evaluate the programs all refer to local and regional economic and social conditions. The data required pertain to many industries as well as to the public sector and must refer to local market conditions rather than simply to local production considerations. And the plans and hence the logic of the demand for the data are written by local, state, or multistate regional bodies.

The demand for statistics implied by national social policy, more than either agricultural or regional policy, refers to the activities of public agencies and to their actual and potential clientele. Since national health, education, and welfare policies all are pursued by the federal government in cooperation with state and local governments, these statistics—like those useful for regional programs—need locational cross-references.

Thus, in contrast to the demand for statistics on commercial agriculture, the demand for social and economic statistics about rural people and areas is fragmented among many federal agencies to the extent that it is focused at the federal level at all, and a large segment of the demand originates at state and local levels. In addition, it is much more comprehensive, spanning many industries and both sides of the markets in which they deal, and is location specific. Finally, it is characterized by observation units composed of public agencies and their clientele as well as private firms.

Another element of the demand for knowledge that has influenced the kind of statistics in demand has been the emphasis on program planning, accountability, and evaluation. These are emphases of the past fifteen to twenty years. Statistics suitable for program justification and planning are those which identify problems and establish need. In the social and regional policy domains, rather rough area summary statistics available from the various censuses plus local unemployment rates have sufficed in the past and remain sufficient for program planning and justification purposes. Statistics useful for program accountability and evaluation are of a totally different sort: information on inputs, input cost, outputs, and the value of outputs are required. The demand may yet be a parent of such statistics and the underlying concepts, but the gestation period is not over and the birth pains may be severe. The demand in the areas of social and regional policy, then, is for new kinds of statistics and has run well ahead of the technical capacity to produce them.

The term "technology" refers to the scientific processes underlying the production of knowledge. In economics this includes theories of behavioral relations, theories of measuring and estimating such relations, data processing technology, and data collection technology. Economic theory, quantitative theory, and data processing and collection technologies are all intertwined.

Any development in one of the four areas of technology raises the marginal products of the others, inducing research and development on them. The rapid growth of neoclassical theory during the first forty years of the twentieth century spawned the work during the 1930s, 1940s, and 1950s which resulted in the quantitative theory by which economic relations might be identified and estimated. These advances, given second- and third-generation computers, allowed the development during the 1960s and early 1970s of algorithms programmed for the computer by which high-quality estimates of economic relations could be obtained at reasonable cost. These three elements—economic theory, quantitative theory, and low-cost estimation programs—have placed great pressure on economic data systems and on data collection technology during the 1970s. And it can be argued that, along with the rapid changes in society and in public policy, they have contributed to the concerns of Leontief [1971], Dunn [1974], Rivlin [1975], Bonnen [1977], and others over the adequacy of our data systems.

Of course, the several parts of economic and quantitative theories have not developed at the same pace, a fact partly related to the kind and nature of the policy problems with which economists have been asked to wrestle. Human capital theory, for instance, developed during the 1950s, in time to help guide the multitude of social programs enacted during the 1960s. It merged with new cost-benefit analysis techniques in evaluations of the programs. The new economic theory of the household has flowered partly as a result of attempts to bring neoclassical household theory to bear on problems revealed by evaluations of the War on Poverty programs and also on recent trends in labor force activity, fertility, marriage, and divorce.

Less progress appears to have been made in regional economics. Vlasin, Libby, and Shelton [1975] noted the confusion of concepts with respect to area growth and development and the disagreements over definitions of the problem, the explanation of it, and appropriate policies to deal with it. Similar statements were made by Leven [1965] more than a decade ago.

The demand for social and economic statistics has grown rapidly since 1960 as the regional growth and development programs of the early 1960s and the subsequent social programs stimulated the demand. The demand has been further stimulated as advances in economic and quantitative theory along with the drastic reduction in computation costs place additional pressure on the nation's data system. Even though national social and economic policies have been major contributors to the demand, they are still less focused at the federal level than is the case for commercial agriculture. Furthermore, the demand at the federal level is spread across many agencies in many departments. With the demand less concentrated than it is for commercial agriculture statistics, demanders have had less control over the quality and quantity of data produced.

The Supply of Economic and Social Statistics

Several features of the supply of economic and social statistics seem to be pertinent in the present context. One is that unit costs of basic statistics have risen rapidly over the past twenty years, the major driving force being labor costs. In response, massive doses of capital have been substituted for labor, especially on the data processing side of statistics production. The last labor intensive place in the system is in data collection itself; enumerative methods of data collection use large amounts of labor. Increasingly, sampling methods have replaced enumeration. The switch to sampling techniques was hastened as systematic under-counts of certain groups in the population came to light during the 1960s (particularly in the categories of central city, nonwhite, and unrelated individuals).[3] A major implication of the switch to sampling methods, combined with strict disclosure laws, has been a reduction in the statistics on social and economic conditions of people in sparsely populated areas with specific location cross-references. Efficient sampling for the purpose of producing national estimates with small errors prohibits the collection of enough sample points in most small rural areas to permit the resulting data to be reported at less than national or census region levels. This, of course, has been the case for years with respect to the Current Population Survey.

Another force has likewise reduced the supply of data for specific segments of the rural population. The repeated redefinitions of "farm" by the USDA and the Bureau of the Census have through time first raised and then eliminated the acreage requirements and raised the minimum gross sales of farm products requirement. These have assuredly improved the quality of agricultural statistics from the standpoint of measuring conditions in commercial agriculture. The same redefinitions, however, by eliminating operations and people no longer considered "commercial farms" and "commercial farm operators," have meant that much less data are now collected by the Census of Agriculture on people on noncommercial farms.[4] Improvement of the concepts underlying the statistics on commercial agriculture, therefore, has come at the expense of data on some rural people.

A more subtle but nonetheless substantial force has to do with the fact that the supply of economic and social statistics is concentrated at the federal level in a very few agencies. The Bureau of the Census, the Bureau of Labor Statistics, the Social Security Administration, and the Treasury Department produce almost all of the statistics about the economic and social conditions of Americans. And, of course, the Office of Management and Budget has ultimate control over what questions may be asked in any survey by a federal agency. The retreat of the USDA from its position as the federal agency for rural people to a federal agency for commercial agriculture has abetted the concentration on the supply side and has resulted in a decline in the demand for statistics about rural people as opposed to farm people. In brief, the supply side of the statistics market is much more concentrated than the demand side and is coordinated at the federal level to a degree unknown in all but the most monopolistic of private markets.

To point out the relative power of the few federal agencies which produce and fund statistics collection is not to ascribe to them any sinister motives. A natural consequence of such power on the supply side, it is argued, is that the statistics collected better serve the goals of federal and national policy than the goals of other areas of demand. It is also the case that no large users of state and local data are represented on statistics advisory committees.[5] Since much of the demand for statistics on rural people and areas emanates from state and local sources, such sources have been less well served than those at the federal level.

The decentralized component of the supply of social and economic statistics is also influenced by federal initiatives and goals. The decentralized system, as Gardner points out [1975], is composed of individual researchers and policy analysts who collect data related to particular issues. Much of the funding of such projects is federal, and the proposals are reviewed by people in relevant federal agencies and congressional committees as well as by others outside the federal establishment. Of course, the judgments of these people about project viability and priorities are influenced by the goals of the agencies in which the reviewers are employed.

A final feature of the supply of economic and social statistics is the fact that the public sector is the primary supplier of social overhead capital via education, health, welfare, and manpower programs. Consequently, a good statistical information system focusing upon the economic and social conditions of people and areas must provide the statistics needed to manage, monitor, and evaluate such programs and their effects on both people and areas. Such programs are, by and large, cooperative ventures among federal, state, and local governments. The statistics collected by each federal agency are those required for the preparation and justification of appropriations requests, and in consequence tend to emphasize the statistics required for program monitoring more than program management and evaluation.

The available statistics are very much better in tracing federal program inputs than state and local program inputs, but in neither case are the statistics suitable for any but the most general kind of program management and evaluation. A part of the problem is the lack of a conceptual base on which to build the production of program output statistics. Another part of the problem is the fact that public agencies are no more willing than private firms to provide the statistics necessary to gauge their performance (Niskanen [1971]).

It is also the case that although program statistics may catalog a few of the characteristics of program participants (typically those on which eligibility is based) statistics to measure the number and characteristics of the eligible population do not exist. Nor do statistics exist to track the extent of program overlap with respect to either participation or eligibility (Daft [1973]). Program managers and policy analysts have only the crudest of notions, therefore, of the extent of the market for the program, and they have little idea of the extent to which the programs they manage and evaluate compete with or complement other programs.

Thus, the rising costs of statistics production and the structure of the statistics producing and using system emphasize the production of statistics to meet narrow federal and national policies at the expense of more diffuse and less organized demands. The demand for statistics on the social and economic conditions of rural people and areas happens to fall in the latter category.

Suggestions for Improvement of the Statistical System

The AAEA Task Force on Social and Economic Statistics produced no specific recommendations for the improvement of the statistical system. Nevertheless, certain common themes connected the papers and the discussion on them. Gardner [1973, 1975] was impressed with the decentralized component of the system. Stinson [1975], who discussed Gardner's 1975 paper at the annual AAEA meeting, agreed and argued that ". . . the strategy with the highest payoff for the future is a relatively more rapid expansion of the decentralized approach coupled with a better system disseminating information about existing data files." Vlasin [1973], C. Edwards [1973], and Daft [1973] all expressed concern with respect to area and regional statistics. In addition, Daft [1973] and Madden [1973] were interested in the development of statistics which could be used to measure public program inputs and outputs and which could also be used by policy analysts and program administrators to evaluate and manage public programs. Edwards [1973] and Vlasin, Libby, and Shelton [1975] were concerned about obsolete area and growth concepts and with continued disagreements over problem specification, concepts, and statistical measures of them.

It is clear that additional emphasis on the decentralized component of the economic and social statistics system is warranted. This could be achieved in a number of ways: (1) increased funding by the National Science Foundation for the purpose of new statistical measurement and data collection efforts on a variety of economic and social topics; (2) increased emphasis within the Economic Research Service, the Statistical Reporting Service, and the Agricultural Research Service of the USDA on relatively small experimental statistical measurement and data collection efforts closely tied with theoretical and applied research work on social and economic problems; (3) the earmarking by the USDA Cooperative State Research Service of Hatch Act funds for experimental statistics gathering by land-grant college researchers engaged in work on particular economic and social problems.

Such emphases are justified on several grounds. Since the individual efforts would be small and would be executed by many different researchers around the country, the chances for innovative research and accompanying data collection would be higher than if the same amount of money were allocated to the federal statistics gathering agencies. The statistics system may become more dynamic, as Bonnen urges. Since each effort would be small, mistakes could be discovered early when they are small and could be eliminated. And an increased emphasis on the decentralized component of the system would tend to right the current imbalance of power in the system in which the supply side is dominant over the demand side.

If there is no agreement on regional and area problems or on area and regional growth concepts, then there should be no coordinated, system-wide effort to collect and systematize statistics in the area and regional domain. Rather, the emphasis should be on diverse small experimental and pilot projects which would simultaneously develop theoretical concepts for area and regional planning and analysis, their empirical statistical analogues, and methods of data collection.[6] Such a strategy fits well with the preceding emphasis on the decentralized component of the system. Indeed, the very fact that area and regional analysis and policy are about areas and regions implies that they are part of the decentralized component and that the problems faced vary from region to region. The strategy invites the innovative solution of theoretical and statistical problems, allows local adaptation to location problems, and enables the inevitable failures to be cut short at least cost.

The allocation of funds for the development of the decentralized system is not enough, however. If the decentralized system is to be an engine of innovation nationally, we need to devise institutional channels through which the work of the system can be communicated, criticized, and made available for incorporation into the national information system. The first and last of these functions can be funded and operated federally. The criticism function is a proper and historical function of professional associations.

In addition to the bibliographies of literature and research work in progress developed by the USDA, the Library of Congress, and others, there is a need for a dynamic computerized bibliography of regional and local data collection efforts. In such a bibliographic system the observation units, content, and accessibility of the data collections would be referenced. Analysts and planners could thus obtain from the system information about the existence of data collections relevant to their purposes and about the method and possible cost of gaining access to the data collections. Similarly, researchers and other groups engaged in primary data collection activities would be encouraged to supply information to the bibliography. Federally funded projects might be required to cooperate in the bibliographic enterprise.

Professional associations, through the offices of their respective journals, have provided means by which books and monographs are subjected to critical review. The reviews serve both to advertise and to evaluate the books. Such scientific scrutiny of the data collection efforts of both the decentralized and centralized data collection systems is needed. A statistics review editor could work in tandem with the book review editor to make sure that the data collection efforts relevant to the profession are given adequate coverage.

At the federal level a review and evaluation of a different sort should be undertaken on a continuing basis. Although professional associations have a responsibility to review critically the data systems on scientific grounds, a federal competence needs to be created in which the data generated by the decentralized system is judged for possible incorporation into the national information system. Such a federal agency or committee would periodically scan the data collection efforts of the decentralized system for the purpose of evaluating any new sampling techniques, new ways of defining and measuring concepts, and possible measurements on new concepts. The criteria used would be related to the possible national demand for such data and to possible improvements in the existing federal statistical system.

Recent proposals by David [1976] appear to meet some of the defects in the statistical system identified by Daft [1973] and Madden [1973]. David correctly argues that statistics on the eligible populations for the various poverty programs do not exist. Furthermore, no means are available by which general population statistics and statistics about federal programs from administrative files may be connected. David's concerns are mainly with respect to the low-income population, but his ideas have wider application. He concentrates on the Current Population Survey and shows how the survey could be changed so that it would possess aspects of a longitudinal panel so that questions about changes through time might be addressed and how common sampling frames and cross-references could be developed between the survey data and samples of administrative records of people and households participating in various governmental programs. If achieved, public program management and evaluative analyses would be easier to make and would bear more fruit. David's proposals are based on deep knowledge of the survey and data collection techniques and appear quite feasible. Such developments require close coordination·between the survey and the various federal agencies. Coordination appears possible because the problem David identifies is clear-cut and seems to have no basic conceptual aspects.

A final suggestion is that heavy users of local and regional information should be represented on federal statistical advisory committees. Such an action would give a voice to a now neglected group of users and would decrease the myopia of the federal statistics establishment.

Conclusion

Statistics for rural people and areas are produced and used in a marketlike system in the United States. The demand and supply sides of the system have been analyzed. The demand is a derived one, emanating principally from public and private decision makers who are forced to make policy and manage programs in an area of uncertainty and yet must bear the responsibility of errors caused by that uncertainty. This demand is characterized as being fragmented among many federal agencies and some state and local agencies. It is comprehensive in origin, spanning many sectors, levels and regions of the economy, public and private. It is also comprehensive in focus in that public and private agencies as well as individuals, all with specific geographic references, are the observation units. It is uncertain in that many of the concepts on which data demands are based are ill-founded and subject to frequent change and also in that many of the public programs which create the demand for such data come and go frequently. The supply is concentrated at the federal level in a few agencies and is focused upon national concerns of federal agencies. Moreover, the supply is subject to rapid escalations in costs which, given the dispersed nature of the demand and the consequent lack of market power, lead to reductions in the supply of the very detail on rural people and areas that is demanded.

The suggestions offered in the preceding section for the improvement of the system recognize these characteristics by advocating increased federal funding of decentralized data-gathering enterprises. A decentralized system encourages innovation, local adaptation, and the early elimination of failures and of data collection efforts serving short-lived demands. Such a system, along with increased representation on federal statistics advisory committees, would serve to buttress the power of the dispersed demand side of the system. Another set of suggestions would provide institutional means by which decentralized data development exercises could be communicated to others, reviewed against scientific criteria, and evaluated for possible inclusion in the centralized part of the system. Finally, work at the federal level is recommended by which data files on federal programs could be merged with data on individuals eligible for the programs, the better to manage and evaluate the programs.

By the late 1960s students graduating from doctoral programs in economics and agricultural economics were expected to have firm control of neoclassical economics and to have quantitative skills which twenty years earlier only a handful of economists possessed. In addition, most have comfortable if not entirely amicable relations with computers. Consequently, the marginal product of sophistication in statistical measurement and data collection techniques is currently high, and interest in such matters is increasing. Since 1968 four large-scale social experiments dealing with cash welfare programs have been mounted along with performance contracting and housing allowance experiments.[7] The resources allocated in these studies to experimental design, to basic data collection, to the training of economists in statistical measurement and data collection techniques, and to training in work with experimental longitudinal panel data are impressive. The 1970s and the 1980s may yet be the "data decades."

Notes

1. The members of the Task Force on Social and Economic Statistics were W. Keith Bryant, D. L. Bawden, L. M. Daft, E. S. Dunn, Jr., C. Edwards, B. Gardner, J. P. Madden, M. Olson, G. S. Tolley (chairman), and R. D. Vlasin.

2. Federal responsibility for welfare policy did not occur until the Great Depression. Federal responsibility for health and education policy with minor exceptions was a development of the 1960s and 1970s.

3. Bonnen [1977] has documented the problems encountered in this switch with respect to the Census of Agriculture.

4. J. T. Bonnen helped to clarify the implications of the changes in definition. See also Hildreth and Worden [1976].

5. This information was supplied by J. T. Bonnen.

6. It should be emphasized that this suggestion is contrary to the spirit of the discussions by Edwards [1973] and Vlasin, Libby, and Shelton [1975]. It is the author's view, however, that until there is agreement on the problem and the conceptual base there can be no coordinated "system" approaches. Where there is no conceptual agreement, there will be no agreement to submit to coordination.

7. See Bawden [1971], U.S. Department of Health, Education, and Welfare [1976], and Pechman and Timpane [1975] for descriptions of the first two cash welfare social experiments. The other two, the Gary Income Maintenance Experiment and the Denver-Seattle Income Maintenance Experiment, are in progress.

Appendix (Part IV). A Brief Review of the Literature by Subject Category

The references at the end of Part IV include, in addition to the sources cited in the text, many sources dealing with various other aspects of agricultural economic information systems and a large number of periodical sources of agricultural economic data. In the present section the major postwar references not cited elsewhere are classified by subject category.

Originally we had hoped to include in Part IV a complete listing of the principal periodical sources of data available to United States agricultural economists. It was our plan to identify the periodicals and to provide information on the sources and data series maintained by each periodical. Constraints on time and the magnitude of the proposed task ruled out this alternative. Although preparation of an exhaustive listing of the principal periodical sources was not feasible, many of these sources are included in the references at the end of Part IV.

An important outgrowth of our inquiry was the discovery that work now being undertaken will eventually fill this gap and will generate new contributions to the agricultural economics information system. In a letter of February 28, 1977, Gaylord E. Worden, then director of the Data Services Center of the Economic Research Service and now with the Statistical Policy Division, Office of Management and Budget, wrote as follows:

> We have our concepts pretty well decided and have started active recruitment for someone to lead this new thrust. The Data Resource Cen-

ter will be a part of our data management services in the Data Services Center, a service division in ERS.

The Data Resource Center would be a computer supported information base containing available and constructed documentation on data used in ERS and other data that would be available to ERS. The information would answer as many as possible of the types of detailed subject matter questions from researchers as well as technical information needed by the data processing staff. The Center would also track statistical and data base activities at the federal level and other key areas to keep the ERS research staff better informed on changing availability of data, etc.

Over time, *the Center could add capability to access bibliographic and information bases needed by the research staff and include more documentation on data uses, data flows, research models and research systems used in ERS.* For example the type of information in Agricultural Handbook No. 365 could be a part of the system and updated fairly routinely and automatically. [Italics added.]

For detailed information on the data series currently maintained by the ERS, the SRS, and the AMS, see USDA Agriculture Handbook 365 and USDA Miscellaneous Publications 1088 and 1308. New publications in agricultural economics from the ERS and the SRS are listed inside the back cover of the ERS monthly periodical, *Agricultural Outlook.*

Information Systems and Purposes

The references in this category include a few publications on the issue of statistical confidentiality and on data interpretation. The remainder of the publications in this category are broad in their approach. Dunn [1974] provides many other useful references on information systems and privacy.

Sources. Bancroft [1972]; Bolling [1956]; Bowman [1968]; Callander [1949]; W. W. Cochrane [1961]; Cox [1962]; Demsetz [1969]; Dunn [1966, 1974]; Fellegi [1972]; E. N. Gilbert [1958]; Hayek [1945]; Hildreth [1967]; Hirshleifer [1971]; Juster [1970]; Klein [1971]; Kuhn [1970]; G. E. Lee and Nicholson [1973]; Lunde [1975]; Marschak [1971]; Orcutt [1970]; Rosenblatt, Glaser, and Wood [1970]; Schnittker [1963]; Shannon and Weaver [1969]; Shoemaker [1962]; Simerl [1962]; Simpson [1966]; Szaniawski [1967]; Trelogan [1962]; Weeks [1972]; Weeks, Schluter and Southard [1974]; Weiner [1974]; Wells et al. [1954]; Wickens [1953]; Wilcox and Ebling [1949].

Theoretical and Operational Concepts

Increased interest in the conceptual foundations of information systems has generated a steady flow of publications, although many more deal with problems in the development of operational concepts or variables than with the development of satisfactory theoretical constructs. Only one reference in this category deals with data interpretation. The development of operational and theoretical constructs receives some attention from writers of articles in the other categories, particularly in "Critical Evaluations."

Sources. Ackerman and Riechen [1964] ; Arrow [undated] ; Bachman et al. [1948] ; Berndt and Christensen [1974] ; Birnbaum [1962] ; Christensen [1975] ; Christensen and Manser [1975] ; Ducoff and Hagood [1947] ; Fritsch et al. [1975] ; Fromm [1973] ; E. N. Gilbert [1958] ; Griliches [1963] ; Herriot and Spiers [1975] ; Hickman [1964] ; Horring [1961] ; Hotelling [1958] ; Houthakker [1968] ; Howe, Handy, and Traub [1975] ; Hulten [1974] ; Hurley [1962] ; Koffsky [1962a] ; Marion and Handy [1973] ; Marshall [1962] ; Masucci [1962] ; Mighell [1969] ; Naive, Cox, and Wiley [1957] ; Nikolitch and McKee [1965] ; Nybroten [1953] ; Pallesen [1962] ; Randall [1968] ; Randall and Masucci [1963] ; Randall and Rojko [1961] ; Rymes [1972] ; Schnittker [1959] ; Shaw [1967] ; Sheehy and McAlexander [1965] ; Sheldon [1960] , Siegel [1956] ; Star [1974] ; Stine [1946] ; USDA, ERS [1972a, 1972b] ; Vining [1953] ; Weeks [1972] ; Weeks, Carlin, et al. [1972] ; Welsch and Moore [1965] ; Winkler [1963] ; Zusman [1967] .

Data Collection Methods

There is a large body of literature on the methodology of data collection, particularly on data obtained from sampling. Many of these studies come from statisticians and economists who are producing numbers, even though they are often focused on methodology, with the methods illustrated by application to numbers. We would characterize them as more constructive than critical.

Sources. ASA, Advisory Committee [1953] ; Backrock and Scable [1967] ; Bailar [1973] ; Bailar and Tepping [1973] ; R. M. Brooks et al. [1974] ; Buse [1973] ; Clausen and Ford [1957] ; R. S. Cochrane [1965] ; Ferber [1966] ; Finkner [1952] ; French and Kranz [1957] ; Grieves [1954] ; Hall [1969] ; Hansen and Hurwitz [1946] ; Hartley [1962, 1965] ; Hendricks [1949] ; Hendricks, Searls, and Horvitz [1964] ; Houseman [1947, 1949, 1950, 1953, 1957] ; Huddleston [1950, 1965, 1968, 1971] ; Hurley and Smith [1951] ; Jebe [1952] ; Jebe and Clifton [1956] ; Jessen [1947, 1955] ; Kelly [1958, 1963] ; Kirkbride [1969] ; Kish [1962] ; Knutson and Harmston [1950] ; McGregor and Frost [1959] ; McVay [1947] ; Neter and Waksberg [1964] ; Reed [1949] ; Rogers [1965] ; Scholl and Burkhead [1949] ; Shaffer [1959a, 1959b, 1959c] ; Shaudys [1969] ; C. C. Smith [1952] ; Stout [1962] ; Sudman and Ferber [1971]; R. G. Thompson [1963]; Trelogan [1966, 1968a, 1968b, 1971]; Tsai [1973]; Vickery [1956]; Vincent [1959]; Vogel [1973, 1975]; Wallace [1955]; West [1965]; W. H. Williams and Mallows [1970].

Evaluations of Methodology

The methodologies employed in information systems are frequently criticized in the literature. Evaluations and suggestions for improvements come from analysts within the information system and elsewhere.

Sources. Abel [1962]; Adelman and Griliches [1961]; Bailey, Muth, and Nourse [1963]; Boxley, Gibson, and Hoffnar [1964]; Budd [1971]; Ducoff and Bancroft [1945]; Edgington [1963]; Ferber [1949]; Foote and Bean [1951]; Foote and Fox [1952]; Foote and Weingarten [1958]; Gale [1968]; Gonzalez [1973]; Houseman [1972]; Houseman and Reed [1954]; Jorgenson [1964]; Light, Mosteller, and Winokur [1971]; McHugh [1961]; Morgan and Sonquist [1963]; Puterbaugh [1961]; Sarle and Robinson [1949]; Selltiz et al. [1964]; Wales and Ferber [1963]; Wigton and Kibler [1972].

Evaluations of Information Systems, Programs, Concepts, and Data

Rarely does the program of the annual meetings of the American Agricultural Economic Association not include a session on agricultural economic data. The peak may have been reached when almost all of the November 1939 issue of *Journal of Farm Economics* was devoted to eleven articles in this area, including several excellent evaluations and several suggestions for improvement.

About half of the representative sources listed in this category are written from the standpoint of information producers (engaging in self-criticism or intramural criticism) and about half from the standpoint of information users. Sometimes the two groups seem to "talk past" each other because they tend to focus on relatively narrow aspects of an information system, not the system as a whole. Nevertheless, nearly every aspect of information has received its share of critical review, and many evaluations offer critiques and suggestions in several areas.

Sources. ASA, Advisory Committee [1948]; Bachman [1958]; Barlowe and Vlasin [1974]; Bawden and Kershaw [1973]; Beck [1955]; Becker [1951]; Becker and Harlan [1939]; Benedict [1939]; Benedict and Kuznets [1958]; Benedict, Tolley, et al. [1944]; Bhatia [1971]; Bodin [1955]; Boger [1961, 1966]; Breimyer [1968]; Burroughs [1950]; Clawson [1966]; Clough [1951]; W. W. Cochrane [1966]; Daly [1963, 1966, 1969]; Denison [1969];

Dyer [1975]; Ebling [1939]; Eisgruber [1973]; Erickson [1971]; Ferris [1962]; Fox [1953]; S. J. Gilbert [1955]; Griliches [1960]; Grove [1967]; Gunnelson, Dobson, and Pamperin [1972]; Halcrow and Hieronymus [1959]; Hale [1939]; Hardin [1946]; Haren [1975]; Harris [1962]; Hathaway [1959, 1963]; Hayenga [1971]; Heflebower [1951]; Hendricks [1955]; Hoffman [1966]; Houk [1957]; Houseman [1955]; Howe and Handy [1975]; Hurley [1965]; Hurley, Jabine, and Larson [1963]; Hurwitz [1962]; Ives [1957]; Jessen [1939, 1942]; D. G. Johnson and Nottenburg [1951]; Jorgenson and Griliches [1967, 1972a, 1972b]; Keith and Purcell [1976]; Kizer [1967]; Koffsky [1947]; Kottke [1964]; Krueger [1963]; Kutish [1955]; I. M. Lee [1952]; Loomis [1957]; Lowenstein [1954]; Luby [1957]; McAllister [1950]; McCormick [1955]; W. K. McPherson [1956]; McVay and Tucker [1950]; Murray [1939]; National Advisory Commission on Food and Fiber [1967]; T. R. Nelson [1967]; Newell [1953, 1957, 1958a, 1958b]; Nordquist [1956]; Paarlberg [1950]; Pearson and Brandow [1939]; Ramsey [1959]; Riley [1956]; Ruttan [1954, 1963]; Sarle [1939]; Sarle, Heimberger, et al. [1953]; Schrader [1951]; Scoville [1959]; Sherr [1960]; Shiskin [1960]; Sinclair [1951]; R. H. Smith [1954]; R. K. Smith [1955]; Snedecor [1939]; Spielman and Weeks [1975]; Stapp [1958]; Stauber [1959b, 1964]; H. C. Taylor [1939]; H. M. Taylor [1950]; Teper [1956]; Timm [1966]; Todd and Ziricle [1952]; Trelogan [1972]; U.S. Congress [1952, 1957, 1960, 1967b, 1971, 1972]; U.S. Congress, Office of Technology Assessment [1976a]; U.S. Department of Commerce, Intensive Review Committee [1954]; U.S. Government [1971]; Upchurch [1974]; W. F. Williams, Bowen, and Genovese [1959]; Woytinsky and Woytinsky [1939]; Wright and Torgerson [1975].

Information and Data Needs

A large and diverse body of literature is devoted to the data and information needed by analysts and decision makers. Some of the suggestions come from data or information users, some from data or information producers. The suggestions range from demands for narrow bands of data to well-thought-out suggestions for large additions to existing information systems.

Sources. Borum [1955]; Bottum and Ackerman [1958]; Bryant [1973]; Budd [1971]; Butz [1966]; Daft [1973]; David [1976]; Ebling and Ahlgren [1954, 1959]; C. Edwards [1969, 1973]; Ewing [1956]; Gardner [1973, 1975]; Gillett [1948]; Grove [1969]; Hathaway [1972]; Houseman [1964]; Hurley [1949, 1954, 1958]; Madden [1970, 1973]; Mayer and Ahalt [1974]; Mendelowitz [1971]; Raup [1959]; Schaars [1955]; Schultze [undated];

J. T. Scott and Heady [1969]; Sturt [1972]; Sundquist [1970]; Thomas [1956]; Vlasin [1973]; Vlasin, Libby, and Shelton [1975]; Webb [1956]; Westcott [1956]; White [1964]; Wilcox [1956].

Reports of Advisory Committees

Sources. AFEA, Agricultural Data Committee [1957]; ASA, Advisory Committee on Statistical Policy [1953]; ASA, Census Advisory Committee [1951]; ASA, Committee on Census Enumeration Areas [1954, 1955]; Fuller, Gillett, et al. [1953]; Rathbun [1972].

Relationship between Agricultural Economic Data and National Economic Data

With the increased interest in aggregate models—including input-output models and econometric models—more attention has been given to the compatibility of agricultural economic data and concepts with the data and concepts used to describe the complete economic system. Similar concern has been focused on income generation and capital formation for the farm and nonfarm sectors. All these forms of interdependence bid fair to occupy a good deal of the time of agricultural economists and macroeconometric model builders.

Sources. Brake [1974]; Brake and Barry [1971]; Christensen and Jorgenson [1973]; de Leeuw [1962]; Denison [1969]; Ducoff and Hagood [1946]; Dunn [1971]; Fabricant [1959]; V. Fuller and Van Vuuren [undated]; Haavelmo [1947]; Jorgenson and Griliches [1967, 1972a,b]; Kendrick [1961, 1972, 1973]; Penson and Baker [1978]; Rice, Hinrichs, Tolley and Hauser [1945]; Robbins [1963]; Ruggles and Ruggles [1971]; UN [1968]; UN, FAO [1973]; UN, FAO [1971]; Wells [1961].

Explanations and Illustrations of Data Series

A considerable body of literature is devoted to explanatory materials on data series (especially on changes therein) and on data systems. Most of the publications reflect the viewpoint of data producers. The explanations usually include data collection procedures as well as information processing procedures.

Sources. Allison, Zwick, and Brinser [1958]; Banks and Shapiro [1971]; Barton and Durost [1960]; Bayton [1950]; Borum [1951]; Bosecker and Ford [1976]; Bowman and Martin [1962]; Boxley [1971]; E. M. Brooks [1949]; Burk [1959]; Burk and Lanahan [1958]; Callander and Sarle [1947]; Caudill [1965]; Cavin [1952]; Ciancio and Tortora [1976]; Eckler and Taeuber [1954]; Grove [1954]; Hansen [1965]; Harlan [1947]; Hendricks [1947,

1963] ; Hendricks and Huddleston [1955] ; Jacobs [1975] ; Knutson [1949] ; Koffsky [1958, 1966] ; Landau and Brandt [1966] ; A. T. M. Lee and Bachman [1953] ; Marsh and Conklin [1953] ; Morton [1969, 1972] ; Nordquist [1952] ; Ogren [1956] ; Parker [1951] ; Parker and Holmes [1958] ; Peterson [1947, 1950] ; Purcell and Raunikar [1971] ; Quackenbush [1954] ; Quackenbush and Shaffer [1960] ; Randall [1968] ; Robinson and Wallrabenstein [1949] ; F. S. Scott, Jr. [1955] ; Sells [1975] ; Senf [1949] ; Simon [1958] ; Stauber [1950, 1959] ; Taeuber [1947, 1957, 1971] ; USDA [1958, 1959] ; USDA, AMS [1957] ; USDA, ERS [1975] ; USDA, FCA [1968] ; USDA, SRS [1967] ; U.S. Department of Labor, BLS [1974] ; Wells [1950, 1958].

Evaluative Techniques

The publications in this category are concerned with the development or use of evaluative techniques on different aspects of information.

Sources. Bullock [1976] ; Fellegi and Krotki [1968] ; Ferber [1955] ; Ingram and Prochaska [1972] ; Marks, Mauldin, and Nisselson [1953] ; H. T. Shapiro [1973].

Economic Forecasting Models

Sources. Barr and Gale [1973] ; Crom [1972] ; Cromarty [1959] ; Daly [1963] ; K. A. Fox [1953] ; Kuznets and Harvey [1953] ; Leuthold et al. [1970] ; Palmer and Schlotzhauer [1950] ; Parr and Calvin [1956] ; Theil [1958].

Foreign Agricultural Economic Information

Sources. Ball and Gardella [1967] ; CIDA [1963] ; Hirsch [1947] ; Koenig [1951] ; United Nations [annual], *Statistical Yearbook*; United Nations, FAO [annual], *Yearbook of Food and Agriculture Statistics*.

References (Part IV)

Abel, M. E. [1962]. "Harmonic Analysis of Seasonal Variation with an Application to Hog Production." *J. Am. Stat. Assoc.* 57:655-667.

Ackerman, J., and T. Riechen [1964]. "Development of Economic Criteria for Classifying Farms." *J. Farm Econ.* 46:1232-1237.

Adelman, I., and Z. Griliches [1961]. "On an Index of Quality Change." *J. Am. Stat. Assoc.* 56:535-548.

Aines, R. O. [1964]. "Farmland Valuation and Farm Programs." *J. Farm Econ.* 46: 1253-1259.

Allen, G., and M. Devers [1973]. *Livestock and Feed Relationships—National and State.* USDA Statistical Bulletin 530 (supersedes 446).

Allen, G., and R. Mighell [1969]. *Urea Consumed by Cattle on Feed, Feeding Year 1965-66.* USDA Agricultural Economic Report 153.

Allison, H. E., C. J. Zwick, and A. Brinser [1958]. "Menu Data and Their Contribution to Food Consumption Studies." *J. Farm Econ.* 40:1-20.

American Agribusiness Associates [1973]. "New Agricultural Data System Needed." Washington, D.C. Mimeo.

American Agricultural Economics Association, Committee on Economic Statistics [1972]. "Our Obsolete Data Systems: New Directions and Opportunities." *Am. J. Agr. Econ.* 54:867-880.

American Bankers Association [monthly]. *Agricultural Banker.* See also the "Special Supplements" and "Special Reports" published in conjunction with the periodical.

AFEA, Agricultural Data Committee [1957]. Unpublished report to USDA and Census Bureau.

ASA, Advisory Committee [1948]. "The Employment Statistics Program of the BLS." *Am. Statistician* 2(2):21-22.

ASA, Advisory Committee on Statistical Policy to the Bureau of the Budget [1953].

428

"Statement of Principles with Respect to Direct Government Collection of Statistical Data." *Am. Statistician* 7(4):28, 33.

ASA, Census Advisory Committee [1951]. "Report." *Am. Statistician* 5(3):10.

ASA, Committee on Census Enumeration Areas [1954, 1955]. "Report." *Am. Statistician* 8(2):21, 10(2):16-17.

Anderson, D. E., L. D. Loftsgard, and L. E. Erickson [1962]. *Characteristics and Changes of Land Ownership in North Dakota, 1945-1958.* North Dakota Agricultural Experiment Station Bulletin 438.

Anderson, E. [1941]. *Per Capita Consumption of Foods, United States, 1909-39.* USDA, BAE. Mimeo.

Andrelenas, P. [1974]. *Farmers' Use of Pesticides in 1971 — Quantities.* USDA Agricultural Economic Report 252.

Andrelenas, P., T. Eichers, and A. Fox [1967]. *Farmers' Expenditures for Pesticides in 1964.* USDA Agricultural Economic Report 106.

Arkin, G. F., R. L. Vanderlip, and J. T. Ritchie [1976]. "A Dynamic Grain Sorghum Growth Model." *Transactions of the ASAE* 19:622-626.

Arnold, C. J., and R. Barlowe [1954]. "The Journal of Farm Economics: Its First 35 Years." *J. Farm Econ.* 36:441-452.

Arrow, K. J. [1974]. "Organization and Information." In *The Limits of Organization.* New York: Norton. Pp. 33-43.

Askew, W. [1969]. "The Many Prices of Wheat." In *Wheat Situation,* USDA, ERS, WS-208, pp. 11-14.

Bachman, K. L. [1958]. "Discussion: Better Basic Data for Agriculture." *J. Farm Econ.* 40:224-227.

Bachman, K. L., J. C. Ellickson, W. D. Goodsell, and R. Hurley [1948]. "Appraisal of the Economic Classification of Farms." *J. Farm Econ.* 30:680-702.

Backrock, S. D., and H. M. Scable [1967]. "Mailed Questionnaire Efficiency: Controlled Reduction of Non-response." *Public Opinion Quarterly* 31:265-276.

Bailar, B. A. [1973]. "A Common Problem in Analysis of Panel Data." In *Abstracts Booklet,* ASA, p. 6.

Bailar, B. A., and B. J. Tepping [1973]. "Enumerator Variance in the 1970 Census." In *Abstracts Booklet,* ASA, p. 127.

Bailey, M. J., R. F. Muth, and H. O. Nourse [1963]. "A Regression Method for Real Estate Price Index Construction." *J. Am. Stat. Assoc.* 58:933-942.

Bailey, W. R., and L. A. Jones [1970]. *Economic Considerations in Crop Insurance.* USDA ERS-447.

Baker, O. E. [1929]. "Changes in Production and Consumption of Our Farm Products and the Trend in Population." In *Annals of the American Society of Political and Social Science,* March 1929 (reprint of 1925 publication).

Ball, D. S., and J. W. Wilson [1968]. "Community Health Facilities and Services: The Manpower Dimensions." *Am. J. Agr. Econ.* 50:1208-1225.

Ball, J., ed., and R. Gardella, compiler [1967]. *Foreign Statistical Documents.* Stanford University, Hoover Institution.

Bancroft, T. A. [1972]. "The Statistical Community and the Protection of Privacy." *Am. Statistician* 26(4):13-16.

Banks, M. J., and G. M. Shapiro [1971]. "Variances of the Current Population Survey, Including within and between PSU Components and the Effect of the Different Stages of Estimation." In *Abstracts Booklet,* ASA, pp. 5-6.

Banks, V. J., and C. L. Beale [1973]. *Farm Population Estimates, 1910-1970*, USDA Statistical Bulletin No. 523.

Banks, V. J., C. L. Beale, and G. K. Bowles [1963]. *Farm Population Estimates for 1910-62*. USDA, ERS-130.

Barlowe, R., and R. D. Vlasin [1974]. "Indicators of Environmental Quality in the Use of Land Resources." Contributed paper presented at AAEA annual meeting, College Station, Texas.

Barr, T. N., and H. F. Gale [1973]. "A Quarterly Forecasting Model for the Consumer Price Index for Food." *Agr. Econ. Res.* 25:1-14.

Barton, G. T., and M. R. Cooper [1945]. *Farm Production in War and Peace*. USDA, BAE Farm Management Report 53.

——— [1948]. "Relation of Agricultural Production to Inputs." *Rev. Econ. and Stat.* 30:117-126.

Barton, G. T., and D. D. Durost [1960]. "The New USDA Index of Inputs." *J. Farm Econ.* 42:1398-1410.

Bawden, D. L. [1971]. "Implications of a Negative Income Tax for Rural People." *Am. J. Agr. Econ.* 53:754-760.

Bawden, D. L., and D. Kershaw [1973]. "Data on the Low Income Population of the U.S." Paper prepared for AAEA Task Force on Social and Economic Statistics.

Bayton, J. A. [1950]. "Consumer Preference Work in the Department of Agriculture." *Agr. Econ. Res.* 2:105-112.

Bean, L. H. [1930]. "Application of a Simplified Method of Correlation to Problems in Acreage and Yield Variations." *J. Am. Stat. Assoc.* 25:428-439.

Beck, F. B. [1955]. "Making Existing Local Data More Available and Useful." *J. Farm Econ.* 37:1030-1037.

Becker, J. A. [1951]. "Discussion: Agricultural Statistics." *J. Farm Econ.* 33:806-807.

Becker, J. A., and C. L. Harlan [1939]. "Developments in Crops and Livestock Reporting since 1920." *J. Farm Econ.* 21:799-827.

Been, R. O., K. Ogren, K. Parr, and B. Deloach [1945]. *Price Spreads between Farmers and Consumers for Food Products, 1913-1944; Supplement* (1947). USDA Miscellaneous Publication 576.

Benedict, M. R. [1939]. "Development of Agricultural Statistics in the Bureau of the Census." *J. Farm Econ.* 21:735-760.

Benedict, M. R., and G. M. Kuznets [1958]. "Better Basic Data for Agriculture: Some Possible Approaches." *J. Farm Econ.* 40:208-221.

Benedict, M. R., H. R. Tolley, F. F. Elliott, and C. Taeuber [1944]. "Need for a New Classification of Farms." *J. Farm Econ.* 26:694-708.

Bergmann, B. R. [1974]. "Have Economists Failed?" Presidential address to the Eastern Economic Association.

Beringer, C. [1961]. *An Economic Model for Determining the Production Function for Water in Agriculture*. California Agricultural Experiment Station, Giannini Foundation Research Report 240.

Berndt, E. R., and L. R. Christensen [1974]. "Testing for the Existence of a Consistent Aggregate Index of Labor Input." *Am. Econ. Rev.* 64:391-404.

Bertrand, A. L., and F. L. Corty, eds. [1962]. *Rural Land Tenure in the United States: A Socio-Economic Approach to Problems, Programs and Trends*. Baton Rouge: Louisiana State University Press.

Beverly, L. H. [1968]. *Status of Water and Sewage Facilities in Communities without Public Systems*. USDA Agricultural Economic Report 143.

Beyer, G. H. [1965]. *Housing and Society*. New York: Macmillan.

Beyer, G. H., and J. H. Rose [1957]. *Farm Housing*. New York: Wiley.

Bhatia, K. B. [1971]. "The USDA Series on Net Investment in Farm Real Estate—A Critique." *J. Am. Stat. Assoc.* 66:492-495.

Bird, A. R. [1964]. *Poverty in Rural Areas of the United States*. USDA Agricultural Economic Report 63.

Bird, R. [1955]. "A Procedure for Estimating State General Sales Taxes Paid by the Farm Population." *Agr. Finance Rev.* 18:29-36.

Bird, R. [1956]. *Taxes Levied on Farm Property in the United States and Methods of Estimating Them*. USDA Statistical Bulletin 189.

Bird, R. [1973]. *Inadequate Housing and Poverty Status of Households, Areas Served by the Farmers Home Administration Programs, 1970, by States*. Rural Development Service. USDA Statistical Bulletin 520.

Bird, R., L. Beverly, and A. Simmons [1968]. *Status of Rural Housing in the United States*. USDA Agricultural Economic Report 144.

Bird, R., and N. Kegley [1971]. "Poor Housing Blights Our Countryside." In *A Good Life for More People—Yearbook of Agriculture, 1971*, USDA, pp. 72-75.

Bird, R., and J. B. Perciful [1972]. *Housing Conditions in Areas Served by Farmers Home Administration Housing Programs, 1970*. USDA Statistical Bulletin 492.

Birnbaum, A. [1962]. "Another View on the Foundations of Statistics." *Am. Statistician* 16(1):17-21.

Bitting, H. W., and R. O. Rogers [1963]. "Utilization of Wheat for Food." *Agr. Econ. Res.* 15:61-69.

Blackman, J. H. [1971]. "The Outlook for Economics." *Southern Econ. J.* 37:385-395.

Blaney, H. F., and W. D. Criddle [1962]. *Determining Consumptive Use and Irrigation Water Requirements*. USDA Technical Bulletin 1275.

Bodin, R. A. [1955]. "A Discussion from the Viewpoint of a State Agricultural Statistician." *J. Farm Econ.* 35:872-875.

Boger, L. L. [1961]. "Economic Indicators in Agriculture—Praised and Appraised." *J. Farm Econ.* 43:430-439.

——— [1966]. "Discussion: Changing Needs in a Changing Agriculture." *J. Farm Econ.* 48:1682-1686.

Bolling, R. [1956]. "The Role of Statistics in Shaping Economic Policy." *Am. Statistician* 10(3):7-9.

Bonnen, J. T. [1966]. "Rural Poverty: Programs and Problems." *J. Farm Econ.* 48:452-465.

——— [1973]. "Statement before the Subcommittee on Census and Statistics." *1974 Census of Agriculture: Hearing of the Committee on Post Office and Civil Service*. House of Representatives, 93rd Congress, 1st Session, pp. 2-6 and 116-125.

——— [1975]. "Improving Information on Agriculture and Rural Life." *Am. J. Agr. Econ.* 57:753-763.

——— [1976]. "An Information System Approach to National Agricultural Data Collection, Analysis and Decision." Paper presented at workshop, Minimum Information Systems for Agricultural Development in Low Income Countries, Oxford, England, December 6-9; to be published by the Agricultural Development Council.

——— [1977]. "Assessment of the Current Data Base for Agricultural Decision Makers: An Information System Approach." (See the table of contents in this volume.)

Borum, C. J. [1951]. "Estimating Flood Damage to the Bean Crop in Michigan." *Agr. Econ. Res.* 3:16-17.

——— [1955]. "Discussion: New Data Requirements by Areas—How Can They Be Met?" *J. Farm Econ.* 37:1056-1057.

Bosecker, R. R., and B. L. Ford [1976]. "Multiple Frame Estimation with Stratified Overlap Domain." In *Abstracts Booklet*, ASA, p. 19.

Bottum, J. C., and J. Ackerman [1958]. "Current and Area Data Progress and Future Needs in the United States." *J. Farm Econ.* 40:1772-1778.

Bowman, R. T. [1968]. "Crossroad Choices for the Future Development of the Federal Statistical System." *J. Am. Stat. Assoc.* 63:801-816.

Bowman, R. T., and M. E. Martin [1962]. "Special Report on Unemployment Statistics: Meaning and Measurement." *Am. Statistician* 16(4):14-22.

Boxley, R. F. [1971]. "Farm Size and the Distribution of Farm Numbers." *Agr. Econ. Res.* 23:87-94.

Boxley, R. F., Jr., W. L. Gibson, Jr., and B. R. Hoffnar [1964]. "The Application of Probability Theory Analysis to Nonrandom Enumeration Data." *J. Farm Econ.* 46:835-840.

Boyne, D. H. [1964]. *Changes in the Real Wealth Position of Farm Operators, 1940-1960*. Michigan Agricultural Experiment Station Technical Bulletin 294.

Brake, J. R. [1974]. "Farm Finance and National Economic Policy—Some Gaps in Knowledge." *Am. J. Agr. Econ.* 56:1056-1062.

Brake, J. R., and P. J. Barry [1971]. "Flow-of-Funds Social Accounts for the Farm Sector: Comment." *Am. J. Agr. Econ.* 53:665-668.

Brandow, G. E. [1976]. *Review and Evaluation of Price Spread Data for Foods*. Report of a task force (G. E. Brandow, chairman), sponsored by the Economic Statistics Committee of the AAEA and by the ERS.

Breimyer, H. F. [1967]. "This is Market News." *Agr. Marketing* (February), 12:8, 9, 13.

——— [1968]. "'Realized' Farm Income: An Outmoded Concept? Comment." *Am. J. Agr. Econ.* 50:432-434.

Brooks, E. M. [1949]. "The General Enumerative Surveys." *Agr. Econ. Res.* 1:37-47.

Brooks, R. M., V. D. Ryan, B. F. Blake, and J. R. Gordon [1974]. *An Explanation and Appraisal of the Methodology Used in the 1973 Indiana Community Preference Study: A Mail Survey*. Purdue University Agricultural Experiment Station Bulletin 53.

Brown, J. D. [1969]. "Effect of a Health Hazard 'Scare' on Consumer Demand." *Am. J. Agr. Econ.* 51:676-678.

Bryant, W. K. [1973]. "The Rising Value of Time and the Demand for Social and Economic Statistics." Paper prepared for AAEA Task Force on Social and Economic Statistics.

Budd, E. C. [1971]. "The Creation of a Microdata File for Estimating the Size Distribution of Income." *Review of Income and Wealth* 17:317-333.

Bullock, J. B. [1976]. "Social Costs Caused by Errors in Agricultural Production Forecasts." *Am. J. Agr. Econ.* 58:76-80.

Burk, M. C. [1956]. "Studies of the Consumption of Food and Their Uses." *J. Farm Econ.* 38:1736-1746.

——— [1959]. "The Study of Regional Food Consumption." *J. Farm Econ.* 41:1040-1049.

────── [1968]. *Consumption Economics: A Multidisciplinary Approach*. New York: Wiley.

Burk, M. C., and T. J. Lanahan, Jr. [1958]. "Use of 1955 Food Survey for Research in Agricultural Economics." *Agr. Econ. Res.* 10:79-99.

Burnham, B. O., and T. L. Jones [1969]. *Housing Costs: Rural-Urban Comparisons*. Ohio Agricultural Research Bulletin 1022.

Burroughs, R. J. [1949]. "Uses and Misuses of the Balance Sheet of Agriculture." *Agr. Finance Rev.* 12:22-32.

────── [1950]. "Balance Sheet of Agriculture—Meaning, Conceptual Limitations, and Uses." *Agr. Econ. Res.* 2:86-95.

Buse, R. C. [1973]. "Increasing Response Rates in Mailed Questionnaires." *Am. J. Agr. Econ.* 55:503-508.

Butz, D. E. [1966]. "Needs of the Agribusiness Community." *J. Farm Econ.* 48:1175-1178.

Callander, W. F. [1949]. "Letter to the Editor—The Agricultural Statisticians and the Program of the A.S.A." *Am. Statistician* 3(4):1.

Callander, W. F., and C. F. Sarle [1947]. "The BAE Program in Enumerative Sampling." *J. Farm Econ.* 29:233-236.

Carlin, T. A., and C. R. Handy [1974]. "Concepts of the Agricultural Economy and Economic Accounting." *Am. J. Agr. Econ.* 56:964-975.

Carlin, T. A., and A. G. Smith [1973]. "A New Approach in Accounting for Our Nation's Farm Income." *Agr. Finance Rev.* 34:1-6.

Carter, H. O., and E. O. Heady [1959]. *An Input-Output Analysis Emphasizing Regional and Commodity Sectors of Agriculture*. Iowa Agricultural Experiment Station Bulletin 469.

Caudill, C. E. [1965]. "Joint Use of Different Sampling Frames." *J. Farm Econ.* 47:1534-1539.

Cavin, J. P. [1952]. "Forecasting the Demand for Agricultural Products." *Agr. Econ. Res.* 4:65-76.

Christensen, L. R. [1975]. "Concepts and Measurement of Agricultural Productivity." *Am. J. Agr. Econ.* 57:910-915.

Christensen, L. R., and D. W. Jorgenson [1973]. "Measuring the Performance of the Private Sector of the U.S. Economy, 1929-1969." In *Measuring Economic and Social Performance*, M. Moss, ed. National Bureau of Economic Research.

Christensen, L. R., and M. E. Manser [1975]. "Cost of Living Indexes and Price Indexes for U.S. Meat and Produce, 1947-71." In *Household Production and Consumption*, N. Terleckyj, ed. National Bureau of Economic Research.

Churchman, C. W. [1971]. *The Design of Inquiring Systems*. New York: Basic Books.

Chryst, W. E. [1965]. "Land Values and Agricultural Income: A Paradox?" *J. Farm Econ.* 47:1265-1273.

Ciancio, N. J., and R. D. Tortora [1976]. "On Unbiased Estimation in the Area and List Frame." In *Abstracts Booklet*, ASA, p. 28.

CIDA (Inter-American Committee for Agricultural Development) [1963]. *Inventory of Information Basic to the Planning of Agricultural Development in Latin America —Regional Report*. Washington: Pan American Union. Reviewed by R. G. Wheeler in *J. Farm Econ.* 46:872-873.

Clark, F., B. Friend, and M. C. Burk [1947]. *Nutritive Value of the Per Capita Food Supply, 1909-45*. USDA Miscellaneous Publication 616.

Clausen, J. A., and R. M. Ford [1957]. "Controlling Bias in Mail Questionnaires." *J. Am. Stat. Assoc.* 42:449.

Clawson, M. [1966]. "Recent Efforts to Improve Land Use Information." *J. Am. Stat. Assoc.* 61:647-657.

——— [1967]. "Rural Poverty in the United States." *J. Farm Econ.* 49:1227-1234.

Clawson, M., and C. L. Stewart [1965]. *Land Use Information: A Critical Survey of U.S. Statistics Including Possibilities for Greater Uniformity.* Washington, D.C.: Resources for the Future.

Clough, M. [1951]. "Changes in Corn Acreage and Production after the Early Indications." *Agr. Econ. Res.* 3:140-146.

Cochran, W. G. [1953]. *Sampling Techniques.* New York: Wiley.

Cochrane, R. S. [1965]. "Multiple Frame Sample Surveys." *J. Am. Stat. Assoc.* 60:656(abstract).

Cochrane, W. W. [1961]. "The Role of Economics and Statistics in the USDA." *Agr. Econ. Res.* 13:69-74.

——— [1966]. "Improvements Needed in Statistics for Making Policy and Program Decisions." *J. Farm Econ.* 48:1654-1666.

Cohen, M. R., and E. Nagel [1934]. *An Introduction to Logic and the Scientific Method.* New York: Harcourt Brace.

Commons, J. R. [1924]. *The Legal Foundations of Capitalism.* New York: Macmillan.

Conklin, M. J., and R. C. McElroy [1966]. *A Survey of Migrant Farmworker Housing in Oregon.* Oregon Agricultural Experiment Station Bulletin 602.

Cook, R. N., and J. L. Kennedy, eds. [1966]. *Proceedings of the Tri-State Conference on a Comprehensive, Unified Land Data System (CULDATA).* University of Cincinnati College of Law.

Cooper, M. R., G. T. Barton, and A. P. Brodell [1947]. *Progress of Farm Mechanization.* USDA Miscellaneous Bulletin 630.

Cox, E. B. [1962]. "Henry Moore and the 'Statistical Complement of Pure Economics.'" *Am. Statistician* 16(2):10-13.

Crawford, T. L. [1974]. "The Bill for Marketing U.S. Farm-Food Products." In *Marketing and Transportation Situation,* USDA, ERS, MTS-194, pp. 15-30.

Crecink, J. C., and H. Hoover [1960]. *Incomes and Resources of Rural Families in the Clay Hills Area of Mississippi.* Mississippi Agricultural Experiment Station Bulletin 604.

Crecink, J. C., and R. Steptoe [1970]. *Human Resources in the Rural Mississippi Delta, with Emphasis on the Poor.* USDA Agricultural Economic Report 170.

Crom, R. J. [1972]. "Economic Projections Using Behavioral Models." *Agr. Econ. Res.* 24:9-15.

Cromarty, W. A. [1959]. "An Econometric Model for United States Agriculture." *J. Am. Stat. Assoc.* 54:556-574.

Crosswhite, M., and G. Vaughn [1962]. *Land Use in the Rural-Urban Fringe: A Case Study of Newcastle County, Delaware.* Delaware Agricultural Experiment Station Bulletin 340.

Crowley, W., Jr. [1972]. *The Influence of Net Real Estate Income and Other Property Characteristics on Prices of Agricultural Properties within and among Selected Areas of Oregon, 1965-69.* Unpublished Ph.D. dissertation, Oregon State University.

Daft, L. [1973]. "Rural Area Public Policy: Some Implications for Social and Economic Statistics." Paper prepared for AAEA Task Force on Social and Economic Statistics.

Daly, R. F. [1957]. "Prospective Demands for Food and Fiber." *Policy for Commercial Agriculture: Its Relations to Economic Growth and Stability.* Joint Economic Committee, 85th U.S. Congress, 1st Session.

—— [1963]. "Long-Run Economic Projections: A Review and Appraisal." *Agr. Econ. Res.* 15:113-121.

—— [1966]. "Current Questions on National Agricultural Outlook." *J. Farm Econ.* 48:1167-1174.

—— [1969]. "Effective Use of Available Data." Paper presented at the National Marketing Service Workshop, Asheville, N.C.

Darr, D. R. [1972]. *Production, Prices, Employment and Trade in the Northwest Forest Industries, Fourth Quarter 1971.* USDA, Forest Service, Pacific Northwest Forest and Range Experiment Station.

David, M. [1976]. "Strategies for Improving Policy-Relevant Data on the Poor." *Am. Statistician* 30:129-133.

Davis, W. D., Jr., and F. Miller [1959]. *Land Price Trends in Missouri.* Missouri Agricultural Experiment Station Research Bulletin 686.

De Leeuw, F. [1962]. "The Concept of Capacity." *J. Am. Stat. Assoc.* 58:826-840.

Demsetz, H. [1969]. "Information and Efficiency: Another Viewpoint." *J. Law Econ.* 12:1-22.

Denison, E. F. [1969]. "Some Major Issues in Productivity Analysis: An Examination of Estimates by Jorgenson and Griliches." *Survey of Current Business* 49(5):1-27 (part 2); reprinted in 1972 in *Survey of Current Business* 52(5):37-63 (part 2).

Dewey, J. [1938]. *Logic, the Theory of Inquiry.* New York: Holt.

Dill, H. W., Jr. [1955]. "Photo Interpretation in Flood Control Appraisal." *Photogrammetric Engineering* 21:112-114.

—— [1967]. *Worldwide Use of Airphotos in Agriculture.* USDA Agriculture Handbook 344.

Dill, H. W., Jr., and R. C. Otte [1970]. *Urbanization of Land in the Western States.* USDA, ERS Report 428.

—— [1971]. *Urbanization of Land in the Northeastern United States.* USDA, ERS Report 485.

Dovring, F., and W. H. Scofield [1963]. *Farm Real Estate Sales in Illinois.* Illinois Agricultural Experiment Station Bulletin 697.

Doyle, Sir Arthur Conan [1930]. "The Adventures of Sherlock Holmes: A Scandal in Bohemia." In *The Complete Sherlock Holmes.* New York: Doubleday. P. 163.

Ducoff, L. J., and G. Bancroft [1945]. "Experiment in the Measurement of Unpaid Family Labor in Agriculture." *J. Am. Stat. Assoc.* 40:205-213.

Ducoff, L. J., and M. J. Hagood [1946]. "Objectives, Uses and Types of Labor Force Data in Relation to Economic Policy." *J. Am. Stat. Assoc.* 41:293-302.

—— [1947]. *Labor Force Definition and Measurement.* Social Science Research Council Bulletin 56.

Dunn, E. S., Jr. [1966]. "Review of Proposals for a National Data Center." *The Computer and the Invasion of Privacy.* Hearings of the Subcommittee, Committee on Government Operations, House of Representatives, 89th Congress, 2nd Session.

—— [1971]. "The National Economic Accounts: A Case Study of the Evolution toward Integrated Statistical Information Systems." *Survey of Current Business* 51(7):45-64 (part 2).

—— [1974]. *Social Information Processing and Statistical Systems—Change and Reform.* New York: Wiley.

Durost, D. D. [1960]. *Index Numbers of Agricultural Production by Regions, 1939-1958.* USDA Statistical Bulletin 273.

Durost, D. D., and G. T. Barton [1960]. *Changing Sources of Farm Output.* USDA, ARS Production Research Report 36.

Dwoskin, P. B., and M. Jacobs [1957]. *Potato Flakes—A New Form of Dehydrated Mashed Potatoes: Market Position and Consumer Acceptance in Binghamton, Endicott and Johnson City, N.Y.* USDA Marketing Research Report 186.

Dyer, D. R. [1975]. "Livestock Capital Formation—A Preliminary Report." *Western Agr. Econ. Assoc. Proceedings,* July, pp. 226-229.

Ebling, W. H. [1939]. "Why the Government Entered the Field of Crop Reporting and Forecasting." *J. Farm Econ.* 21:718-734.

Ebling, W. H., and H. L. Ahlgren [1954]. "Agricultural Data Requirements—National, State, and County." *J. Farm Econ.* 36:1226-1239.

———— [1959]. "Some Needed Developments in Statistical Programs to Obtain Research Data." *J. Farm Econ.* 41:1506-1518.

Eckler, R., and C. Taeuber [1954]. "The Current Statistics of the Census Bureau." *J. Am. Stat. Assoc.* 49:348 (abstract).

Edgington, E. S. [1963]. "Joint Analysis of Differences in Central Tendency and Variability." *Am. Statistician* 17(3):28-30.

Edwards, A. D., and D. G. Jones [1964]. *Housing in South Carolina: Its Socio-economic Context.* South Carolina Agricultural Experiment Station Bulletin 511.

Edwards, C. [1969]. "A Rural Economic Indicator System." *J. Farm Econ.* 51:1202-1205.

———— [1973]. "Local Economic Development." Paper prepared for AAEA Task Force on Social and Economic Statistics.

Egbert, A. C. [1969]. "An Aggregate Model of Agriculture: Empirical Estimates and Some Policy Implications." *Am. J. Agr. Econ.* 51:71-86.

Ehlers, W. F. [1960]. "Economic Implications of Drought Probabilities for Humid Area Irrigation." *J. Farm Econ.* 42:1518-1519.

Eisgruber, L. M. [1967]. "Micro- and Macro-analytic Potential of Agricultural Information Systems." *J. Farm Econ.* 49:1541-1552.

———— [1973]. "Managerial Information and Decision Systems in the U.S.A.: Historical Developments, Current Status, and Major Issues." *Am. J. Agr. Econ.* 55:930-939.

Eley, C. [1971]. "Cost of Packaging Materials for Farm Foods." In *Marketing and Transportation Situation,* USDA, ERS, MTS-182, pp. 17-20.

Elrod, R. H., and P. E. LaFerney [1970]. *Sector Income and Employment Multipliers: Their Interactions on the National Economy.* USDA Technical Bulletin 1421.

Erickson, C. E. [1971]. "Adequacy of Economic Statistics for Agribusiness Planning." *Am. J. Agr. Econ.* 53:912 (abstract).

Evans, J. A., and W. F. Hughes [1971]. *Production Costs, Resource Returns, and Other Economic Characteristics—Commercial Cotton Farms, Southern High Plains, Texas, 1966-69.* USDA, ERS Report 478.

Ewing, J. A. [1956]. "Discussion: Local Data Requirements in Areas of High Agricultural Specialization." *J. Farm Econ.* 38:1471-1474.

Ezekiel, M. [1924]. "A Method of Handling Curvilinear Correlation for Any Number of Variables." *J. Am. Stat. Assoc.* 19:431-453.

Fabricant, S. [1959]. *Basic Facts on Productivity Change.* National Bureau of Economic Research, Occasional Paper 63.

Fellegi, I. P. [1972]. "On the Question of Statistical Confidentiality." *J. Am. Stat. Assoc.* 67:7-18.

Fellegi, I. P., and K. J. Krotki [1968]. "The Testing Programs for the 1971 Census in Canada." *J. Am. Stat. Assoc.* 63:750-751 (abstract).

Ferber, R. [1949]. *Statistical Techniques in Market Research.* New York: McGraw-Hill.

—— [1955]. "On the Reliability of Responses Secured in Sample Surveys." *J. Am. Stat. Assoc.* 50:788-810.

—— [1956]. "On the Interpretation of the Aggregate Savings Ratio." *Am. Statistician* 10(3):10-13.

—— [1966]. "Item Non-response in a Consumer Survey." *Public Opinion Quarterly* 30:399-413.

Ferguson, R. H., and N. P. Kingsley [1972]. *The Timber Resources of Maine.* USDA, Northeastern Forest Research Experiment Station, Resource Bulletin NE-26.

Ferris, J. [1962]. "Unsolved Problems in Data Collection and Analysis." *J. Farm Econ.* 44:1763-1772.

Finkner, A. L. [1952]. "Adjustment for Non-response Bias in a Rural Mailed Survey." *Agr. Econ. Res.* 4:77-82.

Fischer, L. K., R. Burkholder, and J. Muehlbeier [1960]. *The Farm Real Estate Market in Nebraska.* Nebraska Agricultural Experiment Station Bulletin SB-456.

Fisher, J. L., and N. Potter [1964]. *World Prospects for Natural Resources: Some Projections of Demand and Indicators of Supply to the Year 2000.* Baltimore: Johns Hopkins University Press.

Foote, R. J. [1970]. *Concepts Involved in Defining and Identifying Farms.* USDA, ERS Report 448.

Foote, R. J., and L. H. Bean [1951]. "Are Yearly Variations in Crop Yield Really Random?" *Agr. Econ. Res.* 3:23-30.

Foote, R. J., and K. A. Fox [1952]. *Seasonal Variation: Methods of Measurement and Tests of Significance.* USDA Agriculture Handbook 48.

Foote, R. J., and H. Weingarten [1958]. "Alternative Methods for Estimating Changes in Production from Data on Acreage and Condition." *Agr. Econ. Res.* 10:20-27.

Fox, A., T. Eichers, P. Andrelenas, R. Jenkins, and H. Blake [1968]. *Extent of Farm Pesticide Use on Crops in 1966.* USDA Agricultural Economic Report 147.

Fox, K. A. [1953], "Factors Affecting the Accuracy of Price Forecasts." *J. Farm Econ.* 35:323-340.

Freeman, R. E. [1970]. *Rural Housing: Trends and Prospects.* USDA Agricultural Economic Report 193.

Freeman, R. E., and D. D. Miller [1970]. "National Goals for Housing." In *A Good Life for More People,* USDA Yearbook of Agriculture.

French, C. E., and D. C. Kranz [1957]. "Telephone Interview as a Means of Surveying Farmers." *J. Farm Econ.* 39:153-155.

Frey, H. T. [1967]. *Agricultural Application of Remote Sensing—The Potential from Space Platforms.* USDA Agriculture Information Bulletin 328.

Frey, H. T., and H. W. Dill, Jr. [1971]. *Land Use Change in the Southern Mississippi Alluvial Valley, 1950-69: An Analysis Based on Remote Sensing.* USDA Agricultural Economic Report 215.

Frey, H. T., O. K. Krause, and C. Dickason [1968]. *Major Uses of Land and Water in the United States with Special Reference to Agriculture: Summary for 1964.* USDA Agricultural Economic Report 149.

Friend, B. [1963]. "Enrichment and Fortification of Foods." In *National Food Situation*, USDA, ERS, NFS-106, pp. 36-40.

Fritsch, C., et al. [1975]. "Task Force Report: A Working Definition of the Food and Fiber System." USDA, ERS. Mimeo.

Fromm, G. [1973]. "Implications to and from Economic Theory in Models of Complex Systems." *Am. J. Agr. Econ.* 55:259-270.

Frye, R. E. [1962]. *Effect of the Pilot Food Stamp Program on Retail Food Store Sales.* USDA Agricultural Economic Report 8.

Fuller, V., R. Gillett, E. Heady, P. Homeyer, D. G. Johnson [1953]. "Report of the AFEA Committee on Farm Employment Estimates." *J. Farm Econ.* 35:976-987; W. A. Hendricks, "Discussion," p. 988.

Fuller, V., and W. Van Vuuren [undated]. "Farm Labor and Labor Markets." University of California (Davis), Department of Agricultural Economics. Mimeo.

Gabbard, L. P., and R. G. Cherry [1948]. *Trend of Taxes on Farm and Ranch Real Estate in Texas, 1890-1946.* Texas Agricultural Experiment Station Bulletin 702.

Gale, H. F. [1967]. *The Farm Food Marketing Bill and Its Components.* USDA Agricultural Economic Report 105.

——— [1968]. "Industry Output, Labor, Input, Value Added and Productivity Associated with Food Expenditures." *Agr. Econ. Res.* 20:113-133.

Gardner, B. [1973]. "Human Resource Statistics for Rural Areas." Paper prepared for AAEA Task Force on Social and Economic Statistics.

——— [1975]. "Strategies for Long-Run Investment in Rural, Social, and Economic Statistics." *Am. J. Agr. Econ.* 57:892-899.

Garlock, F., and P. Allen [1964]. *Technical Appraisal of the 1960 Sample Survey of Farm Debt.* USDA, ERS Report 167.

Gertel, K. [1962a]. "Water Data for Economic Decisions." International Seminar on Water and Soil Utilization, Brookings, S.D., July 18-August 10.

——— [1962b]. *Water: Uses, Supplies, Projections—An Introduction to Terms and Reference Sources.* USDA, ERS.

Gibson, W. L., Jr., C. J. Arnold, and F. D. Aigner [1962]. *The Marginal Value of Flue-Cured Tobacco Allotments.* Virginia Agricultural Experiment Station Technical Bulletin 156.

Gibson, W. L., Jr., and R. L. Chambliss, Jr. [1966]. "Peanut Allotments and the Price of Farm Land." *Virginia Farm Economics*, No. 196, Virginia Polytechnic Institute.

Gilbert, E. N. [1958]. "An Outline of Information Theory." *Am. Statistician* 12(1):13-19.

Gilbert, S. J. [1955]. "Discussion: Needed Changes in State and Local Crop and Livestock Reports." *J. Farm Econ.* 37:1058-1059.

Gillett, R. L. [1948]. "Data Needs for Agricultural Research and Marketing." *J. Farm Econ.* 30:271-281.

Gilliam, H. C., Jr., and J. W. Hubbard [1971]. *An Analysis of Agricultural Land Values in Selected Cotton Producing Counties of the South Carolina Coastal Plain.* South Carolina Agricultural Experiment Station Bulletin 554.

Gomme, F. R. [1972]. "Buckwheat: A Look at Its Prospects and Problems." In *Wheat Situation*, USDA, ERS, WS-220, pp. 9-11.

Gonzalez, M. E. [1973]. "Use and Evaluation of Synthetic Estimates." In *Abstracts Booklet*, ASA, pp. 41-42.

Goodsell, W. D. [1956]. *Costs and Returns: Commercial Family-Operated Farms by Type and Size, 1930-1951.* USDA Statistical Bulletin 197.

Goodsell, W. D., W. H. Brown, H. C. Fowler, E. Hole, E. B. Hurd, Jr., J. Vermeer, and I.

Jenkins [1956]. *Farm Costs and Returns, 1955 (with Comparisons): Commercial Family-Operated Farms, by Type and Location.* USDA Agriculture Information Bulletin 158.

Grange, G. R. [1967]. "The Changing Face of Market News." *Agr. Marketing* 12:4, 5, 13.

——— [1972]. "The Federal-State Market News Service." *Major Statistical Series of the U.S. Department of Agriculture—How They Are Constructed and Used. Volume 10, Market News.* USDA Agriculture Handbook 365, pp. 1-7.

Grieves, H. C. [1954]. " 'Spot Checks' in Lieu of Complete Censuses." *J. Am. Stat. Assoc.* 49:347 (abstract).

Griliches, Z. [1960]. "Measuring Inputs in Agriculture: A Critical Survey." *J. Farm Econ.* 42:1411-1427.

——— [1963]. "The Sources of Measured Productivity Growth, U.S. Agriculture, 1940-60." *J. Pol. Econ.* 71:331-346.

Grove, E. W. [1939]. "Farm Population, Nonfarm Population, and Number of Farms in the United States, 1910-1939: Section I, Population, Farming, and Farmers." In *Income Parity for Agriculture,* part 5, USDA, BAE. Mimeo.

——— [1954]. "Quarterly Estimates of Realized Gross and Net Farm Income." *Agr. Econ. Res.* 6:65-76.

——— [1967]. "Realized Farm Income: An Outmoded Concept?" *J. Farm Econ.* 49: 795-805.

——— [1969]. "Econometricians and the Data Gap: Comment." *Am. J. Agr. Econ.* 51:184-188.

Guither, H. D. [1970]. *Needs and Preferences for Grain Market News among Illinois Farm Operators.* University of Illinois Agricultural Experiment Station AERR-103.

Gunnelson, G., W. D. Dobson, and S. Pamperin [1972]. "Analysis of the Accuracy of USDA Crop Forecasts." *Am. J. Agr. Econ.* 54:639-645.

Haavelmo, T. [1947]. "The Interdependence between Agriculture and the National Economy." *J. Farm Econ.* 29:910-923.

Hady, T. F. [1970]. "Differential Assessment of Farmland on the Rural-Urban Fringe." *Am. J. Agr. Econ.* 52:25-32.

Hady, T. F., and T. F. Stinson [1967]. *Taxation of Farmland on the Rural-Urban Fringe.* USDA Agricultural Economic Report 119.

Hagood, M. J. [1945]. *General Purpose Sample Survey.* USDA, BAE. Processed Report.

Hagood, M. J., and E. H. Bernert [1945]. "Component Indexes as a Basis for Stratification in Sampling." *J. Am. Stat. Assoc.* 40:330-341.

Hahn, F. H. [1970]. "Some Adjustment Problems." *Econometrica* 38:1-17.

Hair, D., and A. H. Ulrich [1971]. *The Demand and Price Situation for Forest Products, 1970-71.* USDA Miscellaneous Publication 1195.

Halcrow, H. G., and T. A. Hieronymus [1959]. "Parity Prices in their Economic Context." *J. Farm Econ.* 41:1289-1299, 1300.

Hale, R. F. [1939]. "Estimating Local Market Prices and Farm Labor since 1920." *J. Farm Econ.* 21:828-837.

Hall, G. E. [1969]. "Recent Experiences in the Collection of Longitudinal Survey Data." *J. Am. Stat. Assoc.* 64:696 (abstract).

Hamlin, E. T. [1970]. *Financing of Rural Nonfarm Housing in the United States.* USDA, ERS.

Hansen, M. H. [1965]. "Some New Developments Increasing the Availability of Census Information." *J. Am. Stat. Assoc.* 60:662 (abstract).

Hansen, M. H., and W. N. Hurwitz [1946]. "The Problem of Non-response in Sample Surveys." *J. Am. Stat. Assoc.* 41:517-528.

Hansen, H., W. N. Hurwitz, and W. G. Madow [1953]. *Sample Survey Methods and Theory.* New York: Wiley.

Hardin, C. M. [1946]. "The BAE under Fire: A Study in Valuation Conflicts." *J. Farm Econ.* 28:635-668.

Haren, C. C. [1975]. "Today's Metropolitan Areas: The Need for Critical Reevaluation." In *Abstracts Booklet*, ASA, p. 61.

Harlan, C. L. [1947]. "The 1945 Census Enumeration of Livestock on Farms." *J. Farm Econ.* 29:691-710.

Harp, H. H., and D. F. Dunham [1963]. *Comparative Costs to Consumers of Convenience Foods and Home Prepared Foods.* USDA Marketing Research Report 609.

Harris, C. C., Jr. [1962]. "Parity Income Prices." *J. Farm Econ.* 44:141-156.

Hartley, H. O. [1962]. "Multiple Frame Surveys." Paper given at the Minneapolis meetings of the ASA.

—— [1965]. "Discussion, Sampling Frames for Collection of Agricultural Statistics." *J. Farm Econ.* 47:1542-1544.

Hartnett, H. B. [1965]. *Marketing Economics Research Publications.* USDA, ERS Report 205.

Hathaway, D. E. [1955]. *The Effects of the Price Support Program on the Dry Bean Industry in Michigan.* Michigan Agricultural Experiment Station Technical Bulletin 250.

—— [1959]. "Discussion: Supplemental Data from the Forthcoming Censuses." *J. Farm Econ.* 41:1503-1505.

—— [1963]. "Improving and Extending Farm-Nonfarm Income Comparisons." *J. Farm Econ.* 45:367-375.

—— [1969]. "The Economics of Agricultural Economics." *Am. J. Agr. Econ.* 51:1011-1026.

—— [1972]. "Some Special Characteristics of Rural Areas." In *Labor Market Information in Rural Areas.* Center for Rural Manpower and Public Affairs, Michigan State University.

Hathaway, D. E., J. A. Beegle, and W. K. Bryant [1968]. *People of Rural America.* 1960 Census Monograph, U.S. Bureau of the Census, Washington, D.C.

Hayek, F. A. [1945]. "The Use of Knowledge in Society." *Am. Econ. Rev.* 35:519-530.

Hayami, Y., and W. Peterson [1972]. "Social Returns to Public Information Services: Statistical Reporting of U.S. Farm Commodities." *Am. Econ. Rev.* 62:119-130.

Hayenga, M. L. [1971]. "Hog Pricing and Evaluation Methods—Their Accuracy and Equity." *Am. J. Agr. Econ.* 53:506-509.

Heady, E. O., and L. Auer [1966]. "Imputation of Production to Technologies." *J. Farm Econ.* 48:309-322.

Heady, E. O., and L. G. Tweeten [1963]. *Resource Demand and Structure of the Agricultural Industry.* Ames: Iowa State University Press.

Heflebower, R. B. [1951]. "An Economic Appraisal of Price Measures." *J. Am. Stat. Assoc.* 46:461-479.

Hein, C. J. [1960]. "The Function and Finances of Special Districts in Rural Areas." *Agr. Finance Rev.* 22:1-19.

Henderson, H. A. [1960]. *Resources and Incomes of Rural East Tennessee People.* Tennessee Agricultural Experiment Station Bulletin 312.

Hendricks, W. A. [1947]. "Farm Employment Levels in Relation to Supply and Demand as Per Cent of Normal." *J. Am. Stat. Assoc.* 42:271-281.

———— [1949]. "Adjustment for Bias by Non-response in Mailed Surveys." *Agr. Econ. Res.* 1:52-56.

———— [1955]. "Validity of Objective Estimates of Corn Yield." *Agr. Econ. Res.* 7: 69-72.

———— [1963]. "Forecasting Yields with Objective Measurements." *J. Farm Econ.* 45: 1508-1513.

Hendricks, W. A., and H. F. Huddleston [1955]. "A Foundation for Objective Forecasts of Cotton Yields." *Agr. Econ. Res.* 7:108-111.

Hendricks, W. A., D. T. Searls, and D. G. Horvitz [1964]. "A Comparison of Three Rules for Associating Farms and Farmland with Sample Area Segments in Agricultural Surveys." *J. Am. Stat. Assoc.* 59:588 (abstract).

Hendrix, W. E. [1955]. "The Low Income Problem in American Agriculture." In *United States Agriculture: Perspectives and Prospects.* The American Assembly, Graduate School of Business, Columbia University. Pp. 84-101.

Heneberry, W. H., and R. Barlowe [1962]. *Assessment of Farm Real Estate for Property Taxes.* Michigan Agricultural Experiment Station Special Bulletin 439.

Herdt, R. W., and W. W. Cochrane [1966]. "Farm Land Prices and Technological Advance." *J. Farm Econ.* 48:243-263.

Herriot, R., and E. Spiers [1975]. "Measuring the Impact on Family Income Statistics of Reporting Differences between the CPS and Administrative Sources." In *Abstracts Booklet*, ASA, p. 65.

Hickman, B. G. [1964]. "On a New Method of Capacity Estimation." *J. Am. Stat. Assoc.* 59:529-549.

Hiemstra, S. J. [1968]. *Food Consumption, Prices and Explanations.* USDA Agricultural Economic Report 138 (also *Supplements* for 1968, 1970, 1971, 1972, and 1973, all bearing the same report number).

Hildreth, R. J. [1967]. "Discussion: Comprehensive Agricultural Data Systems." *J. Farm Econ.* 49:1558-1560.

———— [1975]. *Report of Task Force on Farm Income Estimates.* Report of a task force (R. J. Hildreth, chairman), sponsored by the Economic Statistics Committee of the AAEA and by the ERS.

Hildreth, R. J., and G. Worden [1976]. "Revisions of Statistical Definitions: What Is a Farm?" In *Proceedings, American Statistical Association, Social Statistics Section*, part I, pp. 42-46.

Hirsch, H. G. [1947]. "1950 World Census of Agriculture." *J. Farm Econ.* 29:564-566.

Hirshleifer, J. [1971]. "The Private and Social Value of Information and the Reward to Inventive Activity." *Am. Econ. Rev.* 61:561-573.

Hoag, H. M. [1970]. *The Use and Need for Livestock Market News: Part II, Personal Interview Survey.* Southern Illinois University, School of Agriculture Publication 34.

Hoffman, A. C. [1966]. "Discussion: Agricultural Economics in the USDA." *J. Farm Econ.* 48:436-439.

Holmes, A. D. [1951]. "Sampling for Agricultural Statistics in Canada." *J. Farm Econ.* 33:780-786.

442   REFERENCES

Holmes, O. W. [1969]. "The Farm Poor: Counted, Miscounted, or Discounted?" *J. Farm Econ.* 51:1557-1560.

Hoover, H., and B. L. Green [1970]. *Human Resources in the Rural Ozarks Region, with Emphasis on the Poor.* USDA Agricultural Economic Report 182.

Horring, J. [1961]. *Concepts of Productivity Measurement in Agriculture on a National Scale.* OECD Documentation in Food and Agriculture 57, Paris.

Hotelling, H. [1958]. "The Statistical Method and the Philosophy of Science." *Am. Statistician* 12(5):9-15.

Houck, J. P., and M. Soliman [1971]. "Revisions of the Major U.S. Agricultural Price Indexes: An Empirical Analysis." USDA, ERS. Unpublished.

Houk, H. J. [1957]. "Discussion: Evaluation of Available Data for Estimating Market Supplies and Prices of Hogs." *J. Farm Econ.* 39:1408-1410.

House, P. [1961]. *State Action Relating to Taxation of Farmland on the Rural-Urban Fringe.* USDA, ERS Report 13.

—— [1967]. *Differential Assessment of Farmland near Cities: Experience in Maryland through 1965.* USDA, ERS Report 358.

Houseman, E. E. [1947]. "The Sample Design for a National Farm Survey by the BAE." *J. Farm Econ.* 29:241-245.

—— [1949]. "Design of Samples for Surveys." *Agr. Econ. Res.* 1:3-10.

—— [1950]. "Sampling Methods in Marketing Research." *Agr. Econ. Res.* 2:73-81.

—— [1953]. "Statistical Treatment of the Nonresponse Problem." *Agr. Econ. Res.* 5:12-19.

—— [1955]. "Some Recent Advances in Statistics in the USDA." *J. Am. Stat. Assoc.* 50:581 (abstract).

—— [1957]. "Sample Design for the Survey of Farm Operators' 1955 Expenditures." *Estadistica* 15:591-600.

—— [1964]. "Sources of Data for Econometric Models." *J. Farm Econ.* 46:1400-1406.

—— [1972]. "The Survey as a Measurement Instrument." *Agr. Econ. Res.* 24:87-92.

Houseman, E. E., and J. A. Becker [1967]. "A Centenary Profile of Methods for Agricultural Surveys." *Am. Statistician* 21(2):15-21.

Houseman, E. E., and H. F. Huddleston [1966]. "Forecasting and Estimating Crop Yields from Plant Measurements." *FAO Monthly Bulletin Agr. Econ. and Stat.* 15(10):1-6.

Houseman, E. E., and T. J. Reed [1954]. *Application of Probability Area Sampling to Farm Surveys.* USDA Agriculture Handbook 67.

Houseman, E. E., and H. C. Trelogan [1967]. "Progress toward Optimizing Agricultural Area Sampling." In *Bulletin of the International Statistical Institute: Proceedings,* 36th Session, vol. 42, 1:293-304.

Houthakker, H. S. [1968]. "'Realized' Farm Income: An Outmoded Concept? Reply." *Am. J. Agr. Econ.* 50:156.

Howe, E. C., and C. R. Handy [1975]. "Inventory and Critique of Productivity Estimates of the U.S. Food and Fiber Sector." *Am. J. Agr. Econ.* 57:916-921.

Howe, E. C., C. R. Handy, and L. G. Traub [1975]. In *Search of an Industry Capital Stock.* USDA, ERS Working Paper.

Huddleston, H. F. [1950]. "Methods Used in a Survey of Orchards." *Agr. Econ. Res.* 2:126-130.

—— [1965]. "A New Area Sampling Frame and Its Uses." *J. Farm Econ.* 47:1524-1533.

—— [1968]. "Point Sampling Surveys in Colorado's San Luis Valley." *Agr. Econ. Res.* 20:1-4.

—— [1971]. "Use of Photography in Sampling for Number of Fruit per Tree." *Agr. Econ. Res.* 23:63-67.

Hulten, C. R. [1974]. "Growth Accounting with Intermediate Inputs." Johns Hopkins University. Mimeo.

Hurlburt, V. L. [1950]. *Buying of Farms in Story County, Iowa, 1940-48.* Iowa Agricultural Experiment Station Research Bulletin 377.

—— [1959]. *On the Theory of Evaluating Farmland by the Income Approach.* USDA, ARS, unnumbered report.

Hurley, R. [1949]. "Plans for the 1950 Census of Agriculture." *J. Farm Econ.* 31:1284-1293. P. J. Crees, "Discussion," pp. 1293-1295; J. R. Motheral, "Discussion," pp. 1295-1296 R. S. Overton, "Discussion," pp. 1296-1297.

—— [1954]. "Plans for the 1954 Census of Agriculture." *J. Farm Econ.* 36:1240-1247.

—— [1958]. "Plans and Publication of State and Local Data for the 1959 Census of Agriculture." *J. Farm Econ.* 40:1782-1786.

—— [1962]. "Census Concepts: Past, Present and Future." *J. Farm Econ.* 44:616-621.

—— [1965]. "Problems Relating to Criteria for Classification of Farms." *J. Farm Econ.* 47:1565-1571.

Hurley, R., and R. K. Smith [1951]. "New Approaches and Methods for the Census." *Agr. Econ. Res.* 3:113-118.

Hurley, R., T. Jabine, and D. Larson [1963]. "Evaluation Studies of the 1959 Census of Agriculture." *J. Am. Stat. Assoc.* 58:554 (abstract).

Hurst, R. L. [1969]. *Rural Housing in the Northeast Coastal Plain Area of South Carolina.* USDA Agricultural Economic Report 163.

Hurwitz, A. [1962]. "Constants and Compromise in the Consumer Price Index." *J. Am. Stat. Assoc.* 57:813-825.

Ingram, J. J., and D. Prochaska [1972]. "Measuring Completeness of Coverage in the 1969 Census of Agriculture." In *Abstracts Booklet*, ASA, p. 69.

Irwin, G. D. [1968]. "Three Myths about the Balance Sheet: The Changing Financial Structure of Farming." *Am. J. Agr. Econ.* 50:1596-1599.

Ives, J. R. [1957]. "An Evaluation of Available Data for Estimating Market Supplies and Prices of Cattle." *J. Farm Econ.* 39:1411-1418.

Jacobs, E. E. [1975]. "Progress Report on the 1972-73 Consumer Expenditure Survey." In *Abstracts Booklet*, ASA, p. 72.

Jebe, E. H. [1952]. "Estimation for Sub-sampling Designs Employing the County as a Primary Sampling Unit." *J. Am. Stat. Assoc.* 47:49-70.

Jebe, E. H., and E. S. Clifton [1956]. "Estimating Yields and Grades of Slaughter Steers and Heifers." *J. Farm Econ.* 38:584-596.

Jennings, R. D. [1958]. *Consumption of Feed by Livestock, 1909-56: Relation between Feed, Livestock, and Food at the National Level.* USDA Production Research Report 21.

Jessen, R. J. [1939]. "An Experiment in Design of Agricultural Surveys." *J. Farm Econ.* 21:855-863.

—— [1942]. *Statistical Investigation of a Sample Survey for Obtaining Farm Facts.* Iowa Agricultural Experiment Station Research Bulletin 304.

—— [1947]. "The Master Sample Project and Its Use in Agricultural Economics." *J. Farm Econ.* 29:531-540.

——— [1949]. "Some Inadequacies of the Federal Censuses of Agriculture." *J. Am. Stat. Assoc.* 44:279-292.

——— [1955]. "Determining the Fruit Count on a Tree by Randomized Branch Sampling." *Biometrics* 11:99-109.

Johnson, D. G., and M. C. Nottenburg [1951]. "A Critical Analysis of Farm Employment Estimates." *J. Am. Stat. Assoc.* 46:181-205.

Johnson, G. L. [1952]. *Burley Tobacco Control Programs: Their Over-All Effect on Production and Prices, 1933-50.* Kentucky Agricultural Experiment Station Bulletin 580.

Johnson, P. L. ed. [1969]. *Remote Sensing in Ecology.* Athens: University of Georgia Press.

Jones, L. A. [1966]. *Rural Home Financing through the Voluntary Home Mortgage Credit Program.* USDA, ERS Report 270.

Jorgenson, D. W. [1964]. "Minimum Variance, Linear, Unbiased Seasonal Adjustment of Economic Time Series." *J. Am. Stat. Assoc.* 59:681-724.

Jorgenson, D. W., and Z. Griliches [1967]. "The Explanation of Productivity Change." *Rev. Econ. Studies* 34:249-283; reprinted with corrections in 1969 in *Survey of Current Business* 49(5):29-64 (part 2); again reprinted with corrections in 1972 in *Survey of Current Business* 52(5):3-36 (part 2).

——— [1972a]. "Issues in Growth Accounting: A Reply to Edward F. Denison." *Survey of Current Business* 52(5): 65-94 (part 2).

——— [1972b]. "Final Reply." *Survey of Current Business* 52(5):111 (part 2).

Juster, F. T. [1970]. "Microdata, Economic Research, and the Production of Economic Knowledge." *Am. Econ. Rev.* 60:138-148.

Keith, K., and W. D. Purcell [1976]. "Possible Implications of Voids in USDA Cattle Slaughter Data." *Am. J. Agr. Econ.* 58:568-571.

Kelly, B. W. [1958]. "Objective Methods for Forecasting Florida Citrus Production." *Estadistica* (journal of the Inter-American Statistical Institute) 58:56.

——— [1963]. "Probability Sampling in Collecting Farm Data." *J. Farm Econ.* 45: 1515-1520.

Kendrick, J. W. [1961]. *Productivity Trends in the United States.* National Bureau of Economic Research, Princeton: Princeton University Press.

——— [1972]. *Economic Accounts and Their Uses.* New York: McGraw-Hill.

——— [1973]. *Postwar Productivity Trends in the United States, 1948-1969.* National Bureau of Economic Research.

King, A. J., and R. J. Jessen [1945]. "The Master Sample of Agriculture." *J. Am. Stat. Assoc.* 40:38-56.

Kirkbride, J. W. [1969]. "Response Problems in Probability Sampling." *Am. J. Agr. Econ.* 51:1214-1217.

Kish, L. [1962]. "Studies of Interviewer Bias for Attitudinal Variables." *J. Am. Stat. Assoc.* 57:92-115.

Kizer, L. G. [1967]. "Discussion: Comprehensive Agricultural Data Systems." *J. Farm Econ.* 49:1553-1556.

Klein, L. R. [1971]. "Whither Econometrics?" *J. Am. Stat. Assoc.* 66:415-421.

Knutson, G. [1949]. "Winter Storm Livestock Loss Surveys." *J. Farm Econ.* 31:1276-1283.

Knutson, G., and F. K. Harmston [1950]. "Problems in Sampling a Heterogeneous Agriculture." *Agr. Econ. Res.* 2:98-100.

Koenig, P. [1951]. "Some Applications of U.S. Experience to Data Problems of Other Countries." *J. Farm Econ.* 33:797-804.

Koffsky, N. M. [1947]. "Some Statistical Problems Involved in Types of Farm Income, by Size." *J. Farm Econ.* 29:1257-1266.

———— [1958]. "Farm Income Estimation Methods and Meaning." *J. Am. Stat. Assoc.* 53:581 (abstract).

———— [1961]. "Potential Demand for Farm Products over the Next Quarter Century." In *Dynamics of Land Use: Needed Adjustments.* Ames: Iowa State University Press.

———— [1962a]. "Analytic Concepts: Changes Induced by Technological Change and Economic Developments." *J. Farm Econ.* 44:625-632.

———— [1962b]. "What the Federal-State Farm Economic Intelligence Service Is and Does." *J. Farm Econ.* 44:1754-1759.

———— [1966]. "Agricultural Economics in the USDA." *J. Farm Econ.* 48:413-421.

Konyha, M. E. [1971]. *Rural Poor Who Could Benefit from Job Retraining in the East North Central States.* USDA Agricultural Economic Report 204.

Kottke, M. W. [1964]. "Discussion: Statistical Bottlenecks to Econometric Analysis." *J. Farm Econ.* 46:1406-1410.

Kramer, R. C., and J. D. Shaffer [1954]. "The Case for the Mail Survey." *J. Farm Econ.* 36:575-589.

Kromer, G. W. [1970]. "Structural Changes in the Soybean Industry." In *Fats and Oils Situation,* USDA, ERS, FOS-253, pp. 16-42.

Kroupa, E. A., and C. Burnett [1973]. *Wisconsin Farmers' Use and Understanding of Broadcast Market News.* University of Wisconsin, College of Agriculture and Life Sciences, Research Report R2506.

Krueger, P. F. [1963]. "Discussion: The Changing World for Agricultural Statistics." *J. Farm Econ.* 45:1506-1507.

Kuhn, T. S. [1970]. *The Structure of Scientific Revolutions.* Second edition. Chicago: University of Chicago Press.

Kutish, F. A. [1955]. "Needed Changes in State and Local Crop and Livestock Reports." *J. Farm Econ.* 37:1050-1053.

Kuznets, G. M., and G. Harvey [1953]. "Forecasting Fruit Production in California." *J. Am. Stat. Assoc.* 48:619 (abstract).

Landsberg, H. H., L. L Fischman, and J. L. Fisher [1962]. *Resources in America's Future, Patterns of Requirements and Availabilities, 1960-2000,* Baltimore: Johns Hopkins University Press.

Landau, E., and C. S. Brandt [1966]. "The Use of Surveys to Estimate Air Pollution Damage to Agriculture." *Biometrics* 22:952 (abstract).

Lavell, R. [1959]. "Introduction of New Regional Indexes for Food Consumption Analysis." In *National Food Situation,* USDA, ERS, NFS-89, pp. 17-40.

LeBovit, C. [1970]. "Foods Eaten away from Home." In *National Food Situation,* USDA, ERS, NFS-132, pp. 25-31.

LeBovit, C., E. Cofer, J. Murray, and F. Clark [1961]. *Dietary Evaluation of Food Used in Households in the United States.* USDA, ARS, Household Food Consumption Survey, 1955, Report 16.

Lee, A. T. M., and K. L. Bachman [1953]. "The 1950 Census of Agriculture as a Source of Basic Data for Economic Research." *Agr. Econ. Res.* 5:45-52.

Lee, G. E., and R. C. Nicholson [1973]. "Managerial Information (Recording, Data, and Decision) Systems in Canada." *Am. J. Agr. Econ.* 55:921-929.

Lee, I. M. [1952]. "A Critical Evaluation of Available Agricultural Statistics." *J. Am. Stat. Assoc.* 47:267-280.

Leiman, M. [1967]. *Food Retailing by Discount Houses.* USDA Marketing Research Report 785.

Leonard, L. A. [1960]. *Assessment of Farm Real Estate in the United States.* USDA, ARS Report 43-117.

Leontief, W. W. [1971]. "Theoretical Assumptions and Non-observed Facts." *Am. Econ. Rev.* 61:1-7.

Leuthold, R. M., A. J. A. MacCormick, A. Schmitz, and D. G. Watts [1970]. "Forecasting Daily Hog Prices: A Study of Alternative Forecasting Techniques." *J. Am. Stat. Assoc.* 65:90-107.

Leven, C. L. [1965]. "Theories of Regional Growth." In *Problems of Chronically Depressed Areas,* Agricultural Policy Institute, North Carolina State University and the Tennessee Valley Authority, API Series 19.

Light, R. J., F. Mosteller, and H. Winokur, Jr. [1971]. "Using Controlled Field Studies to Improve Public Policy." *Report of the President's Commission on Federal Statistics,* vol. 2, Washington.

Loftsgard, L. D., J. E. Johnson, and T. K. Ostenson [1963]. *Taxes Levied on Personal Property in North Dakota.* North Dakota State University, Department of Agricultural Economics. Mimeo.

Loomis, R. A. [1957]. "Effect of Weight-Period Selection on Measurement of Agricultural Production Inputs." *Agr. Econ. Res.* 9:129-136.

Loomis, R. A., and G. T. Barton [1961]. *Productivity of Agriculture, United States, 1870-1958.* USDA Technical Bulletin 1238.

Lowenstein, F. [1954]. "Variations in Crop Forecasts for Cotton." *J. Farm Econ.* 36:674-680.

Luby, P. J. [1957]. "Evaluation of Available Data for Estimating Market Supplies and Prices of Hogs." *J. Farm Econ.* 39:1402-1408.

Lund, L. A., and M. C. Burk [1969]. *A Multidisciplinary Analysis of Children's Food Consumption Behavior.* Minnesota Agricultural Experiment Station Technical Bulletin 265.

Lunde, A. S. [1975]. "Problems in the Establishment of National Data Systems." In *Abstracts Booklet,* ASA, p. 99.

Lutz, E. A. [1960]. *Local and State Financing in the United States and New York State.* New York State College of Agriculture Extension Bulletin 1040.

McAllister, K. J. [1950]. "The Role of Market News in Marketing and Some Problems." *J. Farm Econ.* 32:958-968.

McCormick, F. B. [1955]. "Livestock and Grain Market Report—They Can Be Improved." *J. Farm Econ.* 37:461-470.

McElveen, J. V. [1969]. *Characteristics of Human Resources in the Rural Southeast Coastal Plain ... with Emphasis on the Rural Poor.* USDA Agricultural Economic Report No. 155.

McElveen, J. V., and K. L. Bachman [1953]. *Low Production Farms.* USDA Agriculture Information Bulletin 108.

McElveen, J. V., and B. L. Dillman [1971]. *A Profile of the Rural Poor in the Coastal Plain of Northeastern South Carolina.* USDA Agricultural Economic Report 202.

McGregor, R. A., and O. M. Frost [1959]. "Comparative Methods of Surveying Horticulture Specialty Crops." *Agr. Econ. Res.* 11:106-114.

McHugh, R. B. [1961]. "Confidence Interval Inference and Sample Size Determination." *Am. Statistician* 15(2):14-17.

McPherson, W. K. [1956]. "Improvement of Livestock and Grain Market Reports." *J. Farm Econ.* 38:154-158.

McVay, F. E. [1947]. "Sampling Methods Applied to Estimating Numbers of Commercial Orchards in a Commercial Peach Area." *J. Am. Stat. Assoc.* 42:533-540.

McVay, F. E., and H. Tucker [1950]. *A Study of Agricultural Price Statistics in North Carolina.* Institute of Statistics Mimeo Series 42.

Madden, J. P. [1970]. "Social Change and Public Policy in Rural America: Data and Research Needs for the 1970's." *Am. J. Agr. Econ.* 52:308-314.

―――― [1973]. "On the Measurement of Program Effects." Paper prepared for AAEA Task Force on Social and Economic Statistics.

Madden, J. P., J. L. Pennock, and C. M. Jaeger [1968]. "Equivalent Levels of Living: A New Approach to Scaling the Poverty Line to Different Family Characteristics and Place of Residence." In *Rural Poverty in the United States*, a report by the President's National Advisory Commission on Rural Poverty, Washington, D.C., pp. 545-552.

Maisel, S. J. [1974]. "The Economics and Finance Literature and Decision Making." *J. Finance* 29:313-322.

Marion, B. W., and C. R. Handy [1973]. *Market Performance Concepts and Measures.* USDA Agricultural Economic Report 244.

Marks, E. S., W. P. Mauldin, and H. Nisselson [1953]. "The Post-enumeration Survey of the 1950 Census: A Case History in Survey Design." *J. Am. Stat. Assoc.* 48:220-243.

Marschak, J. [1971]. "Economics of Information Systems." *J. Am. Stat. Assoc.* 66:192-219.

Marsh, M., and H. E. Conklin [1953]. "Farm Variability within Block Samples." *J. Farm Econ.* 35:283-285.

Marshall, J. T. [1962]. "A Comparison of Some of the Census Concepts Used in Canada and the U.S." *J. Am. Stat. Assoc.* 57:494 (abstract).

Martin, L. R. [1970]. "Characteristics of Poverty in the United States, 1970." Public lecture, University of California, Berkeley.

Masucci, R. H. [1959]. *Dollar Volume of Agriculture's Transactions with Industry.* USDA Marketing Research Report 375.

―――― [1962]. "Income Parity Standards for Agriculture." *Agr. Econ. Res.* 14:121-133.

Mathis, A. G. [1968]. "Changing Patterns of Fluid Milk Sales." In *Dairy Situation*, USDA, ERS, DS-322, pp. 24-27.

―――― [1970]. "More Whey Is Coming." In *Dairy Situation*, USDA, ERS, DS-332, pp. 26-32.

Matthews, T. H., and R. Bird [1970]. *Personal Property Taxes Levied on Farmers, 1950 to 1967.* USDA Statistical Bulletin 447.

Mayer, L. V., and J. D. Ahalt [1974]. "Public Policy Demands and Statistical Measures of Agriculture." *Am. J. Agr. Econ.* 56:984-987.

Mead, E. [1926]. *Federal Reclamation: What It Should Include.* Government Printing Office.

―――― [1931]. *The Place of Federal Reclamation in Federal Land Policy.* Government Printing Office.

Melichar, E., and R. J. Doll [1969]. "Capital and Credit Requirements of Agriculture and Proposals to Increase Availability of Bank Credit." In *Reappraisal of the Federal Discount Mechanism* 1:107-112, U.S. Federal Reserve System, Board of Governors.

Mendelowitz, A. I. [1971]. "The Measurement of Economic Depreciation." *J. Am. Stat. Assoc.* 66:140-148.

Mighell, R. L. [1969]. "What are Farms and Who Are Farmers?" Unpublished paper.

Mikesell, J. J. [1971]. *Selected Characteristics of Open Country Mobile Home Residents, East North Central States, 1967.* USDA Agricultural Economic Report 203.

Miklius, W. [1969]. *Economic Performance of Motor Carriers Operating under the Agricultural Exemption in Interstate Trucking.* USDA Marketing Research Report 838.

Miller, R. H. [1968]. "Estimating Domestic Tobacco Use through Regression Methods." Paper presented at 22nd Tobacco Workers Conference, Asheville, N.C., July 22.

Miller, R. R. [1971]. "The Changing U.S. Cheese Industry." In *Dairy Situation,* USDA, ERS, DS-336, pp. 18-33.

Moore, C. V. [1961]. "A General Analytical Framework for Estimating the Production Function for Crops Using Irrigation Water." *J. Farm Econ.* 43:876-888.

Morgan, A. F., ed. [1959]. *Nutritional Status, U.S.A.* California Agricultural Experiment Station Bulletin 769.

Morgan, J. N., and J. A. Sonquist [1963]. "Problems in the Analysis of Survey Data and a Proposal." *J. Am. Stat. Assoc.* 58:415-434.

Morgenstern, O. [1973]. *On the Accuracy of Economic Observations.* Second edition. Princeton: Princeton University Press.

Morton, J. E. [1969]. *On the Evolution of Manpower Statistics.* Kalamazoo: Upjohn Institute.

——— [1972]. "A Student's Guide to American Federal Government Statistics." *J. Econ. Lit.* 10:371-397.

Murray, N. C. [1939]. "A Close-Up View of the Development of Agricultural Statistics from 1900-1920." *J. Farm Econ.* 21:707-717.

Murray, R. A., and R. D. Reinsel [1965]. *The Transfer of Farm and Open Country Real Estate in Six Maryland Counties, 1962.* Maryland Agricultural Experiment Station Miscellaneous Publication 557.

Naive, J. J., C. B. Cox, and J. R. Wiley [1957]. *Accuracy of Estimating Live Grades and Dressing Percentages of Slaughter Hogs.* Indiana Agricultural Experiment Station Bulletin 650.

National Academy of Sciences [1970]. *Remote Sensing: With Special Reference to Agriculture and Forestry.* Committee on Remote Sensing for Agricultural Purposes, National Research Council.

National Advisory Commission on Food and Fiber [1967]. *Food and Fiber for the Future.* Washington, D.C. Pp. 284-292.

National Commission on Food Marketing [1966a]. *Food from Farmer to Consumer: Final Report.* U.S. Government Printing Office.

——— [1966b]. *Organization and Competition in the Poultry and Egg Industries.* Technical Study 2.

——— [1966c]. *Organization and Competition in the Dairy Industry.* Technical Study 3.

——— [1966d]. *Organization and Competition in the Fruit and Vegetable Industry.* Technical Study 4.

——— [1966e]. *Organization and Competition in the Milling and Baking Industries.* Technical Study 5.

——— [1966f]. *The Structure of Food Manufacturing.* Technical Study 8.

——— [1966g]. *Cost Components of Farm-Retail Price Spreads for Foods.* Technical Study 9.

Nelson, P. E., Jr. [1965]. *Market News Dissemination in the Southwest: How the Feed-Grain and Livestock Industries Obtain and Evaluate Market Information.* USDA Agricultural Economic Report 71.

Nelson, T. R. [1967]. "Discussion: Comprehensive Agricultural Data Systems." *J. Farm Econ.* 49:1556-1558.

Neter, J., and J. Waksberg [1964]. "A Study of Response Errors in Expenditures Data from Household Surveys." *J. Am. Stat. Assoc.* 59:18-55.

Newell, S. R. [1953]. "Planning within Agricultural Estimates for a Workable Modernization Program." *J. Farm Econ.* 35:855-864.

——— [1957]. "A Program for Development of Crop and Livestock Estimates." Paper presented at the annual meeting of the ASA, Atlantic City, N.J.

——— [1958a]. "A Program for Development of Crop and Livestock Estimates." *J. Am. Stat. Assoc.* 53:587 (abstract).

——— [1958b]. "Discussion: Present and Future Program for Agricultural Statistics in Canada." *J. Farm Econ.* 40:1769-1771.

Neyman, J. [1934]. "On the Two Different Aspects of the Representative Method: The Method of Stratified Sampling and the Method of Purposive Selection." *J. Royal Stat. Soc.* (Series A) 97:558-606.

Nieto-Ostolaza, Maria Del Carmen [1973]. "Balance Between Statistical Information and Models in Agricultural Research." *International Journal of Agrarian Affairs* 5:458-470.

Nikolitch, R., and D. E. McKee [1965]. "The Contribution of the Economic Classification of Farms to the Understanding of American Agriculture." *J. Farm Econ.* 47:1545-1554.

Niskanen, W. A., Jr. [1971]. *Bureaucracy and Representative Government.* Chicago: Aldine and Atherton.

Nordquist, A. V. [1952]. "Measuring Magnitudes and Trends in the Production of Livestock and Meat." *J. Am. Stat. Assoc.* 47:77-90.

——— [1956]. "Livestock Estimates and the Search for Further Improvement." *Agr. Econ. Res.* 8:128-131.

Nybroten, N. [1953]. "Consumer Choice and Research in Standards for Consumer Grades." *J. Farm Econ.* 35:135-139.

Ogren, K. E. [1956]. "The Farmer's Share: Three Measurements." *Agr. Econ. Res.* 8:43-50.

Ogren, K., F. E. Scott, K. Parr, and H. Rabinowitz [1957]. *Farm-Retail Spreads for Food Products: Costs, Prices.* USDA Miscellaneous Publication 741 (supersedes 576).

Olson, M., Jr. [1970]. "The National Income and the Level of Welfare: Recent Progress in Social Accounts." *Proceedings Am. Stat. Assoc., Business and Economics Section,* pp. 198-207.

Orcutt, G. H. [1970]. "Basic Data for Policy and Public Decisions: Technical Aspects—Data, Research and Government." *Am. Econ. Rev., Papers and Proceedings* 60(2):132-137.

Oury, B. [1965]. "Allowing for Weather in Crop Production Model Building." *J. Farm Econ.* 47:270-283.

Overton, R. S. [1949]. "Sampling to Develop New Statistical Series." *Agr. Econ. Res.* 1:87-92.

Paarlberg, D. [1950]. "Discussion: Agricultural Statistics." *J. Farm Econ.* 32:879-880.

Pallesen, J. E. [1962]. "Discussion: Census Concepts—Past, Present and Future." *J. Farm Econ.* 44:622-624.

Palmer, C. O., and E. O. Schlotzhauer [1950]. "Methods of Forecasting Fruit Production." *Agr. Econ. Res.* 2:10-19.

Palmer, W. C. [1962]. *Meteorological Drought.* U.S. Weather Bureau Technical Paper 45.

Parker, C. V. [1951]. "Organization of Agricultural Statistics Work in Canada." *J. Farm Econ.* 33:787-794.

Parker, C. V., and A. D. Holmes [1958]. "Present and Future Program for Agricultural Statistics in Canada." *J. Farm Econ.* 40:1758-1769.

Parr, R. D., and L. D. Calvin [1956]. "Research on Objective Forecasts of Filbert Production." *Agr. Econ. Res.* 8:92-94.

Parsons, M. S., F. H. Robinson, P. Strickler [1960]. *Farm Machinery: Use, Depreciation, and Replacement.* USDA Statistical Bulletin 269.

Pavelis, G. A. [1965]. "Coordinating Physical and Economic Data in Water Resource Planning." Paper presented to staff conference, USDA, ARS Soil and Water Conservation Research Division, Memphis, Tenn.

Pearson, F. A., and G. E. Brandow [1939]. "Agricultural Price Statistics in the United States and Abroad." *J. Farm Econ.* 21:788-797.

Pechman, J. A., and P. M. Timpane, eds. [1975]. *Work Incentives and Income Guarantees: The New Jersey Negative Income Tax Experiment.* Brookings Institution.

Penson, J. B., Jr. [1972]. "Demand for Financial Assets in the Farm Sector: A Portfolio Balance Approach." *Am. J. Agr. Econ.* 54:163-174.

Penson, J. B., Jr., and C. B. Baker [1978]. *An Aggregative Income and Wealth Simulator for the Farm Sector: Its Description and Analysis.* USDA Technical Bulletin. In process.

Penson, J. B., Jr., D. A. Lins, and G. D. Irwin [1971]. "Flow-of-Funds Social Accounts for the Farm Sector." *Am. J. Agr. Econ.* 53:1-7.

Perkinson, L. B. [1969]. "General Hospital Facilities in Michigan, 1965." *Am. J. Agr. Econ.* 51:1548-1552.

Perrin, R. K. [1968]. *Analysis and Prediction of Crop Yields for Agricultural Policy Purposes.* Unpublished Ph.D. dissertation, Iowa State University.

Peterson, A. G. [1947]. "Agricultural Price Index Numbers." *J. Am. Stat. Assoc.* 42: 597-604.

——— [1950]. "Letter to the Editor—The Parity Price Index of the Department of Agriculture." *Am. Statistician* 4(1):1.

Peterson, G. A., and E. O. Heady [1955]. *Application of Input-Output Analysis to a Simple Model Emphasizing Agriculture.* Iowa Agricultural Experiment Station Research Bulletin 427.

Phelps Brown, E. H. [1972]. "The Underdevelopment of Economics." *Econ. J.* 82:1-10.

Pine, W. H. [1956]. *Farm and City Real Estate Taxes in Kansas.* Kansas Agricultural Experiment Station Bulletin 382.

Pine, W. H., and W. H. Scofield [1961]. *The Farm Real Estate Market in Kansas.* Kansas Agricultural Experiment Station Bulletin 428.

Plaunt, D. H. [1967]. "Canada's Experience in and Aspirations for a Comprehensive Farm Data System." *J. Farm Econ.* 49:1526-1540.

Price, D. W. [1967]. *Specifying the Effects of Household Composition on United States Food Expenditures.* Michigan State University Research Bulletin 16.

Proctor, C. H. [1965]. "Variations in Response Errors Induced by Changing Instructions to Enumerators." *Proceedings, Am. Stat. Assoc. Social Stat. Section,* pp. 51-55.

Proctor, C. H., and B. Stines [1963]. *An Experimental Survey to Study Response Errors in Agricultural Enumerative Surveys.* North Carolina State University, Institute of Statistics, Progress Report 34.

—— [1972]. "Conversational Activity and the Quality of Information from Interviews for Obtaining Farm Facts." *Agr. Econ. Res.* 24:16-20.

Purcell, J. C., and R. Raunikar [1971]. "Price Elasticities from Panel Data: Meat, Poultry, and Fish." *Am. J. Agr. Econ.* 53:216-221.

Puterbaugh, H. L. [1961]. "Purchasing Power of Urban, Rural Nonfarm and Rural Farm Income, 1955." *Agr. Econ. Res.* 13:89-94.

Quackenbush, G. G. [1954]. "Demand Analysis from the M.S.C. Consumer Panel." *J. Farm Econ.* 36:415-427.

Quackenbush, G. G., and J. D. Shaffer [1960]. *Collecting Food Purchase Data by Consumer Panel.* Michigan Agricultural Experiment Station Technical Bulletin 279.

Ramsey, C. E. [1959]. "Discussion: Structural Changes in Agriculture and Research Data Needs." *J. Farm Econ.* 41:1491-1494.

Randall, C. K. [1949]. "Parity Prices." *Agr. Econ. Res.* 1:11-16.

—— [1968]. " 'Realized' Farm Income: An Outmoded Concept? Comment." *Am. J. Agr. Econ.* 50:430-432.

Randall, C. K., and R. H. Masucci [1963]. "Farm and Nonfarm Income." *J. Farm Econ.* 45:359-366.

Randall, C. K., and A. S. Rojko [1961]. "Methods, Assumptions and Results of the Price and Income Projections of the U.S. Department of Agriculture." *J. Farm Econ.* 43:348 356.

Rathbun, D. B. [1972]. "The Report of the President's Commission on Federal Statistics." *Am. Statistician* 26(1):15-18.

Raunikar, R., J. C. Purcell, and J. C. Elrod [1969]. *Spatial and Temporal Aspects of the Demand for Food in the United States — Fluid Milk.* Georgia Agricultural Experiment Station Research Bulletin 61.

Raup, P. M. [1959]. "Structural Changes in Agriculture and Research Data Needs." *J. Farm Econ.* 41:1480-1491.

Ray, R. M., III, and H. F. Huddleston [1976]. "Illinois Crop Acreage Estimation Experiment." In *Symposium Proceedings on Machine Processing of Remotely Sensed Data,* Purdue University.

Reagan, B. B. [1954]. "Condensed vs. Detailed Schedule in Expenditure Survey." *Agr. Econ. Res.* 6:41-53.

Reed, F. K. [1949]. "The Mailed Inquiry and Methods of Increasing Returns." *J. Farm Econ.* 31:1265-1273. R. K. Smith, "Discussion," pp. 1273-1275.

Reinsel, R. D. [1973]. *The Aggregate Real Estate Market.* Unpublished Ph.D. dissertation, Department of Agricultural Economics, Michigan State University.

Reinsel, R. D., and R. D. Drenz [1972]. *Capitalization of Farm Program Benefits into Land Values.* USDA, ERS Report 506.

Renshaw, E. F. [1957]. "Are Land Prices Too High? A Note on Behavior in the Land Market." *J. Farm Econ.* 39:505-510.

Rice, S. A., A. F. Hinrichs, H. R. Tolley, and P. M. Hauser [1945]. "Problems of Integrating Federal Statistics: A Round Table." *J. Am. Stat. Assoc.* 40:237-244.

Riley, H. E. [1956]. "Discussion: A Critique of Federal Statistical Series: Index of Consumer Prices." *J. Farm Econ.* 38:394-395.

Ritz, P. M. [1955]. "Agriculture, a Commodity Producing Segment in the 1947 Interindustry Relations Study." In *Input-Output Analyses, Technical Supplement to Input-Output Analysis: An Appraisal*, vol. 18, Studies in Income and Wealth. Princeton: Princeton University Press (for National Bureau of Economic Research).

Rivlin, A. M. [1975]. "Income Distribution—Can Economists Help?" *Am. Econ. Rev.* 65:1-15.

Robbins, P. R. [1963]. "Developing and Using Input-Output Information." *J. Farm Econ.* 45:831-838.

Roberts, M. J. [1974]. "On the Nature and Condition of Social Science." *Daedalus* 103: 54.

Robinson, T. C. M., and P. P. Wallrabenstein [1949]. "Estimates of Agricultural Employment." *J. Farm Econ.* 31:233-252.

Rogers, C. E. [1965]. "A Random Sample Using Limited Mail Questionnaires and Nonresponse Interviews." *Agr. Econ. Res.* 18:10-12.

Rosenblatt, D., E. Glaser, and M. K. Wood [1970]. "Principles of Design and Appraisal of Statistical Information Systems." *Am. Statistician* 24:10-15.

Ruggles, N., and R. Ruggles [1971]. "Evolution of the National Accounts and the National Data Base." *Survey of Current Business* 51(7), part 2.

Ruttan, V. W. [1954]. "The Relationship between the BAE Level-of-Living Indexes and the Average Incomes of Farm Operators." *J. Farm Econ.* 36:44-51.

—— [1963]. "Discussion: Farm-Nonfarm Income Comparisons." *J. Farm Econ.* 45: 381-384.

Rymes, T. K. [1972]. "The Measurement of Capital and Total Factor Productivity." *Review of Income and Wealth* 18:79-108.

Sanderson, F. H. [1954]. *Methods of Crop Forecasting.* Cambridge: Harvard University Press.

Sargent, R. L., J. R. Davidson, and L. A. Jones [1964]. *Availability of Rural Housing Credit in Montana.* Montana Agricultural Experiment Station Bulletin 586.

Sarle, C. F. [1939]. "Future Improvements in Agricultural Statistics." *J. Farm Econ.* 21:838-845.

Sarle, C. F., J. J. Heimberger, J. R. Wallace, L. Soth, J. D. Baker, Jr., and M. H. Hansen [1953]. "Discussion of Congressional House Committee Report of the Investigation of the Federal Crop Reporting Service." *Agr. Econ. Res.* 5:25-39.

Sarle, C. F., and T. C. M. Robinson [1949]. "Measurement of Agricultural Production." *J. Farm Econ.* 31:213-230; C. Hildreth, "Discussion," pp. 231-232.

Schaars, M. A. [1955]. "Discussion: Local Data Wanted by Business Firms." *J. Farm Econ.* 37:1057-1058.

Schaller, W. N. [1964]. "Data Requirements for New Research Models." *J. Farm Econ.* 46:1391-1399.

Schluter, G. E. [1972]. "Linkages between Agriculture and the U.S. National Income and Product Accounts." *J. Northeastern Agr. Econ. Council* 1:83-93.

Schnittker, J. A. [1959]. "Discussion: Revisions of the Parity Index." *J. Farm Econ.* 41:1300-1302.

—— [1963]. "The Role of Statistics in Formulating the (Proposed) Food and Agriculture Act of 1962." *J. Am. Stat. Assoc.* 58:560 (abstract).

Schnittker, J. A., and E. O. Heady [1957]. *Application of Input-Output Analysis to a Regional Model Stressing Agriculture.* Iowa Agricultural Experiment Station Bulletin 454.

Scholl, J. C., and C. E. Burkhead [1949]. "Interviewing Non-respondents to a Mail Survey." *Agr. Econ. Res.* 1:16-23.

Schrader, F. M. [1951]. "Discussion: Agricultural Statistics." *J. Farm Econ.* 33:794-796.

Schultze, C. L. [undated]. "Governmental and Public Data Needs." Unpublished paper, Brookings Institution.

Scott, F. E., and H. Badger [1970]. "Farm Food Market Basket Statistics." In *Major Statistical Series of the U.S. Department of Agriculture, Vol. 4, Agricultural Marketing Costs and Charges,* USDA Agriculture Handbook 365.

Scott, F. S., Jr. [1955]. "Estimating Cattle on Feed." *J. Farm Econ.* 37:127-129.

Scott, J. T., Jr., and E. O. Heady [1969]. "Econometricians and the Data Gap: Reply." *Am. J. Agr. Econ.* 51:188.

Scoville, O. J. [1959]. "Discussion: Needed Developments in Statistical Programs to Obtain Research Data." *J. Farm Econ.* 41:1519-1521.

Searls, D. T. [1963]. *On the Large Observation Problem.* Unpublished Ph.D. dissertation, North Carolina State College.

Sells, T. [1975]. "Price Spreads for Beef." Contributed paper presented at the annual meeting of the AAEA, Columbus, Ohio.

Selltiz, C., M. Jabada, M. Deutsch, and S. W. Cook [1964]. *Research Methods in Social Relations.* New York: Holt, Rinehart, and Winston.

Senf, C. [1949]. "The General Enumerative Surveys—II." *Agr. Econ. Res.* 1:105-128.

Shaffer, J. D. [1959a]. "Information about Price and Income Elasticity for Food Obtained from Survey Data." *J. Farm Econ.* 41:113-118.

—— [1959b]. "Differences in Costs and Returns of Stamped and Business Reply Envelopes in a Mail Survey." *J. Farm Econ.* 41:268-271.

—— [1959c]. "Estimating Population Characteristics by Mail Survey." *J. Farm Econ.* 41:833-836.

—— [1968]. *A Working Paper Concerning Publicly Supported Economic Research in Agricultural Marketing.* USDA, ERS.

Shannon, C. E., and Warren Weaver [1969]. *The Mathematical Theory of Communication.* Urbana: University of Illinois Press.

Shapiro, H. [1962]. *Taxation of Tangible Personal Property Used in Agriculture.* USDA, ERS Report 86.

—— [1963]. "Economies of Scale and Local Government Finance." *Land Economics* 39:175-185.

Shapiro, H. T. [1973]. "Is Verification Possible? The Evaluation of Large Econometric Models." *Am. J. Agr. Econ.* 55:250-258.

Shaudys, E. T. [1969]. "Farm Panels as a Source of Farm Management Data: The Ohio Plan." *Am. J. Agr. Econ.* 51:1211-1213.

Shaw, L. H. [1967]. "Alternative Measures of Aggregate Inputs and Productivity in Agriculture." *J. Farm Econ.* 49:670-683.

Shaw, L. H., and D. D. Durost [1962]. *Measuring the Effects of Weather on Agricultural Output.* USDA, ERS Report 72.

—— [1965]. *The Effect of Weather and Technology on Corn Yields in the Corn Belt, 1929-1962*. USDA Agricultural Economic Report 80.

Sheehy, S. J., and R. H. McAlexander [1965]. "Selection of Representative Benchmark Farms for Supply Estimation." *J. Farm Econ.* 47:681-695.

Sheldon, H. D. [1960]. "Where We Stand in Urban-Rural and Farm Residence Concepts." *J. Am. Stat. Assoc.* 55:371 (abstract).

Sherr, H. [1960]. "A Basis for the Reconsideration of Wastes and Losses in Food Marketing." *Agr. Econ. Res.* 12:52-57.

Sherr, H., E. A. Power, and R. A. Kahn [1948]. "Supply and Distribution of Fishery Products in the Continental United States, 1930-47." In *National Food Situation*, USDA, ERS, NFS-45, pp. 19-43.

Shiskin, J. [1960]. "How Accurate?" *Am. Statistician* 14(4):15-17.

Shoemaker, K. [1962]. "Unsolved Problems in Dissemination and Application." *J. Farm Econ.* 44:1773-1778.

Siegel, I. H. [1956]. "What Concepts Are Appropriate to Consumer Price Indexes?" *J. Farm Econ.* 38:361-368.

Simerl, L. H. [1962]. "Discussion: Unsolved Problems in Dissemination and Application." *J. Farm Econ.* 44:1778-1780.

Simmons, W. [1949]. *Assessment Procedures in Rural New York*. Cornell University, New York State College of Agriculture, Extension Bulletin 760.

Simon, M. S. [1958]. "Clothing Expenditure Units: A New Time Series." *Agr. Econ. Res.* 10:37-48.

Simpson, G. D. [1966]. "Resources and Facilities for Providing Needed Statistics: The Role of the Statistical Reporting Service." *J. Farm Econ.* 48:1674-1682.

—— [1967]. "The User and the Producer of Agricultural Statistics." Paper presented at the CENTO symposium on Agricultural Statistics, Ankara, Turkey.

Simunek, R. W. [1974]. "National Farm Economic Accounts: Current Analytic Needs, Bookkeeping Requirements, and Future Possibilities." Unpublished paper, USDA, ERS.

—— [1976]. "National Farm Capital Accounts." *Am. J. Agr. Econ.* 58:532-542.

Sinclair, S. [1951]. "Discussion: Agricultural Statistics." *J. Farm Econ.* 33:804-806.

Small, R. P. [1975]. "Modifications of USDA Farm Labor and Wage Rate Estimates Program." *Statistical Reporter* (U.S. OMB) 75-11:184-185.

Smith, C. C. [1952]. "Effects of Personal Visits on Response Rates to Mail Surveys." *Agr. Econ. Res.* 4:126-127.

Smith, R. K. [1954]. "Discussion: Agricultural Data." *J. Farm Econ.* 36:1247-1251.

—— [1955]. "Discussion: Making Existing Local Data More Available and Useful." *J. Farm Econ.* 37:1053-1056.

Snedecor, G. W. [1939]. "Design of Sampling Experiments in the Social Sciences." *J. Farm Econ.* 21:846-855.

Southern, J. H., and W. E. Hendrix [1959]. *Incomes of Rural Families in Northeast Texas*. Texas Agricultural Experiment Station Bulletin 940.

Southern Land Economics Research Committee [1970]. *Farmland Tenure and Farmland Use in the Tennessee Valley*. Report 9.

Spielmann, H., and E. E. Weeks [1975]. "Inventory and Critique of Estimates of U.S. Agricultural Capacity." *Am. J. Agr. Econ.* 57:922-928.

Spurlock, H. H. [1968]. *Rural Housing Conditions in the Arkansas, Missouri and Oklahoma Ozarks*. Arkansas Agricultural Experiment Station Bulletin 736.

—— [1970]. *Rural Housing Quality in the Ozark Region as Related to Characteristics of Housing Units and Occupants, 1966.* Arkansas Agricultural Experiment Station Bulletin 758.

—— [1971]. *Rural Homeowners' Use of Home Mortgage Credit in the Ozark Region, 1966.* USDA Agricultural Economic Report 211.

Stallings, J. L. [1961]. "A Measure of the Influence of Weather on Crop Production." *J. Farm Econ.* 43:1153-1160.

Stapp, P. [1958]. "Discussion: Agricultural Statistics in a Changing World." *J. Farm Econ.* 40:1225-1227.

Star, S. [1974]. "Accounting for the Growth of Output." *Am. Econ. Rev.* 64:123-125.

Stauber, B. R. [1950]. "Current Frontier in Farm Price Data." *J. Farm Econ.* 32:865-877.

—— [1956]. "The Parity Index and the Farm Expenditure Survey." *J. Farm Econ.* 38:369-377.

—— [1959a]. "The 1959 U.S.D.A. Index Revisions and Some Related Policy Questions." *J. Farm Econ.* 41:1272-1288.

—— [1959b]. "Critical Problems of Price Index Construction." *Am. Stat. Assoc. Proceedings Business and Economic Statistics Section*, pp. 184-190.

—— [1964]. "A Report on Research in the Data Collection Program of Prices Received and Prices Paid by Farmers." *J. Farm Econ.* 46:1336-1340.

Stauber, B. R., R. F. Hale, and B. S. Peterson [1959]. "The January 1959 Revision of the Price Indexes." *Agr. Econ. Res.* 11:33-80.

Stauber, B. R., N. M. Koffsky, and C. K. Randall [1950]. "The Revised Price Indexes." *Agr. Econ. Res.* 2:33-62.

Steele, H. A., and G. A. Pavelis [1967]. "Economics of Irrigation Policy and Planning." In *Irrigation of Agricultural Lands*, American Society of Agronomy, Series 11.

Steward, D. D., and P. R. Myers [1972]. *Housing 1970: Differences between SMSA's by Region with State Data.* USDA Agricultural Economic Report 230.

Stiebeling, H. K., and C. M. Coons [1939]. "Present-Day Diets in the United States." In *Food and Life, Yearbook of Agriculture, 1939*, pp. 296-320.

Stigler, G. J. [1961]. "The Economics of Information." *J. Pol. Econ.* 62:213-225.

Stillman, C. W. [1949]. "Rural Health and the Truman Plan." *J. Farm Econ.* 31:391-408.

Stine, O. C. [1946]. "Parity Prices." *J. Farm Econ.* 28:301-305.

Stinson, T. F. [1967]. *Financing Industrial Development through State and Local Governments.* USDA Agricultural Economic Report 128.

—— [1975]. "Comments on: Strategies for Long-Run Investment in Information Systems for Rural, Social, and Economic Statistics." Paper presented at the AAEA annual meeting, Columbus, Ohio.

Stinson, T. F., E. L. Courtney, and R. Bird [1969]. *Revised Estimates of Taxes Levied on Farm Real Estate, 1950-67.* USDA Statistical Bulletin 441.

Stocker, F. D. [1953]. *Local Sales Taxes in New York State.* Cornell University, Department of Agricultural Economics, AE 852.

—— [1955]. *The Impact of Federal Income Taxes on Farm People.* USDA, ARS 43-11.

—— [1956]. "Disposable Income of Farm People." *Agr. Econ. Res.* 8:13-17.

—— [1957]. "Some Effects of Suburban Residential Development on Local Finances." *Agr. Econ. Res.* 9:37-53.

—— [1963]. *Selected Legislative and Other Documents on the Preferential Assessment of Farmland.* USDA, ERS, AER 256.

Stocker, F. D., and J. C. Ellickson [1959]. "How Fully Do Farmers Report Their Incomes? *National Tax J.*, 12:116-126.

Stoner, J. E. [1967]. *Interlocal Government Cooperation.* USDA Agricultural Economic Report 118.

Stout, R. G. [1962]. "Estimating Citrus Production by Use of the Frame Count Survey." *J. Farm Econ.* 44:1037-1049.

Sturt, D. W. [1972]. "The Need for Rural Labor Market Information at the National Level." *Labor Market Information in Rural Areas.* Michigan State University, Center for Rural Manpower and Public Affairs.

Sudman, S., and R. Ferber [1971]. "Experiments in Obtaining Consumer Expenditures by Diary Methods." *J. Am. Stat. Assoc.* 66:725-735.

Sundquist, W. B. [1970]. "Changing Structure of Agriculture and Resulting Statistical Needs." *Am. J. Agr. Econ.* 52:315-320.

Szaniawski, K. [1967]. "The Value of Perfect Information." *Synthese* 17:408-424.

Taeuber, C. [1947]. "Some Aspects of the Statistics Program in the Department of Agriculture." *J. Am. Stat. Assoc.* 42:41-45.

────── [1957]. "Some Results of the 1954 Census of Agriculture." *J. Am. Stat. Assoc.* 52:382 (abstract).

────── [1971]. "Future Structure of Census Data Relating to Agriculture and Rural People." *Am. J. Agr. Econ.* 53:909 (abstract).

Taylor, C. C., G. H. Aull, C. E. Woodall, and W. H. Faver, Jr. [1960]. *Suggested Procedures for the Assessment of Farm Real Estate in South Carolina.* South Carolina Agricultural Experiment Station AE 188.

Taylor, H. C. [1939]. "A Century of Agricultural Statistics." *J. Farm Econ.* 21:697-706.

Taylor, H. M. [1950]. "Discussion: Farm Price Data." *J. Farm Econ.* 32:877-879.

Teele, R. P. [1927]. *The Economics of Land Reclamation in the United States.* Chicago: Shaw.

Teper, L. [1956]. "BLS Consumers' Price Index and the AMS Index of Prices Paid by Farmers for Family Living—A Juxtaposition." *J. Farm Econ.* 38:378-390.

Theil, H. [1958]. *Economic Forecasts and Policy.* Amsterdam: North-Holland.

Thomas, M. D. [1956]. "Data Requirements in Agricultural Administration and Research." *J. Farm Econ.* 38:1452-1454.

Thompson, L. M. [1962]. "Evaluation of Weather Factors in the Production of Wheat." *J. Soil and Water Conservation* 17:149-156.

────── [1963a]. "Evaluation of Weather Factors in the Production of Grain Sorghums." *Agron. J.* 55:182-185.

────── [1963b]. *Weather and Technology in the Production of Corn and Soybeans.* Iowa State University, Center for Agricultural and Economic Development, Report 17.

────── [1966]. *Weather Variability and the Need for a Food Reserve.* Iowa State University, Center for Agricultural and Economic Development, Report 28.

Thompson, R. G. [1963]. "Discussion: Probability Sampling in Collecting Farm Data." *J. Farm Econ.* 45:1520-1521.

Timm, T. R. [1966]. "Proposals for Improvement of the Agricultural Outlook Program of the United States." *J. Farm Econ.* 48:1179-1184.

Todd, A. S., Jr., and J. J. Ziricle, Jr. [1952]. "A Test of Survey Methods for Estimating Stumpage Prices." *Agr. Econ. Res.* 4:115-125.

Tostlebe, A. S. [1957]. *Capital in Agriculture: Its Formation and Financing since 1870.* Princeton: Princeton University Press.

Tostlebe, A. S., D. C. Horton, R. J. Burroughs, H. C. Larsen, L. A. Jones, A. R. Johnson, and N. J. Wall [1945]. *Impact of the War on the Financial Structure of Agriculture*. USDA Miscellaneous Publication 567.

Trelogan, H. C. [1962]. "To Acquire and Diffuse Information." *Agricultural Statisticians in a Changing World*. National conference, Statistical Reporting Service.

—— [1963]. "The Changing World for Agricultural Statistics." *J. Farm Econ.* 45: 1500-1506.

—— [1966]. "Progress with New Techniques in U.S. Agricultural Estimates." Paper presented at the Dominion Bureau of Statistics Federal-Provincial Conference, Ottawa, Canada, February 22.

—— [1968a]. "Cybernetics and Agriculture." *Agr. Econ. Res.* 20:77-81.

—— [1968b]. "Agricultural Statistics in the Next Decade." In *Proceedings of the Statistical Reporting Service Conference*. USDA, SRS.

—— [1971]. "Implications of the Census for Agricultural Statistics." *Am. J. Agr. Econ.* 53:910 (abstract).

—— [1972]. "Future Census Data for Agriculture: Reply." *Am. J. Agr. Econ.* 54:363.

Truesdell, L. [1949]. "The Development of the Urban-Rural Classification in the United States, 1874 to 1949." In *Current Population Reports*, Population Characteristics, Series P-23, No. 1.

Tsai, R. [1973]. "A Method for Correcting the Bias Due to Nonresponse in a Mail Survey." In *Abstracts Booklet*, ASA, pp. 130-131.

Tweeten, L. G., and J. E. Martin [1966]. "A Methodology for Predicting U.S. Farm Real Estate Price Variation." *J. Farm Econ.* 48:378-393.

Tweeten, L. G., and T. R. Nelson [1970]. *Sources and Repercussions of Changing U.S. Farm Real Estate Values*. Oklahoma Agricultural Experiment Station Technical Bulletin T-120.

United Nations [annual]. *Statistical Yearbook*.

—— [1968]. *A System of National Accounts: Studies in Methods*. Series F, No. 2. New York.

United Nations, FAO [annual]. *Yearbook of Food and Agricultural Statistics*.

—— [1954]. *World Pulp and Paper Resources and Prospects*.

—— [1973]. *Provisional Handbook of Economic Accounts for Agriculture*. Rome.

United Nations, FAO, and Inter-American Statistical Institute [1971]. *Economic Accounts for Agriculture*. Report of the 6th Session, Subcommittee on Agricultural Statistics, Washington, D.C.

United Nations, World Food Conference [1974]. *Assessment of the World Food Situation: Present and Future*. Item 8 of the Provisional Agenda, Rome.

U.S. Congress [1952]. *Crop Estimating and Reporting Services of the Department of Agriculture*. Report and recommendations of a special subcommittee, 82nd Congress, 2nd Session, House of Representatives, Committee Print.

—— [1959]. *Water Resource Activities in the United States: Land and Water Potentials and Future Requirements for Water*. Senate Select Committee on National Water Resources, 86th Congress, 1st Session, Committee Print 12.

—— [1960]. *Department of Agriculture Appropriations for 1960*. Hearings before the Subcommittee of the Committee on Appropriations, House of Representatives, Subcommittee on Department of Agriculture and Related Agencies, 86th Congress, 1st Session. Part 1, pp. 85-250.

—— [1967a]. *Parity Returns Position for Farmers*. Senate Document 44, 90th Congress, 1st Session.

―――― [1967b]. *The Coordination and Integration of Government Statistical Programs.* Hearings before the Subcommittee on Economic Statistics, Joint Economic Committee, 90th Congress, 2nd Session.

―――― [1971]. *The Economic and Social Condition of Rural America in the 1970's.* Senate Committee on Government Operations, 1st Session. Parts, 1, 2, 3.

―――― [1972]. *Investigation of Possible Politicization of Federal Statistical Programs.* Subcommittee on Census and Statistics of the House Committee on Post Office and Civil Service, 92nd Congress, 2nd Session, House Report 92-1536.

―――― [1973]. *Agriculture and Consumer Protection Act of 1973, Export Sales Reporting, Sec. 812.* 93rd Congress, 1st Session.

U.S. Congress, House Appropriations Committee [1957]. *Hearings on the Department of Agriculture Appropriations for 1958.* Subcommittee on Appropriations, Part II, pp. 886-894.

U.S. Congress, Joint Economic Committee [1974]. *Government Price Statistics.* Hearings before the Subcommittee on Economic Statistics of the Joint Economic Committee, 87th Congress, 1st Session. Part 1.

U.S. Congress, Office of Technology Assessment [1976a] : *Food Information Systems— Summary and Analysis.* Office of Technology Assessment OTA-F-35.

―――― [1976b]. *Food Information Systems: Hearings before the Technology Assessment Board of the Office of Technology Assessment.*

USDA [annual]. *Changes in Farm Production and Efficiency: A Summary Report.* Statistical Bulletin 233.

―――― [1924]. *Yearbook of Agriculture, 1923.*

―――― [1939]. *Food and Life: Yearbook of Agriculture, 1939.*

―――― [1957-72]. *Major Statistical Series of the U.S. Department of Agriculture—How They are Constructed and Used.* Agriculture Handbook 118 (vols. 1-9, 1957); Agriculture Handbook 365 (revised and updated editions of vols. 1-9, 1969-72; vols. 10 and 11, 1972).

   [1957, 1970]. *Vol. 1, Agricultural Prices and Parity.*

   [1957, 1970]. *Vol. 2, Agricultural Production and Efficiency.*

   [1957, 1969]. *Vol. 3, Gross and Net Farm Income.*

   [1957, 1970]. *Vol. 4, Agricultural Marketing Costs and Charges.*

   [1957, 1972]. *Vol. 5, Consumption and Utilization of Agricultural Products.*

   [1957, 1971]. *Vol. 6, Land Values and Farm Finance.*

   [1957, 1969]. *Vol. 7, Farm Population, Employment and Levels of Living.* (In the 1969 edition the title was revised to *Farm Population and Employment.*)

   [1957, 1971]. *Vol. 8, Crop and Livestock Estimates.*

   [1957, 1970]. *Vol. 9, Farmer Cooperatives.*

   [1972]. *Vol. 10, Market News.*

   [1972]. *Vol. 11, Foreign Trade, Production and Consumption of Agricultural Products.*

―――― [1958]. *The Federal and State Agricultural Outlook Service.*

―――― [1959]. *Agricultural Estimating and Reporting Services of the United States Department of Agriculture.* Miscellaneous Publication 703.

USDA, AMS [1955]. *Measuring the Supply and Utilization of Farm Commodities: New Indices, 1922-54.* Agriculture Handbook 91.

―――― [1957]. *A Program for the Development of the Agricultural Estimating Service.*

―――― [1960]. *Uses of Marketing Information by Farmers in Michigan.* AMS-418.

USDA, AMS, and Bureau of the Census [1958]. *Farmers' Expenditures in 1955, by Regions, for Production and Farm Living with Tables on Off-Farm Income*. Statistical Bulletin 224.

USDA, ARS [1957a]. *Dietary Levels of Households in the United States, Spring*. Household Food Consumption Survey, 1955, Report 6.

—— [1957b]. *Fertilizer Used on Crops and Pasturelands in the United States*. Statistical Bulletin 216.

—— [1958]. *Farm Costs and Returns, Commercial and Family-Operated Farms*. Agriculture Information Bulletin 196.

—— [1960]. *Farm Costs and Returns: Commercial Farms by Type, Size, and Location*. Agriculture Information Bulletin 230 (annual revisions).

—— [1969]. *Dietary Levels of Households in the United States, Spring 1965*. Household Food Consumption Survey, 1965-66, Report 6.

—— [1972]. *Food and Nutrient Intake of Individuals in the United States, Spring 1965*. Household Food Consumption Survey, 1965-66, Report 11.

USDA, BAE [1949]. *Consumption of Food in the United States, 1909-48*. Miscellaneous Publication 691.

—— [1953]. *Consumption of Food in the United States*. Agriculture Handbook 62.

USDA, Bureau of Human Nutrition and Home Economics [1944]. *Family Food Consumption in the United States, Spring 1942*. Miscellaneous Publication 550.

—— [1949]. *Nutritive Value of Diets of Urban Families, United States, Spring 1948, and Comparison with Diets in 1942*. Food Consumption Surveys, 1948, Preliminary Report 12.

USDA, Conservation Needs Inventory Committee [1971]. *Basic Statistics: National Inventory of Soil and Water Conservation Needs, 1967*. Statistical Bulletin 461.

USDA, ERS [annual]. *Farm Real Estate Taxes—Recent Trends and Developments*.

—— [1962-72]. *Farm Costs and Returns: Commercial Farms by Type, Size and Location*. Agriculture Information Bulletin 230 (annual revisions).

—— [1962]. *Farm Population—Revised Estimates for 1941-59*. ERS-90.

—— [1963]. *Agriculture and Economic Growth*. Agricultural Economic Report 28.

—— [1964]. *World Food Budget to 1970*. Foreign Agricultural Economic Report 19.

—— [1965]. *U.S. Food Consumption: Sources of Data and Trends, 1909-63*. Statistical Bulletin 364.

—— [1966]. *Agricultural Markets in Change*. Agricultural Economic Report 95.

—— [1968]. *National Food Situation*. NFS-125.

—— [1970]. *Marketing America's Food*. Report 446 (revised 1972).

—— [1972a]. *Changes in Farm Production and Efficiency*. Statistical Bulletin 233.

—— [1972b]. "Farm Income and Capital Accounting—Findings and Recommendations of a 1972 ERS Task Force." Unpublished report.

—— [1972c]. *Productivity: Index of Total Farm Output and Productivity for Each . Farm Production Region, 1939-71*. Statistical Bulletin 233, supplement 5.

—— [1973a]. *Marketing Economics Research Publications*. Report 205.

—— [1973b]. *Selected U.S. Crop Budgets, Yields, Inputs and Variable Costs. Vol. 1, Southeast Region*, Report 457. *Vol. 2, North Central Region*, Report 458. *Vol. 3, Great Plains Region*, Report 459. *Vol. 4, Northwest Region*, Report 460. *Vol. 5, South Central Region*, Report 461. *Vol. 6, Southwest Region*, Report 514.

—— [1975]. *The Food and Fiber System—How it Works*. Agriculture Information Bulletin 383.

USDA, FCA [1968]. *Production Credit Associations and their Loans*. Bulletin CR-10.

USDA, Forest Service [annual]. *The Demand and Price Situation for Forest Products.* Miscellaneous Publications 953 (1963), 983 (1964), 1009 (1965), 1045 (1966), 1066 (1967), 1086 (1968-69), 1165 (1969-70), 1195 (1970-71), 1231 (1971-72), 1239 (1972-73), 1292 (1973-74), 1315 (1974-75).

———— [1958]. *Timber Resources for America's Future.* Forest Resource Report 14.

———— [1965]. *Timber Trends in the United States.* Forest Resource Report 17.

———— [1974]. *Outlook for Timber in the United States.* Forest Resource Report 20.

USDA, Interbureau Coordinating Committee on Postwar Planning [1945a]. *What Peace Can Mean to American Farmers: Post-war Agriculture and Employment.* Miscellaneous Publication 562.

———— [1945b]. *What Peace Can Mean to American Farmers: Maintenance of Full Employment.* Miscellaneous Publication 570.

———— [1945c]. *What Peace Can Mean to American Farmers: Expansion of Foreign Trade.* Miscellaneous Publication 582.

———— [1945d]. *What Peace Can Mean to American Farmers: Agricultural Policy.* Miscellaneous Publication 589.

USDA, PMA [1947]. *Conversion Factors and Weights and Measures for Agricultural Commodities and Their Products.* Mimeo.

USDA, SCS [1958, 1967]. *A National Inventory of Soil and Water Conservation Needs.* Revised 1967.

———— [1971]. *Soil Survey, Orange County, Virginia.* Prepared in cooperation with Virginia Agricultural Experiment Station.

———— [1972]. *List of Published Soil Surveys.*

USDA, SRS [quarterly]. *Pig Crop Report.*

———— [1964, 1975]. *Scope and Methods of the Statistical Reporting Service.* Miscellaneous Publication 967 (1964); revision issued as Miscellaneous Publication 1308 (1975).

———— [1967]. *Crop and Livestock Estimates.*

———— [1969]. *The Story of U.S. Agricultural Estimates.* Miscellaneous Publication 1088.

———— [1971a]. "Changes in the Program of Reports for Field, Fruit and Nut Crops." *Crop Estimates Memorandum* 1715. Mimeo.

———— [1971b]. "Changes in the Program of Reports for Livestock, Dairy and Poultry." *Crop Estimates Memorandum* 1720. Mimeo.

———— [1972]. "Program Modifications for Fresh Market and Processing Vegetables and Potatoes." *Crop Estimates Memorandum* 1728.

U.S. Department of Commerce [1954]. *Readings in Concepts and Methods of National Income Statistics.*

U.S. Department of Commerce, Bureau of the Census [quinquennial]. *Census of Agriculture.* Vols. 1, 2, 3, 1974, and earlier issues.

———— [1953]. *Revised Estimates of the Farm Population of the United States, 1910-1950.* Farm Population Series, Census-BAE 16.

U.S. Department of Commerce, Bureau of Economic Analysis, Interindustry Economics Division [1974]. "The Input-Output Structure of the U.S. Economy: 1967." *Survey of Current Business* 54(2):24-56.

U.S. Department of Commerce, Intensive Review Committee [1954]. *Appraisals of Census Programs.*

U.S. Department of Commerce, Office of Business Economics, National Economics Division [1969]. "Input-Output Structure of the U.S. Economy: 1963." *Survey of Current Business* 49(11):16-47.

U.S. Department of Commerce, Weather Bureau [1963]. *Selective Guide to Published Climatic Data Sources, Prepared by the U.S. Weather Bureau.*

U.S. Department of Health, Education, and Welfare [1976]. *Summary Report: Rural Income Maintenance Experiment: A Social Experiment in Negative Income Taxation.* Sponsored by the Office of Economic Opportunity and the Department of Health, Education, and Welfare.

U.S. Department of the Interior, Bureau of Outdoor Recreation [1971]. *Selected Outdoor Recreation Statistics.*

U.S. Department of the Interior, Geological Survey. *Periodic Circular Series on Estimated Use of Water in the United States.* Same title: Circular 115, 1950; Circular 398, 1955; Circular 456, 1960; Circular 556, 1965.

—— [1964]. *Long-Range Plan for Resource Surveys: Investigations and Research Programs of the United States Geological Survey.*

U.S. Department of Labor, BLS [1959]. *Trends in Output per Man-Hour in the Private Economy, 1909-58.* Bulletin 1249.

—— [1974]. *Indexes of Output per Man-Hour.* Bulletin 1827.

U.S. Federal Reserve System, Board of Governors [1964]. *Farm Debt—Data from the 1960 Sample Survey of Agriculture.*

U.S. Government [1971]. *Federal Statistics: Report of the President's Commission.* Vol. 1, *Report.* Vol. 2, *Supporting Papers and Documents.*

U.S. Interstate Commerce Commission, Investigation and Suspension Docket 7656 [1963]. *Grain in Multiple-car Shipments—River Crossings to the South.* Decided January 21, 1963; service date, January 1964.

U.S. Office of Management and Budget, Statistical Policy Division [1974]. *Standard Industrial Classification Manual, 1972.*

U.S. Water Resources Council [1968]. *The Nation's Water Resources: The First National Assessment of the Water Resources Council.*

—— [1969]. *The Water Use Data Base: The Report of the Task Force on Water Use Data to the Planning Committee of the Water Resources Council.*

—— [1970]. *Water Resources Regions and Subregions for the National Assessment of Water and Related Land Resources.*

University of New Brunswick, Department of Surveying Engineering [1968]. *Proceedings of a Symposium on Land Registration and Data Banks.*

Upchurch, M. L. [1974]. "Toward a Better System of Data for the Food and Fiber Industry." *Am. J. Agr. Econ.* 56:635-637.

—— [1977]. "Developments in Agricultural Economic Data." (See the table of contents in this volume.)

Van Dress, M. G. [1971]. *The Food Service Industry: Type, Quantity, and Value of Foods Used.* USDA Statistical Bulletin 476.

Van Vuuren, W. [1968]. *Agricultural Land Prices and Returns in an Advanced Urban and Industrial Economy.* Unpublished Ph.D. dissertation, University of California, Berkeley.

Veblen, T. [1914]. *The Instinct of Workmanship and the State of the Industrial Arts.* New York: Kelley.

Vickery, R. E. [1956]. "An Appraisal of Interview Procedures in Farm Surveys." *Agr. Econ. Res.* 8:59-65.

Vincent, W. H. [1959]. "A Farm Panel as a Source of Income and Expenditure Data." *Agr. Econ. Res.* 11:97-102.

Vining, R. [1953]. "Delimitation of Economic Areas: Statistical Conceptions in the Study of the Spatial Structure of an Economic System." *J. Am. Stat. Assoc.* 48: 44-61.

Virginia Conservation Needs Inventory Committee [1970]. *Virginia Conservation Needs Inventory of 1967.* Virginia Polytechnic Institute, Extension Publication 384.

Vlasin, R. D. [1973]. "Substate Regions — Issues and Data Implications." Paper prepared for AAEA Task Force on Social and Economic Statistics.

Vlasin, R. D., L. W. Libby, and R. L. Shelton [1975]. "Economic and Social Information for Rural America: Priorities for Immediate Improvement." *Am. J. Agr. Econ.* 57:900-909.

Voelker, S. W. [1969]. *Selected Publications on County Government Services and Costs of Particular Interest to the Great Plains States.* North Dakota State University, Agricultural Economics Miscellaneous Report 3.

Vogel, F. A. [1973]. "An Application of a Two-Stage Multiple Frame Sample Design." In *Abstracts Booklet*, ASA, p. 132.

―――― [1975]. "Surveys with Overlapping Frames — Problems in Application." In *Abstracts Booklet*, ASA, pp. 162-163.

Wales, H. G., and R. Ferber [1956]. *A Basic Bibliography on Marketing Research.* American Marketing Association, Bibliography Series 2.

―――― [1963]. *A Basic Bibliography on Marketing Research.* Second edition. American Marketing Association.

Walker, F. A. [1883]. *Land and Its Rent.* Boston: Little, Brown.

Wallace, D. [1955]. "A Case for and against Mail Questionnaires." *Public Opinion Quarterly* 18:40-52.

Waugh, F. V. [1964]. *Demand and Price Analysis.* USDA Technical Bulletin 1316 (reprinted 1970).

Webb, L. M. [1956]. "Discussion: The Need for an Expanded Price Research Program." *J. Farm Econ.* 38:390-394.

Weeks, E. E. [1970]. *The Agriculture Industry.* National Agricultural Outlook Conference, Washington. Processed.

―――― [1971a]. *Aggregate National Agricultural Data — Status and Alternatives.* USDA, ERS Progress Report.

―――― [1971b]. "The Data Problem in Agricultural Economics Research." *Am. J. Agr. Econ.* 53:911 (abstract).

―――― [1972]. "The Concept and Measurement of Farm Income and General Welfare in Agriculture." *Western Agr. Econ. Assoc. Proceedings*, pp. 259-266.

Weeks, E. E., T. Carlin, C. Cobb, J. Mikesell, P. Nelson, and A. Smith [1972]. *Farm Income and Capital Accounting — Findings and Recommendations of a 1972 ERS Task Force.* USDA, ERS, unpublished.

Weeks, E. E., G. E. Schluter, and L. W. Southard [1974]. "Monitoring the Agricultural Economy: Strains on the Data System." *Am. J. Agr. Econ.* 56:976-983.

Weiner, N. S. [1974]. "The Report of the President's Commission on Federal Statistics: A Summary of Recommendations, Views, and Counterviews." *Am. Statistician* 28:42-46.

Weisgerber, P. [1971]. *Commercial Wheat Production: World Market, U.S. Production Centers, Costs and Returns Analysis.* USDA, ERS Report 480.

Wells, O. V. [1942]. "America's Changing Food Consumption, 1909-41." *J. Home Econ.* 34:463-467.

—— [1950]. "Agricultural Statistics as an Aid to Research, Service, and Administration." *J. Farm Econ.* 32:858-864.

—— [1958]. "Agricultural Statistics in a Changing World: Adapting Data to New Conditions." *J. Farm Econ.* 40:1214-1227.

—— [1961]. "Discussion: How Well Do the Economic Indicators Indicate What Is Happening in the Major Sectors of the Economy?" *J. Farm Econ.* 43:459-461.

Wells, O. V., J. D. Black, P. H. Appleby, H. C. Taylor, H. R. Tolley, R. J. Penn, and T. W. Schultz [1954]. "The Fragmentation of the BAE." *J. Farm Econ.* 36:1-21.

Welsch, D. E., and D. S. Moore [1965]. "Problems and Limitations Due to Criteria Used for Economic Classification of Farms." *J. Farm Econ.* 47:1555-1564.

Wessel, R. I. [1963]. "Can County Government Costs Still Be Reduced?" *Iowa Farm Science* 18:25-27.

West, V. I. [1965]. "Discussion: Sampling Frames for Collection of Agricultural Statistics." *J. Farm Econ.* 947:1539-1541.

Westcott, G. W. [1956]. "Discussion: Agricultural Data Requirements in Extension Work." *J. Farm Econ.* 38:1468-1470.

White, J. H. [1964]. "Discussion: Statistical Bottlenecks to Econometric Analysis." *J. Farm Econ.* 46:1410-1414.

White, J. P., ed. [1968]. *Proceedings of a Workshop on Problems of Improving the United States System of Land Titles and Records.* Indianapolis Law School, Indiana University and Purdue University. Processed.

Wickens, A. J. [1953]. "Statistics and the Public Interest." *J. Am. Stat. Assoc.* 48:1-14.

—— [1954]. "Prospects for a Federal Statistical System in the U.S." *Am. Statistician* 8(4):12-16.

Wigton, W. H., and W. E. Kibler [1972]. "New Methods for Filbert Objective Yield Estimation." *Agr. Econ. Res.* 24:37-46.

Wilcox, E. C. [1956]. "Local Data Requirements in Areas of High Agricultural Specialization." *J. Farm Econ.* 38:1455-1468.

Wilcox, E. C., and W. H. Ebling [1949]. "Presentation of Agricultural Data in the States." *J. Farm Econ.* 31:309-322; L. M. Carl, "Discussion," pp. 322-324.

Williams, W. F., E. K. Bowen, and F. G. Genovese [1959]. *Economic Effects of U.S. Grades for Beef.* USDA Marketing Research Report 298.

Williams, W. H., and C. L. Mallows [1970]. "Systematic Biases in Panel Surveys." *J. Am. Stat. Assoc.* 65:1338-1349.

Winkler, O. [1963]. "A New Approach to 'Measuring' Agricultural Production." *J. Am. Stat. Assoc.* 58:564 (abstract).

Wollman, N., and G. W. Bonem [1971]. *The Outlook for Water: Quality and National Growth.* Baltimore: Johns Hopkins University Press.

Wooten, H. H., and J. R. Anderson [1957]. *Major Uses of Land in the United States.* USDA Agriculture Information Bulletin 168.

Worswick, G. D. N. [1972]. "Is Progress in Economic Science Possible?" *Econ. J.* 82:73-79.

Woytinsky, E. S., and W. S. Woytinsky [1939]. "Progress of Agricultural Statistics in the World." *J. Farm Econ.* 21:761-787.

Wright, B. H., and R. E. Torgerson [1975]. "Reporting Cash Grain Prices: Issues and Their Possible Resolution." Contributed paper presented at the AAEA annual meeting, Columbus, Ohio.

Zusman, P. [1967]. "A Theoretical Basis for Determination of Grading and Sorting Schemes." *J. Farm Econ.* 49:89-106.

Epilogue

Epilogue

The chapters in this volume emphasize the importance of more fully integrating the array of various quantitative approaches to problem solving and to the testing of theoretical constructs. Whether approached from an econometric, optimization, systems and simulation standpoint, or from a more pragmatic data-dredging standpoint, the applied problems of agricultural economics require specialized analysis if they are to be handled effectively. Accordingly, the authors of each of the chapters look toward the day when the apparently separate tasks associated with problem-oriented research will be more fully and effectively integrated. The compartmentalization typical in the profession and emphasized by the organization of the volume seems more and more artificial as the quantitative methods and approaches to data generation are viewed in their modern and/or generalized forms.

The review of econometric methods by Judge concludes with an evaluation of estimation techniques which support the theme of integration. The various forms of preliminary testing and Stein-rules, Bayesian estimation and inference, adaptive estimation, updating, and variational parameter procedures are all econometric techniques which recognize and emphasize the specialization of method to the problem at hand. Moreover, they point toward a need for the integration of research tasks associated with data gathering, model revision, and applications in policy or optimizing contexts. For example, variational parameter estimation methods are consistent with evolutionary problem specifications and a variety of schemes for obtaining data. Similarly, the comparatively recent results on preliminary tests and adaptive model construction have done much to formalize and lend scientific content to methods of analysis long practiced by applied researchers. Although the results in this instance are somewhat discouraging regarding the information content of the adaptively or sequentially constructed models, they do underline the value of optimizing methods for model revision, the collection of additional data, and policy applications. These methods are at present somewhat demanding computationally and even conceptually, but they indicate the direction in which the modern developments in econometrics are moving.

Day's chapter on the conceptual background of economic optimization is on the surface somewhat less suggestive of the integration theme. Technical aspects of modern optimization methods and problems or structures are surveyed in an expository manner. The connection of these models or methods with economic systems such as market processes and their extensions to dynamic frameworks are key features which support the general theme. Throughout the chapter the reader is reminded that the model, however elegant, is not an end in itself; rather, it is formulated for a specific purpose—to study an economic system. Correspondingly, as perceptions of the economic system being modeled change, perhaps through use of the model itself, the optimizing models can be altered in such a fashion as to capture more accurately or economically those aspects of the problem of interest to the researcher.

Day's chapter also delineates several types of dynamic optimizing models. With command of these formal dynamic optimizing structures, it is natural to initiate the process of formalizing the procedures for model revision to comply with added or developed perspective on the economic system in question. Potential variables for broadly conceived optimizing models are designs for data generation and estimation methods and again must incorporate in an integral fashion the other quantitative approaches and/or problems considered in this volume.

The review of applications of optimizing methods by Day and Sparling surveys past studies and presents a few speculations on directions for future research. The studies are categorized by food and diet, farm and business management, farm development, production response, spatial economies, natural resources, and development. The chapter highlights original contributions or studies which represent the first attempt at the systematic application of optimizing techniques to the selected problem areas. As in the preceding chapters, several methods applied to complex problems which are demanding from a computational viewpoint are identified as important milestones in the evolution of results on optimization methods. Of the applications reviewed, the resource models possibly come the closest to achieving an integration of quantitative techniques along the data-estimation-optimization focus of the present discussion. Attempts to cope with uncertainty about the initial conditions and the economic structure, along with the intrinsic dynamic nature of these problems, place this work in the forefront of advanced modeling applications. Similar problems arise in the construction of models for farm growth management. Largely because of the readily available traditional linear programming methods, however, generalization to an integrated approach was limited by the failure early in the research efforts to formulate the problem in a truly dynamic context.

Woodworth's chapter reviews the extensive theoretical and applied work on production functions. The chapter thus concentrates more on an area of economic substance than on analytical methods or data. For this reason the review is less integrated into the present discussion than are the other chapters. The research on production functions is, however, an area in which theory, data, and estimation methods have been effectively combined. The evolution of specifications to more generalized forms, allowing for variation in the elasticity of substitution, linkages of these models to input-output relationships in fixed coefficient forms, questions of appropriate levels and methods of aggregation, and the estimation of parameters incorporating firm equilibrium conditions are identified as important developments and avenues for further study. As shown by the review, much of the original work in applying and estimating production functions has been done in agricultural economics. For the United States applied activity in this area peaked in the late 1950s and early 1960s, owing in some respects to the adoption of the major concepts in production theory by the technical scientists generating the data (a factor useful in explaining the continued work on estimating production functions in developing economies) and perhaps because the specifications of the models and uses have focused on comparative statics. Following the theme of the earlier comments on adaptive modeling, it would seem apparent that interest in production functions will be renewed when dynamic models of firm behavior are made more complete and accompanying evolutionary specifications for the associated technical relationships are required.

The review of systems and simulation procedures and analyses by Johnson and Rausser focuses on the importance of systematizing the processes of model development, estimation, and application and choice. The initial sections of the chapter provide a framework for integrating these processes and identify their connection with the modern work on adaptive control. Systems and simulation are shown to have been useful in stimulating more general approaches to methods of model construction and application. It is also shown that the implicit optimizing context in which purposeful model development and application are viewed calls for much more structured approaches to the problems of verification, validation, estimation, operation, and revision. A major limitation of the applied work in systems and simulation has been the highly personalized nature of the models. The chapter concludes with a survey of applications, concentrating on those which have been innovative in method and in the formalization of model construction and application processes.

The remaining chapters are a collection of essays on data systems, including their history and implications for future research. Upchurch provides a fairly complete survey of sectorwide data systems. He emphasizes that the various data systems have been typically initiated in response to particular economic problems. Farm surveys and commodity statistics which arose from policy problems faced during the depression years, costs and returns studies to support parity programs, and the more recent concerns with rural development are examples of instances in which data systems have been initiated or greatly expanded in response to an agricultural problem requiring centralized policy action.

From the present perspective this unstructured approach to data collection and the development of an information base for the agricultural sector may seem unfortunate. But is it reasonable to expect anything else? Data and information are expensive, so choices must be made on the bits of information to be included in the system. Current policy problems dictate the relevance of the various existent and possible data systems. These problems tend to change in unpredictable ways. This being the case, it is likely that researchers will continually be dissatisfied with the existing base. What will happen is largely what has happened in the past. The information system will continue to evolve very slowly and adapt to the information needs of the data users, with some improvement in the communication between the people who collect the data and those who use it for research or decision-making purposes.

Trelogan and his associates chronicle the history, evolution, and present status of the Statistical Reporting Service of the USDA. Again the emphasis is on the development and extension of the SRS data system in response to perceived policy problems at the national level. More specifically, the extensions have occurred largely in response to administrative and governmental program needs — for example, the need for data to monitor and implement the various types of governmental programs for agriculture which have been applied over the years.

Of particular interest in this chapter are the observations made on new technologies for data gathering and handling. Advances in multiframe sampling theory, along with the accumulated knowledge on the population, have made possible the development of more reliable estimates for the recorded features of the sector of the economy and the units within it. Similarly, technological advances in data processing have resulted in the cost feasibility of handling and maintaining a much more ambitious data base. Many important possibilities associated with linking data systems on a real-time basis are still to be explored. As these possibilities are recognized and exploited, data systems may begin to focus more on the information content and the economic and social returns of having the information and less on the costs of collection. Finally, remote sensing holds great potential for reducing costs of data gathering. For example, worldwide crop acreage inventories obtained on essentially a real-time basis seem at present almost within our technological grasp. It is interesting to note that remote sensing as applied in modeling has also developed just as the need for policies more effectively linking the agricultural sector to world food and fiber markets has emerged as a major concern in the efficient and purposeful functioning of the sector. Although of course dependent on space technology, the process of obtaining information for more accurately modeling world food production, stocks, and consumption patterns can be viewed as a response of the data system to recent major policy issues involving population dynamics and economic development.

Bonnen explicitly treats the data gathering, storage, and discrimination processes as an evolving system. Problems with the data base, Bonnen argues, are best approached by recognizing that the essential features of the process can be viewed in an information systems context. He stresses that data systems involve management and operationalization of economic concepts, along with institutional and statistical theory. Moreover, data systems feed into a larger structure termed an inquiry system. The scope and content of the inquiry system is to a large extent defined by the informational needs and requirements of the various agricultural decision makers. Within this process we can readily envisage changes in data-gathering techniques, in data base management, and in the focuses for the basic sampling or recording endeavors. It is important that the information system serve current policy needs. Various hallowed data series or concepts on which data gathering has been focused should not be automatically perpetuated. The costs and benefits of the different types of information which can be obtained—not tradition and vested interest—should guide the system. For agriculture, Bonnen argues that vested interest groups have made the data system less flexible than it might otherwise have become. The optimal economic framework for positioning the data or information system must balance benefits and costs on a continual basis, emphasizing the advantages of more accurate or more complete information in existing and contemplated research activities.

The observations made by Bryant in the essay on economic and social statistics for rural people are quite consistent with our general theme and with the chapter on data systems by Bonnen. Specialized experiments on a grand scale are strongly suggested as useful approaches to the generation of data needed for fruitful studies of rural development. Moreover, Bryant recommends the collection of more secondary data on rural populations and economies to support the research suggested by modern development policies. Thus, Bryant's remarks, in the context of the general theme and Bonnen's comments on information systems, are easily understood, given the recent attention of the profession to rural development problems. Bryant's chapter provides a good example of how the process of reorienting and expanding data or information systems occurs in response to changing theoretical concepts with respect to human capital, household production theories, and so on and in response to changing economic problems and policy questions. It is unfortunate that this response cannot be more timely and less costly, but these characteristics are symptomatic of the major decisions on information trade-offs that such changes imply.

Since the systems and simulation chapter necessarily addresses the gamut of activities associated with model development, specialization for applied problems and use, it has anticipated a number of our overall concluding comments. Systems concepts have proved very useful in understanding and modeling highly complex structures. Johnson and Rausser emphasize what has been implicit in all of the chapters—namely, the importance of clearly identifying the purposeful intent of research in developing models and of corroborating the models with the system vis-à-vis data collection and information processing and applying this acquired knowledge in a descriptive, behavioral, forecasting, or decision context. In this regard, it has been illustrated that the theory of adaptive or dual control provides a framework sufficiently general to unify the modeling and research process. With systems concepts and the adaptive control framework, the compartmentalization of quantitative research and teaching processes such as estimation, data gathering, and optimization can be discarded.

Modeling activities and, in fact, research in general involve implicit optimizing processes. Models are constructed and research is conducted with implicit or explicit purposeful intent. Moreover, there are natural and identifiable constraints associated with the modeling process itself and of course with the system under study. Thus, research efforts, whether related to model formulation or to application in a policy context, have identifiable objectives which are approached by strategies for allocating scarce resources. Users of this framework view choices of estimation method, data collection, verification and validation procedures, and analytical construct as potential control variables in a general optimizing process.

The evolutionary nature of the research process underscores the importance and use of the adaptive control framework in guiding and specializing research, which is by design a search and discovery process. Consequently, at various points in the research process increased knowledge of the system in question puts the decision maker in an improved position for identifying the relevant instrument variables and setting optimizing levels of controlled activities. This together with the observation that the agricultural sector and the subunits within it are in a state of continual change further underscores the importance of electing an approach to research activities which can accommodate and adapt to evolutionary processes. Changes in the system, perceived problems, data systems, methods of analysis, and the like are more the rule than the exception and thus require an adaptive mode for decisions regarding research activities.

Agricultural economics has been heavily influenced by the neoclassical paradigm in economics and classical statistical decision theory. Both are constructs which abstract from the evolutionary nature of the processes, economies, agents, and managerial participants interacting with the system under examination. Perhaps this has caused the profession to look too much for "the" optimal data systems and has led to inflexible models and optimization methods which in many cases require perfect knowledge and foresight. Developments in systems and simulation and within the statistical and optimization methods and information processing areas have shown the frailty of these concepts. Such developments argue for a more realistic characterization of the present state of knowledge and for more adaptive research strategies. The world is changing and our perceptions of it are being revised as a result of passive and manipulative intervention in the various subsystems.

The reviews in this volume have stressed that data systems, methods of model construction, model use, and research strategies which do not recognize the integrative features of the information generation process are often ineffective and inefficient. Nevertheless, the progress toward estimation and optimization methods and data generation systems which are more attuned to the evolutionary nature of research problems and activites is reflected in each review.